# MOTOCOURSE

**THE WORLD'S LEADING GRAND PRIX ANNUAL**

HAZLETON PUBLISHING

# CONTENTS

*Motocourse* is published by Hazleton Publishing, 3 Richmond Hill, Richmond, Surrey TW10 6RE. Printed in Holland by drukkerij de lange/van Leer bv, Deventer. Typesetting by Solo Graphics Ltd, Twickenham, Middx. Colour reproduction by Adroit Photo Litho Ltd, Birmingham.

ISBN: 0-905138-45-7

UK Distribution by
**Osprey Publishing Ltd**
12/14 Long Acre
London WC2E 9LP

United States distribution by
**Motorbooks International**
Publishers and Wholesalers Inc.
Osceola, Wisconsin 54020, USA

**Dust-jacket illustration by Don Morley depicts 1986 World Champion, Eddie Lawson, on his 500 cc Marlboro Yahama during the Belgian Grand Prix meeting at Spa.**

**Title page photograph features 1986 Sidecar World Champions Egbert Streuer and Bernard Schnieders at the Dutch TT.**

Photo: Don Morley

PUBLISHER
Richard Poulter

EDITOR
Peter Clifford

EXECUTIVE PUBLISHER
Elizabeth Le Breton

ART EDITOR
Steve Small

PUBLISHING ASSISTANT
Jayne Payton

HOUSE EDITOR
S.G. Spark

SECRETARY
Jane Doyle

ASSISTANT
Joss Hobbs

RESULTS AND STATISTICS
John Taylor

CHIEF PHOTOGRAPHER
Don Morley

Photographs in *Motocourse 1986-87* have been contributed by:
Doug Baird, Nigel Caldecott, Peter Clifford, John Cosgrove, Ray Daniel, Kel Edge, Tomas Gescheidt, Ross MacKay, Phil Masters, John McKenzie, Don Morley, Georg Pickartz, Jonathan Reeves, Tom Riles, Colin Watling.

**ACKNOWLEDGMENTS**
**The Editor would like to thank the following for their help throughout the year:**
E.J., Anne-Marie Gerber (FIM), Charlie Henneken, Henk Keulemans, Hans van Loozenoord, Ian MacKay, Toni Merendino, Paolo Scalera, Gary Taylor, Mike Trimby and Gunther Wiesinger.

# YAMAHA FZR1000
## Proving the genius of Genesis

The Yamaha FZR1000. Four-stroke motorcycling in a new dimension. Proving the genius of Yamaha's "Genesis technology" by totally-integrated development of engine and chassis.

The most powerful, most compact engine in its class in the most-advanced chassis on today's roads . . . the alloy "delta box" chassis from our World Championship and endurance racers.

Four-stroke engineering that leads the world!

Forward-inclined, parallel four-cylinder engine + Downdraft carburation + 20-valve cylinder head + Twin overhead-camshafts + Digital electronic ignition control + Lightweight alloy "delta box" frame + Twin 320mm front disc brakes + Hollow-spoke cast-alloy wheels + Monocross suspension.

**YAMAHA**
A tradition of perfection.

# The choice of the world leaders

## AP RACING
### Lockheed BORG & BECK

Manufacturers of Lockheed brakes and Borg & Beck clutches for race cars and bikes.

Automotive Products plc, AP Racing Division, Leamington Spa, England. Telephone: 0926 312025. Telex: 311571 AP PLGC. Fax: 0926 35983.

# FOREWORD

## by Eddie Lawson

I knew that winning the second World Championship would be no easier than the first. However, if you want something badly enough you can do it. I had *Motocourse* to remind me about my winning year in 1984 and last year as a record of when things did not go my way.

I also had the best team and the motor cycle I needed. Once again they never let me down; the Yamaha was as good as anything else on the track and it was great to be able to exploit its advantages. The team worked better together than ever before and that made things even more enjoyable.

Now I have another *Motocourse* to look back on and I am no less determined that I will be writing the foreword again next year, but there are a lot of other very good guys who are going to try and take the title away from me.

We cannot afford to sit back and think we are the best because we won the championship – there is always someone else who will end up in front as soon as we get complacent. So when next year starts we'll have to go harder than ever and we're already working on it.

Racing is a serious professional sport – at least that is what we keep telling ourselves – but fortunately it is not without its lighter side. The serious business is winning and this year Yamaha were better at that than anyone, completely reversing the results of the previous season. The story of how they managed it, how Egbert Streuer secured his third World Title, and how Aspar Martinez and Luca Cadalora won their first World Championships is contained in later pages. Meanwhile, here are some of the images that had little to do with winning races or championships but are nevertheless vital parts of Grand Prix racing.

Randy Mamola always seems to be having more fun than anyone else and in '86 he had a new Mercedes to play with. It helps when you have someone to do those mundane tasks, like washing it and checking the tyre pressure. He also enjoys wearing a silly hat.

Martin Ogborne displays the latest high technology from the Skoal Bandit Suzuki team – a fine example of their work with composite materials.

Ogborne throwing out the rubbish from a week's work at the Grand Prix – demonstrating that team work is more than just clipboards, stopwatches and champagne.

Jean-François Baldé confirmed the French predilection for the grape by producing his own Bordeaux. Whether or not he pressed every barrel with his own bare feet he was not prepared to say.

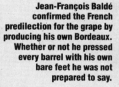

Peter Ingley worked flat-out all year designing, developing and testing Dunlop tyres.

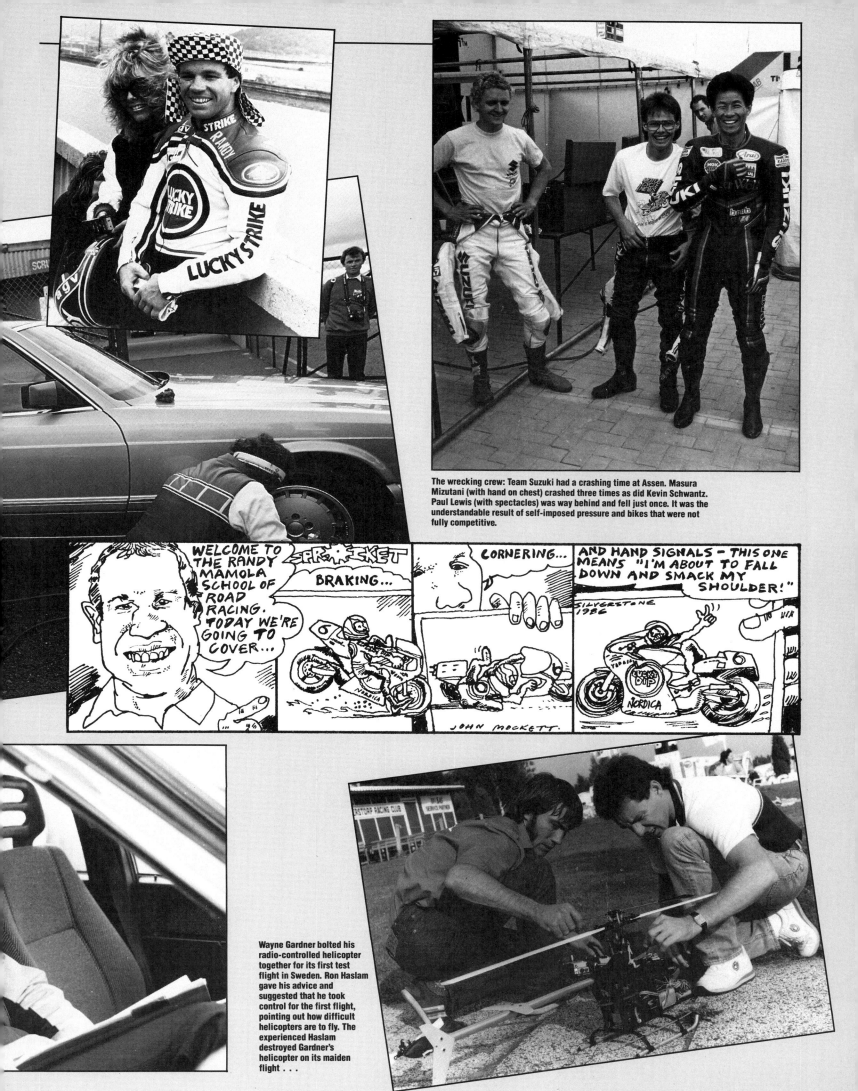

The wrecking crew: Team Suzuki had a crashing time at Assen. Masura Mizutani (with hand on chest) crashed three times as did Kevin Schwantz. Paul Lewis (with spectacles) was way behind and fell just once. It was the understandable result of self-imposed pressure and bikes that were not fully competitive.

WELCOME TO THE RANDY MAMOLA SCHOOL OF ROAD RACING. TODAY WE'RE GOING TO COVER...

SPROCKET

BRAKING...

CORNERING...

AND HAND SIGNALS - THIS ONE MEANS "I'M ABOUT TO FALL DOWN AND SMACK MY SHOULDER!"

SILVERSTONE 1986

JOHN MOCKETT.

Wayne Gardner bolted his radio-controlled helicopter together for its first test flight in Sweden. Ron Haslam gave his advice and suggested that he took control for the first flight, pointing out how difficult helicopters are to fly. The experienced Haslam destroyed Gardner's helicopter on its maiden flight . . .

Yamaha FZ 750.
The smooth unleashing of pure power!

Concentration on the essentials makes the Yamaha FZ 750 a great motorcycle. Flexibility, power to spare, perfect handling. Motion turned into excitement! Proved by Eddie Lawson with victory at Daytona. Sold by your Yamaha dealer! Features: Forward-inclined, parallel four-cylinder engine • Downdraft carburation • 20-valve cylinder head • Twin overhead-camshafts • Digital electronic ignition control • New full fairing • Box-section chassis tubing • Monocross rear suspension.

**◆YAMAHA**
**A tradition of perfection.**

# MIKE TRIMBY & IRTA

## By PETER CLIFFORD

**Eddie Lawson sits in the bare Rijeka pits thinking of something more than the circuit's natural safety and rudimentary facilities.**

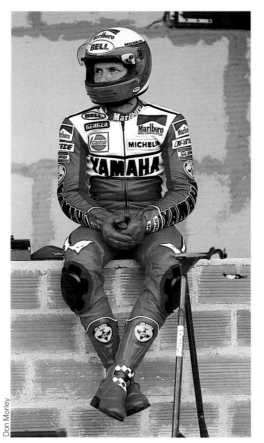

Don Morley

**Spa is a fine track, combining the classic and atmospheric old startline section with a modern, fast, interesting and comparatively safe new roadway** (opposite).

Even readers who study Grand Prix racing closely and know all the details of men and machinery can fail to appreciate how much Grand Prix racing has improved over the last four years. It may not have changed the way the bikes look, the speed or the closeness of the racing, because the revolution has taken place behind the scenes, in the paddock, where most of the competitors and mechanics live. I know; I live there too and after years of being treated like performing animals by organisers (an attitude that extended well before my time in the sport) conditions have altered to the point where life has become more ordered and pleasant. Most importantly, it has meant that at the start of each race you no longer have to face that awful fear that one of your friends might be seriously hurt or killed.

Racing is *still* a very dangerous sport but the risks in Grand Prix racing in particular have become more acceptable since the most dangerous circuits are no longer used and safety standards are much improved at those tracks currently employed. It is no coincidence that this has come about since Mike Trimby has been representing the Grand Prix riders. The next revolution may be much more visible.

By 1982, riders had realised that they needed someone to speak for them as they could not afford to be politicians and riders at the same time. Trimby took on the job experimentally for four Grands Prix at the end of 1982 but soon found that voicing the riders' points of view to organisers was not easy – many organisers simply took no notice. 'The Swedish listened but the others treated me with contempt; there was no co-operation at all. At that time I represented, and was paid by, the ten factory riders. They had realised that they needed someone to work for them and things had come to a head at Nogaro earlier that year when the riders had refused to ride because the track was totally unsuitable', remembers Trimby.

At the end of that year the organisation was changed so that Trimby represented everyone in the 500 class and worked to a budget that was funded by 3 per cent of the 500 cc class prize fund. It was a voluntary contribution and all bar a few competitors gave willingly.

The following season started badly, however, witnessing two fatal accidents at the first European event. That is something that Trimby will never forget: 'It taught me a very harsh lesson – that there can be no compromise as far as safety is concerned. Those riders should not have died and Michel Frutschi was killed simply because he hit a catch fence pole. From that point we insisted that all catch fences be removed. The biggest shock to me when I started was the safety of the circuits, or lack of it. Walking round to do track inspections, I could not believe how dangerous they were, how many things could cause injury and death. At Rijeka in Yugoslavia, for example, there were catch fences and where the poles had come loose in the ground there were steel wires holding them up. A rider could have been decapitated going into one of those. Riders don't see dangers when they are riding unless they are very obvious. When you stop to look

things are very different but in all the time I was racing I never thought too much about circuit safety.'

Trimby himself started racing in 1968 after leaving school to work in a motor cycle shop. He made an arrangement with well-known dealer Sid Lawton that he would work in the evenings for nothing if he could race one of the bikes in the shop. He started on a 1963 250 Aermacchi and eventually raced all over the world, through Europe and from Daytona to Macau. Even after retiring from competition he has continued to help with organising the Macau Grand Prix.

In more than ten years of racing Mike Trimby gained a good idea of what it feels like to be a competitor. Yet, although petty-minded bureaucrats have long been a hated species to him, he recalls how, like everyone else, he never thought of actually changing anything as a rider. 'Just racing took all our time. I remember riding in Formula 750 races at Nogaro and going into town by mini-bike every morning for a coffee just so we could use some decent toilets.'

In fact, although Trimby's position as riders' representative has brought about major changes in Grand Prix racing, non-GP circuits and organisations remain a long way behind as far as safety and facilities are concerned. The Formula 1 and European Championship contenders have to compete at circuits too dangerous for Grands Prix, as though a course that's dangerous for Eddie Lawson or Rob McElnea is somehow safe enough for Anders Andersson or Joey Dunlop. Endurance races are also held at non-GP tracks. The Österreichring can never qualify for a Grand

Prix because the armco barrier is too close to the trackside in several places, yet it has been homologated by the FIM for World Championship events. In the FIM statutes there is no differential between the safety standards for Grands Prix or Endurance ... which brings us to Suzuka and the Japanese Grand Prix of 1987.

Suzuka runs the Eight-Hour Endurance race as part of the FIM World Championship and has been homologated by the FIM to a standard they consider suitable for a Grand Prix. The track inspection was carried out by Luigi Brenni, President of the Road Racing Commission of the FIM, and by far the sanest voice on the FIM regarding safety and track facilities.

'It is an unfortunate situation', admits Trimby. 'Japan should have a Grand Prix, obviously, and we have no wish to stop Japan holding a Grand Prix or to embarrass Brenni, who has been most helpful in the past. But at Silverstone this year we held a meeting to discuss Suzuka because it was after the Eight-Hour and Christian Sarron, Wayne Gardner and Kenny Roberts had ridden there and expressed the opinion that it was not safe to run a GP. We made a report of some nine points on the circuit which had to be altered, as well as organisational changes which are important but relatively easy to put right. I understand that the circuit changes will be expensive but, as Sarron pointed out at the meeting, how can we go back three or four years to the sort of circuit we used to race at in Europe? It will be too late to put things right next year; it has to be done before the Grand Prix. I learnt at Le Mans in '83 that there can be no compromise because I would never be able to live with it if someone got hurt. Circuit inspections are the worst thing to do; that is why I always share them with two riders. That gets them involved and shares the responsibility.'

Apart from inspecting new circuits there has been less for Trimby to do in the last twelve months, now that the early battles of '83 and '84 are in the past. 'Roberts and Uncini were the people that made things happen in those days. Uncini was riders' representative to the FIM and I was his secretary. I had his mandate and my letters had his name on them even when he was critically injured at Assen. If we wanted something and the organisers ignored us, Roberts and Uncini were prepared to say "no race" and the others would follow.

'At first, organisers did try and ignore me as riders' rep, and the FIM shunned me when I attended the FIM as representative from Hong Kong through my Macau commitments. But Brenni pointed out that, although he as the FIM President could not liaise with Mike Trimby, he could as Franco Uncini's secretary as he was elected to the Road Racing Committee. Brenni has always had a sympathetic ear and, while certainly not pro-rider, he is the first even-handed President there has been on the Road Race Committee, the first to weigh up both sides of the argument. He works so hard that no-one approaches the kind of effort he puts in and we have regular unofficial meetings to discuss all sorts of problems.'

This season Trimby found the job of riders' rep-

Don Morley

**McElnea and Lawson, charging hard in practice at Anderstorp. The straw bales in the background are placed in short rows so that a sliding man may knock down several sets before hitting anything firmer** *(left)*.

*Below:* **Mike Trimby occasionally faces criticism because he helps organise the Macau Grand Prix on one of the most dangerous circuits in the world. However, there are no championship points or works contracts at stake, and riders who wish to compete have the nature of the circuit carefully explained – the idea is to put on a show for the crowd. Ron Haslam is an expert at riding fast enough while still keeping a little in hand; here he follows newcomer Didier de Radigues in the 1985 event.**

resentative was running out of substance as most of his work had been done. 'I think that most of the circuits we use are as safe as they can reasonably be while we have to race cars as well as bikes on them. We have had no fatality for two years. The last was Kevin Wretton in '84 at Spa and that corner is being changed for next year. There will always be accidents and deaths, unfortunately, but some like the Brown and Huber crash at Silverstone have nothing to do with trackside safety. I was beginning to wonder how long the job would last and how long I could justify the $1500 that it was costing the riders each race to have me there.'

Fortunately for all, early this year a new organisation was formed – IRTA. At a meeting held in Austria, the idea of inviting Trimby to be Secretary General was formulated and in Yugoslavia he was asked to join. No longer collecting 3 per cent from the riders, he takes a salary and expenses from IRTA, the International Racing Teams Association. This is formed from members of the professional teams from the 500 and 250 classes, as well as the top service companies like Dunlop and Michelin, so it represents the most durable strength of racing. Riders come and go but teams and larger companies last longer. Trimby still looks after rider safety and facilities but while these now move along more smoothly as long as he keeps a watching brief over them, the sport needs a different kind of representative if it is to make the jump from an amateur event watched by a few thousand spectators to a fully

professional sport watched worldwide on television.

The prize money paid at Grands Prix is insufficient to support private riders and while large sponsorship deals finance a few teams there is no depth, particularly in the 500 class where many riders should not qualify and would not were better riders encouraged to compete.

IRTA is looking at ways to move the sport forward. 'It may be that we need Bernie Ecclestone to do with motor cycle racing what he has done with Formula 1 car racing', says Trimby. 'Whether we like it or not, he is getting involved. He will be running the Grand Prix at Jerez next year and perhaps Czechoslovakia because he has promised to pay something like three times the FIM minimum prize fund. In Formula 1 he has the TV rights and the trackside advertising in many cases tied up. He knows that with the TV audience assured he can sell the trackside advertising and this finances the teams that make up the grid.'

In motor cycling there is no one person who has the television rights to all races. This discourages a lot of national television networks because they are unable to show all the Grand Prix races. If they cannot have the continuity of the complete season they are not interested in trying to build up an audience. The FIM thought they owned the television rights but now a court action has been threatened following the discovery by an Italian company which bought the rights from the FIM

that individual circuit organisers owned the rights. The FIM's belief that they were the owners of the television rights has led to threats of a court action. An Italian company, which had paid the FIM for the rights, discovered that these were actually owned by individual circuit organisers. The FIM may have to pay many thousands of dollars in compensation and that will come out of every rider's licence fee.

The sport has benefited considerably and directly from the activities of Mike Trimby since 1983 and of course by those riders who have backed him. He has created some order out of the ideas of the thirty or so individuals that make up the 500 class. The result has been a safer and better sport for everyone. IRTA has the potential to make still greater changes because it has more power, money and continuity. By definition, the team managers that sit on the committee are managers and more used to organising matters than riders.

'IRTA can work with the FIM', says Trimby. 'There is no reason to overthrow the system as long as they are prepared to make changes.' So while the time of the riders' representative has ended, Trimby is at the centre of what promises to be an exciting new era. We who live in the paddock appreciate the improvements and Trimby remembers that one man said it all. 'Gustav Reiner summed it up for me when he said "I can stand crashing, I can stand making no money but I can't stand being treated like an animal".'

Don Morley

# IN THE 500cc AND 250cc 1986 WORLD CHAMPIONSHIP BOTH YAMAHA AND HONDA WERE FIRED ON NGK.

In fact the first six riders in the 500cc World Championship all relied on NGK Spark Plugs. And, if that wasn't reward enough, we also helped win the 250cc world title.

**NGK Copper Core Excellence.**

CBR1000F

power : one hundred and thirty two P.S.

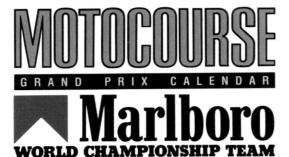

# MOTOCOURSE
## GRAND PRIX CALENDAR
## ▲ Marlboro
### WORLD CHAMPIONSHIP TEAM

## First across the line

Steer your way through 1987 with that proven winning formula – the Marlboro World Championship Team MOTOCOURSE Calendar and Diary.

The large format, 13-leaf calendar vividly captures all the action and atmosphere of Grand Prix bike racing in 25 full-colour photographs.

The 96-page diary combines colour photographs, circuit diagrams, rider profiles, race-by-race results recorder and detailed team information with a generous diary section.

If you enjoy bike racing, send for the Marlboro World Championship Team MOTOCOURSE 1987 Calendar and Diary. Order them separately or together, but do it today – they go fast!

Prices (inc VAT and P&P) are:
Calendar (590 x 420mm) £7.00 each.
Diary (172 x 81mm) £4.60 each.

**SPECIAL OFFER (SAVE £1)**
Calendar and Diary set £10.60.

1986 Prices Held!

Please send your name and address, together with your cheque*/postal order (made payable to Hazleton Publishing) to: Dept 2, MWCT MOTOCOURSE Offer, 3 Richmond Hill, Richmond, Surrey TW10 6RE.

Your Calendar/Diary will be despatched separately in October/November.

*Cheques from outside the UK must be drawn on a London bank in £ Sterling, no Eurocheques.

# YAMAHA'S TECHNICAL ADVANTAGE

Carlos Lavado's HB 250 Yamaha run by the usual Venemotos crew was a perfect half-cylinder replica of the proven 500 and was equally dominant.

Peter Clifford

The changing fortunes of riders, teams and companies that make the sport so interesting, along with the technical developments that extend the envelope of knowledge and machine performance, this year produced enough surprises to make it exciting from start to finish.

Put simply, the story is that the 500 class was dominated by Yamaha because the V-four became the bike that the three-cylinder NS500 Honda had been perhaps three years before. The three had been the most rideable all-round performer and all the top stars could ride it. Yamaha achieved their success in '86 with a bike that was, arguably, even better, having superior top speed and even fewer handling vices than had the Honda in '83 and '84.

One of the most crucial elements in the Yahama's success story is that tyre technology had progressed to a point where riders could make use of this power. Back in '83 and '84, Yamaha

riders complained that the Honda spun its rear wheel and drove forward, whereas the Yamaha spun and went sideways. Now the Yamaha also drives forward, laying great lines of rubber and launching man and machine down the straight at a rate unmatched by any other machine.

Tyre development is discussed elsewhere, but the Yamaha's triumphs cannot be credited simply to rear-wheel rubber. Wayne Gardner had the use of the same rear tyres as Lawson, yet the Honda tended to spin the rear wheel and go sideways, as though it had inherited the Yamaha's problems instead of its three-cylinder forerunner's qualities.

Gardner complained that although the Honda would be fine in the early stages of a race, the tyres were unable to cope with the sudden power delivery once they were past their best. One might point out that this did not seem to prevent Spencer from winning the championship in 1985,

but, remembering more accurately, he did have problems after the first eight or ten laps. By that time he was far enough ahead to be able to defend his lead. This year, Lawson was so much better that Gardner never had that luxury and found he could not fight all the way to the finish.

Whilst there was only one four-cylinder Honda racing for much of the time and Roche had less luck on the bike than Gardner did, it is hard to be 100 per cent certain about the machine's ability. There will always be those who question what would have happened had a fit Spencer ridden it.

No such question can detract from the performance of the Yamaha which hardly changed at all from the 1985 specification but for a revised rear suspension geometry that made life easier for the Öhlins rear unit, as Swedish engineer Lars Östh explained. 'The new linkage is designed to put less load into the frame and to make suspension adjustment easier.' Initially, these alterations

**GRIPPED BY PIRELLI.**

*GRIPPING STUFF*

*Motocourse* Editor Peter Clifford gets the technical details from Kel Carruthers before testing Lawson's World Championship-winning 500 Yamaha.

appeared to have failed when Lawson struck trouble in Spain, but from that point on it worked well, although adjustment seemed to be critical on a bike that otherwise worked so reliably. Lawson would set the suspension up so that the damping was a little too hard at the beginning of the race, knowing that it would come right as it heated up. The spring pre-load can be adjusted while riding thanks to the knurled knob mounted above the left-hand bar, but while this has proved useful in practice for setting the bike up, it has less application during the race. There is little time to pay attention to such adjustments and in any case it is the damping that alters as the unit gets hot rather than the springing. Lawson does soften the spring a little through the race as the fuel load lightens and the rear tyre passes its best.

Power characterstics had also altered over the winter and Kel Carruthers made some tuning modifications of his own to the cylinders on Lawson's bikes. This information was passed on so that other Yamaha riders benefited. The reed valves seemed to be a problem and Yamaha had some special units for Lawson which at first were unavailable to the Lucky Strike team, but when Mike Sinclair enlisted the services of Bernard Hargreves to produce some special reeds in time for Assen, Yamaha did not like the idea of outsiders doing their work and produced enough reed systems to go round.

It was not always Lawson alone who received special treatment, for at Assen the larger diameter cranks arrived and there were parts for Mamola as well as the championship leader. Said to be 92 mm in diameter, these provided more tractability; the engine already had bags of power and looked faster than the Honda on most occasions.

More remarkable even than the performance of the Yamaha has been its unfailing reliability and none of the five riders suffered a machine failure in the eleven Grand Prix series. The only part prone to failure as opposed to normal planned replacement has been the ignition system, and that has had the happy knack of never failing in use. On several occasions the iginition systems started to play up during practice after they had performed perfectly in the previous race or session. It appears that they would work while hot as the bike was running but on cooling they then failed; when the bike was restarted the next day the ignition was inoperative. With a sighting and warm-up lap to give warning before the race, this sort of failure is much more acceptable than an unpredictable disaster.

The Yamaha had been called the OW81 a year earlier but as the YZR 500 in '86 it became a production racer rather than a works special. Honda headed in the other direction and in contrast to the NS three-cylinder, which had been very similar to the RS bike sold to the public, the NSR four was a factory-rider-only special, never intended for mass-production and completely different to its championship-winning predecessor of 1985.

The engine looked the same, retaining the reed-valve induction V-four layout, but in fact it had been completely redesigned. The powerplant was tipped forward because the centre of gravity was thought to be too high and too far back. The new engine was 25 mm narrower than the old version and all the castings and internal parts had to be redesigned to achieve this – the only unchanged component was said to be the clutch. The result was a lighter machine by 5 per cent with a wheelbase 1 cm shorter.

There were three versions of the engine, distinguished by different power characteristics created by different combinations of exhaust pipes and cylinders. The factory found difficulty fitting in four well-designed pipes and had tried to produce a four-into-two system but without achieving the required spread of power.

At Assen, Gardner got the chance to use a new engine with a different exhaust system. The ATAC boxes that had been used since the early NS engines had been dropped because although they varied the exhaust volume they did still not give enough breadth to the power band. The revised powerplant had exhaust valves more closely related to the Yamaha system, in that they effectively altered the exhaust port time, yet without employing the guillotine in the exhaust tract in quite the same way as Yamaha. As turbulence in the exhaust port downwind of the guillotine is known to detract from the scavenging of the Yamaha design, it is logical to assume that Honda have used something like a drawbridge that lowers into the tract to reduce the port height while providing for a more gradual return to the full exhaust tract section. If it has not been done in this way it should be tried, as an exhaust chamber could be included in the same design if required with the drawbridge opening up the chamber as it is lowered.

Suzuki seem committed to their exhaust valving system as it is included in their new V-four as well as the older unit used by both the Skoal Bandit and Suzuki teams this year. Through

# RG 500. NOTHING ON THE ROAD TAKES YOU SO CLOSE TO THE GRAND PRIX EXPERIENCE.

MCN's Mat Oxley.

**SUZUKI**

**SET THE PACE**

HERON A Heron International Company

The Yamaha primary drive shows how both
cranks are geared together so that they turn
in opposite directions.

Peter Clifford

sheer hard work and determination, the British team made great strides with the reed-valve modification to the square-four that Suzuki produced as a stopgap before the V-four became ready.

On arrival from Japan the engine was found to be rather uncompetitive. However, by greatly increasing the intake volume of the reed valves, improving the flow both through the boxes and the inlet tracts, as well as increasing the pumping efficiency of the engine by filling in the crankcases above the flywheels, the engine was made to work very well indeed. I was fortunate to be able to ride it at the end of the season when the engine improvements, coupled with the exceptional handling of the composite frame and well thought-out suspension, made it a very rideable motor cycle and as good as any three-cylinder Honda. I rode it only days after an outing on Lawson's championship-winning Yamaha, and

of course that was just simply more powerful all round. The new V-four Suzuki should bridge that gap and the British team have a new composite frame that is a beautiful creation, making full use of all they have learnt in two years with the old machine.

Honda were unlucky with the 250 as they lost the services of Freddie Spencer and ran up against a better machine at the same time. They did with their 250 what Yamaha did with the OW81: turned it into a limited-production racer for sale while Yamaha did the opposite and produced their 250 as a factory-only special that outclassed the Honda. It was as fast and handled better. Lavado simply had to stay aboard it often enough to ensure there was simply no contest. Wimmer and Taira proved, with their practice performances at least, that anyone should have been able to win with it. Again, I was lucky enough to ride it and it was demonstrably better

than Spencer's championship-winning Honda, if only for the way it handled under heavy braking going into corners and the neutral throttle carburation.

Yamaha made their championship-winning 250 in the simplest manner by splitting the V-four vertically and scaling down the twin-spar aluminium frame. With the twin they had the choice of using the same exhaust-valve system as the 500 or, for maximum power with a little loss of flexibility, non-power-valve cylinders. It was a toss-up as to the best choice for tight circuits, for although the lap times with both engines tended to be the same the power valve made getting through traffic easier.

On a purely personal note, I found myself in the incredibly fortunate position of having ridden the two Yamahas, the Skoal Bandit Suzuki and the Elf, quite obviously the most technically impressive machines of the year.

21

# That day even more people

**appreciated Shell Oils.**

# Eddie Lawson

Lawson developed the art of winning a race before the start by being able to respond to any practice time the opposition might record. It never seemed to be a great effort for him, and even if he suffered defeat in either practice or race there was always an impression that the championship was highest in his mind and nothing would divert him from his course towards it.

The fall at Assen was an extraordinary mistake, not only running off the track but also falling before he could regain the tarmac. Considering the year as a whole, however, all that incident did was to keep the championship contest alive a little longer rather than act as a substantial threat to his eventual triumph.

The confidence that Lawson exuded came of course from the knowledge that the Yamaha would finish the race in good order and that the tyres would be up to the job, no matter what he demanded of them.

# TOP TEN

| | |
|---|---|
| **1** | **EDDIE LAWSON** |
| **2** | **WAYNE GARDNER** |
| **3** | **RANDY MAMOLA** |
| **4** | **MIKE BALDWIN** |
| **5** | **RON HASLAM** |
| **6** | **SITO PONS** |
| **7** | **ROB McELNEA** |
| **8** | **CARLOS LAVADO** |
| **9** | **CHRISTIAN SARRON** |
| **10** | **LUCA CADALORA** |

## THE EDITOR'S EVALUATION OF THE LEADING RIDERS IN 1986

John McKenzie

Marlboro riders were a great force to be reckoned with once again with Eddie Lawson winning the 500 Championship and Luca Cadalora the 125. Martin Wimmer found frustration in the 250 category and despite always being fast, race wins eluded him.

*Photos by Don Morley*

# 2 Wayne Gardner

# 3 Randy Mamola

Freddie Spencer's disastrous season was a mixed blessing for Gardner because it put a great load on his shoulders from the first race. It had the effect of stopping Gardner from racing and acting as he had in the past, with a certain abandon. The riding style changed completely, so the wild slides and appearance of semi-control were gone. Yet the pressure did not force him into making mistakes, and while Lawson slipped in Holland Gardner went on racking up the points. At Silverstone he was back to his old self as the bike slid and onlookers expected him to fall off. He stayed on board, however, and knew exactly what he was doing.

Gardner says that he will beat Lawson as soon as he has a bike that can match the Yamaha. While he would certainly be more competitive on a better machine, he would none the less have to ride better than the World Champion. Despite his three successes over the Lawson this year, there are still things for Gardner to learn and Lawson would have to stop improving for Gardner to have a clear run at the championship.

The ultimate entertainer and the 'if only' champion. Mamola has everything required to be World Champion bar the need to succeed. He even views himself as an entertainer, the wheelie king of Grand Prix racing who developed a new trick, the 'stopie' to perfection in 1986. As fast as anyone on two wheels, the Californian does not consider being World Champion as the most important thing in his life, perhaps because after finishing second so many times he has resigned himself to disappointment. It would be interesting to see how he would react if he was pesented with the chance to be champion rather than always being frustrated.

If next season should begin to go Mamola's way there is little doubt that he has the ability to capitalise on it. The difference between winning and taking second or third, as he has so often done, would seem to lie within Mamola's own determination. A great rider for any team, he could confound the critics in '87 and would then be the most popular champion for a decade.

# 4 Mike Baldwin

Perhaps the surprise of the season was the way Baldwin took the V-four Yamaha and rode it as though he had been born to it. Always fast, hard-riding and dramatic, he looked to be on the ragged edge but in fact only fell in the wet in Belgium. On five occasions he finished third, yet several of the circuits he had never even seen before and he had to contend with some very bad starts.

Baldwin has had a long racing career outside the Grands Prix. When his first attempt at breaking into the World Championship was cut short because of a serious accident in America it looked as though Baldwin had missed the boat. The years spent riding for Honda America in a secure, well-paid position meant that Grand Prix racing as a privateer made little sense, but to Baldwin the chance was worth taking because of his total confidence in his own ability. This year proved that confidence well founded; the experience he has gained with the Yamaha and his familiarisation with new circuits may well help him to chalk up more victories over Gardner and Mamola in 1987. He is unlikely to repeat the tyre choice mistake he made at Spa which cost him a possible third place or even second in the championship.

It was a great year for Haslam and although it was the first time since he started racing at Grands Prix that he had finished lower in the points than in the previous season, he gained considerable respect from competitors and informed observers for the way he turned an untried prototype with unique steering and suspension systems into a competitive Grand Prix machine.

No other rider could have done it; no other top-line rider would have entertained the idea of trying to compete against the best machines and riders in the world using a machine that did not exist when he signed and had grown from another bike that had been a conspicuous failure. The Elf 3 would probably not have fared much better than the original Elf 2 but for Haslam who reflected the determination and effort of the entire Serge Rosset team. Haslam's belief in his own ability meant that he knew he could get the bike right thanks to his great talent and experience in sorting out steering and suspension on a wide variety of machines.

The Spaniard had a dismal season on a rather uncompetitive 500 Suzuki in '85 but a return to the 250 class and a top-line machine achieved more than just a return to his previous form; it showed that Pons could be perhaps the rider most respected in the 250 category. Though not always as fast through every corner as Lavado, Pons showed himself to be more reliable and less prone to mistakes.

It was clear that the Honda was not the equal of the Yamaha. His bad luck in Germany, when the bike refused to run properly and Pons crashed through desperation, and poor starts (for example Austria and Silverstone, where he was forced off the track at the beginning of the race) prevented him from pressing Lavado harder.

Pons still has the idea that he can succeed in the 500 class on the right bike, and certainly the one unsuccessful year does not prove otherwise. Over a season Pons is now a very good bet for the 250 World Championship and can win whatever the weather conditions.

# 5 Ron Haslam

# 6 Sito Pons

**Photos by Don Morley**

# YAMAHA TZR250

## Last year the racetrack.
## This year the road!

Yamaha two-strokes have won over 50 World Championships in thirty years of road-racing. We added to that total this year, courtesy of Eddie Lawson in the 500cc class and Carlos Lavado in the 250. Plus, just for good measure, the World 250 Motocross title for Jacky Vimond. Technology that wins World Championships also makes winners of our road machines. What we prove on the racetracks, we use on the road. Take the Yamaha TZR250. Less than one step removed from our TZ production racers and using much of the YZR technology that helped Lawson and Lavado win their Championship crowns. We say it's the best 250 on the roads today. And who can disagree?

Liquid-cooled, 2-stroke twin + Reed-valve crankcase induction + YPVS exhaust power valves + Alloy "delta box" frame + Hollow-spoke cast-alloy wheels + 320mm front disc brake + Variable Damping front forks + Monocross rear

**YAMAHA**

## 7 Rob McElnea

Kel Carruthers and Eddie Lawson have every confidence that McElnea will be one of the very best riders in the world. His self-confidence has been tested on several occasions this season when things went wrong, when he was unable to beat Baldwin or when he fell as he did at Monza and Misano, but he has what it takes. With a year of experience in the Yamaha team behind him he is likely to prove a greater threat in '87 to the four who finished in front of him in the championship.

He admitted that riding the Yamaha came as rather a shock as the bike had to be ridden as hard as the less powerful Suzuki if he expected to gain results. Jarama was not an easy place to start the Grand Prix season but throughout the year he approached racing with great intelligence and enthusiasm, learning from Lawson who was a willing instructor. He pin-pointed the areas of his riding style that needed development, such as the controlled rear-wheel slide, and worked at it with success.

## 8 Carlos Lavado

No-one rides a motor cycle faster than Carlos Lavado but he cannot deny that luck was with him in '86. It started on the first lap of the first race when he fell, only to be able to restart and win because the race was halted due to another incident. He fell again at Rijeka, Spa and Misano, but when he stayed upright he was only ever beaten twice – by Toni Mang and Dominique Sarron.

Lavado says that his falls have come about because he is unaccustomed to having such a top class machine and has not learnt how to ride at less than 110 per cent. Certainly some of his falls appear to have been caused by a loss of concentration. In Yugoslavia and Italy he was out on his own at the head of the field when he lost the front end going into a corner.

His ride from the back of the field in Yugoslavia was quite the most thrilling spectacle of the season, a ride that had the Lawsons and the Mamolas wondering how they would cope if they were in the 250 class. Lavado can never be counted out in any race or championship for there is none faster and none more brave.

Carlos Lavado had luck when he fell but Sarron got hurt. In Germany and England he was injured even though others walked away from similar falls. The other thing that kept him back was his disastrous starting, which made it almost impossible for him to beat McElnea and Baldwin consistently. His size is no help when it comes to pushing the four, even if his light weight is an advantage once he gets rolling. If clutch starts are introduced for the '87 season, Sarron may well move up the championship table, but he is still prone to fall a little often and always seems to get hurt when he does.

His best rides have often been in the wet and perhaps this is because his 'sit on and lean' riding style does not suit the rear-wheel sliding that works so well on the current top-line bikes and radial tyres. Modifying this approach is likely to be difficult for a rider so used to working the front tyre hardest, but it is probably essential if he is to achieve ultimate success.

Though only seventeenth in the 1985 World Championship, Cadalora attracted the attention of the Garelli team and the moment he got a works ride he responded by proving to be faster than reigning champion Ezio Gianola.

He had needed to work hard in 1985, and just when he seemed to be getting into the points with a fine seventh at Assen he crashed the next week at the beginning of practice for the Belgian GP. He was unlucky to miss out on the points with his eleventh in the rain at Silverstone but he failed to start after another fall in Sweden.

In 1986 he made no such mistakes and proved well capable of withstanding the pressure of leading the World Championship after a cautious start in Spain and Italy. Three straight wins in a row saw him move ahead of Gresini and demonstrated that he was the best rider in a competitive class. The 23-year-old Italian attracted the interest of teams wanting him to ride 250s and 500s for the following season and his smooth style could well translate into those classes with success.

## 9 Christian Sarron

## 10 Luca Cadalora

## BEFORE ANY BMW DEALER SELLS A K100RS, HE NATURALLY TAKE[S]

Some go a little further than others.

To the Isle of Man in the case of Nick Jefferies.

For the last 2 years, Nick has taken a brand new, absolutely standard K100RS and raced it in the 'MCN/Avon Production TT.' (Finishing 8th in 1984 and 7th in 1985.)

With an average field of some eighty machines, it's an impressive performance.

Particularly when a good number of the opposition were thinly disguised race replicas, much more at home on traffic free race tracks than on normal congested public roads.

But what is even more impressive than the final placings of these two BMWs, is their final fate.

### BMW FOR SALE – ONLY ONE CAREFUL PREVIOUS OWNER.

One of Nick Jefferies' own customers bought the 1984 motorbike, and to date ha[s] enjoyed twenty thousand trouble free com[-] muting miles.

The 1985 motorbike has also been sol[d] this time to Nick's race mechanic who use[d] it as the fast but reliable sports road bike [it] was designed to be.

What other motorcycle could inspir[e] such faith?

Indeed, how many other motorcycle[s]

## T FOR A TEST RIDE.

Braddan Bridge · Union Mills · "The Highlander" · Ballacraine · Ballig Bridge · Glen Helen · Cronk-Y-Voddy · Barregarrow · Kirk Michael

WCRS

...ould you dare buy after they'd been used ...s a full blown racer?

The BMW K100RS is designed to be ...ushed to its limits without needing a major ...rip down after every high speed run.

### SMOOTH SURGING POWER RATHER THAN UNCONTROLLABLE BURSTS.

The in-line four cylinder all-alloy engine ...es not need to be revved to the red line ...achieve its full potential.

83% of its fuel injected torque is developed below 3,400 rpm – giving this light bike a 0-60 time of 3.9 seconds.

And with a computer designed fairing, a top speed of 137 mph is easily achieved (but of course only on a race track).

The aerodynamic fairing also produces the lowest front axle lift of any motorcycle in its class – and consequently, one of the highest levels of road holding.

The rear wheel is similarly glued to the tarmac by BMW's unique monolever suspension.

So whether you're planning a trip round the Isle of Man, the British Isles, or just the traffic island at the bottom of the street, only one bike will do them all justice.

The BMW K100RS.

## THE ULTIMATE RIDING MACHINE

...VICE, PO BOX 46, HOUNSLOW, MIDDLESEX, OR TELEPHONE 01-897 6665 (LITERATURE REQUESTS ONLY). FOR TAX FREE SALES: 56 PARK LANE, LONDON, W.1. TELEPHONE 01-629 9277.

Our MR2, we have to confess, has little going for it in the way of luggage space.

The big-hearted engine, however, more than makes up.

Twin overhead camshafts, the sixteen valves and the sixteen hundred c.c's are a formidable combination.

On an autobahn, for example, you could go through the five gears right up to 124 mph.

But it's off the straight and narrow that the car really shows its form. "What Car" in rating the MR2 Coupé of the Year 1986, said: 'Pin-sharp steering and grippy low-

# WHAT YOU LOSE IN BOOT

profile tyres allow the car to be hurled accurately through fast corners in roll-free, neutral fashion'.

Such athleticism is possible because our heart's in the right place.

The MR2 sports what car designers call a mid-engine configuration.

This puts 55% of the car's weight over the back axle and 45% over the front.

The result is anything but middling.

"Fast Lane" magazine put it thus:

'Toyota haven't just produced a superb sports car, they've produced a car that is unrivalled by anything in Europe at the price...'

# YOU GAIN IN WELLIE.

Toyota (GB) Ltd., Head Office & Tax Free Sales, The Quadrangle, Redhill, Surrey. Tel: (0737) 68585. **TOYOTA**

THE MR2 COSTS £11,099. PRICE CORRECT AT TIME OF GOING TO PRESS AND INCLUDES CAR TAX AND V.A.T. BUT NOT NUMBER PLATES OR DELIVERY. D.O.T. FUEL CONSUMPTION FIGURES: URBAN CYCLE — 34.9 MPG (8.1L/100 KM). CONSTANT 56 MPH — 47.1 MPG (6.0L/100 KM). CONSTANT 75 MPH — 36.7 MPG (7.7L/100 KM).

# RUBBER AT WORK
## MICHELIN DEVELOP THE RADICAL RADIAL

Don Morley

A Michelin technician at work during his hectic Grand Prix day.

Squinting down the slightly undulating ribbon of black tarmac towards the start of the Mistral straight, one can see that the road is not quite as flat and level as it appeared at first glance. In fact, the straight runs uphill slightly towards the end but only looking at it from a stationary viewpoint reveals this.

From there the black triangle that originates in the far distance swims a little, distorted by the heat haze. The trail of white dots that marks the centre line weaves down the road not because of the haze but through being painted in a rather lax manner.

Such thoughts disappear as the mind concentrates on that speck in the far distance. Steadily, it grows, with increasing rapidity, until it resolves itself into a motor cycle with a rider crouched behind the screen. The yellow separates from the bright orange to become a front number plate; then the number 2 registers and provides the final confirmation that it is Lawson on the Marlboro Yamaha.

The idea is that the radial tyre should slide so predictably that the rider can maintain control. Juan Garriga did manage to get the better of the Cagiva on this occasion.

Things happen quickly now: a head bobs up, a knee flicks out and the number plate dips. The bike that has been upright since it materialised drops down on its right side and sweeps across the field of vision through the corner, as the background blurs, then disappears. You concentrate only on the machine, trying to watch everything – Lawson, the suspension, the tyres. But there's no time. In a wail of sound as he gets the power on, the back end gives a barely discernable shake as man and bike shoot off down the short straight to the next corner.

Then the pack screams past and concentration on one bike is impossible; it is hard enough to pick out individual riders to get any idea of the order amongst the flashes of colour. Yet one image remains: the sheeer effortless speed of Lawson and the Yamaha. There is enough time before he comes round on the next lap to reflect on how impressive it was before realising that one must concentrate on one thing, such as Lawson's hands or his feet, the front suspension, the back or front wheel. There is no way that anything meaningful can be detected from a general view.

Even this level of concentration can prove frustrating. The rider moves slowly enough in a planned yet apparently casual series of actions; the hands, knees and feet can be watched even if the genius behind it is invisible. The mechanical parts, on the other hand, defeat the eye. Sure, you can pick out the major slide, the big wobble, the bad case of wheel chatter, but the subtleties are too fast – the way the tyre deforms as the bike is leant over cannot be viewed.

Because the activity cannot be studied visually, it seems almost irrelevant. Observers would not even think about tyres but for the frequency with which riders mention them. They speak of the tyres' importance, how they work well or badly, whether they have gone off or are too hard or too soft. One could be left with the idea that tyres are more important than rider and machine put together.

How is it possible to get any idea of how much work the tyre is doing when one is standing at the trackside watching Lawson or any other star sweep through the corner? Consider the forces involved. If that machine leans over at 45 degrees through a corner, maintaining a constant radius without slippage, then it is not hard to image the side force being coped with by the tyres. At that angle, the side force is equal to the weight of the bike and its rider. Imagine picking up Lawson and his Yamaha and concentrate that weight through contact patches the size of your hands, and you have a good idea of the frictional force created by the tyres.

As if coping with that side force is not enough, the tyres have also to cope with braking and acceleration forces. Naturally, maximum braking or acceleration is not attempted while the machine is heeled over at 45 degrees but that front tyre while upright will provide enough grip to raise the back wheel off the ground. Current racing technique puts more stress on the rear tyre than ever before and only a very few can use the best tyres up to their maximum potential.

Lawson gets on the power early while the bike is still on its side, rubbing off fibreglass against the tarmac. He rolls on the throttle as soon as he has stopped braking, is fully committed and at the maximum angle of lean. He is gentle with the throttle and just gets the back end to break away slightly. It spins very slightly; mainly it drives forward but when Lawson is in a real hurry the spinning is enough to lay down a strip of black rubber as the corner unwinds and the bike is gradually straightened up. With his weight shifted back and still hanging to the inside of the bike, the throttle is opened hard as less sideways force is inflicted on the tyre, but the bike is still leaning over. Lawson has the gearing chosen so that a sudden slide and accompanying violent wheelspin will take the engine out of top of the rev band, thus cutting back the power output and giving him a chance to regain control.

That's the way Lawson makes the most of his rear tyre. How do I know? Have I seen it? No; the report comes from Rob McElnea, one of the few to have come close enough, and it impresses him as much as it should anyone capable of comprehending what it takes to feel that combination of side slip, angle, acceleration, engine response and forward drive.

The tyre ties rider and machine to the road, the contact patch is the hinge about which the whole thing pivots. While the most obvious component of the tyre is the rubber that becomes more malleable and sticky as it becomes hot and grips the tarmac, that is only half the story. It is, perhaps, the lesser half because the rubber is only the cladding on a very important structure – the casing, which with its layer of covering rubber creates the profile. The way that the profile varies and is controlled by the casing dictates the area of contact between the rubber and the road. The amount of rubber that is in touch with the road is obviously of fundamental importance to the grip.

The action of the rubber tread is straightforward enough, even if the chemistry of a successful compound mix is something of a magician's secret. Friction generated by the rubber can be split into three parts, although the first, the molecule-to-molecule bonding between a molecule of rubber and an adjacent molecule of tarmac, is almost insignificant and can be largely discounted.

Far more important is the friction created by the rubber as it moulds itself round grains of tarmac, and the force required to make the rubber deform if it is to slip across the irregularities. More force is required if the sharper grains of tarmac are to cut through the rubber. To understand how these forces are resisted by the rubber, one must have a little understanding of the internal structure.

Rubber is made up of long chain molecules. The chains have arms that sometimes form links with other chains. The performance of the rubber depends on the activity of these chains – their length, how they are intertwined, the number of bends in the chain, the stiffness of the bends, the number of side arms and cross-links, and the strength of all the inter-molecular bonds. The chemist who designs the compound can vary all these factors and alter the performance of the rubber accordingly. His work is often referred to as a black art for more than just the reason that carbon is an important ingredient.

Heat has a significant effect on the performance of the compound because heat energy affects the bonds between atoms and between molecules. It changes the stiffness of chains and can break bonds, shortening chains or cutting the number of cross-links. When chains move more easily, the rubber becomes more malleable.

The malleability of rubber increases or reduces grip. Cold rubber cannot mould itself close enough to the tarmac to provide optimum grip. As it warms, the rubber moulds itself better and the grip improves but if the rubber gets too hot the grip decreases because the rubber deforms and flows over the tarmac instead of gripping it. If the bonds are weakened by heat, the tarmac can cut through the rubber. Loss of tread can become too rapid, but the ultimate disaster is when so much heat builds up that the actual mechanics of the tyre begin to fail and the tread may start to detach from the carcass and blister.

Such severe blistering is rare in motor cycle racing but potentially very dangerous. In 1980, when Marco Lucchinelli finished third at Silverstone behind Mamola and Roberts, his rear tyre was badly blistered, but I have seen very few cases like that – remarkable given the constant increase in power output and the pressure on tyre companies to produce ever-lighter tyres with greater grip yet able to last the Grand Prix distance. The next stage beyond blistering is when the tread detaches itself completely; then the carcass soon flies apart. This was blamed as the cause of Barry Sheene's near-fatal Daytona accident in 1975, although this was never proved conclusively.

The compounder has a hard task to create a mix that will respond quickly to the initial input of heat over the first lap yet will retain its characteristics as more heat is fed into the tyre when the rider tries harder.

From this, it becomes obvious that heat input must be controlled. A source of heat is in the flex of the tyre, as well as the friction created within the rubber itself as it moves around. The tyre carcass is important because it holds much of the key to heat build-up, in addition to providing tyre profile. Furthermore, it affects contact patch area and contributes to suspension, while also influencing stability and steering.

A tyre's casing is made up of plies – layers which resemble cloth woven with almost all warp and very little weft. The ply material can be rayon, polyester or a polyamide such as nylon or Kevlar, or a mixture of several different materials depending on the mechanical properties required.

The plies are laid up so that they cross each other at an angle and this angle is vital to the performance of the cross-ply structure. It largely dictates the tyre's contribution to machine stability and to the amount of suspension in the tyre. The smaller the angle between the plies, the nearer they lie to the direction of the tyre circumference and the stiffer the casing.

Christian Sarron rides the immaculate blue
Sonauto Gauloises Yamaha.

The tyre requires a reasonable degree of stiffness in the tread area to maintain the designed
profile against side forces at every lean angle, yet
the sidewall must flex to accommodate small
irregularities in the road. As a compromise, a flexible casing is combined with a stiffer tread section by laying a second series of plies on the
crown of the tyre making that area stiffer than
the sidewalls. This produces the bias-belted tyre.

Cross-ply construction has dominated motor
cycle racing design since the end of the Second
World War. The British companies Avon and
Dunlop fought each other for racing honours
after the war, but by the 1970s Avon had dropped
out. Dunlop was left to rule on its own
with its famous range of trigonic tyres that
had a relatively stiff casing to produce a very
triangulated profile.

This meant that when the bike was upright the
contact patch was small but as the machine leant
over the tyre profile offered a much larger contact
area. These tyres allowed high cornering speeds
but as engine power increased greater demands
were made on the tyre under acceleration.
Dunlop were disinclined to spend a fortune on
development, having a virtual monopoly on the
World Championship, and hence when Michelin
arrived on the scene in the early-Seventies there
was scope for more competition.

The first Michelin racing tyres were simply
road tyres that could be bought in any shop – the
PZ2, and then the PZ3 and PZ4. They were first
raced in 1972 in French Championship events,
then used for World Championships in the 250
and 350 classes. Australian Jack Findlay, one of
the real stars of the continental circus, started to
use these tyres on the 500s and 750s as well.
Much rounder in profile than the triangular
Dunlops they put more rubber on the road at less
radical angles of lean and allowed more grip
when accelerating out of corners.

The PZ tyres contributed to victory in the 1974
125 cc World Championship when Kent Andersson used them at the end of the year, but the first
true Michelin World Title was Paolo Pileri's 1975
125 crown on the Morbidelli.

By then the factory had become involved in the
construction of special racing tyres and Barry
Sheene used Michelins on the works Suzukis. The
first PZ tyres had been road designs and obviously had a tread pattern but the slick tyre was not
far away. Slicks were first raced by Goodyear as
they already had extensive experience of them in
car racing where they were already common. The
American company was to develop its slick
racing technology until it became a great force
in the World Championships but at first problems
arose in trying to find a tyre structure and rubber
compound that would warm up sufficiently
quickly to grip early on yet would last the
distance.

Michelin tested a slick racing tyre at Daytona
in February 1974 and this line of development
was to become a major part of their racing programme. The Sheene connection brought them
the most publicity in Europe as he won the 500 cc
World Championship in 1976 and '77, and he used
the new slicks known as the SV and SB designs.

**WORLD CHAMPIONS 500cc**

**WORLD CHAMPIONS 250cc**

Since 1974, Michelin-shod riders have dominated the World Championships. Their success has been so overwhelming that not a year has passed, during the last dozen, without at least one taking a title.

All in all it's a victory roll that amounts to a staggering 39 Grand Prix World Championships being won on our rubber – a feat that leaves other tyremakers standing.

And never more so than in 1985 and '86 when all four championship classes went to Michelin.

What's more it was our radials, racing onto the scene, that snatched both the 500cc and 250cc categories.

Such a performance says a lot for our desire to win, but much more for our determination to go on producing a better product.

That better product is the shape of things to come.

In other words, a Michelin radial for road, as well as race bikes.

# 'S A MICHELIN

**WORLD CHAMPIONS 125cc**

**WORLD CHAMPIONS 80cc**

# Michelin radials for road bikes.
# The shape of things to come.

These tyres grip so well in the wet that even when the bike had thrown Raymond Roche off at Spa the bike continued down the track until it smacked into the pit barrier *(main picture)*.

A remarkable picture taken from underneath a transparent section of roadway at one of Michelin's test facilities, which shows how a treaded tyre dispels water *(centre right)*.

This simple graph *(far right)* depicts the relationship between lateral force on the vertical axis and slip angle on the horizontal axis.

Tadahiko Taira was fast all year but only savoured victory at Misano *(bottom)*.

Walter Villa also used Michelins to win the 250 and 350 categories on the Aermacchi Harley Davidson, while a Michelin-shod Morbidelli ridden by Pier Paolo Bianchi hung on to the 125 class. The French company's finest hour in the Seventies came in 1977 when they achieved a clean sweep of all solo classes from 50 cc to 500 cc.

Dunlop had certainly been caught napping but competition intensified in 1978 and Michelin could only retain the 50 cc Championship, losing the 125, 250 and 350 Championships to Dunlop with riders Angel Nieto, Toni Mang and Jon Ekerold, with the 500 going to Goodyear after the arrival of Kenny Roberts.

Goodyear supported only Roberts in the World Championship and there were many arguments as to whether this was a blessing or a curse for the Yamaha rider. Riders like Mike Baldwin and Freddie Spencer had occasional rides but in effect it was a one-man team. Opponents said that he had the advantage of the best tyres and individual attention. Kel Carruthers remembers things rather differently, pointing out that every time they went to a new circuit not only had Roberts probably never seen the venue before but he had no tyre experience to draw on. The bewildering variety of compounds and constructions to be tried meant that their lives were spent changing tyres and wheels without any baseline to compare the results against.

They mastered the situation well, however, and for three years Roberts and Goodyear were the 500 cc World Champions while Dunlop kept the 250 and 350 titles through 1979 and 1980. The next year saw Marco Lucchinelli and Michelin triumph over Roberts and Goodyear and the American company pulled out, leaving Roberts to switch to Dunlop in 1981.

That year was also important for it saw Honda and Spencer come together for the first time at a Grand Prix when Spencer rode the NR500 at Silverstone. Although Dunlop had done most of the early work on the NR, Honda now had a strong association with Michelin and this was maintained a year later with the arrival of the NS500 two-stroke, leading to a full attack on the championship.

Franco Uncini kept the championship in Italy in '82 with the Michelin-shod Suzuki but Spencer won his first Grand Prix and the following year took the World Championship, making it three years in a row. Once more, Michelin had all the solo classes.

It began to look as though Michelin had a stranglehold over the Grand Prix scene. What had been an even-handed battle between Dunlop and Michelin in the second half of the Seventies was beginning to look distinctly one-sided. Dunlop was facing severe financial restrictions on research and development, as well as the racing programme.

Dunlop's background of experience and expertise could only hold up for a limited time against the huge effort from France. As the budgetary controls became ever more stringent, Michelin, in contrast, seemed to have more money than ever to spend, thanks to the incredible commercial success of a range of radial tyres for four-wheeled vehicles. This represented a truly revolutionary breakthrough in tyre technology which was to have a tremendous impact on motor cycle racing for two reasons. It boosted the company in general, and hence helped provide the money to go racing, and it formed the basis of radial technology that has since had such an important effect on road racing.

In 1984 Michelin developed the radial tyre with Freddie Spencer, Marco Lucchinelli, Randy Mamola and Franco Uncini, even though Dunlop won the World Championship with Eddie Lawson and conventional cross-ply construction.

Michelin justly claim to have done more than anyone else to bring the advantages of radial design to the world of road car tyres, making the most of the structure that allows the sidewalls to flex enough to absorb road bumps whilst keeping the belt-supported tread firmly in contact with the road. The true radial has a single ply with all the thread running at right angles to the bead of the tyre or rim of the wheel. This can produce a very flexible sidewall indeed and because there is no crossover of plies there is very little build-up of heat. Considerable heat is normally generated where the plies try and work against each other as they cross over.

Michelin were not the first to produce a radial motor cycle tyre and Pirelli decided to follow that line of development in 1981. The following year Graziano Rossi took part in preliminary track tests of a radial slick at Daytona in a private session on the Morbidelli Grand Prix 500. A year later Pirelli were fully committed to radial development and were testing radial road tyres in Australia where much of the high-performance testing is done by Mattich, the local importers.

Although Pirelli used their tyres in the Italian and European road race championships and launched their MP7 radial road tyre, their racing never extended to World Championship success. The bias-belted Phantom range also remains their best road tyre in production racing.

At the time Pirelli claimed that the advantage of the radial was so significant that different compounds for racing would no longer be needed, the radial limiting heat build-up so effectively that a soft compound could be used without fear of overheating.

The Italian company was never able to prove this theory in racing and it was left to the French to draw on their unsurpassed experience with automotive radial tyres. Michelin first tested their radial motor cycle racing tyre at Le Mans at the end of 1982 when Pierre-Etienne Samin tried one on the rear of the works Suzuki Endurance racer. At that time the work was top secret and Michelin did not start discussing it publicly until 1984. A year later their radial design had advanced to such an extent that it won all twelve 500 cc Grands Prix in '85, repeating the performance in '86 as well as adding the 250 class to its sphere of influence.

Dunlop also started to develop the radial and, unusually, changes in internal structure could be seen outside as a generation of very short sidewall tyres appeared on racing machines. Because the sidewall is naturally so flexible, it has to be shortened if sufficient rigidity is to be maintained. This results in reduced weight bringing with it the associated benefits of less heat and less rotating mass. As a result, wheel sizes on the NR500 Hondas, for example, have gone up from 16 in. to 17 in., first on the back and then the front as the short-wall radial tyre has taken over from the cross-ply, keeping the outside diameter of the tyre very much the same.

It is not always easy to pick out the radial tyres, for a cross-ply construction and a radial can be used to produce the same profile and shape of tyre. Indeed, in '86 Michelin had 17-inch front

Don Morley

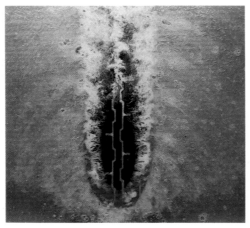

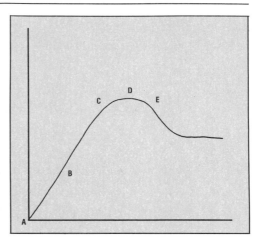

tyres, radial and cross-ply, that were interchangeable. The radial can be made with a high sidewall and the Michelin road radial introduced generally at the end of '86 is a high-sidewall tyre because it must fit existing wheels as a replacement for cross-ply tyres. Nevertheless, the ultimate advantages of low weight and so on are best explored with low-sidewall designs and this is the direction that racing development is taking.

Michelin carry out their motor cycle tyre design at Ladoux in the Central Massif of France, just outside the city of Clermont-Ferrand, which is home for Michelin as well as the Sarron brothers.

Much of the road tyre track testing is done at Ladoux and some racing tests are performed for rain tyres and intermediates because the test circuit incorporates sprinkler systems to control the water level on a variety of surfaces. However, the majority of slick testing must be done at race tracks because of the high speeds required. Recently, Michelin's winter testing has been at either Surfers Paradise in Australia (which Honda prefer because it is close to Japan) or at Goyana in Brazil. Michelin prefer the latter because it is safer and it is where Eddie Lawson, Rob McElnea, Martin Wimmer, Tadahiko Taira and Carlos Lavado did their pre-season testing this year. It obviously paid off as Lavado and Lawson went on to win the 250 and 500 championships.

At Ladoux, motor cycle tyre design is carried out under the watchful eye of chief engineers François Decima and Gérard Martin. The former pointed out during my visit to the test centre that it was the riding style of the current top stars which demanded the development of the radial as much as the increase in power output. 'We had reached the limited of the bias-belted tyre; riders wanted smooth sliding with traction and that is

very difficult with the bias-belted cross-ply tyre. When we made the first radial tyre we used the same mould as for the bias tyre and just changed the internal structure.'

Michelin have found that the radial tyre produces that predictable slide the riders have been looking for and this can best be shown by studying the relationship between side force on the tyre during cornering and the side slip that results from it. If the relationship is depicted graphically (see figure) it can be seen that slip is proportional to lateral force at first.

This is logical, as even if the tyre does not seem to be sliding the squirming of the rubber means that as it rolls forward it will also walk sideways. So the graph runs up from the origin (A) along a straight line (B). Where the lateral force is the vertical axis of the graph and the side slip or slip angle the horizontal axis, the steeper the line the better the grip the tyre is producing.

The racing tyre is asked to perform at very high lateral forces created by the centrifugal forces of high-speed cornering. Towards the limit of adhesion the graph begins to curve down (C) as there is more side slip for each increase in lateral force until the point is reached where no increase in side force still causes side slip (D). At this point the rear wheel is sliding away rapidly but a reduction of lateral force (which could be accomplished by the rider easing off the throttle and widening his line) could still reduce the slip and bring the rear tyre back into line. If the line is followed further, though, it dips back towards the horizontal axis (E). Things are then out of control because the slip angle increases even as the lateral force reduces.

Apart from a steep initial straight line which can be created by a large contact patch and a sticky rubber compound, the racing rider also

needs a very flat curve so that he can have the chance of feeling the increase in slip angle and halting the increase in lateral force before he gets over the crest of the curve – the point of no return.

The curve also changes as the race goes on, thanks initially to changes in temperature and then either because of a further increase in temperature or the degrading effects going on in the tyre structure. All racing tyres reach a peak of performance early in the race, the exact position varying with circuit and machine but usually around lap 5. By lap 8 the performance has deteriorated slightly but the effect is less marked in radial tyres. After the initial peak, the radial has been found to remain very consistent which has endeared them to riders who can rely on stable performance through to the end of the race. Obviously this is as important as the maximum grip and as vital as the steepness of the peak in the force against slip angle graph.

The radial design holds the running temperature of the tyre lower and hence the wear rate is kept down. The radial can run ten or fifteen degrees centigrade lower than a comparable cross-ply and at a high-speed circuit like Daytona where the loads on the banking are extreme the difference is more like twenty degrees, making this a major advance for reasons of safety as well as performance.

Having proved that the radial tyre worked in principle, Michelin still had a great deal of work to do and the radial idea has opened up such a wide field of possibilities that at the moment development seems open-ended. If all avenues of development were to be explored by producing tyres to each possible combination of profile, tread depth, sidewall height, rim width – bias construction as well as compound – then the cost would be prohibitive and testing so time-consuming that few tyres would ever see the race track.

Experienced tyre designers can quite often tell whether a design is likely to succeed by studying a completed drawing of a cross-section and calculating the effect of inflation pressure, load, centrifugal force and side forces. The associated drawings and calculations are also lengthy and involved so Michelin have been using a computer aided design (CAD) system to do much of the donkey work.

Computer aided design is not new and is used for everything from oil rigs to connecting rods but each application requires special softwear. Michelin have spent much time and effort creating a series of programs that enable them to predict the way that modifications to tyre structure and composition will affect peformance.

Each tyre is designed around the steady state curve. This is a theoretical line about which the tyre carcass can be considered to flex as long as there is no extension of the ply material. As the ply is nylon and this does stretch, the computer has to work out how the practical shape varies from this theoretical curve.

On the computer the designer builds his tyre around this line, laying up the cords, plies and rubber, and stipulating the mould shape he

Don Morley

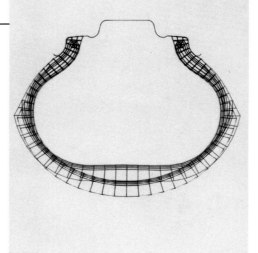

Martin Wimmer and Carlos Lavado stand on the startline in Sweden contemplating the wisdom of their tyre choice *(main picture)*.

The computer can generate diagrams like this which help the engineer to see how the tyre is affected under varying loads *(right)*.

Don Morley

requires. The first thing that the computer calculates is the shape that the tyre will take on once it is removed from the mould.

The computer then mounts the tyre on a rim and the rim shape is laid down in a European standards book, ETRTO. Each time the tyre is drawn on the screen, the variation to its overall shape and to the theoretical steady state curve can be readily seen. Thus a tyre that is obviously going wrong can be quickly discarded or modified in only a few minutes' work, rather than waiting for lengthy calculations by hand and elaborate engineering drawings to be carried out by a draughtsman.

With the tyre mounted on the rim, the designer can check that there will be the correct interaction with the wheel to ensure that the tyre will seal as it is inflated.

Next, the computer can show how the tyre will change shape once inflated at various pressures. All these calculations are done on a section of the tyre and performed over half its width because both halves are symmetrical. The inflated tyre is then examined from the side, looking like a ring or toroid, so as to study its shape when put on the road and loaded to a certain extent with a stipulated inflation pressure.

Up to this point, all sections of the tyre could be considered to act in the same way but now the segments must be treated differently, with some in contact with the road. To this end the tyre is divided into 24 segments, not evenly grouped but more frequent in the lowest quarter – the one most affected by road contact. The segments must be small enough to be considered homogenous, so that variation along the length of each segment is negligible.

In the previous calculations there are 300 points on the tyre drawing which must be plotted using three calculations on each point. Now these must be calculated on each of the 24 segments as the deformation of one segment affects the next. These 21,600 calculations are worked and reworked until the total deformation is drawn by a series of successive approximations. The result is displayed once more on the screen and can be printed out.

Of particular relevance to the design of motor cycle tyres is the facility to lean the wheel over in the computer. When viewed at 90 degrees to the axle, the deformation caused by the road and cornering forces can be studied. Tyres that have been deformed by the road surface provide vital information because the computer can produce a contact patch picture. Furthermore, point loadings across the patch can be shown, which is obviously fascinating and very useful when assessing the grip provided by a particular profile and construction.

The CAD system speeds up the work spectacularly and cuts down the amount of drawing and manual calculation required, as well as making unnecessary wasteful construction of prototype tyres that cannot work. The designer can be warned where the bias plies that run circumferentially under the tread are placed in compression. These are made of polyamide, and although that aramid fibre can withstand very

high tensile stresses and hardly stretches at all, it should not be placed in compression. There are purely practical considerations; Motor Cycle Road Racing Manager Gérard Fayol asserts that, with this sort of information, early-season testing can take place with four possible new tyre designs instead of eight.

The CAD is an advanced system when compared to hand drawing and slide rule calculation but setting up the programs themselves is a time-consuming, complex and highly skilled operation. As yet the softwear falls short of its potential, so it is being developed to provide even more information for 1987. Because it is, as yet, impossible to combine dynamic and static loadings, the centrifugal model cannot be combined with the cornering model to provide data on the contact patch on very high speed corners.

Further development should see the addition of the tyre's elasticity to the dynamic models so that it is possible to study the rate at which it returns to the round after being deformed. Some tyres develop ripples as the deformed tyre bounces back from deformation and goes past its normal shape through lack of damping. Too much damping may result in the tyre being slow to flex as it passes over road surface irregularities; this will have a great effect on the grip provided. Therefore, when it comes, a dynamic elastic model should prove of great value. At the moment this sort of work is done experimentally with wheels rolling on drums, involving the use of high-speed photography to study ripples and so on.

Another very interesting advance would be to study the change in the front tyre contact patch as the wheel leans over and steers into the corner. The contact patch may be considered to move forward around the wheel as the wheel turns in, but the change in patch shape depends on the angle of the steering head, the trail and the tyre profile. If this could be simulated on the computer it would give considerable assistance in the search to find out why, on some machines, the front wheel turns under to a greater or lesser extent, depending on the tyre type and rim width. If loading could be added to this model to simulate braking some real advances could be made in the understanding of handling going into corners. Such models will be complex and taxing on the size of the computer, but development would be very rewarding.

At the moment the effect of the tyre profile and other variables on steering must be tested on the track, and this is both a blessing and a curse. The track is not as precise as the solid state chip and the rider does not think like a computer program. The computer is unaffected by the time of day, arguments with the mechanics or a dislike for the circuit, but on the other hand it is the rider who ultimately has to race and win on the tyre, so the feel it gives him can be more important than theoretical maximum grip.

One thing that the radial tyre has not altered is the design of the rain tyre tread pattern. Michelin found that the old patterns developed on the cross-ply worked well on the new casings, but since they have made the switch to radial they have developed the rain pattern further and

Mamola won on the new design at Spa. This new version is a marked improvement, as Sarron found when he stuck to the tried and tested pattern in Belgium.

In fact, radial construction may have allowed advances in pattern not possible with old carcasses, but the team at Michelin cannot be sure because with the commitment to radial development the new pattern has not been tried on the old tyre. Bearing in mind Mamola's main comment on the performance after the race, it may well be that the radial structure does offer some fundamental advantage. The Californian said that when he first looked at the tyre the tread blocks stood out so markedly that he thought the lack of support for the blocks would make the tyre very unstable. As it was, Mamola found that the bike tracked straight, which can be attributed to good tread design, in which the grooves are placed in the direction of stress. In part, at

least, it may have been attributable to the use of very firm polyamide ply under the tread, made possible by the flexible radial sidewall.

Rain tyres, because of the tread pattern, look very much more like road tyres than do slicks, although internally all racing motor cycle tyres are very close to road designs – much more so than in the car world. Indeed, Michelin's road radial front tyres are true radials, with the ply at 90 degrees to the bead, just like the racing tyre. The racing rear is also a true radial but the different demands placed on the road tyre make this inadvisable. The road tyre has to cope with less power coming out of a corner but the rear tyre must make a considerable contribution to straightline stability. For this reason the radial plies must be at a small angle away from 90 degrees, which helps to damp out weave.

Because the radial tyre works in a very different way to the older designs, several factors

become of greater importance to its performance: inflation pressure and rim width. The rim width used to mount any tyre will have an effect on the profile and its performance, but because the radial sidewall is so flexible the tyre is designed to have a near-vertical sidewall and any departure from the stipulated rim width will obviously alter the orientation of the sidewall to the detriment of the performance. Similarly, the inflation pressure must be precise because of its contribution to the shape of the case.

The fact that Michelin have started to use 17 in. front tyres this season is interesting as they were prime movers in the adoption of the 16 in. front wheel only a few years ago. The larger rim offers more advantages than just reduced total weight of tyre and wheel.

The endurance racing teams hated 16 in. front wheels because of the terrible difficulties encountered when trying to change wheels. The front

discs are now so large that there is precious little room for the calipers and wide 16 in. front tyres made life awkward.

One of the stated advantages of the 16 in. tyre was its lower rotating mass and the lower weight of the radial makes it a better choice than the high-sidewall sixteen. The same is true of the rear tyre; because the tyres rotate at such speed their weight is arguably more important than any other component on the machine.

More important than any other component on the machine? Well, the tyre designers and the race technicians would like to think so, and the riders *do* spend a great deal of time talking about tyres, blaming them perhaps for a disappointing performance. So the next time there's a chance to see Lawson sweep through a corner, knee on tarmac, engine wailing, look hard at that dark area of contact between rubber and road . . . and try and work out what is going on.

## JACKIE STEWART'S PRINCIPLES OF PERFORMANCE DRIVING

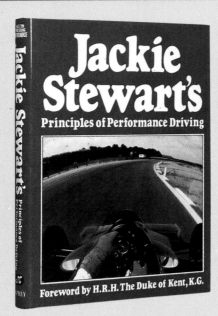

Jackie Stewart's name became a legend in Grand Prix racing when he retired in 1973 with three World Championships and a record of 27 Grand Prix wins to his credit.

Now, in conjunction with Alan Henry, he shares his own personal insights into the essential skills needed to become a champion driver, although this is more than just a 'how to race' book. Share the Stewart philosophy – not only behind the wheel but also in his approach to business and life in general.

29 colour and 120 black & white photographs
ISBN: 0 905138 43 0
Price: £14.95

## THE ART & SCIENCE OF MOTOR CYCLE ROAD RACING

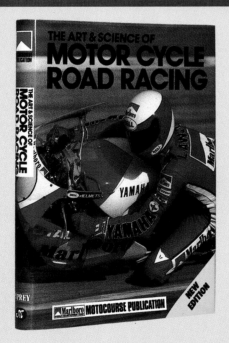

### by Peter Clifford

The second edition of this best-selling book has been acclaimed as the most accurate and authoritative account of the skills and principles involved in motor cycle road racing. Cornering, engines, steering, suspension, frames, tyres – all are explored in detail, and now a completely new chapter covers the latest technical innovations and how these affect the rider.

20 colour and 80 black & white photographs
ISBN: 0 905138 35 X
Price: £12.95

## McLAREN: *The Grand Prix, Can-Am and Indy Cars*

### by Doug Nye

From the early days of McLaren Cars in 1963 to Emerson Fittipaldi's first World Championship title for the team in 1974. Two years later James Hunt did it again, winning his historic season-long battle with Niki Lauda.

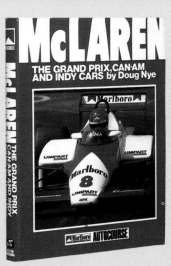

20 colour and over 90 black & white photographs

ISBN: 0 905138 28 7
Price: £12.95

## BRABHAM: *The Grand Prix Cars*

### by Alan Henry

The story of the Brabham Grand Prix team from its early pioneering days in the Sixties through to the takeover of the team by Bernie Ecclestone in 1972 and Nelson Piquet's World Championship titles in 1981 and 1983.

28 colour and 145 black & white photographs

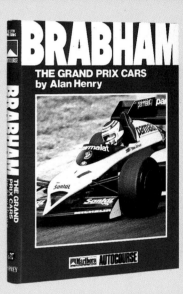

ISBN: 0 905138 36 8
Price: £14.95

## FERRARI: *The Grand Prix Cars*

### by Alan Henry

The history of the most famous racing marque of them all from its first hesitant steps on to the Grand Prix stage in the early post-war years through to Lauda's two World Championship titles in 1975 and 1977 and the highly specialised world of the turbocharged engines of the Eighties.

35 colour and over 100 black & white photographs

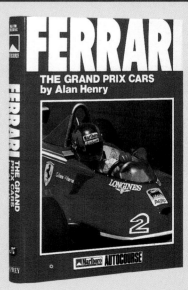

ISBN: 0 905138 30 9
Price: £14.95

## AUTOCOURSE
### *1986-87*

The 1986-87 edition of *Autocourse* will be the most colourful and lavish in its 36-year history with over 100 photographs in superb colour and over 150 excellent black-and-white shots from the very best motor sport photographers. It contains complete coverage of the 1986 Formula 1 season plus full reviews of sports car and US racing, Le Mans and Formulas 3 and 3000 in a new and exciting 272 pages. A major issue – engines – is covered by Doug Nye, while Alan Henry's in-depth feature on Keke Rosberg and a comprehensive results and statistics section complete this collector's edition.

ISBN: 0 905138 44 9
Price: £19.95

## MOTOCOURSE
### *1986-87*

All the action and excitement of the 1986 World Championship season is here in a new, top-quality package featuring 50 per cent more spectacular colour.

As well as his original Grand Prix reports, editor Peter Clifford takes an exclusive look behind the scenes at Michelin and holds an in-depth interview with Mike Trimby who acts on behalf of the riders. Lively coverage of the US scene, Isle of Man TT, detailed statistics and much more makes *Motocourse* a must for all motor cycle enthusiasts.

75 colour and 130 black & white photographs
ISBN: 0 905138 45 7
Price: £17.95

## RALLYCOURSE
### *1986-87*

The fifth edition of *Rallycourse* focuses on the atmosphere and action of a controversial season in World Championship rallying. The story unfolds through the lively reports of editor Mike Greasley, with over 100 dramatic colour photographs from the inimitable Reinhard Klein. A special feature on the Hong Kong– Beijing rally, full results, maps, stage times and much more, make this annual an essential record of the rallying year.

110 colour and 40 black & white photographs
ISBN: 0 905138 46 5
Price: £17.95

## THE AUTOCOURSE HISTORY OF THE GRAND PRIX CAR 1966-85

### *by Doug Nye*

This detailed, well-illustrated historical survey spans the era from the 350-horsepower tube-framed cars to the nearly 800-horsepower turbocharged carbon-composite cars of 1985. Follow the fortunes of the great teams and the not-so-great as Doug Nye reveals the inside technical story of the cars and human story of the men who devised, designed and developed them.

This major production is essential reading for all Formula 1 enthusiasts and an important collector's item.

50 colour and 130 black & white photographs plus 60 line drawings and unique factory blueprints

ISBN: 0 905138 37 6
Price: £19.95

**Published by Hazleton Publishing, 3 Richmond Hill, Richmond, Surrey TW10 6RE.**
**Distributed by Osprey Publishing Ltd and available through your local or specialist bookshop.**

# CBR 1000F

*coefficient of drag: zero point zero, zero one eight*

# FOLLOW THAT ◄

HONDA
**CBR**
NOTHING COMES NEAR

# SPECIFICATIONS

**Eddie Lawson**
***498 cc YZR Yamaha***
**Engine:** 56 mm × 50.6 mm, water-cooled, four-cylinder two-stroke, crankcase reed-valve induction; five transfer and three exhaust ports; one plain piston ring; roller big ends and needle roller small ends; two pressed cranks, four roller bearings each; dry clutch with five friction and six steel plates; six springs. *Gearbox:* six-speed, alternative ratios for all gears; drum selection. *Carburettors:* 34 mm or 35 mm flat-slide Mikuni.
**Frame:** Yamaha twin-spar aluminium, taper roller head bearings; box-section aluminium swing arm, needle roller bearings; lower-end-linked rear suspension, one Öhlins unit, coil-spring plus nitrogen pressure; oil-damping, adjustable; Yamaha forks, coil-springs; oil-damped, adjustable. *Wheels:* Marvic, commonly used sizes 3.5 in. × 17 in. front and 5.5 in. × 17 in. rear. *Tyres:* Michelin. *Brakes:* two Brembo steel discs front and one Yamaha rear; 320 mm front and 220 mm rear; Brembo aluminium calipers front, Nissin rear, Brembo and Nissin pads. *Plugs:* NGK. *Gearbox and engine oil:* Castrol.

**Raymond Roche**
***499 cc NS500 Honda***
**Engine:** 62.6 mm × 54 mm, water-cooled, three-cylinder two-stroke, reed-valve induction; five transfer and one bridged exhaust port and mechanically controlled variable-volume exhaust pipes; one plain piston ring; roller big ends and needle roller small ends; one pressed crank, one ball and three roller bearings each; dry clutch with seven friction and seven steel plates; six springs. *Gearbox:* six-speed, six possible ratios for first and sixth gears, seven for second, nine for third and fourth, and eight for fifth; drum selection. *Carburettors:* 36 mm cylindrical-slide Keihin.
**Frame:** Honda twin-spar rectangular-section aluminium tube, taper roller head bearings; box-section aluminium swing arm, needle roller bearings; Pro-Link rear suspension, one Showa unit, coil-spring plus nitrogen pressure; oil-damping, adjustable; Showa forks, coil-springs, oil-damped, adjustable; mechanical-hydraulic anti-dive. *Wheels:* Comstar aluminium, commonly used sizes 3.5 in. × 17 in. front and 5.5 in. × 17 in. rear. *Tyres:* Michelin. *Brakes:* two Honda steel discs front and one Honda carbon-fibre rear; 305 mm front and 215 mm rear; Nissin calipers, Nissin pads. *Plugs:* NGK. *Gearbox and engine oil:* Total.

**Wayne Gardner**
***494.6 cc NSR500***
**Engine:** 54 mm × 54 mm, water-cooled, four-cylinder two-stroke, crankcase reed-valve induction; five transfer ports and mechanically controlled variable-volume exhaust; one piston ring; needle roller big ends and small ends; single pressed crank, five roller bearings; dry clutch with seven friction and seven steel plates; six springs. *Gearbox:* six-speed, alternative ratios for all gears; drum selection. *Carburettors:* 34 mm cylindrical-slide Keihin.
**Frame:** Honda twin-spar box-section aluminium, taper roller head bearings; triangulated aluminium swing arm, needle roller bearings; 'Pro-Link' rear suspension, one Showa unit, coil-spring plus nitrogen pressure; adjustable damping; Showa forks, coil-springs; oil-damped, adjustable; mechanical-hydraulic anti-dive. *Wheels:* Honda cast-magnesium, commonly used sizes 3.5 in. × 17 in. front and 5.5 in. × 17 in. rear. *Tyres:* Michelin. *Brakes:* two Honda steel discs front and one Honda carbon-fibre rear; 320 mm front and 190 mm rear; Nissin calipers, Nissin pads. *Plugs:* NGK 9.5. *Gearbox and engine oil:* Shell.

**The bare Yamaha YZR 500 aluminium twin-spar frame with the swing arm leaning up against the bench.**

### Niall MacKenzie
**498 cc XR70 Suzuki**

**Engine:** 56 mm × 50.6 mm, water-cooled, four-cylinder two-stroke, crankcase reed-valve induction; seven transfer and one exhaust port; one plain piston ring; needle roller big ends and small ends; two pressed cranks, two ball and two needle roller bearings each; dry clutch with eight friction and eight steel plates; five springs. *Gearbox:* six-speed, six possible ratios for first four gears and five for fifth and sixth; drum selection. *Carburettors:* 36 mm or 38 mm cylindrical-slide Mikuni.

**Frame:** Heron carbon-fibre and aluminium composite box, taper roller head bearings in adjustable angle inserts; composite swing arm, needle roller and shims; adjustable rocker arm rear suspension, one White Power unit, coil-spring; oil-damping, adjustable; White Power forks, coil-springs; oil-damped, not externally adjustable. *Wheels:* Marvic, commonly used sizes 3.5 in. × 17 in. front and 5.5 in. × 17 in. rear. *Tyres:* Michelin. *Brakes:* two cast-iron Lockheed discs front and one carbon-fibre rear; 310 mm front and 210 mm rear; Lockheed aluminium calipers, Ferodo pads. *Plugs:* ND. *Gearbox and engine oil:* Shell.

*Top:* **Christian Sarron's YZR 500 receiving attention. The ignition-generating system is mounted on the left-hand end of the lower crankshaft but the triggers are on the left end of the upper crank, hidden in this picture by the radiator hose. The hose sweeps round the top of the ignition and down to the water pump.**

**The two main photographs show the great similarity between the YZR 500 Yamaha engine** (centre) **and the new XR71 Suzuki** (bottom) **that will be used next season. The clutch actuation system is obviously different, but more importantly the primary drive on the Yamaha is laid out so that the two cranks are geared together and the clutch runs off a smaller gear in the middle of the lower crank. With the Suzuki, both cranks drive the back of the clutch directly and this means that the Suzuki cranks turn in the same direction while the Yamaha's turn in opposite directions.**

The Chevallier team continued to do what they could with the three-cylinder Honda engine but the tubular steel frame seemed to have reached the limit of its strength and rigidity when ranged against the composite or twin-spar aluminium designs *(top)*.

Chevallier tried to examine suspension performance by running a steel tape from the end of the swing arm to a sensor mounted on the seat. Movement of both the front and rear suspension was recorded in this way but results were inconclusive. In this picture the sensor is mounted on the standard RS500 chassis *(above)*.

The Cagiva uses a similar V-four layout to the 500 Yamaha but is not as compact. One problem is that the DellOrto carbs are much bigger than the Mikunis, hence Cagiva cannot get the carbs mounted as close to the cranks as they should; this does not help the power output *(right)*.

The elegant simplicity of the Honda NSR250 twin-spar aluminium frame. The plastic rear wheel fairing is still in place (it is intended to cut down wind resistance rather than act as a mudguard).

### Sito Pons
#### 247.3 cc RS250R-W Honda
**Engine:** 54 mm × 54 mm, water-cooled, twin-cylinder two-stroke, reed-valve crankcase induction; mechanically controlled variable-volume system; one plain piston ring; needle roller big ends and small ends; one pressed crank, three ball bearings; dry clutch; five springs. *Gearbox:* six-speed, alternative ratios for all gears; drum selection. *Carburettors:* two 38 mm cylindrical-slide Keihin.

**Frame:** twin extruded aluminium spars with machined sections in addition, caged ball head bearings; box-section aluminium swing arm, needle roller bearings; Pro-Link rear suspension, one Showa unit, coil-spring; oil-damping, adjustable; Showa forks, coil-springs; oil-damped, adjustable. *Wheels:* Honda cast magnesium, commonly used sizes 3.5 in. × 16 in. front and 4.5 in. × 17 in. rear. *Tyres:* Michelin. *Brakes:* two Nissin steel discs front and one Nissin steel rear; 270 mm front and 190 mm rear; Nissin aluminium calipers. Nissin pads. *Plugs:* NGK 9.5. *Gearbox and engine oil:* Campsa.

### Donnie McLeod
#### 247.3 cc Silverstone Armstrong
**Engine:** 54 mm × 54 mm water-cooled, twin-cylinder two-stroke, disc-valve induction; five transfer and three exhaust ports; one plain piston ring; needle roller big ends and small ends; two pressed cranks, three ball bearings each; dry clutch with six friction and six steel plates; six springs. *Gearbox:* six-speed, two possible ratios for first two gears; drum selection. *Carburettors:* 37.2 mm cylindrical-slide DellOrto.

**Frame:** Armstrong twin-spar carbon-fibre composite, taper roller head bearings; carbon-fibre composite box-section swing arm, needle roller bearings; tension rear suspension, one Armstrong unit, coil-spring; oil-damping, adjustable; Forcia Italia forks, coil-springs; oil-damped, adjustable. *Wheels:* Marvic and Dymag, commonly used sizes 2.75 in. × 17 in. front and 3.0 in. × 18 in. rear. *Tyres:* Dunlop. *Brakes:* two Spondon cast-iron discs front and one Zanzani aluminium rear; 260 mm front and 220 mm rear; Brembo aluminium calipers, Brembo pads. *Plugs:* Champion N82. *Gearbox and engine oil:* Shell.

### Martin Wimmer
#### 249 cc Yamaha
**Engine:** 56 mm × 50.6 mm, water-cooled, twin-cylinder two-stroke, crankcase reed-valve induction; five transfer and three exhaust ports; one plain piston ring; roller big ends and needle roller small ends; two pressed cranks, two roller bearings each; dry clutch with five friction and six steel plates; six springs. *Gearbox:* six-speed, alternative ratios for all gears; drum selection. *Carburettors:* 34 mm flat-slide Mikuni.

**Frame:** Yamaha twin-spar aluminium, taper roller head bearings; box-section aluminium swing arm, needle roller bearings; lower-end-linked rear suspension, one Öhlins unit, coil-spring plus nitrogen pressure; oil-damping, adjustable; Yamaha forks, coil-springs; oil-damped, adjustable. *Wheels:* Marvic, commonly used sizes 3.5 in. × 16 in. front and 4.5 in. × 17 in. rear. *Tyres:* Michelin. *Brakes:* two Brembo steel discs front and one Yamaha rear; 320 mm front and 220 mm rear; Brembo aluminium calipers front, Nissin rear, Brembo and Nissin pads. *Plugs:* NGK. *Gearbox and engine oil:* Castrol.

*Below:* The V-twin 250 Garelli started to go well towards the end of the season and Jan Theil wanted to devote all his time to it but so long as his 125 continues to win championships the company will want to carry on using it. In this photo the 250 has had its rear subframe removed. The rear suspension is hidden by the back end of the monocoque. The unit is mounted vertically and connected to the swing arm through a Pro-Link-style linkage at its lower end.

## Alan Carter
### 249.6 cc Cobas

**Engine:** 54 mm × 54.5 mm, water-cooled, twin-cylinder two-stroke; five transfer and one exhaust port, vacuum-operated exhaust valve; one plain piston ring; needle roller big ends and small ends; two pressed cranks, two roller bearings; dry clutch with five friction and six steel plates; six springs. *Gearbox:* six-speed, four possible ratios for first and second gears; drum selection. *Carburettors:* 38 mm cylindrical-slide DellOrto.
**Frame:** Cobas, triangulated straight chrome moly tube, taper roller head bearings; chrome moly swing arm, roller bearings; rocker arm rear suspension, one White Power unit, coil-spring; oil-damping, adjustable for both compression and rebound; White Power forks, coil-springs; oil-damped, non-adjustable. *Wheels:* Marvic, commonly used sizes 3.5 in. × 16 in. front and 4.5 in. × 17 in. rear. *Tyres:* Michelin. *Brakes:* one Brembo cast-steel disc front and one Zanzani aluminium rear; 280 mm front and 200 mm rear; Brembo aluminium calipers, Brembo pads. *Plugs:* Champion 82 or 84. *Gearbox oil and engine oil:* Castrol.

Jorg Müller continued to look after his baby, the disc-valve Parisienne, but though promising it never quite came up with the results that might have been expected of it. It hurt that Jacques Cornu often beat the machine with his production RS 250 Honda. Müller blamed rider Pierre Bolle and Bolle blamed the machine.

Louise Christen had been asked to produce a monocoque frame for the Parisienne, employing a scaled-up version of the design that August Auinger was using to such great effect in the 125 class. Unfortunately the rearward-facing exhaust made life difficult and the frame was never built.

Fausto Gresini's 125 Garelli, winner of so many World titles. The engine brought Nieto three championships and it won as a Minarelli before that. This season it added another title and it may well remain undefeated until the rules change to single-cylinder at the end of '87.

### Pier Paolo Bianchi
*124.7 cc MBA Elit*

**Engine:** 44 mm × 41 mm, water-cooled, twin-cylinder two-stroke, disc-valve induction; six transfer and three exhaust ports; one plain piston ring; needle roller big ends and small ends; one pressed crank, four ball bearings; dry clutch with seven friction and seven steel plates; five springs. *Gearbox:* six-speed, four possible ratios for each gear; drum selection. *Carburettors:* 29 mm cylindrical-slide Mikuni.

**Frame:** MBA twin-loop, chrome moly, taper roller head bearings; aluminium box-section triangulated swing arm, plain bearings; cantilever rear suspension, one Marzocchi unit, coil-spring; oil-damping, adjustable for compression and rebound; Marzocchi forks, coil-springs; oil-damped, adjustable for both compression and rebound. *Wheels:* Marvic, commonly used widths 2.0 in. front and 2.25 in. rear. *Tyres:* Dunlop. *Brakes:* two Zanzani aluminium discs front and one Zanzani aluminium rear; 230 mm front and 200 mm rear; Brembo aluminium calipers, Brembo pads. *Plugs:* Champion. *Gearbox and engine oil:* Castrol.

### Fausto Gresini
*124.7 cc Garelli*

**Engine:** 44 mm × 41 mm, water-cooled, twin-cylinder two-stroke, disc-valve induction; six transfer and one exhaust port; one plain piston ring; needle roller big ends and small ends; one pressed crank, four ball bearings; dry clutch with seven friction and seven steel plates; five springs. *Gearbox:* six-speed, three possible ratios for each gear; drum selection. *Carburettors:* 29 mm cylindrical-slide DellOrto.

**Frame:** Sheet aluminium monocoque, taper roller head bearings; aluminium box-section swing arm, taper roller bearings; twin-shock rear suspension, two White Power units, coil-springs; oil-damping, adjustable; Ceriani forks, coil-springs; oil-damped, adjustable. *Wheels:* Campagnolo, commonly used sizes 1.85 in. × 18 in. front and 2.5 in. × 18 in. rear. *Tyres:* Michelin. *Brakes:* two Zanzani aluminium discs front and one Zanzani aluminium rear; 220 mm front and rear; Brembo aluminium calipers. Brembo pads. *Plugs:* Champion. *Gearbox and engine oil:* Total.

### Domenica Brigaglia
*124.7 cc Ducados*

**Engine:** 44 mm × 41 mm, water-cooled, twin-cylinder two-stroke, disc-valve induction; eight transfer and three exhaust ports; one plain piston ring; needle roller big ends and small ends; one pressed crank, four ball bearings; dry clutch with seven friction and seven steel plates; six springs. *Gearbox:* six-speed, three possible ratios for first and third gears, five for second and fifth, and four for fourth and sixth; drum selection. *Carburettors:* 29 mm cylindrical-slide DellOrto.

**Frame:** twin-loop chrome moly tubing, taper roller head bearings; aluminium triangulated box-section swing arm, needle roller bearings; cantilever rear suspension, one Zaccaria unit, coil-spring; oil-damping, adjustable; Forcia Italia forks, coil-springs; oil-damped, adjustable. *Wheels:* Technomagnesio, commonly used sizes 1.85 in. × 18 in. front and 2.15 in. × 18 in. rear. *Tyres:* Michelin. *Brakes:* one Disacciati cast-steel disc front and one aluminium rear; 260 mm front and 200 mm rear; Brembo aluminium calipers, Ferodo pads front, Brembo rear. *Plugs:* Champion. *Gearbox and engine oil:* Castrol.

## August Auinger
### 124.7 cc Bartol MBA

**Engine:** 44 mm × 41 mm, water-cooled, twin-cylinder two-stroke, disc-valve induction; eight transfer and three exhaust ports; one plain piston ring; needle roller big ends and small ends; one pressed crank, two ball and two roller bearings; dry clutch with six friction and six steel plates; six springs. *Gearbox:* six-speed, two possible ratios for first three gears; drum selection. *Carburettors:* 31 mm flat-slide Mikuni.
**Frame:** sheet aluminium monocoque, taper roller head bearings; triangulated chrome moly swing arm, taper roller bearings; cantilever rear suspension, one Öhlins unit, coil-spring; oil-damping, adjustable; Forcia Italia or White Power forks, coil-springs; oil-damped, adjustable. *Wheels:* Marvic, commonly used sizes 2.0 in. × 18 in. front and 2.5 in. × 18 in. rear. *Tyres:* Dunlop. *Brakes:* one Brembo cast-steel disc front and one Bartol carbon-fibre rear; 280 mm front and 200 mm rear; Brembo aluminium calipers, Ferodo and Bartol pads. *Plugs:* Champion. *Gearbox and engine oil:* Castrol.

August Auinger's Bartol MBA was cared for by Dave Johnson. This photograph was taken at the Nürburgring where the Forcia Italia forks were used, but later in the season Auinger used White Power forks at Assen, Silverstone and Anderstorp.

Ceriani produced this experimental front fork as their answer to the White Power and Öhlins upside-down front suspension systems. The Italian design is very different in that it has a single external spring and damper system. The design is more rigid because the left and right sides are joined by the wishbone (left).

The generous proportions of the Krauser frame are in contrast to the rest of the machine and explain its good handling. The engine is tiny and the electric water pump sits below it in the bottom of the fairing. The exhaust pipe, which has been removed here, normally runs between pump and engine.

### Stefan Dörflinger
**79.6 cc Krauser**

**Engine:** 49 mm × 42.5 mm, water-cooled, single-cylinder two-stroke, disc-valve induction; six transfer and three exhaust ports; one plain piston ring; needle roller big end and small end; pressed cranks, one ball and one roller bearing; dry clutch with five friction and six steel plates; six springs. *Gearbox:* six-speed, three or four possible ratios for each gear; drum selection. *Carburettors:* 34 mm cylindrical-slide Bing.

**Frame:** LCR sheet aluminium monocoque, taper roller head bearings; chrome moly box-section swing arm, plain bearings; cantilever rear suspension, one White Power unit, air-spring; oil-damping, adjustable; Ceriani forks, coil-springs; oil-damped, adjustable. *Wheels:* Campagnolo, commonly used sizes 1.85 in × 16 in. front and 1.85 × 16 in. rear. *Tyres:* Michelin. *Brakes:* one Zanzani aluminium disc front and one Zanzani aluminium at rear; 220 mm front and 180 mm rear; Mozzi Motor aluminium calipers, Mozzi Motor pads. *Plugs:* Champion. *Gearbox and engine oil:* Shell.

### Jorge Martinez
**79.6 cc Derbi**

**Engine:** 48 mm × 44 mm water-cooled, single-cylinder two-stroke, disc-valve induction; four transfer and one exhaust port; one plain piston ring; needle roller big end and small end; pressed crank, two ball bearings each; dry clutch with four friction and five steel plates; four springs. *Gearbox:* six-speed, four possible ratios for first and sixth gears; drum selection. *Carburettors:* 34 mm cylindrical-slide DellOrto.

**Frame:** Derbi chrome moly four main tube triangulated spine, taper roller head bearings; chrome moly box-section swing arm, needle roller bearings; con rod and rocker arm rear suspension, one White Power unit, coil-springs; oil-damping, adjustable; White Power forks, coil-springs; oil-damped, non-adjustable. *Wheels:* Marvic, commonly used sizes 1.85 in. × 16 in. front and 1.85 in. × 18 in. rear. *Tyres:* Michelin. *Brakes:* two Zanzani aluminium discs front and one Zanzani aluminium rear; 220 mm front and 200 mm rear; Brembo aluminium calipers, Brembo pads. *Plugs:* Champion. *Gearbox and engine oil:* Motul.

### Pier Paolo Bianchi
**79.8 cc Seel**

**Engine:** 46.5 mm × 47 mm, water-cooled, single-cylinder two-stroke, disc-valve induction, six transfer and one exhaust port; one plain piston ring; needle roller big end and small end; one pressed crank, one ball and one roller bearing; dry clutch with four friction and five steel plates; eight springs. *Gearbox:* six-speed, three possible ratios for first and second gears; drum selection. *Carburettors:* 32 mm cylindrical-slide Mikuni.

**Frame:** sheet aluminium twin spine, taper roller head bearings; triangulated aluminium box-section swing arm, ball bearings; single-shock rear suspension, one White Power unit, coil-spring; oil damping, adjustable; Marzocchi forks, coil-springs; oil-damped, adjustable; mechanical anti-dive. *Wheels:* PVM, commonly used sizes 1.6 in. × 18 in. front, 1.85 in. × 18 in. rear. *Tyres:* Michelin. *Brakes:* one Zanzani aluminium disc front and one Zanzani aluminium rear; 260 mm front and 220 mm rear; Brembo aluminium calipers, Brembo pads. *Plugs:* Champion. *Gearbox and engine oil:* Castrol.

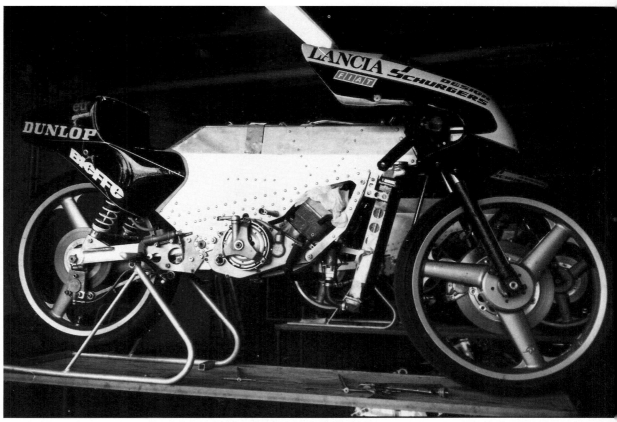

*Above:* the Huvo Casal, as ridden by Hans Spaan and Theo Timmer. It has never quite been able to match the Krauser and Derbi but is very close; another winter of development could see a three-way battle for the championship.

The single-cylinder Derbi *(left)* is as simple as the Krauser and also uses an electric water pump.

Like the other 80 cc machines the Seel uses a single disc valve, this time on the right-hand side of the engine *(below left)*.

### Hans Spaan
#### 79.6 cc Casal

**Engine:** 48 mm × 44 mm, water-cooled, single-cylinder two-stroke, disc-valve induction; eight transfer and three exhaust ports including central bridged port; one plain piston ring; needle roller big ends and small ends; one pressed crank, two ball bearings; dry clutch with four friction and five steel plates; five springs. *Gearbox:* six-speed, two possible ratios for all six gears; drum selection. *Carburettors:* 32 mm cylindrical-slide DellOrto.
**Frame:** Timmer, aluminium monocoque, taper roller head bearings; box-section aluminium swing arm, needle roller bearings; twin-shock rear suspension, two White Power units, coil-spring; oil-damping, adjustable; Marzocchi forks, coil-springs; oil-damped, non-adjustable. *Wheels:* Campagnolo, commonly used sizes 1.85 in. × 16 in. front and 1.85 in. × 18 in. rear. *Tyres:* Dunlop. *Brakes:* one Zanzani aluminium disc front and one Zanzani aluminium rear; 260 mm front and 200 mm rear; Brembo aluminium calipers, Brembo pads. *Plugs:* Champion. *Gearbox and engine oil:* Shell.

The 500 cc Krauser engine uses crankcase reed-valve induction and, while it showed promise, fuel starvation problems ruined Biland's season (above).

The front suspension system on Rolf Biland's LRC outfit (above right).

Kumano's much-modified Yamaha engine uses Muggen motocross cylinders normally fitted to the Honda 125 cc single.

Nick Webster looked after his son's LCR Yamaha expertly throughout the season (far right).

### Alain Michel
**498 cc LCR Yamaha**

**Engine:** 56 mm × 50.6 mm, water-cooled, four-cylinder two-stroke, piston-ported induction; six transfer and three exhaust ports; single plain piston ring; roller big ends and needle roller small ends; four pressed cranks, two needle roller bearings each; dry clutch with seven friction and seven steel plates; six springs. *Gearbox:* six-speed, six possible ratios for first gear, three for second and sixth, four for third, and two for fourth; drum selection. *Carburettors:* 36 mm cylindrical-slide DellOrto.
**Chassis:** LCR sheet aluminium monocoque, riveted and Araldited, adjustable; wishbone rear suspension, one Koni unit, coil-spring; oil-damping, adjustable; parallelogram front suspension, one Koni or one Bilstein unit, coil-spring; oil-damping, adjustable; no sidecar suspension. *Wheels:* Gotti, 13 in. diameter, commonly used sizes 9 in. front, 11 in. or 12 in. rear, 10 in. sidecar. *Tyres:* Yokohama. *Brakes:* cast-iron all round, ventilated 254 mm front, 240 mm rear and side; Lockheed calipers, Mintex pads. *Plugs:* Champion N82. *Gearbox and engine oil:* Elf.

### Steve Webster
**498 cc LCR Yamaha**

**Engine:** 56 mm × 50.6 mm, water-cooled, four-cylinder two-stroke, piston-ported induction; six transfer and three exhaust ports; single plain piston ring; roller big ends and needle roller small ends; two pressed cranks, four needle roller bearings each; dry clutch with seven friction and seven steel plates; six springs. *Gearbox:* six-speed, six possible ratios for bottom gear, three for second and sixth, four for third, and two for fourth; drum selection. *Carburettors:* 38 mm cylindrical-slide Mikuni.
**Chassis:** LCR, sheet aluminium monocoque, riveted and Araldited; wishbone rear suspension, one Koni unit, coil-spring; oil-damping, adjustable; parallelogram front suspension, one Koni unit, coil-spring; oil-damping, adjustable; no sidecar suspension. *Wheels:* Ronal, 13 in. diameter, commonly used widths 8.2 in. front, 10 in. rear, 9 in. sidecar. *Tyres:* Avon. *Brakes:* cast-iron all round; ventilated 254 mm front, 240 mm rear and side; Lockheed calipers, Ferodo pads. *Plugs:* Champion N82. *Gearbox and engine oil:* Silkolene.

### Rolf Biland
**498 cc Krauser**

**Engine:** 56 mm × 50.6 mm, water-cooled, four-cylinder two-stroke, crankcase reed-valve induction; eight transfer and three exhaust ports; single plain piston ring; roller big ends and needle roller small ends; four pressed cranks, two needle roller bearings each; dry clutch with seven friction and seven steel plates; six springs. *Gearbox:* six-speed, three possible ratios for first three gears; drum selection. *Carburettors:* 36 mm cylindrical-slide DellOrto.
**Chassis:** LCR sheet aluminium monocoque, riveted and Araldited, adjustable; wishbone rear suspension, one White Power unit, coil-spring; oil-damping, adjustable; parallelogram front suspension, one White Power unit, coil-spring; oil-damping, adjustable; no sidecar suspension. *Wheels:* BBS, 13 in. diameter, commonly used widths 9 in. front, 11 in. or 12 in. rear, 10 in. sidecar. *Tyres:* Yokohama. *Brakes:* cast-iron all round, ventilated 254 mm front, 240 mm rear and side; Lockheed calipers, Mintex pads. *Plugs:* NGK B10EGV. *Gearbox and engine oil:* Wintershall.

### Egbert Streuer
**498 cc LCR Yamaha**

**Engine:** 56 mm × 50.6 mm, water-cooled, four-cylinder two-stroke, piston-ported induction; six transfer and three exhaust ports; single plain piston ring; roller big ends and needle roller small ends; two pressed cranks, four needle roller bearings each; dry clutch with seven friction and seven steel plates; six springs. *Gearbox:* six-speed, three possible ratios for first three gears; drum selection. *Carburettors:* 38 mm cylindrical-slide Mikuni.
**Chassis:** LCR sheet aluminium monocoque, riveted and Araldited, adjustable; wishbone rear suspension, one Koni unit, coil-spring; oil-damping, adjustable; parallelogram front suspension, one Koni or Bilstein unit, coil-spring; oil-damping, adjustable; no sidecar suspension. *Wheels:* Ronal, 13 in. diameter, commonly used widths 9 in. front, 10 in. rear and sidecar. *Tyres:* Yokohama. *Brakes:* cast-iron all round, ventilated 254 mm front, 240 mm rear and side; Lockheed calipers, Tormos pads. *Plugs:* Champion N84. *Gearbox and engine oil:* Bel Ray.

**Gérard Coudray, Patrick Igoa, Alex Vieira**
_748 cc Honda RVF750_
**Engine:** 70 mm × 48.6 mm, water-cooled four-stroke V4 based on VF750; gear-driven dohc operating four valves per cylinder. _Maximum power:_ 130 bhp at 12,000 rpm (12,500 rpm limit for short races, 12,000 rpm for 24-hour races). _Carburettors:_ 34 mm CV Keihin. _Ignition:_ self-generating CDI. _Clutch:_ wet multi-plate. _Gearbox:_ five-speed.
**Frame:** Fabricated aluminium box-section using engine as stressed member; bolt-on aluminium rear subframe; fabricated aluminium one-sided swing arm with inboard disc and dished wheel; Pro-Link rising-rate rear suspension; Showa unit adjustable for spring pre-load and rebound and compression damping; Showa 41 mm telescopic front fork with spring pre-load and rebound damping adjustment. _Wheels:_ HRC 17 in. × 3.5 in. front, 17 in. × 5.5 in. rear. _Brakes:_ twin semi-floating front discs with four-piston calipers; single rear disc with twin-piston caliper. _Tyres:_ Michelin radials. _Plugs:_ NGK. _Oil:_ Honda. _Weight:_ 166 kg.

**Hervé Moineau, Bruno le Bihan, Eric Delcamp**
_749 cc Suzuki GSX-R750_
**Engine:** 70 mm × 48.7 mm, oil-cooled transverse four-cylinder four-stroke based on GSX-R750; chain-drive dohc operating four valves per cylinder. _Maximum power:_ 132 bhp at 12,000 rpm. _Carburettors:_ 34 mm flat-slide Mikuni. _Compression ratio:_ 12:1. _Ignition:_ Suzuki battery-powered CDI. _Clutch:_ dry multi-plate. _Gearbox:_ six-speed.
**Frame:** aluminium box-section double cradle with bolt-on rear subframe; aluminium rear swing arm; full-floater rising-rate rear suspension; Showa unit adjustable for spring pre-load and rebound and compression damping; Showa 40 mm front fork with adjustable pre-load and rebound damping. _Wheels:_ Campagnolo 17 in. × 3.5 in. front, 17 in. × 5.5 in. rear. _Brakes:_ twin floating front discs with twin-piston Lockheed calipers; one floating rear disc with Suzuki twin-piston caliper. _Tyres:_ Michelin radials. _Plugs:_ NGK. _Oil:_ Ipone. _Weight:_ 156 kg.

The Hondas were dishearteningly reliable and efficient (_above_).

So near and yet so far. The Suzuki was _almost_ a match for the Honda yet somehow never had a real chance of winning the championship (_top_).

**Mat Oxley, Vesa Kultalahti, Geoff Fowler**
*749 cc Harris Yamaha*
**Engine:** 68 mm × 51.6 mm, water-cooled transverse four-cylinder four-stroke based on FZ750; chain-driven dohc operating five valves per cylinder. *Maximum power:* 105 bhp at 10,500 rpm. *Carburettors:* 36 mm CV Mikuni. *Compression ratio:* 11.5:1. *Ignition:* Yamaha CDI. *Clutch:* wet or dry multi-plate. *Gearbox:* six-speed.
**Frame:** fabricated Harris aluminium beam-section frame; bolt-on steel rear subframe; rising-rate rear suspension; Öhlins unit with adjustable pre-load and rebound and compression damping; White Power upside-down telescopic fork. *Wheels:* Dymag 17 in. × 3.5 in. front, 18 in. × 5.5 in. rear. *Brakes:* twin semi-floating front discs with four-piston Lockheed calipers; single rear disc with Brembo twin-piston caliper. *Tyres:* Michelin cross-plies or radials. *Plugs:* NGK. *Oil:* Castrol. *Weight:* 185 kg.

**Christian Sarron, Richard Hubin, Pierre-Etienne Samin/Jacques Cornu**
*749 cc Yamaha FZR750 Genesis*
**Engine:** 68 mm × 51.6 mm, water-cooled transverse four-cylinder four-stroke based on FZ750; chain-driven dohc operating five valves per cylinder. *Maximum power:* 145 bhp at 12,000 rpm. *Carburettors:* 36 mm or 37 mm downdraught Mikuni. *Compression ratio:* 12.3:1 for 24-hour races, 12.8:1 for short races. *Ignition:* Yamaha CDI. *Clutch:* dry multi-plate. *Gearbox:* six-speed.
**Frame:** fabricated aluminium beam-section; bolt-on rear subframe; fabricated aluminium swing arm; rising-rate rear suspension; Öhlins unit adjustable for spring pre-load and rebound and compression damping; 41 mm front fork with adjustable pre-load and compression damping. *Wheels:* Marvic 17 in. × 3.5 in. front, 17 in. × 5.5 in. rear. *Brakes:* twin floating front discs with four-piston calipers; one floating rear disc with twin-piston caliper. *Tyres:* Michelin radial. *Plugs:* NGK. *Oil:* Motul. *Weight:* 166 kg.

The works Yamaha Genesis incorporated a twin-spar aluminium frame and water-cooled FZ750 engine. The carburettor bell-mouths show the near-vertical orientation of the throats *(top)*.

The Harris Yamaha – prettier than a cross-channel ferry and faster *(above)*.

## NEIL ROBINSON

When Neil Robinson was killed on the wooded park circuit at Scarborough in northern England the racing world lost perhaps its most popular character as well as a great rider. That might seem a strong statement as Robinson had yet to become as internationally famous as the Lawsons and Gardners, but in the sport he was well loved by all who met him. His infectious smile and easygoing nature meant you had to like him.

In 1983 he was British 250 Champion and the following year he scored points in the 125 cc World Championship, finishing 22nd at the end of a season which brought him a fine ninth in Holland on a rather slow MBA. A year previously his brother Donny had ended his very promising career in a frightening crash at the Salzburgring, resulting in a badly broken leg.

In '85 Neil tried his hand at riding a 500 but the private team had far too little money and most often he failed to finish. He did score two fine points in the pouring rain at Silverstone, following his recovery from a nasty fall on the first lap of the Italian GP at Misano which broke his ankle.

Robinson decided that there was little point in contesting the Grands Prix in '86 as he had no money to buy competitive machinery so he concentrated on riding a GSX-R 750 Suzuki, mainly in England. Halfway through the summer the Skoal Bandit team did what they should have done at the beginning of the year and signed him to ride their works bikes in the TT Formula 1 World Championship.

In his first ride, the Dutch round at Assen, Robinson was heading for a great win over World Champion Joey Dunlop when the chain broke. Robinson was not be be denied success, however, and he returned to his native Ireland for the Ulster Grand Prix, the most important event in that country's calendar. He won the Formula 1 race, beating Joey Dunlop on home ground.

It looked as though the end of the season was going to end on a high note for the Skoal Bandit team. The Grand Prix squad had found Niall MacKenzie to lead their 500 effort for 1987, while Robinson had the ability to take the F1 World Championship from Honda.

Then came the National meeting at Scarborough and although Robinson had never ridden there before he went with the Suzuki team. Honda have refused to race at this venue for several years because they consider it too dangerous and their riders miss out on the championship points. The circuit is narrow, bumpy and lined with trees.

Keith Huewen was following Robinson when he crashed on his sixth practice lap. According to Huewen, Robinson was riding fast but well in control when suddenly he saw the back wheel slide away. Robinson was thrown off the machine and his head hit the road very hard. He died later in hospital. His accident threw a pall of sadness over the meeting. One of his great rivals, Kenny Irons, won the Superstock race then announced that he would never race there again. His death was a terrible waste and occurred on a circuit that should not be used for any championship races, if at all.

Peter Clifford

# RIDERS' CIRCUIT REPORT

**Criteria have remained unchanged from 1985. However, only 11 Grands Prix have been included; the last event at Hockenheim is not considered a full GP as it lacks the 250 cc and 500 cc classes.**

| | Possible score | SPAIN Jarama | ITALY Monza | WEST GERMANY Nürburgring | AUSTRIA Salzburgring | YUGOSLAVIA Rijeka | NETHERLANDS Assen | BELGIUM Spa | FRANCE Paul Ricard | GREAT BRITAIN Silverstone | SWEDEN Anderstorp | SAN MARINO Misano |
|---|---|---|---|---|---|---|---|---|---|---|---|---|
| **1. Safety** | | | | | | | | | | | | |
| a) Natural safety of circuit | 20 | 16 | 13 | 19 | 8 | 16 | 17 | 5 | 12 | 10 | 13 | 18 |
| b) Temporary safety provisions | 20 | 18 | 12 | 19 | 16 | 12 | 16 | 18 | 2 | 19 | 17 | 18 |
| c) Clerk of Course | 10 | 7 | 7 | 10 | 9 | 2 | 8 | 8 | 9 | 9 | 8 | 10 |
| d) Marshals | 10 | 5 | 9 | 6 | 8 | 3 | 7 | 7 | 8 | 9 | 5 | 10 |
| e) First aid | 10 | 5 | 6 | 8 | 9 | 5 | 8 | 5 | 8 | 9 | 6 | 8 |
| **Total** | 70 | 51 | 47 | 62 | 52 | 38 | 56 | 43 | 39 | 56 | 49 | 64 |
| **2. Facilities** | | | | | | | | | | | | |
| a) Paddock size | 10 | 2 | 1 | 9 | 6 | 5 | 10 | 9 | 8 | 10 | 3 | 8 |
| b) Paddock amenities | 10 | 6 | 2 | 9 | 5 | 6 | 6 | 6 | 6 | 9 | 7 | 2 |
| c) Sanitary arrangements | 10 | 6 | 0 | 8 | 5 | 8 | 9 | 3 | 3 | 9 | 8 | 0 |
| d) Paddock security | 10 | 7 | 0 | 10 | 0 | 9 | 9 | 1 | 3 | 6 | 4 | 0 |
| e) General working conditions | 10 | 7 | 1 | 9 | 5 | 8 | 8 | 5 | 4 | 8 | 4 | 1 |
| **Total** | 50 | 28 | 4 | 45 | 21 | 36 | 42 | 23 | 24 | 42 | 26 | 11 |
| **3. Organisers' co-operation** | | | | | | | | | | | | |
| a) Circuit owners | 10 | 8 | 5 | 10 | 8 | 8 | 9 | 3 | 4 | 9 | 9 | 5 |
| b) Promoters | 5 | 4 | 1 | 5 | 4 | 4 | 5 | 4 | 4 | 3 | 5 | 5 |
| c) Organisers | 5 | 5 | 3 | 5 | 4 | 5 | 5 | 5 | 4 | 3 | 5 | 5 |
| **Total** | 20 | 17 | 9 | 20 | 16 | 17 | 19 | 12 | 12 | 15 | 19 | 15 |
| **4. Spectator facilities** | | | | | | | | | | | | |
| a) Viewing | 10 | 8 | 5 | 6 | 10 | 9 | 7 | 9 | 6 | 5 | 6 | 5 |
| b) Facilities | 10 | 2 | 3 | 7 | 4 | 2 | 7 | 4 | 3 | 8 | 5 | 2 |
| **Total** | 20 | 10 | 8 | 13 | 14 | 11 | 14 | 13 | 9 | 13 | 11 | 7 |
| **5. Location and scheduling** | | | | | | | | | | | | |
| a) Circuit location, travel hassle | 10 | 2 | 7 | 7 | 7 | 5 | 7 | 7 | 7 | 5 | 3 | 7 |
| b) Practice timing, race schedule | 10 | 6 | 5 | 5 | 7 | 7 | 5 | 3 | 1 | 7 | 7 | 3 |
| **Total** | 20 | 8 | 12 | 12 | 14 | 12 | 12 | 10 | 8 | 12 | 10 | 10 |
| **6. Media** | | | | | | | | | | | | |
| a) Press facilities (photo/reporting) | 10 | 8 | 7 | 10 | 6 | 3 | 8 | 7 | 9 | 7 | 7 | 7 |
| b) TV coverage (quality and volume) | 10 | 8 | 9 | 8 | 8 | 7 | 8 | 1 | 8 | 9 | 1 | 8 |
| **Total** | 20 | 16 | 16 | 18 | 14 | 10 | 16 | 8 | 17 | 16 | 8 | 15 |
| **GRAND TOTAL** | 200 | 130 | 96 | 170 | 129 | 124 | 159 | 110 | 109 | 154 | 123 | 122 |
| **RANKING** | | 4th | 11th | 1st | 5th | 6th | 2nd | 9th | 10th | 3rd | 7th | 8th |
| 1985 Ranking | | 11th | 9th* | 1st† | 3rd | 8th | 4th | 10th | 12th‡ | 2nd | 6th | 5th |
| 1984 Ranking | | 12th | 6th** | 3rd | 4th | 10th | 2nd | 11th | 5th | 1st | 9th | 7th* |

*Mugello    ‡Le Mans
†Hockenheim    **Misano

**Compiled from views expressed by regular GP riders throughout the season.**

# COMMENTS ON CIRCUITS
## (*IN RANK ORDER*)

## 1
### WEST GERMANY
#### *NÜRBURGRING*

Without doubt this was the preferred GP of 1986. The organisation was superb and the co-operation received from the organisers was magnificent. This is all the more impressive because the improvement resulted from a change in policy and staff and was instigated as a direct response to criticism of the inaugural event. This is the highest score ever achieved in this survey and will be very hard to beat.

## 2
### THE NETHERLANDS
#### *ASSEN*

Assen has moved up the rankings primarily due to the new, surfaced paddock. There are still a few shortcomings in the facilities and track that need to be resolved before Assen can take the number 1 position in the survey.

## 3
### BRITAIN
#### *SILVERSTONE*

The British event completes the trio of countries that have traditionally dominated the results of this survey. Silverstone was once again plagued by bad weather and this highlighted the shortcomings of the circuit. Next year the British GP moves to Donington and it will be interesting to see if that circuit can maintain the high standards set by the Silverstone organisation.

## 4
### SPAIN
#### *JARAMA*

This is another example of an organiser who has transformed his attitude towards the competitors and now makes a real effort to accommodate their views in the way the meeting is run. Spain has gone from last to fourth place in the three years of this survey but work will have to be done on the paddock before it can climb any higher. This is another case where a new location for the 1987 event (at Jerez) will act as a spur to competition between circuits to improve their events.

## 5
### AUSTRIA
#### *SALZBURGRING*

Whilst significant improvements have been made to the safety of the track since last year the event has dropped down the rankings for two main reasons. Firstly, the organisers tried to cater for more classes and support races than the paddock or timetable could comfortably accommodate. Secondly, the organisers broke FIM rules and offended competitors by selling paddock tickets to the general public.

## 6
### YUGOSLAVIA
#### *RIJEKA*

This event moves up the rankings every year by sheer dogged determination. Despite a lack of funds, the organisers make some improvements to the facilities for each GP. This year a further section of the paddock was surfaced and the water supply was improved – fundamental matters when the paddock is also your home. Good co-operation with riders will keep this event popular but the Clerk of the Course and marshals prevent the event from moving up further.

## 7
### SWEDEN
#### *ANDERSTORP*

Whilst the organisers of this event make every effort to oblige the riders and to raise the standard of their facilities, it is difficult to believe that this event will survive for many more years. The lack of television coverage reduces the event's appeal to the main teams and the Swedish round of the championship cannot match the professionalism and glamour of most other GPs. Urgent work needs to be done on the circuit and the paddock to bring it up to GP standards.

## 8
### SAN MARINO
#### *MISANO*

This event stays off the bottom of the rankings because Misano is naturally a very safe circuit and because Giorgio Campana is an excellent Clerk of the Course with a well-trained team of marshals. However, although co-operation is received from the organisers, the facilities and the paddock conditions in general are prehistoric. Paddock security is non-existent and only the vigilance of the teams stops even greater losses from theft.

## 9
### BELGIUM
#### *SPA*

The very fast and potentially lethal corners at Spa are due to be modified to make them safe for the '87 event. This will enable Spa to move up the rankings on grounds of safety but the lack of security in the paddock and the absence of television coverage will drag the averages down.

## 10
### FRANCE
#### *PAUL RICARD*

The French organisers set themselves the task of running the motor cycle GP just 14 days after the Formula 1 car meeting . . . and failed. An attempt to co-operate with the riders at the last moment could not make up for inadequate planning, an absence of free practice, lack of security in the paddock, and a confusing and misunderstood pass system. Equally, the Ricard circuit can no longer consider itself one of the safest; times and standards have changed and much work must be done on permanent and temporary protection before this event can be more highly rated.

## 11
### ITALY
#### *MONZA*

Without doubt this was the worst Grand Prix of the year. The famous circuit, steeped in history, has been modified to provide a reasonable level of safety but the paddock facilities have been left behind. None of the criticisms of the last Monza GP were rectified and the organisers, on all aspects other than safety, proved completely unco-operative. The Italian GP is the only remaining event where teams find it impossible to get the right number of passes from the organisers so that all team staff can have access. This fact alone illustrates how far the organisation has to improve before the Italian meeting can approach the events that top this poll.

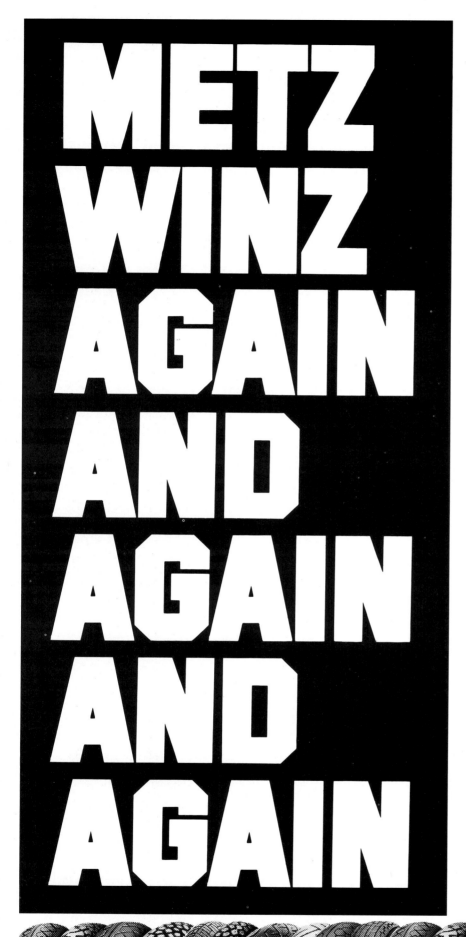

Over the past few years motorcycles fitted with Metzeler tyres have dominated the Production TT races. And this year is no exception, with more riders in the top six in each class than any other tyre manufacturer.

Obviously our competitors have been none too pleased at coming in behind us.

This year they tried even harder. But guess what? We won again and again and again ...

## PRODUCTION TT

| **CLASS A** 751cc 1300cc 4 stroke | **3rd** Brian Morrison **4th** Nick Jeffries **5th** Barry Woodland **6th** Helmut Dahne |
|---|---|
| **CLASS B** 401cc 500cc 2 stroke +601cc 750cc 4 stroke | **1st** Phil Mellor **2nd** Helmut Dahne **4th** Trevor Nation **6th** Andy McGladdery |
| **CLASS C** 250cc 400cc 2 stroke 401cc 600cc 4 stroke | **1st** Garry Padgett **2nd** Malcolm Wheeler **5th** Phil Nicholls |
| **CLASS D** 250cc 2 stroke 400cc 4 stroke | **1st** Barry Woodland **2nd** Graham Cannell **3rd** Matt Oxley **4th** Pete Bateson **5th** Glen Williams |

Congratulations to all riders enjoying yet another successful year at the TT Races.

And remember, you can fit the exact same tyres the winners fit.

Just ask your dealer about Metzeler. If he doesn't give you the right answers ask him again and again and again.

## METZELER
### ADVANCED MOTORCYCLE TYRES

Metzeler Tyres
Unit 9 and 10, Sneyd Industrial Estate,
Burslem, Stoke on Trent, Staffs ST6 2DL
Tel: 0782 826699

A DIVISON OF BELSTAFF INTERNATIONAL LIMITED

# GRANDS PRIX 1986

# Gran Premio de ESPAÑA

Kenny Roberts was watching practice at the first tight left-hander behind the pits. Spencer came through on his own peculiar line, straight up the inside on the left of the track, almost on the ripple strip and braking deep into the turn, still running straight and drifting out across the normal racing line as the corner turned left. Running high out towards the curb he flopped the Honda on its side as he got off the brakes, pulled a sharp U-turn and dropped back on a very late apex, accelerating hard out of the corner almost upright. It was the most accentuated example of the anti-classic line imaginable – a style Roberts was well familiar with, but this example didn't meet with his approval.

'He is very deep on the brakes and late to turn; that makes it hard on him, it takes a lot of effort and allows him no rest.' Roberts was schooling Mamola on a different line – still nowhere near a classic apex but much wider than Spencer –

going in running on the brakes round the outside of the turn until Mamola dropped the Yamaha over and swooped for a late apex not far from Spencer's spot, accelerating relatively upright.

Mamola's high line contributed to one of his practice crashes, allowing him no room for error when he found the back end hopping on the brakes going in. 'We had stiffened up the rear suspension', said Mamola later, 'and the back end started to hop going into the turn and I had to get on the front brake hard; there was no room to go straight on and the front end turned under.'

Mamola fell twice in practice and a further contributory factor was the new range of Michelin tyres riders had to choose from. Along with the popular 16 in. radial front they had developed a 17 in. radial and a 17 in. crossply. Mamola found himself getting off one bike fitted with the radial 17 in. front and on another fitted with the cross-ply and trying to push the front end just as hard

and it would not take it.

Mamola was not that upset by the first crash, at least; he understood what had caused it and was still thrilled with the performance of the 500 Yamaha. 'It is three hundred times better than the Honda triple I rode last year. I am certainly not trying to get at Honda; they were very good to me and the three-cylinder was good but this is just better. When I put in a quick time here on the Honda I felt I was right on the edge of crashing it. With the Yamaha I feel more relaxed; the thing is so strong and sturdy that when you do something stupid it will straighten itself out.'

It sounded as though Mamola had fallen on his feet with the Yamaha, joining the newly formed Lucky Strike team with triple World Champion Kenny Roberts as figurehead and team manager and Paul Butler as organiser. Between them they had put together a very powerful team with New Zealander Mike Sinclair returning to Mamola's

side as technical chief and the Number Two riding spot going to Mike Baldwin. The latter's gamble of Grand Prix racing as a complete privateer in 1985 paid off in the form of better machinery and someone else paying the bills in '86.

Baldwin had been impressed with the performance of the Yamaha and said that it reminded him of the best traits exhibited by the FWS 1000 cc V-four Honda he had raced in the States. The GP Yamaha was of course lighter and Baldwin loved the light way it changed direction. It was a relief that he got to like it so quickly after four years of campaigning the three-cylinder Hondas. 'At first I thought, "this is weird, I cannot lean it over". It was the same feeling the FZ Superbike gave me at Daytona but there I was not prepared to stick my neck out. On the 500 I pushed harder and once I got it laid over I found how stable it is and even when you are going really hard, up to 100 per cent, it is still comfortable and you feel

you are just riding around. It has a lot of weight on the front wheel and is very forgiving. I guess I had got so used to the Honda I didn't realise how much better more weight would feel.'

So while the two new Yamaha men in the Lucky Strike team were thrilled with their new mounts, Rob McElnea was just as pleased with the way things were going for him in the Marlboro team, having signed on to ride beside ex-World Champion Eddie Lawson. Although 1985 had not provided him with exciting results, enough people had been impressed by his considerable riding talent – hampered as it was by a less than competitive Suzuki – to ensure that he was not short of offers for 1986.

In November he was offered a ride by Cagiva after a test session at Misano. He found the bike reasonable, despite the cold weather and the shortness of the session which gave him only a limited idea of the machine's capabilities. The

financial reward offered by the Castiglioni brothers was considerable; their generous funds ensured that Kenny Roberts was paid handsomely to test the bike earlier, with an even larger sum offered if he would race it.

McElnea was tempted and told Cagiva that he was thinking very strongly about riding when out of the blue came an offer from Giacomo Agostini. Less money was involved, but the Cagiva still needed development whereas the Yamaha was proven Grand Prix winner. McElnea did not have to think too long about their relative merits and went for the Yamaha, getting his first ride on the V-four in Brazil at a private test session early in the year.

He had his anxieties though. 'I had worried a lot about riding the Yamaha and what I would do if I just could not get on with it. As soon as I rode it I realised that there was no problem and I enjoyed it.' For the first couple of days of testing McElnea was actually faster than Lawson but in the end the Californian extended himself and bettered the new-boy's best.

McElnea was just as pleased by the good relationship he soon had with the rest of the team; with one French and one Italian mechanic, Australian Kel Carruthers as Technical Manager and Italian Giacomo Agostini as the boss, the easygoing Humbersider found no problems in fitting in to the cosmopolitan atmosphere.

In Brazil, Lawson also had a short ride on the V-twin 250 that Martin Wimmer and Carlos Lavado were testing, very similar to the bikes that Lavado had raced twice in '85. Lawson only did a few laps but his times were close to the 250 specialists, reminding everyone what a fine lightweight rider he has been in the past. Nevertheless, he was not tempted enough to aim for a Spencer-style 250/500 double.

Lawson and McElnea got on well from the start and helped each other out at that Brazilian session. 'We took it in turns to stop on corners and watch each other', said McElnea. 'Eddie was a big help and I tried to get used to sliding the back end, steering with the back wheel. I had tried it with the Suzuki last year but the power band was so narrow that it wasn't easy and it threw me off at Mugello. The Yamaha made it much easier but I am not an expert yet. I am not sure that it is the best way to ride, to slide the back end all the time – it must wreck the tyres and I think you would be a better rider if you could go as fast and not slide all the time.'

By the time Lawson attempted fast laps at Jarama he realised that perhaps the small number of alterations to the 500 Yamaha from the previous year had not made it a better machine. The 1986 bike had revised rear suspension and a modified power curve, while the suspension linkage geometry had been altered to put less load into the frame, thereby improving the rate curve. Lawson was not pleased with the engine modifications. 'It is supposed to have more power but I think that all that has happened is that last year's power has been squeezed into a smaller rev band.'

Already there were rumours that Yamaha were developing a completely new single-crank V-four

Fire mutilated the Chevallier of Didier de Radigues when he crashed (right).

Freddie Spencer (far right) rode the first four laps as he had done throughout his Championship-winning 1985 season . . . but then things went wrong.

Wayne Gardner took full advantage of Freddie Spencer's wrist injury (below).

Carlos Lavado was lucky and fast in equal measure (bottom).

which would appear later in the season. The 1986 V-fours were no longer referred to as OW machines but as YZR500s, indicating that Yamaha no longer considered them factory racing prototypes but production racers. It had long been suggested that to beat the V-four Honda they needed a similar single-crank design because, with eight main bearings to Honda's five, they needed to reduce the internal friction.

Honda's secret development was going into the 250 turbo which was to be their answer to the NR500 four-stroke disaster. The NR project had never been killed off completely but, realising that they could never win with a 500 four-stroke, they had turned to the turbocharged 250 as the only way of winning the 500 Championship with a four-stroke – their stated intention at the beginning of the NR project.

However, they had not been standing still with the two-stroke and although the 1986 NSR500

looked very much like the Championship-winning '85 version, it had been completely reworked. The new frame had only detail changes but they made it lighter and more compact. The more obvious alteration was the use of a new extrusion for the mainframe spars with a chamferred outside top edge so that the rider's knees could fit closer in to the tank. The engine had also been redesigned and tipped further forward in the frame by a few degrees so as to increase the weight on the front wheel. This meant a new set of pipes had to be designed and it turned out to be an even more masterful work of art than the '85 versions, with their fastest section running across the belly of the machine from one side to the other.

The power band had also been broadened and Wayne Gardner commented that the bike actually seemed slower than before because the power was less vicious. Spencer didn't like the new

Don Morley

power band but he only tested the bike for the first time at Jarama the week before the Grand Prix so there was little time to do much about it. He asked that they revert to the 1985-specification power band.

At least Spencer had more time to relax with only a single class to compete in. He was installed in his new $300,000 motorhome – as if putting himself at a distance from the common herd, in a vehicle that no-one else could afford, was part of the image intrinsic to his unapproachability as a rider. It was as if this was part of some psychological plot to defeat his rivals before they even got to the race.

## 125 cc

Angel Nieto's hopes of winning both the 80 cc and 125 cc World Championships and of getting closer to Giacomo Agostini's record number of titles took a knock when he retired on the second lap of the 125 race. The MBA seized, probably because new pistons had been put in after practice and there was only the short morning warm-up session to run them in.

Nieto had already been left in mid-pack at the start as World Champion Fausto Gresini led on the Garelli, closely followed by Domenico Brigaglia, and the two soon increased their distance from the field. Gresini eventually won comfortably when he shook off Brigaglia in the last couple of laps having been tailed all the way up to that point.

Ezio Gianola had a lonely race in third place on his MBA well ahead of the second of the works Garellis riden by Luca Cadalora. The latter had started poorly and had to catch the group battling for fourth in the early stages, which comprised Johnny Wickström, Pier Paolo Bianchi and Willy Perez.

Cadalora had moved into fourth by lap 7 and that split up Perez, Bianchi and Wickström. August Auinger had made a slow start but was in his usual determined mood. He pulled through from fifteenth at the end of lap 1 to move into fifth by lap 12 but then crashed three laps later while chasing Cadalora.

## 80 cc

This was a Derbi demonstration race with Jorge Martinez, Manuel Herreros and Angel Nieto swapping places from beginning to end. World Champion Stefan Dörflinger was out of luck down in fourth place battling with Pier Paolo Bianchi. On lap 19 the Swiss ace crashed the Krauser but remounted to finish ninth, one lap behind the leaders. In the closing stages, Martinez (or 'Aspar' as he is known in Spain) pulled out to win by eight seconds from Nieto who seemed to be clowning around, patting Martinez on the shoulder midway through the race as they went side-by-side down the start-and-finish straight.

Apart from the excitement up front, which gave the patriotic crowd the opportunity to let off huge strings of fireworks, the rest of the race was rather processional. Behind the Dörflinger and Bianchi battle for fourth, Ian McConnachie and Hans Spaan had a quiet contest between themselves until the Dutchman crashed on lap 14; he remounted then called at the pits before finishing 18th.

Juan Bolart got the best of Gerhard Waibel in the closing stages and they were well ahead of Hubert Abold and the remounted Dörflinger whose bike was not running well after the fall.

## 500 cc

There had been doubts about Freddie Spencer's ability to dominate the World Championship against Gardner on a similar V-four and the five hard-ridden Yamahas. For the first ten laps of the race those doubts seemed to fade completely. The double World Champion clicked straight into his paralysing early race pace that left everyone floundering in his wake, just as they had done so many times through 1985. Gardner and Lawson both made good starts but they could not match the way he instantly settled to a flat-out speed.

Raymond Roche was off the line in second place but Lawson was soon past, followed by Gardner. The Frenchman on the three-cylinder NS500 hung on to the two fours, however, as they tried in vain to keep a tail on Spencer. Rob McElnea had also started the second of the Marlboro Yamahas well and slotted himself into fifth place ahead of Didier de Radigues and Christian Sarron.

Slower starting were the two Lucky Strike Yamahas and although Baldwin was up to 13th place on lap 2 Mamola was still in the lower twenties with only Haslam of the usual top runners in a worse position after he had been left on the line.

An impressive privateer was Fabio Biliotti who had said before the race that if he had Spencer's bike he would win. The Italian pushed his way into eighth place on lap 3 but Baldwin was already gaining and Mamola had scythed his way through the pack to 12th position and closing.

Gardner realised that Spencer was getting clean away and dived past Lawson in an attempt to improve the situation. Lawson fought back and repassed the Australian but the Honda rider kept increasing the pressure through laps 4 to 7 and then managed to break free of the Yamaha. With the increase in pace, Roche rather lost touch after doing a great job throughout the opening laps.

As the battle for second split up, the contest for fifth intensified. McElnea had been gradually overhauled by de Radigues and Sarron and although he could hold them at bay a more serious threat was approaching. This took the form of the Lucky Strike crew with Mamola leading, although Baldwin reasserted his advantage on lap 13.

De Radigues had been riding the Chevallier very hard from the beginning and, lacking the power of the Yamahas whose company he was keeping, the effort of getting away from the corners with them required early hard acceleration. Getting it on a little too early from one of the tight hairpins spat him over the top on lap 14; as the bike caught fire he was carried off with a broken collarbone.

There was more drama to come because since lap 10 it had been obvious that Spencer first was not getting any further away from Gardner and then was visibly being caught. It was not that the Young Pretender had suddenly found the secret of Spencer's speed but that the World Champion had trouble. So much so that on lap 15 he stopped at the pits and handed the bike back to his mechanics.

'My forearm had pumped up so badly that it had cut off the blood supply to my right hand. I tried to rest it and to use the back brake instead of the front but it just got worse. It started on lap 6 and my times went up as I had to ease off and I realised that there was no way I could finish in the points. I could hardly hold onto the bike in the end and when I almost ran off the track I realised I had to stop.' Spencer relaxed in his motorhome while the race continued without him.

The tendonitis that had forced him out had affected others before. Jeff Sayle and Kenny Roberts had both needed operations to relieve the pressure in their forearm muscles. Spencer had never suffered this problem and because of personal problems and a severe virus infection he had not tested a bike since the end of 1985. He had only got on the NSR in the week prior to the race and it was then that he realised he had a problem. Although he tried to do as few laps as possible, the precaution was not sufficient to help him in the race.

Having been handed his first Grand Prix win on a plate after trying so hard with the three-cylinder in 1985, Gardner made no mistakes in the closing stages. It was not all plain sailing, because the four was not running perfectly. The weather had changed considerably from practice (which had been hot) and the colder, denser air on race day caused many bikes to run a little lean. It affected the Yamahas which are always critical on carburation and it upset Gardner's Honda sufficiently to make it misfire down the main straight. 'It was so down on power compared with practice that it would not pull top', he said. 'I was worried that it might get worse and on the last lap it seemed to stop completely but then it went again and finished. It nearly gave me a heart attack, though.'

Lawson had his share of difficulties with the Yamaha carburating badly; its viciousness coming out of the corner accentuated a rear suspension problem making it impossible to get enough power to the road to chase Gardner effectively. He closed on him over the last few laps but was still two seconds behind at the flag.

Arguably, it was Baldwin who had the ride of the race, finishing third after keeping up the pace and aggression that he had shown all through practice. He left Mamola behind and passed McElnea and then Roche to be third from lap 24 onwards. McElnea was annoyed at himself for losing what he felt should have been a secure fourth: 'I was a bit inexperienced and I got stuck at the speed I was going and when Baldwin came past I could not speed up.'

By lap 28 Mamola was also through to third and McElnea had a fight on his hands with Sarron and Roche. Or rather he watched the two French arch-rivals fight it out. 'I couldn't believe it; they were kicking each other and going all over

the place in the last few laps.' They crossed the line side by side with Sarron getting the verdict over Roche and McElnea right on their tail.

Eighth went to Juan Garriga who kept the home crowd happy with a great ride on the Cagiva and a race-long battle with Biliotti. They were ahead of Ron Haslam who scored a point for the new Elf 4 after beating off the Suzukis of Paul Lewis and Dave Petersen.

The Elf team were so ecstatic with Ron Haslam's tenth place that you would have thought he had won the World Championship. The reason for their shouting and leaping up and down was not just the excitement of the Elf's first-ever Championship point, no mean achievement for a little-tested machine. They were more than a little relieved that the bike finished at all as they had misread the regulations and thought that the race was to be run over 27, not 37, laps.

They were so sure that Ron would not have enough fuel to finish that Team Manager Serge Rosset was prepared to pull Ron in for more fuel. Ron's wife Anne said that there was little point in showing him signs to stop because he would ignore them. 'If you show him a sign that says "Gas" he will just think you are being cheeky because he is going as fast as he can. There is no way he will stop.'

Ron continued embroiled in his battle with Lewis which he won to claim the point for tenth. The tank was bone dry after the race and he only took the chequered flag because Haslam and Lewis were lapped by Gardner and needed to run just 36 laps.

## 250 cc

Calls for clutch starts at Grands Prix were renewed after a serious accident that started when Tadahiko Tairo could not get the V-twin Marlboro Yamaha off the line quickly. He was hit from behind by Stéphane Mertens coming off the sixth row. Mertens then slewed across the road and collided with Sergio Pellandini and to round things off Bruno Bonhuil ran into the debris.

The race was stopped and the luckiest man at the circuit was Carlos Lavado because he crashed on the first lap at the fast downhill left-hander when the back end slid round as he tried to get the power on early having entered on a shallow line. The bike was wrecked and that would have been the end of his race but for the startline mêlée.

Lavado also benefited from a change in the FIM rules that allow a second machine to be used if the race is stopped for any reason. If that was not enough, the change of bikes put him onto the power-valve engined machine instead of the peakier but slightly more powerful non power-valve version. That was probably to be crucial to his victory.

Reinhold Roth also fell on that first aborted lap but his crash was as a direct result of the red flags suddenly shown at the start-and-finish line. As he swooped through the fast right-hander onto the straight Gary Noel in front of him saw the race being stopped and slowed. Roth clipped his back wheel and shot off the track. He was lucky to

escape serious injury, but both wheels of the bike were destroyed.

Just to show that he was not upset by the first crash, Lavado shot into the lead from the restart followed by Mang and Cornu. Pole-position man Martin Wimmer had been very slow away from the original start but this time he was slightly better placed and completed the first lap in tenth place.

Lavado continued to lead but Sito Pons was through to second ahead of Mang and Cornu. This trio broke away and Cornu was left well clear of Fausto Ricci while Pierre Bolle held sixth but was rapidly overhauled by the advancing Wimmer who relegated him a place on lap 7.

By that time Mang had taken over the lead but could not get away from Lavado and Pons. With Pons providing the nationalistic interest the leading trio had the crowd shouting with excitement. Wimmer's performance was just as entertaining as he carefully calculated the best place to deal with Ricci and then Cornu. The weather was very overcast and a drop of rain fell but it was never more than that and did not dampen the circuit.

As Wimmer moved into fourth on lap 12 Ricci was close to Cornu but although the Italian was on the superior works Honda, Cornu worked his private production bike harder to keep ahead and Ricci's challenge faded. Bolle was a lonely seventh and, behind, Donnie McLeod was doing a

good job of holding back Jean-Michel Mattioli who was to retire on lap 14.

At the head of the field the pace became more furious as each rider was informed that Wimmer was closing. The question was whether or not he would catch them soon enough to win. With ten laps still to go he was getting very close and Lavado took the lead from Mang and increased the pace further. As the Venezuelan started to open out a small lead Pons tried to pass Mang and go with him but the ex-World Champion fought back and Wimmer closed right in on the pair of them with four laps still to go.

Wimmer was on the non power-valve bike and this is where it became a disadvantage. 'With the slightly narrower power band the gearing is critical. That is fine when you are on your own but when you want to pass and have to go off line it is easy to get out of the power band.' Wimmer – never one to be desperate at an overtaking manoeuvre, and certainly not in the first race of the season – was forced to wait and in fact he never did get past Pons who chased Mang across the line to complete the rostrum positions.

Lavado won perhaps the most incredible race of his dramatic career. He had crashed in practice and was sore enough from that, never mind the first-lap incident. His self confidence must have been incredible to come back from such a high-speed fall then go out immediately into the lead and win a Grand Prix.

# Gran Premio de España, 4 May/statistics
# Circuito Permanente del Jarama, 2.058-mile/3.312-km circuit

## 500 cc

**37 laps, 76.15 miles/122.54 km**

| *Place* | *Rider* | *Nat.* | *Machine* | *Laps* | *Time & speed* | *Practice time* | *Grid* |
|---|---|---|---|---|---|---|---|
| 1 | Wayne Gardner | AUS | Honda | 37 | 56m 01.87s 81.593 mph/ 131.311 km/h | 1m 28.81s | 2 |
| 2 | Eddie Lawson | USA | Yamaha | 37 | 56m 03.94s | 1m 29.20s | 3 |
| 3 | Mike Baldwin | USA | Yamaha | 37 | 56m 19.04s | 1m 29.24s | 4 |
| 4 | Randy Mamola | USA | Yamaha | 37 | 56m 30.03s | 1m 29.39s | 5 |
| 5 | Christian Sarron | F | Yamaha | 37 | 56m 31.84s | 1m 30.65s | 9 |
| 6 | Raymond Roche | F | Honda | 37 | 56m 31.93s | 1m 30.22s | 7 |
| 7 | Rob McElnea | GB | Yamaha | 37 | 56m 32.34s | 1m 29.63s | 6 |
| 8 | Juan Garriga | E | Cagiva | 37 | 57m 15.86s | 1m 31.57s | 10 |
| 9 | Fabio Biliotti | I | Honda | 37 | 57m 16.04s | 1m 31.73s | 11 |
| 10 | Ron Haslam | GB | Elf | 36 | 56m 13.49s | 1m 32.24s | 13 |
| 11 | Paul Lewis | AUS | Suzuki | 36 | 56m 13.69s | 1m 32.25s | 14 |
| 12 | Dave Petersen | ZIM | Suzuki | 36 | 56m 24.95s | 1m 32.40s | 15 |
| 13 | Henk van der Mark | NL | Honda | 36 | 56m 47.40s | 1m 33.33s | 18 |
| 14 | Pier Francesco Chili | I | Suzuki | 36 | 57m 02.07s | 1m 33.07s | 16 |
| 15 | Boet van Dulmen | NL | Honda | 36 | 57m 08.16s | 1m 33.13s | 17 |
| 16 | Peter Sköld | S | Honda | 36 | 57m 23.31s | 1m 33.58s | 21 |
| 17 | Simon Buckmaster | GB | Honda | 36 | 57m 23.84s | 1m 34.61s | 24 |
| 18 | Manfred Fischer | D | Honda | 36 | 57m 25.19s | 1m 34.01s | 22 |
| 19 | Marco Gentile | CH | Fior | 36 | 57m 25.94s | 1m 34.14s | 23 |
| 20 | Andreas Leuthe | LUX | Honda | 35 | 56m 24.06s | 1m 33.56s | 20 |
| 21 | Dietmar Mayer | D | Honda | 34 | 56m 47.23s | 1m 38.37s | 27 |
| | Leandro Becheroni | I | Suzuki | 23 | DNF | 1m 33.39s | 19 |
| | Freddie Spencer | USA | Honda | 14 | DNF | 1m 28.48s | 1 |
| | Didier de Radigues | B | Chevallier | 13 | DNF | 1m 30.42s | 8 |
| | Peter Linden | S | Honda | 8 | DNF | 1m 34.78s | 26 |
| | Gustav Reiner | D | Honda | 2 | DNF | 1m 32.19s | 12 |
| | Wolfgang von Muralt | CH | Suzuki | | DNS | 1m 34.77s | 25 |
| | José Parra | E | Honda | | DNQ | 1m 38.88s | |
| | Vincenzo Cascino | RCH | Suzuki | | DNQ | 1m 42.62s | |
| | Carlos Morante | E | Honda | | DNQ | 1m 43.40s | |
| | Stelio Marmaras | GR | Suzuki | | DNQ | 1m 44.11s | |

*Fastest lap:* Gardner, 1m 29.35s, 82.973 mph/133.532 km/h.
*Lap record:* Freddie Spencer, USA (Honda), 1m 28.99s, 83.26 mph/133.99 km/h (1985).

**World Championship: 1** Gardner, 15; **2** Lawson, 12; **3** Baldwin, 10; **4** Mamola, 8; **5** Sarron, 6; **6** Roche, 5; **7** McElnea, 4; **8** Garriga, 3; **9** Biliotti, 2; **10** Haslam, 1.

## 250 cc

**31 laps, 63.80 miles/102.67 km**

| *Place* | *Rider* | *Nat.* | *Machine* | *Laps* | *Time & speed* | *Practice time* | *Grid* |
|---|---|---|---|---|---|---|---|
| 1 | Carlos Lavado | YV | Yamaha | 31 | 47m 50.43s 80.066 mph/ 128.853 km/h | 1m 31.47s | 3 |
| 2 | Anton Mang | D | Honda | 31 | 47m 52.61s | 1m 32.27s | 8 |
| 3 | Alfonso Pons | E | Honda | 31 | 47m 52.80s | 1m 31.55s | 5 |
| 4 | Martin Wimmer | D | Yamaha | 31 | 47m 52.95s | 1m 31.15s | 1 |
| 5 | Jacques Cornu | CH | Honda | 31 | 48m 22.43s | 1m 31.49s | 4 |
| 6 | Pierre Bolle | F | Parisienne | 31 | 48m 27.74s | 1m 32.05s | 6 |
| 7 | Donnie McLeod | GB | Armstrong | 31 | 48m 31.34s | 1m 32.67s | 11 |
| 8 | Jean-François Baldé | F | Honda | 31 | 48m 36.79s | 1m 32.52s | 9 |
| 9 | Fausto Ricci | I | Honda | 31 | 48m 39.29s | 1m 32.08s | 7 |
| 10 | Alan Carter | GB | Kobas | 31 | 48m 41.98s | 1m 32.55s | 10 |
| 11 | Maurizio Vitali | I | Garelli | 31 | 48m 52.32s | 1m 33.56s | 21 |
| 12 | Jean Foray | F | Chevallier | 31 | 48m 52.47s | 1m 34.01s | 29 |
| 13 | Reinhold Roth | D | Honda | 31 | 48m 52.68s | 1m 32.84s | 15 |
| 14 | Manfred Herweh | D | Aprilia | 31 | 48m 58.77s | 1m 33.24s | 19 |
| 15 | Stefano Caracchi | I | Aprilia | 31 | 48m 58.85s | 1m 32.95s | 17 |
| 16 | Dominique Sarron | F | Honda | 31 | 48m 58.93s | 1m 33.44s | 20 |
| 17 | Jean-Louis Guignabodet | F | MIG | 31 | 48m 22.89s | 1m 38.80s | 25 |
| 18 | Antonio Boronat | E | Kobas | 30 | 48m 11.53s | 1m 34.72s | 34 |
| 19 | Roland Freymond | CH | Yamaha | 30 | 48m 17.29s | 1m 33.70s | 23 |
| 20 | Brent Jones | NZ | Yamaha | 30 | 48m 18.85s | 1m 33.82s | 26 |
| 21 | Antonia Garcia | E | Honda | 30 | 48m 31.53s | 1m 35.08s | 36 |
| | Harald Eckl | D | Honda | 29 | DNF | 1m 32.88s | 16 |
| | Ian Newton | GB | Armstrong | 27 | DNF | 1m 33.17s | 18 |
| | Carlos Cardus | E | Yamaha | 21 | DNF | 1m 32.77s | 12 |
| | Fernando Gonzalez | E | Kobas | 18 | DNF | 1m 34.14s | 30 |
| | René Délaby | B | Rotax | 16 | DNF | 1m 33.96s | 27 |
| | Jean-Michel Mattioli | F | Yamaha | 14 | DNF | 1m 32.81s | 13 |
| | Gary Noel | GB | EMC | 13 | DNF | 1m 33.70s | 22 |
| | Jean-Louis Tournadre | F | Yamaha | 8 | DNF | 1m 32.84s | 14 |
| | Urs Luzi | CH | Yamaha | 2 | DNF | 1m 34.00s | 28 |
| | Loris Reggiani | I | Aprilia | 2 | DNF | 1m 34.38s | 33 |
| | Tadahiko Taira | J | Yamaha | | DNS | 1m 31.17s | 2 |
| | Stéphane Mertens | B | Yamaha | | DNS | 1m 33.78s | 24 |
| | Julian Echaide | E | Kobas | | DNS | 1m 34.23s | 31 |
| | Bruno Bonhuil | F | Honda | | DNS | 1m 34.29s | 32 |
| | Eduardo Cots | E | Yamaha | | DNS | 1m 34.96s | 35 |
| | Sergio Pellandini | CH | Honda | | DNQ | 1m 35.59s | |
| | Marcelino Garcia | E | MBA | | DNQ | 1m 35.64s | |
| | Andrea Brasini | I | Garelli | | DNQ | 1m 36.70s | |
| | Ruben del Rio | E | Arbizu | | DNQ | 1m 37.53s | |
| | Johnny Simonsson | S | Honda | | DNQ | 1m 37.82s | |
| | Jean-Luc Guillemet | F | Yamaha | | DNQ | 1m 37.92s | |

*Fastest lap:* Wimmer, 1m 31.05s, 81.424 mph/131.039 km/h (record).
*Previous record:* Freddie Spencer, USA (Honda), 1m 32.05s, 80.49 mph/129.53 km/h (1985).

**World Championship: 1** Lavado, 15; **2** Mang, 12; **3** Pons, 10; **4** Wimmer, 8; **5** Cornu, 6; **6** Bolle, 5; **7** McLeod, 4; **8** Baldé, 3; **9** Ricci, 2; **10** Carter, 1.

## 125 cc

**28 laps, 57.62 miles/92.74 km**

| *Place* | *Rider* | *Nat.* | *Machine* | *Laps* | *Time & speed* | *Practice time* | *Grid* |
|---|---|---|---|---|---|---|---|
| 1 | Fausto Gresini | I | Garelli | 28 | 45m 30.63s 76.020 mph/ 122.342 km/h | 1m 34.50s | 1 |
| 2 | Domenico Brigaglia | I | Ducados | 28 | 45m 35.38s | 1m 35.83s | 3 |
| 3 | Ezio Gianola | I | MBA | 28 | 45m 53.16s | 1m 36.72s | 6 |
| 4 | Luca Cadalora | I | Garelli | 28 | 46m 00.62s | 1m 35.06s | 2 |
| 5 | Johnny Wickström | SF | Tunturi | 28 | 46m 51.88s | 1m 39.22s | 16 |
| 6 | Willy Perez | RA | Zanella | 28 | 47m 03.40s | 1m 38.18s | 10 |
| 7 | Pier Paolo Bianchi | I | Elit | 28 | 47m 09.45s | 1m 38.39s | 12 |
| 8 | Marin Andreas Sanchez | E | Ducados | 28 | 48m 18.87s | 1m 39.05s | 15 |
| 9 | Jussi Hautaniemi | SF | MBA | 27 | 45m 48.97s | 1m 39.69s | 17 |
| 10 | Hakan Olsson | S | Starol | 27 | 46m 14.00s | 1m 40.49s | 23 |
| 11 | Patrick Daudier | F | PMDF | 27 | 46m 25.77s | 1m 41.06s | 25 |
| 12 | Fernando Gonzalez | E | MBA | 27 | 46m 44.82s | 1m 40.43s | 22 |
| 13 | Daniel Mateos | E | MBA | 27 | 47m 22.26s | 1m 40.34s | 20 |
| 14 | Jacques Hutteau | F | MBA | 26 | 45m 41.30s | 1m 42.69s | 31 |
| 15 | Alfred Waibel | D | Real | 26 | 45m 42.49s | 1m 39.79s | 18 |
| 16 | Steve Mason | GB | MBA | 26 | 45m 44.52s | 1m 43.37s | 33 |
| 17 | Antonio Oliveros | S | San Benero | 26 | 45m 47.28s | 1m 41.85s | 29 |
| 18 | Ivan Troisi | YV | MBA | 26 | 45m 47.46s | 1m 43.70s | 35 |
| 19 | Eric Gijsel | B | MBA | 26 | 46m 29.21s | 1m 43.64s | 34 |
| 20 | Peter Balaz | CS | MBA | 26 | 46m 34.71s | 1m 42.48s | 30 |
| | Robin Appleyard | GB | MBA | 23 | DNF | 1m 40.93s | 24 |
| | Thierry Feuz | CH | MBA | 20 | DNF | 1m 36.42s | 4 |
| | Lucio Pietroniro | B | MBA | 18 | DNF | 1m 38.78s | 13 |
| | Manuel Hernandez | E | Benetti | 17 | DNF | 1m 40.37s | 21 |
| | August Auinger | A | Bartol | 14 | DNF | 1m 36.47s | 5 |
| | Esa Kytola | SF | MBA | 11 | DNF | 1m 41.32s | 27 |
| | Willi Hupperich | D | Seel | 9 | DNF | 1m 36.93s | 8 |
| | Michel Escudier | F | MBA | 7 | DNF | 1m 41.77s | 28 |
| | Giuseppe Ascareggi | I | Seel | 6 | DNF | 1m 41.20s | 26 |
| | Bady Hassaine | DZ | MBA | 5 | DNF | 1m 43.95s | 36 |
| | Eric Saul | F | LGM | 4 | DNF | 1m 43.03s | 32 |
| | Bruno Kneubühler | CH | LCR | 3 | DNF | 1m 36.82s | 7 |
| | Angel Nieto | E | Ducados | 2 | DNF | 1m 37.12s | 9 |
| | Jean-Claude Selini | F | MBA | 1 | DNF | 1m 40.23s | 19 |
| | Olivier Liegeois | B | Assmex | 0 | DNF | 1m 38.94s | 14 |
| | Paolo Casoli | I | MBA | 0 | DNF | 1m 38.19s | 11 |
| | Pablo Gamberini | CHI | MBA | | DNQ | 1m 44.78s | |
| | David Simpson | GB | MBA | | DNQ | 1m 45.17s | |
| | Manfred Braun | D | MBA | | DNQ | 1m 47.11s | |

*Fastest lap:* Gresini, 1m 35.47s, 77.654 mph/124.972 km/h (record)
*Previous record:* Pier Paolo Bianchi, I (MBA), 1m 35.55s, 77.54 mph/124.79 km/h (1985).

**World Championship: 1** Gresini, 15; **2** Brigaglia, 12; **3** Gianola, 10; **4** Cadalora, 8; **5** Wickström, 6; **6** Perez, 5; **7** Bianchi, 4; **8** Sanchez, 3; **9** Hautaniemi, 2; **10** Olsson, 1.

## 80 cc

**22 laps, 45.28 miles/72.86 km**

| *Place* | *Rider* | *Nat.* | *Machine* | *Laps* | *Time & speed* | *Practice time* | *Grid* |
|---|---|---|---|---|---|---|---|
| 1 | Jorge Martinez | E | Derbi | 22 | 37m 01.75s 73.411 mph/ 118.143 km/h | 1m 38.45s | 1 |
| 2 | Angel Nieto | E | Derbi | 22 | 37m 09.45s | 1m 38.86s | 2 |
| 3 | Manuel Herreros | E | Derbi | 22 | 37m 10.35s | 1m 39.26s | 4 |
| 4 | Pier Paolo Bianchi | I | Seel | 22 | 37m 41.12s | 1m 40.60s | 6 |
| 5 | Ian McConnachie | GB | Krauser | 22 | 37m 43.92s | 1m 41.01s | 7 |
| 6 | Juan Bolart | E | Autisa | 22 | 38m 22.19s | 1m 41.78s | 9 |
| 7 | Gerhard Waibel | D | Real | 22 | 38m 22.37s | 1m 42.96s | 12 |
| 8 | Hubert Abold | D | Seel | 21 | 37m 20.86s | 1m 42.08s | 11 |
| 9 | Stefan Dörflinger | CH | Krauser | 21 | 37m 25.12s | 1m 39.05s | 3 |
| 10 | Domingo Gil | E | Autisa | 21 | 37m 25.67s | 1m 45.53s | 20 |
| 11 | Reiner Scheidhauer | D | Seel | 21 | 37m 32.50s | 1m 43.45s | 13 |
| 12 | Steve Mason | GB | Huvo | 21 | 37m 40.93s | 1m 46.33s | 21 |
| 13 | Theo Timmer | NL | Huvo | 21 | 37m 41.92s | 1m 41.95s | 10 |
| 14 | Massimo Fargeri | I | MBA | 20 | 37m 05.22s | 1m 49.29s | 26 |
| 15 | Jos van Dongen | NL | Krauser | 20 | 37m 05.80s | 1m 48.06s | 23 |
| 16 | Bertus Grinwis | NL | Krauser | 20 | 37m 07.93s | 1m 49.13s | 24 |
| 17 | Chris Baert | B | Seel | 20 | 37m 23.07s | 1m 49.26s | 25 |
| 18 | Hans Spaan | NL | Huvo | 20 | 37m 38.94s | 1m 39.75s | 5 |
| 19 | Paolo Priori | I | Lusuardi | 20 | 38m 25.47s | 1m 50.87s | 28 |
| 20 | Juan Esteve | E | Autisa | 20 | 38m 57.39s | 1m 52.22s | 30 |
| 21 | Reiner Koster | CH | LCR | 19 | 37m 09.64s | 1m 49.95s | 27 |
| 22 | Ramiro Blanco | E | Krauser | 18 | 38m 27.25s | 1m 56.62s | 35 |
| | Henk van Kessel | NL | Krauser | 20 | DNF | 1m 43.77s | 14 |
| | Serge Julin | B | Huvo | 18 | DNF | 1m 51.97s | 29 |
| | Rainer Kunz | D | Ziegler | 17 | DNF | 1m 41.56s | 8 |
| | Salvatore Milano | I | Krauser | 11 | DNF | 1m 45.45s | 19 |
| | Gerd Kafka | A | Krauser | 7 | DNF | 1m 45.39s | 18 |
| | Luis Reyes | COL | Autisa | 7 | DNF | 1m 43.97s | 15 |
| | Felix Rodriguez | E | Autisa | 6 | DNF | 1m 44.50s | 16 |
| | Javier Arumi | E | Autisa | 4 | DNF | 1m 53.38s | 32 |
| | Ramon Gali | E | Krauser | 4 | DNF | 1m 56.20s | 34 |
| | Alexandre Barros | BR | Autisa | 2 | DNF | 1m 46.76s | 22 |
| | Julian Miralles | E | Huvo | 1 | DNF | 1m 45.26s | 17 |
| | Georges Fissette | B | Huvo | 1 | DNF | 1m 52.78s | 31 |
| | Francisco Torontegui | E | Kobas | | DNS | 1m 54.88s | 33 |
| | Lorenzo Navarro | E | Yamaha | | DNQ | 1m 59.01s | |
| | Jean-François Verdier | F | Derbi | | DNQ | 2m 10.30s | |

*Fastest lap:* Martinez 1m 38.50s, 75.266 mph/121.128 km/h (record).
*Previous record:* Jorge Martinez, E (Derbi), 1m 40.00s, 74.09 mph/119.23 km/h (1985).

**World Championship: 1** Martinez, 15; **2** Nieto, 12; **3** Herreros, 10; **4** Bianchi, 8; **5** McConnachie, 6; **6** Bolart, 5; **7** Waibel, 4; **8** Abold, 3; **9** Dörflinger, 2; **10** Gil, 1.

**Martinez leads Bianchi, Dörflinger and van Kessel early in the 80 cc race** *(opposite page top)*.

**Mike Baldwin** *(above left)* **surprised a few people with his determined riding, and Raymond Roche's form began to recall past rides on the three-cylinder Honda.**

# GranPremio delle
# N A Z I O N I

**From any angle Tony Mang's style is impressive.**

Everyone loves a good piece of gossip; speculation is one of the things that keeps paddock life interesting and speculation about World Champions sends everyone's tongues wagging. 'Did you know?' and 'Have you heard?' remarks were being freely exchanged on Thursday as rumours spread that Freddie Spencer would not be riding at Monza.

Two years earlier, his team would have been certain that he would turn up. A year ago, they would have presented an air of confidence and stated with some conviction 'Yes Freddie will be arriving on this afternoon's plane.' Several non-appearances in recent times had meant that no one took the team's assurances very seriously and it even seemed as if they might be the last to know. This was indeed the case. As unofficial practice started, 'Mac' Mackay, Freddie's Public Relations Manager, asked whether Freddie would be arriving and if would he race, stated: 'Yes, of course, Freddie's out there practising.' Unfortunately, he wasn't, and Mackay later that afternoon made a statement that Freddie would *not* be racing because of the tendonitis that had forced him to pull out of the Spanish Grand Prix.

It can be no fun trying to be a PR man when you are kept in the dark about what is going on. Erv Kanemoto had been to the airport to meet planes expecting Freddie to be on them but the World Champion remained at home in Shreveport. Back at HRC in Japan, eighteen hours after he failed to appear for unofficial practice, Honda were not aware that he was not going to race. Takazumi Katayama waited until 3.0 a.m. (Italian time) on Friday morning to ring the factory (afternoon in Japan) so that he could request that Spencer's V-four be made available for his rider Raymond Roche to use. Honda could not agree to this as they had not been told Spencer would not ride and Roche never got the use of the bikes.

Spencer's stated reason for not competing was that his right forearm, which had swollen up during the opening laps of the Spanish Grand Prix and forced him to retire, was still causing problems. Despite undergoing intensive therapy since flying home after Spain, the problem had not been cured. He had taken a ride on a street bike only to find that after twenty minutes of road riding the tendonitis had again affected his wrist and cut off the blood supply to the arm. He realised it was pointless to try and compete in Italy. It is a pity that his team did not know that until everyone else did.

Not satisfied with the 'Spencer stays at home with arm injury' story, many gossips looked for a more juicy angle and some came up with the idea that he was in the middle of a financial wrangle with Honda or with Rothmans or both. While that seemed plausible there were other fantastical, if not downright slanderous, suggestions that implied Spencer's problems came from his personal life.

While Spencer had reason to feel aggrieved that so few people accepted the physical problem as his sole reason for the non-appearance at Monza, their scepticism of any statement written on Honda notepaper came from a lengthy history of smoke-screens and half-truths.

Whatever the reason, Spencer's absence put the 500 contest in a new light as questions of a possible Lawson mental block about beating Spencer disappeared and he became once more a championship favourite. Gardner suddenly found himself in a highly pressurised position. In the space of a week he had gone from Number Two rider, not expected or expecting to win the championship and happy to learn more before looking for a Grand Prix victory, to championship leader, Number One Honda rider and virtual sole company representative with a chance of being champion. As well as having to accept the possibility of winning the championship, he also felt the responsibility of being probably the only Honda rider capable of doing so.

Gardner tried to look at the situation philosophically but it was difficult. 'Honda have told me not to worry about the fact that I am now their best chance, which is nice of them, but that seems to make it worse somehow.'

The reaction outside the Honda camp was very different and everyone seemed to have an extra bounce in their step – a backhanded compliment if you like to Spencer's apparent riding superiority. There were similar indirect compliments to Gardner's talent, as many were relieved to think that the increased pressure would adversely affect his riding performance. Certainly, through practice he was not as conspicuous at the top of the table as he had been at Jarama, despite starting in great style by being fastest in the opening session on Friday morning.

That afternoon the Marlboro Yamahas came into their own with McElnea and Lawson lapping faster and faster through the session. McElnea had the edge but in the dying moments Lawson chased his team-mate round the parkland circuit to cut nearly half a second off his time and take the lead. Gardner hung on to third thanks to his morning time, but he was coming under pressure from Mamola.

The Californian on the Lucky Strike Yamaha was fractionally ahead of his team-mate Mike Baldwin and both were obviously progressing with each session. Some of this at least could be put down to Kenny Roberts either offering constructive advice or winding his men up to greater effort, whichever seemed appropriate at the time.

Gone was the Mamola trait of setting his fastest time in the first or second session and then slipping back as everyone else improved theirs. There seemed to be a more determined Mamola at work, one who was prepared to try different equipment, lines and techniques to get his times down. He tried the Lockheed twin-piston calipers during practice as both he and McElnea had complained that the Brembos lacked a little in performance.

Baldwin had never ridden at Monza before but he was just as determined as he had been in Spain and needed no prodding from Roberts to spur him to greater effort. The relationship between Roberts and his two riders remained as different as their two personalities. Mamola remained in awe of Roberts' ability and in the winter had taken up temporary residence near his hero's home, outside Modesto. Kenny had taken charge of everything from Mamola's physical training programme, through honing his reaction and skill on dirt bikes, to his diet.

Baldwin, Roberts freely acknowledged, had his own ideas on racing and the best that Roberts could do was provide him with the best machinery and mechanics available and offer advice where it was pertinent. This Baldwin appreciated tremendously as he was to comment after the Italian Grand Prix. 'He understands so much and he can save us time. At Monza I had been altering the gearbox through practice and I was third-fastest. On Saturday morning I thought I'd raise second a bit for the chicanes and it felt much better but when I came in I was two seconds slower. Kenny had been watching and pointed out that though I was a fraction quicker in one section I was losing a tenth going out and by the time that added up all the way down the straight I was a second and a half slower.

'I changed it back and in the race it was perfect, but another year someone might have suggested I change and I would have taken no notice thinking that he did not know what he was talking about. But Kenny has done it; he knows. I would have kept the gearbox and maybe finished sixth in the race telling myself to put it right for the following year, but Kenny save me that year.'

The hand that Christian Sarron had hurt in a pre-season photo session was healing and he put in his quickest time in the last round of practice to move into fifth place behind McElnea. That put him in front of Baldwin who had made the mistake with the gearbox selection and went no faster in the last practice period.

Behind the five Yamahas and the lone V-four Honda came four three-cylinder Honda-powered machines split by the Cagiva of Juan Garriga. Raymond Roche headed the NS Honda stakes but had lost his way a little after setting his fastest time in the second period. De Radigues was less than half a second slower on the Chevallier-framed bike even though he was hampered by the left shoulder that had been pinned after his crash at Jarama. Thierry Espié was on hand in case de Radigues was too badly injured to ride but as de Radigues gritted his teeth the talented Frenchman remained bikeless.

By qualifying ninth Garriga proved that his Jarama performance was no home circuit flash in the pan. For the home crowd Cagiva had prepared a second bike for ex-champion Marco Lucchinelli and he qualified twelfth behind the two British Honda men Roger Burnett and Ron Haslam. Burnett was having one of the year's exploratory outings on his Honda Britain triples and was under half a second quicker than Haslam on the Elf.

Coincidentally both were using Dunlop tyres and Burnett commented that the combination of the latest radials and the long high-speed Monza corners was scary. 'I am leaning over so far that I feel I have to tuck my elbows in to stop them touching the road; I've got my knee hard in against the tank but there are scrape marks all the way down my leg.'

Haslam needed more than just the latest

Stefan Dörflinger *(right)* won a race to the line on the 80 cc Krauser.

Showing his class on the Marlboro Yamaha – Eddie Lawson *(far right)*.

Heartbreak for Ian McConnachie *(below)* whose fall after an engine seizure spoilt a great ride from last place.

Rob McElnea rode hard but trying to get the power on too early on the last lap left him with no points for his effort *(bottom)*.

radials to help him out of a problem the team was encountering with the Elf. No matter what they did the back end chattered alarmingly and to try and compensate Dunlop had produced a very flexible sidewall tyre that, it was hoped, would do some of the work the suspension seemed incapable of. While it was not the complete answer by any means it did ease the problem.

Dunlop made no secret of the fact that they considered the 500 cc World Championship lost to Michelin. Neither of their runners, Haslam or de Radigues, thought of themselves as title candidates. In the 250 class, however, the situation was very different. Though the first blood had gone to Michelin when Lavado won in Spain, Dunlop's hopes were pinned on Toni Mang – and after his comfortable win at Daytona with radials front and back, the first time the 17-inch front had been used on a 250, things looked good. Unfortunately, as far as the weight of numbers went, long-time Dunlop riders Martin Wimmer and Tadahiko Taira had both joined the French as part of the Team Agostini deal. With Mang obviously the man most likely to, Dunlop also had Italian Fausto Ricci on his NSR Honda and the Parisienne team of Pierre Bolle and Jacques Cornu but minus Sergio Pellandini after the Jarama start-

line accident. Dunlop also had the Armstrong team but while Donnie McLeod had the ability to make full use of the best tyres, star youngster Niall MacKenzie remained out of action after his early season Cadwell crash in which he badly broke his leg. Replacement Ian Newton was promising but very much an inexperienced GP newcomer.

Mang was more than capable of shouldering the responsibility of being Dunlop's main hope but, despite finishing second in Spain, he was not thrilled with the way the season had begun. 'I started the year unable to do the testing I wanted because I had only one bike and not enough of the new tyres. I have had to spend practice trying to sort the bike out and that means that I haven't been as fast in training as I should have been. You cannot concentrate on putting in a fast lap time if you are thinking about what the bike is doing all the time.'

That very problem left Mang down in sixth place at the end of practice. Although Ricci was third-fastest ahead of the Aprilia ridden by Manfred Herweh, Honda were worried that the Yamahas had the speed advantage as Wimmer sat on pole a second quicker than their fastest man, while Lavado was second. It was interesting

to see Jacques Cornu and Carlos Cardus on their production RS250 Hondas close behind the NSRs of Sito Pons, Mang and Dominique Sarron. Some suggested that the NSRs were not so superior to the production bike as Spencer's bike had been; others said the difference was Spencer.

Perhaps the truth lay somewhere between as there were certainly differences between the '86 model NSRs and Spencer's own bike. The World Championship-winning machine weighed in at under the minimum 90 kg and needed lead weights in the fork legs to get it through scrutineering. The production bikes came out at 94 kg thanks to aluminium instead of magnesium crankcases, the heavier, more robust clutch off the production bike and separate aluminium carbs instead of the special magnesium-bodied twin-choke unit.

With less titanium in the brackets, nuts and bolts this accounted for the weight increase and was done to save cost when it came to producing the batch to be handed out in '86. Power production was said to be as good as the genuine Spencer model. However, Yamaha now had the upper hand as they were running only two riders on magnesium crankcase factory specials instead of special production bikes as they had in 1985.

Kel Carruthers now had his hands full, and on top of looking after the 500s, he was giving advice to the Lucky Strike and Gauloises teams in addition to tuning cylinders for all and sundry. He put some effort into the 250s at Monza as well as working on the 500s and with Lavado and Wimmer on top it seemed to be having the desired effect.

## 125 cc

After being almost a second faster than anyone else in practice Fausto Gresini was the firm race favourite and true to form he dominated the 18-lap race. Nevertheless he had to battle hard at the start to get clear of what became a race-long battle for second between Angel Nieto, August Auinger, Luca Cadalora, Ezio Gianola and Domenico Brigaglia.

The opening laps were fierce, with Auinger on the Bartol MBA the early leader. Despite being passed by the Garelli-mounted Gresini, he hung onto him until lap 5 and at the same time battling to stave off the attacks of those behind. Both Gianola and Brigaglia retired in the closing stages but Nieto on the Ducados and Auinger fought it out to the line leaving Cadalora a little in the last two desperate laps.

The 250 grid lines up with Wimmer on pole on the far side, while Lavado, Ricci, Herweh and Sarron take subsequent positions (left).

Right: **Out of the last chicane and on to the back straight.**

**Dave Petersen** (below) **brought the HB Suzuki home in eleventh place.**

Auinger had been barged off the track by Cadalora at one stage but he was still able to give Nieto a run for it at the flag. He came off second best, though, when both tried for the same piece of road in one of the chicanes and he had to settle for third.

From lap 7 Gianola had a lonely ride in sixth place until he stopped with crankshaft failure after fifteen laps, two laps after Brigaglia had stopped with a similar ailment. That promoted Pier Paolo Bianchi and Lucio Pietroniro to fifth and sixth and they swapped places until Bianchi opened up a convincing advantage over the last two laps.

Thierry Feuz was seventh after getting the better of a contest with Gastone Grassetti who came under pressure from Johnny Wickström and Willy Perez just two laps from the flag.

### 80 cc

Push starts may be frustrating and unfair but they also occasionally produce heightened excitement as riders are forced to ride from the back of the field after failing to get the engine started with the rest. Unfortunately for Ian McConnachie making bad starts was becoming a habit and as Angel Nieto and Stefan Dörflinger got away cleanly at the head of the field McConnachie was left struggling to get his private Krauser fired up long after the pack had headed for the first chicane.

The disastrous getaway fired up the British lad and he passed fourteen people on the first lap but up front the World Champion had taken the lead on the works Krauser leaving Nieto to try and defend second from 'Aspar' Martinez. The third

Derbi man, Herreros, moved into fourth place and began a race-long contest with Gerhard Waibel who had fitted a manual ignition advance lever to the handlebar of his Real and this enabled him to pull another 500 rpm as he slipstreamed the normally quicker works Derbi.

Dörflinger had been fastest in practice with Nieto second ahead of Martinez, Herreros and McConnachie and therefore it was not surprising to see the Swiss pulling away slightly at the head of the field. The battle for second was crucial for several reasons: firstly, Derbi team orders for the rest of the season were to be decided on championship positions after the first three races and therefore Nieto had to beat Martinez to redress the balance following the Spanish Grand Prix. Secondly, and beyond the Derbi team and the '86 World Championship, the Spanish saw the battle as that of the Old School represented by Nieto against the new order headed by Aspar.

With all this resting on the result there was no quarter asked or given and the advantage changed hands at every turn. Meanwhile McConnachie's rise was meteoric as he went from tenth on lap 3 to eighth and then sixth on lap 50. There was no doubt that not only was he moving up through the field but closing on Dörflinger. He broke the lap record several times as he flicked the little machine through the chicanes visibly faster than anyone else.

Dörflinger was also being overhauled by Martinez and Nieto and crossing the line at the end of lap 8 the veteran led the field with Martinez and Dörflinger right with him going into the first chicane. Through the left-hander Martinez made a play for the lead and into the right both Derbi men tried to use the same piece of road with

Nieto losing out and crashing.

As McConnachie arrived at the chicane (having just passed Herreros and Waibel) and with Nieto down he was in third place. Sadly, he never had the chance to appreciate that, as on arriving at the left-hander the Krauser seized and he slid off.

Neither Nieto or McConnachie could continue and that elevated the Herreros and Waibel battle to one for third and giving Pier Paolo Bianchi fifth ahead of Theo Timmer and Hans Spaan on the Casals. The winner was still to be decided because Dörflinger had lost ground as Nieto fell in front of him and had to push hard to catch Martinez.

The Swiss ace regained the lead a lap later but Aspar fought back again and it came down to a rush for the line won by the World Champion who got the verdict by less than three-tenths of a second. It meant that Nieto was likely to be out of

luck as team orders would surely dictate that he followed Martinez if the situation did not change radically at the Nürburgring.

## 250 cc

Carlos Lavado admitted that he had a 'piccolo trucco' to get the V-twin Yamaha fired up and off the line cleanly but he was not going to admit what that little trick was. The man who needed to know was Martin Wimmer who once more made a mediocre getaway while Lavado chased Fausto Ricci, Toni Mang, Dominique Sarron and Jean-Michel Mattioli into the first chicane.

At the end of the first circuit the race plan began to emerge with Ricci still leading but Mang and Lavado hard on his heels. Carlos Cardus had worked his way into fourth on the RS250 Honda ahead of the NSR ridden by Sarron.

A lap later Mang had taken the lead but Ricci

held off Lavado while Cardus came under pressure from Sarron and Jean-François Baldé became the man to watch as he had moved from eleventh at the end of lap 1 to sixth on lap 3.

Donnie McLeod stopped with a broken crank which was doubly frustrating after his mechanic had shown the dubious unit to the Rotax engineer the night before but was assured it would be fine for the race. His team-mate Ian Newton also stopped but after having completed 15 laps.

On lap 4 Cardus retired with clutch problems as Baldé passed Sarron to gain fourth. He had been down in 17th place on the grid but as he pointed out the night before the race, 'it is easier for me to improve than the others'. True to his word he chopped two seconds off his practice time in the race and said it was all to do with the rear suspension.

'All the springs that Honda offered me seemed

too soft, I was running out of ground clearance in the corners. The night before the race they came up with one very hard spring and we tried it in the free practice on Sunday. We just had to guess at the adjustment but we were exactly right and for the race I think it was perfect.'

Pole-position man Wimmer was down in 13th place at the end of the second lap and as usual was cautious with his progress. On lap 5 he had caught the group behind Baldé and Sarron which included Pierre Bolle on the Parisienne, Sito Pons and Mattioli. As he got to the front of the group another three joined onto the tail: Jacques Cornu, Massimo Matteoni and Reinhold Roth, all on RS Hondas.

Wimmer dragged the group with him as he caught Sarron; with that, Pons became inspired and led the chase after Baldé. By lap 11, Pons, Baldé and Wimmer were wrapped up in a private struggle well clear of Sarron who was trying to

Fausto Gresini leads Luca Cadalora, August Auinger and Angel Nieto through one of the tight chicanes.

retain a steady advantage over Cornu. The latter was pulling away from Bolle who in turn had got clear of Mattioli and Matteoni. Ricci had dropped out of the race on lap 6 with ignition failure leaving Mang to lead Lavado by what appeared to be an increasingly comfortable margin.

Mang's problem was that although he had got away from Lavado he was pushing the bike considerably harder than he had in practice and the bike was not set up for it. The front forks and the front tyre began to protest. The damping of the forks was affected by the loss of performance of the front tyre and equally the loss of suspension performance upset the rubber. Mang had to ease the pace going into the corners and at Monza backing off on the brakes into the chicanes allowed Lavado to close on him.

It became obvious with four laps still to go that it was going to be a very close run thing at the flag as Lavado was narrowing the gap rapidly. On lap 16 of the 18 the Venezuelan was right on Mang's tail and next time round he was in front. Lavado made enough of a mistake to let Mang retake the lead on the final circuit but Lavado lined himself up to take victory on the Parabolica, the last sweeping right-hander.

As the pair braked for the tightening radius section of the corner Lavado pulled alongside to Mang's left. He had made himself take the long way round though and as the corner opened up Mang got on the power and let the Honda drift wide. Lavado had left himself too much to do and was too committed to drop back inside Mang whose experience had the situation covered.

'It is impossible to go round the outside there. The only way to pass is up the inside but I stopped him doing that and when he went for the outside I knew that he could not pass. I knew because I tried to do it to Ekerold in '81.'

The battle for second was just as exciting with Pons, Baldé and Wimmer swapping places five times a lap and juggling for the best position for the slipstreaming run across the line. Baldé won from Wimmer and Pons, well clear of Cornu who took sixth from Sarron on the last lap. Bolle beat off an attack from Matteoni and Mattioli who finished tenth and glad that the bike ran reasonably after breaking the crank in the morning warm-up session and rushing through a complete rebuild before the race.

## 500 cc

'I didn't know what to do, I have never got to the first corner in front before', said Lawson later. None the less, he obviously knew perfectly well what to do at the time and with a clear road ahead of him set about a Spencer-style domination of the 25-lap race that turned the World Championship odds completely around. Gardner was left in agony on the startline having been hit by European Champion Marco Gentile on the Fior.

'I didn't get started properly and as I jumped on I was hit from behind', recalled the Australian later. 'The impact smashed my knee into the footrest and it hurt so bad that I let go of the throttle and the clutch so the engine died. I pulled myself

together and got off to push again but my leg almost gave way underneath me. When I did get the engine started I found I couldn't change gear because the lever and the footrest plate were bent, so I just did a slow lap and pulled into the pits.'

Though he had lost more than a lap Gardner rejoined the race at the tail of the field determined to try and score a point however impossible that seemed. Honda must have been wondering how they had angered the gods for they now had both their stars injured and no-one else with the four-cylinder machinery necessary to enable them to take up the cudgels.

The race became a Yamaha benefit but only after the five V-fours had dealt with the harrying Chevallier ridden with such determination by Didier de Radigues, scarcely mindful of his pinned collarbone. Less of a threat was Ron Haslam who had been practising the starts with the Elf all week after his poor getaway in Spain. For at least two years Haslam had been the fastest starter in Grand Prix racing and he had not lost the knack. What had hindered him was the experimental Elf and the tortuous route the clutch cable took as it left the lever.

Haslam's practice paid dividends because he was on Lawson's tail approaching the first chicane. 'I thought about taking the lead', Haslam said later. 'I could have done but I thought I'd better not take any risks passing Lawson with cold tyres.' Haslam had no ideas of winning; he realised that he was limited by what he could do with the Elf but as always he set about the race in an intelligent fashion and defended every place as he was forced back.

De Radigues hung on to second for two laps and Mamola would later blame the Belgian for the fact that he lost touch with Lawson. Mamola and de Radigues had not seen eye to eye for two years following the collision at Jarama when Mamola pulled across and slowed on the main straight for a plug chop. De Radigues ran into the back of him and Mamola cursed him for always following too close, for waiting during practice until someone fast came past and then tagging on behind. De Radigues was not impressed by Mamola's point of view and blamed him completely for the pain he had suffered at Jarama.

Here de Radigues was not tagging along but staying in front and once more riding the wheels off the Chevallier. it was not until lap 5 that Mamola finally got past and shortly afterwards the Chevallier was overhauled by Baldwin, McElnea, Sarron and Roche. A two-lap contest sorted things out leaving Baldwin, McElnea and Sarron in a group chasing Mamola and dropping Roche who soon pushed de Radigues back to seventh. Eighth was Juan Garriga having a good ride on the Cagiva with Haslam now a lonely ninth fitting the odd slide on the Elf which was not giving the traction it had earlier in practice. 'I don't know what they did to the suspension but it lost all the drive coming out of the corners.' At the end of the race it was remarkable to see the rubber marks round the edge of the bead that showed just how the soft sidewalls had been

flexing.

Up front Lawson rode a masterful race, took things easy passing tail-enders but maintained a comfortable buffer between himself and Mamola. The Lucky Strike rider eventually gave up the chase and settled for a reasonably safe second although he was not that far ahead of the pursuing trio of McElnea, Sarron and Baldwin. With the end of the race approaching it became a question of who would be in front at the flag as none could get clear away.

Unfortunately for McElnea he was deceived into thinking the race was a lap nearer finishing than it was. 'We were in such a tight bunch that I could not see my own pit board. I had to look at the official board at the start-and-finish line but that was a lap out. So when I thought it was the last lap I made my move to lead the other two over the line but there was no chequered flag, and as I realised I had made a mistake the others came past.' With one lap now remaining McElnea repassed Sarron but Baldwin was still several yards ahead through the last chicane with only the back straight and the Parabolica to go. Baldwin's bike had been the quicker of the three throughout the race and McElnea needed a superior drive onto the back straight if he was going to stay with him. He got on the power early and hard but it was too much for the race-weary rear tyre which sent the V-four into a long slide. 'I thought I was going to hold it but then the bitch flicked me', reported McElnea, turning round one of Lawson's favourite sayings; 'Flick the bitch'.

McElnea was lucky to escape with severe bruising after flying through the air and ending up in a heap at the trackside. Sarron picked up the points for fourth but was a little frustrated. 'One day we will get fair starts, that is all I ask; I am fed up with having to make up for bad push starts', he complained. Sarron was 14th at the end of lap 1 and pointed out that this handicapped him later on. 'I asked a lot of my tyres at the beginning of the race when I had to catch up and there was not much I could do at the end. I did my fastest laps catching Baldwin and McElnea but when I did I could not get away. Baldwin's bike was the fastest but he was not quick round some of the corners. At the end McElnea fell off right in front of me so there was nothing I could do to catch Baldwin.'

Lawson reported few problems after his race win. 'It was hot and humid and I was sweating a lot so some ran in my eyes, but that was about my only problem. The bike was perfect and we set the shock up a little slow for the beginning of the race so that it would be good at the end, and it worked out fine. It is far too early to talk about the championship because it is a long season and I could easily have the same problem that Gardner had here – push starts are just stupid.'

It was a good day for picking up unexpected points; apart from McElnea's crash on the last lap, Roche had fallen on lap 16 and then both Haslam and Garriga ran out of fuel with less than a lap to go. Certainly in the case of the Elf the fuel tank was too small even though the team had topped it up on the startline after the warm-up lap. Two fuel dramas in as many races was beyond a joke.

# Autodromo Nazionale di Monza, 3.604-mile/5.800-km circuit

## 500 cc

**25 laps, 90.10 miles/145.00 km**

| *Place* | *Rider* | *Nat.* | *Machine* | *Laps* | *Time & speed* | *Practice time* | *Grid* |
|---|---|---|---|---|---|---|---|
| 1 | Eddie Lawson | USA | Yamaha | 25 | 46m 29.95s 116.260mph/ 187.102 km/h | 1m 49.95s | 1 |
| 2 | Randy Mamola | USA | Yamaha | 25 | 46m 35.63s | 1m 50.30s | 2 |
| 3 | Mike Baldwin | USA | Yamaha | 25 | 46m 37.58s | 1m 51.25s | 6 |
| 4 | Christian Sarron | F | Yamaha | 25 | 46m 39.97s | 1m 50.91s | 5 |
| 5 | Didier de Radigues | B | Chevallier | 25 | 47m 18.95s | 1m 51.91s | 8 |
| 6 | Boet van Dulmen | NL | Honda | 25 | 48m 13.90s | 1m 55.32s | 16 |
| 7 | Pier Francesco Chili | I | Suzuki | 25 | 48m 23.33s | 1m 54.18s | 13 |
| 8 | Fabio Biliotti | I | Honda | 24 | 46m 30.18s | 1m 54.54s | 14 |
| 9 | Paul Lewis | AUS | Suzuki | 24 | 46m 41.06s | 1m 55.77s | 18 |
| 10 | Marco Papa | I | Honda | 24 | 46m 51.97s | 1m 54.61s | 15 |
| 11 | Dave Petersen | ZIM | Suzuki | 24 | 46m 52.41s | 1m 55.33s | 17 |
| 12 | Peter Sköld | S | Honda | 24 | 47m 11.41s | 1m 56.31s | 20 |
| 13 | Henk van der Mark | NL | Honda | 24 | 47m 12.08s | 1m 57.07s | 25 |
| 14 | Manfred Fischer | D | Honda | 24 | 47m 33.90s | 1m 56.51s | 22 |
| 15 | Karl Truchsess | A | Honda | 24 | 47m 44.01s | 1m 58.25s | 29 |
| 16 | Wayne Gardner | AUS | Honda | 24 | 47m 52.24s | 1m 50.71s | 3 |
| 17 | Peter Linden | S | Honda | 24 | 48m 00.99s | 1m 56.81s | 24 |
| 18 | Rob Punt | NL | Honda | 24 | 48m 15.08s | 1m 59.36s | 32 |
| 19 | Marco Marchesani | I | Suzuki | 23 | 47m 43.74s | 1m 56.56s | 21 |
| | Rob McElnea | GB | Yamaha | 24 | DNF | 1m 50.86s | 4 |
| | Ron Haslam | GB | Elf | 24 | DNF | 1m 54.11s | 11 |
| | Juan Garriga | E | Cagiva | 24 | DNF | 1m 52.64s | 9 |
| | Andreas Leuthe | LUX | Honda | 22 | DNF | 1m 59.55s | 33 |
| | Leandro Becheroni | I | Honda | 21 | DNF | 1m 57.77s | 26 |
| | Raymond Roche | F | Honda | 15 | DNF | 1m 51.58s | 7 |
| | Roger Burnett | GB | Honda | 12 | DNF | 1m 53.81s | 10 |
| | Sepp Doppler | A | Honda | 12 | DNF | 2m 00.59s | 35 |
| | Marco Gentile | CH | Fior | 11 | DNF | 2m 00.43s | 34 |
| | Simon Buckmaster | GB | Honda | 10 | DNF | 1m 58.52s | 30 |
| | Armando Errico | I | Suzuki | 6 | DNF | 1m 56.66s | 23 |
| | Alessandro Valesi | I | Honda | 3 | DNF | 1m 56.25s | 19 |
| | Vittorio Scatola | I | Paton | 1 | DNF | 1m 57.95s | 28 |
| | Wolfgang von Muralt | CH | Suzuki | 1 | DNF | 2m 00.84s | 36 |
| | Vinicio Bogani | I | Suzuki | 1 | DNF | 1m 59.11s | 31 |
| | Marco Lucchinelli | I | Cagiva | 1 | DNF | 1m 54.16s | 12 |
| | Georg-Robert Jung | D | Honda | 1 | DNF | 1m 57.86s | 27 |
| | Eero Hyvarinen | SF | Honda | | DNQ | 2m 01.09s | |
| | Dave Griffith | GB | Suzuki | | DNQ | 2m 06.24s | |
| | Vicenzo Cascino | RCH | Suzuki | | DNQ | 2m 13.45s | |

*Fastest lap:* Baldwin, 1m 49.31s, 118.693 mph/191.017 km/h (record).
*Previous record:* Kenny Roberts, USA (Yamaha), 1m 52.80s, 115.021 mph/185.108 km/h (1983).

**World Championship: 1** Lawson, 27; **2** Baldwin and Mamola, 20; **4** Gardner, 15; **5** Sarron, 14; **6** de Radigues, 6; **7** Roche, Biliotti and van Dulmen, 5; **10** McElnea and Chili, 4; **12** Garriga, 3; **13** Lewis, 2; **14** Haslam and Papa, 1.

## 250 cc

**18 laps, 64.87 miles/104.40 km**

| *Place* | *Rider* | *Nat.* | *Machine* | *Laps* | *Time & speed* | *Practice time* | *Grid* |
|---|---|---|---|---|---|---|---|
| 1 | Anton Mang | D | Honda | 18 | 35m 35.76s 109.344 mph/ 175.972 km/h | 1m 58.29s | 6 |
| 2 | Carlos Lavado | YV | Yamaha | 18 | 35m 35.89s | 1m 57.34s | 2 |
| 3 | Jean-François Baldé | F | Honda | 18 | 35m 46.94s | 1m 59.54s | 18 |
| 4 | Martin Wimmer | D | Yamaha | 18 | 35m 47.13s | 1m 56.77s | 1 |
| 5 | Alfonso Pons | E | Honda | 18 | 35m 47.31s | 1m 58.30s | 7 |
| 6 | Jacques Cornu | CH | Honda | 18 | 35m 56.48s | 1m 58.55s | 9 |
| 7 | Dominique Sarron | F | Honda | 18 | 35m 57.03s | 1m 58.28s | 5 |
| 8 | Pierre Bolle | F | Parisienne | 18 | 36m 03.16s | 1m 59.74s | 22 |
| 9 | Massimo Matteoni | I | Honda | 18 | 36m 03.48s | 1m 59.46s | 16 |
| 10 | Jean-Michel Mattioli | F | Yamaha | 18 | 36m 03.62s | 1m 59.27s | 14 |
| 11 | Alan Carter | GB | Kobas | 18 | 36m 09.52s | 1m 59.50s | 17 |
| 12 | Hans Lindner | A | Castrol | 18 | 36m 09.76s | 2m 00.45s | 28 |
| 13 | Stefano Caracchi | I | Aprilia | 18 | 36m 10.49s | 1m 59.92s | 23 |
| 14 | Manfred Herweh | D | Aprilia | 18 | 36m 10.63s | 1m 57.79s | 4 |
| 15 | Reinhold Roth | D | Honda | 18 | 36m 10.89s | 1m 59.55s | 20 |
| 16 | Harald Eckl | D | Honda | 18 | 36m 29.14s | 2m 00.28s | 26 |
| 17 | Stéphane Mertens | B | Yamaha | 18 | 36m 29.33s | 1m 59.64s | 21 |
| 18 | Siegfried Minich | A | Honda | 18 | 36m 30.24s | 2m 01.09s | 32 |
| 19 | Brent Jones | NZ | Yamaha | 18 | 36m 30.43s | 1m 59.02s | 12 |
| 20 | Ivan Palazzese | YV | Rotax | 18 | 36m 30.80s | 2m 00.66s | 30 |
| 21 | Antonio Neto | BR | Yamaha | 18 | 36m 40.36s | 2m 00.41s | 27 |
| 22 | Tadahiko Taira | J | Yamaha | 18 | 36m 53.85s | 1m 58.76s | 10 |
| 23 | Loris Reggiani | I | Aprilia | 18 | 36m 54.04s | 1m 59.08s | 13 |
| 24 | Marcellino Lucchi | I | Cazzaniga | 18 | 36m 55.89s | 2m 00.03s | 25 |
| 25 | Bruno Bonhuil | F | Honda | 18 | 36m 56.08s | 2m 01.17s | 33 |
| 26 | Jean-Louis Guignabodet | F | MIG | 18 | 36m 56.48s | 2m 01.18s | 34 |
| 27 | René Délaby | B | Rotax | 18 | 37m 27.03s | 2m 01.00s | 31 |
| | Ian Newton | GB | Armstrong | 15 | DNF | 1m 59.97s | 24 |
| | Konrad Hefele | D | Honda | 13 | DNF | 2m 01.21s | 35 |
| | Fausto Ricci | I | Honda | 6 | DNF | 1m 57.74s | 3 |
| | Gary Noel | GB | EMC | 5 | DNF | 2m 01.27s | 36 |
| | Carlos Cardus | E | Honda | 3 | DNF | 1m 58.34s | 8 |
| | Jean Foray | F | Chevallier | 3 | DNF | 1m 59.45s | 15 |
| | Alberto Rota | I | Honda | 3 | DNF | 1m 59.52s | 19 |
| | Donnie McLeod | GB | Armstrong | 2 | DNF | 1m 58.96s | 11 |
| | Jean-Louis Tournadre | F | Yamaha | 2 | DNF | 2m 00.53s | 29 |
| | Nedy Crotta | CH | Armstrong | | DNQ | 2m 01.28s | |
| | Maurizio Vitali | I | Garelli | | DNQ | 2m 01.51s | |
| | Fabio Marcaccini | I | Honda | | DNQ | 2m 01.64s | |
| | Roland Freymond | CH | Yamaha | | DNQ | 2m 01.84s | |
| | Urs Luzi | CH | Yamaha | | DNQ | 2m 02.56s | |
| | Johnny Simonsson | S | Honda | | DNQ | 2m 02.80s | |
| | Luis Lavado | YV | Yamaha | | DNQ | 2m 03.20s | |
| | Peter Hubbard | GB | Rotax | | DNQ | 2m 04.18s | |
| | Oscar la Ferla | I | Yamaha | | DNQ | 2m 04.99s | |
| | Marcello Iannata | I | Yamaha | | DNQ | 2m 05.52s | |
| | Andrea Brasini | I | Garelli | | DNQ | 2m 05.65s | |
| | Eilert Lundstedt | S | Rotax | | DNQ | 2m 06.07s | |
| | Gérard Vallée | F | Yamaha | | DNQ | 2m 06.23s | |
| | Miguel Gonzalez | YV | Yamaha | | DNQ | 2m 07.61s | |

*Fastest lap:* Pons, 1m 57.16s, 110.741 mph/178.220 km/h (record).
*Previous record:* Loris Reggiani, I (Aprilia), 1m 59.93s, 108/183 mph/174.103 km/h (1985).

**World Championship: 1** Mang and Lavado, 27; **3** Pons and Wimmer, 16; **5** Baldé, 13; **6** Cornu, 11; **7** Bolle, 8; **8** McLeod and Sarron, 4; **10** Ricci and Matteoni, 2; **12** Carter and Mattioli, 1.

## 125 cc

**18 laps, 64.87 miles/104.40 km**

| *Place* | *Rider* | *Nat.* | *Machine* | *Laps* | *Time & speed* | *Practice time* | *Grid* |
|---|---|---|---|---|---|---|---|
| 1 | Fausto Gresini | I | Garelli | 18 | 37m 51.45s 102.812 mph/ 165.459 km/h | 2m 04.18s | 1 |
| 2 | Angel Nieto | E | Ducados | 18 | 38m 02.03s | 2m 06.45s | 6 |
| 3 | August Auinger | A | Bartol | 18 | 38m 02.22s | 2m 05.07s | 3 |
| 4 | Luca Cadalora | I | Garelli | 18 | 38m 05.10s | 2m 04.97s | 2 |
| 5 | Pier Paolo Bianchi | I | Elit | 18 | 38m 45.90s | 2m 07.49s | 8 |
| 6 | Lucio Pietroniro | B | MBA | 18 | 38m 50.04s | 2m 08.65s | 12 |
| 7 | Thierry Feuz | CH | MBA | 18 | 39m 00.88s | 2m 08.49s | 11 |
| 8 | Gastone Grassetti | I | MBA | 18 | 39m 03.61s | 2m 08.43s | 10 |
| 9 | Johnny Wickström | SF | Tunturi | 18 | 39m 03.79s | 2m 08.84s | 14 |
| 10 | Willy Perez | RA | Zanella | 18 | 39m 04.89s | 2m 08.70s | 13 |
| 11 | Alfred Waibel | D | Real | 18 | 39m 55.66s | 2m 11.54s | 19 |
| 12 | Hakan Olsson | S | Starol | 18 | 39m 55.86s | 2m 10.31s | 17 |
| 13 | Thomas Möller-Pedersen | SF | MBA | 18 | 39m 56.05s | 2m 11.56s | 20 |
| 14 | Adolf Stadler | D | MBA | 18 | 39m 56.53s | 2m 13.95s | 31 |
| 15 | Marin Andreas Sanchez | E | Ducados | 18 | 39m 57.75s | 2m 12.85s | 25 |
| 16 | Jacques Hutteau | F | MBA | 17 | 37m 57.71s | 2m 12.41s | 24 |
| 17 | Patrick Daudier | F | PMDF | 17 | 38m 00.41s | 2m 13.14s | 26 |
| 18 | Robin Appleyard | GB | MBA | 17 | 38m 06.50s | 2m 12.40s | 23 |
| 19 | Peter Balaz | CS | MBA | 17 | 38m 14.11s | 2m 13.22s | 28 |
| 20 | Karl Dauer | A | MBA | 17 | 38m 18.67s | 2m 14.98s | 35 |
| 21 | Manfred Braun | D | MBA | 17 | 38m 21.81s | 2m 14.27s | 33 |
| 22 | Wilhelm Lücke | D | MBA | 17 | 38m 22.18s | 2m 14.18s | 32 |
| 23 | Peter Sommer | CH | MBA | 17 | 39m 16.53s | 2m 14.61s | 34 |
| | Ezio Gianola | I | MBA | 15 | DNF | 2m 05.91s | 5 |
| | Domenico Brigaglia | I | Ducados | 13 | DNF | 2m 05.68s | 4 |
| | Jussi Hautaniemi | SF | MBA | 12 | DNF | 2m 12.26s | 22 |
| | Ivan Troisi | YV | MBA | 12 | DNF | 2m 15.17s | 36 |
| | Mike Leitner | A | LCR | 9 | DNF | 2m 09.73s | 16 |
| | Giuseppe Ascareggi | I | Seel | 5 | DNF | 2m 11.18s | 18 |
| | Bruno Kneubühler | CH | LCR | 3 | DNF | 2m 07.86s | 9 |
| | Olivier Liegeois | B | Assmex | 3 | DNF | 2m 07.19s | 7 |
| | Paolo Casoli | I | MBA | 2 | DNF | 2m 09.47s | 15 |
| | Esa Kytola | SF | MBA | 2 | DNF | 2m 13.35s | 29 |
| | Eric Saul | F | LGM | 2 | DNF | 2m 13.69s | 30 |
| | Janez Pintar | YU | MBA | 2 | DNF | 2m 11.95s | 21 |
| | Manuel Hernandez | E | Benetti | 0 | DNF | 2m 13.22s | 27 |
| | Steve Mason | GB | MBA | | DNQ | 2m 15.21s | |
| | Rune Zaelle | S | MBA | | DNQ | 2m 16.18s | |
| | Robert Hmeljak | YU | MBA | | DNQ | 2m 16.70s | |
| | Thierry Maurer | CH | MBA | | DNQ | 2m 17.02s | |
| | Angelo Scapellato | I | MBA | | DNQ | 2m 17.67s | |
| | Fernando Gonzalez | E | MBA | | DNQ | 2m 18.39s | |
| | Shaun Simpson | GB | MBA | | DNQ | 2m 21.12s | |
| | | | | | DNQ | | |

*Fastest lap:* Gresini, 2m 04.57s, 104.153 mph/167.618 km/h (record).
*Previous record:* Fausto Gresini, I (Garelli), 2m 04.82s, 103.945 mph/167.283 km/h (1985).

**World Championship: 1** Gresini, 30; **2** Cadalora, 16; **3** Brigaglia and Nieto, 12; **5** Gianola, Bianchi and Auinger, 10; **8** Wickström, 8; **9** Perez, 6; **10** Pietroniro, 5; **11** Feuz, 4; **12** Sanchez and Grassetti, 3; **14** Hautaniemi, 2; **15** Olsson, 1.

## 80 cc

**13 laps, 46.85 miles/75.40 km**

| *Place* | *Rider* | *Nat.* | *Machine* | *Laps* | *Time & speed* | *Practice time* | *Grid* |
|---|---|---|---|---|---|---|---|
| 1 | Stefan Dörflinger | CH | Krauser | 13 | 28m 56.58s 97.122 mph/ 156.302 km/h | 2m 11.27s | 1 |
| 2 | Jorge Martinez | E | Derbi | 13 | 28m 56.75s | 2m 12.55s | 3 |
| 3 | Manuel Herreros | E | Derbi | 13 | 29m 23.98s | 2m 13.77s | 4 |
| 4 | Gerhard Waibel | D | Real | 13 | 29m 24.25s | 2m 14.82s | 8 |
| 5 | Pier Paolo Bianchi | I | Seel | 13 | 29m 42.15s | 2m 14.57s | 7 |
| 6 | Theo Timmer | NL | Huvo | 13 | 29m 43.08s | 2m 14.33s | 6 |
| 7 | Hans Spaan | NL | Huvo | 13 | 29m 44.11s | 2m 16.45s | 9 |
| 8 | Gerd Kafka | A | Krauser | 13 | 29m 58.70s | 2m 16.46s | 10 |
| 9 | Rainer Kunz | D | Ziegler | 13 | 30m 33.05s | 2m 19.98s | 19 |
| 10 | Salvatore Milano | I | Krauser | 13 | 30m 39.26s | 2m 20.23s | 20 |
| 11 | Luis Reyes | COL | Autisa | 13 | 30m 40.29s | 2m 19.80s | 18 |
| 12 | Hubert Abold | D | Seel | 13 | 30m 54.03s | 2m 20.37s | 21 |
| 13 | Chris Baert | B | Seel | 13 | 31m 33.45s | 2m 23.11s | 24 |
| 14 | Jos van Dongen | NL | Krauser | 12 | 29m 01.80s | 2m 24.18s | 26 |
| 15 | Lionel Robert | F | Scrab | 12 | 29m 02.21s | 2m 24.36s | 27 |
| 16 | Raimo Lipponen | SF | Keifer | 12 | 29m 03.88s | 2m 24.86s | 28 |
| 17 | Vincenzo Saffiotti | I | UFO | 12 | 29m 04.99s | 2m 26.70s | 34 |
| 18 | Reiner Koster | CH | LCR | 12 | 29m 08.77s | 2m 25.93s | 31 |
| 19 | Richard Bay | D | Rupp | 12 | 29m 16.33s | 2m 26.43s | 33 |
| 20 | Jarmö Piepponen | SF | Keifer | 12 | 29m 16.51s | 2m 25.22s | 29 |
| 21 | Bertus Grinwis | NL | Krauser | 12 | 29m 43.28s | 2m 27.34s | 35 |
| | Mario Stocco | I | Huvo | 12 | DNF | 2m 21.45s | 23 |
| | Felix Rodriguez | E | Autisa | 10 | DNF | 2m 18.52s | 14 |
| | Thomas Engl | D | ESCH | 10 | DNF | 2m 21.34s | 22 |
| | Stefan Brägger | CH | Huvo | 9 | DNF | 2m 27.96s | 36 |
| | Angel Nieto | E | Derbi | 8 | DNF | 2m 11.96s | 2 |
| | Ian McConnachie | GB | Krauser | 8 | DNF | 2m 13.77s | 5 |
| | Reinhard Koberstein | D | Seel | 8 | DNF | 2m 25.95s | 32 |
| | Serge Julin | B | Huvo | 8 | DNF | 2m 25.29s | 30 |
| | Juan Bolart | E | Autisa | 7 | DNF | 2m 17.99s | 13 |
| | Reiner Scheidhauer | D | Seel | 6 | DNF | 2m 19.74s | 17 |
| | Henk van Kessel | NL | Krauser | 6 | DNF | 2m 17.64s | 12 |
| | Alexandre Barros | BR | Autisa | 4 | DNF | 2m 19.41s | 16 |
| | Steve Mason | GB | Huvo | 3 | DNF | 2m 24.14s | 25 |
| | Domingo Gil | E | Autisa | 3 | DNF | 2m 17.21s | 11 |
| | René Dünki | CH | Krauser | 3 | DNF | 2m 18.68s | 15 |
| | Mika-Sakari Komu | SF | Berhard | | DNQ | 2m 28.07s | |
| | Claudio Granata | I | Lusuardi | | DNQ | 2m 31.28s | |
| | Guiliano Tabanelli | I | Mancini | | DNQ | 2m 28.98s | |
| | Nicola Casadei | I | RB | | DNQ | 2m 29.16s | |
| | Georges Fissette | B | Huvo | | DNQ | 2m 29.73s | |
| | Otto Machinek | A | Hummel | | DNQ | 2m 30.09s | |
| | Kees Besseling | NL | Huvo | | DNQ | 2m 31.11s | |
| | Mario Scalinci | I | Huvo | | DNQ | 2m 35.43s | |
| | Jan Vanecek | CS | Kreidler | | DNQ | 2m 38.84s | |

*Fastest lap:* McConnachie, 2m 10.90s, 99.117 mph/159.513 km/h (record).
*Previous record:* Salvatore Milano, I (Huvo), 2m 22.01s, 91.362 mph/147.033 km/h (1985).

**World Championship: 1** Martinez, 27; **2** Herreros, 20; **3** Dörflinger, 17; **4** Bianchi, 14; **5** Nieto and Waibel, 12; **7** McConnachie, 6; **8** Bolart and Timmer, 5; **10** Spaan, 4; **11** Abold and Kafka, 3; **13** Kunz, 2; **14** Gil and Milano, 1.

# Grosser Preis von
# DEUTSCHLAND

'Will he, won't he, will he, won't he, will he join the dance?' There was no fairytale comeback but the Lewis Carroll style saga continued as Spencer's bikes and motorhome were ready at the Nürburgring for him to arrive and race if he was fit enough. Spencer arrived but not to ride as his wrist was still not right and in a light support. He only made the transatlantic trip to explain the position and dispel the mounting rumours that it was a financial argument with Rothmans or Honda rather than any medical problem that was keeping him from racing.

'There has never been an argument and I signed my contract with Honda last October. I am very sorry not to be riding but it is physically impossible at the moment. The pain is not a problem but the wrist just gets to the point where I cannot move it. An operation would not be easy but I am having three hours of treatment every day and I hope to be fit to ride in Austria in two weeks time. I have not yet given up hope of retaining my Championship yet and three years ago I missed out on scoring in three rounds and still won the Championship but it is certainly going to be very hard from here.'

Spencer was not at all happy to be at the Nürburgring. 'I should be at home continuing the treatment which I am working at every day but I just had to come and straighten things out. I am the very worst spectator and I just want to ride as soon as possible.'

Spencer merely gave a press conference before flying back to Louisiana and the truck containing his bikes returned to the European headquarters in Aalst.

At least Wayne Gardner could ride but he was far from a hundred per cent fit and had 50 cc of fluid drained from his injured knee before he could ride. He gave the first untimed practice a miss so that the injury had more time to heal. When he did ride the knee was painful and stiff; he modified his riding style a little to move about the bike less but no-one who rides fast can modify their style that much and still be natural enough to be competitive at the highest level. The Nürburgring is hard work with both high- and medium-speed changes of direction so he could hardly avoid using the main muscles of his legs to push against the footrests working the bike from one direction to the other. The result was that he had to be lifted off the bike after practice.

Gardner knew that he could not really hope to beat Lawson while not fit but equally he knew he would not be handicapped for long and as this was only the third Grand Prix of the season there would be time to try that later. More importantly, he needed to keep accruing points and not let Lawson get too far ahead in the Championship chase.

Lawson had things working very nicely for him and the new carburettors on his bike had improved the engine performance. 'It has cleaned up the carburation', said Lawson. 'But it is not perfect and it does not seem to have helped the starting.' If the carburation had not helped the starting then Lawson had learnt to get the bike off the line himself because he was getting away better than he had in '85.

Team-mate Rob McElnea had good memories of his first ride at the Nürburgring two years before when he had qualified on the front row on his outpowered Suzuki even though he had crashed in the race. He was wary of expecting too much, however: 'The Yamaha has so much power that the circuits are very different to what they were on the Suzuki, and at Jarama it was a bit of a handful.'

Lawson headed practice on the first day with Sarron second ahead of Mamola, Baldwin and McElnea, making it a Yamaha clean sweep, while de Radigues and Roche headed Gardner on the Hondas. Gustav Reiner on his private Honda was ahead of Dave Petersen on the Gallina Suzuki and Ron Haslam on the Elf. That trio gave a hint of the race they would have on Sunday. Reiner had missed the Italian Grand Prix thanks to crashing in practice at the German National meeting at the Nürburgring the week after Spain. He had still ridden in the race and won, only to find later that a bone in his ankle was broken. Reiner took the plaster off just before practice as is his wont and no-one who knows him was surprised at this display of determination.

Reiner had been only one of some fifty fallers at that wet national meeting and there were fears that the track surface had become so smoothed by car testing that the lack of grip would prove disastrous at the Grand Prix. To effect a cure the circuit owners resorted to grinding the surface to produce a rough area on the racing line through the corners. The treated area was good but they were a little conservative with the scope, and the braking and accelerating areas had not been ground. It made the bikes feel unstable at those points and took some getting used to. The fast left-right flick leaving the bottom corner was only treated at the apex. Lawson's reaction was representative. 'Where the surface has been ground it is not bad but feels a little slippery on the old surface and it has only been done on one line right in the corner so it is a bit hard to rush up to the turn and tip it in.'

It was felt that rain would make this section and other places treacherous. There was one wet session on Saturday morning but Gardner elected not to go out and the rest were sufficiently cautious to stay out of trouble.

Paul Lewis was one of the fallers in the dry on Friday and someone following was unkind enough to run over his glasses which had come off in the fall. He was lucky to get a local optician to make him up a new set overnight in time for Saturday's practice and Skoal Bandit team manager Garry Taylor suggested that they were an improvement. 'He can't see anything without his specs, he had to be guided to the opticians. The new glasses must be better than the old ones – Paul realised for the first time this morning that I had a beard.' Unfortunately the glasses were not good enough to stop him falling again on Saturday but he was in good company as Nieto was one of the few other fallers.

In only the second session on Friday Gardner got into the groove and was right with Lawson. The Yamaha team responded and when the track dried on Saturday afternoon Lawson pulled one out of the bag to take pole by 0.27s. While Gardner did not improve on his time, McElnea jumped to third, just 0.17s slower than the Australian. Both Baldwin and Sarron were faster than Mamola who was getting a bit tired of the pressure from his team-mate and passed a few comments about the desperate way he was riding.

As far as Baldwin was concerned he was riding well within himself. 'I have never been further from crashing than I am now. I feel I am riding well again. I have ridden this well before, in '82 and '79, and I am not going out trying to win each race. I would like to win one before the end of the season but when I do it will not be from riding desperately on the edge of disaster; I am riding conservatively.'

Following a good but not spectacular year as a Grand Prix privateer in '85, Baldwin admitted the strength of his desire to get into a works team. 'When Kenny offered me the ride I just

*Above:* **At the start of the 500 race, Manfred Fischer (number 35) gets going on the Heine Gericke RS 500.**

*Left:* **Barry Brindley and Chris Jones work hard on the Fowlers' racing Yamaha.**

**Ricci leads Lavado, Bolle, Cornu, McLeod, Cardus and Herweh through the Nürburgring's smooth sweeping curves** (below).

agreed. The money was fair – not as much as I was earning in the States but it was fair and good by European standards. I would have probably ridden for nothing, though, to get on good bikes.'

After being AMA champion four times in a row, Baldwin had had enough of racing in America where there was little challenge or appreciation. 'It is difficult when you go to some tracks where there are only a thousand people watching, like Pocono and Sears Point. How can you get excited? The bonuses from Honda kept me going there, but when we got to Laguna or Loudon where the people were good and the TV was interested that made up for it. But it is still not like GP racing; you could be sliding both wheels through and out of every turn and no-one would notice. At the Grands Prix at the end of the day someone is going to appreciate it and that is worth more than money.'

Baldwin first rode the 500 Yamaha seriously in

Malaysia where he remembered that to start with he did not get on with the machine after four years with the Honda triple. 'I was out of sorts with the bike but Kenny had been watching practice and he said, "You are riding it like a Honda. I don't want you to ride it like that; ride it like your old Yamaha." When I did ride it like that I was suddenly three seconds a lap quicker and I felt like I was going at half the pace. I was faster than Randy and that gave me a lot of my confidence back.'

Kenny Roberts further boosted his confidence when he suggested that Baldwin would do well in the World Championship. 'Kenny told me that I had an advantage. He said, "You can beat all of those guys because they have the pressure on them and when you get behind them and they get the sign board saying you are closing they won't be able to handle it." '

Roberts signed Baldwin when others ques-

tioned his inclusion in the team. 'At the press conferences you can see what they are thinking and they want to know why Kenny didn't sign Lawson or Gardner but Kenny sees things in a different light. He sees things from the seat and he has ridden against me and all the other guys, and he knows what I can do.

'After Spain and Italy Kenny told me "You could have won those races if you had a better start", but I wasn't thinking about winning those races. I was just riding my own race and not riding on the edge of disaster. It meant I had time to think what I was doing, my strategy and where I could push it a bit harder. In Spain my last three laps of the race were the fastest and in Italy I had the end of the race worked out.'

Alan Carter learnt during practice that his elder brother Kenny had committed suicide yet Alan managed to keep a grip of his own situation and threw himself into the job of sorting out his

Kobas. He had been having difficulties making himself understood to the Spanish mechanics and he did not always agree with the way they worked but he stuck at it. The troubles both personal and professional did not seem to affect his performance adversely on the track, and during untimed training he was unofficially fastest.

When the first timed training began he slipped to fourth but with only Wimmer, Lavado and Pons ahead it was no disgrace. Mang was down in eighth place but that afternoon he jumped to the head of the table leaving Lavado second ahead of Wimmer. Saturday morning was wet but Mang considered that time fast enough and was not concerned when Lavado inched ahead of him in the final session that afternoon. He had no particular plan for the race but said he could comfortably repeat his practice time. 'I was not trying too hard and tomorrow my main plan is not to fall off in front of my home crowd.'

For once, 125 World Champion Fausto Gresini did not have things all his own way in practice and Garelli team-mate Luca Cadalora was consistently quicker from the first session. Gresini struggled to get the suspension on the Garelli to work to his satisfaction and the same problem was probably to cost him the race. Gresini was finding his new team-mate much easier to get along with both on and off the track than Gianola, whom he had found far too excitable. He was dropped from the squad at the end of '85.

### 80 cc

Jorge Martinez got a great start on the works Derbi, determined to win the race and thereby make certain that team orders would dictate that Nieto would have to take a back seat for the rest of the season. The veteran was not far behind in sixth place with his own ideas as to the outcome.

Dörflinger had suffered a handicap from the start and was down in twelfth place at the end of lap 1 while Pier Paolo Bianchi on the Seel hounded Martinez and took the lead on lap 2 with Martinez right behind, ahead of Hans Spaan, Manuel Herreros and Nieto. Dörflinger was up to seventh behind Henk van Kessel but Ian McConnachie was fighting to get into the first twenty after being forced onto the grass in a startline mêlée.

With Dörflinger advancing rapidly, Martinez realised that it was time to open up as much of a lead as possible. By lap 4 Dörflinger was up to second but Martinez had a 2.5-second lead and Bianchi was slowing eventually to retire at the pits.

Martinez could not get away, though, and the World Champion closed, taking Herreros with him. Dörflinger took the lead on lap 6 with Aspar still heading Herreros and Nieto while Spaan was fifth ahead of van Kessel and McConnachie was already up to seventh having just passed Gerhard Waibel.

That was the end for Martinez as his Derbi stopped with electrical problems but Dörflinger was still left with two of the red machines to deal with and Herreros was having one of the best rides of his career. The pair started to pull away from Nieto who had problems of his own as

McConnachie was closing in his usual determined manner, passing van Kessel on lap 8 and Spaan two laps later.

In eighth place by this time was Austrian Mandy Fischer riding in his first Grand Prix. The 21-year-old had won the Austrian 125 Sachs Cup two years in a row and used a Krauser for some Grands Prix and the European Championships.

After opening up a five-second gap over Nieto, Dörflinger and Herreros began to slip back as they swapped places. McConnachie was closing all the time and gaining at more than a second a lap.

On lap 16 he passed Nieto and then had the two leaders in his sights. Dörflinger was having handling problems which made the British privateer wary and he gave up the chance of trying to take second or even first on the final circuit. It was Herreros who crossed the line first taking advantage of some back-markers and as McConnachie was hoping to get some assistance from Krauser he had more sense than to detract from Dörflinger's championship total. McConnachie took the lap record with his well-deserved third.

Nieto was disappointed to be fourth but it put back the question of team orders as it was Herreros, nominally the third rider in the team, who headed the table with 35 points, then Dörflinger on 29, Martinez 27 and Nieto 20 – hardly the time to decide who should go for the championship.

It is doubtful as to whether Nieto would have accepted team orders in any case. His attitude was that he had won five World titles for Derbi in the past and if it ever came to racing in the rain Martinez would not stand a chance. Mindful of his lack of wet-weather ability Martinez had been practising in the rain at every opportunity during the winter.

### 250 cc

Martin Wimmer was very tired of getting bad starts; it had only happened twice but it had certainly cost him championship points and after working so hard to sit on the front row of the grid there was little point in allowing himself to be in midfield going into the first corner.

To guarantee that the engine fired up smartly his mechanics fitted a lever to the left handlebar with a cable running to the throttle so that the opening could be set at the right position for the start and he would not have to rely on the feel of the twistgrip when he was at his most nervous, at the drop of the flag.

Wimmer's Yamaha fired well but his getaway was still not as clean as it should have been and at the end of lap 1 he was tenth as Cornu briefly led from Bolle, Ricci, Lavado and McLeod. Mang had been in a far worse position than Wimmer, and forced his way up to 13th at the end of lap 2 while Wimmer was up to seventh and Lavado had already taken the lead with Ricci second.

Mang's rise was rapid but Lavado had the advantage of a clear road ahead. By lap 5, with Mang seventh, the German Honda rider was looking at an eight-second deficit; Wimmer was also still moving forward but more cautiously and took second from Ricci on lap 8, lying nearly

seven seconds behind Lavado. Mang was still charging and passed both Ricci and Wimmer on lap 9 to second position, over seven seconds adrift of Lavado.

Mang had shattered the lap record with that charge but he never lapped quite as quickly again and from that point Lavado was able to slowly but surely to extend his lead to a comfortable twelve seconds by lap 18. The interest lay more in the tussle for second between Wimmer and Mang. Both took their turn in second but neither could close on Lavado.

Fourth was contested between Fausto Ricci and Pierre Bolle for almost the entire race but Jean-François Baldé caught the pair in the last five laps after a slow start and a very well measured advance through the field. Less fortunate was Virginio Ferrari, Baldé's new team-mate, who had been drafted in to Takazumi Katayama's squad as a replacement for Tereo Fukuda (the Japanese ace who had been injured at Mugello at the end of 1984 and then again at a private test session at Willow Springs in 1985, and still not fit to return to racing).

Ferrari had been asked to fill his place at least temporarily but he had problems adapting to the 250 as the gearchange was on the wrong side and there is no arrangement for modification. The works-issue handlebars did not suit his extremely sloping preference and it was hard to leap into the most competitive of Grand Prix classes after having had virtually a year off since being dropped from the Marlboro Yamaha team at the end of '84.

Baldé left behind a fierce struggle for seventh between Cornu, McLeod and Cardus. The fight for the last points-scoring position hotted up towards the last lap as Tadahiko Taira moved up to challenge Sito Pons, taking Alan Carter with him. Taira had suffered another bad start thanks to his still very sore ankle but closed in on Pons, forcing the Spaniard to make a mistake on the last lap and crash. Cardus also fell on the final circuit but remounted to finish 13th. That gave Taira ninth and Carter tenth. The Englishman had been thinking about passing Taira on the last lap. 'I wanted a point but I didn't think I could get one. I was going to try and pass Taira but when Pons went up the road I was distracted watching him and missed my chance', said Carter, who was lucky to get a race after destroying his best engine in the final practice period.

The win was comfortably Lavado's but second remained at issue right up until the penultimate lap when Mang used a bit of intimidation on Wimmer forcing him to back off enough to take the Honda across the line by three-tenths of a second, though ten seconds behind the Venemotos Yamaha.

As Lavado said, 'It is my birthday today and that is the best birthday present I could have given myself. Everything went just like practice, lap after lap – perfect.'

### SIDECARS

Rolf Biland was worried before practice began. 'I have never started a season in such a state of

Lavado, Wimmer and Mang share the spoils of victory *(right)*.

The V-four Yamaha proved a real force in the hands of Eddie Lawson *(right)* and Mike Baldwin *(below)*.

mind. I just don't know how my new engine is going to compare with the others. I have no way of knowing how much work they have done in the winter and whether or not mine will be fast enough.'

Four days later sitting in pole position he was a good deal more pleased but with only a tenth of a second advantage over Egbert Streuer he was by no means confident. The completely new Krauser engine had its crankcase reed-valve induction into the back of the cases instead of into the front as on the '85 version. It was working well but he was not going to rely on the status quo remaining for the rest of the year and had new streamlining and a bigger reed-valve engine being put in readiness for the Austrian Grand Prix.

Almost from the start of the race he realised that he would need something extra, for, despite leading, Streuer soon passed early second-place man Steve Webster and sat on Biland's tail. Webster lasted for 9 of the 25 laps in a lonely third place while the battle behind him became much more exciting with Steve Abbott swapping places with Alain Michel, Rolf Steinhausen, Derek Jones, Alfred Zurbrügg and Markus Egloff.

Steinhausen got the best of the struggle and, looking more competitive than he has for several seasons with a brand new Busch outfit, he inherited third place as Webster dropped out. Streuer continued to shadow Biland without any apparent difficulty and fourth was passed between Jones, Michel and Egloff. They spurred each other on and began to catch Steinhausen once more. The pace was a little hot for Egloff who was caught by Abbott as the fortunes of the race changed once more.

Steinhausen's good ride ended on lap 19 when he was forced to retire. Jones spun and dropped back to finish fifth, while Michel fell back to sixth on the last lap when part of the sidecar wheel suspension broke and he finished the race with the third wheel being dragged sideways.

Streuer took command with two laps to go; he already had the lap record from lap 3 and he also seized the race record in a comfortable five-second win over Biland. Abbott took advantage of the various dramas and pushed on in the second half of the race to take third ahead of Zurbrügg.

## 500 cc

Several riders complained later that the sidecars had left too much rubber on the road and after the warm-up lap most had picked up great strips of it on their tyres which did their confidence no good at all. It is likely that Mamola was most affected by this because after a bad start caused by his hand slipping off the twistgrip he did not make the rapid progress he had in preceding races.

Rubber on the track made little difference to Lawson who made another great start and soon passed German Manfred Fischer who had shot off the line. Didier de Radigues had also been quicker away and Lawson waited until the end of lap 1 to blast past him. From that moment he was never headed and turned in another faultless performance, increasing his lead carefully by half a second per lap until he had a sixteen-second buffer after 25 of the 30 laps.

De Radigues once more worked hard to defend each place as the more powerful four-cylinder machines came past. The second to flash by was McElnea who had plans to chase Lawson after being less than four-tenths slower in practice. 'I

saw Eddie ahead and thought "this is my chance; just get on his tail and do what he does", but as I pitched it into the fast right-hander leading downhill behind the pits the front end juddered almost out of control. I'd swear the front tyre was coming off the ground it was pattering so bad.'

As McElnea got the Marlboro Yamaha back under control Gardner took the opportunity to go past on the Rothmans Honda. A painful practice starting session on Saturday evening had paid off and even with the still very sore knee he had not been left on the line. McElnea found the juddering occurred on every fast right-hander and had to ease the pace, letting Sarron past on lap 4.

Sarron was flying and soon caught Gardner and passed him on lap 6. Lawson had nearly five seconds on him at that point and any thoughts the Frenchman had of a clear run at the leader had to be shelved as Gardner dived past him once more. They became embedded in a two-way match

that became three-cornered on lap 16 when Baldwin arrived, having fought his way from eighth on lap 1.

McElnea was having to ride the Yamaha as hard as he reasonably could in the circumstances to keep ahead of de Radigues who once more was working marvels with the Chevallier. Some 15 seconds behind him was Mamola who had got past Roche on lap 14 and the interest behind then lay with Dave Petersen, Ron Haslam and Gustav Reiner fighting for the last few points.

Petersen made a mediocre start but caught Reiner and Haslam quickly, putting in his fastest time on lap 6. Once he caught the pair he could not get away, finding the Suzuki too slow compared with the Honda-engined machines. Haslam rode the Elf hard despite poor handling and beat the others over the line.

With Lawson circulating well in control, the battle for second intensified as the end of the race

approached. Gardner and Baldwin collided and both blamed each other and on the second-to-last lap Sarron crashed as the back end of the Sonauto Yamaha came round and spat him off. He was lucky to escape with a cracked bone in his ankle. Gardner managed to hold Baldwin off to take second and McElnea was promoted to fourth ahead of de Radigues and Mamola.

---

### 125 cc

After two demonstration victories by Fausto Gresini in Spain and Italy, his Garelli team-mate Luca Cadalora stepped into the picture. The latter took the win as well as the race and lap records, crossing the line over twelve seconds ahead of Gresini, who was even further ahead of third man Ezio Gianola.

Cadalora had been consistently quicker throughout practice and no-one else came close to

the times set up by the two Garellis. In the race, August Auinger quickly slotted into third place behind the two Italians but could never catch them and on lap 6 the gearchange connecting mechanism broke and he lost a lap in the pits having it repaired.

That left Gianola in third place narrowly ahead of Bruno Kneubühler. There was a good battle for fifth between Thierry Feuz and Willy Perez with Feuz eventually beating the Argentine by just 3½ seconds. They were well clear of the seventh- to ninth-place men, Olivier Liegeois, Paolo Casoli and Johnny Wickström. These were joined on lap 19 of the 23 by Auinger but the Austrian was a lap behind and crossed the line with them but in 25th place.

The third race left Gresini with a handy eleven-point lead over Cadalora with '85 Garelli team-mate Gianola third another eleven points adrift.

Dörflinger has the upper hand over Herreros in their 80 cc battle (top).

He may have been putting on a brave face but Freddie Spencer's bandaged wrist told its own story (above).

# 500 cc

### 30 laps, 84.66 miles/136.26 km

| Place | Rider | Nat. | Machine | Laps | Time & speed | Practice time | Grid |
|---|---|---|---|---|---|---|---|
| 1 | Eddie Lawson | USA | Yamaha | 30 | 52m 11.45s 97.327 mph/ 156.632 km/h | 1m 42.56s | 1 |
| 2 | Wayne Gardner | AUS | Honda | 30 | 52m 24.25s | 1m 42.83s | 2 |
| 3 | Mike Baldwin | USA | Yamaha | 30 | 52m 24.85s | 1m 43.11s | 4 |
| 4 | Rob McElnea | GB | Yamaha | 30 | 52m 40.46s | 1m 42.94s | 3 |
| 5 | Didier de Radigues | B | Chevallier | 30 | 52m 47.23s | 1m 43.85s | 7 |
| 6 | Randy Mamola | USA | Yamaha | 30 | 53m 03.32s | 1m 43.63s | 6 |
| 7 | Raymond Roche | F | Honda | 30 | 53m 34.10s | 1m 44.36s | 8 |
| 8 | Ron Haslam | GB | Elf | 30 | 53m 38.54s | 1m 45.37s | 10 |
| 9 | Gustav Reiner | D | Honda | 30 | 53m 38.52s | 1m 45.75s | 11 |
| 10 | Dave Petersen | ZIM | Suzuki | 30 | 53m 38.94s | 1m 46.07s | 12 |
| 11 | Manfred Fischer | D | Honda | 29 | 52m 31.25s | 1m 47.71s | 17 |
| 12 | Paul Lewis | AUS | Suzuki | 29 | 52m 31.78s | 1m 46.84s | 13 |
| 13 | Boet van Dulmen | NL | Honda | 29 | 52m 32.27s | 1m 47.05s | 15 |
| 14 | Fabio Biliotti | I | Honda | 29 | 52m 32.40s | 1m 47.98s | 18 |
| 15 | Henk van der Mark | NL | Honda | 29 | 52m 32.84s | 1m 47.60s | 16 |
| 16 | Pier Francesco Chili | I | Suzuki | 29 | 52m 45.44s | 1m 46.89s | 14 |
| 17 | Wolfgang von Muralt | CH | Suzuki | 29 | 52m 55.54s | 1m 50.59s | 26 |
| 18 | Simon Buckmaster | GB | Honda | 29 | 53m 25.42s | 1m 49.59s | 23 |
| 19 | Gerold Fischer | D | Honda | 29 | 54m 00.12s | 1m 51.53s | 29 |
| 20 | Rob Punt | NL | Honda | 28 | 52m 16.90s | 1m 49.83s | 24 |
| 21 | Georg-Robert Jung | D | Honda | 28 | 52m 59.05s | 1m 50.45s | 25 |
| 22 | Maarten Duyzers | NL | Suzuki | 28 | 52m 59.64s | 1m 50.85s | 27 |
| 23 | Bernd Steif | D | Honda | 28 | 53m 01.14s | 1m 51.94s | 32 |
| 24 | Andreas Leuthe | LUX | Honda | 28 | 53m 01.94s | 1m 51.74s | 31 |
| 25 | Thomas Lange | D | Suzuki | 28 | 53m 07.17s | 1m 51.22s | 28 |
| 26 | Dietmar Mayer | D | Honda | 28 | 53m 14.69s | 1m 52.58s | 34 |
| 27 | Sepp Doppler | A | Honda | 28 | 53m 51.24s | 1m 52.95s | 35 |
| 28 | Helmut Schütz | D | Honda | 28 | 53m 52.28s | 1m 53.42s | 36 |
| 29 | Philippe Robinet | F | Honda | 26 | 53m 22.96s | 1m 57.27s | 38 |
| | Christian Sarron | F | Yamaha | 28 | DNF | 1m 43.31s | 5 |
| | Mile Pajic | NL | Honda | 24 | DNF | 1m 49.43s | 19 |
| | Bohumil Stasa | CS | Honda | 15 | DNF | 1m 54.12s | 37 |
| | Rolf Aljes | D | Honda | 12 | DNF | 1m 51.67s | 30 |
| | Paval Dekanek | CS | Suzuki | 9 | DNF | 1m 52.31s | 33 |
| | Eero Hyvarinen | SF | Honda | 5 | DNF | 1m 49.44s | 20 |
| | Marco Gentile | CH | Fior | 4 | DNF | 1m 49.47s | 21 |
| | Vincenzo Cascino | RCH | Suzuki | 4 | DNF | 1m 57.47s | 39 |
| | Juan Garriga | E | Cagiva | 1 | DNF | 1m 45.19s | 9 |
| | Friedhelm Weber | D | EB | 1 | DNF | 1m 57.52s | 40 |
| | Karl Truchsess | A | Honda | | DNS | 1m 49.53s | 22 |
| | José Parra | E | Honda | | DNQ | 2m 00.74s | |
| | Josef Ragginger | A | Suzuki | | DNQ | 2m 01.74s | |

Fastest lap: Lawson, 1m 43.24s, 98.403 mph/158.364 km/h (record).
Previous record: Freddie Spencer, USA (Honda), 1m 43.43s, 98.223 mph/158.074 km/h (1984).

**World Championship: 1** Lawson, 42; **2** Baldwin, 30; **3** Gardner, 27; **4** Mamola, 25; **5** Sarron, 14; **6** McElnea and de Radigues, 12; **8** Roche, 9; **9** Biliotti and van Dulmen, 5; **11** Haslam and Chili, 4; **13** Garriga, 3; **14** Lewis and Reiner, 2; **16** Papa and Petersen, 1.

# 250 cc

### 25 laps, 70.55 miles/113.55 km

| Place | Rider | Nat. | Machine | Laps | Time & speed | Practice time | Grid |
|---|---|---|---|---|---|---|---|
| 1 | Carlos Lavado | YV | Yamaha | 25 | 45m 03.00s 93.971 mph/ 151.231 km/h | 1m 47.69s | 1 |
| 2 | Anton Mang | D | Honda | 25 | 45m 13.62s | 1m 47.81s | 2 |
| 3 | Martin Wimmer | D | Yamaha | 25 | 45m 13.94s | 1m 47.87s | 3 |
| 4 | Jean-François Baldé | F | Honda | 25 | 45m 32.16s | 1m 49.09s | 11 |
| 5 | Fausto Ricci | I | Honda | 25 | 45m 33.35s | 1m 50.11s | 23 |
| 6 | Pierre Bolle | F | Parisienne | 25 | 45m 33.69s | 1m 49.04s | 9 |
| 7 | Jacques Cornu | CH | Honda | 25 | 45m 38.89s | 1m 48.63s | 5 |
| 8 | Donnie McLeod | GB | Armstrong | 25 | 45m 41.00s | 1m 48.53s | 4 |
| 9 | Tadahiko Taira | J | Yamaha | 25 | 45m 53.52s | 1m 48.91s | 6 |
| 10 | Alan Carter | GB | Kobas | 25 | 45m 55.64s | 1m 48.98s | 8 |
| 11 | Dominique Sarron | F | Honda | 25 | 45m 56.00s | 1m 49.04s | 10 |
| 12 | Jean Foray | F | Chevallier | 25 | 46m 01.76s | 1m 49.70s | 17 |
| 13 | Carlos Cardus | E | Honda | 25 | 46m 05.10s | 1m 49.53s | 12 |
| 14 | Siegfried Minich | A | Yamaha | 25 | 46m 05.10s | 1m 49.73s | 18 |
| 15 | Stefano Caracchi | I | Aprilia | 25 | 46m 15.98s | 1m 49.97s | 20 |
| 16 | Ian Newton | GB | Armstrong | 25 | 46m 16.32s | 1m 50.58s | 33 |
| 17 | Harald Eckl | D | Honda | 25 | 46m 16.58s | 1m 50.04s | 21 |
| 18 | Stéphane Mertens | B | Yamaha | 25 | 46m 17.01s | 1m 50.07s | 22 |
| 19 | Jean-Michel Mattioli | F | Yamaha | 25 | 46m 20.14s | 1m 49.60s | 13 |
| 20 | Herbert Hauf | D | Honda | 25 | 46m 21.48s | 1m 50.86s | 34 |
| 21 | Maurizio Vitali | I | Garelli | 25 | 46m 29.10s | 1m 51.12s | 36 |
| 22 | Roland Freymond | CH | Yamaha | 25 | 46m 29.51s | 1m 49.89s | 19 |
| 23 | Brent Jones | NZ | Yamaha | 25 | 46m 30.24s | 1m 50.55s | 31 |
| 24 | Virginio Ferrari | I | Honda | 25 | 46m 33.21s | 1m 50.50s | 29 |
| 25 | Antonio Neto | BR | Yamaha | 25 | 46m 35.78s | 1m 50.32s | 25 |
| 26 | Hans Lindner | A | Castrol | 25 | 46m 43.41s | 1m 49.62s | 15 |
| 27 | Herbert Besendörfer | D | Yamaha | 25 | 46m 43.87s | 1m 50.13s | 24 |
| 28 | Josef Hutter | A | Bartol | 25 | 46m 44.46s | 1m 50.46s | 27 |
| 29 | René Délaby | B | Moreno | 25 | 46m 48.53s | 1m 50.57s | 32 |
| 30 | Bruno Bonhuil | F | Honda | 25 | 46m 55.40s | 1m 51.39s | 39 |
| 31 | Jochen Schmid | D | Yamaha | 24 | 45m 03.76s | 1m 51.39s | 40 |
| 32 | Andy Watts | GB | Decorite | 24 | 45m 04.32s | 1m 50.51s | 30 |
| 33 | Gary Noel | GB | EMC | 24 | 45m 26.10s | 1m 51.22s | 38 |
| | Alfonso Pons | E | Honda | 24 | DNF | 1m 48.96s | 7 |
| | Michel Simeon | B | Yamaha | 12 | DNF | 1m 50.48s | 28 |
| | Antonio Garcia | E | Honda | 12 | DNF | 1m 51.16s | 37 |
| | Reinhold Roth | D | Honda | 9 | DNF | 1m 49.68s | 16 |
| | Jean-Louis Tournadre | F | Yamaha | 9 | DNF | 1m 49.61s | 14 |
| | Manfred Herweh | D | Aprilia | 9 | DNF | 1m 50.42s | 26 |
| | Franz Lederer | D | Rotax | 4 | DNF | 1m 50.87s | 35 |
| | Frank Wagner | D | Honda | | DNQ | 1m 51.73s | |
| | Massimo Matteoni | I | Honda | | DNQ | 1m 51.94s | |
| | Loris Reggiani | I | Aprilia | | DNQ | 1m 51.97s | |
| | Reiner Gerwin | D | Rotax | | DNQ | 1m 52.10s | |
| | Nicolas Gonzalez | E | Kobas | | DNQ | 1m 52.24s | |
| | Konrad Hefele | D | Honda | | DNQ | 1m 52.29s | |
| | Urs Lüzi | CH | Yamaha | | DNQ | 1m 52.38s | |
| | Jacky Onda | F | Yamaha | | DNQ | 1m 52.39s | |
| | Cees Doorakkers | NL | Honda | | DNQ | 1m 52.59s | |
| | Reinhard Strack | D | Wiwa | | DNQ | 1m 52.77s | |
| | Eilert Lundstedt | S | MBA | | DNQ | 1m 52.81s | |
| | Roland Busch | D | Yamaha | | DNQ | 1m 53.34s | |
| | Ivan Palazzese | YV | Yamaha | | DNQ | 1m 53.34s | |
| | Peter Hubbard | GB | Rotax | | DNQ | 1m 53.68s | |
| | Eric de Donker | B | Honda | | DNQ | 1m 53.83s | |
| | Gérard Vallée | F | Yamaha | | DNQ | 1m 53.86s | |
| | Nedy Crotta | CH | Honda | | DNQ | 1m 53.91s | |
| | Detlef Karthin | D | Yamaha | | DNQ | 1m 54.03s | |
| | Jean-Luc Guillemet | F | Yamaha | | DNQ | 1m 55.31s | |

Fastest lap: Mang, 1m 46.90s, 95.035 mph/152.944 km/h (record).
Previous record: Manfred Herweh, D (Real) 1m 48.29s, 93.815 mph/150.980 km/h (1984).

**World Championship: 1** Lavado, 42; **2** Mang, 39; **3** Wimmer, 26; **4** Baldé, 21; **5** Pons, 16; **6** Cornu, 15; **7** Bolle, 13; **8** Ricci, 8; **9** McLeod, 7; **10** Sarron, 4; **11** Carter, Matteoni and Taira, 2; **14** Mattioli, 1.

## 125 cc

**23 laps, 64.91 miles/104.47 km**

| Place | Rider | Nat. | Machine | Laps | Time & speed | Practice time | Grid |
|---|---|---|---|---|---|---|---|
| 1 | Luca Cadalora | I | Garelli | 23 | 43m 34.77s 89.367 mph/ 143.822 km/h | 1m 51.62s | 1 |
| 2 | Fausto Gresini | I | Garelli | 23 | 43m 47.14s | 1m 52.07s | 2 |
| 3 | Ezio Gianola | I | MBA | 23 | 44m 01.60s | 1m 53.53s | 4 |
| 4 | Bruno Kneubühler | CH | LCR | 23 | 44m 11.26s | 1m 54.10s | 7 |
| 5 | Thierry Feuz | CH | MBA | 23 | 44m 29.07s | 1m 54.40s | 8 |
| 6 | Willy Perez | RA | Zanella | 23 | 44m 32.59s | 1m 56.41s | 16 |
| 7 | Olivier Liegeois | B | Assmex | 23 | 44m 36.99s | 1m 55.55s | 12 |
| 8 | Paolo Casoli | I | MBA | 23 | 44m 37.91s | 1m 55.46s | 11 |
| 9 | Johnny Wickström | SF | Tunturi | 23 | 44m 38.92s | 1m 56.27s | 14 |
| 10 | Alfred Waibel | D | Real | 23 | 44m 45.56s | 1m 54.79s | 10 |
| 11 | Pier Paolo Bianchi | I | Elit | 23 | 44m 46.61s | 1m 54.57s | 9 |
| 12 | Thomas Möller-Pedersen | DK | MBA | 23 | 45m 06.79s | 1m 56.84s | 17 |
| 13 | Robin Appleyard | GB | MBA | 23 | 45m 13.36s | 1m 58.42s | 29 |
| 14 | Jussi Hautaniemi | SF | MBA | 23 | 45m 20.00s | 1m 59.15s | 36 |
| 15 | Steve Mason | GB | MBA | 23 | 45m 20.25s | 1m 58.19s | 27 |
| 16 | Patrick Daudier | F | PMDF | 23 | 45m 20.69s | 1m 57.25s | 20 |
| 17 | Adolf Stadler | D | MBA | 23 | 45m 27.46s | 1m 57.46s | 21 |
| 18 | Hakan Olsson | S | Starol | 22 | 43m 50.02s | 1m 58.44s | 31 |
| 19 | Norbert Peschke | D | MBA | 22 | 44m 50.29s | 1m 58.05s | 26 |
| 20 | Mike Leitner | A | MBA | 22 | 44m 00.47s | 1m 57.09s | 19 |
| 21 | Manuel Hernandez | E | Benetti | 22 | 44m 10.44s | 1m 57.83s | 23 |
| 22 | Jacques Hutteau | F | MBA | 22 | 44m 10.67s | 1m 58.37s | 28 |
| 23 | Klaus Huber | D | MBA | 22 | 44m 24.93s | 1m 58.43s | 30 |
| 24 | Jan Eggens | NL | LCR | 22 | 44m 25.20s | 1m 59.63s | 37 |
| 25 | August Auinger | A | Bartol | 22 | 44m 35.40s | 1m 53.95s | 6 |
| 26 | Ernst Himmelsbach | D | MBA | 22 | 44m 51.15s | 1m 58.75s | 33 |
| 27 | Marin Andreas Sanchez | E | Ducados | 22 | 44m 52.36s | 1m 57.71s | 22 |
| | Erich Zürn | D | Seel | 19 | DNF | 1m 58.86s | 34 |
| | Heinz Litz | D | MBA | 15 | DNF | 1m 59.72s | 38 |
| | Peter Balaz | CS | MBA | 13 | DNF | 1m 59.82s | 39 |
| | Dirk Hafeneger | D | MBA | 13 | DNF | 1m 55.88s | 13 |
| | Willi Hupperich | D | Seel | 10 | DNF | 1m 56.90s | 18 |
| | Angel Nieto | E | Ducados | 9 | DNF | 1m 53.61s | 5 |
| | Giuseppe Ascareggi | I | Seel | 8 | DNF | 1m 57.99s | 25 |
| | Esa Kytola | SF | MBA | 7 | DNF | 1m 57.92s | 24 |
| | Ivan Troisi | YV | MBA | 6 | DNF | 1m 58.93s | 35 |
| | Domenico Brigaglia | I | Ducados | 1 | DNF | 1m 53.23s | 3 |
| | Lucio Pietroniro | B | MBA | 0 | DNF | 1m 56.36s | 15 |
| | Thierry Maurer | CH | MBA | 0 | DNF | 1m 58.44s | 32 |
| | Peter Sommer | CH | MBA | 0 | DNF | 1m 59.91s | 40 |
| | Josef Bader | D | MBA | | DNQ | 1m 59.96s | |
| | Bady Hassaine | DZ | MBA | | DNQ | 2m 00.07s | |
| | Eric Gijsel | B | MBA | | DNQ | 2m 00.21s | |
| | Wilhelm Lücke | D | MBA | | DNQ | 2m 00.32s | |
| | Boy van Erp | NL | MBA | | DNQ | 2m 00.64s | |
| | Fernando Gonzalez | E | MBA | | DNQ | 2m 00.66s | |
| | Flemming Kistrup | DK | MBA | | DNQ | 2m 02.14s | |
| | Manfred Braun | D | MBA | | DNQ | 2m 02.81s | |
| | Ton Spek | NL | MBA | | DNQ | 2m 03.15s | |

*Fastest lap*: Cadalora, 1m 51.73s, 90.926 mph/146.331 km/h (record).
*Previous record*: Eugenio Lazzarini, I (Garelli), 1m 53.48s, 89.524 mph/144.075 km/h (1984).

**World Championship: 1** Gresini, 42; **2** Cadalora, 31; **3** Gianola, 20; **4** Brigaglia and Nieto, 12; **6** Perez, 11; **7** Wickström, Auinger, Feuz and Bianchi, 10; **11** Kneubühler, 8; **12** Pietroniro, 5; **13** Liegeois, 4; **14** Sanchez, Grassetti and Casoli, 3; **17** Hautaniemi, 2; **18** Olsson and Waibel, 1.

## 80 cc

**18 laps, 50.80 miles/81.76 km**

| Place | Rider | Nat. | Machine | Laps | Time & speed | Practice time | Grid |
|---|---|---|---|---|---|---|---|
| 1 | Manuel Herreros | E | Derbi | 18 | 36m 06.81s 84.401 mph/ 135.830 km/h | 1m 59.50s | 6 |
| 2 | Stefan Dörflinger | CH | Krauser | 18 | 36m 08.13s | 1m 57.96s | 1 |
| 3 | Ian McConnachie | GB | Krauser | 18 | 36m 08.72s | 1m 58.81s | 4 |
| 4 | Angel Nieto | E | Derbi | 18 | 36m 17.56s | 1m 58.53s | 3 |
| 5 | Gerhard Waibel | D | Real | 18 | 36m 34.57s | 2m 01.70s | 9 |
| 6 | Hans Spaan | NL | Huvo | 18 | 36m 35.53s | 1m 58.81s | 5 |
| 7 | Josef Fischer | A | Krauser | 18 | 36m 48.33s | 2m 03.59s | 18 |
| 8 | Henk van Kessel | NL | Krauser | 18 | 36m 50.61s | 2m 03.48s | 15 |
| 9 | Felix Rodriguez | E | Autisa | 18 | 37m 04.23s | 2m 03.15s | 14 |
| 10 | Luis Reyes | COL | Autisa | 18 | 37m 04.60s | 2m 03.88s | 20 |
| 11 | Alexandre Barros | BR | Autisa | 18 | 37m 04.77s | 2m 03.72s | 19 |
| 12 | Gerd Kafka | A | Krauser | 18 | 37m 06.27s | 2m 03.54s | 16 |
| 13 | Michael Gschwander | D | Keifer | 18 | 37m 39.46s | 2m 06.69s | 26 |
| 14 | Salvatore Milano | I | Krauser | 18 | 37m 39.65s | 2m 05.57s | 24 |
| 15 | Steve Mason | GB | Huvo | 18 | 38m 14.48s | 2m 07.96s | 33 |
| 16 | Richard Bay | D | Rupp | 17 | 36m 10.19s | 2m 06.96s | 28 |
| 17 | Gunter Schirnhöfer | D | Krauser | 17 | 36m 12.06s | 2m 05.10s | 22 |
| 18 | Reinhard Koberstein | D | Seel | 17 | 36m 12.29s | 2m 06.87s | 27 |
| 19 | Hans Koopman | NL | Ziegler | 17 | 36m 12.80s | 2m 07.93s | 32 |
| 20 | Chris Baert | B | Seel | 17 | 36m 13.47s | 2m 09.47s | 40 |
| 21 | Francisco Torontegui | E | Kobas | 17 | 36m 15.70s | 2m 08.67s | 37 |
| 22 | Jos van Dongen | NL | Krauser | 17 | 36m 31.25s | 2m 08.83s | 38 |
| 23 | Rainer Partl | D | Huvo | 17 | 36m 38.68s | 2m 09.15s | 39 |
| 24 | Raimo Lipponen | SF | Keifer | 17 | 36m 45.19s | 2m 08.59s | 36 |
| 25 | Bert Smit | NL | Minarelli | 17 | 36m 57.77s | 2m 05.19s | 23 |
| 26 | Aad Wijsman | NL | Huvo | 17 | 36m 59.89s | 2m 09.55s | 41 |
| | Mario Stocco | I | Huvo | 15 | DNF | 2m 07.78s | 29 |
| | Jarmö Piepponen | SF | Keifer | 13 | DNF | 2m 08.52s | 35 |
| | Lionel Robert | F | Scrab | 13 | DNF | 2m 07.87s | 30 |
| | René Dünki | CH | Krauser | 8 | DNF | 2m 04.36s | 21 |
| | Rainer Kunz | D | Ziegler | 7 | DNF | 2m 02.09s | 10 |
| | Theo Timmer | NL | Huvo | 7 | DNF | 2m 02.59s | 12 |
| | Jorge Martinez | E | Derbi | 6 | DNF | 1m 58.17s | 2 |
| | Pier Paolo Bianchi | I | Seel | 5 | DNF | 2m 00.06s | 7 |
| | Juan Bolart | E | Autisa | 4 | DNF | 2m 00.42s | 8 |
| | Domingo Gil | E | Autisa | 1 | DNF | 2m 03.10s | 13 |
| | Reiner Scheidhauer | D | Seel | 0 | DNF | 2m 03.57s | 17 |
| | Thomas Engl | D | ESCH | 0 | DNF | 2m 07.89s | 31 |
| | Hubert Abold | D | Seel | | DNS | 2m 02.59s | 11 |
| | Stefan Prein | D | Loeffler | | DNS | 2m 06.01s | 25 |
| | Josef Lutzenberger | D | ERS | | DNS | 2m 08.29s | 34 |
| | Reiner Koster | CH | LCR | | DNQ | 2m 09.73s | |
| | Karoly Juhasz | H | Huvo | | DNQ | 2m 09.90s | |
| | Serge Julin | B | Huvo | | DNQ | 2m 09.99s | |
| | Bertus Grinwis | NL | Krauser | | DNQ | 2m 10.10s | |
| | Mika-Sakari Komu | SF | Eberhardt | | DNQ | 2m 11.47s | |
| | Kees Besseling | NL | Krauser | | DNQ | 2m 12.45s | |
| | Roland Busch | D | Huvo | | DNQ | 2m 14.85s | |
| | Zdravko Matulja | YU | MTM | | DNQ | 2m 17.07s | |

*Fastest lap*: McConnachie, 1m 57.01s, 86.823 mph/139.728 km/h (record).
*Previous record*: Jorge Martinez, E (Derbi), 2m 01.83s, 83.388 mph/134.120 km/h (1984).

**World Championship: 1** Herreros, 35; **2** Dörflinger, 29; **3** Martinez, 27; **4** Nieto, 20; **5** Waibel, 18; **6** McConnachie, 16; **7** Bianchi, 14; **8** Spaan, 9; **9** Bolart and Timmer, 5; **11** Fischer, 4; **12** Abold, Kafka and van Kessel, 3; **15** Kunz and Rodriguez, 2; **17** Gil, Milano and Reyes, 1.

## Sidecars

**25 laps, 70.55 miles/113.55 km**

| Place | Driver & passenger | Nat. | Machine | Laps | Time & speed | Practice time | Grid |
|---|---|---|---|---|---|---|---|
| 1 | Egbert Streuer/ Bernie Schnieders | NL NL | LCR- Yamaha | 25 | 45m 49.88s 92.360 mph/ 148.639 km/h | 1m 47.88s | 2 |
| 2 | Rolf Biland/ Kurt Waltisperg | CH CH | Krauser | 25 | 45m 55.09s | 1m 47.78s | 1 |
| 3 | Steve Abbott/ Shaun Smith | GB GB | Windle- Yamaha | 25 | 46m 32.22s | 1m 51.13s | 9 |
| 4 | Alfred Zurbrügg/ Martin Zurbrügg | CH CH | LCR- Yamaha | 25 | 46m 50.33s | 1m 49.27s | 6 |
| 5 | Derek Jones/ Brian Ayres | GB GB | LCR- Yamaha | 25 | 46m 55.53s | 1m 50.22s | 8 |
| 6 | Alain Michel/ Jean-Marc Fresc | F F | Krauser- Yamaha | 25 | 47m 03.86s | 1m 49.66s | 7 |
| 7 | Markus Egloff/ Urs Egloff | CH CH | LCR- Yamaha | 25 | 47m 04.50s | 1m 48.11s | 3 |
| 8 | René Progin/ Yves Hunziker | CH CH | Seymaz- Yamaha | 25 | 47m 22.74s | 1m 51.48s | 10 |
| 9 | Theo van Kempen/ Gerardus de Haas | NL NL | LCR- Yamaha | 25 | 47m 28.50s | 1m 52.65s | 12 |
| 10 | Mick Barton/ Fritz Buck | GB D | LCR- Yamaha | 25 | 47m 32.79s | 1m 52.96s | 14 |
| 11 | Hans Hügli/ Markus Fahrni | CH CH | LCR- Yamaha | 25 | 47m 33.56s | 1m 52.98s | 15 |
| 12 | Frank Wrathall/ Simon Birchall | GB GB | LCR- Yamaha | 25 | 47m 33.94s | 1m 53.62s | 18 |
| 13 | Wolfgang Stropek/ Hans-Peter Demling | A A | LCR- Rotax | 24 | 46m 15.39s | 1m 54.50s | 24 |
| 14 | Bernd Scherer/ Adolf Hänni | D CH | BRS- Yamaha | 24 | 46m 16.73s | 1m 53.70s | 20 |
| 15 | Erwin Weber/ Klaus Kolb | D D | LCR- Yamaha | 24 | 47m 43.93s | 1m 53.77s | 21 |
| 16 | Derek Bayley/ Bryan Nixon | GB GB | LCR- Ricardo | 22 | 47m 02.96s | 1m 52.38s | 11 |
| 17 | Dennis Bingham/ Julia Bingham | GB GB | LCR- Yamaha | 21 | 47m 49.39s | 1m 54.40s | 23 |
| 18 | Barry Brindley/ Chris Jones | GB GB | Windle- Yamaha | 19 | 47m 23.48s | 1m 53.45s | 17 |
| | Werner Kraus/ Bernd Schuster | D D | Busch- Yamaha | 22 | DNF | 1m 53.40s | 16 |
| | Amadeo Zini/ Carlo Sonaglia | I I | LCR- Yamaha | 22 | DNF | 1m 53.70s | 19 |
| | Luigi Casagrande/ Hans Egli | CH CH | LCR- Yamaha | 19 | DNF | 1m 54.62s | 25 |
| | Rolf Steinhausen/ Bruno Hiller | D D | Busch | 18 | DNF | 1m 49.07s | 5 |
| | Steve Webster/ Tony Hewitt | GB GB | LCR- Yamaha | 9 | DNF | 1m 48.59s | 4 |
| | Mick Boddice/ Chas Birks | GB GB | LCR- Yamaha | 9 | DNF | 1m 52.79s | 13 |
| | Graham Gleeson/ Dave Elliott | NZ GB | LCR- Yamaha | 6 | DNF | 1m 54.28s | 22 |
| | Egon Schons/ Eckart Rösinger | D D | Busch- Yamaha | | DNQ | 1m 54.74s | |
| | Ray Gardner/ Tony Strevens | GB GB | LCR- Yamaha | | DNQ | 1m 55.42s | |
| | Norbert Wild/ Simon Prior | D GB | Yamaha | | DNQ | 1m 55.46s | |
| | Albert Weber/ Harald Schneidewind | D D | LCR- Yamaha | | DNQ | 1m 56.51s | |
| | Herbert Prügl/ August Dierlinger | A A | HOMA- Yamaha | | DNQ | 1m 56.67s | |
| | Gary Thomas/ Geoff White | GB GB | LCR- Yamaha | | DNQ | 1m 57.24s | |
| | Rudolf Reinhard/ Karl Paul | D CH | LCR- Yamaha | | DNQ | 1m 57.88s | |
| | Judd Drew/ Horst Kowalski | GB NL | BLR- Yamaha | | DNQ | 1m 59.26s | |
| | Axel von Berg/ Thomas Bottemer | D D | Busch- Yamaha | | DNQ | 2m 00.98s | |

*Fastest lap*: Streuer, 1m 47.60s, 94.416 mph/151.947 km/h (record).
*Previous record*: Egbert Streuer/Bernie Schnieders, NL/NL (LCR-Yamaha), 1m 48.21s, 93.884 mph/ 151.091 km/h (1984).

**World Championship: 1** Streuer, 15; **2** Biland, 12; **3** Abbott, 10; **4** Zurbrügg, 8; **5** Jones, 6; **6** Michel, 5; **7** Egloff, 4; **8** Progin, 3; **9** van Kempen, 2; **10** Barton, 1.

**Steve Webster and Tony Hewitt showed great promise on their Silkolene-backed outfit.**

# Grosser Preis von
# ÖSTERREICH

Even though the Austrian Grand Prix did not start until June the weather threatened to make the event a miserable affair. It was cold and wet for much of practice with few dry sessions. The clouds hung around the craggy peaks that look down on the sweeping curves of the Salzburgring and kept people huddled under awnings or in their caravans and motorhomes when not forced to venture outside.

Those sweeping curves had been modified since 1985 and the circuit lengthened by 40 metres, more or less in line with a request by 500 competitors after the previous year's event as concern grew about the ultra high-speed armco-lined circuit.

A chicane was incorporated beyond the start-and-finish, where the track had previously curved right at about 160 mph. The chicane looked narrow and was not liked by all (and particularly detested by Mike Baldwin) but it did reduce speeds at a very dangerous point.

Christian Sarron and Freddie Spencer did a track inspection before practice began and the point was raised about the possibility of first-lap collisions at the chicane if one competitor ran out of brakes as had Sarron when he collected Spencer at Assen last year. 'We had a bit of a laugh about that', said Spencer later, 'but it could obviously happen because there is no room to go and if you miss your braking and cut across the corner on the old surface you are very likely to collide with someone coming out of the chicane.'

In fact it was Sarron who was brought down in this manner in the dying moments of the last practice session as Wayne Gardner later explained. 'Christian had been chasing me trying to get a good time and I was going slowly hoping that he would go away. He hung on, though, and I went faster and he came alongside going down the straight. I was a little late on the brakes and there was not very much room going into the chicane; we both needed the same piece of road and as I was up the inside I'm afraid he ended up in the dirt. It was one of those things. I was sorry it happened and I apologised to him.' Sarron suffered further injury to the same ankle he hurt at the Nürburgring.

The other change actually made the track faster at the top of the hill behind the pits with the virtual removal of a left-hander by cutting the bank back and putting in a much more gentle curve leading to the right-hand loop back to the start.

The armco had been right by the side of the track here and, as Spencer pointed out, this made things faster but safer. 'It means that the entry into the corner is at less of an angle and you can go in a lot smoother and you can see round the corner better.'

Spencer was making his comeback after the disappointment at Jarama and did the first practice session in the rain, which is something that Spencer almost never does. 'Yes it is a long time since we practised in the wet', confirmed Erv Kanemoto. Later Spencer explained why he was out in every session rain or shine. 'We have missed two races and I am now trying things on the bike that we should have tested weeks ago.'

Spencer needed to do a lot of experimentation and as his riding style varied somewhat from Gardner he could not just assume that what Gardner tried and discarded would not suit him. It is also fair to assume that just as Spencer guarded his secrets jealously, Gardner was not likely to reveal everything about the way his bike was set up.

Though Spencer was out in every session he kept the number of laps to a minimum. 'The wrist is still causing me problems, so that I am trying to be easy on it. I think that if the race is cold and wet it will be OK because there will be much less heavy braking and the cold will help keep the swelling down. If it is dry I think I could have trouble but I have a spray that should freeze it before the race and I hope it lasts.'

Suffering problems with both the bike and his forearm, Spencer was not as big a force in practice as in '85. He started off fastest by one-hundredth of a second ahead of Eddie Lawson in the wet but at the end of four sessions he could not pull out that extra bit of magic that has so often put him on pole or at least right behind Lawson. This time it was left to Lawson to scream round the circuit in the closing minutes of the final session, once more chasing Rob McElnea and using his slip-stream to get that extra fraction of top speed to secure pole by over half a second from Randy Mamola. McElnea also benefited from the cat-and-mouse session with a time seven-tenths slower than Lawson and only three-hundredths behind Mamola.

Gardner eased himself into fourth place ahead of Spencer with careful practice periods and only the clash with Sarron to upset things. Sarron was sixth-fastest ahead of Baldwin and Roche, with Japanese newcomer Shungi Yatsushiro ninth. Yatsushiro was riding an NSR500 Honda painted in Moriwaki colours yet it was a full works machine. Mr Yoichi Oguma, Director of HRC, was present to see his first Grand Prix of the season and was taking a keen interest in the newcomer who, Honda were hoping, would develop into the best rider in Japan if they could help with GP experience.

Yatsushiro found the high-speed circuit took some getting used to compared with the Japanese circuits but he was already quite an experienced campaigner having raced in the Australian Swann series in 1984 and the New Zealand winter series on the same Pacific tour.

Yamaha were as secure in the 250 class as they were in the 500 and Honda's run of bad luck continued when Toni Mang crashed his NSR250 after only eight laps in the first session of practice, breaking three bones in his foot. Reinhold Roth was following and saw his fellow German fall. 'He seemed to get on the power too early and as he crossed a change in tarmac the bike slid and threw him off. He slid in front of it but then it caught him up and they got tangled and rolled over.'

Mang went back to his home near Munich to seek treatment and although he stayed there on Friday he turned up for the final practice session on Saturday in an attempt to qualify. Despite trying to cut up boots to get one over his swollen

and supported foot, he could not even stand. He reluctantly had to admit he could not ride and set about trying to get fit for the Yugoslav GP a week later.

The weather was variable all through practice and after the first 250 qualifying session, which took place on a drying circuit during Thursday afternoon with only a narrow dry line, Carlos Lavado was quickest ahead of Jacques Cornu and Martin Wimmer. Conditions improved considerably for Friday morning and Lavado cut his time by nearly four seconds, leaving Wimmer the only other man inside 1m 30s. The pair of them were ahead of Austrians Hans Lindner and Josef Hutter, the former using his usual Schafleitner-tuned Rotax in a Nico Bakker frame. That was a similar arrangement to '85, but the Bakker frame was the latest offering from the Dutch frame-builder using as the main stress-bearing members twin extruded spars, in very much the same way as the Honda 250 design.

Hutter had the twin-cylinder disc-valve Bartol that had been raced by Patrick Fernandez and Graeme McGregor before Bartol was forced to admit that he could not afford to sustain a full GP effort with the tremendous cost of producing spares. The two Austrians put the fastest Honda, that of Fausto Ricci, down in fifth place and that is where he stayed for Friday afternoon as it rained again.

Saturday's single, and final, session was dry and everyone improved their times. Lavado was the only man below 1m 28s with Wimmer 0.25s slower. The two Austrians were pushed back with Lindner tenth and Hutter fifteenth, even though both were nearly a second faster than before. The Hondas took over, with Ricci again the fastest ahead of Jean-François Baldé, Dominique Sarron and Virginio Ferrari. The Italian was obviously getting to grips with the 250 and making people take notice, especially those who had thought Takazumi Katayama's choice of rider rather strange.

Ferrari's old team, Cagiva, were not doing so well, however, and after a great start to the season Juan Garriga was down in sixteenth place and struggling somewhat. The V-four had new cylinders in the hope of finding extra speed but they were causing problems and were to put the bike out of the race with a blown head-gasket. The team had been trying to tidy up the airflow through the fairing by repositioning the ignition boxes and by using plastic ducting. The rear wheel was also covered by a mudguard, as per Yamaha and Honda.

The Austrian time-keeping has often been suspect and in previous years Randy Mamola has benefited. This year it was Pier Francesco Chili's turn and the officials placed him tenth on the grid when he should have been down in fifteenth place with team-mate Dave Petersen. Both their bikes incorporated some modifications which, the factory hoped, would make the reed-valve engines perform more efficiently. Petersen had a new set of cases from the factory and Chili had an old set modified to a similar design.

The Skoal Bandit team had been notified of similar modifications by the factory and had

**Wayne Gardner buckles up.**

added some ideas of their own. These included unashamedly taking a good look at the RS500 Honda which uses similar crankcase reed-valve induction. The Suzuki men noted that the Honda reed-valve boxes were allowed to open much more freely, giving a bigger flow area, so they added plates to the top of the cases, filling in the volume above the flywheels to improve the crankcase pumping.

The theory was that the increased crankcase volume created by adding the reed-valve boxes had reduced the pumping efficiency of the engine. Apart from a single engine seizure, it seemed effective and the team were well pleased with the results of what they freely admitted was more of an educated guess than the result of any dyno development programme. Grand Prix racing mid-season allows no time for that.

The Gallina and Skoal Bandit engines were not the same but Lewis was close to Petersen on the grid, in fifteenth place, a tenth of a second slower. Both had the frustration of seeing Honda privateer Gustav Reiner in front of them and three-quarters of a second quicker.

In front of Reiner was Ron Haslam, twelfth-fastest and very well pleased with the progress that was being made with the Elf Honda. 'The rear wheel pattering problem that has held us back since the bike was built has been cured and I think that the bike is probably better now than my NS500 was last season', said Haslam. That was an important statement as the intention all along was to make the special machine better than a conventional three-cylinder Honda-engined bike. Haslam was convinced in his own mind but he needed to prove it with a race result. He was confident that the Austrian Grand Prix might provide the opportunity.

Haslam's ability to start a racing bike had become almost legendary but it still surprised Alan Carter who was having trouble getting his Rotax-engined Cobas to fire up smartly. 'Ron knew I needed some help so he came over to give me some advice. He had never seen the bike before but he just pushed a couple of steps and it fired perfectly, it was amazing. He just has the touch; it doesn't seem to matter what bike it is.'

Someone else who need a bit of the Haslam starting magic was Randy Mamola but he was disinclined to practice and some other members of his team were not that impressed, especially when he took delight in making fun of team-mate Mike Baldwin while he practised his starting technique when the start of one session was delayed as marshals swept some running water off the track. As one of the team commented, 'He just doesn't take things seriously enough. He went to Germany to buy a new Mercedes not to race and the only reason he can't start the bike is because he can't be bothered to practice.'

The very different personalities of Mamola and Baldwin added to the fact that everyone saw Baldwin as very much the Number Two rider – everyone except the five-times American Champion himself, that is. This was leading to a measurable degree of friction in the Lucky Strike camp. It may well not have been at all harmful in the long run; riders certainly thrive on competi-

tion and perhaps both were riding harder because of it, and with Baldwin second in the World Championship ahead of both Gardner and Mamola there were a few reputations on the line.

In-team rivalry was thriving in the 125 class as well because for the second week running World Champion Fausto Gresini had been pushed out of pole position by Garelli team-mate Luca Cadalora. August Auinger was third-quickest and considerably faster than anyone else in the one totally wet session. Fourth was Ezio Gianola, Gresini's '85 team-mate, who the Champion had found much too excitable and hard to handle. 'I can cope with Cadalora, he is more sensible and a better team-mate', said Gresini, obviously not pleased to have his title very much under pressure. There was little pressure from Nieto on the Ducados for although the Spaniard was fifth his time was two seconds slower than Gresini and another half-second off Cadalora's time.

## 80 CC

Saturday afternoon started with something of a demonstration win for Aspar Martinez on the works Derbi but the battle for second was good compensation. Dutchman Hans Spaan led off the line on his Casal but on the climb up the back of the pits Pier Paolo Bianchi pulled past – as did Martinez, who was well in the lead by the time the pack came back on to the start-and-finish straight. Bianchi was second ahead of Spaan and they had a slight advantage over Gerhard Waibel and Stefan Dörflinger.

The second time round Martinez had a one-second lead, still over Bianchi and Spaan although Dörflinger was closing on them, the Krauser pulling hard up the hill. The private Krauser ridden by Ian McConnachie was well back, not so much because of a bad start (although he was not away with the leaders) but because he was put off-line by someone who broke down in the first chicane. Furthermore, he was taking things easy on new tyres. 'Michelin did not have time to put them on for the free warm-up period so I had to be careful over the first few laps.' What hindered McConnachie even more was that his bike was painfully slow up the back straight and that had contributed to him being only twelfth-fastest in practice though he had set new records at the last two races. It was nothing short of amazing to see him make it a hat-trick at the Salzburgring as he battled against faster machinery.

By lap 4 the Englishman was up to eighth while the struggle for second was becoming much more intense. Bianchi was still ahead of the pack – but only just – from Spaan, who had led him on lap 3, Dörflinger, Herreros, Waibel and Nieto. Herreros had started slowly and was only seventh at the end of lap 2.

Dörflinger could not face being beaten by both Derbis and moved in to second on lap 6, over six seconds behind Martinez. A lap later Herreros was third, just keeping ahead of Spaan and Bianchi. Nieto lay further back in sixth place fighting to stay ahead of Waibel and with McConnachie trying hard to close in on them.

Dörflinger could make no impression on Martinez and, worse still, he began losing out to Herreros, Bianchi and Spaan who were tailing the second Derbi. By lap 10 the three of them had recaught Dörflinger and were themselves being overhauled by McConnachie who had made short work of Nieto and Waibel.

From then on it was slow work for McConnachie; he badly needed to slipstream one of the faster bikes in front but despite inching closer he never got within range. He kept trying, all the same, setting that lap record on the 16th of 18.

Martinez was well away but team-mate Herreros had his work cut out trying to keep in front of Bianchi and Spaan. He beat them in the end by one second after putting in his fastest lap of the race on the final circuit. Bianchi was third, closely followed by Spaan with Dörflinger a very disappointed fifth, still two seconds in front of McConnachie.

## SIDECARS

Also run on Saturday, the sidecar race produced an easy win for World Champions Egbert Streuer and Bernard Schnieders and their theoretical rivals Rolf Biland and Kurt Waltisperg failed to score any points thanks to an ignition fault that was eventually blamed on a faulty rev-counter.

Second place was equally clear-cut, once Steve Webster and Tony Hewitt had got past fast-starting Theo van Kempen and Gerardus de Haas, which they did on the second lap.

There was inspiration from the battle for third which started off being a seven-outfit affair but by the last laps had been pared to three: Alain Michel, Steve Abbott and Derek Jones.

The first crew to lead the third-place pack were Rolf Steinhausen and Bruno Hiller, the veteran German riding better than for many years with a new lease of life. Right on his tail came Michel just ahead of the Zurbrügg brothers, with van Kempen sixth but dropping back and soon to be passed by Abbott, Jones and the Egloff brothers.

On lap 7 Michel pushed to the front of the group, and tried but failed to get away from the rest because Abbott passed Steinhausen and closed the gap on Michel. On lap 10 Abbott took second but for the most part of it just depended on where you were lap scoring because the seven-machine crocodile swapped around as the slipstream made one outfit faster than another.

Halfway through the 23-lap race some form began to emerge and Steinhausen was forced to stop with a water leak. Abbott, Michel, Jones and Egloff finally broke clear of Zurbrügg and van Kempen. The four battling for third swapped places frequently but Egloff was obviously struggling a little to hang on and when he lost the slipstream passing some back-markers on lap 16 he had to settle for sixth. The remaining three traded places right up to the flag but Michel got the decision with Abbott fourth and Jones fifth.

## 125 CC

On Sunday morning the weather did its best to upset the practice form by raining hard before the start of the race. By the time the bikes came

to the line it had stopped raining but the track was soaking wet and all the riders started on full wets. If the track were to dry out that was going to be a worry but in places water was running across the surface and intermediates were out of the question. In any case, 125s were not going to destroy tyres as quickly as 500s.

It was just what Auinger might have prayed for and he wasted no time in taking the lead halfway round the first lap as the pack swept up the hill and into the curves behind the paddock. Esa Kytola had made a great start, and though Pier Paolo Bianchi and Bruno Kneubühler both challenged for the lead on that first half-lap it was the local hero who emerged with a clear lead onto the start-and-finish straight to complete the first circuit.

Kytola hung on to second, but only just, from Bianchi, Pietroniro, Gianola and Kneubühler with Gresini seventh and Cadalora tenth. Auinger stretched his advantage with every circuit and was over four seconds in front after four laps while Gianola had moved into second at that point, displacing Bianchi, whose bike was very slow up the rising back straight. Kytola had been pushed back to fourth ahead of Gresini who had Cadalora on his tail.

The two Garelli men were on the move and nose-to-tail they overhauled Bianchi on lap 7 to take third, then started to close rapidly on Gianola. Too rapidly, in fact, because Gresini lost control in the slippery conditions braking for the new chicane. He fell hard and was briefly knocked unconscious as well as sustaining a broken collarbone.

Cadalora continued to close on Gianola and took second place on lap 14. Gianola fought back but they should have been more concerned with Auinger who at one point had nearly a ten-second advantage. However, as the circuit began to dry out this was cut to only four seconds and they stood a real chance of overhauling him with only 15 of the 23 laps completed.

In fact, they did not even have to try because

Auinger's engine cut out with ignition failure and Cadalora assumed the lead on lap 16. Gianola had no reply and though he tried to hang on to the works Garelli, he lost ground at the rate of nearly one second a lap.

The leading pair were a long, long way off the next man, Bianchi, who experienced the frustration of having all his hard work on a slow bike eaten up on the last lap by Kneubühler who took third nearly forty seconds behind the winner. Domenico Brigaglia was fifth on the Ducados, his team-mate Nieto having retired on lap 2.

### 500 cc

Sarron got a great start thanks to being pushed off the back row of the grid. 'I was almost embarrassed', he admitted later. 'I could have led into the first corner but I slowed down because I thought someone might have objected.' It was Spencer who led down to the first chicane and Lawson, whose Yamaha also fired up well, saw him go. 'I thought, "this is it, I can't let him get away". I went up the inside going into the first chicane and Roche was in second place just as I arrived. We both needed the same bit of road and I guess I kind of used him as a berm on the way through.'

A slight exaggeration on Lawson's part perhaps, because Roche certainly was not troubled by the affair but Lawson exited the corner second after being about seventh on the way in. Haslam followed Lawson on the way in so he, too, was well placed.

More was to come from Lawson on that first lap. 'I got on the power hard going through the bottom corner to get a good drive up the hill and then just drifted past Spencer.' The Yamaha flew past the Honda as though it was standing still on the long climb up the hill. It hardly seemed possible but Lawson had completely turned the tables on Spencer who had made it a habit to destroy the opposition in the opening laps.

Psychologically Lawson went a long way to winning the race there and then but it had been

dawning on him through practice that he had a good chance. 'I thought that Spencer would pull in with his wrist but I wanted to be leading when he did; I didn't want the old story of "I only won because Spencer stopped".'

Spencer has in the past maintained an air of unbeatability, supported by the fact that he almost never practised in the rain, never did Sunday morning warm-up periods and often missed free practice as well as official Honda test sessions, then just disappeared in the first four laps of the race.

Being injured, this programme was difficult to maintain. He had to do the free training as there were aspects of the bike that needed testing. For the same reason, he practised in the rain and obviously there was still work to be done on race day as he turned out for the warm-up session. Add to this Spencer's contention that a dry race would cause problems for his wrist, and the psychological battle was Lawson's before the flag dropped. The top racers are so evenly matched in riding ability that confidence can often be deciding factor. Lawson had it and it showed.

Spencer had an awkward choice to make. He could try to chase Lawson knowing that the Yamaha was very good at the Salzburgring and that his wrist was going to play up if the race was hard. The alternative was to concede victory to Lawson and to try and score some points making life as easy as possible for his wrist. Spencer only really knows how to win but the decision was taken out of his hands when the steering damper bolt pulled out of the Honda's frame.

He had to call into the pits on lap 5. The locking wire was still securing the bolthead; it had not come undone but pulled out of the frame. The thread was ruined and all Spencer's mechanics could do was to nail the bolt back in and hope it stayed there. The fact that it had come out in the first place indicated that the bike was suffering severe handling problems and Gardner's bike was also performing frightening contortions. It seemed to twist as he changed gear and some

suggested that it was because the flywheels on the crank were too tight.

Spencer came out of the pits having lost a lap but in the company of Mike Baldwin and Christian Sarron. They were contesting third some way behind Gardner who was trying but not succeeding in catching Lawson, with his three-second advantage.

Mamola had made a slow start and after being twentieth at the end of lap 1 had forced his way rapidly through the field. At the end of that first circuit he was just behind Rob McElnea whose Yamaha had fired well enough but refused to clear. 'When Randy came past on the third lap I tried to stay with him but I just couldn't stick it past the slower guys as hard as he did. I guess it is something I just have to learn.'

Mamola was up to fifth by lap 5, some way ahead of Yatsushiro and McElnea. When McElnea went past, the Japanese picked up a few of his lines and quickened his pace, repassing him briefly on lap 10. On the same lap, Mamola went past both Sarron and Baldwin; he also overtook Spencer who was running at the same pace but keeping out of their way. 'I just wanted to see if my wrist could stand the pace for the full race distance but it was not right and in the end I had to slow down', a disappointed Spencer reported later. 'There is no point in me continuing like this. I am going back home and will not be racing again until it is completely right; it might need an operation.'

Spencer was not the only well-placed contender to feel frustrated in the race as both Ron Haslam and Raymond Roche retired with crankshaft failure after only a few laps.

Once Mamola had got past Baldwin and Sarron the first three places were decided. Lawson had a comfortable five-second advantage on lap 12 that was gradually increasing and there seemed little prospect of Mamola catching Gardner.

Baldwin and Sarron provided some excitement as both are dramatic to watch. Back wheels waved in the air as they entered the chicane but they kept up a good pace and although McElnea closed on them he needed more than the thirty laps to complete the job. Yatsushiro had a lonely final two-thirds of the race well clear of Gustav Reiner who was promoted to eighth when Didier de Radigues had a nasty fall accelerating out of the bottom corner. The latter rebroke his plated collarbone and was badly knocked about.

Some way behind Reiner was a two-way battle for the last points between Pier Francesco Chili and Boet van Dulmen, in which the Italian finally came out on top. Earlier they had dealt with Fabio Biliotti but the Honda privateer realised he could not hang on when he had to run across the grass after entering the chicane too fast.

Behind him was a four-man battle for twelfth which went in favour of Dave Petersen ahead of Manfred Fischer, Paul Lewis and Wolfgang von Muralt.

Sarron did well to beat Baldwin to the flag, especially considering his injured foot. 'The bike was fast', said Sarron later, 'but I had some handling problems. I made a mistake with the rear suspension adjustment and there was something

## Grosser Preis von Österreich, 8 June/statistics
### Salzburgring, 2.636-mile/4.243-km circuit

### 500 cc

30 laps, 79.08 miles/127.29 km

| Place | Rider | Nat. | Machine | Laps | Time & speed | Practice time | Grid |
|---|---|---|---|---|---|---|---|
| 1 | Eddie Lawson | USA | Yamaha | 30 | 41m 43.79s 113.724 mph/ 183.020 km/h | 1m 22.06s | 1 |
| 2 | Wayne Gardner | AUS | Honda | 30 | 41m 55.29s | 1m 22.88s | 4 |
| 3 | Randy Mamola | USA | Yamaha | 30 | 42m 05.92s | 1m 22.74s | 2 |
| 4 | Christian Sarron | F | Yamaha | 30 | 42m 09.52s | 1m 23.52s | 6 |
| 5 | Mike Baldwin | USA | Yamaha | 30 | 42m 10.15s | 1m 23.63s | 7 |
| 6 | Rob McElnea | GB | Yamaha | 30 | 42m 11.21s | 1m 22.77s | 3 |
| 7 | Shunji Yatsushiro | J | Honda | 30 | 42m 34.17s | 1m 24.03s | 9 |
| 8 | Gustav Reiner | D | Honda | 30 | 43m 08.62s | 1m 25.25s | 13 |
| 9 | Pier Francesco Chili | I | Suzuki | 29 | 41m 55.54s | 1m 24.30s | 10 |
| 10 | Boet van Dulmen | NL | Honda | 29 | 41m 55.76s | 1m 26.64s | 18 |
| 11 | Fabio Biliotti | I | Honda | 29 | 42m 02.33s | 1m 26.69s | 19 |
| 12 | Dave Petersen | ZIM | Suzuki | 29 | 42m 13.19s | 1m 26.02s | 14 |
| 13 | Manfred Fischer | D | Honda | 29 | 42m 14.17s | 1m 26.58s | 17 |
| 14 | Paul Lewis | AUS | Suzuki | 29 | 42m 14.42s | 1m 26.13s | 15 |
| 15 | Wolfgang von Muralt | CH | Suzuki | 29 | 42m 14.90s | 1m 26.87s | 20 |
| 16 | Freddie Spencer | USA | Honda | 29 | 42m 22.63s | 1m 23.01s | 5 |
| 17 | Henk van der Mark | NL | Honda | 29 | 42m 34.96s | 1m 27.13s | 21 |
| 18 | Mile Pajic | NL | Honda | 29 | 42m 55.85s | 1m 27.79s | 24 |
| 19 | Simon Buckmaster | GB | Honda | 29 | 42m 56.05s | 1m 27.54s | 23 |
| 20 | Leandro Becheroni | I | Suzuki | 28 | 41m 58.26s | 1m 28.21s | 26 |
| 21 | Eero Hyvarinen | SF | Honda | 28 | 42m 00.49s | 1m 27.94s | 25 |
| 22 | Georg-Robert Jung | D | Honda | 28 | 42m 03.32s | 1m 28.51s | 27 |
| 23 | Dietmar Mayer | D | Honda | 28 | 42m 43.34s | 1m 29.96s | 30 |
| 24 | Rudolf Zeller | A | Suzuki | 27 | 42m 07.67s | 1m 33.86s | 35 |
| | Didier de Radigues | B | Chevallier | 23 | DNF | 1m 24.32s | 11 |
| | Marco Gentile | CH | Fior | 23 | DNF | 1m 28.90s | 28 |
| | Juan Garriga | E | Cagiva | 18 | DNF | 1m 26.42s | 16 |
| | Helmut Schütz | D | Honda | 8 | DNF | 1m 30.21s | 31 |
| | Sepp Doppler | A | Honda | 7 | DNF | 1m 29.75s | 29 |
| | Raymond Roche | F | Honda | 4 | DNF | 1m 23.72s | 8 |
| | Ron Haslam | GB | Elf | 3 | DNF | 1m 24.40s | 12 |
| | Peter Linden | S | Honda | 2 | DNF | 1m 31.77s | 34 |
| | Peter Sköld | S | Honda | 1 | DNF | 1m 27.43s | 22 |
| | Dietmar Marehard | A | Homa | | DNS | 1m 30.32s | 32 |
| | Andreas Leuthe | LUX | Honda | | DNS | 1m 30.39s | 33 |
| | Vincenzo Cascino | RCH | Suzuki | | DNQ | 1m 35.00s | |
| | Pablo Exposito | E | Honda | | DNQ | 1m 41.53s | |

*Fastest lap:* Lawson, 1m 22.40s, 115.186 mph/185.374 km/h (record for modified circuit).
*Previous circuit record:* Randy Mamola, USA (Suzuki), 1m 18.11s, 121.44 mph/195.44 km/h (1984).

**World Championship: 1** Lawson, 57; **2** Gardner, 39; **3** Baldwin, 36; **4** Mamola, 35; **5** Sarron, 22; **6** McElnea, 17; **7** de Radigues, 12; **8** Roche, 9; **9** Chili and van Dulmen, 6; **11** Biliotti and Reiner, 5; **13** Haslam and Yatsushiro, 4; **15** Garriga, 3; **16** Lewis, 2; **17** Papa and Petersen, 1.

wrong with either the front fork or the front tyre.'

Baldwin was disappointed but philosophical. 'We had problems all through practice trying to get some speed out of the bike. We tried three different engines but still ended up racing with a slow one.'

Gardner had his share of troubles. 'I had cramp in both my knees; I think that is because I have not been able to run since Monza. I had a real big slide early on and realised I had to cool it. I tried everything I knew to catch Eddie but I couldn't.'

**The three-cylinder battle should have raged between Didier de Radigues and Ron Haslam but the Elf's powerplant expired early in the race.**

### 250 cc

In previous years, the Salzburgring has been famous for long chains of bikes battling for the top places but since first Honda and then in response Yamaha produced works machines in limited quantities, even the slipstreaming possibilities of the circuit have not enabled the privateers to keep up.

In 1986 it was Carlos Lavado who dominated the event and the only man who might have given him something to think about, Martin Wimmer, was left struggling off the line and still down in 17th place at the end of the first lap.

Jean-François Baldé got off to a rocket start on his NSR250 Honda and Lavado was fifth on lap 1. One circuit later the Venezuelan was in front and from that moment he was never troubled, while Baldé held off Fausto Ricci, Sito Pons, Manfred Herweh, Dominique Sarron and Siggi Minich.

Lavado opened up his lead cautiously but by lap 5 he had a two-second advantage over Baldé and Wimmer was up to seventh. Second turned into an interesting contest as Ricci seemed to gain the upper hand on lap 7 and Baldé dropped back a little, being overhauled by Pons and Herweh with Wimmer moving through the pack.

It took Wimmer until lap 11 to get through to third, just heading Pons and Baldé. He continued his advance and closed on Ricci, much to the delight of the Bavarian crowd. Baldé stuck to Wimmer's tail and when Wimmer took second on lap 13 Baldé was with him and took third two laps later. Lavado had a three-second advantage when Wimmer moved into second and although the German tried hard he could not stop the gap from increasing. It was only two- or three-tenths per lap but it added up and Wimmer had to accept that he was riding for second.

Baldé secured his third place from Ricci, who in turn had Pons covered. Dominique Sarron and Manfred Herweh engaged in a lengthy battle for sixth which the Frenchman won. Mertens had been chasing them early on but crashed heavily on lap 10. That left the fast-starting Siggi Minich eighth on his private Honda but, riding for most of the second half of the race completely alone, he was eventually overhauled by the front of a thirteen-man group.

He was lucky that the race ended when it did because only Taira (who had started at the back of the field) actually got past before the flag, leaving Minich ninth. Maurizio Vitali got a point for tenth after riding hard on the V-twin Garelli. Out of luck were Roth, Ferrari, Cornu and Besendörfer. Josef Hutter crashed heavily with two laps to go and was lucky to escape serious injury.

**Martin Wimmer** (above) once more got off to a poor start but rode with tremendous determination.

**Mamola puts on the Austrian style, displaying appropriate headgear on the winner's car** (right).

# 250 cc

**25 laps, 65.90 miles/106.08 km**

| Place | Rider | Nat. | Machine | Laps | Time & speed | Practice time | Grid |
|---|---|---|---|---|---|---|---|
| 1 | Carlos Lavado | YV | Yamaha | 25 | 36m 52.68s<br>107.238 mph/<br>172.583 km/h | 1m 27.88s | 1 |
| 2 | Martin Wimmer | D | Yamaha | 25 | 37m 00.69s | 1m 28.13s | 2 |
| 3 | Jean-François Baldé | F | Honda | 25 | 37m 03.62s | 1m 28.51s | 4 |
| 4 | Fausto Ricci | I | Honda | 25 | 37m 08.47s | 1m 28.47s | 3 |
| 5 | Alfonso Pons | E | Honda | 25 | 37m 12.97s | 1m 29.18s | 9 |
| 6 | Dominique Sarron | F | Honda | 25 | 37m 21.31s | 1m 28.52s | 5 |
| 7 | Manfred Herweh | D | Aprilia | 25 | 37m 21.56s | 1m 29.51s | 13 |
| 8 | Tadahiko Taira | J | Yamaha | 25 | 37m 37.51s | 1m 29.59s | 17 |
| 9 | Siegfried Minich | A | Yamaha | 25 | 37m 37.78s | 1m 29.56s | 14 |
| 10 | Maurizio Vitali | I | Garelli | 25 | 37m 38.27s | 1m 29.97s | 23 |
| 11 | Reinhold Roth | D | Honda | 25 | 37m 38.49s | 1m 29.76s | 20 |
| 12 | Virginio Ferrari | I | Honda | 25 | 37m 38.78s | 1m 28.82s | 6 |
| 13 | Jacques Cornu | CH | Honda | 25 | 37m 42.22s | 1m 29.84s | 21 |
| 14 | Herbert Besendörfer | D | Yamaha | 25 | 37m 43.83s | 1m 30.52s | 33 |
| 15 | Andreas Preining | A | Yamaha | 25 | 37m 44.78s | 1m 30.13s | 26 |
| 16 | Pierre Bolle | F | Parisienne | 25 | 37m 45.59s | 1m 29.75s | 19 |
| 17 | Thomas Bacher | A | Dixi | 25 | 37m 45.89s | 1m 30.37s | 30 |
| 18 | Harald Eckl | D | Honda | 25 | 37m 48.04s | 1m 29.58s | 16 |
| 19 | Stefan Klabacher | A | Rotax | 25 | 37m 55.57s | 1m 30.12s | 25 |
| 20 | Hans Becker | D | Yamaha | 25 | 38m 13.78s | 1m 30.21s | 28 |
| 21 | Jochen Schmid | D | Yamaha | 25 | 38m 14.08s | 1m 30.49s | 31 |
| 22 | René Délaby | B | Moreno | 24 | 36m 58.17s | 1m 30.84s | 36 |
| 23 | Antonio Moreno | E | Kobas | 24 | 37m 19.49s | 1m 30.84s | 37 |
| 24 | Werner Felber | A | Rotax | 24 | 37m 25.24s | 1m 30.53s | 34 |
| | Josef Hutter | A | Bartol | 23 | DNF | 1m 29.57s | 15 |
| | Donnie McLeod | GB | Armstrong | 17 | DNF | 1m 29.49s | 11 |
| | Hans Lindner | A | Castrol | 15 | DNF | 1m 29.42s | 10 |
| | Carlos Cardus | E | Honda | 10 | DNF | 1m 30.60s | 35 |
| | Stéphane Mertens | B | Yamaha | 9 | DNF | 1m 29.04s | 7 |
| | Alan Carter | GB | Kobas | 8 | DNF | 1m 29.12s | 8 |
| | Sergio Pellandini | CH | Honda | 7 | DNF | 1m 30.15s | 27 |
| | Massimo Matteoni | I | Honda | 4 | DNF | 1m 29.91s | 22 |
| | Jean-Louis Tournadre | F | Yamaha | 3 | DNF | 1m 30.21s | 28 |
| | Jean Foray | F | Chevallier | 2 | DNF | 1m 29.50s | 12 |
| | Jean-Louis Guignabodet | F | MIG | 2 | DNF | 1m 30.50s | 32 |
| | Franz Lederer | D | Rotax | | DNS | 1m 29.73s | 18 |
| | Niall MacKenzie | GB | Armstrong | | DNS | 1m 30.01s | 24 |
| | Bruno Bonhuil | F | Honda | | DNQ | 1m 31.07s | |
| | Roland Freymond | CH | Yamaha | | DNQ | 1m 31.13s | |
| | Andy Watts | GB | Decorite | | DNQ | 1m 31.50s | |
| | Urs Lüzi | CH | Yamaha | | DNQ | 1m 31.50s | |
| | Engelbert Neumair | A | Helten | | DNQ | 1m 31.53s | |
| | Stefano Caracchi | I | Aprilia | | DNQ | 1m 31.57s | |
| | Jean-Michel Mattioli | F | Yamaha | | DNQ | 1m 31.85s | |
| | Loris Reggiani | I | Aprilia | | DNQ | 1m 32.30s | |
| | Silvo Habat | YU | Yamaha | | DNQ | 1m 32.48s | |
| | Gerard van der Wal | NL | Assmex | | DNQ | 1m 32.60s | |
| | Johnny Simonsson | S | Honda | | DNQ | 1m 33.06s | |
| | Anton Mang | D | Honda | | DNQ | 1m 37.02s | |

*Fastest lap:* Wimmer, 1m 27.18s, 108.871 mph/175.210 km/h (record for modified circuit).
*Previous circuit record:* Freddie Spencer, USA (Honda), 1m 23.27s, 113.86 mph/183.25 km/h (1985).

**World Championship: 1** Lavado, 57; **2** Mang, 39; **3** Wimmer, 38; **4** Baldé, 31; **5** Pons, 22; **6** Ricci, 16; **7** Cornu, 15; **8** Bolle, 13; **9** Sarron, 9; **10** McLeod, 7; **11** Taira, 5; **12** Herweh, 4; **13** Carter, Matteoni and Minich, 2; **16** Mattioli and Vitali, 1.

# 125 cc

**23 laps, 60.63 miles/97.59 km**

| Place | Rider | Nat. | Machine | Laps | Time & speed | Practice time | Grid |
|---|---|---|---|---|---|---|---|
| 1 | Luca Cadalora | I | Garelli | 23 | 38m 03.40s<br>95.603 mph/<br>153.858 km/h | 1m 33.64s | 1 |
| 2 | Ezio Gianola | I | MBA | 23 | 38m 08.74s | 1m 33.95s | 2 |
| 3 | Bruno Kneubühler | CH | LCR | 23 | 38m 43.17s | 1m 35.21s | 5 |
| 4 | Pier Paolo Bianchi | I | Elit | 23 | 38m 45.93s | 1m 36.06s | 7 |
| 5 | Domenico Brigaglia | I | Ducados | 23 | 38m 55.14s | 1m 36.15s | 9 |
| 6 | Olivier Liegeois | B | Assmex | 23 | 38m 55.34s | 1m 36.07s | 8 |
| 7 | Alfred Waibel | D | Real | 23 | 39m 04.73s | 1m 36.51s | 13 |
| 8 | Lucio Pietroniro | B | MBA | 23 | 39m 04.92s | 1m 38.62s | 22 |
| 9 | Esa Kytola | SF | MBA | 23 | 39m 17.88s | 1m 37.80s | 18 |
| 10 | Adolf Stadler | D | MBA | 23 | 39m 21.73s | 1m 36.50s | 12 |
| 11 | Paolo Casoli | I | MBA | 23 | 39m 22.14s | 1m 36.98s | 14 |
| 12 | Jussi Hautaniemi | SF | MBA | 23 | 39m 28.21s | 1m 37.59s | 17 |
| 13 | Thomas Möller-Pedersen | DK | MBA | 23 | 39m 33.34s | 1m 37.36s | 15 |
| 14 | Willy Perez | RA | Zanella | 22 | 38m 08.54s | 1m 36.41s | 11 |
| 15 | Johnny Wickström | SF | Tunturi | 22 | 38m 13.16s | 1m 36.25s | 10 |
| 16 | Thierry Feuz | CH | LCR | 22 | 38m 25.72s | 1m 35.47s | 6 |
| 17 | Robin Appleyard | GB | MBA | 22 | 38m 27.98s | 1m 39.19s | 26 |
| 18 | Norbert Peschke | D | MBA | 22 | 38m 43.96s | 1m 38.00s | 20 |
| 19 | Ton Spek | NL | MBA | 22 | 39m 04.53s | 1m 40.27s | 32 |
| 20 | Karl Dauer | A | MBA | 22 | 39m 22.36s | 1m 38.91s | 23 |
| 21 | Eric Saul | F | LGM | 22 | 39m 31.20s | 1m 40.68s | 34 |
| 22 | Mike Leitner | A | MBA | 22 | 39m 38.31s | 1m 39.33s | 28 |
| 23 | Peter Sommer | CH | MBA | 22 | 39m 38.96s | 1m 40.61s | 33 |
| 24 | Thierry Maurer | CH | MBA | 21 | 38m 59.84s | 1m 40.86s | 35 |
| | Marin Andreas Sanchez | E | Ducados | 17 | DNF | 1m 37.92s | 19 |
| | Steve Mason | GB | MBA | 16 | DNF | 1m 40.99s | 36 |
| | August Auinger | A | Bartol | 15 | DNF | 1m 34.12s | 4 |
| | Josef Bader | D | MBA | 15 | DNF | 1m 39.39s | 29 |
| | Giuseppe Ascareggi | I | Seel | 12 | DNF | 1m 39.56s | 31 |
| | Fausto Gresini | I | Garelli | 9 | DNF | 1m 33.95s | 3 |
| | Willi Hupperich | D | Seel | 9 | DNF | 1m 37.42s | 16 |
| | Hakan Olsson | S | Starol | 8 | DNF | 1m 39.45s | 30 |
| | Jacques Hutteau | F | MBA | 7 | DNF | 1m 39.24s | 27 |
| | Peter Balaz | CS | MBA | 4 | DNF | 1m 39.05s | 25 |
| | Angel Nieto | E | Ducados | 2 | DNF | 1m 38.14s | 21 |
| | Manuel Hernandez | E | Benetti | | DNS | 1m 39.03s | 24 |
| | Karl Bubenicek | A | MBA | | DNQ | 1m 41.23s | |
| | Robert Zwidl | A | MBA | | DNQ | 1m 41.36s | |
| | Fernando Gonzalez | E | Kobas | | DNQ | 1m 43.09s | |
| | Manfred Braun | D | MBA | | DNQ | 1m 47.79s | |

*Fastest lap:* Gianola, 1m 32.28s, 100.67 mph/162.01 km/h (record for modified circuit).
*Previous circuit record:* Fausto Gresini, I (Garelli), 1m 28.13s, 107.59 mph/173.14 km/h (1985).

**World Championship: 1** Cadalora, 46; **2** Gresini, 42; **3** Gianola, 32; **4** Brigaglia, Bianchi and Kneubühler, 18; **7** Nieto, 12; **8** Perez, 11; **9** Wickström, Auinger and Feuz, 10; **12** Liegeois, 9; **13** Pietroniro, 8; **14** Waibel, 5; **15** Sanchez, Grassetti and Casoli, 3; **18** Hautaniemi and Kytola, 2; **20** Olsson and Stadler, 1.

# 80 cc

**18 laps, 47.45 miles/76.37 km**

| Place | Rider | Nat. | Machine | Laps | Time & speed | Practice time | Grid |
|---|---|---|---|---|---|---|---|
| 1 | Jorge Martinez | E | Derbi | 18 | 30m 01.98s<br>94.809 mph/<br>152.580 km/h | 1m 39.84s | 1 |
| 2 | Manuel Herreros | E | Derbi | 18 | 30m 09.08s | 1m 40.86s | 3 |
| 3 | Pier Paolo Bianchi | I | Seel | 18 | 30m 10.14s | 1m 42.81s | 6 |
| 4 | Hans Spaan | NL | Huvo | 18 | 30m 10.67s | 1m 41.91s | 4 |
| 5 | Stefan Dörflinger | CH | Krauser | 18 | 30m 10.90s | 1m 40.23s | 2 |
| 6 | Ian McConnachie | GB | Krauser | 18 | 30m 12.68s | 1m 45.06s | 12 |
| 7 | Gerhard Waibel | D | Real | 18 | 30m 36.86s | 1m 43.63s | 8 |
| 8 | Angel Nieto | E | Derbi | 18 | 30m 37.07s | 1m 43.37s | 7 |
| 9 | Josef Fischer | A | Krauser | 18 | 31m 08.78s | 1m 42.09s | 5 |
| 10 | Juan Bolart | E | Autisa | 18 | 31m 11.47s | 1m 45.15s | 13 |
| 11 | Henk van Kessel | NL | Krauser | 18 | 31m 16.52s | 1m 45.27s | 15 |
| 12 | Felix Rodriguez | E | Autisa | 18 | 31m 18.08s | 1m 47.56s | 22 |
| 13 | Theo Timmer | NL | Huvo | 18 | 31m 19.58s | 1m 44.35s | 10 |
| 14 | Domingo Gil | E | Autisa | 18 | 31m 35.28s | 1m 47.81s | 24 |
| 15 | Salvatore Milano | I | Krauser | 18 | 31m 35.52s | 1m 46.02s | 16 |
| 16 | Reiner Scheidhauer | D | Seel | 18 | 31m 43.57s | 1m 45.04s | 11 |
| 17 | Hubert Abold | D | Seel | 18 | 31m 46.47s | 1m 46.93s | 17 |
| 18 | Thomas Engl | D | ESCH | 17 | 30m 19.58s | 1m 47.17s | 21 |
| 19 | Steve Mason | GB | Huvo | 17 | 30m 21.84s | 1m 50.41s | 30 |
| 20 | Reinhard Koberstein | D | Seel | 17 | 30m 48.15s | 1m 48.55s | 25 |
| 21 | Reiner Koster | CH | LCR | 17 | 30m 51.45s | 1m 48.78s | 26 |
| 22 | Mario Stocco | I | Huvo | 17 | 30m 51.72s | 1m 49.23s | 29 |
| 23 | Alexandre Barros | BR | Autisa | 17 | 31m 11.17s | 1m 47.74s | 23 |
| 24 | Raimo Lipponen | SF | Keifer | 17 | 31m 21.01s | 1m 52.02s | 34 |
| 25 | Johann Auer | D | Krauser | 17 | 31m 24.70s | 1m 53.90s | 35 |
| 26 | Jarmö Piepponen | SF | Keifer | 17 | 31m 25.15s | 1m 51.36s | 32 |
| 27 | Richard Bay | D | Rupp | 16 | 30m 07.67s | 1m 51.42s | 33 |
| 28 | Steve Lawton | GB | Eberhardt | 16 | 31m 27.99s | 1m 56.81s | 36 |
| | Rainer Kunz | D | Ziegler | 16 | DNF | 1m 44.18s | 9 |
| | Jos van Dongen | NL | Krauser | 15 | DNF | 1m 46.93s | 18 |
| | Gerd Kafka | A | Krauser | 9 | DNF | 1m 47.16s | 19 |
| | René Dünki | CH | LCR | 8 | DNF | 1m 45.25s | 14 |
| | Chris Baert | B | Seel | 8 | DNF | 1m 47.16s | 20 |
| | Francisco Torontegui | E | Kobas | 7 | DNF | 1m 48.93s | 27 |
| | Mika-Sakari Komu | SF | Eberhardt | 6 | DNF | 1m 51.25s | 31 |
| | Luis Reyes | COL | Autisa | | DNS | 1m 48.95s | 28 |
| | Otto Machinek | A | MH | | DNQ | 2m 02.41s | |
| | Erich Reuberger | A | Hummel | | DNQ | 2m 33.21s | |

*Fastest lap:* McConnachie, 1m 38.25s, 96.604 mph/155.469 km/h (record for modified circuit).
*Previous circuit record:* Stefan Dörflinger, CH (Zundapp), 1m 36.22s, 98.52 mph/158.56 km/h (1984).

**World Championship: 1** Herreros, 47; **2** Martinez, 42; **3** Dörflinger, 35; **4** Bianchi, 24; **5** Nieto, 23; **6** Waibel, 22; **7** McConnachie, 21; **8** Spaan, 17; **9** Bolart and Fischer, 6; **11** Timmer, 5; **12** Abold, Kafka and van Kessel, 3; **15** Kunz and Rodriguez, 2; **17** Gil, Milano and Reyes, 1.

# Sidecars

**23 laps, 60.63 miles/97.59 km**

| Place | Driver & passenger | Nat. | Machine | Laps | Time & speed | Practice time | Grid |
|---|---|---|---|---|---|---|---|
| 1 | Egbert Streuer/<br>Bernie Schnieders | NL<br>NL | LCR-<br>Yamaha | 23 | 34m 22.56s<br>105.840 mph/<br>170.332 km/h | 1m 29.32s | 1 |
| 2 | Steve Webster/<br>Tony Hewitt | GB<br>GB | LCR-<br>Yamaha | 23 | 34m 32.37s | 1m 30.93s | 3 |
| 3 | Alain Michel/<br>Jean-Marc Fresc | F<br>F | Krauser-<br>Yamaha | 23 | 34m 47.11s | 1m 31.66s | 4 |
| 4 | Steve Abbott/<br>Shaun Smith | GB<br>GB | Windle-<br>Yamaha | 23 | 34m 47.88s | 1m 34.02s | 13 |
| 5 | Derek Jones/<br>Brian Ayres | GB<br>GB | LCR-<br>Yamaha | 23 | 34m 49.12s | 1m 34.51s | 14 |
| 6 | Markus Egloff/<br>Urs Egloff | CH<br>CH | LCR-<br>Yamaha | 23 | 34m 58.62s | 1m 32.45s | 6 |
| 7 | Alfred Zurbrügg/<br>Martin Zurbrügg | CH<br>CH | LCR-<br>Yamaha | 23 | 35m 18.42s | 1m 30.86s | 2 |
| 8 | Theo van Kempen/<br>Gerardus de Haas | NL<br>NL | LCR-<br>Yamaha | 23 | 35m 23.80s | 1m 32.09s | 5 |
| 9 | Masato Kumano/<br>Helmut Diehl | J<br>D | LCR-<br>Yamaha | 23 | 35m 50.79s | 1m 40.93s | 20 |
| 10 | Barry Brindley/<br>Chris Jones | GB<br>GB | Windle-<br>Yamaha | 23 | 35m 52.08s | 1m 32.81s | 8 |
| 11 | René Progin/<br>Yves Hunziker | CH<br>CH | Seymaz-<br>Yamaha | 23 | 35m 52.37s | 1m 32.84s | 9 |
| 12 | Yoshisada Kumagaya/<br>Kazuhiko Makiuchi | J<br>J | LCR-<br>Yamaha | 22 | 34m 31.93s | 1m 39.93s | 17 |
| 13 | Luigi Casagrande/<br>Hans Egli | CH<br>CH | LCR-<br>Yamaha | 22 | 34m 43.76s | 1m 41.56s | 21 |
| 14 | Erwin Weber/<br>Klaus Kolb | D<br>D | LCR-<br>Yamaha | 22 | 34m 44.29s | 1m 34.81s | 15 |
| 15 | Wolfgang Stropek/<br>Hans-Peter Demling | A<br>A | LCR-<br>Rotax | 22 | 34m 59.97s | 1m 32.96s | 11 |
| 16 | Herbert Prügl/<br>August Dierlinger | A<br>A | HOMA-<br>Yamaha | 22 | 35m 38.06s | 1m 40.41s | 18 |
| 17 | Graham Gleeson/<br>Dave Elliott | NZ<br>GB | LCR-<br>Yamaha | 20 | 35m 25.24s | 1m 35.66s | 16 |
| | Mick Barton/<br>Fritz Buck | GB<br>D | LCR-<br>Yamaha | 20 | DNF | 1m 41.64s | 22 |
| | Rolf Steinhausen/<br>Bruno Hiller | D<br>D | Busch | 13 | DNF | 1m 33.64s | 12 |
| | Hans Hügli/<br>Markus Fahrni | CH<br>CH | LCR-<br>Yamaha | 6 | DNF | 1m 32.85s | 10 |
| | Rolf Biland/<br>Kurt Waltisperg | CH<br>CH | Krauser | 6 | DNF | 1m 32.48s | 7 |
| | Frank Wrathall/<br>Phil Spendlove | GB<br>GB | LCR-<br>Yamaha | | DNS | 1m 40.48s | 19 |
| | Dennis Bingham/<br>Julia Bingham | GB<br>GB | LCR-<br>Yamaha | | DNQ | 1m 41.99s | |
| | Derek Bayley/<br>Bryan Nixon | GB<br>GB | LCR-<br>Ricardo | | DNQ | 1m 45.66s | |

*Fastest lap:* Streuer, 1m 28.39s, 107.380 mph/172.811 km/h (record for modified circuit).
*Previous circuit record:* Egbert Streuer/Bernie Schnieders, NL/NL (LCR-Yamaha), 1m 23.56s, 113.47 mph/182.62 km/h (1984).

**World Championship: 1** Streuer, 30; **2** Abbott, 18; **3** Michel, 15; **4** Biland, Jones, Webster and Zurbrügg, 12; **8** Egloff, 9; **9** von Kempen, 5; **10** Progin, 3; **11** Kumano, 2; **12** Barton and Brindley, 1.

# *Grand Prix de*
# YOUGOSLAVIE

Very few people look forward to the Yugoslav Grand Prix. There is only one good thing about this event and that is the ribbon of tarmac that winds its way round the sides of the dried-up river bed. The circuit is interesting and demanding and one of the best on the calendar but at the edge of the asphalt one runs out of good things to say – even the run-off areas are strewn with rocks, the armco rusts and the pits remain quarter-finished.

Should you ever want to teach someone a lesson in anti-communism, take them to the Yugoslav Grand Prix, where the local acceptance of power failure, a diabolical telephone system and the rarity of good fresh food testifies to the country's backwardness. The decaying buildings left over from the days of Austrian administration only serve to remind of what might have been. But the people are not Austrian; their lack of organisation mimics the Italians but they are without any Latin flair or enthusiasm.

The lengthy queue for scrutineering guaranteed, as in previous years, that everyone was fed up with the Yugoslav organisers even before official practice started. The dusty, overcrowded and half-paved paddock did not make work a pleasure and nor was there any compensation from the weather, as although the sun shone the wind also blew with a vengeance. It came tumbling over the backdrop of mountains, swirling and gusting across the paddock, destroying awnings and work tents, and forcing the first day of timed practice on Friday to be abandoned.

The wind blew even more strongly at night, so most of the experienced teams took down their awnings at the end of the day, re-erecting them each morning when there were people on hand to hold on to them. The Rothmans Honda hospitality bus lost its awning one night – the guy ropes remained tied, unused in neat bows. That morning, before the owners arrived from their hotel, riders and mechanics posed for photographs in the ruins. Friday was strange as practice was first delayed and not finally abandoned until the afternoon, providing the rare sight of mechanics and riders standing around chatting and laughing in a relaxed, holiday-like atmosphere. For once, there were no bikes to prepare and no distant circuit to race off to.

With no practice on Friday, Saturday was rescheduled, giving each of the three classes three sessions, each of forty minutes duration. It created a lot of work for the mechanics and left them travailing well into Saturday night. The wind still blew on Saturday and by the afternoon many thought it was as bad as Friday but no-one protested. No practice meant no race ... and above all everyone wanted to race. The wind contributed to a few crashes and Gustav Reiner was once more out of luck when he suffered a nasty injury to his elbow. Pier Paolo Bianchi broke a finger and Shungi Yatsushiro, Stéphane Mertens, Simon Buckmaster, Boet van Dulmen, Alan Carter and Gerhard Waibel were all fallers.

The bike that Yatsushiro fell from was one of Spencer's, out of use because the triple World Champion was at home in America undergoing a carpal tunnel operation on his right wrist. The news on Friday was that the operation had gone well and Spencer hoped to be back in action at Paul Ricard. Yatsushiro had the use of both bikes and that gave him the chance to find out how Spencer had them set up. It also helped HRC out with some engine testing they needed to do. There were three engine specifications available so that with different exhaust pipes and cylinders the riders could choose which combination would suit any particular circuit. Little difference could be seen on the outside but the high-speed pipes had larger bore tailpipes. These had been used in Austria and were tried again in Yugoslavia.

At the other end of the scale, Ian McConnachie finally got the use of a works Krauser – not quite the same as Dörflinger's but his spare number three bike. At least it did not cost him anything to run and the engine was better than his own even if McConnachie found the handling was not to his liking. He sorted that out to a certain extent during practice and was certain that at least the works engine would enable him to get a good start. 'No problem, you just watch – one push and I'll be gone, you'll be amazed', he insisted, with manifest confidence. At least he was getting some help and with two free sets of Michelins at each meeting and some regular prize money, life was looking up. At Rijeka, too, it was confirmed that he would ride Dr Joe Ehrlich's single-cylinder Rotax-engined EMC at Assen. While the single could not really be competitive against the current twins it was interesting in view of the impending rule change to single-cylinder 125s.

New machines had been thin on the ground and the new Suzuki V-four had been so long talked about that some began to wonder if it would ever appear. There was a false alarm on Wednesday when a V engine was spotted being smuggled into Roberto Gallina's work tent but in fact it was a 250 Yamaha which required some welding work on the frame. The Suzuki remained just a rumour with the latest twist being the suggestion that Mizutani, the Japanese test rider, would campaign one at Assen.

Roberto Gallina did not expect to have a new V-four for his riders at Assen but a new rolling chassis was waiting for the team back at La Spezia. The frame had been raced in Japan by Mizutani and was a twin-spar type, something between the Yamaha and Honda designs. Dave Petersen said that the bike certainly needed improvements to the handling as well as more engine power. Gallina received yet more parts and information from the factory and built a special reed-valve engine for Rijeka. The parts arrrived late so while the engine was being built on Wednesday Petersen went out on the spare bike, the old disc-valver, just to refresh his circuit knowledge. The revised reed-valve engine was worth waiting for, though, and performed well on Saturday, only being let down by pattering from both the front and back wheels.

The rumours of a new single-crank Yamaha engine had subsided and the latest piece of gossip was that there would be a new frame. Yamaha did not really seem to need it, as Lawson was in tremendously confident mood, more outgoing than ever before. The air of confidence probably had more to do with the way he overtook Spencer on the first lap in Austria than with winning the race and leading the championship by a handsome margin.

The team were at last getting the better of the carburation problems on the 500s – no easy task as the carburettors had no pilot jetting system and the single main jet and needle made separate adjustment of the low, mid and upper rev range carburation extremely inconvenient. The special carbs that Lawson had been trying from the beginning of the year had never been used for a race and were finally abandoned, but the original units were at last responding to Kel Carruthers' efforts.

With things going well on the 500s he was also able to devote some more time to the 250s and particularly to Martin Wimmer's dreadful starting problems. By the time Wimmer arrived on Wednesday evening, Carruthers had already completed his own private test session. 'I took your special starting lever off and I've altered the jetting a little; it starts just fine for me.' Wimmer knew he had to try it for himself, because whether his troubles were caused by nerves on the startline or a deficiency in his technique, it had to be sorted out. He practised in the paddock before every practice session and each time he called at the pits during practice he push-started his machine. Sometimes it went and sometimes it didn't but by Saturday afternoon he was confident that he was getting the hang of it.

Lawson was almost equally diligent, as was McElnea. Lawson would set off from his pit, cruise up past the working area towards the exit, stop, dismount and perform a practice start complete with clutch-slipping full-speed exit. It worked but why he had not done it four years before was harder to understand. Baldwin practised his starting but Mamola did not. He apparently was going to do his winning by lapping faster than anyone else and his times were impressive. In the first session he was half a second quicker than Lawson, with McElnea third ahead of Baldwin and Haslam. Unfortunately, that time for Haslam was pure imagination on the part of the timekeepers, as was that for Fabio Biliotti who they declared seventh behind Sarron and in front of Gardner. Lawson cut exactly a second off his time for the second session to move ahead; Mamola was seven-hundredths slower as Gardner pushed McElnea out of third place.

Rijeka is a tricky circuit and there are many ways of tackling it. Mamola has his own method and never uses first or second gear. To stay in third through two important sections he has to keep his corner speed high and when Randy told McElnea of this the Englishman tried to do the same. In fact, he lapped fractionally slower than he had in the morning when he had been following Lawson's advice. For the final session he went out and did his own thing, perhaps borrowing a little from each of the others, and went faster than Gardner's second session time. The Australian also went quicker, however, and remained nearly four-tenths ahead. Mamola jumped onto pole with a time three-tenths under Lawson's, who did not improve on his

Lawson was smooth and so much faster than anyone else that the championship looked to have been decided on the spot.

Ron Haslam lost his distinction as the fastest starter in Grand Prix racing to Manfred Fischer because the Englishman was hampered by the Elf's awkwardly routed clutch cable *(below)*.

second period time.

It was difficult to go quick in that final session as the wind had increased in strength and Mamola was a tenth of a second slower than Spencer's pole time of 1985 set in much better conditions. Mamola was faster than Lawson's lap record although Lawson himself was not.

Way down in fourteenth place was Didier de Radigues, obviously having problems with his collarbone. His accident at the Salzburgring was nasty; not only did he rebreak the plated collarbone and bend the plate but he also fell heavily on his head and for a while thought he had lost the feeling in his legs. That turned out to be a false alarm but while he practised at Rijeka he said there was no way he could last the race distance with the collarbone in such a bad way. 'We have some handling problems with the bike', he said. 'I want to use the time to get that sorted out if I can.'

Another injured rider who practised with no intention of racing was Niall MacKenzie. Still recovering from the broken leg he had plated after falling at Cadwell Park before the Grand Prix season began, the Scottish ace was walking and riding with just his lower leg in plaster. He was still quick enough to qualify eleventh on the Armstrong, just ahead of similarly Rotax-powered Manfred Herweh, although they were some way behind the fastest Rotax man, Hans Lindner, who was up in sixth place behind Jean-François Baldé and Sito Pons, the Spaniard being the fastest of the Honda men.

Practice was dominated by the Yamahas, though, with Lavado over half a second quicker than Wimmer after the first session and Taira in third place nearly a second down. The second session was very windy but in the final period Wimmer got to within eight-hundredths of Lavado's time and both were faster than Spencer's

pole time of a year ago. Taira was nearly a second slower than Wimmer but over half a second better than Pons.

Yamaha had certainly taken a grip of the 250 class and the rumours were strong that the V-twins would be for sale in '87. Honda must have been beginning to wish they had not brought works bikes into the 250 class but fate was to smile on them for the race.

## 80 cc

True to his word McConnachie got a great start and was second into the first corner behind Pier Paolo Bianchi and ahead of Manuel Herreros. Derbi team leader Jorge Martinez was fifth at the end of lap 1 as Herreros took the lead. Nieto was last off the line and Dörflinger also had his work cut out and was tenth after lap 1.

Herreros started to pull away as McConnachie

tried to hold on to second against increasing pressure from Martinez. Dörflinger was moving slowly and Hans Spaan took over fourth from Bianchi.

Martinez was the fastest man on the circuit and took the lead from Herreros on lap 4 leaving McConnachie third ahead of Spaan. Dörflinger got into his stride and was up to fifth by lap 5 but Martinez was well away and Herreros started to slow and stopped at the pits on lap 7.

McConnachie was left in a lonely second well clear of Spaan but Dörflinger was slowly catching and took over third place on lap 9, with Nieto fifth ahead of Bianchi and Waibel.

McConnachie had to give way to Dörflinger, not because of team orders but because of tyres. 'I made the wrong choice and when they started sliding I had to slow down,' admitted McConnachie. He lost second to Dörflinger on lap 11 of the 18 but remained well ahead of Nieto who gave Spaan a bit of a push and a shove as he went past on lap 11.

Spaan chased him and the pair closed on McConnachie. By lap 14 they were on his tail but he managed to increase the pace enough to ride

home a secure third. Martinez won by a clear 11 seconds with Dörflinger almost as secure in second.

## 250 cc

It was probably the most remarkable race of the year, one of those events that is a true privilege to watch for a display of riding that was astounding. Carlos Lavado for the first time in the year made a disastrous start. While Jean-Michel Mattioli led into the first corner he and Martin Wimmer had only just got the V-twin Yamahas started. Tadahiko Taira was only a little better off.

Ricci started second but took the lead on the first lap with Stéphane Mertens second on his private Yamaha. Mattioli was third but dropping back. Jean-François Baldé was right there, with Dominique Sarron, Carlos Cardus and Reinhold Roth a solid block of Hondas.

Two of the works-issue NSRs were well down – not quite as far back as the Yamahas, but Toni Mang and Sito Pons were battling well down the field. The lower-placed riders were hindered when Maurizio Matteoni fell while braking heavily for the first corner at the end of lap 1. The debris and

dirt came onto the circuit from the inside and Pons was one of those that had to go off the track to avoid it, which put him back with Lavado.

Lavado was still down in 17th place at the end of lap 5 but from then on he really started to move. Wimmer and Taira had tried to do the same but both crashed trying to pass slower men; their experiences were similar. Taira had been trying to move forward with Mang: 'Mang went to pass a slower rider who picked the bike up as he went past. Mang had to pick his bike up and there was no room for me – I had to go off the track.'

Wimmer went off the circuit trying to pass a group who moved over leaving him no room and he ended up hitting a tyre-protected barrier. He ended his race with a twisted knee. 'This time the engine didn't even fire but at least Carlos had the same problem, which shows it isn't just me.'

Lavado leap-frogged up the field as Baldé took over the lead from Ricci. He was taking two or even three seconds off the gap between himself and Baldé or passing as many as four or five riders. It was astonishing to watch and on his sixth lap he took a second and a half off Freddie Spencer's lap record.

Don Morley

*Below:* **At the height of the 250 battle Cardus fights to stay ahead of Sarron, Baldé and Ricci.**

**Randy Mamola and Wayne Gardner** *(above)* **battled for second and third position respectively behind Lawson.**

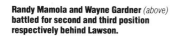

**Ian McConnachie** *(right)* **was becoming the hero of the 80 cc class.**

Don Morley

**Shungi Yatsushiro** *(left)*: a new name in Grand
Prix racing and a real character.

**Ferrari and Mang lead Herweh, Bolle and Roth
through Rijeka's sweeping curves** *(bottom)*.

On lap 10, Baldé led from Cardus, Ricci and
Sarron but Lavado was closing and next time
round he was in front and nearly two seconds
ahead. For one more lap he extended his lead still
further . . . but then he crashed. 'I don't understand it', said a tearful Lavado later. 'I was having
a small problem with the front tyre but I was
only going at the same pace as I had all through
and it went away from me. I picked the bike up
and I thought I had only lost a few seconds but
after a couple of laps my team hung out the board
saying "stop".'

In fact Lavado had lost 46 seconds to leader
Baldé and was back down to 26th place. He still
gained on the leaders at a rate of over a second a
lap but the time spent picking up the bike and
scraping the worst of the rocks out of the fairing
had meant that he could score few if any points
and his team concluded it was too dangerous to
let him continue.

When Lavado crashed, Pons had got as far as
sixth place, progressing more cautiously than
Lavado but gaining all the time. Up front, Baldé
led by a small margin from Cardus, Sarron and
Ricci. Mertens had been riding the wheels off his
Yamaha and set the second-fastest lap of the race,
just under Spencer's record, but the bike was no
match for the Hondas, and Pons closed in.

Mertens was relegated to sixth on lap 19 and
Pons started to catch the leading four. By lap 21
he was among them and while Baldé led Pons
was obviously going to get the best of any contest.
He hit the front on lap 23 and Baldé was
reduced to holding off Sarron while Ricci and
Cardus were left to contest fourth.

Pons pulled away at over half a second per lap.
The group closed up once more behind him and
Sarron took over second. Ricci got another burst
of life and also passed Baldé but Cardus was on
the production bike and struggled a little, having
to settle for fifth.

Pons was a good clear winner and on the last
lap Baldé got the better of the battle with Sarron,
thanks at least in part to them coming upon some
back-markers, but it was a great ride from the
endurance expert and brother of the ex-250 World
Champion. Virginio Ferrari scored points for
seventh after a good hard ride, beating off

Herweh, Bolle and Roth.

## 500 cc

Lawson was beginning to be boring. The speed at
which he disappeared off into the lead meant
that after two laps the result was not in doubt.
Manfred Fischer led into the first corner with
Haslam and Roche right behind. Roche took the
lead almost immediately but Lawson lay in sixth
place into the first corner, behind von Muralt and
van Dulmen. By the time the field appeared down
the hill across the circuit from the pits, the Californian was challenging Roche for the lead.
Through the esses at the lowest point of the circuit he eased past the Frenchman. 'I don't know
where Raymond was going but I went past as he
headed off across the track.'

Roche tried to hang on and for the first five laps
he was second but no matter how hard he rode
the Yamaha went away at over two seconds a lap.
Third place was entertaining and Sarron took
over from Gardner. McElnea was determined and
passed Gardner on lap 3, then chased Sarron and
took third on lap 5.

The group was getting bigger and more fiercely
fought as Gardner, Sarron, McElnea and Mamola
closed in on Roche. On lap 6 he was absorbed and
Gardner was the first to go past. The Australian
was over twelve seconds behind Lawson as he
drew Mamola away from Sarron and McElnea.
Roche could not keep up with the fours, further
hindered by the fact that he had suffered a severe
bout of flu the night before.

Gardner and Mamola were battling wheel to
wheel and as they passed some tail-enders the
pair got squeezed together going into the corner
at the end of the main straight. A shower of
sparks thrown out from between the two bikes
showed that something was making contact but
both stayed upright.

McElnea got the better of Sarron but there was
nothing he could do about catching Mamola and
Gardner. 'I still have a bit to learn', admitted the
Englishman later. 'When the tyres started to slide
I had to ease off. I've got to learn how to get on the
power early and drift it through the corner; at the
moment I am getting on the power too hard and it

goes sideways.'

Baldwin had made a bad start and having
never ridden at the circuit he had still to
acquaint himself with it. 'I had hoped to follow
someone and pick up a few points where I had not
got things completely sorted out in practice but
the bike did not start and the fast guys had all
gone. I was pleased, though, and I learnt a lot. If I
finish at all the tracks that are new to me it won't
be at all bad.'

Baldwin passed Roche on lap 14 and on the
next lap Haslam retired at the pits with front
brake problems and a split fuel tank. It took
Baldwin until lap 23 of the 32 to pass Sarron and
the Frenchman was not impressed with himself. 'I
was not riding very well at all and I found that I
could not turn my head to see round some of the
corners. I think I must have hurt it when I fell in
Austria.'

Shungi Yatsushiro had a very lonely ride into
eighth place and Dave Petersen had a good ride
from a bad start to take ninth. Because he was
caught out by the indecisive starter, Petersen had
to work hard after being 20th off the line. By the
end of lap 3 he was up to 13th and a few laps later
had closed on Italian Fabio Biliotti riding an
RS500 Honda. Petersen got past but Biliotti hung
to the tail of the Suzuki. 'He was pretty desperate
on the brakes and every lap at the end of the back
straight he was coming alongside. I started going
deeper and deeper into the corner and he just
kept braking later. I was just thinking that one
lap he is going to leave it too late when down the
road he went.' Biliotti was not hurt when this
happened on lap 22. For the remaining ten laps,
Petersen was alone and nearly half a minute in
front of Paul Lewis in tenth place on the Skoal
Bandit Suzuki.

Lawson was conspicuously the man of the race
and obviously had few problems. 'The bike ran
perfectly; we now seem to have the carburation
sorted out and it started well and pulled strongly
out of the corners. We had the suspension set hard
from the start and at first it was a little too hard
but as the shock heated up it worked perfectly. It
was hard work, though', said Lawson, sweating
profusely after stripping off his leathers, 'and I
was glad the race finished when it did.'

# Grand Prix de Yougoslavie, 15 June/statistics
## Rijeka, 2.590-mile/4.168-km circuit

## 500 cc

**32 laps, 82.88 miles/133.38 km**

| Place | Rider | Nat. | Machine | Laps | Time & speed | Practice time | Grid |
|---|---|---|---|---|---|---|---|
| 1 | Eddie Lawson | USA | Yamaha | 32 | 49m 55.81s 99.591 mph/ 160.275 km/h | 1m 31.85s | 2 |
| 2 | Randy Mamola | USA | Yamaha | 32 | 50m 06.55s | 1m 31.55s | 1 |
| 3 | Wayne Gardner | AUS | Honda | 32 | 50m 07.17s | 1m 32.09s | 3 |
| 4 | Rob McElnea | GB | Yamaha | 32 | 50m 20.13s | 1m 32.47s | 4 |
| 5 | Mike Baldwin | USA | Yamaha | 32 | 50m 28.13s | 1m 33.04s | 5 |
| 6 | Christian Sarron | F | Yamaha | 32 | 50m 33.15s | 1m 33.28s | 6 |
| 7 | Raymond Roche | F | Honda | 32 | 50m 45.72s | 1m 34.24s | 11 |
| 8 | Shunji Yatsushiro | J | Honda | 32 | 51m 15.06s | 1m 33.97s | 8 |
| 9 | Dave Petersen | ZIM | Suzuki | 31 | 49m 59.96s | 1m 34.48s | 12 |
| 10 | Paul Lewis | AUS | Suzuki | 31 | 50m 26.78s | 1m 35.36s | 16 |
| 11 | Wolfgang von Muralt | CH | Suzuki | 31 | 50m 28.43s | 1m 37.36s | 22 |
| 12 | Juan Garriga | E | Cagiva | 31 | 50m 39.96s | 1m 34.17s | 10 |
| 13 | Boet van Dulmen | NL | Honda | 31 | 50m 49.24s | 1m 35.63s | 17 |
| 14 | Eero Hyvarinen | SF | Honda | 31 | 51m 05.52s | 1m 37.47s | 24 |
| 15 | Marco Gentile | CH | Fior | 31 | 51m 09.24s | 1m 36.50s | 20 |
| 16 | Marco Papa | I | Honda | 31 | 51m 13.12s | 1m 36.50s | 19 |
| 17 | Fabio Barchitta | I | Honda | 31 | 51m 26.64s | 1m 38.15s | 27 |
| 18 | Mile Pajic | NL | Honda | 30 | 50m 01.58s | 1m 37.83s | 26 |
| 19 | Georg-Robert Jung | D | Honda | 30 | 50m 12.98s | 1m 38.87s | 30 |
| 20 | Andreas Leuthe | LUX | Honda | 30 | 50m 20.61s | 1m 38.56s | 29 |
| 21 | Marco Marchesani | I | Suzuki | 30 | 50m 36.24s | 1m 38.26s | 28 |
| 22 | Paval Dekanek | CS | Suzuki | 30 | 51m 19.10s | 1m 39.08s | 31 |
| 23 | Maarten Duyzers | NL | Suzuki | 30 | 51m 19.56s | 1m 39.75s | 34 |
| 24 | Leandro Becheroni | I | Suzuki | 30 | DNF | 1m 37.14s | 22 |
| | Sepp Doppler | A | Honda | 24 | DNF | 1m 40.26s | 35 |
| | Helmut Schütz | D | Honda | 23 | DNF | 1m 39.64s | 33 |
| | Fabio Biliotti | I | Honda | 22 | DNF | 1m 34.02s | 9 |
| | Henk van der Mark | NL | Honda | 17 | DNF | 1m 37.73s | 25 |
| | Ron Haslam | GB | Elf | 15 | DNF | 1m 33.86s | 7 |
| | Pier Francesco Chili | I | Suzuki | 10 | DNF | 1m 35.34s | 15 |
| | Manfred Fischer | D | Honda | 6 | DNF | 1m 36.50s | 18 |
| | Armando Errico | I | Suzuki | 4 | DNF | 1m 40.68s | 36 |
| | Gustav Reiner | D | Honda | | DNS | 1m 34.94s | 13 |
| | Didier de Radigues | B | Chevallier | | DNS | 1m 35.24s | 14 |
| | Simon Buckmaster | GB | Honda | | DNS | 1m 37.38s | 23 |
| | Dietmar Marehard | A | Homa | | DNS | 1m 39.29s | 32 |
| | Rudolf Zeller | A | Suzuki | | DNQ | 1m 40.78s | |
| | Dimitrios Papandreou | GR | Yamaha | | DNQ | 1m 41.59s | |
| | Detlef Vogt | D | Suzuki | | DNQ | 1m 42.14s | |

*Fastest lap:* Lawson, 1m 32.12s, 101.211 mph/162.883 km/h.
*Lap record:* Eddie Lawson, USA (Yamaha), 1m 31.78s, 101.586 mph/163.487 km/h (1985).

**World Championship: 1** Lawson, 72; **2** Gardner, 49; **3** Mamola, 47; **4** Baldwin, 42; **5** Sarron, 27; **6** McElnea, 25; **7** Roche, 13; **8** de Radigues, 12; **9** Yatsushiro, 7; **10** Chili and van Dulmen, 6; **12** Biliotti and Reiner, 5; **14** Haslam, 4; **15** Garriga, Lewis and Petersen, 3; **18** Papa, 1.

## 250 cc

**30 laps, 77.70 miles/125.04 km**

| Place | Rider | Nat. | Machine | Laps | Time & speed | Practice time | Grid |
|---|---|---|---|---|---|---|---|
| 1 | Alfonso Pons | E | Honda | 30 | 48m 34.73s 95.964 mph/ 154.438 km/h | 1m 35.27s | 4 |
| 2 | Jean-François Baldé | F | Honda | 30 | 48m 37.65s | 1m 35.32s | 5 |
| 3 | Dominique Sarron | F | Honda | 30 | 48m 37.85s | 1m 36.14s | 12 |
| 4 | Fausto Ricci | I | Honda | 30 | 48m 38.99s | 1m 35.98s | 10 |
| 5 | Carlos Cardus | E | Honda | 30 | 48m 41.26s | 1m 36.44s | 20 |
| 6 | Stéphane Mertens | B | Yamaha | 30 | 48m 54.03s | 1m 35.79s | 9 |
| 7 | Virginio Ferrari | I | Honda | 30 | 48m 55.51s | 1m 36.88s | 24 |
| 8 | Manfred Herweh | D | Aprilia | 30 | 48m 56.18s | 1m 36.14s | 13 |
| 9 | Pierre Bolle | F | Parisienne | 30 | 48m 56.54s | 1m 36.30s | 16 |
| 10 | Reinhold Roth | D | Honda | 30 | 48m 59.77s | 1m 36.67s | 22 |
| 11 | Herbert Besendörfer | D | Yamaha | 30 | 49m 06.59s | 1m 35.69s | 8 |
| 12 | Jean-Michel Mattioli | F | Yamaha | 30 | 49m 07.43s | 1m 35.68s | 7 |
| 13 | Jean Foray | F | Chevallier | 30 | 49m 09.74s | 1m 37.89s | 33 |
| 14 | Jacques Cornu | CH | Honda | 30 | 49m 10.02s | 1m 36.19s | 15 |
| 15 | Donnie McLeod | GB | Armstrong | 30 | 49m 10.28s | 1m 36.38s | 19 |
| 16 | Siegfried Minich | A | Yamaha | 30 | 49m 10.69s | 1m 36.62s | 21 |
| 17 | Harald Eckl | D | Honda | 30 | 49m 11.64s | 1m 36.96s | 25 |
| 18 | Hans Lindner | A | Castrol | 30 | 49m 47.79s | 1m 35.34s | 6 |
| 19 | Marcellino Lucchi | I | Malanca | 30 | 49m 53.54s | 1m 37.16s | 27 |
| 20 | Roland Freymond | CH | Yamaha | 30 | 49m 59.66s | 1m 38.45s | 37 |
| 21 | Hans Becker | D | Yamaha | 30 | 50m 04.36s | 1m 37.86s | 32 |
| 22 | Thomas Bacher | A | Dixi | 30 | 50m 09.53s | 1m 37.24s | 29 |
| 23 | Helmut Bradl | D | Honda | 30 | 50m 13.14s | 1m 37.70s | 31 |
| 24 | René Délaby | B | Moreno | 29 | 48m 38.53s | 1m 36.85s | 23 |
| 25 | Bruno Bonhuil | F | Honda | 29 | 48m 38.73s | 1m 38.36s | 35 |
| 26 | Maurizio Vitali | I | Garelli | 29 | 48m 45.33s | 1m 36.15s | 14 |
| 27 | Antonio Garcia | E | Honda | 29 | 48m 55.87s | 1m 37.23s | 28 |
| | Anton Mang | D | Honda | 24 | DNF | 1m 36.33s | 17 |
| | Carlos Lavado | YV | Yamaha | 17 | DNF | 1m 33.76s | 1 |
| | Alan Carter | GB | Kobas | 8 | DNF | 1m 36.37s | 18 |
| | Jean-Louis Tournadre | F | Yamaha | 7 | DNF | 1m 37.14s | 26 |
| | Andreas Preining | A | Wiwa | 4 | DNF | 1m 38.19s | 34 |
| | Tadahiko Taira | J | Yamaha | 1 | DNF | 1m 34.81s | 3 |
| | Massimo Matteoni | I | Honda | 0 | DNF | 1m 37.64s | 30 |
| | Martin Wimmer | D | Yamaha | 0 | DNF | 1m 33.84s | 2 |
| | Niall MacKenzie | GB | Armstrong | | DNS | 1m 36.12s | 11 |
| | Jean-Louis Guignabodet | F | MIG | | DNS | 1m 38.41s | 36 |
| | Urs Lüzi | CH | Yamaha | | DNQ | 1m 38.69s | |
| | Silvo Habat | YU | Yamaha | | DNQ | 1m 39.44s | |
| | Fernando Gonzalez | E | Kobas | | DNQ | 1m 39.56s | |
| | Sergio Pellandini | CH | Honda | | DNQ | 1m 39.64s | |
| | M. Sraj | YU | Yamaha | | DNQ | 1m 39.72s | |
| | Daniel Amatrain | E | Kobas | | DNQ | 1m 39.96s | |
| | Franz Lederer | D | Rotax | | DNQ | 1m 39.97s | |
| | Gerard van der Wal | NL | Assmex | | DNQ | 1m 40.50s | |
| | Eilert Lundstedt | S | MBA | | DNQ | 1m 40.60s | |
| | Oscar la Ferla | I | Yamaha | | DNQ | 1m 40.87s | |
| | Massimo Sirianni | I | Yamaha | | DNQ | 1m 41.20s | |
| | Jean-Luc Guillemet | F | Yamaha | | DNQ | 1m 41.30s | |
| | Andrea Brasini | I | Garelli | | DNQ | 1m 42.30s | |
| | S. Tsalikis | GR | Yamaha | | DNQ | 1m 45.13s | |

*Fastest lap:* Lavado, 1m 33.43s, 99.792 mph/160.599 km/h (record).
*Previous record:* Freddie Spencer, USA (Honda), 1m 34.80s, 98.350 mph/158.278 km/h (1985).

**World Championship: 1** Lavado, 57; **2** Baldé, 43; **3** Mang, 39; **4** Wimmer, 38; **5** Pons, 37; **6** Ricci, 24; **7** Sarron, 19; **8** Cornu and Bolle, 15; **10** McLeod and Herweh, 7; **12** Cardus, 6; **13** Taira and Mertens, 5; **15** Ferrari, 4; **16** Carter, Minich and Matteoni, 2; **19** Mattioli, Vitali and Roth, 1.

## 80 cc

**18 laps, 46.62 miles/75.02 km**

| Place | Rider | Nat. | Machine | Laps | Time & speed | Practice time | Grid |
|---|---|---|---|---|---|---|---|
| 1 | Jorge Martinez | E | Derbi | 18 | 31m 09.33s 89.778 mph/ 144.483 km/h | 1m 41.23s | 1 |
| 2 | Stefan Dörflinger | CH | Krauser | 18 | 31m 20.53s | 1m 42.32s | 2 |
| 3 | Ian McConnachie | GB | Krauser | 18 | 31m 25.49s | 1m 43.05s | 3 |
| 4 | Angel Nieto | E | Derbi | 18 | 31m 25.86s | 1m 43.39s | 6 |
| 5 | Hans Spaan | NL | Huvo | 18 | 31m 28.63s | 1m 44.99s | 9 |
| 6 | Pier Paolo Bianchi | I | Seel | 18 | 31m 48.05s | 1m 44.72s | 8 |
| 7 | Rainer Kunz | D | Ziegler | 18 | 31m 56.64s | 1m 45.20s | 10 |
| 8 | Josef Fischer | A | Krauser | 18 | 31m 57.77s | 1m 47.24s | 15 |
| 9 | Gerhard Waibel | D | Real | 18 | 31m 59.31s | 1m 46.30s | 11 |
| 10 | Luis Reyes | COL | Autisa | 18 | 31m 59.64s | 1m 46.38s | 12 |
| 11 | Hubert Abold | D | Seel | 18 | 32m 28.52s | 1m 47.54s | 16 |
| 12 | Henk van Kessel | NL | Krauser | 18 | 32m 30.24s | 1m 47.05s | 14 |
| 13 | Chris Baert | B | Seel | 18 | 32m 32.12s | 1m 51.18s | 28 |
| 14 | Salvatore Milano | I | Krauser | 18 | 32m 32.40s | 1m 47.73s | 17 |
| 15 | Reiner Scheidhauer | D | Seel | 18 | 32m 32.64s | 1m 46.93s | 13 |
| 16 | Gerd Kafka | A | Krauser | 18 | 32m 42.78s | 1m 47.75s | 18 |
| 17 | Mario Stocco | I | Huvo | 17 | 31m 16.60s | 1m 50.21s | 27 |
| 18 | Jos van Dongen | NL | Krauser | 17 | 31m 16.88s | 1m 51.47s | 29 |
| 19 | Raimo Lipponen | SF | Keifer | 17 | 31m 25.09s | 1m 49.76s | 24 |
| 20 | René Dünki | CH | Krauser | 17 | 31m 52.46s | 1m 47.91s | 19 |
| 21 | Thomas Engl | D | ESCH | 17 | 31m 59.01s | 1m 52.09s | 30 |
| 22 | Reiner Koster | CH | LCR | 17 | 32m 19.31s | 1m 53.33s | 33 |
| 23 | Richard Bay | D | Rupp | 17 | 32m 19.55s | 1m 49.96s | 26 |
| 24 | Zdravko Matulja | YU | MTM | 17 | 32m 34.28s | 1m 52.38s | 31 |
| 25 | Francisco Torontegui | E | Kobas | 16 | 32m 15.62s | 1m 48.27s | 21 |
| | Janez Pintar | YU | Eberhardt | 15 | DNF | 1m 49.93s | 25 |
| | Serge Julin | B | Huvo | 11 | DNF | 1m 54.22s | 35 |
| | Alexandre Barros | BR | Autisa | 9 | DNF | 1m 44.71s | 7 |
| | Domingo Gil | E | Autisa | 9 | DNF | 1m 48.29s | 22 |
| | Theo Timmer | NL | Huvo | 8 | DNF | 1m 48.24s | 20 |
| | B. Rokavec | YU | Seel | 8 | DNF | 1m 53.67s | 34 |
| | Manuel Herreros | E | Derbi | 7 | DNF | 1m 43.13s | 4 |
| | Peter Balaz | CS | Huvo | 7 | DNF | 1m 52.55s | 32 |
| | Mika-Sakari Komu | SF | Eberhardt | 5 | DNF | 1m 54.53s | 36 |
| | Juan Bolart | E | Autisa | 4 | DNF | 1m 43.16s | 5 |
| | Felix Rodriguez | E | Autisa | 3 | DNF | 1m 49.60s | 23 |
| | Kees Besseling | NL | Huvo | | DNQ | 1m 55.78s | |
| | Jarmo Piepponen | SF | Keifer | | DNQ | 1m 56.39s | |
| | Jan Vanecek | CS | Kreidler | | DNQ | 2m 02.69s | |
| | Zdravko Leljak | YU | Sever | | DNQ | 2m 09.29s | |
| | U. Tomanovic | YU | Sever | | DNQ | 2m 09.56s | |

*Fastest lap:* Martinez, 1m 40.16s, 93.087 mph/149.808 km/h (record).
*Previous record:* Stefan Dörflinger, CH (Krauser), 1m 42.04s, 91.372 mph/147.048 km/h (1985).

**World Championship: 1** Martinez, 57; **2** Herreros and Dörflinger, 47; **4** Nieto and McConnachie, 31; **6** Bianchi, 29; **7** Waibel, 24; **8** Spaan, 23; **9** Fischer, 9; **10** Bolart and Kunz, 6; **12** Timmer, 5; **13** Abold, Kafka and van Kessel, 3; **16** Rodriguez and Reyes, 2; **18** Gil and Milano, 1.

**The 80s climb through the fast S-bend across the circuit from the pits.**

# Grote Prijs van NEDERLAND

It is not difficult to see how the Dutch TT makes money. Hundreds of thousands of people come for race day, many of whom arrive during the preceding week to watch practice and soak up the atmosphere of race week at Assen. To extend the period in which people spend their time and money in the town and its environs, the European Championship was incorporated into race week with practice starting on Monday morning at nine o'clock. From that moment there was a full programme of either practice or racing until Saturday afternoon. The European Championship races were held on Tuesday afternoon and as soon as they finished practice started for the TT Formula 1 World Championship. The race was run at seven o'clock on Thursday evening and a large crowd that had turned out to see the first day of timed practice for the Grand Prix proper stayed on to watch Joey Dunlop win after Neil Robinson stopped with a broken chain.

It was a great week of sport, helped by glorious weather and the various improvements made by the circuit owners to facilities, including paving much of the paddock. Even the grass is well mown and how many circuits can boast a flower bed at the entrance to the paddock? There could be few complaints, with a great paddock restaurant and well-timed organisation.

The well-attended grass was a touch too inviting and there were numerous fallers in practice. Two Japanese campaigners in the 500 class fell three times before the race was over. That must be put down to self-applied pressure between the two of them. Shungi Yatsushiro was having his third Grand Prix outing on the NSR500 Honda and had ridden very well to score points in Austria and Yugoslavia. New on the scene was Masaru Mizutani riding for Suzuki. Not only was Mizutani Suzuki's test rider but also their number one man in the important Japanese 500 cc Championship. What made the first clash of the

pair in Europe so charged was that Mizutani had beaten Yatsushiro at the most recent Japanese Championship meeting, so while the Suzukis were getting blown off in Europe Mizutani had managed to put one over on the NSR in Japan. He came to Assen with the firm idea that he would beat Yatsushiro again. If Austria and Yugoslavia were true reflections of Yatsushiro's ability that meant Mizutani would have to finish in the top six, far higher than Petersen, Chili or Lewis had been able to achieve.

It had been rumoured that Mizutani would be riding the long-awaited V-four but that was far from ready and he appeared with an ageing square-four – and the disc-valve engine at that, rather than the stopgap reed-valver that both the Skoal Bandit team and Gallina had got going rather well (at least, they were better than the private RS500 Hondas at Assen).

Mizutani preferred the disc-valver and the trip to Europe was more of a thank you to him from the factory for good service than an R & D project, so he used the machine he liked with the standard aluminium rectangular tubular frame as used by Petersen. Mizutani fell before the time-keepers even got a time for him in the first session, damaging the bike so badly it could not be ridden that afternoon. He went out on Pier Francesco Chili's machine because the Italian was unable to ride after injuring a foot in an Italian meeting the week before. The time-keepers still got no time as he fell again.

The bike was repaired overnight and after 12 laps on Friday Mizutani was up to 24th-fastest. In the final session that afternoon he recorded one more lap, fell again and slipped to 25th on the grid. Meanwhile, Yatsushiro was up in 16th place but he had been having his moments as well, having fallen off in the first session and then again on Friday morning, hurting his wrist which meant he had to miss the afternoon outing. The first fall was on one of Spencer's machines and it ended up in a dyke which filled it with water.

That did not impress Spencer's mechanics. Erv Kanemoto and George Vukmanovitch, who, together with the bike, were on loan and unused to repairing crash-damaged motor cycles.

Yatsushiro was not the only additional Suzuki rider at Assen as Texan Kevin Schwantz was making his debut on one of the British-framed Suzukis not under the Skoal Bandit banner. It sported standard Suzuki blue and white, with the team's new backer, Rizla, as the biggest visible sponsor.

Schwantz only started racing in 1984 and while riding an FJ600 Yamaha and RZ350 at club races was spotted by John Ulrich, now editor of the American weekly *Cycle News*, as Schwantz recalled. 'The club races I was doing were sometimes on the same weekend as an endurance race and John was riding for Team Hammer so he got to see me ride. At the end of '84 I went to Road Atlanta for the Grand National final and a friend of mine got hurt in the endurance race so he offered me the chance of riding his 900 Ninja in the sprint race. I did two laps of practice then won the race. The only trouble was, I got disqualified because I rode under his name because I hadn't even qualified for the final.

'After that, John told me that Yoshimura were looking for a new rider if I was interested. I said I sure was and he arranged a try-out at Willow Springs. He gave me a go on the Team Hammer bike the day before because I'd only ridden street bikes and on the Sunday I rode the Yoshimura and won the Formula 1 and the 750 Superbike races. They signed me up for '85.'

In 1985 Schwantz only did four Nationals on the West Coast but he won at Willow Springs, Seattle and Sears Point. He broke down at Laguna Seca, as he had done at Daytona, when he qualified third on the air-cooled Suzuki but had the clutch disintegrate on the line.

That first year of Superbike racing was impressive to say the least because after breaking down in Florida, Schwantz took on Fred Merkel, the reigning Superbike champion at Willow

Gardner rode a very well-judged race to win his second GP of the season.

Sunshine and crowds are part of the TT atmosphere.

Springs. He beat him in the heat race and then in both legs of the final. So when pressed on the issue of how Schwantz compared himself with the other Americans who race back home, he replied: 'Merkel beat me for the first time the other weekend at Pocono. I made the wrong choice of tyre and it was just too soft. I guess Wayne Rainey and I are pretty equal at the moment, we've raced nose-to-tail. He has more experience than I have and it shows in practice when he seems to have more idea setting the bike up.'

That does not mean that Schwantz finds himself in any way out of his depth riding different machines. 'I don't always know how to sort out the steering and suspension but I can alter my riding and change the way the bike works instead.' Trying to ride both the Formula 1 bike and the Grand Prix 500 at the demanding, tight and twisty Assen circuit was a lot to ask even from Schwantz and he crashed both. By the end of four sessions he was 12th-fastest behind Petersen and Burnett but had completed only 24 laps, compared with the usual highest scorer Christian Sarron who had 47 to his name.

Sarron was fourth-fastest with Lawson on pole ahead of Gardner and McElnea. Gardner had been pleased with the way things were going in practice until perhaps the final session. 'We have had some problems with the bike that needed sorting out – you must have seen the way it was handling in Yugoslavia. Something had to be done and they have come up with some new parts, changing the suspension and geometry. It seems to work.'

Gardner led Lawson after the second session by two-tenths of a second but on Friday afternoon the Californian was in sensational form and without doubt did the definitive lap of the circuit to date in a time that the lap-scorers did not believe. While they gave him 2m 12.7s some five private but very reliable watches scored him a full second faster than that. That axed two

seconds off his previous best, more than two seconds off Spencer's practice lap record of 2m 13.91s set in 1985's single dry session, and four seconds quicker than his own lap record set in '84 of 2m 15.75s.

It was not just the Marlboro Yamaha timing computer that recorded the effort. Sonauto Yamaha had it, as did Suzuki and HRC. Gardner did not believe it possible. 'I know how fast I was going to do thirteens, I know how hard he must have been going to do twelves, and I certainly wouldn't have liked to be on the back if he did elevens.' Gardner's chief mechanic, Jerry Burgess, backed him up. 'No, it was too much of a jump to cut a full second off the other times he had been doing in that session just in one lap.'

It remained an impressive performance if one believes the weight of evidence but it turned out to be entirely irrelevant to the race as Lawson never got to complete a single circuit. It only served to remind Lawson later of his potential speed advantage over everyone else on race day, and that must have made him curse his first-lap impetuosity even more.

If there was ever a race he had won before it started this was it, but he certainly realised how it could all go wrong so easily – a fear he voiced on Friday evening, though referring more to his championship chances than to individual races. 'I haven't begun to think that the championship has been won. I could go out there tomorrow and get taken out at the first corner.'

He was well aware of how crucial the start would be, particularly at Assen where the narrow track makes passing so difficult. 'We spend all our

time practising to get a good place on the grid then have to push start so some guys from the back of the grid can lead us into the first corner. The Yamaha is not starting so well here, the carburation is not quite as good as it was in Yugoslavia and when I've been practising it has not been picking up just right. I'll have to take another couple of steps in the race.'

Lawson's starting had improved greatly over previous years but even more significant was his pace over the opening laps. For sure, there was no Spencer to compare him with, but the rate at which he left the rest behind was stunning and he had passed Spencer on the first lap in Austria. Lawson admitted that he now viewed the opening laps differently. 'When I first came to Europe I didn't want to make mistakes. I couldn't go diving past Roberts and Spencer; I looked up to them. Now it is different: I've learnt over the last three years and I've got more of an idea what I am doing, how far you can push the tyres on the first lap. You can push them hard, they'll grip real good from cold . . . but only up to a point, and you had better know where that point is because when they let go they'll spit you off. It's not like when they are warm – after two laps you can slide them like a dirt-tracker. When they are cold it is real sudden. Now I've got a bit more of an idea where that limit is on the first lap – or at least I think I have – and I'm prepared to push it. Now I don't hold back from passing others; if I have to take the stickers off their fairings on the way past then I'll do it.'

Lawson felt more than ready to race Spencer any time he showed up. If you wanted to dramatise it 'High Noon style', here was Lawson waiting

**Coming and going – Carlos Lavado looked like a World Champion** (far right).

**Wayne Gardner was smooth and consistent all the way to the rostrum for his second well-deserved Grand Prix victory of the season** (centre).

**Close action from Herreros and Spaan in the 80 cc race** (right).

in town, his town; having the occasional skirmish with the locals whom he dominated, still waiting for final showdown with the absent head honcho Spencer. 'I think Spencer will always have a problem of some sort: I don't think he is prepared to race and lose. I'll race wheel-to-wheel with him all race, I don't care. I don't think he is prepared to do that. If it comes to a fight where he might finish second I think some sort of problem will come up again; he won't race me.

'I don't think anyone else saw what was going on last year. I had him beaten in the rain in Austria by two seconds, then in the last half-lap someone got in the way and he won by three-hundredths of a second. He got off the line first in Belgium and I had to fight my way past Sarron but I still set the fastest lap of the race. I just never got with him to give him a race. He won in the wet at Silverstone but you know how much of an advantage it was to ride the 250 race before that so he knew what the track was like.'

## 80 cc

As always, things started early at Assen on race morning and by ten o'clock the 80s were preparing for the start of their 12-lap race. It was to provide just as much drama and excitement as any other in the day and a display of riding from Ian McConnachie that left spectators and competitors with one of the more memorable impressions of the event.

It was yet another poor start from the Englishman that initiated the dramatic ride and while Pier Paolo Bianchi led off the line, followed by Jorge Martinez and Manuel Herreros, McConnachie was well down the field and only completed the first lap in 15th place.

During that first circuit Martinez took the lead, taking his team-mate Herreros past Bianchi, who hung onto third place ahead of Hans Spaan, Mandy Fischer and Stefan Dörflinger. Martinez was riding well and soon started to open up a lead while Herreros struggled to hold off Spaan and Dörflinger as the three pulled away from Bianchi and Fischer. McConnachie had jumped to tenth at the end of lap 2 and by lap 4 was fourth.

Martinez was extending his lead over the second-place trio but it was obvious to all that he was not getting away from McConnachie. On lap 5 he flew past Dörflinger and Spaan, crossing the line on the tail of the second Derbi. Martinez was well aware of the Englishman's progress and continued to lap at 2m 33s which was as fast as he had managed in practice, but he could not cope with the fact that McConnachie (who had qualified third behind Dörflinger at 2m 34s) was now lapping nearly four seconds faster than he had then. He was more than nine seconds under the lap record and only one second off Nieto's 125 lap record. On lap 8, McConnachie was three seconds behind Aspar; a lap later he was half a second behind and lap 10 saw him pass and open out a 2.7-second advantage over the Spaniard.

The rest of the field seemed pedestrian in comparison, though Nieto had pulled through from a start as bad as McConnachie's to take fifth place behind Spaan and ahead of Dörflinger. The lat-

ter's championship chances were beginning to look a little sad and, to make matters worse, McConnachie was showing what could be done with a works Krauser.

Unfortunately the British rider did not realise that he had opened up a five-second lead over Martinez as they raced round the last lap and, coming into the ninety-degree right-hander made famous by Sarron's skittling of Spencer a year before, the front tyre of McConnachie's bike let go. He picked it up immediately and set off again but in too much of a hurry while still on the grass. He fell again and this time the ignition was damaged and the little machine would not restart. 'I really feel a fool', admitted McConnachie later. 'I was not trying any harder than I had before but I had not eased off because I had only passed Martinez a lap or so before and I thought he must be still on my tail.'

Martinez could not believe his luck with the gift of a win, nearly ten seconds ahead of Herreros, who beat Spaan to the line well ahead of Nieto and Dörflinger.

## 250 cc

Wimmer's long saga of poor starts continued when the Marlboro Yamaha fired instantly but as the West German leapt aboard and tucked down behind the screen the little V-twin just gasped, spluttered and crawled off the line while the pack flew past him.

Carlos Lavado had no such trouble and although Fausto Ricci led on the Honda Italy NSR250, the Venezuelan was soon into second place ahead of Donnie McLeod, Sito Pons and Jacques Cornu. By the end of lap 2 Lavado had taken the lead and quickly started to open up an advantage over Ricci who came under pressure from Pons and McLeod. Wimmer was 21st at the end of lap 1 and not much better off was Mang in 15th place.

Mang advanced rapidly, however, and by lap 5 was up to eighth, having just passed Dominique Sarron, and slipped in behind Siggi Minich on his private RS250 Honda. While Lavado continued to extend his lead, Pons took second from Ricci on lap 6 while McLeod held fourth only a little way behind. It was obvious that these three battling for second were going to come under pressure from Mang as he moved into sixth place on that lap, with only Cornu between himself and McLeod.

On lap 7 Mang passed Cornu but two laps later Ricci crashed when he lost the front end on the brakes. That promoted McLeod temporarily to third before being demoted once more by Mang on lap 10. In one circuit the German passed McLeod and Pons but was so far behind Lavado that there was no chance of winning unless the Yamaha made a mistake. Lavado was trying to make sure he did no such thing. 'I dare not fall off because my mechanic told me he would cut my xxxxs off if I did.' By halfway through the race he had an eight-second lead and comfortably held it at that.

The three behind were much closer, and while Mang led he could not get away from Pons.

McLeod hung on well despite the lack of speed from the Rotax-engined Armstrong.

The battle for fifth was led by Cornu and Baldé but Tadahiko Taira, who had started behind Mang, passed them on lap 12. Just behind him came Sarron and Wimmer, so a five-way battle developed for a few laps until Taira, Wimmer and Sarron broke away from Cornu and Baldé on the sixteenth lap.

The battle for the last point was between Siggi Minich, Reinhold Roth and Stéphane Mertens. There was nothing to choose between them but Mertens crashed on the last lap and Roth got the point, which seemed rather hard luck on Minich who had also ridden well.

Mang held off Pons to take second behind Lavado and McLeod dropped back over the last few laps when he realised that beating the Hondas was impossible. He was far enough ahead of Wimmer and Taira not to be concerned. Wimmer got the better of his Japanese team-mate on the last lap and they both finished well ahead of Sarron. Cornu did a masterly job of beating Baldé on the run-in to the line.

## SIDECARS

Alain Michel and Jean-Marc Fresc rode a perfectly consistent and well-judged race to win the 16-lap event from Steve Webster and Tony Hewitt with Masato Kumano and Helmut Diehl a very good third after a poor start.

Rolf Biland and Kurt Waltisperg led off the line but the Krauser soon hit trouble and the crowd came to their feet as Egbert Streuer and Bernard Schnieders took over to lead across the line at the end of lap 1. Biland retired at the pits with clutch trouble. Michel was then a close second but keen to conserve his tyres as pole-man Streuer opened up a five-second lead. It stretched to nine seconds before the Barclay outfit came to a halt with ignition failure on lap 11 and Michel took over. 'I had planned to save the tyres for the last five laps, but I did not have to', said Michel later.

Webster stayed behind Michel throughout the

race and although he was never in a position to challenge the French crew, equally he was never threatened from behind. Kumano was down in tenth place halfway round the first lap and gradually worked his way up. He was eighth on lap 2 but was then repassed by Mick Barton who moved quickly up through the field until he got to fifth place on lap 8, only to go off the track trying to catch the Egloff brothers. They regained the circuit back in eighth place and managed to get back to sixth by the flag. Streuer's eleventh-lap retirement promoted the Egloffs to third but by then Kumano was fourth ahead of Abbott and Biggs as Jones and Ayres crashed in spectacular fashion. On lap 14 Kumano took third and was able to pull out a nine-second advantage over the Egloffs before the flag.

## 500 cc

There is no room at Assen for even the smallest mistake, as Lawson proved on the first lap when he braked too late in the sharp right-hander, two-thirds of the way round the circuit – the same corner where Christian Sarron brought down Freddie Spencer twelve months before. At many tracks he would have got away with it, running wide but staying on the tarmac. At Assen there is no room to run wide and he ended up on the grass. As he tried to regain the tarmac he fell and that was the end of his race and his domination of the championship.

Typically, Lawson made no excuse for his first-lap mistake. 'I was trying to go round some other guys and I ran out of road and got onto the grass. I tried to get going again but the marshals would not let me.' Eye-witnesses say that Lawson approached the corner too fast and it is possible that he did not make enough allowance for the bike being brimful of fuel under braking for the almost dead-stop ninety-degree turn. Carruthers always sends his team riders out for the race day morning warm-up session with full tanks of fuel so that they go into the race aware of the weight.

Kevin Schwantz fell at the same corner as Lawson after being fourth going into the chicane

at the end of lap 1. He didn't intend to be, though, and had shot past McElnea and de Radigues going in because the Suzuki's throttles appeared to be sticking. He ran across the dirt but regained the circuit in seventh place, only to fall at Lawson's corner half a lap later. He still remounted and continued at the back of the field but pulled out once lapped by Gardner after half-distance.

Gardner did not even know that Lawson had crashed until the race was over. 'I thought that he was behind me all the time. I had a pit board early on saying "Lawson out" but I could see a Marlboro bike behind me and I thought that was him instead of Rob. I expected him to come past but I kept reading the lap boards and managed to keep a distance. I played the back-markers to my advantage and put in an effort when the gap went down from three and a half seconds to under one. I got it back to three and I knew I could put in a quick one at the end if I had to.'

Ron Haslam made his usual great start and led the field off the line. He flew round the first lap to open up quite a lead before Gardner settled in and passed him during lap 2. Haslam began to slip back with brake problems, being passed first by Raymond Roche then McElnea, Mamola and Baldwin. He finally finished seventh, putting in a concerted effort over the last quarter of the race to stay ahead of Roger Burnett on the Honda Britain machine.

McElnea and Mamola attempted to chase Gardner and seemed to be closing but the Australian increased his pace, held them off and made sure of his lead. Mamola took second from McElnea on lap 7 and started to pull away, but despite getting to within a second of the leading Honda Gardner always seemed to have the answer. By lap 16 of the 20, the gap had grown to 3.3s. Mamola managed to cut that back to 2.3s going on to the last lap.

Mamola pulled a wheelie and was waving to the crowd on the final circuit, admitting that he could not catch Gardner. Later he claimed he could have beaten Gardner. 'I thought I had it covered on the second-to-last lap but he got a better run through traffic while I got held up and there was nothing I could do. I came up behind this back-marker in the fast section and I thought "If I get past him here I'm going to win the race", but there was no way. If I had tried to get by I would have crashed.'

Mamola is no stranger to disappointment and considered the result to have been a good end to a bad week. 'My girlfriend had to go into hospital for an operation here and that made it difficult for me to concentrate during practice. I was back and forwards to the hospital and I only qualified sixth. The bike was not quite right; it was too rich but if we lean it out it loses power. We were using the new big-crank engine but we need to get the carburation sorted. We don't go running down to Kel and ask him what he is doing, like he doesn't come round here. We try to sort our own things out.'

McElnea was a great deal more frustrated at the way his race ended. Halfway round the last lap he had almost a one-second advantage over Baldwin but lost out in the last few yards as the

dejected Englishman subsequently explained. 'I looked behind me on the last lap and saw he was there so I knew I had to make the effort. I was a bit held up by Marco Papa but that wasn't a big problem. I went into the last chicane hard because I thought he might try to come up the inside. When he didn't I thought I had made it but he must have come out of the turn better and beat me to the line.' McElnea ended the race with a large seagull stuck in the fairing after hitting it with two laps to go.

Baldwin had made a poor start and completed lap 1 in 11th place and admitted that it had been hard work catching McElnea. 'I was catching up OK until I got behind Roche and Rob got away a little as it took me time to get by and I made a few small mistakes that cost me time. With eight laps to go I said to myself, 'I don't care how I am going to do it but I'm going to catch him'. I could see I was catching all the time and then on the last lap he got baulked by a back-marker and I thought about going up the inside because I had ten mph on him. But there wasn't enough room and we would have touched for sure. I sat back and coming into the chicane I just flicked it in there and hoped, because I had been gaining on him before coming out and I hoped it would be enough.'

Christian Sarron finished fifth after making his usual bad start. 'I did not ride that well. I had a poor morale after such a bad start because the best I thought I could do was finish sixth or seventh.' Roche finished sixth, the first of the three-cylinder Hondas home, and Didier de Radigues was ninth on the Chevallier, a long way ahead of Juan Garriga on the Cagiva.

## 125 cc

Although the 500 race had been interesting and dramatic thanks to Lawson's fall, the 125 race was a much closer contest. It turned into an Auinger versus Garelli struggle which the Austrian lost when he fell, leaving team-mates Luca Cadalora and Fausto Gresini to battle to the flag. Cadalora eventually won by a quarter-second after the pair had swapped places all the way round the circuit. At the end of the 16 laps they were nearly half a minute ahead of third-place man Ezio Gianola.

Right from the start it was a three-way battle and fourth-place man Alfred Waibel was left well behind. By lap 3 Gianola, who had completed lap 1 in 15th place, was up to seventh, but by the time he took fourth on lap 4 the leading trio were so far ahead that he had no chance of catching them.

It was great stuff up front with no favours being given either way, but Auinger's fall on lap 7 rather took the sting out of it. He later blamed the Garellis, which have no catch tanks, for blowing fuel out of their tank breather pipes.

Gianola was then in a secure third ahead of Domenico Brigaglia but Bruno Kneubühler was making steady progress and the Swiss veteran tried to beat Brigaglia for fourth. He almost succeeded when he got in front but it was not when it counted, on the run-in to the flag. Johnny Wickström was a lonely sixth while Paolo Casoli just held off Thierry Feuz for seventh.

## Circuit van Drenthe, Assen 3.812-mile/6.134-km circuit

## 500 cc

**20 laps, 76.24 miles/122.68 km**

| *Place* | *Rider* | *Nat.* | *Machine* | *Laps* | *Time & speed* | *Practice time* | *Grid* |
|---|---|---|---|---|---|---|---|
| 1 | Wayne Gardner | AUS | Honda | 20 | 45m 17.78s 100.975 mph/ 162.503 km/h | 2m 13.39s | 2 |
| 2 | Randy Mamola | USA | Yamaha | 20 | 45m 21.41s | 2m 14.49s | 6 |
| 3 | Mike Baldwin | USA | Yamaha | 20 | 45m 27.84s | 2m 14.41s | 5 |
| 4 | Rob McElnea | GB | Yamaha | 20 | 45m 27.92s | 2m 13.70s | 3 |
| 5 | Christian Sarron | F | Yamaha | 20 | 45m 38.21s | 2m 14.08s | 4 |
| 6 | Raymond Roche | F | Honda | 20 | 45m 50.42s | 2m 14.98s | 7 |
| 7 | Ron Haslam | GB | Elf | 20 | 45m 57.74s | 2m 15.99s | 8 |
| 8 | Roger Burnett | GB | Honda | 20 | 46m 05.03s | 2m 16.99s | 11 |
| 9 | Didier de Radigues | B | Chevallier | 20 | 46m 25.48s | 2m 16.74s | 9 |
| 10 | Juan Garriga | E | Cagiva | 20 | 46m 52.10s | 2m 17.53s | 13 |
| 11 | Marco Gentile | CH | Fior | 20 | 47m 09.18s | 2m 19.02s | 20 |
| 12 | Boet van Dulmen | NL | Honda | 20 | 47m 12.89s | 2m 18.88s | 18 |
| 13 | Wolfgang von Muralt | CH | Suzuki | 20 | 47m 39.15s | 2m 19.98s | 24 |
| 14 | Masaru Mizutani | J | Suzuki | 19 | 45m 19.15s | 2m 20.38s | 25 |
| 15 | Simon Buckmaster | GB | Honda | 19 | 45m 19.93s | 2m 21.13s | 30 |
| 16 | Mile Pajic | NL | Honda | 19 | 45m 20.85s | 2m 19.84s | 23 |
| 17 | Manfred Fischer | D | Honda | 19 | 45m 24.08s | 2m 19.02s | 19 |
| 18 | Marco Papa | I | Honda | 19 | 45m 30.31s | 2m 19.68s | 22 |
| 19 | Eero Hyvarinen | SF | Honda | 19 | 45m 46.74s | 2m 20.52s | 27 |
| 20 | Rob Punt | NL | Honda | 19 | 45m 58.01s | 2m 20.50s | 26 |
| 21 | Esko Kuparinen | SF | Honda | 19 | 46m 36.25s | 2m 22.02s | 33 |
| 22 | Dietmar Mayer | D | Honda | 19 | 46m 48.50s | 2m 23.54s | 36 |
| | Kevin Schwantz | USA | Suzuki | 12 | DNF | 2m 17.22s | 12 |
| | Peter Sköld | S | Honda | 12 | DNF | 2m 21.20s | 31 |
| | Mark Phillips | GB | Suzuki | 12 | DNF | 2m 20.68s | 28 |
| | Maarten Duyzers | NL | Suzuki | 11 | DNF | 2m 23.02s | 35 |
| | Peter Linden | S | Honda | 9 | DNF | 2m 20.98s | 29 |
| | Massimo Messere | I | Honda | 5 | DNF | 2m 18.83s | 17 |
| | Dave Petersen | ZIM | Suzuki | 5 | DNF | 2m 16.96s | 10 |
| | Gustav Reiner | D | Honda | 4 | DNF | 2m 18.11s | 15 |
| | Ray Swann | GB | Suzuki | 3 | DNF | 2m 22.22s | 34 |
| | Kenny Irons | GB | Yamaha | 2 | DNF | 2m 19.03s | 21 |
| | Shunji Yatsushiro | J | Honda | 2 | DNF | 2m 18.28s | 16 |
| | Paul Lewis | AUS | Suzuki | 2 | DNF | 2m 18.01s | 14 |
| | Karl Truchsess | A | Honda | 1 | DNF | 2m 21.92s | 32 |
| | Eddie Lawson | USA | Yamaha | 0 | DNF | 2m 12.70s | 1 |
| | Henny Boerman | NL | Assmex | | DNQ | 2m 23.68s | |
| | Dave Griffith | GB | Suzuki | | DNQ | 2m 24.17s | |
| | Andreas Leuthe | LUX | Honda | | DNQ | 2m 25.45s | |
| | Bohumil Stasa | CS | Honda | | DNQ | 2m 26.06s | |
| | Helmut Schütz | D | Honda | | DNQ | 2m 26.93s | |
| | Philippe Robinet | F | Honda | | DNQ | 2m 29.70s | |

*Fastest lap:* Gardner, 2m 14.28s, 102.185 mph/164.450 km/h (record).
*Previous record:* Eddie Lawson, USA (Yamaha), 2m 15.75s, 101.08 mph/162.67 km/h (1984).

**World Championship: 1** Lawson, 72; **2** Gardner, 64; **3** Mamola, 59; **4** Baldwin, 52; **5** Sarron and McElnea, 33; **7** Roche, 18; **8** de Radigues, 14; **9** Haslam, 8; **10** Yatsushiro, 7; **11** Chili and van Dulmen, 6; **13** Biliotti and Reiner, 5; **15** Garriga, 4; **16** Lewis, Petersen and Burnett, 3; **19** Papa, 1.

## 250 cc

**18 laps, 68.62 miles/110.41 km**

| *Place* | *Rider* | *Nat.* | *Machine* | *Laps* | *Time & speed* | *Practice time* | *Grid* |
|---|---|---|---|---|---|---|---|
| 1 | Carlos Lavado | YV | Yamaha | 18 | 42m 13.19s 97.500 mph/ 156.91 km/h | 2m 18.18s | 1 |
| 2 | Anton Mang | D | Honda | 18 | 42m 17.78s | 2m 20.37s | 7 |
| 3 | Alfonso Pons | E | Honda | 18 | 42m 19.14s | 2m 20.01s | 4 |
| 4 | Donnie McLeod | GB | Armstrong | 18 | 42m 21.06s | 2m 20.05s | 5 |
| 5 | Martin Wimmer | D | Yamaha | 18 | 42m 27.63s | 2m 18.70s | 2 |
| 6 | Tadahiko Taira | J | Yamaha | 18 | 42m 28.96s | 2m 19.66s | 3 |
| 7 | Dominique Sarron | F | Honda | 18 | 42m 32.06s | 2m 20.12s | 6 |
| 8 | Jacques Cornu | CH | Honda | 18 | 42m 34.19s | 2m 21.59s | 17 |
| 9 | Jean-François Baldé | F | Honda | 18 | 42m 34.46s | 2m 20.41s | 8 |
| 10 | Reinhold Roth | D | Honda | 18 | 42m 55.56s | 2m 20.90s | 11 |
| 11 | Siegfried Minich | A | Honda | 18 | 42m 57.24s | 2m 21.07s | 12 |
| 12 | Niall MacKenzie | GB | Armstrong | 18 | 43m 06.47s | 2m 20.66s | 10 |
| 13 | Hans Becker | D | Yamaha | 18 | 43m 15.59s | 2m 22.33s | 25 |
| 14 | Hans Lindner | A | Castrol | 18 | 43m 21.45s | 2m 21.73s | 19 |
| 15 | Alan Carter | GB | Kobas | 18 | 43m 21.81s | 2m 22.02s | 23 |
| 16 | Maurizio Vitali | I | Garelli | 18 | 43m 22.10s | 2m 23.17s | 28 |
| 17 | Cees Doorakkers | NL | Honda | 18 | 43m 22.40s | 2m 23.60s | 31 |
| 18 | Gary Noel | GB | EMC | 18 | 43m 29.84s | 2m 23.48s | 29 |
| 19 | Jochen Schmid | D | Yamaha | 18 | 43m 37.96s | 2m 21.57s | 16 |
| 20 | Urs Lüzi I | CH | Yamaha | 18 | 43m 43.16s | 2m 23.99s | 35 |
| 21 | Gerard van der Wal | NL | Assmex | 18 | 43m 47.64s | 2m 24.79s | 36 |
| 22 | Antonio Garcia | E | Kobas | 18 | 43m 54.53s | 2m 23.80s | 33 |
| | Stéphane Mertens | B | Yamaha | 17 | DNF | 2m 21.95s | 22 |
| | Harald Eckl | D | Honda | 11 | DNF | 2m 22.12s | 24 |
| | Fausto Ricci | I | Honda | 8 | DNF | 2m 20.46s | 8 |
| | Jean Foray | F | Chevallier | 8 | DNF | 2m 21.73s | 20 |
| | Mar Schouten | NL | Honda | 8 | DNF | 2m 24.91s | 37 |
| | Roland Freymond | CH | Yamaha | 6 | DNF | 2m 23.91s | 34 |
| | Jean-Michel Mattioli | F | Yamaha | 6 | DNF | 2m 21.94s | 21 |
| | Virginio Ferrari | I | Honda | 5 | DNF | 2m 21.59s | 18 |
| | Pierre Bolle | F | Parisienne | 4 | DNF | 2m 21.25s | 14 |
| | Herbert Besendörfer | D | Yamaha | 2 | DNF | 2m 21.07s | 13 |
| | Andreas Preining | A | Wiwa | 2 | DNF | 2m 23.55s | 30 |
| | Carlos Cardus | E | Honda | 1 | DNF | 2m 21.39s | 15 |
| | Andy Watts | GB | EMC | 0 | DNF | 2m 22.84s | 26 |
| | Manfred Herweh | D | Aprilia | 0 | DNF | 2m 22.94s | 27 |
| | René Délaby | B | Moreno | | DNS | 2m 23.65s | 32 |
| | Bruno Bonhuil | F | Honda | | DNQ | 2m 25.09s | |
| | Jean-Louis Guignabodet | F | MIG | | DNQ | 2m 25.14s | |
| | Gary Cowan | GB | Honda | | DNQ | 2m 25.28s | |
| | Svend Andersson | DK | Yamaha | | DNQ | 2m 25.95s | |
| | Joey Dunlop | GB | Honda | | DNQ | 2m 26.39s | |
| | Ian Newton | GB | Armstrong | | DNQ | 2m 28.15s | |
| | Luis Lavado | YV | Yamaha | | DNQ | 2m 28.23s | |
| | Sergio Pellandini | CH | Honda | | DNQ | 2m 30.03s | |
| | Manuel Gonzalez | YV | Yamaha | | DNQ | 2m 30.18s | |

*Fastest lap:* Wimmer, 2m 19.07s, 98.665 mph/158.786 km/h (record).
*Previous record:* Edwin Weibel, CH (Yamaha), 2m 24.12s, 95.15 mph/153.13 km/h (1984).

**World Championship: 1** Lavado, 72; **2** Mang, 51; **3** Pons, 47; **4** Baldé, 45; **5** Wimmer, 44; **6** Ricci, 24; **7** Sarron, 23; **8** Cornu, 18; **9** Bolle and McLeod, 15; **11** Taira, 10; **12** Herweh, 7; **13** Cardus, 6; **14** Mertens, 5; **15** Ferrari, 4; **16** Carter, Matteoni, Minich and Roth, 2; **20** Mattioli and Vitali, 1.

## 125 cc

**16 laps, 60.99 miles/98.14 km**

| *Place* | *Rider* | *Nat.* | *Machine* | *Laps* | *Time & speed* | *Practice time* | *Grid* |
|---|---|---|---|---|---|---|---|
| 1 | Luca Cadalora | I | Garelli | 16 | 39m 30.04s 92.632 mph/ 149.077 km/h | 2m 26.55s | 1 |
| 2 | Fausto Gresini | I | Garelli | 16 | 39m 30.30s | 2m 27.01s | 3 |
| 3 | Ezio Gianola | I | MBA | 16 | 39m 57.29s | 2m 27.63s | 4 |
| 4 | Domenico Brigaglia | I | Ducados | 16 | 40m 02.98s | 2m 28.31s | 5 |
| 5 | Bruno Kneubühler | CH | LCR | 16 | 40m 03.38s | 2m 29.82s | 10 |
| 6 | Johnny Wickström | SF | Tunturi | 16 | 40m 16.72s | 2m 30.03s | 12 |
| 7 | Paolo Casoli | I | MBA | 16 | 40m 32.88s | 2m 30.76s | 15 |
| 8 | Thierry Feuz | CH | LCR | 16 | 40m 33.35s | 2m 29.78s | 9 |
| 9 | Gastone Grassetti | I | MBA | 16 | 40m 52.82s | 2m 31.34s | 16 |
| 10 | Angel Nieto | E | Ducados | 16 | 41m 01.89s | 2m 30.49s | 13 |
| 11 | Willy Perez | RA | Zanella | 16 | 41m 04.60s | 2m 30.52s | 14 |
| 12 | Paul Bordes | F | MBA | 16 | 41m 04.88s | 2m 33.26s | 26 |
| 13 | Marin Andreas Sanchez | E | Ducados | 16 | 41m 23.70s | 2m 33.13s | 25 |
| 14 | Robin Appleyard | GB | MBA | 16 | 41m 32.22s | 2m 35.09s | 36 |
| 15 | Jan Eggens | NL | LCR | 16 | 41m 32.71s | 2m 34.37s | 30 |
| 16 | Norbert Peschke | D | MBA | 16 | 41m 53.15s | 2m 32.37s | 20 |
| 17 | Esa Kytola | SF | MBA | 16 | 41m 53.63s | 2m 33.85s | 28 |
| 18 | Robin Milton | GB | MBA | 16 | 41m 56.28s | 2m 32.75s | 22 |
| 19 | Patrick Daudier | F | PMDF | 15 | 39m 55.03s | 2m 31.89s | 17 |
| 20 | Thierry Maurer | CH | MBA | 15 | 40m 00.73s | 2m 33.37s | 27 |
| 21 | Thomas Möller-Pedersen | DK | MBA | 15 | 40m 01.67s | 2m 32.37s | 21 |
| 22 | Ton Spek | NL | MBA | 13 | 39m 46.37s | 2m 34.84s | 35 |
| | Anton Straver | NL | MBA | 14 | DNF | 2m 32.84s | 23 |
| | Hakan Olsson | S | Starol | 13 | DNF | 2m 34.78s | 34 |
| | Jussi Hautaniemi | SF | MBA | 12 | DNF | 2m 30.01s | 11 |
| | Mike Leitner | A | Bartol | 11 | DNF | 2m 32.08s | 19 |
| | Alfred Waibel | D | Real | 10 | DNF | 2m 28.87s | 7 |
| | Jacques Hutteau | F | MBA | 10 | DNF | 2m 33.11s | 24 |
| | Janez Pintar | YU | MBA | 9 | DNF | 2m 35.32s | 37 |
| | August Auinger | A | Bartol | 6 | DNF | 2m 26.91s | 2 |
| | Pier Paolo Bianchi | I | Elit | 6 | DNF | 2m 29.39s | 8 |
| | Lucio Pietroniro | B | MBA | 5 | DNF | 2m 28.69s | 6 |
| | Willi Hupperich | D | Seel | 4 | DNF | 2m 34.49s | 31 |
| | Peter Sommer | CH | MBA | 4 | DNF | 2m 34.10s | 29 |
| | Steve Mason | GB | MBA | 1 | DNF | 2m 34.51s | 32 |
| | Adolf Stadler | D | MBA | | DNS | 2m 31.98s | 18 |
| | Matti Kinnunen | SF | MBA | | DNS | 2m 34.65s | 33 |
| | Olivier Liegeois | B | Assmex | | DNQ | 2m 35.71s | |
| | Manfred Braun | D | MBA | | DNQ | 2m 35.82s | |
| | Manuel Hernandez | E | Benetti | | DNQ | 2m 36.41s | |
| | Eric Gijsel | B | MBA | | DNQ | 2m 36.44s | |
| | Michel Escudier | F | MBA | | DNQ | 2m 37.73s | |
| | Giuseppe Ascareggi | I | Elit | | DNQ | 2m 38.04s | |
| | Peter Balaz | CS | MBA | | DNQ | 2m 38.07s | |
| | Fernando Gonzalez | E | MBA | | DNQ | 2m 38.36s | |
| | Ivan Troisi | YV | MBA | | DNQ | 2m 39.03s | |
| | Rune Zaelle | S | MBA | | DNQ | 2m 40.03s | |
| | Jean-Claude Selini | F | ABF | | DNQ | 2m 41.96s | |
| | Boy van Erp | NL | MBA | | DNQ | 2m 42.66s | |

*Fastest lap:* Gresini, 2m 26.43s, 93.209 mph/150.005 km/h (record).
*Previous record:* Angel Nieto, E (Garelli), 2m 29.63s, 91.70 mph/147.58 km/h (1984).

**World Championship: 1** Cadalora, 61; **2** Gresini, 54; **3** Gianola, 42; **4** Brigaglia, 26; **5** Kneubühler, 24; **6** Bianchi, 18; **7** Wickström, 15; **8** Nieto and Feuz, 13; **10** Perez, 11; **11** Auinger, 10; **12** Liegeois, 9; **13** Pietroniro, 8; **14** Casoli, 7; **15** Grassetti and Waibel, 5; **17** Sanchez, 3; **18** Hautaniemi and Kytola, 2; **20** Olsson and Stadler, 1.

## 80 cc

**12 laps, 45.74 miles/73.61 km**

| *Place* | *Rider* | *Nat.* | *Machine* | *Laps* | *Time & speed* | *Practice time* | *Grid* |
|---|---|---|---|---|---|---|---|
| 1 | Jorge Martinez | E | Derbi | 12 | 31m 03.05s 88.380 mph/ 142.234 km/h | 2m 33.15s | 1 |
| 2 | Manuel Herreros | E | Derbi | 12 | 31m 12.42s | 2m 35.45s | 5 |
| 3 | Hans Spaan | NL | Huvo | 12 | 31m 14.73s | 2m 35.00s | 4 |
| 4 | Angel Nieto | E | Derbi | 12 | 31m 21.60s | 2m 36.44s | 6 |
| 5 | Stefan Dörflinger | CH | Krauser | 12 | 31m 22.60s | 2m 33.36s | 2 |
| 6 | Gerhard Waibel | D | Real | 12 | 31m 35.88s | 2m 37.04s | 10 |
| 7 | Josef Fischer | A | Krauser | 12 | 31m 53.11s | 2m 39.05s | 13 |
| 8 | Domingo Gil | E | Autisa | 12 | 32m 08.48s | 2m 40.47s | 15 |
| 9 | Gerd Kafka | A | Krauser | 12 | 32m 28.15s | 2m 40.23s | 14 |
| 10 | Felix Rodriguez | E | Autisa | 12 | 32m 31.83s | 2m 42.25s | 23 |
| 11 | Henk van Kessel | NL | Krauser | 12 | 32m 40.34s | 2m 41.54s | 21 |
| 12 | Francisco Torontegui | E | Kobas | 12 | 32m 40.75s | 2m 41.67s | 22 |
| 13 | Chris Baert | B | Seel | 12 | 32m 42.97s | 2m 46.23s | 34 |
| 14 | Bert Smit | NL | BZ | 12 | 32m 47.56s | 2m 43.62s | 27 |
| 15 | Gunter Schirnhöfer | D | Krauser | 12 | 32m 47.86s | 2m 42.44s | 24 |
| 16 | Reiner Scheidhauer | D | Seel | 12 | 32m 48.31s | 2m 40.88s | 18 |
| 17 | Kees Besseling | NL | CJB | 12 | 32m 48.58s | 2m 44.47s | 29 |
| 18 | Rainer Kunz | D | Ziegler | 12 | 32m 50.72s | 2m 36.80s | 9 |
| 19 | Hans Koopman | NL | Ziegler | 12 | 33m 12.04s | 2m 46.39s | 35 |
| 20 | Mario Stocco | I | Huvo | 12 | 33m 24.72s | 2m 44.97s | 30 |
| 21 | Stefan Prein | D | Huvo | 12 | 33m 47.22s | 2m 44.33s | 28 |
| 22 | Raimo Lipponen | SF | Kiefer | 12 | 33m 47.71s | 2m 45.88s | 33 |
| 23 | Reiner Koster | CH | LCR | 12 | 33m 49.00s | 2m 46.58s | 36 |
| 24 | Janez Pintar | YU | Eberhardt | 11 | 31m 19.05s | 2m 45.82s | 32 |
| | Ian McConnachie | GB | Krauser | 11 | DNF | 2m 34.25s | 3 |
| | Salvatore Milano | I | Krauser | 11 | DNF | 2m 42.48s | 25 |
| | Jos van Dongen | NL | Krauser | 9 | DNF | 2m 43.36s | 26 |
| | Luis Reyes | RCH | Autisa | 8 | DNF | 2m 36.51s | 7 |
| | Pier Paolo Bianchi | I | Seel | 7 | DNF | 2m 36.69s | 8 |
| | Stefan Brägger | CH | Huvo | 6 | DNF | 2m 45.00s | 31 |
| | Bruno Casanova | I | Unimoto | 5 | DNF | 2m 37.36s | 12 |
| | Theo Timmer | NL | Huvo | 3 | DNF | 2m 40.54s | 16 |
| | Juan Bolart | E | Autisa | 3 | DNF | 2m 40.93s | 19 |
| | Alexandre Barros | BR | Autisa | 0 | DNF | 2m 37.11s | 11 |
| | René Dünki | CH | Krauser | 0 | DNF | 2m 41.13s | 20 |
| | Wilco Zeelenberg | NL | Huvo | 0 | DNF | 2m 40.58s | 17 |
| | Thomas Engl | D | ESCH | | DNQ | 2m 47.00s | |
| | Mika-Sakari Komu | SF | Eberhardt | | DNQ | 2m 48.62s | |
| | Serge Julin | B | Huvo | | DNQ | 2m 48.90s | |
| | Richard Bay | D | Rupp | | DNQ | 2m 49.06s | |
| | Jarmö Piepponen | SF | Kiefer | | DNQ | 2m 49.09s | |
| | Steve Mason | GB | Huvo | | DNQ | 2m 50.75s | |
| | Otto Machinek | A | MH | | DNQ | 2m 54.00s | |
| | Steve Lawton | GB | Eberhardt | | DNQ | 2m 56.86s | |

*Fastest lap:* McConnachie, 2m 30.79s, 90.997 mph/146.445 km/h (record).
*Previous record:* Jorge Martinez, E (Derbi), 2m 39.98s, 85.77 mph/138.03 km/h (1984).

**World Championship: 1** Martinez, 72; **2** Herreros, 59; **3** Dörflinger, 53; **4** Nieto, 39; **5** Spaan, 33; **6** McConnachie, 31; **7** Waibel and Bianchi, 29; **9** Fischer, 13; **10** Bolart and Kunz, 6; **12** Timmer and Kafka, 5; **14** Gil, 4; **15** Abold, van Kessel and Rodriguez, 3; **18** Reyes, 2; **19** Milano, 1.

## Sidecars

**16 laps, 60.99 miles/98.14 km**

| Place | Driver & passenger | Nat. | Machine | Laps | Time & speed | Practice time | Grid |
|---|---|---|---|---|---|---|---|
| 1 | Alain Michel/ | F | Krauser– | 16 | 38m 44.55s | 2m 22.30s | 3 |
|  | Jean-Marc Fresc | F | Yamaha |  | 94.445 mph/ |  |  |
|  |  |  |  |  | 151.994 km/h |  |  |
| 2 | Steve Webster/ | GB | LCR– | 16 | 38m 54.65s | 2m 23.09s | 4 |
|  | Tony Hewitt | GB | Yamaha |  |  |  |  |
| 3 | Masato Kumano/ | J | LCR– | 16 | 39m 19.19s | 2m 25.08s | 11 |
|  | Helmut Diehl | D | Yamaha |  |  |  |  |
| 4 | Markus Egloft/ | CH | LCR– | 16 | 39m 27.74s | 2m 23.47s | 5 |
|  | Urs Egloff | CH | Yamaha |  |  |  |  |
| 5 | Steve Abbott/ | GB | Windle– | 16 | 39m 30.54s | 2m 25.50s | 12 |
|  | Vince Biggs | GB | Yamaha |  |  |  |  |
| 6 | Mick Barton/ | GB | LCR– | 16 | 40m 25.22s | 2m 28.11s | 17 |
|  | Eckart Rösinger | D | Yamaha |  |  |  |  |
| 7 | Barry Brindley/ | GB | Windle– | 16 | 40m 31.05s | 2m 27.52s | 15 |
|  | Chris Jones | GB | Yamaha |  |  |  |  |
| 8 | Bernd Scherer/ | D | BSR– | 16 | 40m 36.27s | 2m 28.83s | 20 |
|  | Wolfgang Gess | D | Yamaha |  |  |  |  |
| 9 | Alfred Zurbrügg/ | CH | LCR– | 16 | 40m 44.14s | 2m 24.41s | 8 |
|  | Martin Zurbrügg | CH | Yamaha |  |  |  |  |
| 10 | Graham Gleeson/ | NZ | LCR– | 16 | 40m 44.99s | 2m 28.57s | 19 |
|  | Dave Elliott | GB | Yamaha |  |  |  |  |
| 11 | Dennis Bingham/ | GB | LCR– | 16 | 40m 50.54s | 2m 28.28s | 18 |
|  | Julia Bingham | GB | Yamaha |  |  |  |  |
| 12 | René Progin/ | CH | Seymaz– | 16 | 41m 02.23s | 2m 26.20s | 13 |
|  | Yves Hunziker | CH | Yamaha |  |  |  |  |
| 13 | Hans Hügli/ | CH | LCR– | 16 | 41m 16.52s | 2m 26.31s | 14 |
|  | Markus Fahrni | CH | Yamaha |  |  |  |  |
| 14 | Mick Boddice/ | GB | LCR– | 13 | 40m 00.94s | 2m 27.75s | 16 |
|  | Don Williams | GB | Yamaha |  |  |  |  |
| 15 | Rolf Biland/ | CH | Krauser | 13 | 40m 53.98s | 2m 22.20s | 2 |
|  | Kurt Waltisperg | CH |  |  |  |  |  |
| 16 | Derek Bayley/ | GB | LCR– | 12 | 39m 20.68s | 2m 24.79s | 10 |
|  | Bryan Nixon | GB | Ricardo |  |  |  |  |
|  | Egbert Streuer/ | NL | LCR– | 10 | DNF | 2m 21.59s | 1 |
|  | Bernie Schnieders | NL | Yamaha |  |  |  |  |
|  | Derek Jones/ | GB | LCR– | 10 | DNF | 2m 23.79s | 6 |
|  | Brian Ayres | GB | Yamaha |  |  |  |  |
|  | Theo van Kempen/ | NL | LCR– | 8 | DNF | 2m 24.76s | 9 |
|  | Gerardus de Haas | NL | Yamaha |  |  |  |  |
|  | Rolf Steinhausen/ | D | Busch | 3 | DNF | 2m 24.21s | 7 |
|  | Bruno Hiller | D |  |  |  |  |  |
|  | Yoshisada Kumagaya/ | J | LCR– |  | DNQ | 2m 28.88s |  |
|  | Kazuhiko Makiuchi | J | Yamaha |  |  |  |  |
|  | Frank Wrathall/ | GB | LCR– |  | DNQ | 2m 29.13s |  |
|  | Kerry Chapman | GB | Yamaha |  |  |  |  |
|  | Wolfgang Stropek/ | A | LCR– |  | DNQ | 2m 29.50s |  |
|  | Hans-Peter Demling | A | Yamaha |  |  |  |  |
|  | Luigi Casagrande/ | CH | LCR– |  | DNQ | 2m 30.72s |  |
|  | Hans Egli | CH | Yamaha |  |  |  |  |
|  | Erwin Weber/ | D | LCR– |  | DNQ | 2m 31.72s |  |
|  | Klaus Kolb | D | Yamaha |  |  |  |  |
|  | Cor van Reeuwijck/ | NL | Yamaha |  | DNQ | 2m 32.41s |  |
|  | Hans Blaauw | NL |  |  |  |  |  |
|  | Egon Schons/ | D | Yamaha |  | DNQ | 2m 32.51s |  |
|  | Eckart Rösinger | D |  |  |  |  |  |
|  | Amadeo Zini/ | I | LCR– |  | DNQ | 2m 34.94s |  |
|  | Vittorio Montanelli | I | Yamaha |  |  |  |  |

*Fastest lap:* Biland, 2m 20.27s, 97.821 mph/157.428 km/h (record).
*Previous record:* Steve Webster/Tony Hewitt, GB/GB (LCR-Yamaha), 2m 22.45s, 96.32 mph/155.02 km/h (1985).

**World Championship: 1** Streuer and Michel, 30; **3** Abbott and Webster, 24; **5** Egloff, 17; **6** Zurbrügg, 14; **7** Biland, Jones and Kumano, 12; **10** Barton, 6; **11** Brindley and van Kempen, 5; **13** Progin and Scherer, 3; **15** Gleeson, 1.

**Steve Webster and Tony Hewitt continued a great series of rides, finishing second to Alain Michel and Jean-Marc Fresc** (bottom).

**Raymond Roche changes direction on the David Earl camera-carrying Rothmans Honda.**

# *Grand Prix de* BELGIQUE

The circuit of Spa can be the most glorious place. When the sun shines there is no better Grand Prix circuit; it is very demanding, varied and scenic. There remain a couple of corners where safety provision needs to be improved (and it should be sorted out for 1987), but above all the track is magnificent. For once one can honestly use that hackneyed phrase, 'a true test of man and machine'.

Unfortunately the weather can let the rest of the picture down rather badly and though practice was superb the rain hung in the valley on race day as it can only do in the Ardennes and it just rained and rained and rained. 'Trop d'eau à la Source', said the French weekly *Moto Journal* as its headline. Literally, that meant 'too much water at the source', Spa being a water spring and La Source the hairpin where many falls occurred.

In such conditions the circuit becomes even more difficult to cope with. Corners that are fast and off-camber in the dry, demanding that the bike's suspension be jacked up to increase ground clearance, are still fast in the wet but the rider has to have an uncompromised faith in his front tyre. He must trust it through those downhill sweepers where the water runs across the tarmac in rivulets, threatening to ferry the front wheel and thereafter the rest of the machine off into the mud at the trackside.

Randy Mamola won the 500 race on faith in his tyres, particularly the front, and on the assumption that, while second place had been sufficient, it was vital for him to win a Grand Prix soon as the second half of the season was beginning. He had faith in the front tyre from the start was telling himself to 'Push the front, push the front'. He trusted the new 17-inch diameter Michelin wet, despite his first impressions of it. 'I didn't like the look of the pattern compared with the old one but I tried it in practice when it was wet in Austria and it was real good, just perfect. It has got big grooves in it to move the water and normally you'd expect that the blocks would move around and squirm even in a straight line but this tyre doesn't do anything like that; it is dead stable.'

the old pattern and Baldwin cursed himself for employing an intermediate. The difference with Lawson was that he preferred not to make a fool of himself at Spa by falling off as he had not forgiven himself for crashing on the first lap in Assen. Lawson cannot excuse crashes, whether his own or anyone else's. For him it is not an accepted part of racing that just happens; it is a mistake that should never be allowed to occur. You don't go faster and faster until you fall off and then try and go almost as quick next time; you go faster and faster but never quite get to the point of falling off. Perhaps Assen is Lawson's bogey circuit; he was not going to let the same thing happen at Spa. On the other hand, Mamola is an exceptional wet-weather rider and, just as he had been distracted in Holland by his girlfriend's hospitalisation, his head was clear at Spa thanks to her recovery and he was clearly the best man on the day.

Mamola was on the boil throughout practice except during the first session, managing only 2m

32.24s while Lawson and Sarron were both into the 29s. 'We discussed things after the first session and I could not understand how the guys were going that fast. Mike Sinclair suggested that I was standing on the brink looking for the door and would then make the breakthrough and go a lot faster. That afternoon I was three seconds faster so I guess I found the door handle.'

Throughout, Sarron remained slightly faster than Mamola and at first was even quicker than Lawson. Mamola explained that the track suited the Frenchman's riding style. 'He doesn't hang off much and is more or less straight up and down. That works here because he keeps up a high corner speed and that is what you need; it is not one of those tracks where you can square the corners off and get the gas on hard and early. That is the mistake that Rob is making, rushing in and getting on the gas hard. I was following and I saw him do it.'

There are corners at Spa that suit the usual American square-off style but they are not the crucial ones – the fast corners leading on to the high-speed sections. This is where Lawson, Sarron, Mamola and Baldwin were making their time, all four grouped at the front, almost a full second quicker than Gardner on the four-cylinder Honda. Many suspected that the handling problems said by the Australian to have been sorted out in Holland had only been eased by the nature of the circuit, and at Spa they were back.

The Yamaha was proving to be an all-round better motor cycle and was beginning to look an almost guaranteed passport to success. McElnea was struggling a little at Spa and only heard Mamola's constructive criticism after practice was over. 'He often gives me advice,' said McElnea. 'I need something here. I'm trying like hell but I'm way off the pace.' It might have come to him in the race but when it rained he did not have the chance to try a different approach.

Didier de Radigues was ahead of McElnea on the grid but the opposition did not agree with the time-keepers' version of his practice times and the time-keepers at Spa are not very reliable. They revised both the Sidecar and 250 qualifying sheets after issuing supposed final times.

Roche qualified behind McElnea in eighth place, having his first ride on the four-cylinder Honda. With Spencer's continued absence, Honda decided that someone might as well use the machines and Roche might be the one to stem the Yamaha tide. He was the only other rider on a Rothmans Honda.

Referring to qualifying positions at previous Grands Prix indicated that the Frenchman would probably have been better off on his three but he wanted to use the four in two weeks time at his home Grand Prix at Paul Ricard. Therefore he decided to persevere with it at Spa, despite the fact that the characteristics did not suit him. 'The front is too heavy; it is built for Spencer and he slides the back. I don't and it doesn't work for me.' Rider preference clearly plays an important role, Roche extolling the lightness of the triple's front end which almost every other rider in the world has condemned as the machine's major vice.

Yamaha had just as much of a grip on the 250

class during practice as they had on the 500, with Wimmer and Lavado battling for pole between them. Lavado was remarkably consistent, putting in a quick time in session one and cutting a second off that time in two out of three remaining periods so that he was never headed.

It seemed a great shame that he could not repeat that consistency in races. Freddie Spencer could have walked off with the 1986 250 cc World Championship with one hand tied behind his back when, after the '85 Dutch TT (the seventh race in the series) he had 89 points. After the same number of races in '86, Lavado only had 72 points following Belgium, and that was without having Spencer to contend with.

After falling off in Spain, Yugoslavia and Belgium Lavado explained that he was finding it difficult to adjust to having such a fast bike. 'For six or eight years I have not had a good bike. I am used to having a slow machine and I have always

*Above:* **At the start of the 250 race, the pack splashes through Eau Rouge in the wake of McLeod and Pons.**

**Paul Lewis gets crossed up while chasing Raymond Roche. Both were to fall in separate incidents at the same spot.**

had to ride so hard round the corners to make up for it. For the first time this year I have a perfect bike but I can't change my riding overnight. I still tend to ride on the limit. Some places I take it a bit easy but corners I like, for example at Eau Rouge at Spa, I still ride 100 per cent.

'Mang's Honda is still good; it has the same acceleration and perhaps 3 kph more top speed but last year he had 15 kph so I don't mind at all because at Spa last year I could still stay with him. I think that Toni's problem is that at the beginning of the year he did not take me seriously – he expected me to crash at every Grand Prix like I did in '80 and '81.'

Though Lavado was not crashing at every event he was having more than his fair share of falls which he had managed to avoid almost completely when he won his first title in 1983. Mang, who started a little slowly but came back to win the Italian GP at Monza, had faded again,

perhaps regretting that his confidence after winning the Daytona 250 race so comfortably in March had led him to do no development before the Spanish GP in May. He was back on the ball in Belgium, second after three sessions ahead of Wimmer, Sarron and Taira, but slipped to third in the final session.

Wimmer put in the big effort on Saturday afternoon to record a time almost as fast as Lavado's Friday best but the Venezuelan also went quicker and was over a second faster than Wimmer at the end of the day. The time-keepers messed around with their times as they tend to do at Spa and after Donnie McLeod's Armstrong team complained that they had not recorded his fastest lap correctly he was promoted to third ahead of Mang. There was no way that McLeod was under any illusion that he had been third-fastest as the Rotax-engined Armstrong is just not powerful enough, and with two tough climbs

the Spa circuit demands power from the engine.

Nevertheless, the Armstrong was rather better off for power than it had been a week previously, thanks to some new cylinders from Rotax that gave a significant boost. The new cylinders, which were available only to the Armstrong and Aprilia teams, had revised porting and Aprilia were not even bothering with the Belgian GP until they tested the cylinders at the Salzburgring early in the week. Team leader Loris Reggiani lapped two and a half seconds faster than he had at the GP and hence the team packed up and headed for Spa. They arrived just in time for the first practice session and did not even have the chance to erect their awning until it was over. The Italian qualified fifteenth.

Armstrong raced with the new cylinders and Schafleitner's crankshafts, and the bikes were better than they had been all year. Despite the fact that he had only just got rid of the plaster

*Left:* **Randy Mamola gave a wet-weather riding demonstration to the spectators, some of whom had a very close look.**

**Kevin Schwantz** (*below*) **showed how not to ride in the wet but got away with it.**

**Ron Haslam almost never makes a mistake in the wet, but this proved to be the exception to his rule** (*bottom*)**.**

cast from his leg, Niall MacKenzie was up in sixth place after two sessions of practice, even though he was forced back to ninth in the final reckoning.

Former World Champion Jean-Louis Tournadre had a nasty fall cresting the rise after Eau Rouge in the third session and was lucky to escape with concussion and a cracked shoulder. He was not having a great deal of luck in his comeback season. Another man making a return was Guy Bertin, who had been out of Grand Prix racing thanks to a lack of backing and sponsorship. He got the use of a French-framed Rotax special called a Defi, featuring a nice twin-spar aluminium frame. He qualified in 24th place, two places ahead of Manfred Herweh who was continuing to have the unhappiest of seasons and did not receive the new cylinders from Rotax. He also suffered a gearbox seizure when he went out with no oil.

## 125 cc

In 1985, Fausto Gresini had dominated both practice and the race. His pole-position time was two seconds better than anyone else and he ran away with the race after the first mile. This time things were very different, with his team-mate Luca Cadalora setting fastest time and Gresini being pushed back to third by August Auinger. A year before, Cadalora had not even raced after falling on the first day of practice and being too badly bruised to ride, but now he was three-tenths quicker than Gresini, although only three-hundreths faster than Auinger. It was a time the young Italian had pulled out of the bag in the final session after trailing Auinger and Gresini through practice.

After the brilliant sunshine of practice, Auinger must have thought matters had moved in his favour as race day dawned wet with the

dreary weather firmly established. He is so much faster than anyone else in such conditions that the result must have been in little doubt but for the failure of his ignition system.

Auinger was third off the line behind Cadalora and Gresini but the ignition started to malfunction almost immediately and he slipped to sixth at the end of the first lap. Auinger had experienced a similar problem in the '85 German Grand Prix when spray from other bikes caused a misfire until he got in front. He persevered but this time things did not improve even as he avoided the spray from other machines, and despite battling on for a couple more circuits and an attempt to rectify the problem at the pits, it was pointless. He retired at the end of lap 4.

There had been more drama at the front on lap 1 as Cadalora crashed the Garelli at La Source hairpin. He remounted and returned to the pits but although he rejoined the race at the rear of

**Pons and McLeod: worthy occupiers of the top rostrum positions.**

the field he was soon back in to retire.

Pier Paolo Bianchi, meanwhile, had seized the lead fractionally from Gresini with local hero Lucio Pietroniro third. On lap 2 Gresini briefly ousted Bianchi but the old master was in front again a lap later as Gresini had his hands full trying to hold off Pietroniro and Willy Perez. Rising up through the field were Domenico Brigaglia and Olivier Liegeois and behind them Ezio Gianola and Paolo Casoli.

Bianchi hung on to the lead but came under increasing pressure from the pack behind as Pietroniro, Gresini, Brigaglia, Perez, Gianola and Liegeois swapped places behind in a cloud of spray. On lap 8 the face of the race altered as Bianchi and Brigaglia started to get away a little. Then Bianchi slipped back and it was Gresini who challenged Brigaglia at the front of the field. By lap 10 Brigaglia still held the lead but now Gianola was looking the strongest of his pursuers and moved into second place as Gresini slipped back to come under pressure from Pietroniro and Casoli.

Lap 11 was Brigaglia's fastest and he even pulled away from Gianola. That was too much for the second man who fell on lap 12 but remounted in seventh place just in front of Bianchi whose fortunes had faded in the second half of the race. While Brigaglia established a commanding lead over the last few laps, second place was full of excitement. Pietroniro was having trouble with Casoli until the latter fell on the final lap, giving second to Pietroniro and third to Perez who had passed Gresini on the last lap.

## 250 cc

The rain continued to fall but that did nothing to dampen Alan Carter's enthusiasm for the race and the week he spent practising the starting of his Cobas bore fruit when he was quickly off the line. As the pack arrived at La Source hairpin at the end of lap 1 Carter was right on the tail of Sito Pons, with Donnie McLeod making it a trio.

From that point the race was between the three of them as a little way back Pierre Bolle on the Parisienne tried to hold off Fausto Ricci, Jacques Cornu and Toni Mang. The race had already turned into a disaster for Yamaha as Carlos Lavado fell at La Source at the end of lap 1 and shortly afterwards retired at the pits. Wimmer was to fare little better as he soon got bogged down with water in his electrics.

Mang could not capitalise on the misfortunes of his two main opponents as he dropped to tenth on lap 2 following a huge slide. He was dragged alongside the machine before he could get it back under control and when he had another bad slide later he concluded that it was not his day.

## 500 cc

If the rain eased for the start of the 500 race it was not enough to let the track dry at all and with the clouds stuck firmly in the valley there was no chance that the surface would dry enough to destroy full wet-weather tyres.

There was drama before the start of the race. When the machines were completing the sight-ing lap and forming up on the grid before the warm-up lap, Kevin Schwantz crashed the Rizla Suzuki at La Source hairpin. The fairing bottom needed changing and the mechanics did what they could to check that dirt had not got past the carbs. Schwantz missed the warm-up lap while this was being done but more importantly he had hurt the collarbone injured recently at Brainerd.

Mamola had no such worries and led off the line on the Lucky Strike Yamaha. Lawson was quickly into second place, chased by de Radigues, McElnea, Gardner and Baldwin, but none had the measure of Mamola who immediately started to extend a noticeable advantage.

As easily as Mamola pulled away from Lawson the championship leader opened up a gap over Gardner who had seized third though still closely pursued by McElnea and Baldwin. De Radigues would later complain of tyre problems and drop-ped back to be absorbed by the next group, which included Christian Sarron, Ron Haslam, Raymond Roche, Pier Francesco Chili and Paul Lewis. Their numbers were to be reduced by fal-lers. First to go was Haslam, then Roche and Lewis. All went down as they left La Source hairpin.

Mamola was getting away at the rate of two seconds a lap for the first ten laps, never looking troubled but there was enough water about to have him spinning the back tyre every time on acceleration.

On lap 4 Gardner had a minor off-track excur-sion that dropped him from third to seventh when he over-braked at the downhill horseshoe right-hander. 'We have some new large-diameter discs and with a 16-inch front wheel they give just too much braking – I was locking up the front every-where. It was very difficult to control and I was lucky only to go off once.'

McElnea would have inherited third but was passed by Baldwin on lap 4. The American Cham-pion was putting in maximum effort as always but had made the wrong choice of front tyre. 'I guess you could say it was pretty stupid. I put on the intermediate front like I had at Assen last year thinking the track might dry a bit but it was no good at all.' He lost the front on the brakes going in to La Source on lap 11, and although he remounted he kept going for just two more laps before the bike seized. 'I lost the footrest in the crash but that was no problem; I just put my boot on the exhaust pipe, but I must have split the radiator because the engine seized.'

When he fell, Baldwin was being caught by Sarron, the Frenchman having already passed McElnea. Next was Gardner, who had been catch-ing up after his mistake and had saved the trou-ble of passing many riders by having them fall off before that became necessary. Mamola at this point was twenty seconds clear of Lawson as Sar-ron kept his distant third ahead of McElnea, who was coming under pressure from Gardner. Riding superbly in sixth was Chili, followed by de Radigues.

On lap 15 Gardner moved past McElnea, who was not pleased with his own performance on a circuit with which he has not yet completely come to grips. 'I'm glad we are leaving', was his comment after the race. By lap 17 Mamola had eased off and his advantage over Lawson had slipped to fifteen seconds but it was a comfortable margin and the result was never in doubt.

From that point on the rest of the placings were well defined as Lawson maintained a gap of over thirty seconds between himself and Sarron and even when Gardner closed on the Frenchman he was still six seconds behind at the flag. McElnea was a further five seconds adrift but a minute ahead of Chili. De Radigues finished a frustrated seventh and it was a long race for him lasting 4½ seconds over the hour.

The Dutchmen Pajic and van Dulmen were eight and ninth ahead of Schwantz – lucky to finish at all after some wild moments in the open-ing laps, having crashed twice at La Source yet without coming off the bike. He finished 14 seconds ahead of Wolfgang von Muralt who as usual rode well and was unlucky not to score a point.

Mamola reported that he had suffered few problems. 'The bike was great and I only had to ease off a bit in the middle of the race when the visor misted a bit while I was passing slower rid-ers but it was not a big problem. I had a couple of slides out of the hairpin but nothing real bad.'

## SIDECARS

With the circuit still soaking wet the sidecar race was not as exciting as it should have been. For the second time in a week Streuer hit trouble, stopping at the end of the first lap with ignition failure. That left Steve Webster and Tony Hewitt in the lead, followed by Derek Bayley and Bryan Nixon, with Alain Michel and Jean-Marc Fresc third just ahead of Rolf Steinhausen and Bruno Hiller.

Biland was out of luck once more as he got water in the carbs on the first lap thanks to the spray kicked up by his own and the other outfits. As he lost ground he tried to make it up in the braking for the hairpin but left it too late, giving away further places. After that, he had to battle up from the back of the field.

On lap 3, Michel swept past Bayley but the British crew hung on to the tail of the French outfit and fended off Steinhausen. The three teams ran nose-to-tail for a couple of laps before Steinhausen got past, and then slowly but surely Michel, tailed by Steinhausen, pulled away from Bayley.

Michel tried hard to catch Webster but after several worrying slides realised that it was not on; as he was twelve seconds behind by lap 8 he contented himself with staying clear of Steinhausen.

Biland was pulling through the field and, from seventh place on lap 8, passed Steve Abbott and Vince Biggs one lap later and then the Egloff brothers. It took until lap 12 for Biland to catch and pass Bayley by which time Steinhausen was too far ahead to be caught.

Webster and Hewitt cruised to a convincing and well-judged win only to find that there was not even a trophy for winning. It must have been rather disappointing not to have a piece of silver-ware for their first GP victory.

# Grand Prix de Belgique, 6 July/statistics
# Spa-Francorchamps Circuit, 4.312-mile/6.940-km circuit

## 500 cc

**20 laps, 86.24 miles/138.80 km**

| *Place* | *Rider* | *Nat.* | *Machine* | *Laps* | *Time & speed* | *Practice time* | *Grid* |
|---|---|---|---|---|---|---|---|
| 1 | Randy Mamola | USA | Yamaha | 20 | 57m 25.02s 90.126 mph/ 145.044 km/h | 2m 29.27s | 3 |
| 2 | Eddie Lawson | USA | Yamaha | 20 | 57m 42.45s | 2m 28.28s | 1 |
| 3 | Christian Sarron | F | Yamaha | 20 | 58m 27.84s | 2m 28.69s | 2 |
| 4 | Wayne Gardner | AUS | Honda | 20 | 58m 33.30s | 2m 30.31s | 5 |
| 5 | Rob McElnea | GB | Yamaha | 20 | 58m 38.65s | 2m 30.76s | 7 |
| 6 | Pier Francesco Chili | I | Suzuki | 20 | 59m 48.69s | 2m 36.65s | 17 |
| 7 | Didier de Radigues | B | Chevallier | 20 | 60m 04.26s | 2m 30.51s | 6 |
| 8 | Mile Pajic | NL | Honda | 19 | 57m 30.80s | 2m 37.61s | 19 |
| 9 | Boet van Dulmen | NL | Honda | 19 | 57m 31.32s | 2m 37.71s | 20 |
| 10 | Kevin Schwantz | USA | Suzuki | 19 | 57m 39.83s | 2m 32.02s | 11 |
| 11 | Wolfgang von Muralt | CH | Suzuki | 19 | 57m 53.88s | 2m 36.05s | 15 |
| 12 | Mark Phillips | GB | Suzuki | 19 | 57m 59.93s | 2m 39.24s | 25 |
| 13 | Masaru Mizutani | J | Suzuki | 19 | 58m 39.96s | 2m 36.47s | 16 |
| 14 | Peter Sköld | S | Honda | 19 | 59m 07.60s | 2m 38.62s | 23 |
| 15 | Georg-Robert Jung | D | Honda | 19 | 59m 09.68s | 2m 39.46s | 28 |
| 16 | Gary Lingham | GB | Suzuki | 19 | 59m 10.41s | 2m 43.61s | 33 |
| 17 | Paul Ramon | B | Suzuki | 19 | 59m 34.88s | 2m 40.46s | 31 |
| 18 | Dave Griffith | GB | Suzuki | 18 | 58m 40.53s | 2m 48.05s | 36 |
| | Andreas Leuthe | LUX | Honda | 17 | DNF | 2m 40.32s | 30 |
| | Alessandro Valesi | I | Honda | 17 | DNF | 2m 39.25s | 26 |
| | Mike Baldwin | USA | Yamaha | 12 | DNF | 2m 29.44s | 4 |
| | Dietmar Marehard | D | Suzuki | 9 | DNF | 2m 44.12s | 34 |
| | Raymond Roche | F | Honda | 7 | DNF | 2m 31.65s | 8 |
| | Bernard Denis | B | Suzuki | 7 | DNF | 2m 38.62s | 22 |
| | Juan Garriga | E | Cagiva | 7 | DNF | 2m 33.31s | 13 |
| | Paul Lewis | AUS | Suzuki | 5 | DNF | 2m 33.03s | 12 |
| | Fabio Biliotti | I | Honda | 5 | DNF | 2m 35.50s | 14 |
| | Maarten Duyzers | NL | Suzuki | 4 | DNF | 2m 41.84s | 32 |
| | Manfred Fischer | D | Honda | 3 | DNF | 2m 37.06s | 18 |
| | Marco Gentile | CH | Fior | 3 | DNF | 2m 37.79s | 21 |
| | Ron Haslam | GB | Elf | 3 | DNF | 2m 31.82s | 9 |
| | Eero Hyvarinen | SF | Honda | 3 | DNF | 2m 39.35s | 27 |
| | Roger Burnett | GB | Honda | 2 | DNF | 2m 31.87s | 10 |
| | Leandro Becheroni | I | Honda | 2 | DNF | 2m 39.98s | 29 |
| | Sepp Doppler | A | Honda | 1 | DNF | 2m 45.47s | 35 |
| | Simon Buckmaster | GB | Honda | 1 | DNF | 2m 39.10s | 24 |
| | Harry Heutmekers | NL | Suzuki | | DNQ | 2m 53.46s | |

*Fastest lap:* Mamola, 2m 48.99s, 91.866 mph/147. 843 km/h.
*Lap record:* Eddie Lawson, USA (Yamaha), 2m 28.35s, 104.647 mph/168.412 km/h (1985).

**World Championship: 1** Lawson, 84; **2** Mamola, 74; **3** Gardner, 72; **4** Baldwin, 52; **5** Sarron, 43; **6** McElnea, 39; **7** Roche and de Radigues, 18; **9** Chili, 11; **10** Haslam and van Dulmen, 8; **12** Yatsushiro, 7; **13** Biliotti and Reiner, 5; **15** Garriga, 4; **16** Lewis, Petersen, Burnett and Pajic, 3; **20** Papa and Schwantz, 1.

## 125 cc

**14 laps, 60.37 miles/97.16 km**

| *Place* | *Rider* | *Nat.* | *Machine* | *Laps* | *Time & speed* | *Practice time* | *Grid* |
|---|---|---|---|---|---|---|---|
| 1 | Domenico Brigaglia | I | MBA | 14 | 43m 21.59s 83.542 mph/ 134.447 km/h | 2m 45.78s | 6 |
| 2 | Lucio Pietroniro | B | MBA | 14 | 43m 39.79s | 2m 48.60s | 11 |
| 3 | Willy Perez | RA | Zanella | 14 | 43m 47.94s | 2m 49.46s | 14 |
| 4 | Fausto Gresini | I | Garelli | 14 | 43m 48.88s | 2m 44.99s | 3 |
| 5 | Olivier Liegeois | B | Assmex | 14 | 43m 52.42s | 2m 47.80s | 8 |
| 6 | Ezio Gianola | I | MBA | 14 | 43m 53.67s | 2m 45.42s | 5 |
| 7 | Pier Paolo Bianchi | I | Elit | 14 | 44m 03.73s | 2m 48.34s | 9 |
| 8 | Paolo Casoli | I | MBA | 14 | 44m 21.09s | 2m 49.41s | 13 |
| 9 | Jussi Hautaniemi | SF | MBA | 14 | 44m 33.14s | 2m 50.40s | 15 |
| 10 | Thierry Feuz | CH | MBA | 14 | 44m 39.01s | 2m 48.40s | 10 |
| 11 | Johnny Wickström | SF | Tunturi | 14 | 44m 40.70s | 2m 49.16s | 12 |
| 12 | Robin Appleyard | GB | MBA | 14 | 44m 45.78s | 2m 51.50s | 20 |
| 13 | Anton Straver | NL | MBA | 14 | 45m 03.83s | 2m 51.77s | 22 |
| 14 | Jean-Claude Selini | F | MBA | 14 | 45m 14.76s | 2m 52.38s | 24 |
| 15 | Willi Hupperich | D | Seel | 14 | 45m 22.92s | 2m 53.91s | 33 |
| 16 | Alain Kempener | B | MBA | 14 | 45m 36.02s | 2m 54.02s | 34 |
| 17 | Peter Sommer | CH | MBA | 14 | 45m 45.29s | 2m 52.72s | 28 |
| 18 | Patrick Daudier | F | PMDF | 14 | 46m 06.09s | 2m 53.66s | 30 |
| 19 | Robin Milton | GB | MBA | 14 | 46m 06.60s | 2m 53.84s | 32 |
| 20 | Ton Spek | NL | MBA | 14 | 46m 28.21s | 2m 54.44s | 35 |
| 21 | Jan Eggens | NL | MBA | 13 | 44m 06.58s | 2m 52.48s | 25 |
| 22 | Ivan Troisi | YV | MBA | 13 | 44m 31.50s | 2m 52.72s | 27 |
| 23 | Hakan Olsson | S | Starol | 12 | 43m 31.18s | 2m 52.61s | 26 |
| | Eric Gijsel | B | MBA | 7 | DNF | 2m 53.71s | 31 |
| | Mike Leitner | A | Bartol | 6 | DNF | 2m 51.39s | 19 |
| | Marin Andreas Sanchez | E | Ducados | 5 | DNF | 2m 51.58s | 21 |
| | Bruno Kneubühler | CH | LCR | 4 | DNF | 2m 45.30s | 4 |
| | August Auinger | A | Bartol | 4 | DNF | 2m 44.72s | 2 |
| | Manfred Braun | D | MBA | 4 | DNF | 2m 52.83s | 29 |
| | Jacques Hutteau | F | MBA | 3 | DNF | 2m 51.32s | 18 |
| | Luca Cadalora | I | Garelli | 3 | DNF | 2m 44.69s | 1 |
| | Esa Kytola | SF | MBA | 2 | DNF | 2m 52.20s | 23 |
| | Alfred Waibel | D | Real | 2 | DNF | 2m 46.83s | 7 |
| | Boy van Erp | NL | MBA | 2 | DNF | 2m 54.72s | 36 |
| | Paul Bordes | F | MBA | 1 | DNF | 2m 50.47s | 16 |
| | Angel Nieto | E | Ducados | 0 | DNF | 2m 51.01s | 17 |
| | Michel Escudier | F | MBA | | DNQ | 2m 54.79s | |
| | Thierry Maurer | CH | MBA | | DNQ | 2m 54.80s | |
| | Christian le Badezet | F | MBA | | DNQ | 2m 54.95s | |
| | Giuseppe Ascareggi | I | Elit | | DNQ | 2m 55.01s | |
| | Manuel Hernandez | E | Benetti | | DNQ | 2m 55.29s | |
| | Thomas Möller-Pedersen | DK | MBA | | DNQ | 2m 55.39s | |
| | Flemming Kistrup | DK | MBA | | DNQ | 2m 55.65s | |
| | Peter Balaz | CS | MBA | | DNQ | 2m 56.62s | |
| | Gary Noel | GB | EMC | | DNQ | 2m 57.17s | |
| | Alain Trippaers | B | MBA | | DNQ | 2m 57.82s | |
| | Eric Saul | F | LGM | | DNQ | 2m 57.88s | |
| | Bady Hassaine | DZ | MBA | | DNQ | 2m 59.54s | |
| | Freddy Blaise | B | MBA | | DNQ | 3m 05.32s | |
| | Shaun Simpson | GB | MBA | | DNQ | 3m 06.35s | |
| | Jean-Claude Collard | B | MBA | | DNQ | 3m 11.00s | |

*Fastest lap:* Brigaglia, 3m 02.05s, 85.275 mph/137.237 km/h.
*Lap record:* August Auinger, A (Monnet), 2m 45.36s, 93.882 mph/151.088 km/h (1985).

**World Championship: 1** Gresini, 62; **2** Cadalora, 61; **3** Gianola, 47; **4** Brigaglia, 41; **5** Kneubühler, 24; **6** Bianchi, 22; **7** Perez, 21; **8** Pietroniro, 20; **9** Wickström and Liegeois, 15; **11** Feuz, 14; **12** Nieto, 12; **13** Auinger and Casoli, 10; **15** Grassetti and Waibel, 5; **17** Hautaniemi, 4; **18** Sanchez, 3; **19** Kytola, 2; **20** Olsson and Stadler, 1.

## 250 cc

**16 laps, 68.99 miles/111.04 km**

| *Place* | *Rider* | *Nat.* | *Machine* | *Laps* | *Time & speed* | *Practice time* | *Grid* |
|---|---|---|---|---|---|---|---|
| 1 | Alfonso Pons | E | Honda | 16 | 47m 43.42s 86.746 mph/ 139.604 km/h. | 2m 37.16s | 7 |
| 2 | Donnie McLeod | GB | Armstrong | 16 | 47m 54.39s | 2m 36.03s | 3 |
| 3 | Jacques Cornu | CH | Honda | 16 | 48m 19.39s | 2m 38.68s | 16 |
| 4 | Dominique Sarron | F | Honda | 16 | 48m 19.71s | 2m 37.08s | 6 |
| 5 | Alan Carter | GB | Kobas | 16 | 48m 20.88s | 2m 38.56s | 14 |
| 6 | Carlos Cardus | E | Honda | 16 | 48m 34.21s | 2m 39.86s | 25 |
| 7 | Jean Foray | F | Chevallier | 16 | 48m 35.67s | 2m 39.39s | 21 |
| 8 | Niall MacKenzie | GB | Armstrong | 16 | 48m 35.99s | 2m 37.35s | 9 |
| 9 | Tadahiko Taira | J | Yamaha | 16 | 48m 38.76s | 2m 36.79s | 5 |
| 10 | Hans Lindner | A | Castrol | 16 | 48m 39.03s | 2m 38.96s | 18 |
| 11 | Fausto Ricci | I | Honda | 16 | 48m 50.05s | 2m 37.90s | 10 |
| 12 | Michel Simeon | B | Yamaha | 16 | 48m 56.42s | 2m 38.38s | 13 |
| 13 | Hans Becker | D | Yamaha | 16 | 48m 59.10s | 2m 40.54s | 30 |
| 14 | Alberto Rota | I | Honda | 16 | 49m 00.49s | 2m 41.33s | 32 |
| 15 | Gary Noel | GB | EMC | 16 | 49m 00.88s | 2m 39.31s | 20 |
| 16 | Reinhold Roth | D | Honda | 16 | 49m 01.49s | 2m 38.37s | 12 |
| 17 | Martin Wimmer | D | Yamaha | 16 | 49m 09.19s | 2m 35.45s | 2 |
| 18 | Anton Mang | D | Honda | 16 | 49m 09.47s | 2m 36.37s | 4 |
| 19 | Cees Doorakkers | NL | Honda | 16 | 49m 32.44s | 2m 41.96s | 35 |
| 20 | Maurizio Vitali | I | Garelli | 16 | 50m 17.27s | 2m 42.32s | 36 |
| 21 | Bruno Bonhuil | F | Honda | 16 | 50m 20.89s | 2m 39.91s | 27 |
| 22 | Roland Freymond | CH | Yamaha | 16 | 50m 21.79s | 2m 41.40s | 33 |
| 23 | Guy Bertin | F | Defi | 16 | 50m 31.12s | 2m 39.60s | 24 |
| | Jean-Michel Mattioli | F | Yamaha | 15 | DNF | 2m 39.52s | 22 |
| | Christian Boudinot | F | Kobas | 14 | DNF | 2m 40.17s | 28 |
| | Pierre Bolle | F | Parisienne | 11 | DNF | 2m 37.27s | 8 |
| | Manfred Herweh | D | Aprilia | 9 | DNF | 2m 39.90s | 26 |
| | Harald Eckl | D | Honda | 7 | DNF | 2m 40.60s | 31 |
| | Loris Reggiani | I | Aprilia | 7 | DNF | 2m 38.63s | 15 |
| | Virginio Ferrari | I | Honda | 6 | DNF | 2m 39.58s | 23 |
| | René Délaby | B | Morena | 4 | DNF | 2m 41.90s | 34 |
| | Jean-François Baldé | F | Honda | 4 | DNF | 2m 38.21s | 11 |
| | Jean-Louis Guignabodet | F | MIG | 2 | DNF | 2m 40.44s | 29 |
| | Siegfried Minich | A | Yamaha | 1 | DNF | 2m 38.97s | 19 |
| | Carlos Lavado | YV | Yamaha | 1 | DNF | 2m 34.34s | 1 |
| | Stéphane Mertens | B | Yamaha | 0 | DNF | 2m 38.76s | 17 |

*Fastest lap:* Sarron, 2m 55.97s, 88.222 mph/141.979 km/h.
*Lap record:* Freddie Spencer, USA (Honda), 2m 36.12s, 99.438 mph/160.030 km/h (1985).

**World Championship: 1** Lavado, 72; **2** Pons, 62; **3** Mang, 51; **4** Baldé, 45; **5** Wimmer, 44; **6** Sarron, 31; **7** Cornu, 28; **8** McLeod, 27; **9** Ricci, 24; **10** Bolle, 15; **11** Taira, 12; **12** Cardus, 11; **13** Carter, 8; **14** Herweh, 7; **15** Mertens, 5; **16** Ferrari and Foray, 4; **18** MacKenzie, 3; **19** Matteoni, Minich and Roth, 2; **22** Mattioli, Vitali and Lindner, 1.

## Sidecars

**15 laps, 64.68 miles/104.10 km**

| *Place* | *Driver & passenger* | *Nat.* | *Machine* | *Laps* | *Time & speed* | *Practice time* | *Grid* |
|---|---|---|---|---|---|---|---|
| 1 | Steve Webster/ Tony Hewitt | GB GB | LCR– Yamaha | 15 | 45m 05.42s 86.074 mph/ 138.522 km/h | 2m 37.81s | 4 |
| 2 | Alain Michel/ Jean-Marc Fresc | F F | Krauser– Yamaha | 15 | 45m 13.48s | 2m 37.50s | 3 |
| 3 | Rolf Steinhausen/ Bruno Hiller | D D | Busch | 15 | 45m 16.33s | 2m 41.47s | 7 |
| 4 | Rolf Biland/ Kurt Waltisperg | CH CH | Krauser | 15 | 45m 39.63s | 2m 36.57s | 1 |
| 5 | Derek Bayley/ Bryan Nixon | GB GB | LCR– Yamaha | 15 | 45m 50.66s | 2m 42.78s | 10 |
| 6 | Markus Egloff/ Urs Egloff | CH CH | LCR– Yamaha | 15 | 45m 53.71s | 2m 38.23s | 5 |
| 7 | Steve Abbott/ Vince Biggs | GB GB | Windle– Yamaha | 15 | 45m 54.67s | 2m 41.76s | 8 |
| 8 | Masato Kumano/ Helmut Diehl | J D | LCR– Yamaha | 15 | 46m 13.88s | 2m 41.42s | 6 |
| 9 | René Progin/ Yves Hunziker | CH CH | Seymaz– Yamaha | 15 | 46m 33.44s | 2m 44.40s | 14 |
| 10 | Yoshisada Kumagaya/ Kazuhiko Makiuchi | J J | LCR– Yamaha | 15 | 46m 46.43s | 2m 43.92s | 13 |
| 11 | Derek Jones/ Brian Ayres | GB GB | LCR– Yamaha | 15 | 46m 51.84s | 2m 42.85s | 11 |
| 12 | Frank Wrathall/ Simon Birchall | GB GB | LCR– Yamaha | 15 | 47m 06.98s | 2m 43.08s | 12 |
| 13 | Graham Gleeson/ Dave Elliott | NZ GB | LCR– Yamaha | 15 | 47m 27.06s | 2m 46.73s | 25 |
| 14 | Hans Hügli/ Markus Fahrni | CH CH | LCR– Yamaha | 15 | 47m 36.22s | 2m 45.31s | 18 |
| 15 | Ray Gardner/ Tony Strevens | GB GB | LCR– Yamaha | 15 | 47m 37.35s | 2m 45.78s | 22 |
| 16 | Barry Brindley/ Chris Jones | GB GB | Windle– Yamaha | 15 | 47m 39.40s | 2m 45.78s | 21 |
| 17 | Werner Kraus/ Dieter Schuster | D D | Busch | 15 | 47m 41.65s | 2m 45.20s | 16 |
| 18 | Dave Hallam/ Mark Day | GB GB | LCR– Yamaha | 15 | 47m 58.63s | 2m 52.84s | 30 |
| 19 | Cor van Reeuwijck/ Hans Blaauw | NL NL | Yamaha | 14 | 46m 03.75s | 2m 50.10s | 28 |
| 20 | Albert Weber/ Harald Schneidewind | D D | LCR– Yamaha | 14 | 46m 40.37s | 2m 46.46s | 23 |
| 21 | Dennis Bingham/ Julia Bingham | GB GB | LCR– Yamaha | 14 | 46m 53.62s | 2m 48.81s | 26 |
| 22 | Alfred Zurbrügg/ Martin Zurbrügg | CH CH | LCR– Yamaha | 14 | 47m 07.83s | 2m 42.65s | 9 |
| 23 | Egon Schons/ Eckart Rösinger | D D | Busch– Yamaha | 14 | 47m 13.94s | 2m 50.83s | 29 |
| 24 | Benny Lysen/ Ole Moller | DK DK | LCR– Yamaha | 13 | 45m 53.29s | 2m 49.70s | 27 |
| | Mick Boddice/ Don Williams | GB GB | LCR– Yamaha | 12 | DNF | 2m 45.24s | 17 |
| | Egbert Streuer/ Bernie Schnieders | NL NL | LCR– Yamaha | 1 | DNF | 2m 37.21s | 2 |
| | Bernd Scherer/ Manfred Sturm | D D | LCR– Yamaha | 1 | DNF | 2m 45.71s | 19 |
| | Wolfgang Stropek/ Hans-Peter Demling | A A | LCR– Yamaha | 0 | DNF | 2m 46.54s | 24 |
| | Theo van Kempen/ Gerardus de Haas | NL NL | LCR– Yamaha | 0 | DNF | 2m 44.40s | 15 |
| | Mick Barton/ Graham Rose | GB GB | LCR– Yamaha | 0 | DNF | 2m 45.77s | 20 |

*Fastest lap:* Steinhausen, 2m 57.06s, 87.689 mph/141.105 km/h.
*Lap record:* Egbert Streuer/Bernie Schnieders, NL/NL (LCR–Yamaha), 2m 36.05s, 99.483 mph/160.102 km/h (1985).

**World Championship: 1** Michel, 42; **2** Webster, 39; **3** Streuer, 30; **4** Abbott, 28; **5** Egloff, 22; **6** Biland, 20; **7** Kumano, 15; **8** Zurbrügg, 14; **9** Jones, 12; **10** Steinhausen, 10; **11** Barton and Bayley, 6; **13** Progin, van Kempen and Brindley, 5; **16** Scherer, 3; **17** Gleeson and Kumagaya, 1.

# Grand Prix de
# FRANCE

That smell of dry heat and pine needles is peculiar to Paul Ricard. The long cool midsummer evenings under an infinite blue sky make the paddock barbecues perhaps the most pleasurable of the year as the racing world is put to rights against a background of chattering cicadas. The week started with Bastille Day but as there was no untimed practice most of the paddock community did not assemble until Wednesday or Thursday.

Some of the evening talk concerned the circuit and the inadvisability of running a motor cycle Grand Prix only two weeks after a Formula 1 car race. Not only had the F1 cars left copious supplies of rubber on the tarmac, and particularly stuck to the white lines, but they had also torn up the surface round the apex of the last tight right-hander onto the start-and-finish straight.

The organisers were working on the circuit but not with any great urgency and were slow to take down the catch fencing which, on balance, does more harm than good to riders. It can slow a man safely unless he hits a fence post – as Gustav Reiner found out when he hit one of the few rows of catch fencing not removed. He twisted his leg badly at the hip socket and was lucky not to break leg and hip for the umpteenth time.

Other fireside discussions concerned Freddie Spencer and his intended comeback at Ricard, although this had now been put back two weeks to Silverstone. Spencer was due to arrive at the circuit for a press conference. More news arrived from America and it concerned Spencer's arch-rival, Lawson. Just when the Californian seemed to be running away with the title he had crashed at the non-championship Laguna Seca meeting.

It was a crash that might have altered the course of the 500 cc World Championship. From a few metres behind, Mamola saw it all happen, as he recalled later at Paul Ricard. 'That is a 100 mph left-hander if you get it exactly right. I had just got into second place as we came up behind this group of four slower riders. I went to go inside as Eddie went round the outside. I couldn't get past them all so I braked and pulled up behind the first two, and one of them moved over on Eddie as he was outside. In that corner you are committed, you can't change line. If you go in two feet wide you'll be five feet wide coming out. This guy pushed Eddie over about five feet, onto the dirty tarmac. There was no way to get it back and there's hardly any run-off there – you go straight into the guard rail. I didn't see him hit it because I was still going round the corner; I just saw him off on the grass.'

Lawson remembers what it felt like going off the track. 'There are bales there on the barrier but it's a third-gear corner and I knew they weren't going to help much. I thought "this is going to hurt"; I even thought I was going to die – and when I'd hit it I wished I could die, it hurt so much. The first thing was, I couldn't breathe at all. The fall knocked all the air out of me.'

In fact Lawson was relatively lucky as the injuries could have been worse. His collarbone became detached from where it sits in the sternum, but that dislocation went back immediately. What caused more lasting pain was the hairline

fracture at the other end of the collarbone where it joins the shoulder.

The first doctor to treat him said he should not race for six weeks, but Lawson was not going to let the championship slip through his fingers and set off for France. To try to cope with the pain and the injury, Lawson flew with a personal physician from California and between practice periods at Paul Ricard received electrically controlled muscle treatment on the affected shoulder.

The treatment itself hurt. Lying on the couch of the motorhome with one large electrical contact pad between his back and the couch, and other pads bandaged to the shoulder, he was clearly not enjoying it and his face was stern. The physician twiddled the knobs of the control unit trying to lessen the pain yet give the best treatment.

Although he was still fast the injury clearly took its toll of his riding. 'It hurts like hell when I have to turn left because I have to push on the left bar and that kills the shoulder. Luckily there are more right-handers here than left.'

With no free practice, the first time Lawson tried the bike after the accident was on Friday morning and immediately he tried to put the crash behind him, managing third-fastest time behind Christian Sarron and Randy Mamola. Sarron was obviously out to make an impression at his home Grand Prix. While Sarron produced a lap time of 2m 3.28s, Lawson was three-tenths slower but a second and a half faster than Gardner, none the less. The effort had a price, however, and Lawson had to be helped off the bike at the end of the session.

It rained at the start of practice that afternoon and although it was only a short shower the circuit was damp, so Lawson just completed one lap before stopping at the pits. He decided not to do any more and got changed. The rain cleared and at the end of the session most riders were in action so Lawson decided to take his girlfriend out to one of the corners on a scooter to have a look.

Arriving at one of the gates the pair did not have the correct pass but Lawson still wanted to go through, telling the official who he was. The official took no notice and kept him back. The confrontation escalated and when Lawson held the man by the throat, the Frenchman hit Lawson across the top of the eye. The two had to be separated by observers.

The ruckus caused quite a stir in the Marlboro camp, with Lawson suffering a cut eyebrow and the marshal a tattered tee-shirt. Things were soon calmed down, however, and Lawson's shoulder injury had not been aggravated. All the same, he didn't feel in the mood to attend the Marlboro dinner that night and went to bed on Friday, thinking about his injured collarbone and how to cope with it during the final day of practice.

Mamola had moved to the top of the practice table after waiting for the track to dry at the end of the Friday afternoon session but on Saturday morning Sarron was determined to get back in front and got into the two-minute bracket with a time of 2m 0.96s. Mamola managed 2m 1.43s, with Lawson only two-hundredths slower.

Saturday lunchtime before the last session saw

Lawson lying once more on the motorhome couch. As usual, three men came to see him together: Kel Carruthers, to discuss the engine and the bike in general; Lars Osth, the Öhlins man, to talk about suspension; and the Michelin technician to discuss the tyres.

Kel started the conversation. 'Did you get to plug chop the bike before you stopped?'

'No', replied Lawson.

'Did you run it real slow because it looks rich?', asked Carruthers.

'No, I stopped it pretty quick.'

'Well', continued Carruthers, 'That might be it. We can lean up the mixture and that might get rid of the flat spot.'

'Yes we've go to get rid of that; it's terrible, I hate it', Lawson assured him firmly.

With the engine sorted out Lawson had a word about the suspension. Everything seemed fine there, but the tyres needed some discussion.

Mamola – the ultimate showman.

'I don't like the feeling from the front, it just doesn't feel safe', Lawson informed the Michelin technician. 'What does it look like?'

'The wear pattern looks fine', the Frenchman replied. 'What about the rear?'

'Not bad,' asserted Lawson. 'But we still have a bad vibration on the one bike. I don't know where it is coming from but I can hardly see the rev-counter in some places.'

'I think that is the rear tyre; we had it with Wimmer yesterday', admitted the Michelin man. 'I'll put a new one on and I think that will sort it out.'

With that the three men left and Lawson was allowed to concentrate on the treatment to his shoulder before going out for the final session on Saturday.

That afternoon he settled to his work but did not complete many laps. He waited until the end of the session before fitting new tyres to the num-ber one bike and setting out for that fast lap. Sarron was lapping slower than he had in the morning and Lawson surprised him with a blis-tering time of 2m 0.74s to take pole.

Afterwards he explained that Kel's alterations to the carburation made all the difference. 'I didn't try any harder at all and when I came in and Kel said we had done that time I didn't believe him; it wasn't hard. When he leaned out the mid-range and got rid of the flat spot it cleaned it up and made it better all the way up through the rev range; the engine ran a lot stronger.

'The shoulder has not been too much of a prob-lem. It hurts but it doesn't get any worse after a few laps and in fact every day it gets a bit better. I think I can manage in the race. I would like to go out and just ride round taking it easy but there is no way I can afford to do that with such a small lead in the championship. I have to go out and try to win it. I have not tried starting the bike yet and I think that is going to be a problem. I can prob-ably push it OK but I don't know how I can bump my weight on the tank to turn the engine over. The start may be real bad.'

With crashes, painful treatment and a minor ruckus it was an up-and-down sort of week for Lawson but it turned out all right in the end. Spencer did come to France to explain his medi-cal situation and stated that he would not be rid-ing until the end of the year at the earliest. 'The operation showed that the problem was worse than the doctor thought. Nerves and tendons do not show up on X-rays so it was not until he started operating that he could see the problem. Until a week ago I could not move my wrist. I have been doing a lot of physiotherapy and exercising now but I have only been using an exercise bike indoors because I could not hang onto the bars out in the street.

'I cannot ride a motor cycle now and I am not

**Sarron looks over his left shoulder as Baldwin tries to climb over his right while accelerating onto the start-and-finish straight ahead of Gardner and Mamola.**

sure when I will be able to race. I am going to try and ride at the last Grand Prix at Misano but I don't want to race until the arm is right. I have been lifting some weights on that arm but at the moment I can only manage one or two pounds.'

The French were thrilled with Christian Sarron and his obvious competitiveness. He headed practice after three sessions with only Lawson managing to go faster at the last minute. Roche was fourth-quickest but still needed to find one second in the race because he had pinned his hopes on a good result at Ricard to show his ability on the V-four, having completed many hundreds of laps at the circuit in 24-hour races. With McElnea fifth ahead of Baldwin that left Gardner seventh on the second V-four, obviously encountering a few problems in getting the machine to work on a circuit which Gardner had never seen before the start of practice.

Haslam was eighth and the Elf team had worked incredibly hard to get another machine ready for Christian le Liard to ride so that two bikes could start, and the Frenchman qualified twelfth. The machine was very similar to that used by Ron Haslam but with castings replacing many of the aluminium fabrications. The bike was built as a second for Haslam but he chose to ride the older machine and Elf very much wanted to have a second machine out at their home Grand Prix.

It was said that a 1987 version of last year's twin swing-arm Elf was being built in Paris which le Liard was due to ride at some time in the year. However, that remained a separate project to the Elf machines being built by Serge Rosset. So there were now two Elf teams, both spending considerable sums of money, and the rumours continued to grow that Elf might pull out altogether at the end of the season.

Rosset was doing his best to keep the sponsor happy and although the castings only arrived the day before practice started his men produced a machine for le Liard after working all through the night. And it worked.

## 125 cc

Lucio Pietroniro got a great start but it was Luca Cadalora on the Garelli who took the lead at the end of the first lap. August Auinger was right on his tail, splitting the Italian team, for Gresini was third, and the trio had already started to pull away from Pietroniro. The latter headed a tight bunch of Gianola, Bianchi, Hautaniemi and Kneubühler. The Swiss was the fastest man on the circuit during those opening laps as he jumped to the front of that group and everyone took notice as Kneubühler latched onto the back of the leading trio. All four then began their race-long battle, trading places at every turn.

The field dropped behind but their battles were no less exciting as Brigaglia fought his way through to fifth ahead of Pietroniro, Feuz, Bianchi, Nieto and Hautaniemi. By lap 6 the fifth-place struggle had split up, Pietroniro and Brigaglia forging ahead as Feuz, Nieto and Bianchi dropped back a little. The situation was changing all the time and by lap 10 all five were together again.

Up front, everyone took a turn leading and the advantage went back and forth. Kneubühler's bike looked fastest but the slipstreaming at Ricard can confuse top-speed advantage. According to the speed trap, the fastest bike all week was Auinger's MBA at 226 km/h or 140 mph, but they were all very close and none of the top four could break away.

On lap 12 of the 16, Gresini took his turn at leading and Cadalora dropped back to third, and as he failed to pass second-place Auinger out of his slipstream it looked as though Gresini might increase his slender championship lead. Cadalora proved himself a champion though and by lap 14 had regained the lead. It was still anyone's race on the last lap but when the leading quartet ran across a back-marker on the last lap Cadalora was through first, ahead of Gresini, Auinger and Kneubühler. Brigaglia was a good fifth, opening out a lead over Pietroniro in the last four laps, Bianchi coming in a lonely seventh.

This meant that Cadalora regained the championship lead from team-mate Gresini, while Gianola did nothing to help his points score as he retired at the pits after five laps. Brigaglia equalled the latter's points total with his fifth-place finish.

## SIDECARS

Alain Michel was not looking forward to his home Grand Prix with any great confidence, having blown up two engines in practice including one in the final session. Nevertheless, once the race started all that was behind him. Biland led and Streuer was second off the line ahead of

Michel and Webster. Down the Mistral straight for the first time Streuer took the lead with Webster second followed by Michel, as Biland swept into the pits with yet another engine failure – the holed piston syndrome had struck again. He had holed three pistons in practice, including the warm-up, and changed the ignition system for the race and removed the rev-counter completely.

From that point there was never any doubt but that the race would be between the first three. Initial fourth-place men Theo van Kempen and Gerardus de Haas were soon relegated, first by Masato Kumano and Helmut Diehl and then by the Zurbrügg brothers.

By lap 5 Michel had secured a small advantage as Webster tried as best he could, possibly holding up Streuer. The Dutchman saw the way things were going and realised that he had to get on the tail of the French crew, so he passed Webster on lap 6 and put in enough of a burst to close on Michel.

Once he had lost the slipstream of the faster machines Webster was unable to hang on, finding that the pace of his engine dropped off after a few laps, probably because the crankcase temperature had risen considerably. Lap 10 saw him ten seconds behind the leading pair. By that time the Zurbrüggs had passed Kumano, who was soon to come under pressure from the Egloff brothers, and not far behind were Jones and Ayres, Bayley and Nixon, and Abbott and Smith.

Streuer and Michel swapped the lead between them but on lap 11 Michel started to get away from Streuer a little and he opened up an advantage of almost a second and a half by lap 14 of the

17. Streuer had left himself a great deal to do but settled to the task over the last three laps. Going onto the last lap, however, Michel still had a half-second advantage. As he powered down the Mistral straight, Streuer was sucked into Michel's slipstream and swept past on the turn-in to the fast right-hander at the end. Michel had no reply and contented himself with the twelve points for second that preserved his position in the championship. The Frenchman had been revving the engine to 13,500 rpm in practice but by raising the gearing he only used 12,000 rpm in the race, thus preserving the engine. Webster was a distant third, well ahead of Zurbrügg, with Kumano a distant fifth and Egloff sixth.

## 500 cc

The opening laps of the 500 race were all action with Rob McElnea providing a fair proportion of the fireworks. Haslam was first off the line, followed by Gardner, but the Elf's three-cylinder power was no match for the fours and Haslam dropped a handful of places going down the Mistral straight for the first time. The pack was headed by Gardner but Roche, Lawson, Haslam and McElnea were all fighting for the same piece of road. Later, Lawson recalled the action at the end of the straight. 'I think Rob must have got sucked into the slipstream and arrived at the corner going faster than he should. He came round me and Ron going into the corner and was gaining on Roche. I thought 'go for it Rob' but halfway round the turn he started to drift wide and had to back off. I was slow through that corner all the way through the race. I don't know why but every

time I'd get in there and realise I was going too slow and have to get on the gas.'

To the delight of the crowd Roche was leading at the end of lap 1 but the glory was shortlived as Lawson took the number one position early on the next lap with Roche second ahead of Gardner, McElnea and Haslam. Roche was desperate to do well on his own back doorstep but overdid things and fell on lap 3. The confusion that the fall caused gave Lawson a small breathing space and from that point there was little doubt about the outcome. Gardner's second and McElnea's close third could not disguise the fact that Lawson was every bit as dominant as he had been in Yugoslavia — if the injured shoulder caused him any problems they certainly didn't show. By lap 5 the Californian had a near five-second advantage.

Gardner pulled away from McElnea and Haslam could not hold on to fourth because of his lack of speed. The first two to go past were Christian Sarron and Mike Baldwin. Both had midfield starts but were well ahead of Randy Mamola who had discovered a serious clutch problem on the sighting lap. Mike Sinclair sent the rider away on the warm-up lap while the crew collected together a new set of clutch plates. Mamola was held on the back of the grid while the repair was carried out and the countdown to the start continued. As the lights turned to green the mechanics replaced the side of the fairing and Mamola pushed off, at the back of the field, though not too far behind. 'I just went mad on the first few laps', said Mamola later. He was twelfth on lap 2 and eighth by lap 3. As Sarron and Baldwin went past Haslam, Mamola was closing rapidly on the three of them.

By lap 7, Baldwin and Sarron's personal contest had brought them past McElnea. He was spurred by their arrival and the three closed on Gardner who was 8.5s behind Lawson. Mamola had overtaken Haslam but hung behind the four as fireworks erupted once more. McElnea was having a hard time of it. 'I found the bike just so slow down the straight that I had to try and make it all up at the end.' He tried too hard on lap 10 and ran wider than he had on lap 1, running off the track and making full use of the generous rough hardstanding and the lack of catch fences which had thoughtfully been removed.

The excursion dropped McElnea to a distant sixth behind Mamola and it ruined his confidence for he never left that position. The action was not over, however, because although Baldwin and Sarron had overcome Gardner they continued to fight with each other to the flag. Mamola kept climbing, passing Gardner on lap 12 and seizing second on lap 14 (with seven laps to go).

It was the Baldwin/Sarron battle that endured, despite an interlude between laps 15 and 17 in which it seemed as if Baldwin had secured his ten points. Sarron had made a mistake with the handlebar suspension adjustment, turning it the wrong way when the unit got hot, with the result that the performance went off badly before the Frenchman got things sorted out.

When he did, Sarron attacked Baldwin once more and with great determination, this time taking the lead on the last lap. Baldwin still fol-

lowed him into the last turn hoping for a mistake. 'He passed me at the end of the straight and though I had ridden round him a couple of times there I thought that he was pretty desperate so I'd better not try it on the last lap. I had a look up the inside going into the last corner but thought better of it', declared Baldwin later.

Haslam was out on his own in seventh and de Radigues finished an equally distant eighth. The battle for ninth was more interesting, between the Suzukis of Dave Petersen and Paul Lewis. They swapped places up to lap 17 when, as Petersen explained, he tricked Lewis. 'On the brakes at the bottom of the circuit I sat up early but did not brake, hoping he would think I was stopping early and try to go past. He obviously did because when I looked round he had dropped right back.' Lewis explained that he thought the engine had seized when in fact the chain had tried to jam itself between the tyre and the swing arm. Petersen took the two points, with Lewis tenth. Wolfgang von Muralt was unlucky enough to miss out with his hard-ridden eleventh.

## 250 cc

This was another great 250 race, at least partly because the circuit lends itself to slipstreaming. Sito Pons led on the first lap from Pierre Bolle and Jacques Cornu, but the two Parisienne riders dropped back on the second tour as Dominique Sarron took over second with Mang third. The German could not hang on to Pons and Sarron though and had to be content with staying in front of Bolle, Baldé, Lavado and Wimmer.

Lavado had been slower off the line than usual and was down in tenth place on lap 1, Wimmer being a little further back. The championship leader went onto the dirt on lap 5 as he struggled to make up ground and dropped from sixth to ninth but that only delayed his progress for a couple of laps. Sarron and Pons were thrilling the crowd with their two-way Honda battle, while Lavado pushed the Yamaha back through the third-place pack.

By lap 8 he was in front of it, taking the lead from Wimmer, but Mang did not want to let him go. They were five seconds behind the leading duo and the presence of Bolle and Baldé turned the group into a volatile package. On lap 10, Lavado made the break and started cutting down the gap between himself and Pons and Sarron.

It took Lavado just two laps to catch the leading pair and a lap later he was in front. That was lap 12 and, surprisingly, Lavado did run away with the race from there. Pons made another bid for the lead but Lavado had the upper hand and by the end of 18 laps enjoyed almost two seconds' advantage.

The fourth-place contest continued up to the flag with Baldé crossing the line first just ahead of Mang, Wimmer and Bolle. Virginio Ferrari had been on the tail of that group but dropped back and was passed by Maurizio Vitali on lap 14, proving that the V-twin Garelli could be a force to be reckoned with. After yet another disastrous start Tadahiko Taira fought his way through to finish tenth.

**Grand Prix de France, 20 July/statistics**
**Circuit Paul Ricard, 3.610-mile/5.810-km circuit**
**500 cc**

**21 laps, 75.81 miles/122.01 km**

| Place | Rider | Nat. | Machine | Laps | Time & speed | Practice time | Grid |
|---|---|---|---|---|---|---|---|
| 1 | Eddie Lawson | USA | Yamaha | 21 | 42m 57.01s 105.909 mph/ 170.444 km/h | 2m 00.74s | 1 |
| 2 | Randy Mamola | USA | Yamaha | 21 | 43m 09.36s | 2m 01.43s | 3 |
| 3 | Christian Sarron | F | Yamaha | 21 | 43m 11.47s | 2m 00.96s | 2 |
| 4 | Mike Baldwin | USA | Yamaha | 21 | 43m 11.83s | 2m 01.67s | 6 |
| 5 | Wayne Gardner | AUS | Honda | 21 | 43m 19.27s | 2m 01.84s | 7 |
| 6 | Rob McElnea | GB | Yamaha | 21 | 43m 23.18s | 2m 01.64s | 5 |
| 7 | Ron Haslam | GB | Elf | 21 | 44m 02.04s | 2m 03.65s | 8 |
| 8 | Didier de Radigues | B | Chevallier | 21 | 44m 23.08s | 2m 04.05s | 9 |
| 9 | Dave Petersen | ZIM | Suzuki | 21 | 44m 38.19s | 2m 05.26s | 10 |
| 10 | Paul Lewis | AUS | Suzuki | 21 | 44m 49.96s | 2m 05.92s | 11 |
| 11 | Wolfgang von Muralt | CH | Suzuki | 21 | 44m 54.03s | 2m 06.48s | 13 |
| 12 | Marco Gentile | CH | Fior | 21 | 45m 00.66s | 2m 08.09s | 21 |
| 13 | Fabio Biliotti | I | Honda | 21 | 45m 01.71s | 2m 07.33s | 19 |
| 14 | Boet van Dulmen | NL | Honda | 20 | 43m 07.29s | 2m 06.90s | 17 |
| 15 | Christian le Liard | F | Elf | 20 | 43m 12.74s | 2m 06.25s | 12 |
| 16 | Mile Pajic | NL | Honda | 20 | 43m 18.73s | 2m 07.80s | 20 |
| 17 | Simon Buckmaster | GB | Honda | 20 | 43m 22.69s | 2m 09.82s | 26 |
| 18 | Alessandro Valesi | I | Honda | 20 | 43m 35.95s | 2m 08.39s | 22 |
| 19 | Dietmar Mayer | D | Honda | 20 | 44m 29.25s | 2m 11.84s | 28 |
| 20 | Juan Garriga | E | Cagiva | 19 | 45m 00.40s | 2m 06.59s | 15 |
| | Lothar Spiegler | D | Suzuki | 15 | DNF | 2m 12.38s | 29 |
| | Raymond Roche | F | Honda | 14 | DNF | 2m 01.60s | 4 |
| | Louis-Luc Maisto | F | Honda | 11 | DNF | 2m 09.30s | 24 |
| | Manfred Fischer | D | Honda | 10 | DNF | 2m 07.32s | 18 |
| | José Parra | E | Honda | 6 | DNF | 2m 21.09s | 31 |
| | Pier Francesco Chili | I | Suzuki | 6 | DNF | 2m 06.68s | 16 |
| | Philippe Robinet | F | Fior | 4 | DNF | 2m 14.86s | 30 |
| | Leandro Becheroni | I | Honda | 3 | DNF | 2m 09.70s | 25 |
| | Gustav Reiner | D | Honda | | DNS | 2m 06.54s | 14 |
| | Josef Ragginger | A | Suzuki | | DNS | 2m 08.73s | 23 |
| | Henk van der Mark | NL | Honda | | DNS | 2m 09.86s | 27 |
| | Stelio Marmaras | GR | Suzuki | | DNQ | 2m 30.53s | |

*Fastest lap:* Lawson, 2m 01.52s, 106.951 mph/172.120 km/h (record).
*Previous record:* Freddie Spencer, USA (Honda), 2m 01.97s, 106.551 mph/171.477 km/h (1984).

**World Championship: 1** Lawson, 99; **2** Mamola, 86; **3** Gardner, 78; **4** Baldwin, 60; **5** Sarron, 53; **6** McElnea, 44; **7** de Radigues, 21; **8** Roche, 18; **9** Haslam, 12; **10** Chili, 11; **11** van Dulmen, 8; **12** Yatsushiro, 7; **13** Biliotti, Reiner and Petersen, 5; **16** Garriga and Lewis, 4; **18** Burnett and Pajic, 3; **20** Papa and Schwantz, 1.

**Little time to look at the rev counter for Dominique Sarron.**

**Egbert Streuer and Bernie Schnieders pause for thought** (opposite).

## 250 cc

**18 laps, 64.98 miles/104.58 km**

| Place | Rider | Nat. | Machine | Laps | Time & speed | Practice time | Grid |
|---|---|---|---|---|---|---|---|
| 1 | Carlos Lavado | YV | Yamaha | 18 | 38m 35.62s 101.027 mph/ 162.586 km/h | 2m 06.67s | 2 |
| 2 | Alfonso Pons | E | Honda | 18 | 38m 37.45s | 2m 08.13s | 5 |
| 3 | Dominique Sarron | F | Honda | 18 | 38m 40.65s | 2m 07.29s | 3 |
| 4 | Jean-François Baldé | F | Honda | 18 | 38m 45.88s | 2m 07.64s | 4 |
| 5 | Anton Mang | D | Honda | 18 | 38m 46.55s | 2m 08.60s | 10 |
| 6 | Martin Wimmer | D | Yamaha | 18 | 38m 47.01s | 2m 06.58s | 1 |
| 7 | Pierre Bolle | F | Parisienne | 18 | 38m 47.56s | 2m 09.22s | 13 |
| 8 | Maurizio Vitali | I | Garelli | 18 | 39m 06.06s | 2m 09.29s | 14 |
| 9 | Virginio Ferrari | I | Honda | 18 | 39m 06.30s | 2m 10.11s | 23 |
| 10 | Tadahiko Taira | J | Yamaha | 18 | 39m 11.34s | 2m 08.17s | 6 |
| 11 | Jacques Cornu | CH | Honda | 18 | 39m 16.95s | 2m 08.58s | 9 |
| 12 | Stefano Caracchi | I | Aprilia | 18 | 39m 17.92s | 2m 08.31s | 7 |
| 13 | Loris Reggiani | I | Aprilia | 18 | 39m 18.36s | 2m 09.54s | 18 |
| 14 | Hans Lindner | A | Castrol | 18 | 39m 19.07s | 2m 10.46s | 30 |
| 15 | Reinhold Roth | D | Honda | 18 | 39m 19.29s | 2m 09.62s | 19 |
| 16 | Jean Foray | F | Chevallier | 18 | 39m 20.38s | 2m 10.86s | 33 |
| 17 | Carlos Cardus | E | Honda | 18 | 39m 30.88s | 2m 11.29s | 36 |
| 18 | Bruno Bonhuil | F | Honda | 18 | 39m 31.35s | 2m 09.41s | 15 |
| 19 | Harald Eckl | D | Honda | 18 | 39m 31.65s | 2m 09.75s | 21 |
| 20 | Alan Carter | GB | Kobas | 18 | 39m 34.61s | 2m 09.02s | 11 |
| 21 | Niall MacKenzie | GB | Armstrong | 18 | 39m 35.16s | 2m 09.09s | 12 |
| 22 | Massimo Matteoni | I | Honda | 18 | 39m 46.49s | 2m 10.46s | 29 |
| 23 | Alberto Rota | I | Honda | 18 | 39m 47.82s | 2m 10.24s | 27 |
| 24 | Jean-Michel Mattioli | F | Yamaha | 18 | 40m 03.33s | 2m 09.43s | 16 |
| 25 | Konrad Hefele | D | Honda | 18 | 40m 08.38s | 2m 10.99s | 34 |
| 26 | Stéphane Mertens | B | Yamaha | 17 | 38m 49.70s | 2m 10.19s | 25 |
| 27 | Fausto Ricci | I | Honda | 17 | 39m 48.38s | 2m 10.16s | 24 |
| 28 | Siegfried Minich | A | Honda | 17 | 39m 52.81s | 2m 09.66s | 20 |
| | Manfred Herweh | D | Aprilia | 10 | DNF | 2m 10.83s | 32 |
| | Christian Boudinot | F | Kobas | 9 | DNF | 2m 10.22s | 26 |
| | Marcellino Lucchi | I | Malanca | 8 | DNF | 2m 10.59s | 31 |
| | Gary Noel | GB | EMC | 4 | DNF | 2m 10.33s | 28 |
| | Jean-Louis Guignabodet | F | MIG | 3 | DNF | 2m 08.56s | 8 |
| | Etienne Quartararo | F | Honda | 2 | DNF | 2m 09.44s | 17 |
| | Donnie McLeod | GB | Armstrong | 1 | DNF | 2m 10.02s | 22 |
| | Jochen Schmid | D | Yamaha | 0 | DNF | 2m 11.13s | 35 |
| | Hans Becker | D | Yamaha | | DNQ | 2m 11.40s | |
| | Philippe Pagano | F | Yamaha | | DNQ | 2m 11.44s | |
| | Guy Bertin | F | DEFI | | DNQ | 2m 11.67s | |
| | Julian Echaide | E | Kobas | | DNQ | 2m 11.89s | |
| | Jean-Philippe Ruggia | F | Yamaha | | DNQ | 2m 11.99s | |
| | Jacky Onda | F | Yamaha | | DNQ | 2m 12.19s | |
| | Xavier Cardelus | AND | Yamaha | | DNQ | 2m 12.23s | |
| | Roland Freymond | CH | Yamaha | | DNQ | 2m 12.23s | |
| | Herbert Besendörfer | D | Yamaha | | DNQ | 2m 12.77s | |
| | Hervé Duffard | D | Honda | | DNQ | 2m 12.97s | |
| | Antonio Garcia | E | Kobas | | DNQ | 2m 13.08s | |
| | René Délaby | B | Moreno | | DNQ | 2m 13.61s | |
| | Gérard Vallée | F | Yamaha | | DNQ | 2m 13.74s | |
| | Alain Bronec | F | Honda | | DNQ | 2m 14.16s | |
| | Bernard Andrault | F | Arakel | | DNQ | 2m 14.33s | |
| | Jean-Luc Guillemet | F | Yamaha | | DNQ | 2m 15.60s | |
| | Luis Lavado | YV | Yamaha | | DNQ | 2m 16.45s | |
| | Manuel Gonzalez | YV | Yamaha | | DNQ | 2m 18.00s | |
| | Henri Chimera | F | Yamaha | | DNQ | 2m 19.60s | |

*Fastest lap:* Carlos Lavado, 2m 06.95s, 102.376 mph/164.758 km/h (record).
*Previous record:* Anton Mang, D (Yamaha), 2m 08.60s, 101.057 mph/162.635 km/h (1984).

**World Championship: 1** Lavado, 87; **2** Pons, 74; **3** Mang, 57; **4** Baldé, 53; **5** Wimmer, 49; **6** Sarron, 41; **7** Cornu, 28; **8** McLeod, 27; **9** Ricci, 24; **10** Bolle, 19; **11** Taira, 13; **12** Cardus, 11; **13** Carter, 8; **14** Herweh, 7; **15** Ferrari, 6; **16** Mertens, 5; **17** Vitali and Foray, 4; **19** MacKenzie, 3; **20** Matteoni, Minich and Roth, 2; **23** Mattioli and Lindner, 1.

## 125 cc

**16 laps, 57.76 miles/92.96 km**

| Place | Rider | Nat. | Machine | Laps | Time & speed | Practice time | Grid |
|---|---|---|---|---|---|---|---|
| 1 | Luca Cadalora | I | Garelli | 16 | 36m 08.81s 95.880 mph/ 154.304 km/h | 2m 14.67s | 1 |
| 2 | Fausto Gresini | I | Garelli | 16 | 36m 09.81s | 2m 15.01s | 2 |
| 3 | August Auinger | A | Bartol | 16 | 36m 10.24s | 2m 15.51s | 4 |
| 4 | Bruno Kneubühler | CH | LCR | 16 | 36m 10.84s | 2m 15.23s | 3 |
| 5 | Domenico Brigaglia | I | Ducados | 16 | 36m 38.69s | 2m 16.23s | 5 |
| 6 | Lucio Pietroniro | B | MBA | 16 | 36m 42.52s | 2m 17.51s | 9 |
| 7 | Pier Paolo Bianchi | I | Elit | 16 | 36m 45.12s | 2m 16.77s | 6 |
| 8 | Johnny Wickström | SF | Tunturi | 16 | 36m 57.50s | 2m 18.25s | 11 |
| 9 | Angel Nieto | E | Ducados | 16 | 36m 58.70s | 2m 19.45s | 17 |
| 10 | Thierry Feuz | CH | MBA | 16 | 36m 59.01s | 2m 17.25s | 8 |
| 11 | Jussi Hautaniemi | SF | MBA | 16 | 37m 05.66s | 2m 18.31s | 12 |
| 12 | Paul Bordes | F | MBA | 16 | 37m 05.67s | 2m 18.44s | 13 |
| 13 | Willy Perez | RA | Zanella | 16 | 37m 41.87s | 2m 19.59s | 19 |
| 14 | Patrick Daudier | F | PMDF | 16 | 37m 50.15s | 2m 19.21s | 16 |
| 15 | Hakan Olsson | S | Starol | 16 | 37m 50.16s | 2m 22.06s | 32 |
| 16 | Jacques Hutteau | F | MBA | 16 | 37m 54.96s | 2m 19.50s | 18 |
| 17 | Manuel Hernandez | E | Beneti | 16 | 37m 56.48s | 2m 21.40s | 29 |
| 18 | Eric Gijsel | B | MBA | 16 | 38m 07.54s | 2m 22.74s | 36 |
| 19 | Jan Eggens | NL | LCR | 16 | 38m 08.24s | 2m 21.72s | 30 |
| 20 | Anton Straver | NL | MBA | 16 | 38m 16.11s | 2m 21.33s | 28 |
| 21 | Peter Balaz | CS | MBA | 16 | 38m 35.53s | 2m 21.21s | 27 |
| 22 | Esa Kytola | SF | MBA | 15 | 36m 12.02s | 2m 22.44s | 34 |
| 23 | Mike Leitner | A | LCR | 14 | 36m 50.37s | 2m 20.32s | 23 |
| | Olivier Liegeois | B | Assmex | 13 | DNF | 2m 17.83s | 10 |
| | Jean-Claude Selini | F | MBA | 13 | DNF | 2m 19.97s | 21 |
| | Norbert Peschke | D | MBA | 12 | DNF | 2m 20.15s | 22 |
| | Christian le Badezet | F | MBA | 10 | DNF | 2m 19.82s | 20 |
| | Bady Hassaine | DZ | MBA | 8 | DNF | 2m 20.68s | 26 |
| | Adolf Stadler | D | MBA | 8 | DNF | 2m 18.84s | 15 |
| | Marin Andreas Sanchez | E | Ducados | 5 | DNF | 2m 22.25s | 33 |
| | Ezio Gianola | I | MBA | 5 | DNF | 2m 16.80s | 7 |
| | Alfred Waibel | D | Real | 4 | DNF | 2m 20.36s | 24 |
| | Paolo Casoli | I | MBA | 3 | DNF | 2m 18.55s | 14 |
| | Robin Appleyard | GB | MBA | 2 | DNF | 2m 22.06s | 31 |
| | Peter Sommer | CH | Vollmer | 1 | DNF | 2m 22.44s | 35 |
| | Gilles Payraudeau | F | MBA | | DNS | 2m 20.63s | 25 |
| | Ivan Troisi | YV | MBA | | DNQ | 2m 22.84s | |
| | Boy van Erp | NL | MBA | | DNQ | 2m 23.16s | |
| | Ton Spek | NL | MBA | | DNQ | 2m 23.33s | |
| | Nicolas Gonzalez | E | MBA | | DNQ | 2m 23.54s | |
| | Michel Escudier | F | MBA | | DNQ | 2m 23.81s | |
| | Flemming Kistrup | DK | MBA | | DNQ | 2m 24.27s | |
| | Manfred Braun | D | MBA | | DNQ | 2m 24.46s | |
| | Karl Dauer | D | MBA | | DNQ | 2m 25.40s | |

*Fastest lap:* Cadalora, 2m 13.35s, 97.462 mph/156.850 km/h (record).
*Previous record:* Angel Nieto, E (Garelli), 2m 14.27s, 96.790 mph/155.768 km/h (1984).

**World Championship: 1** Cadalora, 76; **2** Gresini, 74; **3** Brigaglia and Gianola, 47; **5** Kneubühler, 32; **6** Bianchi, 26; **7** Pietroniro, 25; **8** Perez, 21; **9** Auinger, 20; **10** Wickström, 18; **11** Nieto, Feuz and Liegeois, 15; **15** Grassetti and Waibel, 5; **17** Hautaniemi, 4; **18** Sanchez, 3; **19** Kytola, 2; **20** Olsson and Stadler, 1.

Don Morley

## Sidecars

**17 laps, 61.37 miles/98.77 km**

| Place | Driver & passenger | Nat. | Machine | Laps | Time & speed | Practice time | Grid |
|---|---|---|---|---|---|---|---|
| 1 | Egbert Streuer/ Bernie Schnieders | NL NL | LCR– Yamaha | 17 | 36m 40.76s 100.394 mph/ 161.568 km/h | 2m 08.10s | 2 |
| 2 | Alain Michel/ Jean-Marc Fresc | F F | Krauser– Yamaha | 17 | 36m 41.16s | 2m 07.64s | 1 |
| 3 | Steve Webster/ Tony Hewitt | GB GB | LCR– Yamaha | 17 | 37m 01.57s | 2m 10.48s | 6 |
| 4 | Alfred Zurbrügg/ Martin Zurbrügg | CH CH | LCR– Yamaha | 17 | 37m 19.03s | 2m 09.52s | 5 |
| 5 | Masato Kumano/ Helmut Diehl | J D | LCR– Yamaha | 17 | 37m 24.37s | 2m 11.90s | 7 |
| 6 | Markus Egloff/ Urs Egloff | CH CH | LCR– Yamaha | 17 | 37m 33.89s | 2m 09.13s | 4 |
| 7 | Derek Jones/ Brian Ayres | GB GB | LCR– Yamaha | 17 | 37m 40.25s | 2m 12.25s | 9 |
| 8 | Derek Bayley/ Bryan Nixon | GB GB | LCR– Yamaha | 17 | 37m 45.33s | 2m 12.80s | 10 |
| 9 | Steve Abbott/ Vince Biggs | GB GB | Windle– Yamaha | 17 | 37m 47.21s | 2m 12.94s | 11 |
| 10 | Frank Wrathall/ Kerry Chapman | GB GB | LCR– Yamaha | 17 | 37m 57.61s | 2m 13.47s | 13 |
| 11 | Theo van Kempen/ Gerardus de Haas | NL NL | LCR– Yamaha | 17 | 38m 06.61s | 2m 13.38s | 12 |
| 12 | Graham Gleeson/ J. Janin | NZ F | LCR– Yamaha | 17 | 38m 32.02s | 2m 16.83s | 21 |
| 13 | Dennis Bingham/ Julia Bingham | GB GB | LCR– Yamaha | 17 | 38m 34.31s | 2m 15.40s | 16 |
| 14 | Ivan Nigrowski/ Frédéric Meunier | F F | Seymaz– Yamaha | 17 | 38m 34.89s | 2m 15.02s | 15 |
| 15 | Pascal Larratte/ Jacques Corbier | F F | LCR– Yamaha | 17 | 38m 52.03s | 2m 17.41s | 24 |
| 16 | Bernd Scherer/ Wolfgang Gess | D D | BSR– Yamaha | 17 | 38m 52.70s | 2m 20.22s | 28 |
| 17 | Amadeo Zini/ Claudio Sonaglia | I I | LCR– Yamaha | 16 | 37m 15.85s | 2m 15.60s | 18 |
| 18 | Erwin Weber/ Klaus Kolb | D D | LCR– Yamaha | 16 | 37m 17.02s | 2m 19.43s | 26 |
| 19 | Jean-Louis Millet/ Claude Debroux | F F | Seymaz– Yamaha | 16 | 37m 21.71s | 2m 17.49s | 25 |
| 20 | Henry Golemba/ Alain-Robert Barrillon | F F | Busch– Yamaha | 15 | 36m 42.00s | 2m 21.07s | 30 |
| | Wolfgang Stropek/ Hans-Peter Demling | A A | LCR– Yamaha | 16 | DNF | 2m 16.18s | 20 |
| | René Progin/ Yves Hunziker | CH CH | Seymaz– Yamaha | 11 | DNF | 2m 13.60s | 14 |
| | Jacques Heriot/ Jean-Louis Heriot | F F | Seymaz– Yamaha | 8 | DNF | 2m 20.06s | 27 |
| | Ray Gardner/ Tony Strevens | GB GB | LCR– Yamaha | 6 | DNF | 2m 15.90s | 19 |
| | Rolf Steinhausen/ Bruno Hiller | D D | Busch | 4 | DNF | 2m 12.03s | 8 |
| | Hans Hügli/ Markus Fahrni | CH CH | LCR– Yamaha | 3 | DNF | 2m 15.42s | 17 |
| | Clive Stirrat/ Simon Prior | GB GB | BLR– Yamaha | 2 | DNF | 2m 16.91s | 22 |
| | Rolf Biland/ Kurt Waltisperg | CH CH | Krauser | 1 | DNF | 2m 08.99s | 3 |
| | Mick Barton/ Graham Rose | GB GB | LCR– Yamaha | 0 | DNF | 2m 16.98s | 23 |
| | Norbert Wild/ Andreas Räcke | D D | OW– Yamaha | 0 | DNF | 2m 20.54s | 29 |
| | Herbert Prügl/ August Dierlinger | A A | HOMO– Yamaha | | DNQ | 2m 27.77s | |

*Fastest lap:* Webster, 2m 07.46s, 101.967 mph/164.099 km/h (record).
*Previous record:* Rolf Biland/Kurt Waltisperg, CH/CH (LCR–Yamaha), 2m 08.19s, 101.381 mph/163.156 km/h (1984).

**World Championship: 1** Michel, 54; **2** Webster, 49; **3** Streuer, 45; **4** Abbott, 30; **5** Egloff, 27; **6** Zurbrügg, 22; **7** Kumano, 21; **8** Biland, 20; **9** Jones, 16; **10** Steinhausen, 10; **11** Bayley, 9; **12** Barton, 6; **13** Progin, van Kempen and Brindley, 5; **16** Scherer, 3; **17** Gleeson, Kumagaya and Wrathall, 1.

# SHELL OILS
# BRITISH
# Grand Prix

At the beginning of the week Niall MacKenzie had an exploratory outing on the Skoal Bandit Suzuki at Donington Park and his long-awaited debut on the 500 was set for Silverstone. He had ridden the bike for about four laps at Oran Park in Australia during the 1985 Swann series when Rob McElnea had been racing the machine, but Suzuki's intention to sign him for '86 was thwarted because he had already agreed to ride for the Armstrong team. Thus he stayed in the 250 class.

The idea was then hatched for him to contest the British Grand Prix as a one-off event alongside regular rider Paul Lewis on the machine that had been prepared for Kevin Schwantz to use at Assen and Spa. His employers, Armstrong, were not impressed with the idea, pointing out that the British Grand Prix was important for both themselves and team sponsors Silverstone. Nor did they wish to detract from the effort that MacKenzie could put into riding the 250.

MacKenzie was so keen to ride the 500 that on returning from the French Grand Prix he asked again, and sportingly the Armstrong hierarchy agreed not to stand in the way of his career. Their acceptance livened up the tail end of the season and sparked the emergence of a new star in the blue riband class. MacKenzie was on the boil from the word go at Silverstone, apparently unaffected by the increased size, power and weight of the 500.

MacKenzie found the bigger machine easy to get on with. 'I'm surprised at how light it is to steer. It corners well and it is very rideable. There is a lot more throttle control involved than with the 250 because you have to be careful with the extra power and you have to be smoother getting on the power in the corner, but it isn't too difficult. I would love to get into the top ten on the 500 and I think I could if the race is dry and clear. I still want to do well on the 250, though, and get in the top six if I can. As for next year I'd like to ride in the 500 class but I'd rather be on a competitive 250 than an uncompetitive 500.'

Untimed practice on the Thursday saw him lapping as fast as anyone but problems on Friday kept him down in 14th place, just ahead of Dave Petersen on the Gallina Suzuki, while Lewis was tenth. Petersen had crashed in that session, however, and was later to lose the little finger from his left hand. It had been trapped under the bike as it slid across the circuit when he fell going through the left-hander onto Hanger Straight.

'I can't really understand it; that should be flat-out, no problem. It was like last year on my Honda but that is not the first time I've crashed after we have softened up the rear suspension.' The rear suspension had been causing problems all season and it seems very likely that the geometry was wrong, causing the chain tension under acceleration to compress the suspension and reduce the downward force on the rear tyre, encouraging it to lose grip. The Skoal Bandit Suzukis, with their composite frames, used a completely different rear suspension system that was far more effective than the standard aluminium chassis issued by the factory in Japan and employed by the Gallina Team.

The weather then made its contribution and ruined the afternoon session. Gardner was fastest ahead of Mamola, Lawson and Sarron. Gallina's misery was completed when Pier Francesco Chili crashed at high speed coming through Woodcote. It could have been a very serious fall but he escaped relatively lightly, only injuring his ankle and shoulder. That left the team without a rider for the Grand Prix and would rule them out of the Swedish as well. The team returned to Italy to prepare for the San Marino Grand Prix at Misano.

Gardner said that there was nothing special about his pole-position time but for once he seemed to have things sorted out early in practice. 'Normally we seem to be dragging the chain a bit and trying to sort the bike out and catch up late in practice. This time the bike was quite good from the start and although I can go a bit quicker I would have been happy to race after the first session', Gardner reported. Since Assen the team had been able to use a new engine with no ATAC boxes in the exhaust pipe. Instead, it featured a valving system more like Yamaha's which alters the exhaust port height, lower at low rpm and higher as the revs rise. It made the engine more flexible with better mid-range power. The harshness of the power band had been causing Gardner problems and when it was clear that the race would be wet the team decided to race with it for the first time at Silverstone.

Lawson was third-quickest and explained that he was not really in the groove early in practice. 'I'm just not into it at all at the moment and this is one of those circuits where you have to be right there to go fast. It is no good just trying too hard; you just have to go round and round, pushing a little harder all the time, and then it will come. And when it clicks you suddenly go much quicker, like you've switched into race gear.'

As practice progressed, the weather merely got more inclement. What had started as a pleasant week deteriorated into one of high winds or rain or both. Rob McElnea was one of those to be reminded of the effect of side winds at Silverstone when he dropped the Marlboro Yamaha in fifth gear at about 150 mph through Abbey Curve and was lucky to escape with a bruising. The bike was in a sorry state and the aluminium frame had to be written off.

McElnea was not the only Yamaha rider to fall in practice and Mamola slipped off his Lucky Strike machine when he wandered onto the kerb approaching Becketts while warming up the tyres. Keeping out of the way of other riders and not watching where he was going, as can often be the case, he was injured because the fall was awkward rather than frightening. He staggered off the track with a very painful shoulder which turned out to have two cracks in it. Mamola needed nine injections to kill the pain before he could race. By the end of practice there was a long list of fallers which included Baldé, Spaan, van Kessel, Carter, Roth, Gianola, Spek, Lindner and Schirnhöfer.

In all, the practice for the 500 race was distinctly inconclusive as Juan Garriga was the only rider in the top twenty who managed to improve his position after the first session. The last session saw most others 1.5s or 2.0s slower than their grid time yet Garriga pushed the Cagiva hard enough to improve his time by over half a second, despite the wind. If calm weather had given him another second and a half, he might have got into the top ten. As it was, he lay 16th between non-starters Petersen and Chili.

Mike Baldwin was riding at Silverstone for the first time having missed the '85 Grand Prix because he was chasing the American championship. Learning new circuits like the Nürburgring scarcely seemed to hold him up at all but the poor practice conditions at Silverstone proved a handicap and at first he found the wide open circuit disconcerting. 'The last corner is the worst because it is so hard to find the right line. It opens up as you go in and it is like driving into the parking lot at K-Mart, with all the grid markings like parking spaces and no idea where the road goes.' Nevertheless, that did not prevent him from lapping fifth-fastest behind Sarron and ahead of McElnea. All three were battling for fourth place in the championship.

Roche was once more out on the Honda four, qualifying seventh ahead of Roger Burnett on the NS500 three-cylinder Honda Britain machine. Barry Sheene had made a personal phone call to Erv Kanemoto at HRC in Belgium to try to get Burnett the use of Spencer's NSR 500 four, but Kanemoto could not or would not oblige.

Kanemoto was helping to look after the bike loaned to Roche and the machine used by Shungi Yatsushiro, but life was proving a little boring in comparison to working with Spencer. Two years ago, after all, they had been running two classes and actually clinched the 250 World Championship at the British Grand Prix.

Kanemoto's involvement with Yatsushiro was slight and the Japanese ace was having a tougher time than when he made his impressive start to his Grand Prix career in Austria and Yugoslavia. Part of the problem lay in genuine homesickness. At least at Silverstone he had the company of another member of the Moriwaki team, Osamu Hiwatashi, who was riding in his first 250 cc Grand Prix on a special Honda with a remarkable frame featuring two horizontal aluminium side spars running forward from the swing-arm pivots either side of the engine and then up to the steering head. Mamuru Moriwaki was present for this one-off outing from Japan, hoping to mount a full-season Grand Prix campaign in 1987.

There was plenty of talk concerning the proposed sixteen-event Grand Prix calendar and particularly the first round in Japan. Some riders had just returned from the Suzuka Eight-Hour endurance race and many described the circuit as too dangerous for a Grand Prix — or an endurance event for that matter. Mike Trimby held a meeting to decide what approach should be made to the Suzuka circuit owners concerning improvements before the Grand Prix could be run at the beginning of the coming season.

The riders present at the meeting were Kenny Roberts, who had ridden at Suzuka and would speak for his team, Wayne Gardner and Christian

Randy Mamola (*right*) fell from the Lucky Strike Yamaha in practice and injured his shoulder.

Wayne Gardner used the new, more flexible non-ATAC exhaust-valve engine to great effect in the rain.

Sarron. The Frenchman had fallen in the endurance race, while his brother Dominique had won, partnering Gardner. The rider were in agreement that some drastic changes were necessary because run-off areas were inadequate with steel barriers too close to the track in most places. They pointed to some nine places on the circuit where alterations would have to be made, involving moving one section of track because there was no room to increase the run-off in its present position. Organisational changes were requested as well but the track alterations would be hardest to execute; it was estimated that these would cost in the region of $250,000. As Sarron asserted, an acceptance of the circuit in its present state would mean stepping back four or five years to the safety standards of old circuits in Europe that had been improved during the period or were no longer in use.

It was announced that the 1987 British Grand Prix would be held at Donington Park. Most thought that, as the best-appointed circuit in England, it deserved the chance to run a Grand Prix, even if it would require resurfacing before the event. Unlike Spa or Assen, Silverstone has no special atmosphere and a change should be interesting, despite Kel Carruthers' doubts about the move. 'Silverstone is different because it is so fast; Donington is like all the other new Grand Prix circuits.'

Looking forward to the coming season was not confined to dates and circuits, and the silly season started as rumours began which suggested Tadahiko Taira would leave the 250 class and ride a 500 as part of Team Agostini. The Italian ex-champion said that, should Yamaha want to run Taira on the 500s, he would still have Lawson and McElnea; running three men would not be a prob-

lem. A more significant question concerned the 250 team, as the names of Juan Garriga, Maurizio Vitali and Luca Cadalora were mentioned as possible riders and even as replacements for Wimmer who was having such a frustrating season.

Gerd Kafka was having an equally frustrating year in the 80 cc class. After winning in Holland and finishing third overall in the championship the previous season, he was languishing in twelfth place in the '86 table after only scoring points twice. He complained that every time he took the private Krauser out it hit trouble and was just too slow on most occasions. Things were beginning to look up at Silverstone, however, for he had a new ignition system that produced extra power and extended rpm. Dörflinger reported that it made the private Krauser impossible to catch, even on his works machine.

**August Auinger's performance fulfilled all one's expectations.**

**Manfred Fischer made another fine start to lead the pack into the spray** *(main picture)*.

Don Morley

## SIDECARS

After having to abandon the race in '85 because of the rain, the three-wheeled brigade had the good fortune to run on Saturday. It was a first-class affair with Webster and Hewitt leading first from Rolf Biland and Kurt Waltisperg before the latter pair's engine failed on the second lap. It was yet another repeat of the seizures caused apparently by fuel supply problems that had dogged them for much of the season including practice at Silverstone.

Egbert Streuer and Bernard Schnieders had been fourth at the end of the initial lap but, in passing Alain Michel and Jean-Marc Fresc, they were able to take second on lap 2. By then the flying British crew had a 200-metre lead and appeared to have no trouble extending that advantage until lap 5 when the World Champions began to close on Webster and Hewitt.

By that point, Markus and Urs Egloff had caught Michel. Their brief dice with the championship leader ended when the Frenchman suffered a collapsed piston and stopped on lap 7. 'I can't understand it. I put in new pistons for the warm-up because some were showing cracks and normally they should be perfect for the race but this time one failed.' Michel was bitterly disappointed to see his championship chances apparently slipping away as he watched his two rivals, Streuer and Webster, race to the finish.

That left the Zurbrügg brothers, Alfred and Martin, in fourth place, just ahead of the Japanese/German pairing of Masato Kumano and Helmut Diehl, and British duo Frank Wrathall and Kerry Chapman. Behind them, Derek Jones and Brian Ayres were pulling through from a poor start and doing battle with Graham Gleeson and Ian Colquhoun and Rolf Steinhausen and Bruno Hiller.

Through laps 5 and 6 Streuer closed rapidly on on Webster, finally pulling out in front on lap 7. The two crews then put on a great show for the crowd, slipstreaming nose-to-tail and swapping places, far ahead of the Egloffs in an isolated third place. Meanwhile, the Zurbrügg twins, benefiting from three days of tuning work done on their engine by Horst Seel before the Grand Prix, pulled away from Kumano and thereafter things became rather processional behind the leaders. Further back, Jones caught and passed Wrathall on lap 13, while Gleeson was getting the better of Steinhausen who was encountering problems which dropped him back to finish 11th.

Up front, Webster and Streuer were fully occupied lapping other outfits in addition to their own battle for the lead, and Webster was proving the more forceful. He regained the lead and opened up a small advantage on lap 15. However, Streuer seemed to have a little in hand because once the road was clear he closed once more, taking the premier position for the final time with two laps to go. He opened out the gap sufficiently to put him a second ahead at the flag, setting a new lap record on the final circuit as he fought to stay in front of a determined Webster.

The Egloffs were a clear third, even though the Zurbrüggs were closing all the way and keeping well clear of Kumano. Jones took sixth with Wrathall having another go in the closing laps. Jones reported a smooth untroubled race. 'It's getting a bit boring; no hairy moments. We'll have to try and liven things up in Sweden.' The Zurbrügg brothers were a little frustrated, as Alfred explained. 'One or two more laps and we would have caught the Egloffs but we messed the start up as usual.'

## 80 cc

Although Ian McConnachie set fastest time in the first practice session, Dörflinger, Martinez and Spaan all improved on this and McConnachie qualified fourth. He was still confident that he could win his first Grand Prix and declared that problems in practice had held him back. Saturday's weather threatened to be as much of a problem as the opposition; during the day the wind increased so much that the 80s would have been blown off the circuit. The time of the race was altered to allow the production bikes and sidecars to go first, in the hope that the wind would die down. The organisers were prepared to run the event on Sunday if the conditions did not improve.

The wind did reduce in strength as the afternoon wore on and when the race eventually started at 6.30 p.m., it had ceased to present a problem. The first 80 cc Grand Prix in Britain was a good advertisement for the class and Dutchman Wilco Zeelenberg led off the line, closely followed by Gerhard Waibel, Dörflinger, McConnachie, Spaan, Martinez and Herreros.

Don Morley

121

Kenny Roberts was there to wave the Lucky Strike flag and to motivate his team, but it was not their best race of the year.

Dominique Sarron (right) won his first Grand Prix with a perfectly measured ride in dreadful conditions.

Niall MacKenzie (below right) finally got his chance to race a 500 and astonished everyone.

Alan Carter overtakes Lavado, but he was to fall on the last lap while trying to beat Sarron (far right).

Angel Nieto continued his unhappy season by starting second-to-last. Things went from bad to worse when, at the end of the first lap, Mandy Fischer crashed in front of him at Woodcote and Nieto ran over the unfortunate German. Neither was seriously hurt.

At the end of the first circuit, McConnachie was the leader, followed by Spaan, Herreros, Martinez and young Brazilian Alexandre Barros on his Autisa. Theo Timmer retired at the pits. Lap 2 saw the leading quartet of McConnachie, Herreros, Martinez and Dörflinger break away, leaving Spaan a clear fifth as he tried to hang on ahead of Barros, who, in turn, was in front of Gerd Kafka and Waibel.

Dörflinger made a mistake on lap 4 which dropped him to fifth temporarily but a lap later he was right back in the action, passing Spaan, Martinez and Herreros to regain second behind McConnachie who was increasing the pace. Dörflinger was capable of hanging on to the British rider but had to set the fastest lap of the race to do so. The others found the pace too hot and a gap opened up to Martinez who held third just ahead of Herreros and Spaan. Back in sixth place, Kafka had taken over from Barros and then on lap 10 the Brazilian was relegated one more place by Waibel.

Martinez had said before the race that he intended to ride cautiously. 'Last year I won four Grands Prix and Dörflinger two, yet he was champion. I don't want that to happen again.' Whether he wanted to let him or not, Dörflinger was getting away and closed right up on McConnachie with three of the 15 laps still to go. Dörflinger needed the 15 points to keep his championship hopes alive but McConnachie was not about to ease off and hand them to the Swiss Krauser team leader. He wanted to win in front of his home crowd and flashed across the line less than half a second in front.

Martinez sorted matters out with his teammate on the final circuit and took third from Herreros as Spaan came in behind in fifth after a fine ride. Waibel got the better of Kafka to take sixth and Barros reached eighth to score his first World Championship points.

Dörflinger was unimpressed by McConnachie's victory as he apparently considered that the Englishman should have let him win. Despite looking a little grim, he declined to complain in public, however. McConnachie was naturally ecstatic and thanked his parents who had sacrificed everything to enable him to go racing. Proof that it had been a close-fought race in the opening laps was the black mark down the right leg of his leathers, visible evidence of the nearness of Martinez's front tyre.

## 250 cc

Rain rain rain . . . that was Sunday at Silverstone. The sidecar and 80 cc competitors avoided it, and the former were well on their way to Sweden by the time the weather turned sour. The only things that varied through the afternoon were the intensity of the downpour and the depth of the puddles.

Pierre Bolle left the line at the head of the field but fell on the first lap. Sito Pons was right behind him at the time and lost a great deal of ground avoiding man and machine, leaving him right at the back of the field at the end of lap 1. Baldé and Mattioli were also badly affected.

Jacques Cornu headed the field at the end of the first circuit, Dominique Sarron on his tail, closely pursued in turn by Virginio Ferrari, Alan Carter, Carlos Lavado, Stéphane Mertens and Reinhold Roth. Carlos Cardus lay ninth ahead of Martin Wimmer and Carl Fogarty.

Lap 2 saw Carter take the lead. He seems to have the conviction that while he might be beaten in the dry he can win any wet-weather Grand Prix. Sarron kept up with him in second, still followed by Ferrari as Cornu dropped to fourth ahead of Lavado and Wimmer. The German was flying and a lap later had passed Lavado and Cornu to move into fourth place but then went sliding down the road after losing the front end of the Marlboro Yamaha. The bike was saved from damage by sliding across the tarmac on Wimmer's right leg. He restarted in 20th place and commenced the long climb back as Sarron took the lead from Carter. His brother was watching at Copse. 'Dominique is either very fast in the wet or too slow', he commented. 'Today he looks fast.'

Lavado had moved into third place on lap 4 and Ferrari began to slip back, being passed a lap later by Cardus and coming under pressure from Roth. The Italian was in trouble because the tape he had over his nose was getting in his eyes. By lap 6 Roth was fifth, but a lap later the leading trio of Carter, Sarron and Lavado started to pull away from the fourth-place group of Roth, Cardus and Ferrari, who continued to swap places for the next few laps.

Carter could not get away from the other two but on lap 10 Lavado moved into second and Sarron dropped back a little. Two laps later, the Cobas rider made a mistake which sent him down to third, while Lavado led. Lap 13 saw Sarron press Lavado hard though Carter seemed to be losing touch, but he refused to give in and fought his way back while Sarron took over at the head of the field. By lap 16 Carter had displaced Lavado, but despite his best efforts the Honda was just too fast to catch. Two laps from the end, Carter was three seconds adrift, though well clear of Lavado.

On lap 23 (one lap to go) Carter was obviously closing but still over a second behind the leader. He threw caution to the wind on the final circuit in an all-or-nothing attempt to win. Sadly, for him it resulted in nothing because he slid off, leaving Lavado the grateful recipient of 12 points.

Sito Pons did brilliantly to take third coming from the back of the field after that first-lap incident. He was 18th on lap 3 but pegged away until he passed Roth on lap 23. Cornu had crashed on lap 4, Mang and Minich on lap 8, Baldé on lap 9, Taira on lap 17. Wimmer received a little compensation for his fall in the form of two points for ninth place, just ahead of Niall MacKenzie who refused to give up when his engine seized after three laps and ran poorly for the rest of the race.

## 125 cc

When it rains August Auinger just disappears into the spray, and once more he obliged with the most predictable display of first-class wet-weather riding. The Bartol MBA ran faultlessly thanks to Dave Johnson's preparation, and after tailing championship leader Luca Cadalora for the first lap to check out the positions of the biggest puddles, Auinger moved into the lead and soon opened up a healthy advantage. Four seconds at the end of lap 3 became six and then ten by lap 5. When he was more than 14 seconds ahead he eased off.

Cadalora was keen to conserve his championship lead and saw no sense in trying to chase Auinger. By lap 5, though, he was under pressure from Johnny Wickström and, a lap later, from Jussi Hautaniemi as well. The only man in the class who can ride anything like as fast as Auinger in the wet is Domenico Brigaglia, winner of the Belgian GP, but he had suffered a bad start and was 11th at the end of lap 2. By lap 7 he was four places further on, having fought his way through the group comprising Lucio Pietroniro, Alfred Waibel, Thierry Feuz, Willy Perez and Jamie Whitham. Whitham's bike expired at the end of lap 10 but by then the group had split up, with Pietroniro in sixth place ahead of Perez and Feuz.

By lap 9 it looked as though Wickström had a firm hold on second, successfully maintaining his advantage over Cadalora and Hautaniemi, but Brigaglia was still on the move. The latter caught and passed Cadalora, the Garelli rider tucking in behind. By lap 13 Wickström was coming under pressure, with Brigaglia the first to go past. Two laps later Wickström had been relegated to fourth by Cadalora, though he stayed well clear of the next man Pietroniro, who had passed Hautaniemi.

The finishing positions were then set except for Perez, who was determined to make the best of the last quarter, passing Hautaniemi on lap 19 and almost catching Pietroniro before the flag. Feuz had crashed on lap 12 but pole-position man Bruno Kneubühler's contribution to the race ended much earlier when he fell on lap 1. Fausto Gresini pulled out on the fifth lap with front brake problems having already paid one visit to the pits to see if the trouble could be sorted out.

## 500 cc

There were two starts to the 500 race because Paul Lewis crashed on leaving the first corner. Nil visibility and the pressure on Lewis to perform well against the new man in the Skoal Bandit Team, MacKenzie, caused the crash. 'I couldn't see because of the spray and when I thought I had track to spare I was actually on the white line', said Lewis later.

Lewis only injured his ankle but the doctor's car was following the pack on the first lap and stopped to give assistance, partially blocking the circuit to protect Lewis. The restart did not help Mamola who was having a hard time pushing the Yamaha and after the first effort needed more treatment before going to the line again. His

team asked for a starter on the precedent gained by Christian Sarron in Austria but was refused.

Once more, Manfred Fischer was first off the line but Wayne Gardner was close behind with Lawson, de Radigues, Haslam, McElnea and Roche all in close attendance. Gardner quickly took the lead, using the more flexible power of his new exhaust-valve engine and finding drive where others found only wheelspin. He opened an advantage remarkably quickly, very much in the manner of Spencer a year earlier.

Lawson was into second place from lap 1 but never looked like catching Gardner, once more balancing the requirement of holding on to his points lead against the risk of falling. Gardner knew that only winning would keep his championship chances alive but could not have reasonably expected Lawson to be pushed back to third. Nevertheless Belgian Didier de Radigues obliged with an inspired ride on the Chevallier.

Initially it seemed as if the threat to Lawson's second place would come from Sarron, who was obviously after a unique brotherly double and rapidly rose through the field from a poor start. Twelfth on the initial lap, he caught de Radigues six laps later but, as he passed next time round, he fell while sweeping through Woodcote in third place, smashing his elbow as he slid across the

concrete ripple strips at the edge of the circuit.

By lap 9 de Radigues had closed on Lawson's tail but the Californian put in extra effort and opened up a small advantage. Halfway through the 28-lap race, the rain fell harder and puddles grew deeper. Lawson eased off as the chance of aquaplaning increased and de Radigues took over second on lap 15.

McElnea in a lonely fourth also closed on his team-mate at this point but had no intention of passing and reducing the potential champion's points score. As the rain eased slightly Lawson accelerated again into a secure third, McElnea had nothing to fear from behind for although Mamola took fifth on lap 14 he was well behind and hindered by his shoulder.

Mamola's ride was impressive. Tenth on lap 2 he had worked hard to pass Haslam and Roche to secure fifth, surviving a near crash on lap 16, sliding through Woodcote and hanging half off the bike as he fought for control. Haslam was having dreadful problems with rear wheelspin, a tyre and suspension problem, while Roche would have felt more at home on the three-cylinder as he did not have a new engine with the exhaust valves as fitted to Gardner's powerplant.

As Roche maintained his isolated sixth, Haslam was overtaken by privateer Gary Lingham

who was having a great ride but hit typical misfortune when his engine seized on lap 22 because there was too much tape over the radiator and it overheated. Haslam returned to seventh place but only temporarily because three riders, Niall MacKenzie, Kenny Irons and Wolfgang von Muralt, were closing. Lap 24 saw MacKenzie and Irons get past but Haslam managed to hold off von Muralt until the flag. They were the last riders not to be lapped by Gardner. Von Muralt was more than a little pleased with tenth after three 11th places in previous races.

Lawson had closed rapidly over the last few laps but just failed to catch de Radigues. From ten seconds adrift with three laps to go he cut the deficit to seven then to five going on to the last lap, but could not quite catch the Belgian who finished just over a second in front.

The most disappointed rider was perhaps Mike Baldwin. He had started slowly then found he could not see, having used a dark visor for the race because in the first start his special non-mist clear visors had misted up immediately. He also was wet and cold but kept going because he could not read his pit board and had no idea where he was. Had he realised he was 18th and nearly two laps adrift he might have thought differently.

## 500 cc

**28 laps, 81.96 miles/131.91 km**

| Place | Rider | Nat. | Machine | Laps | Time & speed | Practice time | Grid |
|---|---|---|---|---|---|---|---|
| 1 | Wayne Gardner | AUS | Honda | 28 | 51m 24.03s 95.66 mph/ 153.94 km/h | 1m 28.16s | 1 |
| 2 | Didier de Radigues | B | Chevallier | 28 | 51m 33.39s | 1m 30.80s | 9 |
| 3 | Eddie Lawson | USA | Yamaha | 28 | 51m 34.66s | 1m 29.00s | 3 |
| 4 | Rob McElnea | GB | Yamaha | 28 | 51m 46.38s | 1m 29.43s | 6 |
| 5 | Randy Mamola | USA | Yamaha | 28 | 52m 11.59s | 1m 28.69s | 2 |
| 6 | Raymond Roche | F | Honda | 28 | 52m 30.36s | 1m 30.52s | 7 |
| 7 | Niall MacKenzie | GB | Suzuki | 28 | 53m 04.28s | 1m 32.07s | 14 |
| 8 | Kenny Irons | GB | Yamaha | 28 | 53m 05.14s | 1m 33.15s | 19 |
| 9 | Ron Haslam | GB | Elf | 28 | 53m 08.27s | 1m 32.00s | 13 |
| 10 | Wolfgang von Muralt | CH | Suzuki | 28 | 53m 13.34s | 1m 33.51s | 21 |
| 11 | Roger Burnett | GB | Honda | 27 | 51m 25.81s | 1m 30.74s | 8 |
| 12 | Boet van Dulmen | NL | Honda | 27 | 51m 28.25s | 1m 32.78s | 18 |
| 13 | Ray Swann | GB | Suzuki | 27 | 52m 22.18s | 1m 35.70s | 35 |
| 14 | Maarten Duyzers | NL | Suzuki | 27 | 53m 10.22s | 1m 35.18s | 32 |
| 15 | Henk van der Mark | NL | Suzuki | 26 | 51m 27.15s | 1m 34.19s | 27 |
| 16 | Glen Williams | NZ | Suzuki | 26 | 51m 27.17s | 1m 35.47s | 34 |
| 17 | Dave Griffith | GB | Suzuki | 26 | 51m 32.41s | 1m 36.89s | 38 |
| 18 | Mike Baldwin | USA | Yamaha | 26 | 51m 36.60s | 1m 29.37s | 5 |
| 19 | Manfred Fischer | D | Honda | 26 | 51m 38.13s | 1m 33.80s | 25 |
| 20 | Barry Woodland | GB | Suzuki | 25 | 51m 38.55s | 1m 35.79s | 37 |
| 21 | Steve Manley | GB | Suzuki | 25 | 51m 52.75s | 1m 35.42s | 33 |
| 22 | Alan Jeffery | GB | Suzuki | 25 | 52m 56.98s | 1m 34.84s | 30 |
| 23 | Helmut Schütz | D | Honda | 23 | 52m 50.96s | 1m 38.72s | 40 |
| | Gary Lingham | GB | Suzuki | 22 | DNF | 1m 35.12s | 31 |
| | Chris Bürki | CH | Honda | 19 | DNF | 1m 37.96s | 39 |
| | Christian le Liard | F | Elf | 14 | DNF | 1m 33.66s | 23 |
| | Dennis Ireland | NZ | Suzuki | 14 | DNF | 1m 34.74s | 29 |
| | Henny Boerman | NL | Assmex | 13 | DNF | 1m 35.72s | 36 |
| | Juan Garriga | E | Cagiva | 13 | DNF | 1m 32.51s | 16 |
| | Mile Pajic | NL | Honda | 10 | DNF | 1m 33.73s | 24 |
| | Simon Buckmaster | GB | Honda | 10 | DNF | 1m 33.24s | 20 |
| | Fabio Biliotti | I | Honda | 8 | DNF | 1m 33.51s | 22 |
| | Trevor Nation | GB | Suzuki | 7 | DNF | 1m 34.02s | 26 |
| | Christian Sarron | F | Yamaha | 7 | DNF | 1m 29.15s | 4 |
| | Shunji Yatsushiro | J | Honda | 6 | DNF | 1m 31.45s | 11 |
| | Marco Gentile | CH | Fior | 6 | DNF | 1m 34.66s | 28 |
| | Roger Marshall | GB | Honda | 4 | DNF | 1m 31.94s | 12 |
| | Lars Johansson | A | Suzuki | 2 | DNF | 1m 40.26s | 41 |
| | Paul Lewis | AUS | Suzuki | | DNS | 1m 31.00s | 10 |
| | Dave Petersen | ZIM | Suzuki | | DNS | 1m 32.41s | 15 |
| | Pier Francesco Chili | I | Suzuki | | DNS | 1m 32.69s | 17 |

*Fastest lap:* Gardner, 1m 44.21s, 101.11 mph/162.69 km/h.
*Lap record:* Kenny Roberts, USA (Yamaha), 1m 28.20s, 119.47 mph/192.27 km/h (1983).

**World Championship: 1** Lawson, 109; **2** Gardner, 93; **3** Mamola, 92; **4** Baldwin, 60; **5** Sarron, 53; **6** McElnea, 52; **7** de Radigues, 33; **8** Roche, 23; **9** Haslam, 14; **10** Chili, 11; **11** van Dulmen, 8; **12** Yatsushiro, 7; **13** Biliotti, Reiner and Petersen, 5; **16** Garriga, Lewis and MacKenzie, 4; **19** Burnett, Pajic and Irons, 3; **22** Papa, Schwantz and von Muralt, 1.

## 250 cc

**24 laps, 70.25 miles/113.06 km**

| Place | Rider | Nat. | Machine | Laps | Time & speed | Practice time | Grid |
|---|---|---|---|---|---|---|---|
| 1 | Dominique Sarron | F | Honda | 24 | 44m 41.76s 94.30 mph/ 151.74 km/h | 1m 34.42s | 9 |
| 2 | Carlos Lavado | YV | Yamaha | 24 | 44m 57.21s | 1m 31.50s | 1 |
| 3 | Alfonso Pons | E | Honda | 24 | 45m 02.87s | 1m 33.07s | 3 |
| 4 | Reinhold Roth | D | Honda | 24 | 45m 04.40s | 1m 34.98s | 18 |
| 5 | Carlos Cardus | E | Honda | 24 | 45m 12.51s | 1m 35.44s | 23 |
| 6 | Virginio Ferrari | I | Honda | 24 | 45m 15.28s | 1m 36.87s | 39 |
| 7 | Jean-Michel Mattioli | F | Yamaha | 24 | 45m 35.82s | 1m 34.62s | 10 |
| 8 | Stéphane Mertens | B | Yamaha | 24 | 45m 47.28s | 1m 34.92s | 16 |
| 9 | Martin Wimmer | D | Yamaha | 24 | 45m 57.12s | 1m 32.34s | 2 |
| 10 | Niall MacKenzie | GB | Armstrong | 24 | 46m 18.74s | 1m 35.43s | 22 |
| 11 | Carl Fogarty | GB | Yamaha | 23 | 44m 54.17s | 1m 36.27s | 31 |
| 12 | Maurizio Vitali | I | Garelli | 23 | 44m 58.36s | 1m 34.31s | 7 |
| 13 | Osamu Hiwatashi | J | Honda | 23 | 45m 00.42s | 1m 36.15s | 29 |
| 14 | Jean Foray | F | Chevallier | 23 | 45m 27.25s | 1m 35.99s | 26 |
| 15 | Donnie McLeod | GB | Armstrong | 23 | 45m 32.54s | 1m 36.18s | 30 |
| 16 | Herbert Besendörfer | D | Yamaha | 23 | 46m 33.61s | 1m 36.53s | 36 |
| 17 | Gary Cowan | GB | Honda | 23 | 46m 33.75s | 1m 35.85s | 25 |
| 18 | Harald Eckl | D | Honda | 22 | 45m 22.31s | 1m 34.26s | 6 |
| 19 | René Délaby | B | Morena | 22 | 46m 06.40s | 1m 37.03s | 40 |
| 20 | Jean-Louis Guignabodet | F | MIG | 22 | 46m 16.17s | 1m 35.37s | 21 |
| 21 | Steve Chambers | GB | Yamaha | 21 | 45m 23.26s | 1m 36.62s | 37 |
| 22 | Rob Orme | GB | Yamaha | 21 | 45m 52.23s | 1m 36.41s | 35 |
| | Alan Carter | GB | Kobas | 23 | DNF | 1m 36.03s | 27 |
| | Gary Noel | GB | EMC | 17 | DNF | 1m 34.63s | 11 |
| | Tadahiko Taira | J | Yamaha | 16 | DNF | 1m 34.74s | 14 |
| | Nigel Bosworth | GB | Yamaha | 14 | DNF | 1m 36.41s | 34 |
| | Jean-Louis Tournadre | F | Yamaha | 10 | DNF | 1m 34.41s | 8 |
| | Fausto Ricci | I | Honda | 9 | DNF | 1m 36.09s | 28 |
| | Mar Schouten | NL | Honda | 9 | DNF | 1m 36.35s | 32 |
| | Jean-François Baldé | F | Honda | 8 | DNF | 1m 34.22s | 5 |
| | Anton Mang | D | Honda | 7 | DNF | 1m 34.96s | 17 |
| | Siegfried Minich | A | Honda | 7 | DNF | 1m 34.69s | 13 |
| | Christian Boudinot | F | Kobas | 6 | DNF | 1m 35.48s | 24 |
| | Peter Hubbard | GB | Rotax | 5 | DNF | 1m 36.65s | 38 |
| | Loris Reggiani | I | Aprilia | 5 | DNF | 1m 35.24s | 19 |
| | Jacques Cornu | CH | Honda | 4 | DNF | 1m 34.66s | 12 |
| | Hans Becker | D | Yamaha | 3 | DNF | 1m 37.05s | 41 |
| | Roland Freymond | CH | Yamaha | 1 | DNF | 1m 35.30s | 20 |
| | Stefano Caracchi | I | Aprilia | 1 | DNF | 1m 34.87s | 15 |
| | Pierre Bolle | F | Parisienne | 0 | DNF | 1m 33.17s | 4 |
| | Bruno Bonhuil | F | Honda | | DNS | 1m 36.36s | 33 |
| | Kevin Mitchell | GB | Yamaha | | DNQ | 1m 37.10s | |
| | Ian Newton | GB | Honda | | DNQ | 1m 37.19s | |
| | Cees Doorakkers | NL | Honda | | DNQ | 1m 37.66s | |
| | Philippe Pagano | F | Yamaha | | DNQ | 1m 37.71s | |
| | Guy Bertin | F | Rotax | | DNQ | 1m 38.06s | |
| | Massimo Matteoni | I | Honda | | DNQ | 1m 38.20s | |
| | Darren Dixon | GB | Honda | | DNQ | 1m 38.20s | |
| | Eric de Donker | B | Honda | | DNQ | 1m 39.18s | |
| | Gerard van der Wal | NL | Assmex | | DNQ | 1m 39.78s | |
| | Tony Head | GB | Armstrong | | DNQ | 1m 39.83s | |
| | Steve Patrickson | GB | Rotax | | DNQ | 1m 40.10s | |
| | Keith Huewen | GB | EMC | | DNQ | 1m 40.15s | |

*Fastest lap:* Carter, 1m 49.24s, 96.45 mph/155.19 km/h.
*Lap record:* Christian Sarron, F (Yamaha), 1m 33.40s, 112.81 mph/181.55 km/h (1984).

**World Championship: 1** Lavado, 99; **2** Pons, 84; **3** Mang, 57; **4** Sarron, 56; **5** Baldé, 53; **6** Wimmer, 51; **7** Cornu, 28; **8** McLeod, 27; **9** Ricci, 24; **10** Bolle, 19; **11** Cardus, 17; **12** Taira, 13; **13** Ferrari, 11; **14** Roth, 10; **15** Carter and Mertens, 8; **17** Herweh, 7; **18** Mattioli, 5; **19** Vitali, Foray and MacKenzie, 4; **22** Matteoni and Minich, 2; **24** Lindner, 1.

**Irons, MacKenzie and Haslam splash round the soaking Silverstone track.**

## 125 cc

**20 laps, 58.54 miles/94.22 km**

| Place | Rider | Nat. | Machine | Laps | Time & speed | Practice time | Grid |
|---|---|---|---|---|---|---|---|
| 1 | August Auinger | A | Bartol | 20 | 38m 54.57s 90.27 mph/ 145.26 km/h | 1m 38.43s | 3 |
| 2 | Domenico Brigaglia | I | Ducados | 20 | 39m 03.55s | 1m 40.12s | 7 |
| 3 | Luca Cadalora | I | Garelli | 20 | 39m 06.28s | 1m 38.34s | 2 |
| 4 | Johnny Wickström | SF | Tunturi | 20 | 39m 14.74s | 1m 41.20s | 10 |
| 5 | Lucio Pietroniro | B | MBA | 20 | 39m 25.48s | 1m 41.45s | 16 |
| 6 | Willy Perez | RA | Zanella | 20 | 39m 25.67s | 1m 42.34s | 22 |
| 7 | Jussi Hautaniemi | SF | MBA | 20 | 39m 32.26s | 1m 42.05s | 18 |
| 8 | Olivier Liegeois | B | Assmex | 20 | 39m 44.33s | 1m 40.65s | 8 |
| 9 | Ezio Gianola | I | MBA | 20 | 39m 46.21s | 1m 38.97s | 4 |
| 10 | Pier Paolo Bianchi | I | Elit | 20 | 39m 46.69s | 1m 41.59s | 17 |
| 11 | Hakan Olsson | S | Starol | 20 | 40m 14.05s | 1m 42.26s | 21 |
| 12 | Alfred Waibel | D | Real | 20 | 40m 30.97s | 1m 41.39s | 15 |
| 13 | Jacques Hutteau | F | MBA | 20 | 40m 54.50s | 1m 41.21s | 11 |
| 14 | Wilhelm Lücke | D | MBA | 19 | 38m 55.56s | 1m 42.69s | 25 |
| 15 | Jean-Claude Selini | F | MBA | 19 | 39m 38.26s | 1m 42.49s | 24 |
| 16 | Mick McGarrity | IRL | MBA | 19 | 39m 49.08s | 1m 45.30s | 36 |
| 17 | Ton Spek | NL | MBA | 19 | 40m 01.32s | 1m 44.65s | 33 |
| 18 | Fernando Gonzalez | E | MBA | 19 | 40m 38.58s | 1m 45.08s | 35 |
| 19 | David Read | GB | MBA | 18 | 39m 59.16s | 1m 46.45s | 38 |
| 20 | Boy van Erp | NL | MBA | 18 | 40m 20.50s | 1m 42.82s | 27 |
| | Bady Hassaine | DZ | MBA | 16 | DNF | 1m 46.67s | 39 |
| | Jan Eggens | NL | LCR | 13 | DNF | 1m 42.99s | 28 |
| | Shaun Simpson | GB | MBA | 13 | DNF | 1m 46.69s | 40 |
| | Thierry Feuz | CH | LCR | 11 | DNF | 1m 39.54s | 6 |
| | Marin Andreas Sanchez | E | Ducados | 11 | DNF | 1m 42.24s | 20 |
| | Jamie Whitham | GB | MBA | 10 | DNF | 1m 41.31s | 13 |
| | Ivan Troisi | YV | MBA | 9 | DNF | 1m 42.73s | 26 |
| | Patrick Daudier | F | PMDF | 8 | DNF | 1m 44.73s | 34 |
| | Thierry Maurer | CH | MBA | 7 | DNF | 1m 44.58s | 32 |
| | Robin Milton | GB | MBA | 6 | DNF | 1m 42.07s | 19 |
| | Fausto Gresini | I | Garelli | 5 | DNF | 1m 39.32s | 5 |
| | Angel Nieto | E | Ducados | 5 | DNF | 1m 41.11s | 9 |
| | Paolo Casoli | I | MBA | 4 | DNF | 1m 41.22s | 12 |
| | Anton Straver | NL | MBA | 2 | DNF | 1m 41.34s | 14 |
| | Esa Kytola | SF | MBA | 2 | DNF | 1m 43.41s | 29 |
| | David Lowe | GB | MBA | 2 | DNF | 1m 42.36s | 23 |
| | Dirk Hafeneger | D | LCR | 1 | DNF | 1m 44.57s | 31 |
| | Eric Gijsel | B | MBA | 1 | DNF | 1m 43.58s | 30 |
| | Bruno Kneubühler | CH | LCR | 0 | DNF | 1m 37.69s | 1 |
| | Giuseppe Ascareggi | I | Elit | 0 | DNF | 1m 46.01s | 37 |
| | Gary Buckle | GB | MBA | | DNQ | 1m 46.93s | |
| | Allan Scott | USA | EMC | | DNQ | 1m 46.94s | |
| | Steve Mason | GB | MBA | | DNQ | 1m 47.48s | |
| | Ken Beckett | GB | MBA | | DNQ | 1m 48.47s | |
| | Tim Salveson | GB | MBA | | DNQ | 1m 49.54s | |

*Fastest lap:* Auinger, 1m 52.17s, 93.93 mph/151.13 km/h.
*Lap record:* Angel Nieto, E (Garelli), 1m 38.41s, 107.07 mph/172.31 km/h (1984).

**World Championship: 1** Cadalora, 86; **2** Gresini, 74; **3** Brigaglia, 59; **4** Gianola, 49; **5** Auinger, 35; **6** Kneubühler, 32; **7** Pietroniro, 31; **8** Bianchi, 27; **9** Wickström and Perez, 26; **11** Liegeois, 18; **12** Nieto and Feuz, 15; **14** Casoli, 10; **15** Hautaniemi, 8; **16** Grassetti and Waibel, 5; **18** Sanchez, 3; **19** Kytola, 2; **20** Olsson and Stadler, 1.

## 80 cc

**15 laps, 43.91 miles/70.67 km**

| Place | Rider | Nat. | Machine | Laps | Time & speed | Practice time | Grid |
|---|---|---|---|---|---|---|---|
| 1 | Ian McConnachie | GB | Krauser | 15 | 26m 20.70s 99.99 mph/ 160.90 km/h | 1m 44.88s | 4 |
| 2 | Stefan Dörflinger | CH | Krauser | 15 | 26m 21.09s | 1m 43.14s | 1 |
| 3 | Jorge Martinez | E | Derbi | 15 | 26m 41.01s | 1m 43.80s | 2 |
| 4 | Manuel Herreros | E | Derbi | 15 | 26m 41.17s | 1m 46.63s | 8 |
| 5 | Hans Spaan | NL | Huvo | 15 | 26m 41.59s | 1m 44.59s | 3 |
| 6 | Gerhard Waibel | D | Real | 15 | 27m 15.21s | 1m 46.24s | 6 |
| 7 | Gerd Kafka | A | Krauser | 15 | 27m 17.36s | 1m 47.23s | 9 |
| 8 | Alexandre Barros | BR | Autisa | 15 | 27m 25.36s | 1m 47.56s | 11 |
| 9 | Wilco Zeelenberg | NL | Huvo | 15 | 27m 35.34s | 1m 49.30s | 10 |
| 10 | Domingo Gil | E | Autisa | 15 | 27m 35.49s | 1m 49.55s | 19 |
| 11 | Rainer Kunz | D | Ziegler | 15 | 27m 42.95s | 1m 49.49s | 18 |
| 12 | Reiner Scheidhauer | D | Seel | 15 | 27m 47.42s | 1m 48.00s | 13 |
| 13 | Francisco Torontegui | E | Kobas | 15 | 27m 47.60s | 1m 50.44s | 21 |
| 14 | Chris Baert | B | Seel | 14 | 26m 27.40s | 1m 48.65s | 17 |
| 15 | Gunter Schirnhöfer | D | Krauser | 14 | 26m 28.54s | 1m 51.13s | 23 |
| 16 | Jos van Dongen | NL | Krauser | 14 | 26m 36.66s | 1m 50.32s | 20 |
| 17 | Jamie Whitham | GB | Wicks | 14 | 26m 36.88s | 1m 53.76s | 31 |
| 18 | Stefan Brägger | CH | Huvo | 14 | 26m 36.90s | 1m 52.76s | 28 |
| 19 | Felix Rodriguez | E | Autisa | 14 | 26m 42.74s | 1m 48.50s | 15 |
| 20 | Thomas Engl | D | ESCH | 14 | 27m 16.43s | 1m 53.41s | 30 |
| 21 | Aad Wijsman | NL | Special | 14 | 27m 17.13s | 1m 52.98s | 29 |
| 22 | Steve Lawton | GB | Eberhardt | 14 | 27m 25.36s | 1m 54.80s | 34 |
| 23 | Dennis Batchelor | GB | Krauser | 14 | 27m 54.58s | 1m 57.90s | 35 |
| 24 | Richard Bay | D | Ziegler | 14 | 28m 34.73s | 1m 51.89s | 26 |
| 25 | Steve Dale | GB | Huvo | 13 | 26m 23.04s | 1m 58.43s | 36 |
| | René Dünki | CH | Krauser | 13 | DNF | 1m 52.62s | 27 |
| | Bertus Grinwis | NL | Krauser | 12 | DNF | 1m 54.01s | 32 |
| | Luis Reyes | COL | Autisa | 10 | DNF | 1m 46.45s | 7 |
| | Kees Besseling | NL | PM | 10 | DNF | 1m 51.55s | 24 |
| | Henk van Kessel | NL | Krauser | 6 | DNF | 1m 47.60s | 12 |
| | Juan Bolart | E | Autisa | 6 | DNF | 1m 50.49s | 22 |
| | Stuart Edwards | GB | Huvo | 3 | DNF | 2m 03.61s | 37 |
| | Steve Mason | GB | Huvo | 2 | DNF | 1m 54.50s | 33 |
| | Theo Timmer | NL | Huvo | 1 | DNF | 1m 48.53s | 16 |
| | Reiner Koster | CH | LCR | 1 | DNF | 1m 51.88s | 25 |
| | Angel Nieto | E | Derbi | 0 | DNF | 1m 45.71s | 5 |
| | Josef Fischer | A | Krauser | 0 | DNF | 1m 48.24s | 14 |
| | John Cresswell | GB | Lusuardi | | DNQ | 2m 06.53s | |

*Fastest lap:* Dörflinger, 1m 43.13s, 102.17 mph/164.39 km/h (record).
*No previous record.*

**World Championship: 1** Martinez, 82; **2** Herreros, 67; **3** Dörflinger, 65; **4** McConnachie, 46; **5** Nieto and Spaan, 39; **7** Waibel, 34; **8** Bianchi, 29; **9** Fischer, 13; **10** Kafka, 9; **11** Bolart and Kunz, 6; **13** Gil and Timmer, 5; **15** Abold, van Kessel, Rodriguez and Barros, 3; **19** Reyes and Zeelenberg, 2; **21** Milano, 1.

**The crowd were thrilled by the effort put in by Steve Webster and Tony Hewitt as they did their best to keep ahead of Egbert Streuer and Bernie Schnieders. However, the Dutchmen triumphed yet again in the race they have made their own.**

## Sidecars

**20 laps, 58.54 miles/94.22 km**

| Place | Driver and passenger | Nat. | Machine | Laps | Time & speed | Practice time | Grid |
|---|---|---|---|---|---|---|---|
| 1 | Egbert Streuer/ Bernie Schnieders | NL NL | LCR– Yamaha | 20 | 31m 14.83s 112.40 mph/ 180.88 km/h | 1m 31.00s | 2 |
| 2 | Steve Webster/ Tony Hewitt | GB GB | LCR– Yamaha | 20 | 31m 16.05s | 1m 31.89s | 3 |
| 3 | Markus Egloff/ Urs Egloff | CH CH | LCR– Yamaha | 20 | 31m 38.15s | 1m 32.28s | 5 |
| 4 | Alfred Zurbrügg/ Martin Zurbrügg | CH CH | LCR– Yamaha | 20 | 31m 40.65s | 1m 33.33s | 6 |
| 5 | Masato Kumano/ Helmut Diehl | J D | LCR– Yamaha | 20 | 31m 51.15s | 1m 34.31s | 8 |
| 6 | Derek Jones/ Brian Ayres | GB GB | LCR– Yamaha | 20 | 31m 59.83s | 1m 34.59s | 9 |
| 7 | Frank Wrathall/ Kerry Chapman | GB GB | LCR– Yamaha | 20 | 32m 00.17s | 1m 34.62s | 11 |
| 8 | Graham Gleeson/ Ian Colquhoun | NZ GB | LCR– Yamaha | 20 | 32m 16.36s | 1m 34.63s | 12 |
| 9 | René Progin/ Yves Hunziker | CH CH | Seymaz– Yamaha | 20 | 32m 27.44s | 1m 35.04s | 13 |
| 10 | Mick Barton/ Graham Rose | GB GB | LCR– Yamaha | 20 | 32m 31.41s | 1m 36.66s | 21 |
| 11 | Rolf Steinhausen/ Bruno Hiller | D D | Busch | 20 | 32m 34.93s | 1m 35.54s | 17 |
| 12 | Dennis Bingham/ Julia Bingham | GB GB | LCR– Yamaha | 19 | 31m 15.09s | 1m 36.55s | 20 |
| 13 | Bernd Scherer/ Wolfgang Gess | D D | BSR– Yamaha | 19 | 31m 19.81s | 1m 35.27s | 14 |
| 14 | Wolfgang Stropek/ Hans-Peter Demling | A A | LCR– Yamaha | 19 | 31m 26.48s | 1m 35.36s | 16 |
| 15 | Lowry Burton/ Geoff Leitch | GB GB | Ironside– Yamaha | 19 | 31m 35.24s | 1m 37.87s | 23 |
| 16 | Werner Kraus/ Bernd Schuster | D D | Busch– Yamaha | 19 | 31m 55.77s | 1m 38.90s | 29 |
| 17 | Clive Stirrat/ Simon Prior | GB GB | BLR– Yamaha | 19 | 32m 16.19s | 1m 38.69s | 27 |
| 18 | Gary Thomas/ Geoff White | GB GB | LCR– Yamaha | 19 | 32m 52.37s | 1m 38.46s | 26 |
| 19 | John Evans/ Geoff Wilbraham | GB GB | LCR– Yamaha | 18 | 31m 20.69s | 1m 38.74s | 28 |
| | Dave Hallam/ Mark Day | GB GB | LCR– Yamaha | 14 | DNF | 1m 38.30s | 25 |
| | Ray Gardner/ Tony Strevens | GB GB | LCR– Yamaha | 12 | DNF | 1m 38.29s | 24 |
| | Derek Bayley/ Bryan Nixon | GB GB | LCR– Ricardo | 8 | DNF | 1m 34.06s | 7 |
| | Alain Michel/ Jean-Marc Fresc | F F | Krauser– Yamaha | 7 | DNF | 1m 31.98s | 4 |
| | Barry Brindley/ Chris Jones | GB GB | Windle– Yamaha | 6 | DNF | 1m 35.80s | 18 |
| | Mick Boddice/ Don Williams | GB GB | LCR– Yamaha | 4 | DNF | 1m 35.97s | 19 |
| | Christian Graf/ Rudolf Ammann | CH CH | LCR– Yamaha | 3 | DNF | 1m 39.29s | 30 |
| | Yoshisada Kumagaya/ Kazuhiko Makiuchi | J J | LCR– Yamaha | 1 | DNF | 1m 37.36s | 22 |
| | Rolf Biland/ Kurt Waltisperg | CH CH | Krauser | 1 | DNF | 1m 30.35s | 1 |
| | Theo van Kempen/ Gerardus de Haas | NL NL | LCR– Yamaha | 1 | DNF | 1m 35.34s | 15 |
| | Steve Abbott/ Vince Biggs | GB GB | Windle– Yamaha | 0 | DNF | 1m 34.62s | 10 |
| | Benny Lysen/ Ole Möller | DK DK | BLR– Yamaha | | DNQ | 1m 39.61s | |
| | Alfred Weber/ Harald Schneidewind | D D | LCR– Yamaha | | DNQ | 1m 39.72s | |
| | Judd Drew/ Dave Elliott | GB GB | BLR– Yamaha | | DNQ | 1m 40.64s | |
| | Warwick Newman/ Eddie Yarker | GB GB | Ireson– Yamaha | | DNQ | 1m 41.29s | |
| | Stewart Rich/ Steve Groves | GB GB | | | DNQ | 1m 41.91s | |
| | Dennis Holmes/ Steve Bagnall | GB GB | LCR– Yamaha | | DNQ | 1m 43.04s | |
| | Axel von Berg/ Eckart Rösinger | D D | Busch– Yamaha | | DNQ | 1m 44.73s | |

*Fastest lap:* Streuer, 1m 31.64s, 114.98 mph/185.00 km/h (record).
*Previous record:* Rolf Biland/Kurt Waltisperg (LCR–Yamaha), 1m 32.01s, 114.52 mph/184.30 km/h (1984).

**World Championship: 1** Webster 61; **2** Streuer, 60; **3** Michel, 54; **4** Egloff 37; **5** Abbott and Zurbrügg, 30; **7** Kumano, 27; **8** Jones, 21; **9** Biland, 20; **10** Steinhausen, 10; **11** Bayley, 9; **12** Progin and Barton, 7; **14** Brindley, van Kempen and Wrathall, 5; **17** Gleeson, 4; **18** Scherer, 3; **19** Kumagaya, 1.

# SWEDISH
## TT

It is a long haul to Anderstorp from Silverstone and there's a variety of routes to choose from. You can cross the Channel by the shortest route, Dover to Calais, and drive from France through Belgium, Holland, Germany and Denmark, with two short ferry journeys to bring you into Sweden. Variations on the long-drive route can be to replace the Danish section by a ferry crossing to southern Sweden from Germany, or by using one of the England to Holland ferry services. But the most relaxing way is to take the ferry from Harwich to Göteborg, leaving just a short drive in Sweden, to Gislaved. The 24-hour crossing provides a rare opportunity for mechanics, riders and others to enjoy a chat between races with no work to do.

There was much talk of the British Grand Prix, the weather and the hope that things would be better in Scandinavia. There were signs of an improvement at Anderstorp as the paddock assembled in what is still more like a rough clearing in a pine forest with an airstrip than an international racing circuit.

Eddie Lawson was reflecting on the British Grand Prix. 'My brain wasn't in gear to go fast. All I kept thinking was "you'd better not screw up or they'll xxx you". It's hard going round like that; it's easier to be behind so that you have to go out and go for it. Wayne will be going for the win here. I don't know what I will do in the race; it depends on the start a bit and how Wayne rides. If he sets it on maniac – and I wouldn't blame him if he did – it might be better to keep clear. I still have to think of the championship.'

There were many people thinking of championships as all were at a crucial stage, not least the sidecars whose title race had turned round at Silverstone as leader Alain Michel failed to score and was overhauled by Streuer and Webster. After the bitter disappointment in Britain Michel was trying to be philosophical about things in Sweden. 'I would rather be second or third in the championship than be World Champion just because the others broke down. Egbert should be champion because he is the best but of course if I won I would not be stupid enough to be sorry about it, but it will be very difficult from here. I will just try and go as fast as I can and see what happens.'

Fellow Frenchman Alain Chevallier was hard at work trying to make his three-cylinder Honda handle after a year-long battle in which everything had come under suspicion – the frame, the tyres and the rider. The frame was altered before the French Grand Prix to include an adjustable steering head angle and during practice at Silverstone the team had tried a suspension measuring system that recorded suspension travel both front and rear as the machine was ridden round the circuit. The results traced out on a pen recorder showed how the suspension was responding but a few problems with the stability of the trace made the results difficult to read; while in theory the system can offer a great deal it requires more development.

Carlos Lavado continued on his precarious road towards the championship and crashed the HB Yamaha on Thursday afternoon. Once more

he was lucky to escape unhurt and good fortune looked set to shine on him long enough to help the Venezuelan to his second world title. The cause of the accident was a seized gearbox. Lavado had stopped at the pits when it locked for the first time but when nothing seemed to be wrong he thought he must have caused the slide and went out again, only to be thrown up the road when the gearbox nipped again.

Randy Mamola, on the other hand, seems fated always to have enough bad luck to keep him from being champion. His practice crash at Silverstone was going to affect him through to the end of the season, despite the fact that he had enlisted the help of Willi Dungl who had aided Niki Lauda's recovery after his near-fatal Nürburgring crash. Mamola missed Thursday's practice as he was receiving treatment and the doctor came to the circuit to keep up the work through the weekend. Dungl practised a special form of treatment developed in China that worked on pressure points to relieve pain. It still meant that Mamola considered the championship a lost cause. 'I'm not worried about winning here; I'm just going to have to ride out the season and wait till next year.'

Practice for the 500s started in the dry on Thursday afternoon but after a few minutes it began to rain so only those who had attacked early got good times and Raymond Roche headed the leaderboard from Wayne Gardner, Eddie Lawson and Ron Haslam. A dry track on Friday morning saw everyone go much quicker and Lawson took the lead from Gardner, Baldwin and McElnea. However, the surprise was Niall MacKenzie who sat in fifth place, ahead of Roche, Haslam, de Radigues and Mamola.

MacKenzie had become very much the star performer in the Skoal Bandit team after Silverstone and as Lewis was too sore to ride from the broken bones in his foot, MacKenzie had two bikes to work with. The third machine was given to Paul Iddon for the weekend. Iddon who had just finished second in the Formula 1 championship had a ride on the 500 as part of his contract agreement. He needed to get accustomed to riding a 500 again and was 18th-fastest after the first dry session.

MacKenzie was certainly impressive and the team obviously had the reed-valve engine working well after a good deal of experimentation with special reed-valve boxes, crankcase stuffers and much-modified inlet tracts. Ex-Suzuki rider Rob McElnea warned MacKenzie that if he slipstreamed the Yamaha down the main straight and outbraked him into the following corner he would never speak to the Scotsman again.

In fact McElnea had his arch-rival Baldwin to worry about, for the Silverstone result had made it possible for McElnea to take fourth in the championship if both Baldwin and Sarron failed to score. Sarron was not in Sweden because his elbow needed an operation but Baldwin was there and faster in practice.

Friday afternoon was exciting as it saw Gardner take pole even though Lawson also went quicker. McElnea also found some extra speed to move into third place as he and Baldwin improved their times, both maintaining that they

could go faster still in the next session. Baldwin explained that his best bike had been playing up since Silverstone and McElnea said that he could find perhaps another second in the last session because he had ruined the practice tyre too soon. 'I was trying hard and kept getting baulked by other riders. I got a bit wound up and ruined the tyre before I got a clear run. If I get it right tomorrow I think it is possible to get into the 35s.'

A big effort from Roche put him in front of MacKenzie in that third session notwithstanding the Scot's improved time. The weather ruined the final session for the 500s on Saturday so Gardner hung on to pole from Lawson, McElnea, Baldwin, Roche and MacKenzie. Ron Haslam was seventh-fastest on the Elf. In that wet final session Mamola was quickest, indicating that he might still present a threat in the race despite his ninth-place grid position. 'I'm feeling better all the time', declared Mamola. 'I've been trying not to

NGK TÄNDSTIFT  NGK TÄNDSTIFT  NGK TÄNDSTIFT  NGK TÄNDSTIFT  NGK

AGP

ÄMPARE

Atlas

Gardner chased Lawson as hard as he could but in the end the choice was between settling for second or risking a crash.

do too much because it gets inflamed again but it should be all right for the race.'

MacKenzie was just as impressive on the 250 Armstrong, second-quickest behind Lavado in the first session, with team-mate Donnie McLeod third ahead of Wimmer and Mang. He moved to the top of the table after the second session only to be relegated to second on Friday as Wimmer found the fastest line. Then in the final session the Scot slipped to fourth as Lavado and Vitali went quicker. McLeod moved himself back into fifth place and the Armstrong pair pointed out that their bikes were more competitive than usual because the circuit meant little time was spent in fifth and sixth gear where they normally lose out badly.

Wimmer was glad to be on pole again and was the only other rider to take pole positions apart from Lavado. The Venezuelan's tally for the season so far stood at six: Germany, Austria, Yugosla-

via, Holland, Belgium and Britain. Wimmer's four were in Spain, Italy, France and now Sweden. Wimmer knew that grid positions did not count for much at the end of the day. 'I have to prove that I can win races and not just set the fastest lap in practice. I haven't got much time left so I have to do well here. Since Silverstone I feel that at least I can get the bike started. I wanted another pole position though so I was watching the lap times in that last session not sure if I should go out again. Luckily I didn't have to. If I can't be champion, and I can't now, then Carlos certainly deserves it.'

The competition in the sidecar class was obviously going to be between the four great names – Biland, Streuer, Michel and Webster – but the Swiss ex-champion was still having engine problems and the outfit stopped just two laps into the second session after he had been fastest in the first outing. The third and fourth

periods were better, with Biland fastest both times and ending up on pole position ahead of Streuer, Michel and Webster.

August Auinger dominated 125 training, starting off a second quicker than Gianola and Cadalora and continued to be fastest in the wet second session. Although the opposition went faster in the third session he was able to shave a fraction off his time which put him on pole because the final session was wet again. It was impressive to see him fastest in all sessions in such varying conditions. He had to be firm favourite for the race even though Ezio Gianola ended up only just over one-tenth slower, with Bruno Kneubühler third.

### 250 cc

Here was one of those races that either 'sorts the men from the boys', or just depends on a lucky

Cadalora, Gresini and Brigaglia ensured there was Italian domination of the 125 race.

Despite the rain blowing across the track Lavado kept going faster.

The use of the chequered flag to bring an early end to the 250 race proved controversial.

choice of tyres, according to your point of view. In truth, whichever tyres a rider chose for Saturday's race they would have been right for about a quarter of the distance and wrong the rest of the time. Carlos Lavado had made several mistakes throughout the year but when it came to the season's most difficult conditions as his championship hung in the balance, he was superb and looked easily capable of winning the race had it finished in snow and sleet.

The track was damp and spots of rain had started to fall again after a break in the clouds had threatened to dry the track when the field swept off the line. Lavado soon claimed the lead ahead of Stéphane Mertens, Sito Pons, Jean-Michel Mattioli and Martin Wimmer.

Lavado was using a cut slick on the rear and an intermediate Michelin on the front so he knew they would warm up quickly and work well on a track that was barely wet. He was soon extending his lead over Mertens, who likewise pulled away from the third-place group headed by Siggi Minich. The latter had come through from seventh on lap 1 to lead the group from Maurizio Vitali (who had been 11th) and Mattioli and Baldé. Wimmer had dropped right down to the rear, the result of an excursion at the end of the back straight on lap 1, and the same reason had dropped Pons to 11th. A lap later Mattioli also ran off the track and went to the tail of the field while Wimmer tried to make his way up from 21st.

Lavado continued unobstructed as the battle behind changed players all the time, with Baldé joining Minich and Mertens in a fight for second but obviously having a speed advantage over the two privateers along the back straight. By lap 5 he had got away from them and as the track continued to dry a little his slick tyres front and rear started to be the most appropriate, enabling him to close on Lavado.

The Venezuelan knew that he had to be careful or he would destroy the intermediate on the front and tear up the cut slick rear which had to last the 25-lap race. Lavado knew that Baldé could not threaten his championship position and was not concerned when Baldé took the lead on lap 7. Lavado held a secure second ahead of Minich while Mertens had dropped back to be embroiled in a fourth-place battle with Stefano Caracchi on the Aprilia, Vitali, and Pons, who had been working his way forward since that early mistake.

Baldé was extending his lead and by lap 10 Pons was up to third with his slick rear and intermediate front tyres. He closed rapidly on Lavado and this was more crucial to the championship, but Lavado, determined not to make another mistake, let Pons past. As Pons overtook Lavado on lap 13 it started to rain again and Baldé ran into problems with his slick tyres.

As Baldé was forced to ease off, Pons quickly caught the Frenchman, being more sure at least that his front tyre would not slide away uncontrollably, and prepared to risk a slide from the slick rear. Lap 16 saw Pons threaten Baldé for the lead, with Lavado now a distant third being caught by an aggressive Virginio Ferrari who had passed Vitali. Tony Mang had been improving after a poor first half but then fell, as did Caracchi. The rain made the circuit suddenly very slippery indeed and Gary Noel and Harald Eckl also disappeared at the same time. Ferrari fell as well and seized the oil flag to warn other riders that the last right-hander onto the start-and-finish straight was very dangerous.

With the circuit decidedly wet Lavado found his choice of tyres correct once more and started to close on Baldé who was doing well to keep his bike on two wheels. Amazingly, he had beaten off the attack from Pons who was himself caught and passed by Lavado on lap 19. By this time there was a new name in fourth place, Dominique Sarron, who had started well down at the bottom of the top 20 but had cautiously worked his way forward. He passed Vitali and the pair started to pull away from Jacques Cornu who had also been a slow starter and not keen to repeat his wet-weather fall at Silverstone. Cornu had Mertens to contend with as they secured an advantage over Jean Foray on the Chevallier who had passed Minich. The Austrian had the intermediates that should have suited the wet but they had been ruined in the dry section of the race and all Minich could do was try and hold off Alan Carter.

The circuit was getting steadily wetter and Baldé could not keep up his amazing speed. Lavado was back in front by lap 20 and a lap later Pons was passing Baldé to relegate the Frenchman to third, though well ahead of the Vitali/Sarron battle. Guy Bertin, riding as a temporary replacement for the injured Pierre Bolle, fell on lap 23, as did Tadahiko Taira. The Clerk of the Course decided that too many were falling off and decided to stop the race. He hung out the chequered flag after Lavado had gone through to start his 24th lap. In fact, he should have used the red flag to finish the race prematurely. The first result announced after 23 laps was later revised to give the finishing order after 22 laps, including Taira and Bertin as finishers and putting Vitali in front of Sarron.

Following an afternoon and evening of argument, the Clerk of the Course, Jan-Erik Sallqvist, was fined £2000 by the FIM and lost his licence. The first three positions were not really affected by the premature end and Lavado was certainly a deserving winner. He looked a worthier World Champion than he had at any time before.

## 125 cc

August Auinger started from pole position and just maintained his place from Ezio Gianola, Johnny Wickström, Luca Cadalora, Lucio Pietroniro and Fausto Gresini. Willy Perez crashed on lap 2, breaking his wrist, while Cadalora moved into second behind Gianola. It was exciting stuff as Gresini and Wickström rubbed the paint off each other's fairings round the long right-hand loop ending the pit straight.

On lap 2 Gianola took over at the front and Gresini dispensed with Wickström which allowed him to close on the leading trio. Gianola's run at the front ended on lap 4 when he toured into the pit and Auinger returned to the front position by the narrowest of margins from Cadalora and Gresini. The race pace was still down on practice times, however. Behind, Domenico Brigaglia was making up ground lost in a slow start, up to fifth on the fourth lap and closing on Wickström, while Pietroniro tried to hold off Kneubühler who had started 10th.

On the sixth lap Auinger crashed: he was still not riding as hard as in the morning warm-up session and later the front tyre was found to have a poor profile. Fortunately he was unhurt but it left the race to the two Garellis. Cadalora was content to follow Gresini home rather than risk losing his championship lead.

Brigaglia took third on lap 6 and soon secured a comfortable advantage over Kneubühler who had taken both Wickström and Pietroniro. The last two battled together for the next six laps and caught Kneubühler again on lap 13.

Further back, Thierry Feuz had secured seventh after a long struggle with Pier Paolo Bianchi, Adolf Stadler, Hakan Olsson, Marin Andreas Sanchez and Jacques Hutteau. That was the best battle of the race and it carried on to the flag.

Things were more predictable at the front and Cadalora was happy to finish second to Gresini with Brigaglia third. Kneubühler put in an extra effort on the last lap and made use of some backmarkers to beat Pietroniro, while Wickström faded a little in the dying moments.

## 500 cc

Lawson had said that his plans for the race depended on his start and the way that Gardner played it. The start was good and while de Radigues led, the World Champion-elect was second ahead of Gardner, Haslam, Roche and McElnea.

By lap 2 the shape of the race was forming with Lawson leading and Gardner right on his tail. De Radigues on the three-cylinder was holding up Roche on the NSR, McElnea had Baldwin to contend with, while Haslam had slipped to seventh ahead of Biliotti, MacKenzie, van Dulmen, von Muralt and Mamola.

Briefly, things settled to three duos, Lawson/Gardner, de Radigues/Roche and McElnea/Baldwin. By lap 4 the last four names were all fighting for third with Roche leading and McElnea trying to get de Radigues and Roche between himself and Baldwin. The American would have none of it and emerged in front of the group on lap 7 ahead of the Marlboro Yamaha with Roche fifth and de Radigues dropping back on the triple. MacKenzie was up to seventh, Mamola a distant eighth and Haslam held on to ninth despite the failure of the Elf's front suspension unit – it was all he could do to keep the machine on the road.

Lawson's advantage over Gardner remained at less than a second yet it became obvious that, scratch as Gardner might on the brakes and round the corners, the Honda was no match for the Yamaha. Whereas Gardner was on the limit and running wide on occasions, Lawson had no need to dig into his reserves of aggression. Push as Gardner might, he could not force Lawson into making the kind of mistake required to open up the championship once more.

The sidecar race started out as the most exciting battle of the year but witnessed mechanical mayhem as Webster, Biland and Streuer all suffered failures, leaving Michel with the championship lead.

First-bend action from the 500 race *(bottom)*.

There was a similar battle of wits taking place in their tyre tracks. Baldwin's third place fell on lap 16 when McElnea passed the American champion. He held on until lap 22 but was never able to get away as first one and then the other would gain the advantage while lapping back-markers. As he did so, Gardner lost track of Lawson. With his lines spoilt, the Australian had no reply to the Yamaha's speed and, without extending himself, Lawson opened up a lead at a second every lap from lap 16 to 21. The difference then settled down to between four and five seconds for the rest of the race.

The last point was squabbled over for almost the entire race by Wolfgang von Muralt, Marco Gentile and Fabio Biliotti. Biliotti fell unhurt on lap 21 of the 30 and von Muralt ran out of brakes but still managed to secure that valuable tenth from an unlucky Gentile who had his best ride of the season.

McElnea hounded Baldwin to the end without being close enough to make a last-lap passing effort. Roche was fifth and de Radigues came close enough to keep his interest up, so he did not fade as usual towards the end of the race. That meant that MacKenzie had to be satisfied with seventh, despite setting the fifth-fastest lap of the race. Mamola was eighth with his sore shoulder and the last man not to be lapped.

## SIDECARS

Potentially, this was to be the best sidecar race of the year. Alain Michel and Jean-Marc Fresc, Egbert Streuer and Bernard Schneiders, and Steve Webster and Tony Hewitt all had a chance of the World Championship with Rolf Biland and Kurt Waltisperg determined to prove that they

would have been in with chance too had not the Krauser engine proved so dreadfully unreliable.

There were remarkably few retirements in the race, four in total, but two of them were Streuer and Biland. Add to that the fact that Webster completed only 21 of the 23 laps and you can see how the race's potential evaporated.

Michel had thought his chances of winning the championship were a little slim after the disappointments of Silverstone but he was prepared to aim for victory if possible. He reasoned that tyres were going to be a problem late in the race so he was not keen to make the pace. On lap 1 he was third behind Biland and Webster but dropped to fourth as Streuer came past. Fifth was Masato Kumano and Helmut Diehl just ahead of René Progin and Yves Hunziker, Derek Bayley and Bryan Nixon, and Alfred and Martin Zurbrügg, who went off the track before the end of the first lap.

The leading quartet looked like the classic high-speed train – not so much passing at every corner as cat-and-mouse, each waiting to see what the other would do. Biland stayed in front with his fingers crossed, hoping the thing would keep going.

Fifth place was taken up by Bayley on lap 2 but the battle was a good deal more cut-and-thrust. Theo van Kempen and Gerardus de Haas had moved in behind him, ahead of Markus and Urs Egloff who had started badly.

On lap 3 Webster took over the lead and by lap 6 the leaders started to pass back-markers, but as Webster tried to make a getaway the gearbox started to play up. Unknown to him at the time, a piece of gear had broken off. As it washed around in the gearbox oil it occasionally got in the way of the selector. He pulled into the pits on lap 7, to see if the selection problem could be rectified, leaving Biland to lead once more from Streuer and

Michel. Egloff had just moved into fourth ahead of Bayley and van Kempen, who was driving wildly to say the least – real opposite-lock slides round the long horseshoe corners.

Webster came out of the pits a lap adrift and continued in and out of the pits hoping that enough crews would drop out to let him pick up at least one point. Behind van Kempen, Kumano was coming under pressure from Derek Jones and Brian Ayres, forcing their way through after a slow start.

The next act of the drama unfolded on lap 14 when Biland's engine packed up once more, giving the lead to Michel. Streuer immediately dropped back, apparently unable to hold on to the French crew, and the Yamaha engine rattled to a halt on lap 18 with a broken con rod.

That left Michel with a large lead over the Egloffs who had passed Bayley on lap 14 but could not get away. With Jones latching on as well, the three crews developed an exciting struggle that lasted to the flag, with Webster also having a hand in the final placings, as Jones later explained. 'Egloff was in front but I thought I could pass Bayley at the end of the straight on the last lap. I pulled out of the slipstream but there was Webster touring right where I wanted to go so I had no chance.'

Kumano finished a lonely fifth and Frank Wrathall and Kerry Chapman did well to take sixth in the closing stages from Progin and van Kempen who were forced to slow because their sidecar wheel fairing disappeared after rubbing on the wheel. Ninth were Steve Abbott and Shaun Smith ahead of Graham Gleeson who was passengered by Peter Linden for the day. The Swedish fighter pilot went on to win the Superbike race on his VFR 750 Honda and had already finished a fine twelfth on his RS 500 in the Grand Prix, a unique achievement.

# Swedish TT, 9/10 August/statistics
# Anderstorp Circuit, 2.505-mile/4.031-km circuit

## 500 cc

**30 laps, 75.15 miles/120.03 km**

| Place | Rider | Nat. | Machine | Laps | Time & speed | Practice time | Grid |
|---|---|---|---|---|---|---|---|
| 1 | Eddie Lawson | USA | Yamaha | 30 | 48m 59.33s 92.04 mph/ 148.12 km/h | 1m 36.64s | 2 |
| 2 | Wayne Gardner | AUS | Honda | 30 | 49m 15.37s | 1m 36.35s | 1 |
| 3 | Mike Baldwin | USA | Yamaha | 30 | 49m 17.77s | 1m 36.90s | 4 |
| 4 | Rob McElnea | GB | Yamaha | 30 | 49m 18.89s | 1m 36.86s | 3 |
| 5 | Raymond Roche | F | Honda | 30 | 49m 41.57s | 1m 37.70s | 5 |
| 6 | Didier de Radigues | B | Chevallier | 30 | 49m 49.06s | 1m 38.69s | 8 |
| 7 | Niall MacKenzie | GB | Suzuki | 30 | 49m 57.79s | 1m 37.73s | 6 |
| 8 | Randy Mamola | USA | Yamaha | 30 | 50m 08.74s | 1m 38.94s | 9 |
| 9 | Ron Haslam | GB | Elf | 29 | 49m 06.62s | 1m 38.36s | 7 |
| 10 | Wolfgang von Muralt | CH | Suzuki | 29 | 49m 22.54s | 1m 41.33s | 13 |
| 11 | Marco Gentile | CH | Fior | 29 | 49m 29.48s | 1m 42.18s | 16 |
| 12 | Peter Linden | S | Honda | 29 | 49m 36.53s | 1m 41.08s | 12 |
| 13 | Boet van Dulmen | NL | Honda | 29 | 49m 41.76s | 1m 42.97s | 20 |
| 14 | Shunji Yatsushiro | J | Honda | 29 | 49m 59.53s | 1m 41.92s | 14 |
| 15 | Paul Iddon | GB | Suzuki | 29 | 50m 00.17s | 1m 42.28s | 18 |
| 16 | Manfred Fischer | D | Honda | 29 | 50m 06.42s | 1m 43.04s | 21 |
| 17 | Henk van der Mark | NL | Honda | 29 | 50m 06.76s | 1m 43.05s | 22 |
| 18 | Simon Buckmaster | GB | Honda | 29 | 50m 10.35s | 1m 42.85s | 19 |
| 19 | Eero Hyvarinen | SF | Honda | 29 | 50m 15.11s | 1m 42.22s | 17 |
| 20 | Alan Jeffery | GB | Suzuki | 29 | 50m 15.28s | 1m 43.38s | 23 |
| 21 | Mile Pajic | NL | Honda | 29 | 50m 39.23s | 1m 45.27s | 33 |
| 22 | Maarten Duyzers | NL | Suzuki | 29 | 50m 42.70s | 1m 44.37s | 29 |
| 23 | Esko Kuparinen | SF | Honda | 28 | 49m 09.23s | 1m 43.44s | 24 |
| 24 | Paul Ramon | B | Suzuki | 28 | 49m 43.39s | 1m 44.28s | 28 |
| 25 | Claus Wulff | DK | Suzuki | 28 | 49m 49.02s | 1m 44.03s | 26 |
| 26 | Ake Dahli | S | Suzuki | 28 | 49m 54.09s | 1m 46.14s | 35 |
| | Fabio Biliotti | I | Honda | 20 | DNF | 1m 40.87s | 11 |
| | Peter Sköld | S | Honda | 19 | DNF | 1m 42.07s | 15 |
| | Dietmar Mayer | D | Honda | 18 | DNF | 1m 45.23s | 32 |
| | Ari Rämö | SF | Suzuki | 17 | DNF | 1m 46.30s | 36 |
| | Christian le Liard | F | Honda | 13 | DNF | 1m 40.46s | 10 |
| | Lars Johansson | S | Suzuki | 13 | DNF | 1m 46.59s | 37 |
| | Helmut Schütz | D | Honda | 8 | DNF | 1m 45.51s | 34 |
| | Chris Bürki | CH | Honda | 6 | DNF | 1m 45.11s | 31 |
| | Sepp Doppler | A | Honda | 6 | DNF | 1m 44.91s | 30 |
| | Mark Phillips | GB | Suzuki | 1 | DNF | 1m 44.01s | 25 |
| | Marco Papa | I | Honda | | DNS | 1m 44.18s | 27 |
| | Geir Hestmann | N | Suzuki | | DNQ | 1m 48.55s | |
| | Gunnar Bruhn | S | Yamaha | | DNQ | 1m 51.77s | |
| | Patrick Salles | F | Honda | | DNQ | 1m 53.36s | |

*Fastest lap:* Lawson, 1m 36.59s, 93.36 mph/150.25 km/h (record).
*Previous record:* Kenny Roberts, USA (Yamaha), 1m 37.11s, 92.83 mph/149.40 km/h (1983).

**World Championship: 1** Lawson, 124; **2** Gardner, 105; **3** Mamola, 95; **4** Baldwin, 70; **5** McElnea, 60; **6** Sarron, 53; **7** de Radigues, 38; **8** Roche, 29; **9** Haslam, 16; **10** Chili, 11; **11** MacKenzie and van Dulmen, 8; **13** Yatsushiro, 7; **14** Biliotti, Reiner and Petersen, 5; **17** Garriga and Lewis, 4; **19** Burnett, Pajic and Irons, 3; **22** von Muralt, 2; **23** Papa and Schwantz, 1.

## 250 cc

**22 laps, 55.11 miles/88.68 km**

| Place | Rider | Nat. | Machine | Laps | Time & speed | Practice time | Grid |
|---|---|---|---|---|---|---|---|
| 1 | Carlos Lavado | YV | Yamaha | 22 | 39m 13.54s 84.30 mph/ 135.67 km/h | 1m 39.77s | 2 |
| 2 | Alfonso Pons | E | Honda | 22 | 39m 17.44s | 1m 40.87s | 6 |
| 3 | Jean-François Baldé | F | Honda | 22 | 39m 18.74s | 1m 41.42s | 9 |
| 4 | Maurizio Vitali | I | Garelli | 22 | 39m 30.35s | 1m 40.23s | 3 |
| 5 | Dominique Sarron | F | Honda | 22 | 39m 30.80s | 1m 41.65s | 12 |
| 6 | Stéphane Mertens | B | Yamaha | 22 | 39m 34.62s | 1m 41.57s | 11 |
| 7 | Jacques Cornu | CH | Honda | 22 | 39m 38.82s | 1m 41.86s | 14 |
| 8 | Jean Foray | F | Chevallier | 22 | 39m 40.62s | 1m 43.44s | 27 |
| 9 | Siegfried Minich | A | Honda | 22 | 39m 54.83s | 1m 42.01s | 17 |
| 10 | Alan Carter | GB | Kobas | 22 | 39m 57.99s | 1m 42.16s | 18 |
| 11 | Niall MacKenzie | GB | Armstrong | 22 | 40m 35.94s | 1m 40.28s | 4 |
| 12 | Martin Wimmer | D | Yamaha | 22 | 40m 36.39s | 1m 39.73s | 1 |
| 13 | Tadahiko Taira | J | Yamaha | 22 | 40m 39.59s | 1m 40.89s | 7 |
| 14 | Guy Bertin | F | Parisienne | 22 | 40m 51.23s | 1m 42.65s | 24 |
| 15 | Roland Freymond | CH | Yamaha | 22 | 41m 06.55s | 1m 43.47s | 28 |
| 16 | Herbert Besendörfer | D | Yamaha | 21 | 39m 09.23s | 1m 43.93s | 32 |
| 17 | Philippe Pagano | F | Yamaha | 21 | 39m 25.29s | 1m 44.70s | 34 |
| 18 | Jean-Michel Mattioli | F | Yamaha | 21 | 40m 41.52s | 1m 41.28s | 8 |
| 19 | Carlos Cardus | E | Honda | 20 | 39m 22.85s | 1m 42.43s | 22 |
| 20 | Jean-Louis Guignabodet | F | MIG | 20 | 39m 26.06s | 1m 41.54s | 10 |
| | Reinhold Roth | D | Honda | 19 | DNF | 1m 42.28s | 21 |
| | Stefano Caracchi | I | Aprilia | 16 | DNF | 1m 42.21s | 19 |
| | Virginio Ferrari | I | Honda | 15 | DNF | 1m 41.92s | 16 |
| | Harald Eckl | D | Honda | 15 | DNF | 1m 41.91s | 15 |
| | Anton Mang | D | Honda | 15 | DNF | 1m 41.81s | 13 |
| | Gary Noel | GB | EMC | 15 | DNF | 1m 44.03s | 33 |
| | Christian Boudinot | F | Rotax | 11 | DNF | 1m 42.78s | 26 |
| | Massimo Matteoni | I | Honda | 10 | DNF | 1m 43.97s | 32 |
| | Jean-Louis Tournadre | F | Yamaha | 9 | DNF | 1m 42.77s | 25 |
| | Fausto Ricci | I | Honda | 9 | DNF | 1m 42.24s | 20 |
| | Loris Reggiani | I | Aprilia | 7 | DNF | 1m 42.48s | 23 |
| | René Délaby | B | Moreno | 7 | DNF | 1m 43.57s | 29 |
| | Donnie McLeod | GB | Armstrong | 6 | DNF | 1m 40.47s | 5 |
| | Bobby Issazadhe | S | Chimoto | 3 | DNF | 1m 43.67s | 30 |
| | Hakan Olsson | S | Rotax | 1 | DNF | 1m 44.72s | 36 |
| | Hans Becker | D | Yamaha | 1 | DNF | 1m 44.70s | 35 |
| | Olivier Liegeois | B | Yamaha | | DNQ | 1m 44.98s | |
| | Anders Skov | DK | Yamaha | | DNQ | 1m 45.07s | |
| | Gérard Vallée | F | Yamaha | | DNQ | 1m 45.44s | |
| | Markku Kivi | SF | Yamaha | | DNQ | 1m 45.47s | |
| | Johnny Simonsson | S | Honda | | DNQ | 1m 46.41s | |
| | Eilert Lundstedt | S | MBA | | DNQ | 1m 47.69s | |
| | Hasse Gustavsson | S | ESW | | DNQ | 1m 49.09s | |
| | Jarmö Lilitiä | SF | Rotax | | DNQ | 1m 50.61s | |
| | Peter Granath | S | Harris | | DNQ | 1m 52.81s | |

*Fastest lap:* Pons, 1m 41.72s, 88.66 mph/142.68 km/h.
*Lap record:* Anton Mang, D (Honda), 1m 41.64s, 88.72 mph/142.78 km/h (1985).

**World Championship: 1** Lavado, 114; **2** Pons, 96; **3** Baldé, 63; **4** Sarron, 62; **5** Mang, 57; **6** Wimmer, 51; **7** Cornu, 32; **8** McLeod, 27; **9** Ricci, 24; **10** Bolle, 19; **11** Cardus, 17; **12** Taira and Mertens, 13; **14** Vitali, 12; **15** Ferrari, 11; **16** Roth, 10; **17** Carter, 9; **18** Herweh and Foray, 7; **20** Mattioli, 5; **21** Minich and MacKenzie, 4; **23** Matteoni, 2; **24** Lindner, 1.

## 125 cc

**23 laps, 57.62 miles/92.71 km**

| Place | Rider | Nat. | Machine | Laps | Time & speed | Practice time | Grid |
|---|---|---|---|---|---|---|---|
| 1 | Fausto Gresini | I | Garelli | 23 | 40m 40.50s 85.00 mph/ 136.79 km/h | 1m 46.18s | 6 |
| 2 | Luca Cadalora | I | Garelli | 23 | 40m 43.47s | 1m 45.70s | 5 |
| 3 | Domenico Brigaglia | I | Ducados | 23 | 41m 07.22s | 1m 45.59s | 4 |
| 4 | Bruno Kneubühler | CH | LCR | 23 | 41m 12.09s | 1m 45.56s | 3 |
| 5 | Lucio Fietroniro | B | MBA | 23 | 41m 12.41s | 1m 47.68s | 9 |
| 6 | Johnny Wickström | SF | Tunturi | 23 | 41m 15.26s | 1m 46.93s | 7 |
| 7 | Thierry Feuz | CH | MBA | 23 | 41m 39.96s | 1m 47.37s | 8 |
| 8 | Adolf Stadler | D | MBA | 23 | 41m 53.52s | 1m 50.56s | 29 |
| 9 | Pier Paolo Bianchi | I | Elit | 23 | 41m 56.97s | 1m 48.62s | 13 |
| 10 | Hakan Olsson | S | Starol | 23 | 41m 57.14s | 1m 51.26s | 33 |
| 11 | Marin Andreas Sanchez | E | Ducados | 23 | 41m 57.38s | 1m 50.14s | 25 |
| 12 | Thomas Möller-Pedersen | DK | MBA | 23 | 42m 20.93s | 1m 49.22s | 18 |
| 13 | Esa Kytola | SF | MBA | 23 | 42m 22.04s | 1m 49.11s | 17 |
| 14 | Robin Milton | GB | MBA | 23 | 42m 23.09s | 1m 49.95s | 24 |
| 15 | Peter Sommer | CH | MBA | 23 | 42m 23.28s | 1m 49.81s | 22 |
| 16 | Mike Leitner | A | MBA | 22 | 40m 59.47s | 1m 49.86s | 23 |
| 17 | Jorgen Ask | S | MBA | 22 | 41m 09.53s | 1m 51.28s | 34 |
| 18 | Mogens Johansen | DK | MBA | 22 | 41m 11.27s | 1m 51.08s | 32 |
| 19 | Ivan Troisi | YV | MBA | 22 | 41m 18.27s | 1m 51.96s | 36 |
| 20 | Ton Spek | NL | MBA | 22 | 41m 18.99s | 1m 52.45s | 37 |
| | Jacques Hutteau | F | MBA | 21 | DNF | 1m 48.81s | 14 |
| | Paul Bordes | F | MBA | 19 | DNF | 1m 49.76s | 21 |
| | Gastone Grassetti | I | MBA | 18 | DNF | 1m 50.14s | 26 |
| | Paolo Casoli | I | MBA | 16 | DNF | 1m 48.60s | 12 |
| | Jean-Claude Selini | F | MBA | 12 | DNF | 1m 48.23s | 10 |
| | Garcia Marcelino | E | Ducados | 11 | DNF | 1m 50.33s | 27 |
| | Olivier Liegeois | B | Assmex | 7 | DNF | 1m 49.04s | 16 |
| | Claudio Macciotta | I | MBA | 7 | DNF | 1m 48.58s | 11 |
| | Hannu Kallio | SF | MBA | 7 | DNF | 1m 49.28s | 19 |
| | August Auinger | A | Bartol | 6 | DNF | 1m 45.19s | 1 |
| | Christian le Badezet | F | MBA | 5 | DNF | 1m 50.48s | 28 |
| | Willi Hupperich | D | Seel | 5 | DNF | 1m 50.82s | 30 |
| | Ezio Gianola | I | MBA | 4 | DNF | 1m 45.33s | 2 |
| | Bady Hassaine | DZ | MBA | 2 | DNF | 1m 51.29s | 35 |
| | Willy Perez | RA | Zanella | 1 | DNF | 1m 49.74s | 20 |
| | Boy van Erp | NL | MBA | 1 | DNF | 1m 50.97s | 31 |
| | Jussi Hautaniemi | SF | MBA | | DNS | 1m 48.94s | 15 |
| | Mikael Nielsen | DK | MBA | | DNQ | 1m 52.67s | |
| | Giuseppe Ascareggi | I | Seel | | DNQ | 1m 52.98s | |
| | Fernando Gonzalez | E | MBA | | DNQ | 1m 53.26s | |
| | Manfred Braun | D | MBA | | DNQ | 1m 53.71s | |
| | Flemming Kistrup | DK | MBA | | DNQ | 1m 54.04s | |
| | Dario Marchetti | I | MBA | | DNQ | 1m 54.71s | |
| | Rune Zälle | S | MBA | | DNQ | 1m 54.80s | |
| | Thierry Maurer | CH | MBA | | DNQ | 1m 55.67s | |
| | Frede Jensen | DK | MBA | | DNQ | 1m 56.48s | |
| | Jan Eggens | NL | LCR | | DNQ | 1m 59.18s | |

*Fastest lap:* Cadalora, 1m 45.01s, 85.88 mph/138.21 km/h (record).
*Previous record:* Ricardo Tormo, E (MBA), 1m 46.94s, 84.33 mph/135.72 km/h (1983).

**World Championship: 1** Cadalora, 98; **2** Gresini, 89; **3** Brigaglia, 69; **4** Gianola, 49; **5** Kneubühler, 40; **6** Pietroniro, 37; **7** Auinger, 35; **8** Wickström, 31; **9** Bianchi, 29; **10** Perez, 26; **11** Feuz, 19; **12** Liegeois, 18; **13** Nieto, 15; **14** Casoli, 10; **15** Hautaniemi, 8; **16** Grassetti and Waibel, 5; **18** Stadler, 4; **19** Sanchez, 3; **20** Olsson and Kytola, 2.

## Sidecars

**23 laps, 57.62 miles/92.71 km**

| Place | Driver & passenger | Nat. | Machine | Laps | Time & speed | Practice time | Grid |
|---|---|---|---|---|---|---|---|
| 1 | Alain Michel/ Jean-Marc Fresc | F F | Krauser- Yamaha | 23 | 39m 19.73s 87.90 mph/ 141.46 km/h | 1m 40.09s | 3 |
| 2 | Markus Egloff/ Urs Egloff | CH CH | LCR– Yamaha | 23 | 39m 43.83s | 1m 41.10s | 6 |
| 3 | Derek Bayley/ Bryan Nixon | GB GB | LCR– Ricardo | 23 | 39m 45.26s | 1m 41.78s | 8 |
| 4 | Derek Jones/ Brian Ayres | GB GB | LCR– Yamaha | 23 | 39m 45.60s | 1m 42.36s | 11 |
| 5 | Masato Kumano/ Helmut Diehl | J D | LCR– Yamaha | 23 | 39m 55.49s | 1m 41.53s | 7 |
| 6 | Frank Wrathall/ Kerry Chapman | GB GB | LCR– Yamaha | 23 | 40m 05.35s | 1m 42.53s | 12 |
| 7 | René Progin/ Yves Hunziker | CH GB | Seymaz– Yamaha | 23 | 40m 07.02s | 1m 42.27s | 10 |
| 8 | Theo van Kempen/ Gerardus de Haas | CH NL | LCR– Yamaha | 23 | 40m 11.68s | 1m 42.94s | 14 |
| 9 | Steve Abbott/ Vince Biggs | GB GB | Windle– Yamaha | 23 | 40m 33.22s | 1m 42.57s | 13 |
| 10 | Graham Gleeson/ Peter Linden | NZ S | LCR– Yamaha | 23 | 40m 41.37s | 1m 43.01s | 15 |
| 11 | Yoshisada Kumagaya/ Kazuhiko Makiuchi | J J | LCR– Yamaha | 23 | 40m 46.65s | 1m 43.89s | 17 |
| 12 | Dennis Bingham/ Julia Bingham | GB GB | LCR– Yamaha | 23 | 41m 04.96s | 1m 45.19s | 20 |
| 13 | Wolfgang Stropek/ Hans-Peter Demling | A A | LCR– Yamaha | 22 | 40m 12.10s | 1m 44.86s | 19 |
| 14 | Benny Lysen/ Ole Moller | DK DK | LCR– Yamaha | 22 | 41m 08.05s | 1m 45.85s | 21 |
| 15 | Steve Webster/ Tony Hewitt | GB GB | LCR– Yamaha | 21 | 40m 09.94s | 1m 40.71s | 4 |
| 16 | Billy Gallros/ A. Nordi | S S | LCR– Yamaha | 20 | 39m 26.57s | 1m 50.18s | 22 |
| 17 | Rolf Steinhausen/ Bruno Hiller | D D | Busch | 19 | 39m 48.21s | 1m 42.15s | 9 |
| 18 | Barry Brindley/ Chris Jones | GB GB | Windle– Yamaha | 17 | 41m 54.93s | 1m 43.62s | 16 |
| | Mick Barton/ Fritz Buck | GB D | LCR– Yamaha | 22 | DNF | 1m 44.74s | 18 |
| | Egbert Streuer/ Bernie Schnieders | NL NL | LCR– Yamaha | 18 | DNF | 1m 39.92s | 2 |
| | Rolf Biland/ Kurt Waltisperg | CH CH | Krauser | 13 | DNF | 1m 39.35s | 1 |
| | Alfred Zurbrügg/ Martin Zurbrügg | CH CH | LCR– Yamaha | 0 | DNF | 1m 40.72s | 5 |

*Fastest lap:* Webster, 1m 40.27s, 89.94 mph/144.74 km/h (record).
*Previous record:* Rolf Biland/Kurt Waltisperg, CH/CH (Krauser), 1m 40.59s, 89.47 mph/143.99 km/h (1985).

**World Championship: 1** Michel, 69; **2** Webster, 61; **3** Strueur, 60; **4** Egloff, 49; **5** Kumano, 33; **6** Abbot, 32; **7** Zurbrügg, 30; **8** Jones, 29; **9** Biland, 20; **10** Bayley, 19; **11** Progin, 11; **12** Steinhausen and Wrathall, 10; **14** van Kempen, 8; **15** Barton, 7; **16** Gleeson and Brindley, 5; **18** Scherer, 3; **19** Kumagaya, 1.

# *Gran Premio di*
# SAN MARINO

With both the 250 cc and 500 cc World Championships decided there remained the 80 cc and 125 cc classes to be sorted out, though those competitors also had the final rounds to face at Hockenheim for the Baden-Württemberg GP. The 125 battle was obviously between the two Garellis and while Cadalora had demonstrated his ability to beat Gresini on several occasions, the reigning champion still had two chances to get his own back. The 80 title was heading Aspar's way, and Dörflinger had McConnachie to worry about as well as the two Derbis.

For the 500s and the 250s the lesser places had yet to be finalised and the question as to whether or not Lawson and Lavado could carry on the Yamaha domination of both classes was not yet answered. Two years before, Lawson had finished fourth in his last race behind the Hondas of Mamola, Roche and Haslam with the title already wrapped up. There were several similarities between that situation and this, as in 1984 Freddie Spencer was also resting and not present at the last event of the year.

Lawson obviously had the ability to win but did he have the drive? Without the need to win, would he put in the effort required? 'Things were different then. I had rear tyre problems that year and when I got a bad start it just wasn't possible to catch up at Mugello.'

Observers might also suggest that Lawson was also a very different rider in '86 to the Lawson that won in '84. It was relatively simple to follow the evolution of Lawson's career but less easy to determine how Carlos Lavado had changed since he first won the championship in 1983. He is one of the most popular men in the paddock, despite speaking little English, and one of the most respected riders who obviously enjoys his sport to the full.

'I still love racing just as much as I did when I started', said Lavado sitting in the Misano paddock outside his modest Italian motorhome after qualifying on pole position. 'More, in fact, because I love being successful and this year's Yamaha is a great bike to ride.'

He had already won the 250 World Championship but that did not make him ease off and his time at Misano would have qualified him on the second row of the grid for the 500 race. 'Things don't get any easier, though, just because the bike is fast this year. There are still a lot of good riders – Wimmer, Taira, Mang and of course Pons. In fact, it has not been that easy for me to adjust to having a quick bike after struggling for the last few years. I still ride just as hard round the corners as I did with the slower bikes and that is why I have crashed a few times this year. I always seem to lose the front end and I have not really worked out why it is.'

Although Martin Wimmer has a reputation for being a technically minded rider, Lavado does not. He tends more to ride with his heart and bravery, yet Lavado maintained he lacked little as a development rider. 'I don't think that I can be too bad because you have to have a reasonable bike to win the World Championship, and I know that Martin thinks a lot about the technical side of racing, but in fact I think he worries too much

about it. He goes very fast when everything is right but if he thinks that something is a bit wrong with the bike or perhaps he thinks he doesn't have the right tyre then he will be too slow. I'm more inclined just to get out there and do my best and not think too much about the bike once the race has started.'

Even Lavado cannot ignore the conditions on some occasions and this year at Anderstorp the varying wet and dry surface of the circuit made things very tricky. 'For me that was the hardest race of the year. I had a cut slick on the rear and an intermediate on the front. They were good at the start of the race when the tarmac was damp but when it started to dry out I had a few problems and I had to slow up because I thought that the tyres would overheat and I might be in big trouble. Then it started to rain again and the tyres were right for the end of the race.

'The best race I think was Silverstone because it was most important that I did not crash and I rode carefully in the wet but I still scored good points. I think that someone was looking after me there. I am religious, a catholic, and I always cross myself before the start.'

After riding in Japan after the end of the Grand Prix season Lavado planned to take things easy. 'I want to sit on the beach and eat and generally take things easy with no worries.' Lavado is not as active as some Grand Prix stars who water-ski or ride moto cross at every opportunity. 'I don't have to train to stay in shape. I do a little bit of work but very little in fact because I just seem to be able to ride a Grand Prix distance without getting too tired.'

At the end of the year Lavado intended to spend a few weeks in Venezuela where he shares a house with his mother, although his home for most of the season is now in Italy. His time in Venezuela would include some testing at San Carlos, the old Grand Prix circuit, and there was bound to be a big crowd as Lavado is a national hero.

Vito Ipolito, the son of Andreas Ipolito, now looks after Venemotos, the company that his father started to import Yamahas into Venezuela. 'Carlo has done a tremendous amount for both Yahama and motor cycling in general at home. Yamaha is the biggest selling brand, ahead of Suzuki and Honda. In fact we have 50 per cent of the market. The biggest bike we sell is the RZ 250 and I am thinking about putting out a special version, the Lavado replica.

'We do not have too many successful athletes in Venezuela so a World Champion is certainly big news. Of course it started with Johnny Cecotto and things were different then because we had never had a motor cycling World Champion. But Carlo is different again because he is so consistent and has been at the top for several years. All his races are shown on television at home and when he goes back there after Japan there will be many TV and press interviews.'

Ipolito hopes that Carlos will not be the last good rider from his country. 'We have some good racing at home but mainly on production bikes because it is difficult and expensive to get good machinery. I am hoping to find sponsorship to get

some of the good riders to come to Europe but since 1983 the exchange rate has become so bad that Venezuelan sponsorship does not go very far in Europe. For the moment then we have to depend on Carlo and I think he just gets better and better. It is amazing; his heart is always so strong and he has such a determination to win that never seems to fade.'

Lavado is determined to win the championship for the third time. 'I want to win the title again next year and I will enjoy racing with the number one on the front of the bike. I would then like to try the 500 class. I have only ridden a 500 once, at Imola in '83 when I crashed, but I was not ready. I might try the 500 when I go to Japan this time; I am not sure. At the moment I am sticking to the 250 and enjoying it.

'I think that I could have beaten Freddie Spencer last year on the 250 Yamaha I have now. The V-twin is as fast as the Honda almost everywhere. If it is five kilometres slower in some places I don't mind because last year the Yamaha was thirty kilometres slower. As for rumours that Freddie will race in both classes next year, well, that would be good but I don't think he can do it. He picked the right time to try it, when he knew he would have the best bike on the track. Now I don't think he could; the competition is much stronger.'

Spencer's plans for '87 were unclear but Kanemoto said that when he spoke to the triple Champion on the phone after his visit to the French Grand Prix, he had spoken enthusiastically of racing in both classes. Spencer had said to others that until he had been put out for most of the season he did not realise just how many things he would miss once he was away from Grand Prix racing.

His fitness remained an important question and although he planned to race in Japan at the end of the season there was no guarantee that he would be able to ride because he still had to work on his injured wrist.

The whole question of the '87 Honda team was up in the air as Wayne Gardner wanted everyone to be aware that he was not committed to staying with the same team for the coming season. He took great pains to point out that he didn't think that the '86 NSR had any merits and that he would be quite happy to ride a Yamaha for the next season and had already been approached by one of the teams. Naturally, he wanted to increase his options, stir Honda into greater effort to redesign the 500, increase the financial offer he might get from them and advertise himself in the market place. He pointed out that he had done a good job in what should have been just a learning year.

'I won three Grands Prix, which is more than anyone else but Lawson, and I think I got more publicity this year than Lawson did winning the championship. Honda have got to improve the bike for next year because this one is useless. They are going to have to make more changes than they did last year. The engine characteristics are wrong, the power band is too narrow and it upsets the handling. The chassis also has to be improved.'

Honda had announced that their method of

**A titanic 250 struggle takes place behind Lavado as Sarron fights off Baldé, Ricci, Mang and Mattioli.**

team organisation would change for '87 and while they intended to run a full works squad, the same bikes would also be available for well-backed private teams in limited numbers. A lease package of two bikes, a spare engine and a year's spare parts, as well as technical back-up, would be expensive and only available in very limited numbers, but it meant that there could be more teams with competitive bikes than in '86, as long as the machinery was competitive with the Yamahas which were already leased to the three squads.

Making matters still more interesting was the unveiling of the V-four Suzuki, which looked very much like a three-year-old Yamaha with primary drive taken directly to the large gear on the back of the clutch so that both cranks rotated in the same direction instead of being geared together as on the current Yamaha model. The same arrangement of two pairs of twin-choke carbs feeding direct into the crankcase through reed valves completed the Yamaha replica appearance, but this is hardly surprising considering the success of the Yamaha unit. Before they pulled out of Grand Prix racing at the end of '83, Suzuki headed a similar design pattern with their disc-valve square-four as at one time both Kawasaki and Yamaka had identical layouts.

The Skoal Bandit team were desperately keen to sign MacKenzie and spread the rumour that he had already signed. MacKenzie denied this, stating that the letter of intent he had given Suzuki was subject to contractual agreements and nothing was sealed at all. In fact he had received several other very interesting approaches.

Paul Lewis had started the year as the only Skoal Bandit rider but his season ended badly. The crash in Silverstone had left him with broken bones in his foot which had not healed in time for Misano. He could ride the bike but starting would present a problem, worsened by a nasty practice crash.

Kevin Schwantz arrived for his third GP of the season but he had crashed several times in recent outings including the last round of the American Championship so he was not brimming over with confidence. When MacKenzie lapped six seconds faster in the first official session and was still going two seconds a lap quicker at the end of practice, his confidence took a further knock.

## 80 cc

The 80 cc machines may not seem to be heavy pieces of machinery to heave around but nothing is easy at Misano as there is little rest and a lot of work. In heatwave conditions several of the riders were feeling the worse for wear after the 22-lap race.

Pier Paolo Bianchi had found the Elit Seel painfully slow for most of the season but he managed to overcome that with pure riding skill, aggression and experience at Misano.

Bianchi led virtually from the start, ahead of Manuel Herreros, Hans Spaan, Stefan Dörflinger, Gerhard Waibel, Angel Nieto, Wilco Zeelenberg and Hubert Abold. McConnachie made yet another poor start but after his recent perform-

**Lawson hung back long enough for everyone to imagine he would have a race on his hands . . . but then he simply disappeared.**

*Below:* **A scene in the early stages. Gardner and de Radigues have just passed; Haslam leads Roche, Lawson, McElnea and Mamola.**

ances his supporters must have hoped he could fight his way to the front and break the lap record in the process, having set four in seven races so far through the year, although his only win had been in Britain.

Bianchi kept Spaan at bay as Herreros and Dörflinger swapped places just behind. Martinez had also been slow away but soon got into his stride, closing on fifth-placed Angel Nieto by lap 4. He went past immediately and began to reel in Dörflinger. It took him four more laps before he could get past and he tucked in behind team-mate Martinez to join battle with both Spaan and Bianchi. The four-way struggle left Dörflinger to try and hold off Nieto.

By lap 9 McConnachie had passed Waibel and moved into seventh place but could go no further. Later he explained that getting that far had taken so much out of him physically that there was nothing more he could do.

Martinez's front position lasted only for laps 11 and 12. Bianchi thereafter resumed control and by the end of the 22 laps had opened up a seven-second lead. Martinez took the second place that made him World Champion, comfortably ahead of team-mate Herreros, who similarly was well clear of Hans Spaan.

Nieto's fifth place was the crowning frustration for Dörflinger and the two Krausers were sixth and seventh, ahead of Brazilian Alexandre Barros on the Autisa and Waibel on the Real.

## 125 cc

The 125 cc race was a personal triumph for August Auinger who has a reputation for being able to win any race in the wet but who lacks the edge in the dry. He didn't make a great start on the Bartol MBA and Pietroniro was the beneficiary, leaving the line in front of Cadalora and Gresini. At the end of the first circuit, Cadalora led from Gresini, with Bianchi third ahead of Kneubühler, Brigaglia, Pietroniro, Feuz and Auinger.

The Austrian was on top form and while the two Garellis consolidated their positions at the head of the field a third-place contest involved Bianchi, Kneubühler, Brigaglia and Auinger. It only lasted a lap because Auinger went through with ease and only Kneubühler made any attempt to follow.

By lap 5 Auinger had closed on Gresini who was losing track of Cadalora and a lap later he went past. He was then 13 seconds behind the leading Garelli and at first the task looked difficult, if not impossible, especially as Cadalora obviously wanted to win in front of his home crowd.

Gresini tried to hang on to the Austrian, while in fourth place Kneubühler had Brigaglia to deal with since Bianchi had dropped back. It took Auinger until lap 13 of the 28 to catch Cadalora but two laps later saw him safely past. The Italian tried to fight back but the pair were working their way through the tail-enders and on lap 18 Auinger put twelfth-placed Hutteau between himself and Cadalora. It gave him the break he needed and he started to open a useful lead.

Tadahiko Taira was a surprising but brilliant winner in the 250 race.

Gresini came in a lonely third and Brigaglia seemed to have got the better of Kneubühler, but on lap 24 the Swiss veteran had caught him again and took over fourth place with two laps to go and held it to the flag. Bianchi was out on his own in sixth, the last man on the same lap as Auinger.

## 250 cc

This was one of the most remarkable races of the season and Tadahiko Taira rode brilliantly in oppressive heat on his Marlboro Yamaha after a bad start made a nonsense of his second-position qualifying time. It was not until lap 5 that he appeared on the leaderboard at all (in 15th place), and by then Carlos Lavado on the HB Yamaha had established a commanding lead ahead of Dominique Sarron, Jean-Michel Mattioli on his private Yamaha (who had been the initial leader) and the Rothmans Hondas of Jean-François Baldé and Toni Mang.

By lap 7 Lavado had a six-second advantage over Baldé and Sarron who were battling for second and Fausto Ricci had moved into fourth just ahead of Mattioli and Mang. A tardy start had left Pons seventh once he had passed Virginio Ferrari, Stéphane Mertens and Pierre Bolle.

Lap 10 saw Taira in eighth place but Lavado had an eight-second lead over Ricci, who was riding on top of his form and headed the second-place group from Sarron, Mang, Baldé, Mattioli and Pons on his Campsa Honda.

Taira set about cutting back their advantage but it was not until lap 18 that he overhauled Baldé and Mattioli, who had dropped out of the

group. The group of four battling for second – Sarron, Mang, Ricci and Pons – were caught on the 24th lap. As he did so there was a sensation in the race. The back end of Lavado's bike had started hopping badly under heavy braking and when he tipped it in to the tight left-hand horseshoe, the front end slid away and he crashed.

Taira was then battling for the lead and relentlessly he picked off the group to take first place on lap 29. In the remaining distance he pulled away from Pons, Sarron and Mang, while Ricci came home a more distant fifth ahead of Wimmer. The German rider had started as badly as Taira on the second Marlboro Yahama and then found himself further frustrated when Alan Carter crashed in front of him.

Taira could hardly believe he had won his first Grand Prix. 'At the start of the race I was sure it was not possible to win. I was 22nd at the end of lap 1 but after a year of bad starts I have a lot of practice at passing the other riders and I just kept trying. It was not too hard until I got up to the leading group and our bikes seemed to be the same speed. The only place I could really overtake was on the braking so I tried hard there every time.'

## 500 cc

Although the championship had been decided there were plenty of reputations at stake and once more de Radigues made a lightning start, getting the edge over Gardner and Haslam. Lawson was not far behind but he was just one of a hard-fighting group contesting third, headed by Haslam, then Roche, Lawson, McElnea and

Fausto Gresini tries in vain to keep August Auinger at bay.

Aspar Martinez won the 80 cc World Championship for Derbi (below).

Mamola. Down in 11th place Sarron was being chased by Baldwin as they moved through the field from poor starts.

Gardner took the lead on lap 2 and pulled away from de Radigues and it was not until lap 4 that Lawson reached the head of the third-place group. As he recalled later, he realised it was time for action. 'I knew that Gardner was getting away and I was still behind de Radigues. I thought it was time I got my finger out and got going.'

When Lawson passed the Belgian on lap 6 he was five seconds behind Gardner and at first he seemed to make little impression because on lap 9 he was still over four seconds adrift. There was plenty of action behind as the chasing group had consumed de Radigues on the sixth lap. Next time round, McElnea had broken away and looked set to make third place his own. No sooner had he achieved that than he crashed. Just past the start-and-finish line the front end slipped away

on the brakes. 'I couldn't believe it. I thought, "this isn't happening".'

McElnea walked away dejected but unscathed as Roche briefly assumed third before being passed by Mamola. The group had grown to include Sarron and Baldwin, but as Mamola cleared off from lap 10 it split up to leave Roche engaged in an all-French struggle against Sarron. Meanwhile, Baldwin had work still to do but he was ahead of de Radigues, who was now being threatened by MacKenzie.

Lap 12 saw Lawson come up to within three seconds of Gardner and he then closed very quickly, tailing the Australian from lap 15. Back-markers let Gardner get ahead a couple of times but Lawson shadowed him almost incessantly. Baldwin had passed Roche and Sarron by lap 14 and set off to catch Mamola, which he did on lap 21 of the 35.

Lawson swept past Gardner on lap 20 and in

spite of the Honda rider's best attempts to stick to his back wheel, a gap started to open until the World Champion crossed the line almost ten seconds ahead. Baldwin got in front of Mamola a couple of times but not when it counted. With Sarron recovering from his broken elbow Roche managed to finish sixth, despite having had to make do with his old triple after Spencer's machines had been sent back to Japan.

De Radigues was seventh, 2.5s ahead of a dis-appointed MacKenzie. He had seen the best of his rear tyre in the early stages and found repeating his practice times for 35 laps very hard. Neverthe-less, he was still in front of Haslam and Kevin Schwantz who had been hampered by his start. Dave Petersen received a Sportsman of the Day award from the organisers for a spirited ride that had him heading for a championship point before being forced to retire after 24 laps because his injured hand had twice slipped off the bar.

# Gran Premio di San Marino, 24 August/statistics
# Autodromo Santamonica, Misano, 2.167-mile/3.488-km circuit

## 500 cc

**35 laps, 75.85 miles/122.08 km**

| *Place* | *Rider* | *Nat.* | *Machine* | *Laps* | *Time & speed* | *Practice time* | *Grid* |
|---|---|---|---|---|---|---|---|
| 1 | Eddie Lawson | USA | Yamaha | 35 | 47m 30.83s 95.791 mph/ 154.161 km/h | 1m 19.31s | 1 |
| 2 | Wayne Gardner | AUS | Honda | 35 | 47m 40.70s | 1m 19.73s | 2 |
| 3 | Randy Mamola | USA | Yamaha | 35 | 47m 49.79s | 1m 20.30s | 5 |
| 4 | Mike Baldwin | USA | Yamaha | 35 | 47m 51.57s | 1m 20.74s | 6 |
| 5 | Raymond Roche | F | Honda | 35 | 48m 08.49s | 1m 21.07s | 7 |
| 6 | Christian Sarron | F | Yamaha | 35 | 48m 12.12s | 1m 21.27s | 9 |
| 7 | Didier de Radigues | B | Chevallier | 35 | 48m 13.67s | 1m 21.21s | 8 |
| 8 | Niall MacKenzie | GB | Suzuki | 35 | 48m 21.81s | 1m 20.13s | 3 |
| 9 | Ron Haslam | GB | Elf | 35 | 48m 35.11s | 1m 21.47s | 10 |
| 10 | Kevin Schwantz | USA | Suzuki | 34 | 47m 31.32s | 1m 22.05s | 13 |
| 11 | Shunji Yatsushiro | J | Honda | 34 | 47m 34.40s | 1m 21.59s | 11 |
| 12 | Leandro Becheroni | I | Honda | 34 | 47m 53.83s | 1m 22.37s | 14 |
| 13 | Wolfgang von Muralt | CH | Suzuki | 34 | 48m 15.30s | 1m 23.43s | 21 |
| 14 | Vittorio Gibertini | I | Cagiva | 34 | 48m 23.69s | 1m 22.98s | 18 |
| 15 | Christian le Liard | F | Elf | 34 | 48m 25.94s | 1m 23.37s | 20 |
| 16 | Andreas Leuthe | LUX | Honda | 34 | 48m 26.99s | 1m 23.78s | 22 |
| 17 | Fabio Barchitta | I | Honda | 34 | 48m 36.28s | 1m 24.84s | 32 |
| 18 | Boet van Dulmen | NL | Honda | 34 | 48m 42.79s | 1m 23.85s | 23 |
| 19 | Manfred Fischer | D | Honda | 33 | 47m 31.15s | 1m 24.06s | 26 |
| 20 | Karl Truchsess | A | Honda | 33 | 47m 35.44s | 1m 25.64s | 36 |
| 21 | Vinicio Bogani | I | Honda | 33 | 47m 40.02s | 1m 24.75s | 31 |
| 22 | Eero Hyvarinen | SF | Honda | 33 | 47m 50.69s | 1m 24.64s | 30 |
| 23 | Mile Pajic | NL | Honda | 33 | 48m 06.64s | 1m 25.44s | 35 |
| 24 | Marco Greco | BR | Honda | 33 | 48m 16.55s | 1m 25.39s | 34 |
| | Simon Buckmaster | GB | Honda | 28 | DNF | 1m 25.00s | 33 |
| | Juan Garriga | E | Cagiva | 27 | DNF | 1m 21.95s | 12 |
| | Dave Petersen | ZIM | Suzuki | 24 | DNF | 1m 22.72s | 16 |
| | Marco Marchesani | I | Suzuki | 20 | DNF | 1m 23.98s | 24 |
| | Armando Errico | I | Suzuki | 14 | DNF | 1m 24.09s | 27 |
| | Fabio Biliotti | I | Honda | 13 | DNF | 1m 23.22s | 19 |
| | Vittorio Scatola | I | Paton | 12 | DNF | 1m 24.25s | 28 |
| | Alessandro Valesi | I | Honda | 12 | DNF | 1m 24.53s | 29 |
| | Rob McElnea | GB | Yamaha | 7 | DNF | 1m 20.14s | 4 |
| | Paul Lewis | AUS | Suzuki | 6 | DNF | 1m 22.65s | 15 |
| | Marco Gentile | CH | Fior | 1 | DNF | 1m 22.95s | 17 |
| | Massimo Messere | I | Honda | | DNS | 1m 23.98s | 25 |
| | Henk van der Mark | NL | Honda | | DNQ | 1m 25.80s | |
| | Chris Bürki | CH | Honda | | DNQ | 1m 26.08s | |
| | Claus Wulff | DK | Suzuki | | DNQ | 1m 26.51s | |
| | Andres Rubio | E | Suzuki | | DNQ | 1m 27.18s | |
| | Sepp Doppler | A | Honda | | DNQ | 1m 27.67s | |
| | Dietmar Marehard | D | Suzuki | | DNQ | 1m 28.77s | |
| | Stelio Marmaras | GR | Suzuki | | DNQ | 1m 29.59s | |

*Fastest lap:* Lawson, 1m 20.20s, 97.287 mph/156.569 km/h (record).
*Previous record:* Eddie Lawson, USA (Yamaha), 1m 20.46s, 96.973 mph/156.063 km/h (1985).

Final 500 cc World Championship points are on pages 178-9.

## 250 cc

**30 laps, 65.01 miles/104.64 km**

| *Place* | *Rider* | *Nat.* | *Machine* | *Laps* | *Time & speed* | *Practice time* | *Grid* |
|---|---|---|---|---|---|---|---|
| 1 | Tadahiko Taira | J | Yamaha | 30 | 41m 52.62s 93.159 mph/ 149.924 km/h | 1m 21.67s | 2 |
| 2 | Alfonso Pons | E | Honda | 30 | 41m 54.16s | 1m 23.28s | 12 |
| 3 | Dominique Sarron | F | Honda | 30 | 41m 54.41s | 1m 23.00s | 9 |
| 4 | Anton Mang | D | Honda | 30 | 41m 54.81s | 1m 22.70s | 6 |
| 5 | Fausto Ricci | I | Honda | 30 | 42m 01.20s | 1m 23.44s | 13 |
| 6 | Martin Wimmer | D | Yamaha | 30 | 42m 05.90s | 1m 22.01s | 3 |
| 7 | Jean-Michel Mattioli | F | Yamaha | 30 | 42m 06.19s | 1m 22.66s | 5 |
| 8 | Virginio Ferrari | I | Honda | 30 | 42m 18.64s | 1m 24.23s | 24 |
| 9 | Pierre Bolle | F | Parisienne | 30 | 42m 22.11s | 1m 23.72s | 15 |
| 10 | Stéphane Mertens | B | Yamaha | 30 | 42m 27.72s | 1m 23.46s | 14 |
| 11 | Jean Foray | F | Chevallier | 30 | 42m 29.79s | 1m 24.83s | 32 |
| 12 | Donnie McLeod | GB | Armstrong | 30 | 42m 30.06s | 1m 23.21s | 10 |
| 13 | Gary Noel | GB | EMC | 30 | 42m 30.34s | 1m 24.01s | 19 |
| 14 | Reinhold Roth | D | Honda | 30 | 42m 40.71s | 1m 23.77s | 16 |
| 15 | Marcellino Lucchi | I | Rotax | 30 | 43m 04.30s | 1m 24.49s | 28 |
| 16 | Jean-Louis Tournadre | F | Yamaha | 30 | 43m 06.80s | 1m 24.85s | 33 |
| 17 | Roland Freymond | CH | Yamaha | 30 | 43m 08.45s | 1m 24.72s | 31 |
| 18 | Harald Eckl | D | Honda | 30 | 43m 11.48s | 1m 24.40s | 26 |
| 19 | Urs Lüzi | CH | Yamaha | 30 | 43m 15.08s | 1m 24.38s | 25 |
| 20 | Bruno Casanova | I | Honda | 30 | 43m 17.04s | 1m 24.16s | 20 |
| 21 | Alberto Rota | I | Honda | 29 | 41m 53.10s | 1m 24.17s | 21 |
| 22 | Gilberto Gambelli | I | Honda | 29 | 42m 21.00s | 1m 25.01s | 34 |
| 23 | Oscar la Ferla | I | Yamaha | 29 | 42m 35.82s | 1m 25.41s | 36 |
| | Carlos Lavado | YV | Yamaha | 23 | DNF | 1m 20.83s | 1 |
| | Jean-François Baldé | F | Honda | 21 | DNF | 1m 23.22s | 11 |
| | Philippe Pagano | F | Yamaha | 15 | DNF | 1m 25.39s | 35 |
| | Stefano Caracchi | I | Aprilia | 11 | DNF | 1m 24.21s | 22 |
| | Massimo Matteoni | I | Honda | 9 | DNF | 1m 23.84s | 17 |
| | Carlos Cardus | E | Honda | 9 | DNF | 1m 24.22s | 23 |
| | Christian Boudinot | F | Kobas | 8 | DNF | 1m 24.46s | 27 |
| | Alan Carter | GB | Kobas | 3 | DNF | 1m 24.68s | 30 |
| | Maurizio Vitali | I | Garelli | 3 | DNF | 1m 22.41s | 4 |
| | Jacques Cornu | CH | Honda | 2 | DNF | 1m 22.99s | 8 |
| | Jean-Louis Guignabodet | F | MIG | 2 | DNF | 1m 24.58s | 29 |
| | Niall MacKenzie | GB | Armstrong | 1 | DNF | 1m 23.88s | 18 |
| | Loris Reggiani | I | Aprilia | | DNS | 1m 22.82s | 7 |
| | René Délaby | B | Moreno | | DNQ | 1m 25.66s | |
| | Bruno Bonhuil | F | Honda | | DNQ | 1m 25.90s | |
| | Siegfried Minich | A | Honda | | DNQ | 1m 26.45s | |
| | Stefan Klabacher | A | Rotax | | DNQ | 1m 26.88s | |
| | Marc Gial | F | Fior | | DNQ | 1m 27.19s | |
| | Daniel Amatrain | E | Kobas | | DNQ | 1m 28.96s | |

*Fastest lap:* Lavado, 1m 22.20s, 94.905 mph/152.734 km/h (record).
*Previous record:* Carlos Lavado, RA (Yamaha), 1m 22.46s, 94.621 mph/152.277 km/h (1985).

Final 250 cc World Championship points are on pages 178-9.

## 125 cc

**28 laps, 60.68 miles/97.66 km**

| *Place* | *Rider* | *Nat.* | *Machine* | *Laps* | *Time & speed* | *Practice time* | *Grid* |
|---|---|---|---|---|---|---|---|
| 1 | August Auinger | A | Bartol | 28 | 40m 08.62s 90.702 mph/ 145.971 km/h | 1m 24.85s | 2 |
| 2 | Luca Cadalora | I | Garelli | 28 | 40m 25.04s | 1m 25.55s | 3 |
| 3 | Fausto Gresini | I | Garelli | 28 | 40m 40.43s | 1m 24.71s | 1 |
| 4 | Bruno Kneubühler | CH | LCR | 28 | 40m 55.58s | 1m 26.90s | 5 |
| 5 | Domenico Brigaglia | I | Ducados | 28 | 40m 55.87s | 1m 26.65s | 4 |
| 6 | Pier Paolo Bianchi | I | Elit | 28 | 41m 25.39s | 1m 27.19s | 8 |
| 7 | Gastone Grassetti | I | MBA | 27 | 40m 34.43s | 1m 29.15s | 21 |
| 8 | Hakan Olsson | S | Starol | 27 | 40m 36.57s | 1m 29.02s | 17 |
| 9 | Mike Leitner | A | MBA | 27 | 40m 36.75s | 1m 28.24s | 11 |
| 10 | Adolf Stadler | D | MBA | 27 | 40m 37.52s | 1m 29.57s | 22 |
| 11 | Marco Pirani | I | MBA | 27 | 40m 50.01s | 1m 29.11s | 19 |
| 12 | Jacques Hutteau | F | MBA | 27 | 41m 05.23s | 1m 29.66s | 26 |
| 13 | Jean-Claude Selini | F | MBA | 27 | 41m 09.78s | 1m 29.62s | 24 |
| 14 | Ivan Troisi | YV | MBA | 27 | 41m 10.04s | 1m 30.89s | 32 |
| 15 | Patrick Daudier | F | PMDF | 27 | 41m 16.18s | 1m 29.58s | 23 |
| 16 | Manfred Braun | D | MBA | 27 | 41m 26.86s | 1m 30.55s | 29 |
| 17 | Thierry Maurer | CH | MBA | 27 | 41m 37.08s | 1m 30.66s | 30 |
| 18 | Marco Cipriani | I | MBA | 26 | 40m 08.84s | 1m 30.22s | 27 |
| 19 | Roberto Dova | I | MBA | 26 | 40m 18.26s | 1m 30.80s | 31 |
| 20 | Josef Bader | D | MBA | 26 | 40m 23.50s | 1m 31.11s | 34 |
| 21 | Peter Balaz | CS | MBA | 26 | 41m 01.97s | 1m 28.85s | 16 |
| | Lucio Pietroniro | B | MBA | 18 | DNF | 1m 27.53s | 9 |
| | Johnny Wickström | SF | Tunturi | 16 | DNF | 1m 28.84s | 15 |
| | Thierry Feuz | CH | LCR | 12 | DNF | 1m 27.59s | 10 |
| | Norbert Peschke | D | MBA | 10 | DNF | 1m 29.06s | 18 |
| | Marin Andreas Sanchez | E | MBA | 10 | DNF | 1m 29.14s | 20 |
| | Giuseppe Ascareggi | I | MBA | 8 | DNF | 1m 31.01s | 33 |
| | Angel Nieto | E | Ducados | 7 | DNF | 1m 28.83s | 14 |
| | Paolo Casoli | I | MBA | 6 | DNF | 1m 27.02s | 6 |
| | Olivier Liegeois | B | Assmex | 5 | DNF | 1m 27.63s | 25 |
| | Michel Escudier | F | MBA | 3 | DNF | 1m 31.34s | 36 |
| | Vincenzo Sblendorio | I | MBA | 3 | DNF | 1m 28.60s | 13 |
| | Bady Hassaine | DZ | MBA | 3 | DNF | 1m 28.39s | 12 |
| | Flemming Kistrup | DK | MBA | 1 | DNF | 1m 30.37s | 28 |
| | Ezio Gianola | I | MBA | 0 | DNF | 1m 27.09s | 7 |
| | Esa Kytola | SF | MBA | | DNS | 1m 31.25s | 35 |
| | Nicolas Hernandez | E | Benetti | | DNQ | 1m 31.45s | |
| | Thomas Möller-Pedersen | DK | MBA | | DNQ | 1m 31.64s | |
| | Boy van Erp | NL | MBA | | DNQ | 1m 31.70s | |
| | Mogens Johansson | DK | MBA | | DNQ | 1m 32.35s | |
| | Karl Dauer | A | MBA | | DNQ | 1m 32.49s | |
| | Eric Saul | F | LGM | | DNQ | 1m 32.62s | |
| | Ton Spek | NL | MBA | | DNQ | 1m 33.31s | |

*Fastest lap:* Auinger, 1m 24.73s, 92.071 mph/148.174 km/h (record).
*Previous record:* Bruno Kneubühler, CH (LCR), 1m 25.14s, 91.643 mph/147.484 km/h (1985).

**World Championship: 1** Cadalora, 110; **2** Gresini, 99; **3** Brigaglia, 75; **4** Auinger, 50; **5** Gianola, 49; **6** Kneubühler, 48; **7** Pietroniro, 37; **8** Bianchi, 34; **9** Wickström, 31; **10** Perez, 26; **11** Feuz, 19; **12** Liegeois, 18; **13** Nieto, 15; **14** Casoli, 10; **15** Grassetti, 9; **16** Hautaniemi, 8; **17** Olsson, Waibel and Stadler, 5; **20** Sanchez, 3; **21** Kytola and Leitner, 2.

## 80 cc

**22 laps, 47.67 miles/76.74 km**

| *Place* | *Rider* | *Nat.* | *Machine* | *Laps* | *Time & speed* | *Practice time* | *Grid* |
|---|---|---|---|---|---|---|---|
| 1 | Pier Paolo Bianchi | I | Seel | 22 | 33m 24.60s 85.628 mph/ 137.807 km/h | 1m 31.65s | 6 |
| 2 | Jorge Martinez | E | Derbi | 22 | 33m 31.46s | 1m 29.70s | 1 |
| 3 | Manuel Herreros | E | Derbi | 22 | 33m 33.45s | 1m 31.53s | 5 |
| 4 | Hans Spaan | NL | Huvo | 22 | 33m 36.55s | 1m 30.52s | 3 |
| 5 | Angel Nieto | E | Derbi | 22 | 33m 54.59s | 1m 32.25s | 7 |
| 6 | Stefan Dörflinger | CH | Krauser | 22 | 33m 57.81s | 1m 29.72s | 2 |
| 7 | Ian McConnachie | GB | Krauser | 22 | 34m 14.79s | 1m 31.28s | 4 |
| 8 | Alexandre Barros | BR | Autisa | 22 | 34m 15.13s | 1m 33.53s | 13 |
| 9 | Gerhard Waibel | D | Real | 22 | 34m 20.02s | 1m 32.56s | 9 |
| 10 | Francisco Torontegui | E | Kobas | 22 | 34m 36.84s | 1m 34.13s | 16 |
| 11 | Hubert Abold | D | Krauser | 22 | 34m 37.89s | 1m 33.59s | 14 |
| 12 | Salvatore Milano | I | Krauser | 22 | 34m 43.88s | 1m 33.04s | 11 |
| 13 | Vincenzo Sblendorio | I | Faccioli | 22 | 34m 49.43s | 1m 33.92s | 15 |
| 14 | Josef Fischer | A | Krauser | 22 | 34m 49.69s | 1m 32.50s | 8 |
| 15 | Wilco Zeelenberg | NL | Huvo | 22 | 34m 52.89s | 1m 34.32s | 18 |
| 16 | Chris Baert | B | Seel | 21 | 33m 43.89s | 1m 36.49s | 27 |
| 17 | Gerd Kafka | A | Krauser | 21 | 33m 56.32s | 1m 34.40s | 19 |
| 18 | Gunter Schirnhöfer | D | Krauser | 21 | 34m 21.67s | 1m 35.50s | 23 |
| 19 | Paolo Priori | I | Lusuardi | 21 | 34m 25.92s | 1m 36.60s | 28 |
| 20 | Raimo Lipponen | SF | Keifer | 21 | 34m 26.05s | 1m 35.85s | 24 |
| 21 | Richard Bay | D | Ziegler | 21 | 34m 45.47s | 1m 36.14s | 25 |
| 22 | Otto Machinek | A | Krauser | 21 | 34m 49.00s | 1m 37.89s | 34 |
| 23 | Thomas Engl | D | ESCH | 21 | 35m 00.40s | 1m 37.72s | 33 |
| 24 | Claudio Granata | I | Lusuardi | 20 | 33m 34.89s | 1m 37.13s | 30 |
| 25 | Jos van Dongen | NL | Krauser | 20 | 33m 38.44s | 1m 37.40s | 31 |
| | Luis Reyes | COL | Autisa | 16 | DNF | 1m 33.42s | 12 |
| | Rainer Kunz | D | Ziegler | 16 | DNF | 1m 32.79s | 10 |
| | Massimo Fargeri | I | Uvo | 14 | DNF | 1m 36.63s | 29 |
| | Felix Rodriguez | E | Autisa | 10 | DNF | 1m 34.97s | 21 |
| | René Dünki | CH | Krauser | 10 | DNF | 1m 35.29s | 22 |
| | Nicola Casadei | I | RB | 10 | DNF | 1m 39.12s | 37 |
| | Mario Stocco | I | Huvo | 6 | DNF | 1m 36.18s | 26 |
| | Theo Timmer | NL | Huvo | 5 | DNF | 1m 34.62s | 20 |
| | Reiner Koster | CH | Kroko | 4 | DNF | 1m 39.96s | 38 |
| | Reiner Scheidhauer | D | Seel | 2 | DNF | 1m 34.16s | 17 |
| | Stefan Brägger | CH | Huvo | 1 | DNF | 1m 38.45s | 36 |
| | Gabriele Gnani | I | Gnani | | DNS | 1m 37.55s | 32 |
| | Vincenzo Saffiotti | I | UFO | | DNS | 1m 38.22s | 35 |
| | Peter Balaz | CS | Huvo | | DNQ | 1m 40.18s | |
| | Jarmo Piepponen | SF | Kiefer | | DNQ | 1m 40.29s | |
| | Zdravko Matulja | YU | MTM | | DNQ | 1m 42.50s | |
| | Bertus Grinwis | NL | Krauser | | DNQ | 1m 42.90s | |
| | Jan Vanecek | CS | Huvo | | DNQ | 1m 45.97s | |
| | Luciano Pagliaroli | I | UFO | | DNQ | 1m 46.30s | |

*Fastest lap:* Bianchi, 1m 29.65s, 87.018 mph/140.042 km/h (record).
*Previous record:* Ian McConnachie, GB (Krauser), 1m 30.99s, 85.751 mph/138.002 km/h (1985).

**World Championship: 1** Martinez, 94; **2** Herreros, 77; **3** Dörflinger, 70; **4** McConnachie, 50; **5** Spaan, 47; **6** Nieto, 45; **7** Bianchi, 44; **8** Waibel, 36; **9** Fischer, 13; **10** Kafka, 9; **11** Bolart, Kunz and Barros, 6; **14** Gil and Timmer, 5; **16** Abold, Rodriguez and van Kessel, 3; **19** Reyes and Zeelenberg, 2; **21** Milano and Torontegui, 1.

# BADEN-WÜRTTEMBERG

Although there was still a mathematical possibility that Luca Cadalora could lose the 125 World Championship to Fausto Gresini, he was bound to hang on to it so long as his Garelli kept going. The real interest lay with the sidecars where the stage was set for the grand finale. Alain Michel led the series by eight points but the Frenchmen had been unlucky so often that one wondered what might go wrong at the last moment. He could certainly not afford a mechanical failure. That kind of problem had played a great part in the season, knocking Rolf Biland and Kurt Waltisperg out of the picture altogether and having such a severe effect on Egbert Streuer's and Bernard Schnieder's points total that they were still only third in the championship despite winning every race in which they finished. The Dutchmen lay behind Alain Michel and Jean-Marc Fresc and Steve Webster and Tony Hewitt.

Webster had also suffered mechanical problems. In Germany the outfit lasted for just 9 of the 25 laps and lost a likely third place, and in Sweden a gearbox problem forced him to limp home out of the points. Michel had not had a trouble-free season either for he only just made the finish in Germany when the collapse of a sidecar wheel mounting left the tyre askew and dragging. His only failure to finish was registered in Silverstone after the piston collapsed.

Careful examination of the piston later revealed that it had seized and this precipitated the failure. Michel was glad to have discovered this for it explained what he had previously been unable to work out: why the piston should have failed when his experience suggested it ought to have lasted the distance without any problems.

In the lull after the Swedish Grand Prix he had tested his outfit on Elf's rolling road dynamometer. Their elaborate test equipment, which includes sensors to test inlet and exhaust gasses and combustion chamber temperature, established that his carburation had been out some way up the rev range and the piston had seized as it ran weak. Modification to the carburation left him confident that the problem would not recur.

Michel claimed to have helped Biland sort out his lengthy and disastrous problems with the Krauser engine. The Frenchman had used a Krauser engine himself at the Schwanenstadt international meeting, proving that it could run well and finish without problems. He had suggested that the solution to Biland's problem was to use a different fuel pump and to modify the fuel tank pick-up. It was not surprising that Michel wanted to help Biland out because the Swiss ace's performance at Hockenheim was likely to be of vital importance to the championship result.

If either Webster or Streuer crossed the line first, Michel had to secure fourth place or better to win his first World Title. Assuming that all the top men kept going, Michel would need to finish behind Streuer, Webster and Biland. That was not too tall an order, unless he was forced to detune the engine too much to ensure reliability. On the other hand, if Biland won Michel would only need

to come sixth – he could surely manage that so long as his outfit held together.

Practice provided little support for Michel's confidence as he was only fifth-fastest behind the Zurbrügg brothers with Streuer taking pole ahead of Biland and Webster. A finish in that position would mean that Michel would miss the championship. Although he would have the same number of championship points as the Dutchman, reigning champion Streuer would take the title on number of wins.

Webster, down in third place, knew that he was going to have to pull out something a little special in the race if he was to beat both Streuer and Biland and win the race and the championship. He found himself down on power, just as he had been throughout the year, so the only way to match the others was to gear the outfit high, hoping to make full use of the slipstream and beat his rivals through the infield. Webster was not disheartened to find himself nearly two seconds slower than the Dutch crew after the last session. 'I always seem to find a bit when it comes to the race, so as long as we can get the slipstream I think I can hang in there.'

Streuer had not coasted to that fastest time either and during that final session the outfit slid wildly through the infield as he tried to demoralise the opposition. Things looked worse for the bearded champion in the morning warm-up on Sunday when the electrode fell off a spark plug and wrecked a piston. It was good fortune that this happened in practice rather than the race.

The surprise of practice in the 80 cc class was Gerhard Waibel who got the use of a works Krauser engine and went faster than anyone else. Dörflinger was quickest over the first three sessions but Waibel jumped from third to first in the final period. That did not improve Ian McConnachie's chances of joining the Krauser team on a permanent basis as Krauser preferred for publicity reasons to have German-speaking team members. McConnachie's bike struck trouble early on and the time he recorded in the first session was the best it could manage; after seizing it just kept getting slower.

Angel Nieto qualified seventh and announced his retirement after twenty years of Grand Prix racing. 'I am glad to finish racing at Hockenheim where I started my Grand Prix career but I wish that the Derbi had finished the race. It was my plan to beat Ago's record of World Championship wins but I can't do that now and I want to stop while I am still riding well.'

Forty-year-old Nieto won 92 Grands Prix in his career and although he won thirteen championships he always said he won twelve plus one because he thought the number thirteen unlucky. Perhaps he was proved right as he never got past it. He said he might go into team management but he had no firm plans. He intended to race three more times in Spain before the end of the season.

As an added attraction to the three Grands Prix and the final round of the German Superbike Championship, Toni Mang, Manfred Fischer, Klaus Klein, Helmut Dahne, Peter Rubato and Hubert Abold took part in what the Germans

called an 'all-round race'. This was similar to the American Superbikers' event, using parts of the Hockenheim stadium section, artificial jumps and some grass track. The motocrossers were much more competitive and the event was won by Alois Niedermayer, while the best that Mang could do was a pair of 18th positions using his ex-André Malherbe Honda.

The ex-World Champion was being pretty cagey about his plans for 1987 but there were plenty of rumours. It seems that, unlike '86, he will have to pay for the lease of the works 250 Hondas in '87 and although he has had the offer of some sponsorship from Camel in Germany this would be insufficient to run the entire team. He also had discussions with both Dunlop and Michelin, trying to decide which tyres to use. He denied rumours that he might retire.

In the supporting German Championship Superbike race, Martin Wimmer did what he had been unable to do on the 250 all year and shot away from the start into a commanding lead. Even though it was a one-off ride he was in a class of his own, just easing off in the closing stages to let Mitsui Germany's usual rider, Michael Galinski, past. With the win Galinski won the championship.

## 125 cc

The last race of the season provided a great five-way battle, despite the fact that the championship had almost been decided in favour of Luca Cadalora who would win the title if the bike did not fail him. Not wanting to make a silly mistake he kept out of the heat of the contest that raged between reigning champion Fausto Gresini on the other works Garelli and the two privateers August Auinger and Ezio Gianola, who were battling for fourth place in the championship. Bruno Kneubühler joined in but without the power to join battle effectively with the other four.

From the first lap to the last the struggle went on, with great use of slipstreaming tactics down the long straights and cornering heroics in the stadium. To the delight of the crowd, Austrian Auinger took the lead at the end of lap 1, fractionally ahead of Gresini, Gianola, Cadalora, Kneubühler and the German Adolf Stadler.

Lap 2 saw Gresini dive inside Auinger in the stadium area to snatch the leading position, while Kneubühler had moved up to third. Stadler dropped back to eighth as Domenico Brigaglia and Paolo Casoli took sixth and seventh. On lap 3 Gianola became the first to break the lap record as he moved into the lead while the leading five pulled clear. Brigaglia and Casoli were left well in front of Stadler who came under pressure from Johnny Wickström and Olivier Liegeois.

The leaders continued to swap places many times each lap and had the small but enthusiastic crowd shouting their approval. Kneubühler seemed to have the most trouble hanging on and it was Gianola and Auinger who dived in and out of the works Garellis trying to get ahead. Several times the pair tried to use the same piece of road in their private battle for fourth place in the championship.

After winning thirteen World Championships, Angel Nieto announced his retirement at Hockenheim (left).

Angel Nieto gets down to it in his last Grand Prix (below).

Gerhard Waibel (bottom), won the last 80 cc race of the year with by far his best ride of the season.

Fausto Gresini's victory after an extraordinary 125 race was small consolation for having lost the championship.

The battle for eighth continued with Liegeois, Wickström and Stadler exchanging places almost as often as the leaders. Behind them, the eleventh-place battle was getting exciting between Mike Leitner, Claudio Macciotta and Willy Perez. On lap 8 things got too hot and Macciotta and Perez tangled going on to the start-and-finish straight. Perez ended up once more breaking his wrist, in the same place he had in Sweden. Leitner was left on his own and, able to catch Liegeois, Stadler and Wickström, he made it a four-way battle for the last few points. One of the four would be unlucky.

Gresini found a little extra on the last lap to lead into the stadium. Gianola was second but Cadalora had grown tired of watching and passed his fellow Italian going into the first left-hander in the stadium. Then Auinger went inside Gianola going into the last corner, securing third in the race and fourth in the championship. The lap record finally went to Cadalora who had looked so comfortable all through the race.

## 80 cc

New World Champion 'Aspar' Martinez crashed the Derbi on lap 4 as he chased Gerhard Waibel (the latter having a one-off ride on a works Krauser). Waibel was in unbeatable form and took the lead from the start while Stefan Dörflinger and Ian McConnachie were left struggling at the back of the field. Martinez was feeling in a confident mood and took the lead on lap 2 as Angel Nieto moved into second in his last Grand Prix, with Hans Spaan fourth well ahead of Manuel Herreros.

It looked at first as though it might develop into a Derbi demonstration ride but lap 3 saw Waibel retake the lead and he soon started to pull away as Dörflinger charged through the field. Krauser team-mate McConnachie, however, retired with a seized engine after one slow lap. 'We never recovered from the seizure in practice', said the disappointed Englishman. 'The bike wouldn't go properly for the rest of practice and in the race it was sick and just stopped.'

When Martinez crashed Waibel was left with a three-second lead over Nieto, Spaan having slipped to a distant third with Dörflinger closing on Herreros. Sixth place was being contested between Wilco Zeelenberg, Hubert Abold and Reiner Scheidhauer. These three kept up their contest right to the flag with Zeelenberg getting the verdict.

By the last lap Dörflinger had passed both Herreros and Spaan but was only presented with second place when Nieto's Derbi died on the final circuit. It was a good win for Waibel who jumped to fifth in the championship and must consider Hockenheim his own circuit for it was the scene of his first GP triumph in 1979. McConnachie was frustrated by dropping two places to sixth in the championship as he was also passed by Spaan. He was fortunate that Nieto did not finish. Derbi succeeded in their plan to see Herreros second in the title chase, three points ahead of Dörflinger.

## SIDECARS

This was a classic confrontation to decide the title. Michel had to finish fourth if Streuer or Webster won but if Biland won he could afford to finish sixth. From the start the lead was contested between Rolf Biland and Kurt Waltisperg. Egbert Streuer and Bernard Schnieders and Steve Webster and Tony Hewitt.

Either Hewitt or Streuer could be champion if they won the race. Therefore, Hewitt decided that as he was down on power he had to gear the engine high and look for a slipstream from Biland and Streuer. That worked well for 10 of the 14 laps but when back-markers got in the way he lost touch and without the slipstream could not catch up.

Michel started in fourth place but his helmet became unclipped. As he battled with that he slipped behind the Zurbrügg brothers and by lap 5 they had started to get away from him. He came under pressure from Masato Kumano and Helmut Diehl as well as the British/New Zealand pairing of Frank Wrathall and Kerry Chapman. These three outfits were joined by Steve Abbott and Shaun Smith so Michel had a real battle on his hands to stand any chance of taking the title even if Biland could beat Streuer across the line – at one time he dropped back to seventh place.

The Zurbrügg brothers looked well out of the Frenchman's grasp and as the race ran towards the 10th of the 14 laps it became increasingly obvious that all the outfits were going to finish for the first time in the season. In fact Steinhausen was the only competitive rider to retire.

Fortune smiled a little on Michel as he came into the stadium at the head of the fifth-place battle on lap 12 as his pursuers were held up by a back-marker. It was the break he needed and he set out to see if he could close the two-second gap on Zurbrügg.

The crowd waited in anticipation for Biland and Streuer to appear, knowing that their finishing order was likely to decide the championship. A gasp went up as Biland passed Streuer coming into the stadium. It looked as if Michel would take the title but at the next left-hander Streuer rushed up the inside and bounced off Biland's outfit to enter the corner first. He held on to win the race and took the title because he had more wins than Michel who had been unable to close on the Swiss outfit in the final circuit.

# Preis von Baden–Württemberg, 28 September/statistics
# Hockenheimring, 4.2183-mile/6.7886-km circuit

## 125 cc

**14 laps, 59.06 miles/95.04 km**

| Place | Rider | Nat. | Machine | Laps | Time & Speed | Practice time | Grid |
|---|---|---|---|---|---|---|---|
| 1 | Fausto Gresini | I | Garelli | 14 | 33m 46.46s 104.920 mph/ 168.852 km/h | 2m 22.94s | 1 |
| 2 | Luca Cadalora | I | Garelli | 14 | 33m 47.29s | 2m 23.71s | 2 |
| 3 | August Auinger | A | Bartol | 14 | 33m 47.52s | 2m 24.04s | 3 |
| 4 | Ezio Gianola | I | MBA | 14 | 33m 47.72s | 2m 24.85s | 5 |
| 5 | Bruno Kneubühler | CH | LCR | 14 | 33m 48.69s | 2m 24.34s | 4 |
| 6 | Domenico Brigaglia | I | Ducados | 14 | 34m 18.45s | 2m 26.21s | 6 |
| 7 | Paolo Casoli | I | MBA | 14 | 34m 33.92s | 2m 28.11s | 10 |
| 8 | Olivier Liegeois | B | Assmex | 14 | 34m 39.31s | 2m 27.18s | 7 |
| 9 | Johnny Wickström | SF | Tunturi | 14 | 34m 39.53s | 2m 28.84s | 15 |
| 10 | Adolf Stadler | D | MBA | 14 | 34m 39.85s | 2m 28.20s | 12 |
| 11 | Mike Leitner | A | MBA | 14 | 34m 40.24s | 2m 27.18s | 8 |
| 12 | Norbert Peschke | D | MBA | 14 | 35m 12.20s | 2m 29.74s | 19 |
| 13 | Lucio Pietroniro | B | MBA | 14 | 35m 12.49s | 2m 28.89s | 16 |
| 14 | Jussi Hautaniemi | SF | MBA | 14 | 35m 12.85s | 2m 30.76s | 25 |
| 15 | Marin Andreas Sanchez | E | MBA | 14 | 35m 13.37s | 2m 29.18s | 17 |
| 16 | Jan Eggens | NL | LCR | 14 | 35m 37.92s | 2m 30.79s | 26 |
| 17 | Willi Hupperich | D | Seel | 14 | 35m 38.39s | 2m 32.81s | 36 |
| 18 | Dirk Hafeneger | D | LCR | 14 | 35m 38.99s | 2m 29.59s | 18 |
| 19 | Flemming Kistrup | DK | MBA | 14 | 35m 48.60s | 2m 31.19s | 28 |
| 20 | Josef Bader | D | MBA | 14 | 35m 51.70s | 2m 31.60s | 30 |
| 21 | Christian le Badezet | F | MBA | 14 | 35m 57.50s | 2m 32.40s | 35 |
| 22 | Peter Balaz | CS | MBA | 14 | 35m 58.38s | 2m 33.16s | 43 |
| 23 | Heinz Litz | D | MBA | 13 | 33m 51.16s | 2m 33.16s | 42 |
| 24 | Helmut Hovenga | D | Seel | 13 | 33m 52.42s | 2m 32.90s | 41 |
| 25 | Peter Sommer | CH | MBA | 13 | 34m 20.24s | 2m 31.67s | 31 |
| 26 | Thomas Möller-Pedersen | DK | MBA | 13 | 34m 21.69s | 2m 33.29s | 44 |
| 27 | Robin Milton | GB | MBA | 13 | 35m 20.03s | 2m 31.46s | 29 |
| | Stefan Prein | D | MBA | 12 | DNF | 2m 32.27s | 33 |
| | Hakan Olsson | S | Starol | 9 | DNF | 2m 30.10s | 21 |
| | Jean-Claude Selini | F | MBA | 9 | DNF | 2m 30.37s | 22 |
| | Claudio Macciotta | I | MBA | 7 | DNF | 2m 28.14s | 11 |
| | Willy Perez | RA | Zanella | 7 | DNF | 2m 27.83s | 9 |
| | Karl Dauer | D | MBA | 7 | DNF | 2m 32.89s | 39 |
| | Nicholas Hernandez | E | Beneti | 6 | DNF | 2m 32.90s | 40 |
| | Bady Hassaine | DZ | MBA | 4 | DNF | 2m 32.37s | 34 |
| | Erich Zürn | D | Seel | 3 | DNF | 2m 32.86s | 38 |
| | Angel Nieto | E | Ducados | 3 | DNF | 2m 31.04s | 27 |
| | Patrick Daudier | F | PMDF | 3 | DNF | 2m 32.82s | 37 |
| | Ernst Himmelsbach | D | Ziegler | 2 | DNF | 2m 32.24s | 32 |
| | Thierry Feuz | CH | LCR | 2 | DNF | 2m 28.46s | 13 |
| | Alfred Waibel | D | Real | 1 | DNF | 2m 30.10s | 20 |
| | Jacques Hutteau | F | MBA | 1 | DNF | 2m 30.45s | 24 |
| | Paul Bordes | F | MBA | 0 | DNF | 2m 30.39s | 23 |
| | Pier Paolo Bianchi | I | Elit | | DNS | 2m 28.66s | 14 |
| | Thierry Maurer | CH | MBA | | DNQ | 2m 33.61s | |
| | Klaus Huber | D | MBA | | DNQ | 2m 34.10s | |
| | Boy van Erp | NL | MBA | | DNQ | 2m 34.24s | |
| | Lothar Zürn | D | MBA | | DNQ | 2m 34.41s | |
| | Wilhelm Lücke | D | MBA | | DNQ | 2m 34.60s | |
| | Esa Kytola | SF | MBA | | DNQ | 2m 34.64s | |
| | Uwe Heider | D | Morbidelli | | DNQ | 2m 34.64s | |
| | Michel Escudier | F | MBA | | DNQ | 2m 34.67s | |
| | Robert Hmeljak | YU | MBA | | DNQ | 2m 36.61s | |
| | Uwe Mahl | D | MBA | | DNQ | 2m 37.41s | |
| | Eric Gijsel | B | MBA | | DNQ | 2m 38.00s | |
| | Giuseppe Ascareggi | I | MBA | | DNQ | 2m 38.01s | |
| | Harald Wiedemann | D | MBA | | DNQ | 2m 38.13s | |
| | Horst Elsenheimer | D | MBA | | DNQ | 2m 40.40s | |
| | Fritz Koch | D | MBA | | DNQ | 2m 45.24s | |
| | Lars-Eric Kallesoe | S | Kantarelli | | DNQ | 2m 46.74s | |
| | Steve Mason | GB | MBA | | DNQ | 2m 50.33s | |
| | Gerd Münch | D | MBA | | DNQ | 3m 00.49s | |
| | Carlo Sieben | D | MBA | | DNQ | 3m 10.98s | |
| | Hugo Vigneti | RA | MBA | | DNQ | 3m 17.30s | |

*Fastest lap:* Cadalora, 2m 22.14s, 106.837 mph/171.937 km/h (record).
*Previous record:* Angel Nieto, E (Garelli) 2m 26.00s, 103.98 mph/167.34 km/h (1983).

Final 125 cc World Championship points are on page 180.

## 80 cc

**11 laps, 46.40 miles/74.67 km**

| Place | Rider | Nat. | Machine | Laps | Time & Speed | Practice time | Grid |
|---|---|---|---|---|---|---|---|
| 1 | Gerhard Waibel | D | Real | 11 | 27m 58.50s 99.517 mph/ 160.157 km/h | 2m 30.93s | 1 |
| 2 | Stefan Dörflinger | CH | Krauser | 11 | 28m 20.07s | 2m 31.10s | 2 |
| 3 | Hans Spaan | NL | Huvo | 11 | 28m 23.52s | 2m 34.01s | 5 |
| 4 | Manuel Herreros | E | Derbi | 11 | 28m 44.95s | 2m 34.73s | 6 |
| 5 | Wilco Zeelenberg | NL | Huvo | 11 | 29m 04.78s | 2m 37.86s | 13 |
| 6 | Hubert Abold | D | Krauser | 11 | 29m 05.12s | 2m 38.58s | 14 |
| 7 | Reiner Scheidhauer | D | Seel | 11 | 29m 06.27s | 2m 37.56s | 11 |
| 8 | Alfred Waibel | D | Real | 11 | 29m 18.62s | 2m 37.70s | 12 |
| 9 | Henk van Kessel | NL | Krauser | 11 | 29m 21.38s | 2m 39.37s | 16 |
| 10 | Theo Timmer | NL | Huvo | 11 | 29m 23.58s | 2m 42.14s | 23 |
| 11 | Salvatore Milano | I | Krauser | 11 | 29m 39.26s | 2m 40.97s | 21 |
| 12 | Günter Schirnhöfer | D | Krauser | 11 | 29m 39.42s | 2m 40.01s | 18 |
| 13 | René Dünki | CH | Krauser | 11 | 29m 48.79s | 2m 40.23s | 19 |
| 14 | Michael Gschwander | D | Kiefer | 11 | 29m 59.78s | 2m 44.18s | 33 |
| 15 | Paul Bordes | F | Scrab | 11 | 29m 59.96s | 2m 46.36s | 39 |
| 16 | Bert Smit | NL | Minarelli | 11 | 30m 04.70s | 2m 43.65s | 30 |
| 17 | Richard Bay | D | Ziegler | 11 | 30m 05.18s | 2m 41.39s | 22 |
| 18 | Reiner Koster | CH | LCR | 11 | 30m 05.81s | 2m 43.32s | 28 |
| 19 | Ralf Waldmann | D | ERK | 11 | 30m 06.00s | 2m 44.27s | 34 |
| 20 | Chris Baert | B | Seel | 11 | 30m 06.18s | 2m 42.23s | 24 |
| 21 | Josef Lutzenberger | D | Eberhardt | 11 | 30m 19.95s | 2m 42.33s | 27 |
| 22 | Peter Ottl | D | Eberhardt | 11 | 30m 20.30s | 2m 43.73s | 31 |
| 23 | Rainer Partl | D | Huvo | 11 | 30m 33.08s | 2m 46.17s | 37 |
| 24 | Johann Auer | D | Auer | 11 | 30m 35.78s | 2m 46.83s | 42 |
| 25 | Kees Besseling | NL | Ziegler | 11 | 30m 37.20s | 2m 47.25s | 45 |
| 26 | Aad Wijsman | NL | Harmsen | 10 | 28m 08.13s | 2m 46.34s | 38 |
| 27 | Raimo Lipponen | SF | Kiefer | 10 | 28m 16.55s | 2m 45.13s | 35 |
| 28 | Oliver Friedrich | D | Ziegler | 10 | 28m 34.99s | 2m 46.91s | 44 |
| | Angel Nieto | E | Derbi | 10 | DNF | 2m 35.30s | 7 |
| | Serge Julin | B | Huvo | 9 | DNF | 2m 46.02s | 36 |
| | Josef Fischer | A | Krauser | 6 | DNF | 2m 36.45s | 9 |
| | Stefan Prein | D | Loffler | 4 | DNF | 2m 42.33s | 26 |
| | Felix Rodriguez | E | Autisa | 4 | DNF | 2m 43.92s | 32 |
| | Jorge Martinez | E | Derbi | 3 | DNF | 2m 32.29s | 3 |
| | Rainer Kunz | D | Ziegler | 3 | DNF | 2m 37.34s | 10 |
| | Roland Bosch | D | Kiefer | 3 | DNF | 2m 46.86s | 43 |
| | Hagen Klein | D | Ziegler | 2 | DNF | 2m 43.42s | 29 |
| | Jos van Dongen | NL | Krauser | 2 | DNF | 2m 42.29s | 25 |
| | Reinhard Koberstein | D | Seel | 2 | DNF | 2m 46.55s | 41 |
| | Ian McConnachie | GB | Krauser | 1 | DNF | 2m 33.79s | 4 |
| | Pier Paolo Bianchi | I | Seel | | DNS | 2m 35.58s | 8 |
| | Jörg Seel | D | Seel | | DNS | 2m 38.77s | 15 |
| | Alexandre Barros | BR | Autisa | | DNS | 2m 39.78s | 17 |
| | Thomas Engl | D | ESCH | | DNS | 2m 40.48s | 20 |
| | Brane Rokavec | YU | Seel | | DNS | 2m 46.43s | 40 |
| | Jarmo Piepponen | SF | Kiefer | | DNQ | 2m 47.67s | |
| | Mario Stocco | I | Huvo | | DNQ | 2m 47.77s | |
| | Nicola Casadei | I | RB | | DNQ | 2m 48.23s | |
| | Stefan Brägger | CH | Huvo | | DNQ | 2m 48.24s | |
| | Hans Koopman | NL | Ziegler | | DNQ | 2m 48.39s | |
| | Robin Milton | GB | Wicks | | DNQ | 2m 48.87s | |
| | Otto Machinek | A | M+H | | DNQ | 2m 49.13s | |
| | Petra Gschwander | D | Kiefer | | DNQ | 2m 49.18s | |
| | Jan Verheul | NL | JVM | | DNQ | 2m 50.18s | |
| | Bertus Grinwis | NL | Krauser | | DNQ | 2m 50.27s | |
| | Stuart Edwards | GB | Huvo | | DNQ | 2m 51.24s | |
| | Mika-Sakari Komu | SF | Eberhardt | | DNQ | 2m 52.27s | |
| | Kasimir Rapczynski | D | Eigenbau | | DNQ | 2m 53.97s | |
| | Hans-Jürgen Erk | D | ERK | | DNQ | 2m 55.88s | |
| | Georg Landthaler | D | Ziegler | | DNQ | 2m 55.96s | |
| | Terho Kauhanen | SF | Huvo | | DNQ | 2m 56.91s | |
| | Siegfried Lohmann | D | Seel | | DNQ | 2m 58.94s | |
| | Jan Vanecek | CS | Huvo | | DNQ | 3m 00.13s | |
| | Willi Haas | D | Eberhardt | | DNQ | 3m 01.53s | |
| | Steve Mason | GB | Huvo | | DNQ | 3m 06.29s | |
| | Wolfgang Engels | D | Huvo | | DNQ | 3m 15.35s | |

*Fastest lap:* Dörflinger, 2m 30.72s, 100.755 mph/162.149 km/h (record).
*Previous record:* Stefan Dörflinger, CH (Zundapp), 2m 39.84s, 94.95 mph/152.81 km/h (1983).

Final 80 cc World Championship points are on page 180.

## Sidecars

**14 laps, 59.06 miles/95.04 km**

| Place | Rider | Nat. | Machine | Laps | Time & speed | Practice time | Grid |
|---|---|---|---|---|---|---|---|
| 1 | Egbert Streuer/ Bernie Schnieders | NL NL | LCR– Yamaha | 14 | 31m 50.37s 111.295 mph/ 188.467 km/h | 2m 13.62s | 1 |
| 2 | Rolf Biland/ Kurt Waltisperg | CH CH | Krauser | 14 | 31m 50.57s | 2m 14.52s | 2 |
| 3 | Steve Webster/ Tony Hewitt | GB GB | LCR– Yamaha | 14 | 31m 54.62s | 2m 25.64s | 3 |
| 4 | Alfred Zurbrügg/ Martin Zurbrügg | CH CH | LCR– Yamaha | 14 | 32m 12.94s | 2m 16.54s | 4 |
| 5 | Alain Michel/ Jean-Marc Fresc | F F | Krauser– Yamaha | 14 | 32m 14.41s | 2m 16.96s | 5 |
| 6 | Masato Kumano/ Helmut Diehl | J D | LCR– Yamaha | 14 | 32m 17.43s | 2m 18.02s | 7 |
| 7 | Steve Abbott/ Shaun Smith | GB GB | Windle– Yamaha | 14 | 32m 17.83s | 2m 18.71s | 8 |
| 8 | Frank Wrathall/ Kerry Chapman | GB GB | LCR– Yamaha | 14 | 32m 20.34s | 2m 18.83s | 9 |
| 9 | Markus Egloff/ Urs Egloff | CH CH | LCR– Yamaha | 14 | 32m 55.01s | 2m 17.74s | 6 |
| 10 | Derek Bayley/ Bryan Nixon | GB GB | LCR– Ricardo | 14 | 32m 56.23s | 2m 19.75s | 11 |
| 11 | Theo van Kempen/ Gerardus de Haas | NL NL | LCR– Yamaha | 14 | 33m 21.92s | 2m 21.97s | 14 |
| 12 | Luigi Casagrande/ Adolf Hänni | CH D | LCR– Yamaha | 14 | 33m 34.41s | 2m 23.18s | 19 |
| 13 | Mick Boddice/ John Hennigen | GB GB | LCR– Yamaha | 14 | 33m 45.23s | 2m 24.22s | 21 |
| 14 | Erwin Weber/ Eckart Rösinger | D D | LCR– Yamaha | 13 | 32m 00.27s | 2m 23.07s | 18 |
| 15 | Kurt Hock/ Kuno Hock | D D | Hock– Yamaha | 13 | 32m 02.28s | 2m 25.49s | 24 |
| 16 | Egon Schons/ Andreas Schröder | D D | Busch– Yamaha | 13 | 32m 45.07s | 2m 26.13s | 27 |
| 17 | Albert Weber/ Günter Quanz | D D | LCR– Yamaha | 13 | 33m 06.01s | 2m 26.12s | 26 |
| 18 | Fritz Stölzle/ Hubert Stölzle | D D | LCR– Yamaha | 13 | 33m 31.08s | 2m 27.85s | 29 |
| | Dennis Bingham/ John Gibbard | GB GB | LCR– Yamaha | 11 | DNF | 2m 25.39s | 23 |
| | Amadeo Zini/ Claudio Sowaglia | I I | Yamaha | 10 | DNF | 2m 25.70s | 25 |
| | Norbert Wild/ Andreas Räcke | D D | Yamaha | 10 | DNF | 2m 26.75s | 28 |
| | Rolf Steinhausen/ Bruno Hiller | D D | Busch | 8 | DNF | 2m 19.46s | 10 |
| | Hans Hügli/ Markus Fahrni | CH CH | LCR– Yamaha | 5 | DNF | 2m 20.74s | 13 |
| | Barry Brindley/ Simon Birchall | GB GB | Windle– Yamaha | 4 | DNF | 2m 20.20s | 12 |
| | Graham Gleeson/ Ian Colquhoun | NZ GB | LCR– Yamaha | 3 | DNF | 2m 22.29s | 16 |
| | Wolfgang Stropek/ Hans-Peter Demling | A A | LCR– Yamaha | 2 | DNF | 2m 22.15s | 15 |
| | Werner Kraus/ Oliver Schuster | D D | Busch | 1 | DNF | 2m 22.35s | 17 |
| | René Progin/ Yves Hunziker | CH CH | Seymaz– Yamaha | 0 | DNF | 2m 23.59s | 20 |
| | Derek Jones/ Brian Ayres | GB GB | LCR– Yamaha | | DNS | 2m 24.76s | 22 |
| | Axel von Berg/ Thomas Bottcher | D D | Busch | | DNQ | 2m 28.02s | |
| | Alfred Heck/ Marlow Sturm | D D | LCR– Yamaha | | DNQ | 2m 29.44s | |
| | Friedel Reinhard/ Karl Paul | D CH | LCR– Yamaha | | DNQ | 2m 30.61s | |
| | Rolf Süess/ Werni Villiger | CH CH | Seymaz– Yamaha | | DNQ | 2m 31.76s | |
| | Rudolf Reinhard/ Karin Sterzenbach | D D | LCR– Yamaha | | DNQ | 2m 32.25s | |
| | Reinhard Link/ Walter Link | D D | LCR– Yamaha | | DNQ | 2m 35.60s | |
| | Erwin Eimermann/ Gerhard Gutfeld | D D | EES– Yamaha | | DNQ | 2m 50.06s | |

*Fastest lap:* Biland, 2m 14.61s, 112.814 mph/181.556 km/h (record).
*Previous record:* Jock Taylor/Benga Johansson, GB/S (Yamaha), 2m 21.94s, 106.93 mph/172.09 km/h (1981).

Final Sidecar World Championship points are on page 181.

# SCHWANTZ *Versus* MERKEL

It's always the individual stars that shine out through the Easter gloom when you come to look back at the Match Races. Who, after all, can recall a particular team performance in the history of the event?

People don't remember who won the series in 1980 but many do recall a slim young American from the Southern States who blitzed the best in the world at Brands Hatch and went on to become a triple World Champion. Now Freddie Spencer has gone on to other things. The Transatlantic Challenge was just another step on the way to superstardom.

But the series itself can still throw up new heroes, future champions who see the nation-versus-nation struggle as a convenient way to sample what the European scene has to offer without the pressure of a GP commitment.

This year's new-look series was no exception. Two fresh jewels shone in the otherwise lack-lustre American crown, even though their combined efforts couldn't save national pride. Individual brilliance counts for little in the Match Races. Though Kevin Schwantz and Fred Merkel were the stars of the show the Americans were trounced by a British team who had complete mastery of the midfield.

For the first time the Match Race format outlawed Grand Prix machinery and plumped for the American superbike formula that's set to become a World Championship class in 1988. This had several effects. Most importantly, it should have ensured that the Americans to a man had better machinery than the Brits. The American superbike formula differs from our superstock system by allowing what are essentially F1 engines in standard chassis. They are wolves in sheep's clothing.

For the third year running there was to be no traipsing around Britain, as the lengthened Donington Park circuit was to be the venue for all three days of the competition. Once again, there was to be a different points-scoring formula. Only one thing was certain about *that* – the public wouldn't understand it.

Two teams of twelve riders apiece lined up for the 16th running of the Match Races with the score to date 10 to 5 in favour of the home side. The organisers had expected only ten men a side and two extras had to be called up for Britain when all twelve invited Americans made the trip.

All the predictions were for an American land-slide with their superior machinery making the difference. How wrong everyone was.

There were high hopes, though, that the British team skipper would be on equal terms, riding the Daytona-winning superbike of Eddie Lawson. And it was McElnea who led the way in the first race of the 1986 contest, winning by two seconds to head a British stampede into the first five places.

But his bike hadn't turned out to be quite the beast he'd expected. 'I reckon the only thing that raced at Daytona was the mudguard', said a disappointed British skipper. The engine had been swapped after the Daytona victory and a standard Yamaha substituted for the bike's trip to the UK.

The Americans hadn't got their US Superbike Championship mounts either. Texan Schwantz, who led the first race in the rain before his wet tyres gave out and he was dumped in the mud at Redgate, rode an ex-Tony Rutter Suzuki that he hadn't even seen until two days before the race. And American works Honda Number One, Merkel, was forced to use the bike ridden at Daytona in 1985 by Jeff Haney. Jeff who?

Ron Haslam, too, had bike problems. There was a wrangle involving Haslam, the organisers, Suzuki, Honda Britain and Elf over what Haslam was or was not allowed to ride. Suzuki originally agreed to him racing the ex-Tony Rutter bike and Elf raised no objection. For some reason Suzuki changed their minds – possibly due to pressure from Haslam's former employers, Honda Britain – and Haslam was left riding a standard VFR 750 Honda. When he first tested the bike Haslam wanted to pull out of the event but was prevailed upon to persevere.

As has so often been the case for the Match Races the weather played a vital role as the teams lined up for the first race. It was wet but not wet enough for full wet tyres. Schwantz opted for rain tyres and so did his compatriots to a man. The Brits supressed their smiles and picked either intermediates or hand-cut slicks. The Americans were beaten before they started.

The Texan led off the line from new Mitsui Yamaha signing Kenny Irons but lasted just three laps before his wets gave out. Irons led for a lap until McElnea came through to score his first win on a Marlboro Yamaha. 'I chose a cut slick for the rear and it was perfect', said McElnea, with high hopes of a clean sweep on the Yamaha. However, it was destined to be his last race win of the series as well as his first.

Merkel was the first American home, behind Honda's Roger Burnett, Irons, Steve Parrish and Suzuki's new signing Chris Martin. Canadian Michel Mercier in eighth and Yamaha's Dan Chivington in tenth were the only other American scorers.

So after one race the pattern had been set. America were 57–9 down and there wasn't much prospect of a close contest.

But if the actual team contest was lacking in sparkle the spectacle provided by certain individuals was simply stunning. The US won Race 2 on points, with Schwantz and Merkel dishing out a dose of the old one-two despite an impressive challenge from Irons.

The sheer exuberance of the two Americans delighted the crowds. Englishmen smile and wave to the crowds when they win a race. By contrast, Schwantz lets out a huge 'rebel yell' and stands on the footrests punching both fists in the air as he does his lap of honour.

'That was more like it', he said after win number one. 'We're on our way. Six more like that and we'll be in business.' Merkel was less modest. 'We smoked 'em', he said.

Chris Martin wasn't so jubilant. He had crashed at the new Melbourne hairpin and was taken to hospital suffering from concussion. Later there were criticisms from public and riders about the way the incident was dealt with, for

Martin lay unconscious on the track for several minutes.

And Martin's team-mate Paul Iddon was in trouble, too, after chucking away his Suzuki on the last corner of the race. Nor was Rothmans Honda Britain's Roger Marshall happy with his series at the end of the first day. In Race 1 he had been plagued with ignition trouble and was near-ly knocked off by team-mate Martin. The ignition trouble still hadn't been sorted out by Race 2.

As the Americans prayed for the rain to go away it fell steadily throughout the night and turned to snow for the start of the second day. Once again their inexperience showed as rider after rider had trouble with steamed-up visors. For Roger Burnett there was no such trouble and he had a convincing win from Marshall and Has-lam, with Merkel the best American in fourth.

As Britain continued on the way to victory – the score standing at 177 to 87 – Burnett decided he would aim for the £5000 cash first prize and blow the team-racing. Two Americans were out to

Kevin Schwantz and Fred Merkel were the stars of the weekend, riding harder than anyone else in the cold and wet conditions.

Schwantz (34) and Irons (8) lead the rest into the first corner.

stop him and the next race showed they weren't going to be put off for long by a little dampness.

Schwantz and Merkel were a joy to watch as they put the showbiz back into superbikes and played to the tv cameras. Californian Merkel led for three laps until his misting visor affected him and he waved Schwantz by into the lead. While Burnett and Marshall were having a private dice for third Schwantz powered away; by lifting his visor on the straights Merkel managed to hold second easily. Then, on the last lap Schwantz slowed to walking pace, allowed Merkel to catch him and led a joint wheelie across the line.

But their show wasn't over yet. The best was to come. In Race 5 it looked like it was going to be a Schwantz/Merkel one-two again but it didn't quite work out that way. As they raced side by side, surviving slide after slide, Schwantz and Merkel had the simultaneous 'moment' of the decade.

Both back ends went away but as Merkel took to the grass at Starkey's Bridge, Schwantz treated

millions of tv viewers to a rodeo display that would have outshone anything in his native Texas. He was thrown virtually off the machine with only his hands and right foot still in contact as he heaved himself back aboard. Schwantz isn't a man to let that sort of thing bother him. He simply opened the throttle, regained the lead he'd lost to Rob McElnea and won the race. 'I don't know how I stayed on but once I'd saved it I just had to get back into the lead', said the talented 22-year-old Texan.

Merkel wasn't so lucky. He too rejoined the race but crashed at the new Goddard turn trying to get back on terms with Schwantz, who took the chequered flag on one wheel with his fist in the air.

On Monday it was Merkel's turn for glory in the dry first race, winning it by a street from Schwantz while the consistent Brits filled the midfield placings and plodded onwards to victory. Schwantz made virtually certain of the individual honours by wining the penultimate race

from Merkel as Burnett crashed out of the reckoning after three laps.

There was a bit of drama in the British camp when Haslam was given Marshall's works bike after the British champion had crashed in a support race. However, as Haslam had never ridden the bike before and it was set up wrongly for him, its usefulness was limited.

The final race was a definite anticlimax. Merkel knew he had to win to get the top cash. Schwantz knew he only had to finish second. And that's what happened. Haslam, after making some changes to the Marshall bike, took third. The final scoreline credited Britain with 314 points and the USA with 214.

The dazzling display by the two American team-riders was in vain. There's no substitute for strength in depth when it comes to team races like the Transatlantic. But ask any one of the 14,000 spectators at Donington over Easter who won this year's Match Races and they are likely to answer Schwantz and Merkel.

# TALES OF MYSTERY AND IMAGINATION

### by John Cutts, *Superbike Magazine*

A popular explanation of how the Isle of Man got its name is that it comes from *Mannanan*, a wizard who kept the island's 227 square miles shrouded in mists when marauders threatened. The genealogy is appropriate. The place is often covered in an all-pervading fog both physically and figuratively. The TT races are both myth and mystery. History and heroism and death are its hallmarks, and it's all hidden away on a tiny island in the Irish Sea where they race on public roads over the longest, most difficult course in the world. The last of the great road races: invisible and inviolable; shrouded by the fog.

So many people still come to the Isle of Man TT races. This year the ferries steaming out of Heysham, Dublin, Stranraer and Belfast carried 9500 solo motor cycles and 40,000 TT fans to Mona's Isle. Add to these an army of marshals, officials and organisers, as well as interested local inhabitants, and you have a captive audience of around 60,000. That's slightly less than you'd get at an average European Grand Prix, though there's one important difference. They haven't come for a day out to watch some 40-minute sprint racing: a lot of them will be on the island for a fortnight and the rest will stay for as long as they can.

The costs of travelling and staying there are prohibitive. Yet still they come, enthusiasts and local supporters sworn to two weeks in June and a feast of motor cycling. So many people that it would be quite wrong to question the event's integrity as a spectacle or to cast doubt on its future. Its status as an international race meeting, however, is quite another matter.

The Isle of Man's commitment to the TT is assured. It costs the tourist board £500,000 to stage, a figure which includes £150,000 in prize money but excludes the £480,000 they spent on building a new grandstand this year. Moreover, the racing entry list is still consistently oversubscribed. Nearly 1000 riders apply to take part yet only about 600 can be accepted.

It is now exactly 75 years since they started racing on the 37.7-mile public road Snaefell Mountain Course. The tourist board has dubbed 1986 as Heritage Year in the island and certainly the TT races figured prominently in its publicity. History and heroism mingle along narrow country lanes between the walls and the hedgerows.

The course has changed much since 1911 although the challenge remains much the same. In the early years it used to be largely a dirt track with little tar and plenty of waterlogged sand and gravel all the way up, over and down the mountain. In those pioneering days, the machines were really bicycles fitted with small engines and pedal assistance was often needed for the ascent up the 1384 ft of Snaefell. This tested stamina, endurance and machine reliability among the major manufacturers, and the bikes were road-going tourers (hence 'Tourist Trophy'). The 1911 Senior winner was O. C. Godfrey, riding an Indian at an average speed of 47 mph, while the Junior went to P. J. Evans on a Humber.

The first 50 mph lap was achieved in 1920. By 1933 and the spirited era of Stanley Woods and Norton, it was up to 80 mph for a seven-lap aver-

age. During the TT's golden age of the Fifties and Sixties, the speeds began to soar. Geoff Duke was the first to set a 90 mph race average, on a Norton. Bob McIntyre on a Gilera ran the first 100 mph lap in 1957 and, two years later, John Surtees achieved a 100 mph average during a six-lap Senior on his MV Agusta. They were all certainly riding the same course as in 1911 but it was now fully tarred and racers had replaced bicycles.

John Williams was the first man to crack a 110 mph lap on a factory Suzuki RG500 in 1976. A decade later, as was proved conclusively this year, a 110 mph lap had become commonplace among the street-legal, production 750 cc and 1100 cc riders, not on slicks but on standard treaded tyres. Even a dizzy 113 mph lap is attainable on a bike available from any high street dealership. Not exactly a tourer, you understand, but a road bike all the same. Capable of such unbelievable performance, the feat added further force to the argument that the TT is finally returning to its glorious roots – road bikes racing on public roads in the supreme test of ability and reliablity.

It is ten years now since the island lost the World Championship 500 cc round and had to create its own Formula 1 and 2 World Championships to take the GP's place. Now it seems certain that by 1988 there will be a new Superbike World Championship to replace the dying formula races. It is what the manufacturers want – production racing at the highest level with machines that look stock yet perform and sound like racers. Yet the island will be but one round in a series of 15 and not all the rounds will count towards the title. The likelihood is that the series will be dominated by short-circuit experts who can afford in advance to discard the TT as a points-scoring round. Thus what the Isle of Man has done so much to encourage, by reintroducing production racing, threatens to diminish it still further.

Production machinery is already perhaps beginning to diminish it as a spectacle. Far too many privateer GSX-Rs are being used as all-purpose Formula 1, Senior and Production machines. Just change the number plates and the exhaust system and away you go.

Of the factories present at the TT this year, all of Suzuki's and Yamaha's racing was based on generally available road bikes. Suzuki had a most successful year winning all four production classes. Only Honda Britain entered real works racers like their all-conquering F1 RVF and they also gave a tantalising glimpse of what the future holds by allowing Geoff Johnson to use an expensive prototype superbike during practice week. Popularly named the 6X, Johnson's bike was an ex-Wayne Gardner Suzuka special, a 135 hp/350 lb missile based around the VFR road bike and bristling with factory one-offs. Like a set of rare and precious 34 mm magnesium Keihin carbs that had to be sent back to Japan midweek accompanied by a man from the factory. The bike was geared for 188 mph, nearly 15 mph faster than reigning World Champion Joey Dunlop's machine, and Johnson stated plainly that it was too quick coming down the mountain and had scared him. It was so powerful, he said, the front

end was getting light everywhere. For the race proper they replaced the prototype engine with a race-kitted one which was still good enough to allow Johnson to achieve two second places in the Formula 1 and Senior. In its practice specification, however, it was possibly the fastest bike the Isle of Man has ever seen. Its sheer speed along the fast straight sections was astounding.

It is quite naturally the assorted pleasures and perils of the 37.7-mile course that dominates events. It remains the ultimate in concentration, the most demanding and difficult track to learn and it has, undeniably, the most blunt and objective dangers. The course is unique. Things happen on it that wouldn't occur elsewhere. Like when the fog comes down on the mountain in the middle of a race or there are unexpected wet patches under the trees. Alternate wet and dry surfaces are the worst conditions for racing, yet at the TT they are par for the course. Worst of all is the risk of machine failure at high speed through a walled or wooded section. There just aren't that many places left to go on a course lined with cottages, dry-stone walls and bus stops.

Riding a TT is not supposed to be a test of bravery and anybody who thinks so (some of the old timers lean towards this view) has partial paralysis of the brain.

The TT Mountain Course is certainly a challenge. And there are those who accept it and sign up and those who decide the risks are too high. One respects both camps but instinctively admires those who can race the TT *and* the GPs as being well-rounded professionals. Sadly, there are pitifully few of them left. There was nobody at the TT this year who could be identified as a regular GP campaigner. How could there be when the dates clashed with the Austrian GP? Instead, the TT has become home for the Irish road specialists, the holiday racers and a curious, still-emerging new breed: the proddie experts.

Four racers died this year taking the total to 140 since the races began in 1907. One of them, Gene McDonnell of Ireland, died in an accident so terrible that even the seasoned hacks from the national papers found no need for sensationalism, the bare facts were horrible enough. McDonnell was killed instantly when he hit a horse on the race track at 100 mph. His death was awful. It should never have happened. Regrettably, it is also necessary to say that it could only have happened at the TT.

In the long and treacherous chain of cause and effect, the inquest concluded that, during the 250 cc Junior race, a child's pony had been spooked by the landing of a helicopter being used to carry away Formula 2 World Champion, Brian Reid, to Nobles Hospital after his bike had seized at Ballaugh Bridge. So frightened was the pony by the whirring rotors, it sought escape across the fields and over four fences before finally finding itself on the TT course in the gaze of hundreds of spectators at one of the most popular viewing spots. McDonnell, lying fifth in the race, burst upon the scene at maximum wick. He saw the horse and hit the brakes aiming away from it but the horse walked into him. The bike subsequently

Brian Reid leaps to victory in the Formula 2 race but the same spot was to be the scene of tragedy later.

hit a parked car and burst into flames in a garage forecourt. Riders passing through afterwards (the race was never stopped) recall it was like riding into and through a nightmare. The spectators' faces were white even though many had turned away.

What can you say about such an incident? It almost defies belief. With respect to the unlucky McDonnell, maybe it really is just a thing best forgotten about. Hidden in the fog ... until the next time. Or the time when a sidecar goes into the crowd; then it will be well and truly over.

Although I have been going to the TT for many years, I still find the body count and the serious, multiple-injury racing accidents hard to accept and harder to swallow. I guess it must be the same for all supporters of the TT, the very last of the great road races.

In a good year there are no fatalities, the races are thrilling and the lap records get shattered. In a bad year the fatalities simply overshadow everything else.

Last year the racing was excellent. This time round it was like the weather – varied and unpredictable, mist and fog with occasional sunny patches. Practice week was the worst hit. Only a dozen or so riders topped 110 mph in the available sessions. Yet the number of riders who then went on to race round Mona faster than ever before increased dramatically, mostly mounted on production machines and *flying*. This in itself is promising. There is a big difference between lapping at 105 mph and at 110 mph, and there are more riders than ever before, most only in their second or third year, capable of doing it.

The TT will always be more than just the racing. It is a sacred and profound celebration of the motor cycling life. The fans come for the island's alternative attractions as much as they do for the races. They come for the rallies and owners' meets, for the pubs that stay open all day, and the Douglas Prom *camaraderie* that goes on all night. They come for the electric mountain railway and the horse-drawn trams, for Mad Sunday, for the Ramsey Sprint along the cobblestones and the Red Arrows over Douglas Bay. They are inevitably seduced by the island's considerable and irresistible charm and by its breathtaking beauty. The whole place is very much like it was in the fifties: unspoilt and unhurried, enchanting, enduring and unchanging. That's a good description of the course itself: a long and winding public road, largely without a speed limit, along which you're free to ride and follow the same path on your own machine as the racers do on theirs. The Isle of Man during TT has a timeless, otherworldly appeal.

What is certain is that despite the popularity of the fringe activities, the legions of fans wouldn't come without the races. The racing perfectly complements and completes the rich fortnight-long festival of motorcycling that goes on around them. Although in a bad year, it has to be said, it is a precariously maintained balance.

### Formula 1

Joey Dunlop came to the TT behind on points in the World Championship to Anders Andersson, a

Swedish Suzuki GSX-R-mounted privateer. Nobody seriously doubted that Dunlop would win the race and regain the championship lead because Andersson was making his TT debut and had made it quite clear that if it wasn't for the precious championship points at stake, he wouldn't be racing at the TT at all.

Andersson practised hard, worked hard and took a pragmatic, realistic attitude to the course.

'I don't like racing here although it isn't as bad as I expected. It is obviously dangerous. If there was no Isle of Man there would be less deaths in motor cycle racing. I can accept the dangers but it is a big risk and if I could avoid taking that risk I would.'

The race was postponed for two days because of persistent fog and drizzle. The organisers, faced with wholesale rescheduling of the week's races, took a gamble in declaring an 11.0 Monday morning start since there was still swirling mist on the mountain reducing visibility to 100 yards in places, with wet patches everywhere. Hedging their bets, they shortened the race to four laps.

In the event, all the racers except Dunlop were circumspect in the fog of the first lap and surprised to come round a lap later and find ideal conditions.

Joey opted to ride the proven 1985 bike rather than the new '86-spec RVF and won the race at a canter. He started with a front intermediate and a hand-cut slick on the back but by lap 2 had established enough of a cushion to call in for fresh, slick rubber. Unlike the rest of the field, Dunlop had been pouring it on from the off. He won by a minute from Geoff Johnson with a fastest lap of 113.9 mph set on dry roads. It was Yer Man's fourth consecutive F1 TT win.

Geoff Johnson felt that finishing second to Joey was as good as winning. Indeed, he rated his fine second place, at an average 111 mph, more of an achievement than his two previous TT proddie wins.

Andy McGladdery was third, plagued by misfires on his GSX-R. John Weeden was fourth on the RG500, the first two-stroke home. Anders Andersson was 12th, only a handful of seconds short of the championship points he desperately craved. He managed a 109 mph circuit, an exceptional lap speed for a rookie, but said the fog on the first lap had detuned him.

'I didn't know where I was going and I thought about retiring. By the next lap you could see perfectly, so I lost because of inexperience. I am not used to the track or racing in the fog.'

Suzuki took ten of the first twelve places.

## Formula 2

This was another race shortened because of uncertain weather. The World Champion, Brian Reid, made no mistakes and stormed to a well-deserved victory over four laps, upping the lap record to 111.7 mph on his 350 Yamaha.

He said afterwards that he had been very determined to make amends for the previous year's heartache when he had run out of petrol less than two miles from the flag while leading the race. This time he cruised the last lap, taking no chances.

John Weeden was second, one minute behind. Neil Tuxworth, riding in his 60th TT, was third. In fourth spot was the first four-stroke, Ray Swann's Kawasaki 600.

Robert Dunlop had a bad spill at the 13th Milestone which forced the withdrawal of elder brother Joey from the afternoon production race. Gene McDonnell walked away from a heavy crash at Cruickshanks, thanking his luck and looking forward to another day's racing.

## Junior

The first six-lapper of the week was a race eagerly anticipated by the crowds as likely to be a cracker. No proddie bikes, just real lightweight 250 racers and at least a dozen riders, mostly Irish, in with a chance of the spoils.

Unfortunately, the 1986 Junior will be remembered as a race devastated at half-distance by the tragic death of Gene McDonnell. Certainly the joy of the winner, Steve Cull, on a Honda, was heavily laced with sadness and remorse at the loss of a friend and a fellow-countryman.

Joey Dunlop on his own Honda had set the pace early on but crashed at Sulby Bridge thanks to a leaky fuel cap that had been dribbling petrol onto the rear tyre. Nobody could remember Joey ever crashing on the island before. He remounted only to go out soon afterwards with a split exhaust.

The first lap witnessed a titanic battle between Dunlop, Cull and Brian Reid. Cull had problems from the off. On lap 1 he flew so high at Ballaugh Bridge he nearly crashed on landing. On lap 2, at the same spot, he almost ploughed into Brian Reid whose Kimoco had seized on the approach.

Cull led from lap 4 onwards but was pushed all the way by Phil Mellor on an EMC, Graham Cannell (Honda) and Dave Leach (Yamaha). More than anything else, Cull's gritty determination under pressure won the race for him.

Phil Mellor ran the quickest lap on the ill-fated third at 111.4 mph.

## Sidecars

The first three-wheeler race went to the very first Irish winners, Lowry Burton and Pat Cushnahan, who beat Warwick Newman and Eddie Yarker by 50 seconds after the early leader, Dick Greasley, had retired.

Dave Saville took the 350 cc F2 honours by a long way, finishing 12th overall and embarrassing a whole bunch of bigger-engined outfits and crews.

The second sidecar race was pure storybook. Nigel Rollason has been campaigning a British-made Barton Phoenix 4 for years at the TT and this year, against all odds, he won, becoming the first British-powered sidecar winner in the last 20 years. The motor, made famous as the power-plant in the film Silver Dream Racer, was nine years old and carried the original barrels, cases and cranks.

Early leader Mick Boddice lost his passenger Chas Birks at Greeba Castle while dicing for the lead with Dave Hallam. By Kirk Michael on lap 1, Hallam had retired and given the lead to Derek Plummer and Brian Marris.

Plummer led into the last lap but was hampered by a misfire. Rollason got past and promptly lost top gear at Rhencullen. Over the mountain on the last there was nothing in it. Rollason had to fight all the way to hold off the plucky Plummer who might well have stolen it in the last six miles had his engine been chiming on all four cylinders for the downhill run to the flag.

In the closest sidecar finish in years, Rollason won by six seconds and became the first man to win both solo and sidecar races over the TT Mountain Course (he won the 1971 Senior Manx GP before switching to three-wheelers).

Third-placed Warwick Newman and Eddie Yarker took the overall aggregate honours. Jock Taylor's 1982 lap record of 108 mph remained untouched and untouchable.

## Production

Four races; four lap records. Each of the fiercely contested three-lappers contained as many surprises as foregone conclusions.

The tiddlers class was among the most keenly competitive. Two brand new bikes, never seen elsewhere, made their racing debut on the island and were a joy to behold. They were Yamaha's beautiful TZR250 two-stroke, a gem of a GP replica, and Suzuki's GSX-R400, a scaled-down, rev-crazy variation of their successful oil-cooled GSX-R four-stroke formula. The 250 had acceleration, the 400 had a slight advantage in top end. Both Mat Oxley (Yamaha) and Barry Woodland (Suzuki) had topped 100 mph in practice.

A 100 mph lap on a production 250? They would have said it was impossible ten years ago. The wonderful thing about modern proddie racing is that most of us would have said it was unlikely a mere twelve months in the past.

It was a smashing race. Oxley held the advantage by a smattering of seconds throughout, head on tank, braking later than seemed possible.

Although some distance apart on the roads, Woodland stalked his shadow on corrected time.

The last lap decided it. Oxley ran into the 750 cc tail-enders (they run two classes in each race and let the bigger capacity bikes get away first) and they held him up in the slower sections. It was frustrating because Oxley could outride them only to have the 750s come back past on the straights and block his path again.

By the mountain ascent, his signallers told him Woodland had crept ahead and was forging on apace. Oxley crashed at Governor's Bridge trying to catch up. He remounted to take third behind Graham Cannell on another TZR. Woodland won by 17 seconds. Oxley set the fastest lap at 100.8 mph.

The Production C class for 250–400 cc strokers and 401–600 cc thumpers was new to the TT and ended with the fourth-closest victory of all time. Gary Padgett on a Suzuki RG400 (another previously unseen scaled-down version of a popular bike) won by one second from Malcolm Wheeler on a Kawasaki GPZ600. The race went to the wire with furious action on the mountain descent, the lead changing hands twice in the last two miles.

Steve Lindsell finished an excellent third on a Yamaha XJ600, a decidedly unfashionable eight-valve, air-cooled machine. He had actually led onto the last lap but slowed to conserve fuel. Joey Dunlop was fourth on a Honda NS400. Padgett established a lap record of 104.4 mph.

The 750 cc race was outstanding. On lap 1, the first 15 were all inside the lap record from a standing start. Fourteen riders had race averages better than the old lap record and three of them didn't even make the cut for a silver replica.

The winning bike was the same as in 1985 – Suzuki's GSX-R – but conditions were better and the record book was comprehensively rewritten.

Phil Mellor took the laurels thanks to a blistering second lap of 110.6 mph which cut deep into the early lead of Helmut Dahne (another GSX-R). Canadian Kevin Wilson was third, Trevor Nation fourth (both GSX-Rs). Dave Leach was a commendable fifth on Honda's new VRF but there was no doubt which manufacturer held the edge in the hyper-sports league.

Exactly the same was true of the Mr Big class, the 1100 cc ultimates in street superbiking. In a field of 48 there were 30 GSX-R1100s. Most of them had been experiencing misfire problems in practice but come race day there were enough good 'uns to swamp the places. Suzuki 1100s took the top eight places.

Trevor Nation romped home in fine style to complete Suzuki's utter domination of production racing proceedings. He ran 113.26 mph on his second lap which was the first time a street bike on street rubber has lapped in under 20 minutes. I took a look at his Michelin tyres afterwards and it was hard to see where the sidewalls began let alone where the tread had once been.

Some final thoughts. There can be no finer test of a road bike's performance and reliability than the TT. Moreover, the organisers had the foresight to reintroduce production racing at a time when it was neither profitable nor popular on the main-

land. In three years of proddie TT racing there have been no fatalities and few big accidents. The racing has been exciting and excellent and has attracted the support of nearly all the major manufacturers and tyre companies. Whatever happens with the proposed World Championship Superbike series, the Isle of Man will remain the most important date in the production racing calendar.

### Senior

In perfect weather, the early laps of the last race of TT week suggested a battle of the giants. Dunlop, Nation, Roger Marshall and Roger Burnett were in close company from the start, together on time and on the roads.

Up front, Dunlop and Nation swapped the lead many times in the first three laps. Nation on a Mk11 RG was flying, undoubtedly pumped up from his scorching victory in the morning's production race. Dunlop had unwisely chosen to ride his Formula 1 750 instead of his 500 but was giving no quarter.

Behind them on the roads, but actually slightly ahead on corrected time, came Honda team-mates Marshall and Burnett on identical bikes and seemingly inseparable as they diced the first 113 miles together, the one shadowing the other.

Unfortunately, what was shaping up to be the fastest, most exciting six-lapper for years was suddenly beset by mechanical gremlins and retirements. Dunlop lost three minutes in the pits replacing a steering damper. Could Joey pull back a minute a lap on Nation, Marshall and Burnett, who had all run the third at 116 mph?

Nation, alone at the front, was the man to catch, having run the fastest lap of the week at 116.5 mph. But zooming down the mountain on the fourth, Dunlop's bike spluttered to a halt at the 32nd Milestone, the tank dry and his race over. He later calculated that he had used 3.3 gallons in one lap. That's 11 mpg.

Marshall dropped down the field after drive-chain problems. Burnett inherited the lead on the fourth and never surrendered it, fortunately surviving an encounter with a swarm of bees on the last.

Geoff Johnson was second on his experimental F1 Honda VFR lookalike. Perhaps the most underrated performance of the week was that of Dave Leach. In a race without a capacity ceiling he finished 7th on a 320 cc Yamaha.

Sadly, four racers were killed during this year's TT.

Ian Ogden sustained fatal injuries during practice week when he lost control of his RG500 at the end of the Cronk-y-Voddee straight. A former Max GP runner-up, he was the first Manxman to be killed in the TT races.

Alan Jervis, a sidecar passenger, died following a practice crash at the bottom of Bray Hill.

Gene McDonnell was killed instantly when he collided with a horse at Ballaugh Bridge during the 250 cc Junior race (see text).

Andy Cooper, a former Manx GP Winner, died at Doran's Bends after crashing on the fourth lap of the Senior race.

Mat Oxley produced the first 100 mph production 250 lap.

Roger Burnett on the Rothmans Honda heads for his first TT victory having passed Phil Mellor on the four-stroke Suzuki.

# FLYIN' FRED MERKEL'S YEAR

## by JOHN ULRICH

It was Fred Merkel's year in US road racing, despite the pundits' contention that Merkel couldn't possibly compete with Honda team-mate Wayne Rainey. Merkel won just two races in the modified street bike Superbike class against Rainey's six Superbike wins. Merkel also sat out Grand Prix-style Formula 1 races which Rainey entered, winning once. But when it was all over, Merkel had won the Camel Pro Series Road Racing Championship, a title and a Number One plate earned with a curious combination of Superbike and Formula 1 points. When the final race ended, Merkel had 146 points to Rainey's 144.

By all reasoning, it shouldn't have been that way. Certainly the powers that be at Team Honda didn't expect it. When the team arrived at races with the giant Honda tractor-trailer truck, Rainey's crew of three mechanics set up three or four machines under two large tents directly in front of the trailer.

Merkel and his two mechanics set up a single tent, with a single bike, off to one side, near the rear of the trailer.

The contrast between the two operations was instantly recognisable. And when Rainey rolled to win after win, convincingly beating Merkel time after time, it seemed to outsiders that the only people at the racetrack who maintained their faith in Merkel were mechanics Mike Velasco and Merlyn Plumlee – nicknamed 'The Burner Brothers'.

The situation was a comedown for Merkel. He had completely dominated Superbike racing for two straight seasons, streaking to a record number of wins (13) in the class, beating the win totals amassed by Eddie Lawson (12), Freddie Spencer (12), Mike Baldwin (10), Wes Cooley (8), and Rainey (7).

Even *after* the 1986 season, Merkel retained the win record, holding 15 wins as against Lawson's and Rainey's 13 wins apiece with the others unchanged.

Merkel had won races and two Superbike Championships. Yet his wins came against weak competition, for Lawson, Spencer and Rainey had been away in Europe in 1984, while Rainey had sat out the 1985 Superbike season in favour of a Formula 1 ride with wealthy privateer Bob MacLean's MacLean Racing.

Lawson and Spencer won their races competing against each other. Baldwin and Rainey raced each other in 1983.

But Honda had fielded the only strong, well-organised, consistently well-prepared team in US racing in 1984 and 1985. And Merkel had been the only rider on that team. Kawasaki had dropped out of US racing completely following Rainey's victory in the Superbike Championship in 1983. Yamaha had not yet committed themselves to Superbike racing in America, and US Suzuki-backed Yoshimura struggled along with air-cooled GS 750s that were no match for the Hondas.

Merkel's winning lap times on the updated V-four Hondas in 1984 and 1985 were slower, the same or scarcely faster than the lap times turned by Rainey in 1983 on the air-cooled Kawasaki GPZ 750.

After two long years of glory and huge win bonuses, Merkel didn't face the prospect of being the number two man on the Honda team for 1986. Instead, Merkel faced the prospect of being without a ride at all. Rainey had been signed to a three-year contract, and Merkel was out.

Merkel scrambled, talking to Yoshimura and US Suzuki and calling executives at Honda Racing Corporation in Japan. Only strong objections from Japan saved Merkel's Honda ride, over American management's objections. But even with his ride intact, Merkel faced 1986 as an exile in his own team.

The strain was evident, but in all Merkel bore it well. He became a little more flamboyant, his hairstyle looking as if it had come straight from the pages of a trendy men's fashion magazine, complete with greasy spikes. He used shoe polish to emblazon a huge '1' on the side of a rental car. He talked big and seemed to work at exuding confidence.

But most of all, Merkel finished races. Racked up points. Kept finishing. Kept racking up points. Race after race after race.

And when it came right down to it, finishing races and racking up points counted a whole lot more than did superior numbers of bikes or mechanics or tents or wins.

In theory, there should have been more threats to Merkel than simply from team-mate Rainey. But as the season progressed, it became evident that one or the other of the two Honda pilots would win the championship.

Suzuki's Kevin Schwantz, coming off three wins in 1985 on outclassed machines, looked set for a full assault on the championship with Yoshimura-prepared GSXR 750s. But Schwantz, although fastest in qualifying at several events, spent most of his time blowing up bikes or crashing or recovering from crashes – never completely – or working on new combinations of the above.

Yamaha got back into US road racing in a big way, spending enough money to win but hiring two riders – veteran Jimmy Filice and newcomer John Kocinski – who were outclassed against Rainey, Merkel and Team Honda. At the right track, on the right day, given the right circumstances, Kocinski could run with Merkel. But most of the time, Kocinski had his hands full dealing with team-mate Filice, and both were breaking, crashing or racing for third or fourth place.

So the race for the new, single combined Camel Pro Series Road Racing Championship (which replaced the separate-but-equal Superbike and Formula 1 championships of the past) came down to Merkel and Rainey.

The championship, based on combined points, was one more step towards the replacement of Formula 1 by Superbike as the premier class in American road racing. A Superbike win paid 20 points; so did a Formula 1 win. Eight events on the season's schedule included both a Superbike race and a Formula 1 race, and, in those cases, only a rider's best finish for the weekend counted towards the championship, and a rider could not use the same machine in both races. If a rider won

both races, he would still only have 20 points awarded towards the championship.

One event – the season-starting Daytona 200 – featured Superbikes with no Formula 1 event at all. That meant there were nine points-paying Superbike races versus eight points-paying Formula 1 races.

The argument against Formula 1 lay in the lack of available Grand Prix machines and the high initial cost of those machines. Four-stroke Superbikes were cheaper to acquire, said Superbike supporters, and the racing was closer. Grand Prix bikes were cheaper to maintain and run for a season, gave privateers a chance to win and didn't break as often, Formula 1 supporters said.

No matter what the arguments, the 1986 season was structured so a Superbike pilot was virtually certain to win the combined championship, with little or no recognition for the Formula 1 man with the most points.

Formula 1 riders complained but soldiered on, many accepting as fact a rumour that the two-leg Formula 1 Nissan 200 at Laguna Seca would pay full points for each 100-kilometre segment, becoming in effect a double-points event to even the chances. The AMA denied the rumour and declined to award double points. The source of the rumour was never pinpointed.

The question that remained was, who would win? Rainey had two chances to every one of Merkel's to score 20 points on a given weekend. On the other hand, racing two distinctly different machines on one weekend – and often on one day – made Rainey's task more difficult.

Merkel had to make every Superbike race count. But Merkel only had to deal with one machine (a VFR 750 Superbike like Rainey's) without having to worry about a three-cylinder two-stroke RS 500 Grand Prix race bike as well.

At Daytona for the first race, Merkel and Rainey had their hands full with more than each other. Lawson returned to Superbike racing for the first time since winning the Superbike Championship in 1981 and 1982, heading to Florida with a Yamaha FZ 750 Superbike. Lawson qualified fastest, set a new lap record and ran with Rainey and Schwantz in tow for the first several laps in the 57-lap, 200-mile race. But Schwantz couldn't keep up the pace on the Suzuki he had used to qualify third-fastest, and fell behind. Rainey could keep up and did, until his bike chunked a Michelin rear tyre on the 15th lap, forcing him to call into the pits. Rainey would have one more rear tyre chunk before the flag and struggled home to finish fourth.

Merkel battled against Baldwin until the latter's works FZ 750 Yamaha blew up. Lawson cruised out in front; Schwantz held off a challenge by Yoshimura team-mate Satoshi Tsujimoto until Tsujimoto's GSXR 750 broke. At the finish, the order was Lawson, Schwantz, Merkel and Rainey, the tyre problems providing a disappointing start to the season for Rainey. Lawson, running the same tyre, experienced no such problems. Schwantz and Merkel ran Dunlops.

Schwantz led the points after Daytona. Marlboro-sponsored Lawson didn't wear a Camel patch however, and was declared ineligible for

**Jim Filice high on the banking** (right).

**The empty grandstands were discouraging but the Superbike Daytona 200 started all the same.**

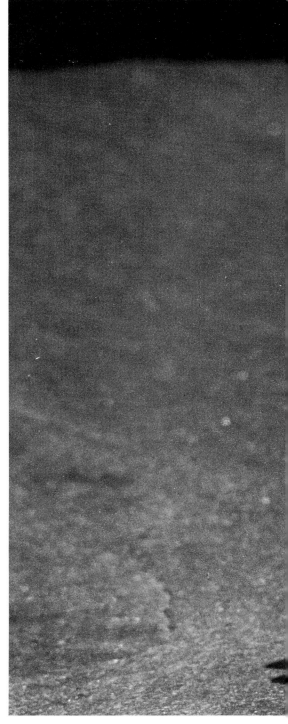

points, although he was able to hold on to his share of the prize money.

Schwantz was the fastest man in both classes at Sears Point in northern California, riding a pair of Superbikes. But Schwantz's bike quit running while he led the Formula 1 race, turning conservative lap times a full second slower than he had in one of his heat races. That made the battle for the lead a struggle between four-times World Champion Kork Ballington, now riding an RS 500 Honda for MacLean Racing, privateer Randy Renfrow and Rainey. With Schwantz out, Rainey led, then faded with a wrong tyre choice. Ballington won, with Renfrow second and Rainey third.

In the Sears Point Superbike race, Merkel was given the win even though he finished far behind Rainey and Schwantz after crashes caused the race to be stopped and restarted. Before the red flag, Rainey and Schwantz passed lapped riders under a waving yellow flag at a crash site. Under AMA rules, no passing is allowed under a waving yellow; Rainey and Schwantz argued that to attempt *not* to pass lapped riders in that particular section of track (fast esses) would have been more dangerous than to just go ahead and pass. So they did. And they were docked a lap each. With Merkel earning first-place points and Rainey taking a third, Merkel led the points, 33 to Rainey's 24.

Schwantz was again the fastest man in both classes at Brainerd International Raceway in far-north Minnesota, once more using a pair of Superbikes. But this time rider error, not machine failure and not a rules violation, took Schwantz out of contention. Schwantz went out in the first practice session early on an overcast race day morning on brand new tyres and threw away his Suzuki in the fourth corner of the course. He broke his collarbone, just as he had done on two occasions in 1985.

Renfrow won the Formula 1 race at Brainerd, Rainey's RS 500 breaking while leading. Ballington was second, Dale Franklin third on an ageing TZ 750.

Rainey won the Superbike race, Merkel finishing second, and the points gap narrowed to three points.

Schwantz sat out the races at Road America in Wisconsin and at Bryar Motorsports Park in Loudon, New Hampshire. Rainey won both races at Road America, Formula 1 and Superbike, and never looked better. Renfrow was second in Formula 1, Ballington third. Merkel was second in Superbike.

At Loudon, Renfrew barely beat Ballington in Formula 1 and Rainey was third after last-minute changes he ordered to be made to his RS 500 backfired. Rainey won the Superbike race, with Merkel second. That gave Rainey the points lead, 84 to 81.

At Pocono International Raceway in the mountains of Pennsylvania, Renfrow won another close Formula 1 race, this time with Rainey just behind and Ballington, suffering from flu, third.

Rainey led every lap of the Superbike race at Pocono, though, with Merkel second and Schwantz, in his first race since his crash at

Brainerd, third. Rainey left Pocono with a seven-point advantage over Merkel.

There were three events left to decide the championship: at Laguna Seca Raceway in California, at Mid-Ohio Sports Car Course in Ohio and at Road Atlanta in Georgia.

The Superbike race was held first at Laguna Seca, and Rainey won again. Schwantz's Suzuki blew up on the main straight, in full view of most of the many Suzuki executives on hand to see Schwantz battle against Team Honda. And Bubba Shobert, Honda's lone dirt track team rider and a part-time road racer, finished second on a 1985 VF 750F-based Superbike, beating Merkel for the first time, although he had finished one position behind Merkel at both Sears Point and Loudon.

The Formula 1 race at Laguna Seca is the closest thing America has to a Grand Prix, and spectators have flocked to the scenic California course to watch American stars like Kenny Roberts, Spencer, Randy Mamola and Lawson return from Europe to race. This year Lawson, Mamola and Baldwin came back, with Roberts managing Baldwin and Mamola under Kool cigarette colours instead of the Lucky Strike banner the team runs under in Europe. Roberts' sponsors don't own the Lucky Strike brand in America but do own Kool.

Lawson, Mamola and Baldwin brought with them their frontline Grand Prix race bikes and a batch of radial Michelin tyres not available in the US. Baldwin qualified fastest at 1m 6.109s, 0.04 seconds per lap faster than Lawson, with Mamola another 0.04 seconds behind Lawson. Ballington was fourth-fastest at 1m 7.723s, over one second a lap faster than Rainey at 1m 8.449s and Renfrow at 1m 8.748s.

Rainey rode on second-string radial Michelins, as sold in Europe. Ballington and Renfrow ran on radial Dunlops.

About 40,000 spectators showed up to watch a race and were not disappointed. Baldwin, Lawson and Mamola ran at a pace faster than qualifying, disappearing from the field, until the race was red-flagged due to a crash. Mamola and Roberts complained that the front runners should hang together and stage a show, doing wheelies for the crowd. The restart saw that happen, with Rainey able to stay close behind, for about ten laps. Then the pace dropped again to 1m 6s and Lawson flew past Baldwin to take the lead. Lapping back-markers at near-record pace, Lawson got wide and went off the track, ramming head-on into a steel barrier protected by hay bales. The crash nearly ended not only Lawson's race but his Grand Prix season. He was badly bruised and one shoulder was severely strained.

Mamola won that first segment, with Baldwin second. In the second segment, Mamola set a new lap record but Baldwin won, racing the whole way, lapped traffic keeping Mamola in second in the closing laps. Rainey started the second segment on one of Lawson's European radials but crashed, breaking his collarbone. In overall scoring Baldwin won, Mamola taking second and Ballington third ahead of Renfrow. Rainey left Laguna Seca with a 14-point lead over Merkel.

The Formula 1 race three weeks later at Mid-

Ohio was, in a word, weak. Renfrow was nervous, leading Formula 1 points and knowing that he could make that lead an insurmountable one with careful riding, albeit aware that the championship he sought was no longer an official one.

Rainey, meanwhile, was in a position to tie up the official title, the overall Camel Pro Series Road Racing Championship, and, with his collarbone bothering him, elected to concentrate on the Superbike race.

The track was peculiarly slick. Renfrow gambled that a radial Dunlop would heat up and work even though it hadn't in practice. Ballington chose a soft bias-ply Dunlop. It turned out that Ballington's choice was perfect, Renfrow's terrible.

Ballington led early and pulled away, seemingly on course for certain victory. But he was so far ahead that he slowed down, declaring later that the reduced pace made his Honda work differently through one bumpy corner. Ballington lost the front wheel and crashed.

Renfrow inherited the lead, slipping and sliding, trying to stay upright and to avoid making a mistake so he could be sure of those points. He was pursued by a motley band of privateer-ridden street bikes and Grand Prix machines. Closest

behind were Dan Chivington on a stock (except for pipe and carbs) Suzuki GSXR 750 and Gary Goodfellow on a similar GSXR 750 LTD. They caught Renfrow, Goodfellow leading Chivington, poised ready to stuff his way past underneath as they entered a downhill right-hander. Renfrow snapped his Honda into the curve, taking a line directly across the path chosen by Goodfellow, who, unseen by Renfrow, was committed. Goodfellow tapped the brakes, lost it, and was flung over the bars. Renfrow won, with Chivington following close behind. Larry Shorts, a dedicated low-dollar privateer known to sleep in his van year-round, was third on another close-to-stock GSXR 750, ahead of Boonie Knott on a Grand Prix RG 500 and Russ Paulk – riding with a collarbone broken in practice at Laguna Seca – on his RS 500.

That stockers could run so far up front, let alone make the winner's circle, in an AMA Formula 1 race was the harshest indictment of the class to date.

It came down to the Superbike class. Again, there was a tyre choice dilemma. Merkel chose the same Dunlop tyre Ballington had used with success in Formula 1. Rainey, committed to Michelin, had a smaller selection and opted for a

bias-ply tyre that was softer than the Dunlops used by Merkel and Ballington; Rainey's only other choice was a far harder Michelin.

Rainey's tyre didn't work. He led, slowed as the tyre overheated dramatically, was caught and passed by Merkel. If Rainey had accepted that, had worked to hold onto second, he could have been champion. But as soon as Merkel got by, Rainey charged, and, grabbing a big handful of throttle off one of the last turns on the course, Rainey slid sideways, caught and flew off the highside, landing face down, hard.

Merkel was on top form, setting a new lap record and winning by a wide margin, Schwantz was a distant second, complaining of handling problems but also in pain with a collarbone rebroken when he crashed a MacLean Racing RS 250 while leading the class at Laguna Seca. Chivington took third place.

Those results gave Merkel the points lead, 130 to Rainey's 124, with one event and 20 points left. If Rainey won and Merkel was third at Road Atlanta, Rainey would be champion. If Merkel was second, Merkel would be champion.

Merkel was running fourth at Atlanta for some laps, behind Rainey, Schwantz and Kocinski. But

Schwantz crashed his Suzuki while running just behind Rainey after falling back, catching up and making a charge. Schwantz said later that the bike jumped into neutral as he ran into a Road Atlanta corner. The result was the same no matter what the cause of the crash. After finally disposing of Kocinski with more effort than he would have liked, Merkel finished second and was champion.

Ballington ended his year in America the same way he started it – winning, passing Renfrow with a daring move, stuffing underneath in traffic on the last lap. Paulk was third on his home track, in what is certain to be the last Camel Pro Series Formula 1 race, despite the class providing some of the closest, most brilliant riding of the year.

The Burner Brothers, Velasco and Plumlee, and Merkel were vindicated, having taken their one tent and one bike and two wins and turned them into a championship and huge bonuses.

Against all odds; in spite of all the doubters; despite what everyone who should have known had said . . . Fred Merkel is champion.

One more time.

Kork Ballington made a welcome return to racing at Daytona and then signed to stay on for the season with Bob MacLean.

Fred Merkel trying to defend his Superbike title *(main picture)*.

# RACING IN THE SOUTHERN HEMISPHERE

**SOUTH AFRICA** *BY JOHN BENTLEY*

The Suzuki GSX Show . . . that was the main attraction for bike fans in the South African track racing series during 1986.

Tight economic times and dwindling sales saw local importers reduce their involvement, bringing about drastic cuts in the sizes of starting grids. Even Mario Rademeyer, back in the country after his abortive crack at Grand Prix racing, was forced to sit out the season.

But, although there was a drop in quantity, there was no decline in the quality of the competition and the standard of riding.

A case in point was the 750 cc Production category. With nothing to touch the Suzuki GSXs, the class developed into a one-make battle. But what a fight – with New Zealander Dave Hiscock and South African Wayne Heasman battling it out for the title, and John Clark, Lawrence Boshoff and the back-from-retirement Rod Gray waiting to pick up the pieces.

Hiscock started the season slowly, and Heasman had two wins under his belt, with Clark taking Round Three, before the New Zealander scored his first victory of the year, at Kyalami in May. From then on, however, the pair swapped places at the head of the table, with wins by Clark (Killarney) and Gray (East London) adding to the interest.

With two rounds to go, it looked as if the title was in the Kiwi's hands, but Heasman fought back, took two wins and secured the championship in the final round.

A string of wins in the poorly supported Superbike class brought Hiscock and the Suzuki GSX1100 a consolation championship victory, even though similarly mounted Rod Gray, back in the groove after an initial settling-down period, handed his opponent three defeats as the season drew to a close.

Suzuki also dominated the 400 cc Production category, with 1985's unofficial 'champion' Gavin Ramsay again taking the honours in this year's officially sanctioned series. Yamaha's Jean d'Assonville was the early-season pace-setter, but a bad fall in Port Elizabeth at the end of September was the final blow to his fading hopes.

Honda were supreme once more in the 600 Production class, with Danny Bristol (NS400), getting the drop on Robbie Petersen (riding similar machinery). Although Petersen was usually quicker while his machine lasted, a series of four retirements as a result of mechanical failure left Robbie an unhappy man.

Lack of reliability also bugged the Petersen/Honda RS250 effort in the 250 racing motor cycle series. The battle for the title was a cliff-hanger to the wire between 1985 Champion Russell Wood and Kevin Hellyer, both on Yamaha TZs.

**Nevil Algie was the surprise of the season in New Zealand, winning the national 250 cc Production title on what was one of only a few KR250s in the face of a determined Suzuki and Yamaha challenge.**

**Dave Hiscock continued to be a great force in South African Superbike Production racing and he was helped by the fact that he rode for Suzuki whose machines proved to be the best available.**

While Kiwi Denis Ireland was finding that he could no longer compete successfully in Europe yet remained competitive at home on his 500 Suzuki *(bottom)*, Brent Jones was conspicuously on top of his class in New Zealand on the 250 Yamaha and therefore packed his bags for a brief but very promising World Championship attempt *(below)*.

## NEW ZEALAND ROAD RACING *BY ROSS MacKAY*

Newcomers Nevil Algie and Lance O'Conner had the pressure taken off them when the Auckland Motorcycle Club was forced to cancel its final round of New Zealand's 1985/86 Road Race Championship. Kawasaki KR 250 rider Algie 'won' the 250 cc Production class with eight points in hand, Yamaha RZ 350R rider O'Conner the victor in the 251–651 cc Production class by a scant two points.

With the Formula 1, Formula 2, Open Production and the Sidecar Championship titles already decided by the fourth and penultimate round of the series, interest centred on Algie and O'Conner and their small-bore Production class competition, teenager Aaron Slight and Neil Smith and Rob Lewis.

Slight and Smith had both beaten their respective rivals in the three-round 'Extra-National' Series held over the Christmas/New Year vaca-tion break and Lewis, the sensation of the 1984/85 National and Extra-National Series, had logged up some impressive 1985/86 performances. A bitter sponsorship disagreement between the Auckland Club and the Auto Cycle Union saw the final, and crucial, round cancelled, however. Algie and O'Conner were the class champions and that was that.

Sponsorship, or perhaps the lack of it, meant that New Zealand's 1985/86 National and Extra-National Road Racing Series were not the spec-tacles they could have been. The racing might have been as close, exciting and intense as ever in the smaller production classes, but reigning rac-ing class champions Dr Rodger Freeth and Brent Jones had little real competition.

Freeth and his McIntosh-framed Suzuki 1100 might not have had it all their own way in the Extra-National Series had it not been for the departure of RGB 500-riding Australian Steve Trinder and similarly-mounted Dennis Ireland competing in only one round. A fifth National ti-tle was Freeth's for the taking, therefore.

International Brent Jones found himself in a similar position and despite an eye injury forcing him to sit out the 'Extra-National' Series, his TZ 250 Yamaha was unbeatable in the 'National' Formula 2 Series. Adaptable Aucklander Paul Pavletich took a Honda CR-barrelled TZ 250 Yamaha to a Formula 2 win in the Extra-National Series but a lack of money meant he could not take Jones on in the National.

Wellington Motorcycle Suzuki team-mates Robert Holden and Bob Toomey held sway over the 'Open' Production Championship races, and the Howard Gregory/Tony Price, Andrew Kippen/Anne Kippen combinations were just as domi-nant in the sidecar ones.

**Malcolm Campbell showed once more his unrivalled determination on all machines, from the 500 two-stroke triple to the 750 superbike and production racing Hondas.**

From an outsider's viewpoint, the Swann Insurance Series would no doubt appear to be the major event in Australian road racing. Yet that is far from being the case.

Sure, the Swann Series provides Australian race fans with a chance to see several top internationals strut their stuff, and, yes, the six races are televised nationally. But, for all that, few locals actually take part. In fact, there's a greater depth of talent on the sidelines than in the races!

There are several reasons for this; the main one being that the Swann Series organisers, like the controlling body of motor cycle sport, the Auto Cycle Council of Australia, have been slow to move with the times.

For the past five years, modified Production machines – Superbikes – have been the major spectator attraction at most race circuits around the Australian continent.

Yet the ACCA has stuck with the traditional classes – 125, 250, 350 and 500 – for the Australian Road Racing Championships. The fact it has retained the 350 cc class well after it was axed at World Championship level speaks volumes about the controlling body's myopic view of racing.

In fact, it was only after strong lobbying from Superbike supporters that a set of national rules was drafted back in the late-1970s. Yet even after that, the ACCA still couldn't see the point of a national Superbike Championship.

As a result, a group of interested Superbike supporters banded together, found outside sponsorship and started their own series. Over the years, this has grown into the _de facto_ Australian Superbike Championship and for the past three years has been sponsored by Western Underwriters Insurance.

Meanwhile, Production racing has also been strongly supported, with all the major distributors fielding teams in the numerous long-distance races run throughout the year.

And again, the ACCA failed to realise that by linking these together, it had a ready-made Australian Production Championship. However, the fortnightly publication _REVS Motorcycle News_ took the initiative and awarded points for each of the major Production races. Thus the _REVS_ Production Championship was born.

In late-1985, Shell Oils announced it would back four of the major races for the coming season. These would be known as the Shell Oils Production Series, and it took over from the _REVS_ Series.

As a consequence, the Western Underwriters Series and Shell Oils Series became the major events on the Australian racing calendar, completely overshadowing the poorly promoted Australian Championships.

So while Grand Prix veteran Jeffrey Sayle was busy wrapping up the Australian 250 Championship with a winning streak unequalled in that event's history, the headlines were being dominated by Malcolm Campbell and Rob Phillis with their battle for the Superbike Series.

In 1985, Team Honda Australia achieved a major ambition when Campbell wrested the Superbike crown away from Phillis, a four-time series winner. For 1986, Phillis set out to get the title

## AUSTRALIAN RACING
### by MIKE ESDAILE

back. To that end, long-time sponsor, Melbourne Suzuki dealer Mick Hone, imported a Yoshimura GSX-R750 engine for Phillis to pit against the works-engined VFR 750 Honda Australia machine provided for Campbell.

After winning the '85 title with a locally modified VF 1000, Honda Australia was eager to retain it and the bike Campbell received for the '86 season was a very close cousin to the special VFR 750 HRC built for Wayne Gardner to race at Suzuka in March, and later used at the TT by Geoff Johnson.

At the first round of the six-round, twelve-race Western Underwriters Series, Campbell qualified the Honda on pole but crashed while leading when the steering stem broke on the second lap of Tasmania's Symmons Plains Raceway. Phillis was then left to play with the Marlboro Yamaha FZ 750 of up-and-coming youngster Kevin Magee, flashing past with ease on the last lap to win the first leg. He backed that up with a harder-fought win over Magee's Marlboro team-mate Michael Dowson in the second leg.

After watching the wreckage of his VFR 750 get trucked away, Campbell could only stand and watch.

However, three months later, Campbell returned to the fray with two stunning wins at the second round, held at Victoria's Winton Raceway. Phillis scored third and second placings to maintain his series lead, but with the best five rounds out of six counting towards the title, Campbell was very much in the hunt.

At the next two rounds, Phillis and Campbell scored two wins apiece, but Campbell crashed in the first leg at Oran Park trying to stay with his Yoshimura Suzuki rival. Phillis was really fired up for that one and trimmed more than a second off Campbell's 1985 lap record although he seemed content to follow the Honda man across the line in the second leg.

At Surfers Paradise for the fourth round, Campbell won the first leg while Phillis finished third behind Honda Australia's number two rider, Iain Pero. In the second leg, Phillis stormed back with a win over Campbell.

But Campbell closed the gap further at the fifth round back at Oran Park with two brilliant wins. In the first leg, Phillis made a wrong choice of front tyre and finished fourth before working his way to second in the second leg. That left the series wide open – just two points (on corrected scores) separating the two, with Phillis leading.

So it all came down to the final round at the Winton Raceway in northern Victoria; a tight, bumpy, narrow and winding circuit that has been the scene of many a close Superbike contest. The race on 14 September 1986 was no exception.

Campbell gave Honda team boss Clyde Wolfenden cause for concern when word got back to Australia that he had crashed one of the HB Suzukis in Yugoslavia and cracked a collarbone.

With just two weeks to go for the Superbike Showdown, Honda needed a rider who was fully fit. But while Campbell admitted his shoulder was still painful, and was suffering from a bout of influenza, his biggest concern at Winton centred on a machine that wasn't carburating properly. Despite the best efforts of the Honda crew, his VFR 750 wasn't running as well as it should in the first leg, and Phillis scorched away to another win.

Everything now depended on the final race. Some more attention to his Honda's carburettors helped Campbell to take an early lead. But the big surprise came from his team-mate Iain Pero. On a VFR 750 down on power compared to Campbell's, Pero slotted into second place and held Phillis off lap after lap.

As the laps ticked away, Phillis became desperate. A third-place finish would nullify his five-point lead, the series would be tied on points and Campbell would win on a countback of race wins. But no matter what he tried, Pero was always in the way. Phillis got past once, but was off-line and Pero snatched the position back.

The battle continued down to the last lap as Phillis still worked away on Pero while Campbell scooted away to a strong lead. Phillis knew what he had to do, and if Pero got in the way, too bad. Going into the final series of turns, Phillis made his move and lunged at Pero. Simultaneously, the Honda man missed a gearchange. That was it. Phillis was through, fist raised in triumph as he took the chequered flag behind Campbell.

It was a fitting end to a hard-fought series; Phillis won his fifth Superbike title on the last corner of the last lap in the final race!

Two weeks later, Campbell had the consolation of winning the Shell Oils Production Series on his more standard VFR 750 in a brilliant three-hour ride at Surfers Paradise. That seemed just reward for missing out on the Superbike crown; it also underlined the standings of Phillis and Campbell at the top of Australian racing.

There was no better illustration of that than in their domination of the Shell Two-Hour Production race at Oran Park in June.

Phillis led from the start, with Campbell working through to second. Through the first hour, Campbell was never more than seven seconds adrift of his great rival, then took over in the second hour. Lap after lap they ran virtually nose-to-tail at a pace that saw them lap riders as far as fourth-placed Wayne Clarke.

Right down to the penultimate lap, they were still seemingly tied together. Neither would given an inch. Phillis wanted to win, Campbell wanted to put the Production Honda into winner's circle for the first time during the year.

After sizing up the situation, Phillis tried for an outside pass at the end of Oran Park's 230 km/h main straight. It didn't work; he pulled the brakes on a little too hard, locked the front wheel and was down, cart-wheeling into the sand trap. And Campbell won.

All season long it was like that, both men so evenly matched that only small differences in their machinery on the day could determine the outcome.

# MESSERE SHINES

After seven rounds, thousands of miles, and much hard work on and off the track, the 500 cc European Championship title was eventually decided in the final round of the series on the very last 2.5-mile lap of the Donington Park circuit. 29-year-old 'Team Italia' rider Massimo Messere had worked his way through to third place on one of the many RS500 Hondas competing in the 1986 championship. New Zealander Richard Scott was leading, performing competently on the three-year-old ex-Roger Burnett Honda after a serious challenge from Mark Phillips had crumbled when his Padgetts Suzuki sustained a broken con rod. It was down to Simon Buckmaster, therefore, and he pursued Scott as Messere's team-mate Fabio Barchitta was receiving desperate pit signals to pass championship leader Alessandro Valesi for fifth place which would enable Messere to take the title. Barchitta responded superbly, and his final-corner manoeuvre guaranteed Messere's glory.

On paper, Messere looked the deserving winner from his opening home-ground victory at the Vallelunga circuit. But an undoubted star of the future, 21-year-old Valesi, took third that day, confirming his threat to the experienced Messere for the forthcoming rounds. Mark Phillips finished sixth in Italy and John Brindley was tenth on the outdated 500 cc Yamaha, but 500 cc Suzuki-mounted Alan Jeffrey had worked through to fourth before crashing out unhurt.

The feature class moved to the splendid Hockenheim venue in West Germany for round 2 and another Italian, Marco Papa, become involved in the championship tussle when he convincingly won from Messere, while Valesi came in third. Experienced campaigner Papa put up a flawless display in front of the massive crowd, the majority of which occupied the unique stadium at the German venue. Phillips improved on his first result by taking fourth place at Hockenheim which consolidated his position behind the three runaway Italians, whilst Ray Swann worked hard for seventh place on the Colin Aldridge Suzuki. Alan Jeffrey just missed out on opening his European account by finishing 11th, while John Brindley reached a hard-earned 13th.

When a certain Swedish bank withdrew the credit guarantee of the Organisers' Account, it forced the cancellation of the scheduled round 3 for 500 cc machines. The inaugural Assen 'speedweek' therefore staged the third round of the now seven-part series.

With the European series running alongside the Formula 1 World Championship and Grand Prix in Holland it gave Britain's Simon Buckmaster the opportunity of a second ride during the colourful week-long event. Fifth overall in 1985, Buckmaster, now on the Sid Griffith's/Duckham's Oils-backed 500 cc Honda, showed his formidable experience and obvious talent to finish second in the race behind Messere who had fought through from his habitual poor start. Papa came home third while close rival Valesi's fifth place kept alive his claim to the coveted title and that all-important guaranteed start in the 1987 Grand Prix.

A strong British contingent at Assen had a dis-

astrous time with the exception of Phillips who finished sixth despite making the wrong tyre choice for the unpredictable Dutch weather. Alan Jeffrey crashed out whilst still in search of his opening points, John Brindley failed to start the Yamaha, whilst Steve Manley retired on lap 4 after anticipating rain but being caught out with intermediate tyres on his 500 cc Suzuki as the weather improved, ending any possibilities of a dream European debut for the Clacton-on-Sea rider.

The series moved to the Imatra circuit in Finland where victory went to 1984 Championship winner Eero Hyvarinen to continue Honda's success on his home circuit. Fellow Finnish rider Esko Kuparinen made his second appearance in the series to snatch second place from Swede Peter Linden. Valesi was the best of the serious contenders in fifth place, Papa took sixth while Messere was the unfortunate victim of a sudden rain shower which resulted in him crashing out of round 4. Britain's Mark Phillips was the only home rider to make the long trip but it only brought more problems for the 24-year-old when a broken big-end forced him out whilst lying fourth.

Czechoslovakia's Brno circuit gave Buckmaster a new opportunity to aim for ultimate victory despite missing three rounds. Second place for the Potters Bar rider launched him into fifth position, whereas rivals Valesi and Messere failed to score and Papa finished a lowly sixth in a race won by German Manfred Fischer.

The penultimate Spanish round at Jerez saw Valesi take his first win and the championship lead when Messere crashed out, but Buckmaster and Papa also increased their chances with second and third places respectively. This left the series poised for a showdown at Donington's seventh and final round. It proved to be just that.

On a three-year-old Honda – first raced and crashed (on the same day) by Wayne Gardner – talented New Zealander Richard Scott celebrated his 27th birthday in superlative fashion with a victory that certainly won't harm his future chances of a GP career. Buckmaster tried hard but had no answer to Scott as he took his fourth 12-points result in as many rounds.

Messere rode a race worthy of a champion to finish third and take the title, with special thanks to team-mate Barchitta for his efforts down in fifth place. Alessandro Valesi, a closest-ever second in the championship need not feel despondent, however. The 21-year-old student from Parma looks forward to a full Grand Prix season with the type of backing that has succeeded in Italy and never matured in Britain.

Not surprisingly Brits flooded the leaderboard at Donington and Trevor Nation's superb fourth was achieved in the face of a severe dose of flue and handling problems on the RG 500 cc Suzuki. A determined Alan Jeffrey eventually hit the points table with an impressive seventh place while Ray Swann took eighth and Steve Manley completed the happy ending for the host nation with tenth spot.

The ultra-competitive 250 cc class was also won and lost at Britain's exciting finish to the

1986 series.

Austrian Josef Hutter on a Bartol-prepared machine took first blood in Vallelunga from Italian Felice Randazzo – having a one-off International ride. The interest centred on third-placed Frenchman Philippe Ruggia for he was soon to become a dominant force in the championship. Sole GB representative Kevin Mitchell took eighth spot at the Italian round under the John Davies Cars racing banner.

In the freezing cold at Zolder, a new name, Hans Lindner from Austria, stormed onto the scene, taking victory from Belgian Eric de Donker, who impressed at his home round. Another Austrian, in the shape of Andreas Preining, finished third while Ruggia showed consistency by coming fourth, sporting the elegant colours of Sonauto Yamaha. Kev Mitchell came of age at Zolder, taking fifth place after demonstrating his potential in practice by setting third-quickest time.

Experienced Grand Prix campaigner Stéphane Mertens took a comfortable victory at the West German round at Hockenheim, but Ruggia's second place brought with it a position at the head of the championship table. Mitchell's race ended on the startline with clutch trouble forcing him out. Lindner took advantage of Ruggia's failure to score at Assen by finishing third behind winner Herbert Hauf of Germany and fellow-German Jochen Schmid.

Mitchell had led in the early stages, but a main bearing seizure caused the Lancashire lad to crash at the halfway stage. Nigel Bosworth and Gary Cowan marked their first European outings with tremendous results. Bosworth finished seventh and Cowan ninth, showing a glimmer of hope to other talented British riders with their sights set on success at the highest level.

Lindner took his second victory of the series at Brno; venue of the Czechoslovakian round. Preining added to his third in Belgium with second place at Brno; Belgian winner Hutter finished third and thereby improved his championship chances.

The new Spanish venue at Jerez hosted the penultimate round and witnessed Ruggia's return to victory after his Czechoslovakian disaster. But winning in the Spanish heat was too late, because even though 22-year-old Lindner was recovering from a broken foot from the British GP, the Austrian third place ensured he was five points clear prior to Donington. 'Team Italia' 250 cc representative Alberto Rota took second place at the new Jerez circuit and his consistency in previous rounds promoted him to fifth in the series before the final outing.

As the vital British round got underway it was a determined Ruggia who set the pace, hotly pursued by Gary Cowan, Rob Orme, Nigel Bosworth and Alberto Rota. Rota, with quite a reputation for his erratic style, rode true to form by crashing and hitting Ruggia at Redgate Corner in an effort to take the lead. Amazingly, Ruggia rejoined the race in ninth place before crashing at the hairpin.

After a fierce battle Bosworth got the better of Cowan (Rob Orme having crashed out whilst in second place). A superb victory for 'Bos' then; but

*By CHRIS HERRING*

1986 winner Massimo Messere leads ex-Champion Eero Hyvarinen at Brno, whilst two more Grand Prix regulars, Manfred Fischer and Simon Buckmaster, make this a Honda-dominated scene.

Hans Lindner was in a class of his own in the 250 European Championship with his Rotax.

what of the championship? Lindner's fifth place was enough to guarantee him the title, with Ruggia maintaining second place despite his misfortune, and Swiss rider Urs Lüzi took third overall after finishing second behind Bosworth. Andy Machin finished ninth in the race, just ahead of Cowan in tenth who had struggled in the latter part of the race with a broken exhaust.

As usual, British crews had dominated the European sidecar battle, but at the top of the table the German pairing of Bernd Scherer and Wolfgang Gess rode consistently through the year, taking second places in Holland, Czechoslovakia and Britain whilst adding a third in Germany to secure the title from undoubted stars of the future Yoshisada Kumagaya and Kazuhiko Makiuchi. The adopted Japanese pairing had obtained ACU licences and almost brought the European title back to Britain in their first full year on the continent. Failing to score in Belgium's opening round, the likeable duo led in Germany until they entertained the Hockenheim crowd with a spectacular crash on entering the stadium section.

'Team Kumagaya' put everything behind them and won at Holland's third round, they won at Czechosolvakia's fourth round and declared war

on next year's Grand Prix three-wheeler class by snatching victory at the final Donington Park round, ironically the home of the 1987 British Grand Prix.

Throughout the year British crews had threatened to overwhelm the series. In Belgium Dave Hallam and Mark Day were victors, John Barker and Steve China were third, John Evans and Geoff Wilbraham fourth, Gary Thomas and Geoff White sixth, Dennis Holmes and Kevin Morgan ninth, and Mick Turrel and Stuart Barlow tenth.

Again, in Germany it was Thomas leading the way for Britain his second place, Ray Gardner and Tony Strevens came fifth, Barker seventh, and Clive Stirrat and Simon Prior tenth.

Keen to compete at Assen, the British contingent was led by Kumagaya to an impeccable victory; John Barker was sixth, Hallam seventh, Thomas eighth and Stirrat ninth. In Czechoslovakia, too, it was Kumagaya's success over Scherer that showed the way for a rather depleted contingent of British pairings, of whom the highest placed were John Barker in ninth and Dennis Holmes in tenth.

ton, but Scherer's very comfortable second place made sure of the title by one point from the

Japanese crew. Gardner finished third, Thomas fifth (for third place overall), Mick Burcombe and Derek Knapp sixth, George Hardwick and Keith Fieldhouse seventh, Tony Baker and Peter Harper ninth with Barker tenth. Yet on the home-built chassis, glory really belonged to 28-year-old Scherer and passenger Gess from Balingen near Stuttgart.

The 125 cc class belonged to Claudio Macciotta on the 'Team Italia' MBA, following some consistent riding with a win in Italy, three second places and third place at Brno to take the title from Frenchman Paul Bordes. Some inspirational riding from Huddersfield's Jamie Whitham gave him fourth place in Italy after leading for the first seven laps. Whitham was second in Belgium before retiring, as he did in Germany, though Rob Milton took ninth in Holland to keep the British involvement alive.

Yet another 'Team Italia' rider, Bruno Casanova, took the 80 cc title with wins at Hockenheim and Brno on the Unimoto machine. Despite the increase in popularity in the 80 cc class, British riders failed to leave their mark on the series which is undoubtedly the best possible stepping stone to a Grand Prix career.

# REID & DUNLOP AGAIN

There could hardly be two more different stories than the tales of the two World Championship formulas. One turned into a saga of woe as the cancelled rounds and lack of development stigmatised the F2 category as the 'who cares?' class of racing. But on the other hand, we were able to enjoy a Formula 1 class with better fields, more rounds than last year and tougher competition than ever.

It's ironic that just when the World F1 Championship is at its strongest, it is being phased out to make way for the American Dream – superbike racing. And the irony is compounded when, after five World Championship wins on the trot, Honda have decided not to field a works team in the series in 1987.

This year Honda and Joey Dunlop were given a scare. The seemingly invincible talents of the undisputed King of the Roads was given a knock by two unlikely F1 heroes in the early stages.

It wasn't until the action switched from Europe to the Isle of Man that Dunlop regained control of the title he's entitled to regard as his personal property following his five-year tenure.

The two new stars were as different from each other as the Mountain Circuit is from Misano and each was as different again to Dunlop – the world's greatest pure road-racer.

Who would have thought that the wayward and excitable Marco Lucchinelli would win the opening round of the World F1 Championship? Probably not even Marco himself. Much less remarkable was the fact that he scored in just one more round of the series and never again gave Joey Dunlop MBE cause for concern.

The second threat to Dunlop's chances came from an even more unlikely quarter: a deep-thinking Swede whose engineering expertise, methodical approach and consistency made him a surprised and surprising leader of the World Championship after two rounds.

But Anders Andersson, whose second and third places in the opening two rounds of the series had put him on top of the world, knew it wasn't going to last. He knew there was a round where he wouldn't score. He knew that Dunlop would make up 15 points. And he knew that the Isle of Man TT would be the turning point. He's a very bright boy. He was absolutely right.

The Isle of Man TT, round 3 of the World Championship, was won by Joey Dunlop. His win there virtually sealed the fate of his rivals' championship aspirations. Not one of the points-scorers in the previous two rounds got a point from the TT; Dunlop went into the lead in the series and was never headed again.

But if Dunlop was on top of the world after the TT, he was in the depths of despair at the end of the opening round of the series at a chilly and windy Misano in the first week in April.

The chill in the air was nothing to the frosty atmosphere in the Rothmans Honda Britain camp at the end of a pointless race for Dunlop who had run out of petrol while about to challenge for the lead on the final lap of the race.

Ex-500 cc World Champion Lucchinelli had led for 51 of the 75 laps round the 2.14-mile circuit near the Adriatic seaside resorts of Rimini and

Riccioni, but going into the final lap it looked like Dunlop was going to begin 1986 in the same style that he had completed the 1985 season.

The Ulsterman was just a couple of lengths behind as they started lap 75. 'I had it all worked out. I was going to tail him through the first few bends then go by on the straight.

'But just as I prepared to make my move the bike spluttered and gave out. I tried everything to squeeze a bit of juice into the carbs but she was completely empty', recalled the World Champion, who had been 27 seconds down at one point after opting to change his rear tyre at the 35th-lap fuel stop.

Lucchinelli lived up to his 'Lucky' nickname. In rubber trouble after deciding against a tyre swap at the stop, Lucchinelli had also lost an exhaust and would have been powerless to prevent Dunlop passing him.

Andersson, whose main interest is in endurance racing, treated it just like a long-distance race and concentrated on consistent laps. It paid off. He was the only other rider to complete the full 160-mile race distance. Australian Rob Phillis took third spot, then promptly disappeared back to Australia never to score again.

It was a curious list of points-scorers: Ottoeson, Cussigh, Orban, Moran and Mönsch – even the Rubatto brothers are hardly household names. But the absence of the Brits who once dominated completely shows the burgeoning European interest in the class.

For most of the fancied British runners Misano was a disaster. Up and coming Ulsterman Neil Robinson went out when he sheared a sprocket bolt on his private Suzuki, and the two Skoal Bandit works Suzukis both blew up.

Paul Iddon's crank failure brought disaster for privateer Andy McGladdery who crashed on the oil slick and broke a collarbone. And Martin's blow-up five laps from the end sent lap-scorers diving for cover as the shrapnel flew.

Any doubts that Dunlop was losing his grip were blasted clean away in Germany a month later as 'Yer Maun' proved he's no mean rider on the artificial circuits.

At Hockenheim he was in stunning form, crossing the line eight seconds ahead of Suzuki's Paul Iddon on time but a street ahead in style and class. Dunlop demonstrated his true talent in the opening couple of laps.

After being caught adjusting his kneepads at the start, Dunlop was 20th as the pack disappeared out of the famous Hockenheim arena, but by the time they reappeared out of the forest he had blasted his RVF 750 Rothmans Honda up to seventh. A lap later he was second to German Ernst Gschwender and by lap 3 he was leading.

He stayed out in front until a perfect pit stop after the 16th of the 23 laps put him 20 seconds down on Iddon. The latter was in form at last on the Skoal Bandit bike that had started the season in ominously unreliable form.

But Dunlop wasn't to be led for long and in the space of a single lap he turned a deficit into a three-second advantage. From there on it was all plain sailing. No fuel problems, just a display of superb riding as he extended his lead to eight

seconds and kept it there. The evidence of Dunlop's superiority is in the lap times. His 113.25 mph fastest lap was a full two seconds quicker than Iddon's best.

Although he was no match for the leaders, Andersson's cool and steady ride gave him third on his immaculate private Suzuki and put him at the top of the title table.

Once more the Brits were in trouble with just two other representatives among the points-scorers. Kenny Irons, after borrowing a motor from team boss Steve Parrish, was first Yamaha home in fifth place, despite suffering from clutch trouble right from the start. And John Weeden made history as the first two-stroke rider to score World F1 points. He finished in eighth spot but was hoping for even better things aboard his RG500 Suzuki at the TT. There was no such good fortune for Mark Phillips, also on a Gamma; after breaking a gear in the warm-up he had to use a spare engine and retired after a lap with ignition problems.

The problems continued too for Skoal Bandit Suzuki's Chris Martin who went out after nine laps when his GSX-R seized a piston while he was lying fifth. Andy McGladdery, still recovering from a broken collarbone sustained in the first round, continued his run of ill-luck by breaking a gear lever.

Just as Andersson had predicted, the Isle of Man proved to be a turning-point. The Swede arrived there hoping to salvage a point or two but in his heart of hearts he knew it was a lost cause. Nevertheless, the championship leader came closer than even he had hoped. He did two laps at over 109 mph and averaged over 108, but in the 'Joe Show' he was just another supporting player and could only finish 12th.

Lord of the Island, Dunlop was in complete control of the race from the off. Shortened from six to four laps after being postponed from Saturday to Monday, it was all too easy for Dunlop, who complained afterwards that the race had been too

*By* **PAUL FOWLER**

Assen found Dunlop under more pressure than usual. Here he leads Kevin Schwantz on the RG500 road bike-based racer on the inside, with the 750 Suzuki under the control of Neil Robinson no. 56 on the outside. Also chasing are Paul Iddon, riding the second Skoal Bandit Suzuki, and Kenny Irons on the Loctite Yamaha.

short. 'I was just getting warmed up when they put out the flag', he protested.

The biggest tribute was paid by a delighted runner-up Geoff Johnson. 'Joey's in a class of his own, so whoever finishes second is as good as a winner.' Johnson's second was ahead of a lucky-at-last Andy McGladdery, with John Weeden piloting his stroker to a remarkable fourth place.

There was to be no fairytale first TT win for Roger Marshall, so often Dunlop's World Championship rival but now forced to sit out the majority of the series, a victim of Rothmans Honda Britain cutbacks. His Honda expired at Braddan Bridge on the last lap while he was holding third. There were no points either for Suzuki's main runners as Neil Robinson finished 11th and Chris Martin only reached 16th place, taking silver replicas, while Iddon's 23rd only entitled him to a bronze.

On the Island, Dunlop was king, but his Thursday evening victory at the Dutch TT was due more to his stock of Irish luck than anything else. Well beaten into second place by Robinson, thanks to the Suzuki's better fuel consumption overcoming the need for a stop, the gods smiled on Dunlop when his young Ulster rival skidded to a halt, his rear chain jamming the back wheel.

As Dunlop celebrated his third win in a row it wasn't all doom and despondency for Suzuki who picked up second and third. Furthermore, they discovered two new stars in Robinson and American Kevin Schwantz, who pipped Iddon for the runner-up spot riding the RG500 which had been used by Weeden at the TT.

However, Andersson slipped further behind, finishing fifth behind Irons, and that allowed Dunlop to go 17 points clear at the top of the table. Most thought it was all over bar the shouting at the halfway stage of the championship. Iddon and Suzuki had other ideas and Dunlop's own team played its part too.

Rothmans Honda Britain could hardly have

shot themselves in the foot more embarrassingly or more publicly. Returning from the victory celebrations at Assen, a car, containing among others Dunlop and Robinson and driven by the Rothmans Honda Britain F1 team manager Dave Sleat, crashed in the small hours of the morning as it failed to complete a high-speed lap of the Assen circuit.

The 80 mph crash left Dunlop with five broken ribs, a twisted ankle and needing stitches in a cut above his left eye. He, and the other six people in the car, were lucky to escape with their lives.

The accident took its toll in the stiffling 100-degree heat of Jerez. As Iddon and the Skoal Bandit Suzuki finally found form, Dunlop slipped to sixth place, hardly able to breathe due to the pain from his broken ribs.

That put Iddon up to second in the series ahead of Andersson who had finished fourth behind Robinson on the second Skoal Bandit bike. Suzuki may have hoped that their first F1 win since Rob McElnea won the 1983 TT would prove a turning point but their optimism was destined to be shortlived. Reliability had been improved by opting for a higher proportion of standard engine parts but they couldn't cope with their biggest problem – Dunlop.

At Vila Real in Portugal he bounced back from his pain in Spain and showed Iddon who was boss. At one stage in the 25-lap street race Iddon got ahead with his best display of riding so far, but on the penultimate lap Dunlop just turned up the wick, sliced a second and a half off his own lap record, and powered away to win by three seconds.

Andersson was third and Robinson finished fifth after a flapping fairing forced him to lose second spot in an unexpected pit stop.

With a 17-point cushion Dunlop was poised to take the title at the infamous Imatra street circuit in Finland, back in the calendar after an absence of a year. He only needed a position in the top five but in true Dunlop style he did better than that, winning from the Skoal Bandit duo of

Iddon and Robinson. And, characteristically, he didn't know he'd done it. After losing track of the race in the closing stages he thought he had finished second to Robinson who had led until forced to slow with tyre trouble.

Often the scene of controversy in the past, Imatra lived up to its reputation in a frightening incident just 50 yards from the start when Iddon, Dunlop, German rider Klaus Klein and several others banged into each other. Four riders crashed including Eire's Ron Sherry, who broke a wrist.

With the series clinched, Dunlop blew his chance to shine on home ground when he picked the wrong tyres for the wet Ulster GP. Neil Robinson made no such mistake and romped away from the start to score the best win of his promising career. Sadly it was to be his last; at Scarborough three weeks later F1 racing lost its newest talent and its nicest guy.

Dunlop and Iddon finished as the top two in the series with Andersson grabbing third and Robinson fourth (his 41 points all scored in the last three rounds).

In 1987 it looks as if there will be no official works Honda team and Dunlop will be forced to do it himself on a semi-works basis, or switch to Suzuki or Yamaha who would both love to wrest the championship from the Big Red. Honda have nothing left to prove. Neither, for that matter has Dunlop, but while the one plans to pull out the other intends to carry on. And if this year's F1 success story is anything to go by, the growing grids and greater number of points-scorers than ever (40 in the eight rounds), could make things all the tougher for him in 1987.

If things are looking healthy in F1, the same cannot be said for Formula 2. The scheduled five rounds ended up as just three and the supremacy of the Yamahas confirmed it as a class that's going downhill fast – but nowhere else.

Despite the brave effort of Colin Aldridge to make Ray Swann's 600 Kawasaki a competitive alternative and Graeme McGregor soldiering on aboard the 600 Ducati, 350 Yamahas filled all but three of the points-scoring places in the series.

Ulsterman Brian Reid was the predictable winner of round 1 on the Island but a crash at Ballaugh Bridge in the 250 race left him with a broken wrist which kept him down in seventh place in the second round. The Spanish event was won in emphatic style by Aussie Graeme McGregor on his Ducati.

A second place behind surprise winner Eddie Laycock at the Ulster GP gave Reid his title in a lacklustre series which saw only himself and Laycock score in all three rounds.

In Ulster, both Reid and Dunlop are sporting heroes to rank with Dennis Taylor and Barry McGuigan. In the rest of the world their brand of racing is viewed with curiosity rather than the fanaticism it attracts back at home where the riders are regarded as a breed apart. Next year looks like being the last for the Formula championships. It will be a shame if they are both forced to disappear just when one championship is riding high and the other is dying its own natural death.

# HONDA ENDURE

**Hondas in front of a lone works Suzuki at Spa. Despite the best efforts of Suzuki and others, there was no-one to touch the reliability and speed of the works Hondas.**

After Suzuki's promising showing in the latter half of 1985 and the arrival on the scene of Yamaha's FZR Genesis, the 1986 Endurance season promised much.

But despite moving ever closer to long-distance Grand Prix racing, the year delivered less than before with factory Hondas dominating every race of the six-round series. Incredibly it was a Ducati that got closest to toppling the mighty V-four at the final round at Jerez. For the rest of the season no-one got within two laps of the Hondas in any race result.

It seemed that only Honda possessed that delicate blend of ingredients to produce the perfect Endurance team: fast, reliable bikes with fast, reliable riders supported by fastidious mechanics and a dedicated crew who understand the intricacies of the long-distance slog.

Suzuki suffered from unpredictable machinery and riders who gradually gave up the struggle against the far superior Hondas.

Yamaha meanwhile preferred to blanket the 500 cc GP grids with factory OW81s rather than commit themselves to a full Endurance season. And they paid the price for it – they had the bikes and riders but not the knowledge to sustain them hour after hour. The result was three painful defeats at Le Mans, Suzuka and the Bol d'Or at the hands of the RVFs.

For the privateers, 1986 was another year spent vainly chasing the factory teams with real glory only possible as a result of factory crashes or breakdowns. It was also the year when qualifying actually began to mean something. At the more hotly contested races, training periods began to resemble GPs in their intensity with mere seconds separating much of the grid. Teams that lined up on the grids of '85 with ease often found themselves non-starters in '86.

Pierre-Etienne Samin was one of the riders who tried so hard to get the Yamaha Genesis its first win.

## 24 Heures du Mans
### 12–13 April

The teams that assembled in the overcrowded Le Mans paddock for the first round of the '86 series could hardly believe it was the beginning of the season. It was so cold that weathermen were predicting temperatures below freezing for the night of the race. And that was going to cause the hardiest of Endurance men some real problems.

Rothmans Honda, with their two RVF-mounted teams (Patrick Igoa/Gérard Coudray/Alex Vieira and Dominique Sarron/Pierre Bolle/Jean-Louis Battistini), considered running 30-minute riding sessions during the night instead of the usual one-hour stints to prevent potentially dangerous numbed fingers and bodies.

Some teams fixed extra sections to the bike fairings to deflect the icy blast from their riders' hands. Others spent small fortunes in the Le Mans Damart shop hoping their investment would give their riders a real advantage as temperatures plummeted after dark.

But even the best prepared couldn't have predicted the scene at the start. As riders gathered for the warm-up lap it was snowing!

The ultra-cold conditions were not just affecting the riders either. Dominique Sarron led the warm-up lap only to crash entering the esses, his tyres not even warmed to the task. Only frantic work by Honda mechanics got the lightly damaged bike onto the grid in time, but Sarron took no further part in the race. He had aggravated an elbow injury sustained in an earlier 250 practice crash at Jarama and despite acupuncture was unfit to ride.

World Champion Gérard Coudray took the initial lead with Christian Sarron well down after the Genesis had refused to start on cue from pole position. Though much detuned from its fragile 1985 spec, and at 162 mph just one mile an hour faster than the RVFs, the Yamaha was already ahead after four laps. But few gave it much

chance of lasting the distance.

In its third big race it was the riders and not the bike that decided the fate of the Genesis. As the rain came down after five hours, first Pierre-Etienne Samin and then Richard Hubin crashed. Even with the helmeted Christian Sarron desperately helping to effect pit repairs, the team lost a lot of time. Four hours later the Yamaha was placed ninth with the number one Honda holding the lead.

Meanwhile, Bolle and Battistini had been hampered by a faulty temperature gauge but the Honda camp's race was otherwise uninterrupted.

As Yamaha fought to catch the leaders, the Kenwood Suzuki of Hervé Moineau, Bruno le Bihan and Eric Delcamp was the only other threat to a Honda whitewash. Suzuki lost their number two bike when Eric Sabatier destroyed it on the ultra-fast Garage Rouge curve in the dark.

The night, as continual rain showers and temperatures toppled towards freezing, went down as one of the toughest in Le Mans history. At dawn Yamaha were still chipping away at the Hondas' advantage and moved up to fourth with three hours to go.

Then further disaster struck as the bike's cush-drive started to break up. That caused several frustrating stops and pushed the Team MCN Harris Yamaha of Mat Oxley, Vesa Kultalahti and Kenny Irons up to fourth. With one hour to go, the tables turned again when an electrical fault dropped Team MCN back to seventh, though not before the Le Mans crowd had been amazed by the riding of Endurance newcomer Kenny Irons. In one night session he passed all five factory bikes.

In the end, however, the works bikes won through, with Honda continuing as they had left off in 1985 with a one-two followed by Suzuki and Yamaha.

## 6 Stunden Motorrad-Marathon Österreichring
### 22 June

The Österreichring held bad memories for the Honda squad. In 1985 they were beaten there by a private Suzuki and they had no plans to let that happen again. Coudray qualified fastest in practice, two seconds ahead of Moineau's Suzuki and a further two seconds ahead of the Team MCN Yamaha.

At the start it was a trio of privateers who led, Dirk Brand's Bakker Yamaha being pursued by Eric Dejonghe's Honda VFR and Oxley. Two laps later Coudray and Moineau pulled through while Dejonghe crashed as he diced desperately with Brand for fourth spot. After one hour Coudray led Moineau, leaving only Oxley and Kultalahti on the same lap.

Moineau and le Bihan hung on grimly in second until halfway when the Honda pitted with a gaping hole blown in its exhaust collector. As Rothmans mechanics swept into action the factory Suzuki took over the lead, but only by 13 seconds. That wasn't much of a handicap for the Coudray/Igoa RVF.

'I was gaining by over a second a lap after the stop so it was no problem catching up', declared Coudray, who left black slide-marks around the ultra-fast circuit as he chased Moineau.

That brief moment of glory was Suzuki's only look-in at the front – which was hardly surprising when Honda revealed they had developed another pit lane time-saver to put them even further out of Suzuki's reach. The new contraption was a pneumatic wheel stand designed by Chief Mechanic Guy Coulon, taking full advantage of the RVF's single-side swinging arm. Thus equipped Honda were able to change rear wheels, refuel and swap riders in just ten seconds.

In the second half of the race, Coudray and Igoa rapidly reasserted themselves in front of the Suzuki. Team MCN seemed secure in a comfortable third until their Harris FZ sprung an oil leak two hours from the end.

The British mechanics lost three minutes as they mopped up the mess and stuffed a few rags round the motor. That hasty repair allowed Oxley and Kultalahti to hang onto their rostrum spot from Dutch ex-Le Mans winner Brand and partner Gerard Flameling.

Team MCN at work on the Harris Yamaha: 'Howard says he's sure he dropped five centimes down here somewhere.'

Mainstays of the works Honda team, Gérard Coudray *(right)* and Patrick Igoa *(far right)* in action.

## Suzuka Eight Hours
### 27 July

The World Endurance Championship always takes a strange twist when it changes its stage to play to the massive crowds at Suzuka, Japan.

The Eight-Hour race is no normal Endurance event. With a mere handful of European teams able to afford the trip halfway round the world (only four made the journey this year), Suzuka becomes more of a long-distance GP.

In 1986 that was more true than ever. With Mike Baldwin partnering Kenny Roberts, Wayne Gardner joining Dominique Sarron, Tadahiko Taira wearing Tech 21 colours with Christian Sarron, Thierry Espié riding with Christian le Liard and Kevin Schwantz teaming up with Satoshi Tsujimoto, the front of the grid looked like a fully fledged GP field.

The pressure showed too, for there were scores of crashes during practice and racing. Baldwin went down twice as did Christian Sarron. Little Dominique also succumbed to the very hot and slippery Suzuka tarmac along with Schwantz, Mal Campbell, Kork Ballington (twice), Kevin Magee, Mike Dowson, Igoa, Moineau and numerous Japanese riders.

With 273,000 Japanese fans attending, Yamaha and Honda especially were taking things very seriously. Honda rolled out their new six-speed RVF for the first time, backed up by Igoa and Coudray, plus Keiji Kinoshita and Mal Campbell (deputising for the injured Wayne Rainey) on the five-speed V-fours.

Yamaha's three-team effort of Roberts/Baldwin, Taira/Sarron and Shinichi Ueno/Shoji Hiratsuka wasn't enough to give them the much-prized pole position. Roberts reckoned that the '86 Genesis wasn't nearly as fast as the bike he had ridden a year before and frankly admitted there was no way he could match Gardner's time on the aston-ishingly fast RVF.

Gardner led from the start, chased hard by Roberts, Sarron, Tsujimoto, Igoa and Magee. As the Honda gradually extended its advantage, only the Lucky Strike Yamaha of Roberts and Baldwin stayed in touch. The rest of the field were suffering problems in the dreadfully humid 95-degree heat.

Moineau crashed the Kenwood Suzuki heavily, losing 30 minutes as a swinging arm was replaced, Igoa dropped the Honda when a rear tyre punctured in the fourth hour. Neither finished in the points and Taira and Sarron retired when a terminal misfire struck their Yamaha at the same time.

After six hours only Roberts and Baldwin were on the same lap as Gardner but after pitting to fit a new fuel tank Baldwin stopped round the back of the circuit with a dead motor. The Lucky Strike mechanics had knocked off a fuel pump wire, starving the motor of petrol. Baldwin pushed back but by then the race was lost. Minutes later, in a futile pursuit of the leaders, the Californian crashed and ended his race.

While Gardner and Sarron afforded themselves the luxury of easing the pace, Kevin Magee and Mike Dowson piled on the coals. The Aussie pairing were performing brilliantly on a superbike-spec FZ750 that was way down on power against the full factory bikes. They lost any chance of outright victory when the gear lever came off in the closing stages but they held off Tsujimoto and Schwantz in third spot with Ueno and Hiratsuka fourth.

The race was Gardner's second Eight Hour win in a row and his ninth consecutive Suzuka victory – enough to confirm his pop star status in Japan and make him HRC's favourite son.

## 24 Heures de Liège
### 16–17 August

After Suzuka the championship returned to the relative calm and sanity of the Spa 24 Hours in Belgium. Neither the championship-leading Honda nor the Suzuki had scored points in Japan so the race had no effect on the championship standings.

Although Honda ran their usual two-team squad at Spa they raced without Dominique Sarron who had been reserved exclusively for 250 GP duties following his Silverstone win earlier in the month.

Honda signed up ex-Belgian World Champion Richard Hubin to act as a replacement on the number two bike while Thierry Espié was to stand in for the injured Pierre Bolle. The choice of Hubin for the Spa outing came as no surprise. The veteran Endurance man had won the '85 race for Suzuki when he lapped extraordinarily fast during the foggy night. If the usual Spa fog descended again Hubin would prove invaluable to the Rothmans team.

Despite the Belgian's home knowledge, Coudray qualified fastest and took only a few laps to overhaul the Kenwood Suzuki of Moineau. With the Kenwood Suzuki of Moineau, le Bihan and Eric Delcamp chasing at a respectful distance, the pattern was set for most of the race.

Suzuki's hopes were dashed when Delcamp crashed on oil in daylight. After fighting back to third Delcamp went down in a big way during the night, dropping them right down to 20th spot.

Although Coudray, Igoa and Vieira looked to be well in control they couldn't shake off the close attentions of the number two Honda until Espié crashed soon after dawn. Repairs put them ten laps behind the leaders and from then on there could be little doubt about the outcome.

Meanwhile Team MCN had been making a superb recovery from a first-hour disaster that lost them nine laps and placed them last. Oxley, Kultalahti and Geoff Fowler fought back after an oil leak was repaired to take third at 7.30 a.m., only for the gearbox to break four hours later.

That returned Frenchmen Patrice More, Patrick Braud and André Lussiana to third as the Kenwood Suzuki still struggled back up the leaderboard. They could only manage seventh spot by the end.

For the last few hours Coudray and Co. cruised round to save their machine, allowing their Rothmans team-mates to close the gap to seven laps at the flag.

The Spa victory effectively gave Coudray and Igoa their third World title in a row. Only third-place men Hubin and Battistini (with points from Le Mans and Spa) and Espié (points from Le Mans, Suzuka and Spa) could mathematically overhaul the French pairing but none of them had rides planned for the last two short races.

Hervé Moineau was as fast as usual but the Hondas always had the advantage in the long run.

### Hockenheim 1000 Kms
### 31 August

Honda's joy was shortlived. In the very last lap of timed practice for the Hockenheim 1000 Kms Coudray crashed at one of the circuit's fast chicanes. There was no excuse for the tumble; Honda were comfortably on pole but Coudray simply lost concentration.

The extensive damage to the RVF was no problem for the Honda crew but Coudray's dislocated shoulder was. The big Frenchman rode in the following morning's pre-race warm-up session but after a few laps he returned to the pits doubled up in pain.

The decision to let Vieira take over the ride was a big one because it meant that Igoa, if Honda won as expected, would be the only true World Champion. As ever, it was team manager Jean-Louis Guilloux who hatched the solution. If Coudray partnered Vieira at the last round in Spain, all three riders would finish the year on equal points as World Champions and that had never happened before.

There was to be no easy walkover this time, however. A short burst of drizzle shortly before the race ensured that the grid started the race on a full range of tyres from wets to slicks.

Early leader was local superbike ace Peter Rubatto on his Heine Gericke GSX-R. But Rubatto and partner Klaus Klein were running a full-house F1 motor after blowing up their milder endurance mill in practice. The strain told and the Suzuki's gearbox broke 30 minutes later.

That left Martin Wimmer (aboard the bike that took second at Suzuka), Moineau, Kultalahti and Christian Monsch to fight for the lead, while Igoa struggled to stay in the top ten on wets.

Once on the right tyres the Honda was soon through to the front after Wimmer had led briefly before suffering clutch problems. This time, though, Honda weren't able to pull out their accustomed lead. Moineau and le Bihan held on grimly and actually began to close up in the late stages of the race.

Third place was hard-fought too. Oxley and Kultalahti had installed themselves there shortly after the halfway point but Dutchmen Brand and Flameling were also catching in the closing stages.

With little more than 30 minutes to go, the Suzuki had closed the gap on Igoa and Vieira to just 30 seconds. Then cruel fate took a hand. Moineau cruised into the pits with a broken gearbox delivering another body blow to Suzuki's already flagging morale.

Even then the drama wasn't entirely over. Fourteen laps before the flag was due, a German monsoon flooded the circuit. Knowing full well how lethal the ultra-fast Hockenheim straights can be in a flood, the organisers acted wisely and put out the red flag. With the second to seventh teams within a single lap of each other it was a sensible decision – no-one wanted to risk losing a place by changing to wets despite the conditions.

### Bol d'Or
### 20-21 September

Although the Bol d'Or wasn't a championship round it retained sufficient prestige to produce the season's third appearance of Yamaha's Genesis.

This time Honda were fully prepared for the challenge with Dominique Sarron partnering Bolle and Battistini aboard the new six-speed RVF. The new bike wasn't actually faster than Coudray and Co.'s five-speed version but it fired out of corners much more strongly.

Christian Sarron's Genesis that he shared with Hubin and Jacques Cornu was a shadow of what it had been a year before. While the RVFs were touching 178 mph on the Mistral, the Genesis could only manage 174 mph. Practice times showed the difference. Once again the Sarron brothers held the first two grid positions but this time it was little Dominique who took pole.

Within a lap of the start the Rothmans rider had opened up a massive advantage as brother Christian struggled to make up time after his usual poor start. The Genesis took over second spot when Coudray crashed at Signes and pushed in. Repairs didn't take long but the engine had ingested gravel and only managed a lap before stopping.

Suzuki men Anders Andersson, Vesa Kultalahti and Graeme McGregor held second briefly before their full-house F1 motor blew at the end of the Mistral straight at 10.0 p.m. The Suzuki's oil brought down three other bikes and came perilously close to skittling Sarron on the Genesis.

Hubin finally fell foul of an oil slick at 5.0 a.m. which lost Yamaha six laps when they had managed to close the gap to the leading Honda to little more than a lap.

Moineau, riding with le Bihan and Jean-Pierre Oudin, was the second in his team to suffer a crash when he also went down on oil early in the morning while third. Le Bihan had crashed in practice and set the team's training bike ablaze. Without a functioning extinguisher in the vicinity the GSX-R had been totally destroyed.

Shortly after dawn Honda also lost time with a fuel leak allowing the Yamaha to get within striking distance again. From then on only Sarron and Cornu rode in a desperate attempt to win for the Genesis its first major success.

But the task was too great. After settling for second, Christian Sarron cruised round with his brother until the crowd invaded the track stopping the race 15 minutes early.

There was no time for such luxuries in the race for the last rostrum position. Eric Delcamp, Jean Monin and Eric Sabatier had to work hard to keep the second factory Suzuki ahead of the Japauto RVF of Guy Bertin, Roger Sibille and Christian Berthod. Japauto had been delayed by a crash in the early stages and were down in 19th after four hours.

Fifth-place finishers Christian le Liard, Thierry Espié and Hervé Guilleux had also crashed. Indeed, there were few finishers who avoided falling foul of the slippery Ricard surface.

### Jerez Eight Hours
### 28 September

Honda's planned triumvirate was a non-starter before the Jerez Eight Hours had even got to the grid. Still suffering from his Hockenheim and Bol d'Or crashes, Coudray could only manage a few practice laps of the tortuous track at a time.

Igoa took over his ride to join Vieira but it wasn't enough to prevent a Ducati taking pole position. The Bologna factory had entered Juan Garriga and Marco Lucchinelli on their four-valve V-twin, not the eight-valver which had been introduced at the Bol d'Or with Virginio Ferrari.

With a bike totally suited to the track, Garriga put himself in front and managed to open a small lead over the pursuing Suzuki and Honda. But Moineau took over at the head of the field after twenty minutes, only to relinquish the position when he pitted his thirstier Suzuki for fuel.

Local hero Garriga made the running until Igoa took over in the second hour. Shortly afterwards Oxley crashed Team MCN out of fourth spot and the race settled into a pattern.

With Ducati doing 80-minute sessions and Honda and Suzuki only putting in 45-minute stints, it took Igoa and Vieira a long time to get a decent lead on the Duke. After five hours Honda finally put a lap between themselves and the Ducati pairing but there was no room for relaxation in the 100-degree heat.

Suzuki were struggling hard to keep the flying Ducati in sight because a rear shock had lost its damping from the second hour onwards – as ever Dominique Meliand and his men were not having the best of luck.

Neither were Dutchmen Brand and Flameling who were holding a strong fourth until they had to push in with a broken fuel pump. Their misfortune elevated Germans Franz-Willi Rösnick and Anton Heiler into their best position ever, while Spanish millionaire's son, Jorge Cavestany, and Juan Cano chased in fifth place aboard a Yamaha which had been flown over for the race from Japan.

In the one race where they could never have imagined that they might have to struggle, Honda came closer to defeat than they had all year. Of course they still won by a lap but the fact that the trouble came from a Ducati made the surprise all the greater.

Next year the Endurance series starts at Jerez. Expect Ducati to be there again to give Honda a little to worry about.

**Virginio Ferrari was stylish and the new water-cooled Ducati looked impressive, but only Italian enthusiasts dream of them beating the Japanese.**

# IRONS TAKES STOCK

After a season in which their team had once again proved almost unbeatable in the British Championship, Honda UK's decision to withdraw from frontline competition – instead opting to put their race budget into largely production-based dealer support packages – was a clear indication of the gradual shift of emphasis in British racing.

Where until recently the 250 cc class was the obvious choice for an ambitious National rider, these days it's the Superstock race for modified road bikes which often needs heats to give everyone a ride. Box-stock production racing is gaining in popularity, too, especially in the Isle of Man. Even in this year's British Championship 1300 cc races there were often only a handful of RG500s – and a bunch of Superstock/F1 bikes – taking on the two Rogers and their RS500s.

Real racing bikes have simply become too expensive for the majority. Production-based machines can be bought for a few thousand pounds. They are relatively easy and cheap to keep running and their success on the track is seen by many manufacturers and importers as highly relevant to road bike sales. 'When I looked through the cuttings from the last year it was obvious that press coverage was very heavily weighted towards production-based racing', said Honda motor cycle chief Roger Etcell, at pains to emphasise that the money saved on the race team would be used for the new scheme.

Financial help would be available for all classes, Etcell said, and Honda would be aiming to get involved, through dealers, with riders on RS125s, 250s and even 500s as well. 'After ten years of success with the race team we decided it was time for a change of emphasis towards the grass roots. At the moment there's a big gap between club level and the factory teams. We are trying to get our dealers involved, in all classes of racing, and it should give more people the chance to prove themselves.'

As redundant team manager Barry Symmons was quick to point out, the glamorous incentive of a Honda works ride is now gone, and with it the chance to be schooled in the art of riding and setting-up a Grand Prix bike. It is possible that this will stem the flow of talent moving to GPs – Gardner and Burnett are just the most recent to pass through Symmon's hands. But it's also true that only a very few aspired to such heights, and that British racing might well be better served by an injection of money and interest at a lower level. If fewer talented riders drop out of the sport for financial reasons, perhaps we'll end up producing more champions anyway.

The Honda team was not present at Scarborough in September when Neil Robinson's shocking yet tragically predictable death highlighted one serious problem in British racing. Robinson had never before raced at the narrow, bumpy track with its boundaries of fences and trees; nor, it must be said, did he much care to. People have been dying regularly for years.

But Neil was a newly signed works rider now, and Suzuki were not going to turn down championship points even if Honda were. Neil Robinson might not have wanted to race at Scarborough but he wanted a job, he wanted to climb the racing ladder, he needed the championship points. He rode off for his first practice session and never came back.

There were five National championship rounds that weekend, which meant a lot of reluctant riders racing – and racing hard – because they needed the points. And this was just one example of the general disregard for riders' safety shown all too often by race promoters and administrators. Championship points do not have to be awarded at circuits like Oliver's Mount, which present, by their nature, an almost insoluble problem. Safety-related improvements are much needed at many other British racetracks, too, and these improvements need money. But most of all they need an *attitude*; a recognition that riders' safety is important. Why does a household name always have to be injured or killed before anything is done?

Injuries played a big part in sharing out the spoils too, in a year when most of the major championships went right to the final round. Trevor Nation led four series in July but crashed and subsequent missed races meant he ended up losing them all. Kenny Irons suffered his share of breaks and bruises, but he was able to make almost sure of his Superstock title at Donington with another victory before returning to its medical centre for attention to the finger he had broken earlier in the day. And at Cadwell, Phil Mellor gritted his teeth to win two production championships with his recently broken wrist in a cast. It's a tough job, racing motorbikes for a living.

## Shell Oils/ACU Transnational Championship

Before the start of this season, Roger Burnett's win in the 1985 Brands Powerbike race was the only time the younger Honda rider had beaten his team-mate Roger Marshall in a trouble-free race. By the season's end it was Marshall who had grown used to coming in second and Burnett who had wrapped up the British 1300 cc Championship, changed in format once again to comprise ten different meetings with two races at each.

The rest of the field were nowhere, although Trevor Nation often chased the all-conquering three-cylinder RS500s hard on his private Suzuki. At the wintry Cadwell season-opener, too, Nial MacKenzie gave the Honda men a hard time on his 350 Armstrong. The Scot was a close third in the damp first leg and managed fourth, behind Nation, in the second. Burnett won close dices with Marshall in both but the other Roger turned the tables to win at the second leg of the Brands round three weeks later.

Before then, both Hondas had been humbled by a first-leg Armstsrong one-two, MacKenzie winning from McLeod as the two Rogers made a wrong tyre choice and finished third and fourth. The Hondas were missing from Oulton's next round, leaving MacKenzie to win again from Scot Howard Selby. And with MacKenzie blowing up and McLeod running out of petrol in the second leg, Selby fended off Joey Dunlop to take the win on his RG500.

**By ROLAND BROWN,** *BIKE MAGAZINE*

Niall MacKenzie and Donnie McLeod on the Silverstone Armstrongs dominated 250 racing whenever they returned from the continent.

Kenny Irons was 'Man of the Year' and dominated the Superstock Championship on his Loctite Yamaha.

The 750 and 1100 Suzukis proved to be the most powerful tools readily available to the privateer, both for production racing and Superstocks. Here, Trevor Nation and Phil Mellor eye the starter.

Burnett was back on top when the series returned to Brands in May, taking the first leg ahead of Neil Robinson and Gary Lingham after Nation and early leader Marshall had crashed. Neither rider was hurt, and they went on to finish third and second in the next leg. Burnett's win showed that the Rothmans rider had lost any lingering doubts he might have had about his ability to beat his former employer.

A Honda won the next race too, at Donington – but much to everyone's surprise it was the awesome '6X' four-stroke Formula 1 bike ridden by New Zealander Richard Scott, who held off Kenny Irons' Suzuki-with-a-Yamaha-badge in the tricky damp conditions. Trevor Nation's third place gained him a few points on Burnett and Marshall, who were downfield after ill-advisedly choosing wet tyres. But while Kenny won again in the second leg, with Nation fourth, Marshall and Burnett finished second and third respectively to take a still firmer grip on the championship.

At the half way point Burnett was 19 points clear of this team-mate, who was another 15 ahead of Nation. But Honda's rising star turned meteorite in the next round at Snetterton, crashing to earth while his closest challengers took first and second to move right back into contention. Although Burnett showed his steel by coming back with broken toes and a dislocated finger to win the second leg – and also the non-championship Race of Aces with a new lap record – he finished the weekend with his lead over Marshall cut to just seven points.

Mallory the next weekend saw Burnett hold off Marshall and Mark Phillips in both legs for a painful double victory. And at Oulton he put one hand on the championship trophy, winning the second race while Roger Marshall slid off and slipped to 24 points adrift with only two rounds left. Burnett had led the wet first race too, but slowed with a misted visor to let past Marshall and Neil Robinson, who took the championship's second four-stroke victory on his GSX-R Suzuki. Trevor Nation finished fifth, but after missing the Mallory round he was right out of contention.

Everyone was out of contention following the display at Thruxton by Roger Burnett. Not only did he win both legs, setting new lap records each time and making sure of his British Championship, but he proved a point by beating returning Grand Prix hero Niall MacKenzie and his Suzuki. 'I was glad to beat Niall because that stamps me as the best 500 rider in Britain', Burnett said afterwards, and underlined it by dominating both the final championship legs at Silverstone and also the non-championship Powerbike International at Brands, where Paul Lewis was the Suzuki GP man who couldn't keep up.

Messrs Haslam, McElnea and even Gardner might have something to say about that next year, when the British Championship format is changed yet again – this time to a late-season series aimed at attracting the big-name Grand Prix riders. But in 1986 Burnett was on top of the domestic pile. Fast and smooth on the track, agreeable and even smoother off it, he has advanced immeasurably in his two years with Honda Britain. 'People forget that I haven't been racing all that long', Burnett said. 'I just feel that I'm getting better and better and I hope I can keep improving.'

Team-mate Roger Marshall was suitably impressed, and quick to deny that Burnett's domestic success was due to his own slowing down. 'People keep asking me why Roger was beating me this year – it's just that he rode very fast. I *know* I'm riding better than I've ever done. When Wayne Gardner was racing here everyone said he was a sensation but we've been breaking lap records everywhere this year on basically the same bikes.' It will be interesting to see whether Burnett can make a Wayne-style impression on the Grands Prix.

Despite missing two of the ten rounds due to Grand Prix commitments, the Silverstone Armstrong pairing of Niall MacKenzie and Donnie McLeod dominated the 250 cc Championship in much the same way as the Honda pair did the bigger class. The difference was that this time the title fight went right to their home circuit, Silverstone, and a last-race dice that could have gone either way.

MacKenzie started the season better. He won the first Cadwell leg from McLeod and, in the second, broke the lap record in his charge from the back to fourth place, behind McLeod, MacKenzie and Kevin Mitchell. He struggled to third and fourth in the Brands legs, choosing wrong tyres in one and crashing but remounting in the other, to leave wins to Darren Dixon and Gary Noel. But at Oulton's third round the Scot won twice, McLeod crashing in a hard-fought first race before coming back to take second place in the next.

With his leg injuries keeping him out of the following Brands round, MacKenzie must have expected his lead to disappear. But after winning the first leg from Darren Dixon, Donnie McLeod broke down in the second to let in Nigel Bosworth and Carl Fogarty. By Donington, MacKenzie was fit again, and he proved it by taking both legs from McLeod and Kevin Mitchell. That increased his slender half way series lead to 11 points.

Both Armstrong riders missed the Snetterton round, where Andy Watts took his EMC to a pair of victories over Carl Fogarty's Yamaha. And although MacKenzie won the first Mallory leg with a new lap record, his second-leg sixth allowed winner McLeod to close the series gap to just four points. Carl Fogarty was a close second in the race but a distant third in the championship, just ahead of Darren Dixon, Watts and Nigel Bosworth.

All three leaders missed Oulton's next round – the Scots with a Grand Prix and Fogarty with injury – and the racing up front was typically fierce 250 cc stuff. Kevin Mitchell won the first race from Rob Orme, then threw his Yamaha down the track while leading the second. That left Orme, Ian Newton, Bosworth and Dixon in a frantic four-way scrap which eventually ended in that order.

To Thruxton and back to normality at first: Niall MacKenzie returned to take the first leg from McLeod and Nigel Bosworth. But the Arm-strong riders didn't have it all their own way for long. The fast-improving Bosworth beat them both to win the second leg on his Yamaha, and with Gary Noel riding his EMC to third between McLeod and MacKenzie's Armstrongs, Niall's series lead was down to three points with one round to go.

If it was MacKenzie who had made all the headlines and been courted by the factory 500 cc teams in recent months, it was 29-year-old Donnie McLeod, always the unsung hero, who had brought the Armstrong team most of their success in 250 cc Grands Prix, more than once qualifying on the front row and reaching the rostrum with a third place at Spa. He'd beaten his younger team-mate a few times at home too, and went into the Silverstone showdown with guns blazing, winning the first leg from MacKenzie to draw level in the series and set up a brilliant finale.

But it was not to be for the unlucky Donnie McLeod. For four laps the two Armstrongs were neck-and-neck, harried too by Gary Noel. The race and the championship was open to either man – and it was McLeod who drew the short straw, slowing with a cracked piston to hand the title to his team-mate. Donnie finished third, ahead of a monumental nine-way dice for fourth place, and with the demise of the Armstrong team it's to be hoped that for 1987 he finds a Grand Prix ride worthy of his ability. The brilliant MacKenzie, of course, had no such difficulty; his rapid rise to fame and fortune will doubtless hearten hopefuls like Mitchell, Dixon and Bosworth, who were separated by just two points for third and fifth places in the championship.

The British Sidecar Championship was a far less hectic affair for World Title contenders Steve Webster and Tony Hewitt, who won 12 of the 18 races they contested to end up on top by 42 points. Derek Bayley and Bryan Nixon got the better of them in a three-way thriller at Cadwell's first round, though; Webster holding off Steve Abbott and Shaun Smith for second after winning the opening leg. But although Abbott and Smith took second-leg wins at both Brands and the following Oulton rounds, Webster and Hewitt won the first race on both occasions. They then scored a double at the Brands fourth round, Bayley heading Abbott for second both times.

Steve Abbott's title chances took a big dive on the first lap of the first leg when he clipped the Starkey's Bridge kerb at Donington, breaking passenger Shaun Smith's knee. Webster and Hewitt took full advantage by winning the race from Bayley and Nixon, although the championship leaders seized in the second. Bayley won that with a lap record, moving equal second with Abbott at the series' half way stage: 96 points to Webster's 124.

The leading crews were at the French Grand Prix while Japanese pair Yoshida Kumagaya and Kazuhiko Makiuchi were busy winning the Snetterton round. With the exception of the injured Shaun Smith they were all back for Mallory and it was Smith's partner Steve Abbott, with Vince Biggs in the chair, who won the first race from

Roger Marshall and Roger Burnett were usually in a class of their own on the 500 Hondas, the last season contested by Honda Britain.

Bayley and the husband-and-wife Bingham team. Webster and Hewitt went out with broken suspension while leading, then came back to win Race Two from Bayley/Nixon and Abbott/Biggs.

That was the last anyone saw of Steve Webster and Tony Hewitt. Confident and consistently fast, they retained their British title in fine style by winning all four remaining races. Three more second placings at Thruxton and Silverstone were enough to put Derek Bayley and Bryan Nixon clear runners-up ahead of Steve Abbott: the Japanese crew ended the year fourth and might one day make the stangest-sounding British Champions of all.

## MCN/EBC Brakes Superstock Championship

Fast, loud and almost always close, the Superstock series attracted still more interest and more competitors in its second year. Purists may not have approved of a glorified production race becoming the feature even of most meetings but, with seven works riders and leading privateers like Nation, Huewen and Mellor taking part, no-one could deny that this was the most competitive racing in Britain.

After struggling in 1985 with a slow bike, Honda were confident that their new VFR750 V4 – lighter and more powerful than the old VF, while the Suzukis and Yamahas stayed basically the same – would prove to be the machine for the job. That's how it looked as the first round got under way at Brands Hatch: Roger Burnett shot into the lead and put daylight between his growling Rothmans-coloured Honda and the rest of the pack.

Honda's joy was shortlived. Burnett, running slicks, found a still-damp patch at Paddock and crashed, leaving Suzuki-mounted Dale Robinson to make a name for himself by leading the next few laps. 'I didn't dare look back', said the Geordie, and a few laps later he didn't need to. The professionals were right behind and it was Suzuki's privateers who came past first – Trevor Nation followed by Phil Mellor and Keith Huewen – then Roger Marshall on the second VFR.

Nation had won last season's final round at Brands and he won this one too, holding off Mellor in a frantic last lap. Marshall beat Huewen for third; Dale Robinson finished a delighted fifth ahead of another man who had not raced at Brands before: New Zealander proddie ace Richard Scott, who had brought his factory-provided Honda through the field after starting almost last.

Trevor Nation's win meant that the Hampshire rider had won four of the last five Superstock rounds he had contested, having dominated the tail-end of the previous season. And Nation came out on top again at Mallory, picking off the country's leading riders one by one after a poor start. Kenny Irons, who had trailed new Mitsui Yamaha team-mate Steve Parrish home to eighth at Brands, beat Suzuki privateers Neil Robinson and Keith Huewen for second. Honda-mounted Richard Scott came fifth after another slow start but Rothmans VFR men Marshall and Burnett,

struggling to seventh and tenth places respectively, were beginning to realise that their new bikes were not as fast as they had hoped.

If Brands and Mallory had seen a continuation of Nation's recent superiority, then the Snetterton Superstock round was the season's turning point. The fast-improving Kenny Irons won the race, passing Keith Huewen at half-distance and pipping him by a wheel at the line. And Nation, dicing for third with Phil Mellor while struggling with a new-construction rear Michelin tyre, crashed out of the race two bends from the end. Scott and John Lofthouse passed Mellor, who ran off the track but stayed on his bike for fifth.

Instead of having a clear advantage, Nation now shared the championship lead with Irons, and Huewen was just four points behind. The Hampshireman's troubles deepened when he came to the next round nursing a hand injured in another crash the week before. Few riders could understand why Cadwell's tiny Woodland circuit was being used but it made for a close race: there make in the first three with tenths of a second between them as Keith Huewen (Suzuki) beat Richard Scott (Honda) and Kenny Irons (Yamaha).

As light rain began to fall Trevor Nation – 'the hand was hurting and I was just hoping the race

would end' – dropped back to fourth, finishing inches ahead of Mellor and Steve Parrish. Still in pain, fourth was all Nation could manage at Oulton Park's next round. Again, there were three makes in the frame but this race was a walkover by Superstock standards, Irons winning by three seconds from Scott and Suzuki's Neil Robinson in a race that had to be re-run after a pile up at the head of the field.

Kenny Irons won at Thruxton too, first taking a big lead but then having to fight all the way as Richard Scott once again proved the speed of both his Honda and himself. The lead changed hands several times on the last two laps, Irons power-sliding out of the last bend to win. Roger Hurst's Yamaha cruelly blew up on the last lap to let Nation sweep past for third; Suzuki-riding John Lofthouse, who with Hurst was the discovery of the series, beat Neil Robinson for fourth and was to end the year an impressive fifth overall.

Irons' second win in a row opened up a 14-point lead over Scott and established him as the man to beat in Superstocks. After years of riding two-strokes, always acting as his own mechanic, the Luton rider was finding that the change to four-strokes had rekindled his enthusiasm for racing. 'Learning to ride the Superstock bike hasn't been a problem, though on a big bike you have to be

The Honda VF 500 Cup was a big success and although Dave Leach (no. 6) won at Thruxton, Jeff Johnson (no. 17) won the Championship.

much smoother.' He puts much of his success down to practice. 'Because I've had less to do I've been getting more riding – and I like a lot of riding. I don't have to work on the FZ so often, though when a four-stroke goes wrong it does it in a big way.'

Prophetic words, because Irons blew up his FZ750 before the Scarborough Superstock round and was forced to borrow Mitsui team-mate Steve Parrish's Yamaha to score yet another win. The day, of course, was marred by Neil Robinson's fatal accident, not to mention a Superstock crash which saw Trevor Nation's bike (and luckily not its rider) go careering off the narrow track and smash into a tree. Kenny Irons left vowing never to return, and Kiwi Scott, third behind Mellor, had not enjoyed himself either.

Sunday 28 September is a day at Donington that will live long in the memory of Kenny Irons. Having crashed at Redgate twice already that day, in pain from a broken little finger and bruises all over his body, Kenny came out of the same corner inside Keith Huewen to take a first-lap lead which was never headed. He broke the lap record, finished the race in agony and became an almost certain champion: 29 points ahead of fifth-finisher Scott with only the double-scoring final round to come. Huewen finished second ahead of Parrish and Nation, whose faint championship hopes were now gone.

Huewen finally got his year's first Superstock victory, taking third in the championship from Nation as he led almost from the start at a typically damp Brands. But the race was all about two men: Scott, who came from almost last once again to take second place in the race and series; and Irons, who cruised to fifth and an emphatic championship victory. 'If it wasn't for the Superstocks I'd be in the position now of every other 250 rider I was up against last year', he'd said earlier in the season. Instead Irons ended an eventful year by signing to partner Roger Marshall on works Suzukis, with the promise of some Grand Prix rides.

Honda's end-of-season announcement was a blow for the impressive Scott, who alone had held up the company's Superstock effort. Ron Grant's tuning technique, which included adding weld to the piston crown to increase compression (the VFR's gear-driven cams means it's the only Superstock-legal way to do it), had not been copied by Honda GB but had made the bike competitive, and better starting would surely have seen him improve on his four second places. 'We've had the bike apart after each race, and each race it's got better and better. It's largely down to Ron's enthusiasm for the job', said a grateful Scott before heading back Down Under for the winter. Let's hope he and the Honda are back next year. With Kawasaki's new 750 joining in, the Superstock series could be even more competitive than ever.

Phil Mellor ended the Superstock year disastrously by falling off on the warm-up lap at Brands. But a fortnight earlier at Cadwell Park he had battled against the pain of a broken wrist to take a third and a fourth place – enough to win him both 1300 cc and 750 cc Metzeler Production

Championships. Trevor Nation had won both races, pipping Brian Morrison on the last bend in the big class, but those mid-season crashes had forced him to miss crucial proddy rounds at Silverstone and Scarborough, losing his lead in both series to the consistent Mellor who had known just what was needed for victory.

The production bike success meant the little Yorkshireman had come full circle; he started racing ten years ago on a production Yamaha RD350. 'I've raced little bikes and all sorts in between but I prefer the big four-strokes now – they're much more enjoyable', he said at Cadwell. 'I've enjoyed this season as much as ever and I just hope I can do the same sort of thing next year.'

Another experienced north-countryman, Geoff Johnson, used all his guile to take the year's other main production-based title, the Honda VF500 Cup. Supported by the importers through their network of dealers, the series followed in the tracks of similar set-ups for the V4 roadster in other European countries. The obvious comparisons with the one-bike Yamaha RD350LC series were not all favourable – the racing was rarely as close or as crash-happy, and the early rounds were marred by a nasty rash of gearbox failures. But the riders had a lot of fun and were glad of generous prize money that went right down to 20th place. That was one thing no other championship could boast.

## Shell Oils/ACU Formula 1 Championship

For a class which looked to be all but dead at the start of the season, Formula 1 racing came through the year strongly to finish with a Big Bang in its final year. Honda's pre-season withdrawal gave an indication of what can be expected in other classes in 1987. The series lost some glamour and credibility but produced a more open fight than before, with a wonderful final round at which six different riders could have taken the title.

Ray Swann splashed round Thruxton to take the first round from Nation, Martin Taylor and Steve Bonhomme, all riding private Suzukis. And it was Suzuki-riding Mark Phillips, fifth in that race, who brought the series to life at Mallory when he became the first two-stroke victor in the history of British F1. Phillips's bike comprising a square-four 500 Gamma road bike engine in a Mk 10 race chassis, won comfortably from Paul Iddon, Kenny Irons and Nation.

But Phillips had not intended to take the F1 Championship seriously – he was only riding the Padgett's Suzuki following family star Gary's death in a road crash – and was away at a European Championship round while Kenny Irons held off team-mate Steve Parrish to win at Donington. Trevor Nation took third place and the series lead, then finished fifth at Scarborough to increase the advantage when race leader Iron's Yamaha blew up. Phillips lost second gear there but he scraped a fourth behind the hard-riding Andy McGladdery, Keith Huewen and Phil Mellor.

Works-bike horsepower showed its advantage at the next round on Silverstone's flat straights: Paul Iddon won on the factory Suzuki, from Richard Scott's Honda and the Loctite Yamahas of Parrish and Irons. Phillips's 500 was struggling for speed at the top end but sixth place gave him 34 points to Nation's 36. With nine points separating the top six of those two, Irons, Parrish, Huewen and Iddon, the scene was set for a classic Cadwell Park finale.

If Mark Phillips could have chosen any track for such a crucial race then Cadwell would surely have been the one. The 23-year-old is a local, from a village a few miles from Lincoln, and first accompanied his bike-racing father to the track in John Cooper's heyday – at the age of 13 months, his mum recalled. Now he was back and riding for the British F1 Championship on a tight circuit which suited his lightweight two-stroke down to the ground.

Kenny Irons led at the start from Trevor Nation, opening up a small gap until Phillips got past Nation and began reeling in the red-and-white Yamaha. Kenny was riding hard but was in pain from the hand injury he had sustained the week before. Struggling to hold on to the handlebars, Irons could do nothing as Phillips took the lead at half way and pulled away to win. Young, fast and very self-confident, Mark would have finished well up in the 500 cc European Championship, too, had he not broken down repeatedly towards the end of the season. He plans to tackle the serie again in '87 – hopefully on a Mk 12 RG500 – and will take a lot of beating.

Trevor Nation finished sixth at Cadwell on his outpaced Superstock bike, trailing home behind Irons, Iddon, Scott and Parrish. In one day Nation had lost three of the major championships he'd been leading earlier in the year, having already lost his chance in the Superstocks. 'I feel a bit fed up about it but what can you do?' he said. 'I've had too many bikes this year – I don't know anybody who's run four bikes before and I find it really hard work. You can get 95 per cent out of them but you can't concentrate and get everything right on them all. I doubt if I'll run so many next year but I would like a good Superstock bike . . . I must have done 12,000 miles on this Suzuki now.' Nation got what he wanted most of all, in the form of a works Yamaha ride for 1987.

It was ironic that, at the same Cadwell meeting that a two-stroke was showing up the diesels in the Formula 1 race, a lone four-stroke was all but sewing up the Formula 2 Championship ahead of a pack of screaming strokers. But then Scot Steve Hislop hurled his 350LC-based Yamaha past Ray Swann's 600 Kawasaki to win the race and close the points gap to a catchable 12 with the final Darley Moor round to come.

Hislop, who had missed the first round but won at Scarborough and Silverstone, had to make it four in a row to have any chance of the title. But instead he crashed out early on, leaving Kenny Irons' former Pro-Am sparring partner to complete a good year for Bedfordshire. With the pressure off, Swann finished in style. He shadowed Tony Head before making a last-lap, last-bend pass to take the championship with a win.

# MCA RESCUE

### By BRIAN CALDECOTT

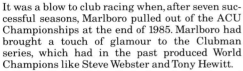

It was a blow to club racing when, after seven successful seasons, Marlboro pulled out of the ACU Championships at the end of 1985. Marlboro had brought a touch of glamour to the Clubman series, which had in the past produced World Champions like Steve Webster and Tony Hewitt.

For 1986, the Motor Cycle Association stepped in, sponsoring a ten-round series in a new deal aimed at spreading the rewards wider. There was attractive prize money and the promise of support for 1987 for the top riders in each of the eight championship classes.

However, the MCA did not have the style of the highly professional and publicity-orientated Marlboro organisation and the series lost some of its sparkle. The image was not enhanced when the final round at Aintree was cancelled through lack of entries.

Nevertheless, this should in no way detract from the efforts of the riders who did support the series, for once again they turned in some splendid performances.

Remarkable consistency was the hallmark of Southport sidecar team Matt Nelson and John Wilson. Although beaten in the opening round at Snetterton by Kieron Kavanagh and John Sleight from Kent, they were runners-up at the first five meetings before coming good at Cadwell Park, where Kavanagh crashed. Nelson and Wilson underlined their right to the championship with a fine win at Mallory Park, the last of the seven rounds.

Another consistent performer was Kettering's Mark Carkeek. It took him until the third round at Brands Hatch to get into his stride on his 125 Honda. But a win there was followed by six more – a record for the Clubman's Championships.

Stu McDonald made good progress during the season and pinched second in the table from Dave Collinson, while 17-year-old Jamie Hitter (from Lowestoft) shone in both 250 and 350 classes. He did the double at Carnaby and won the 350, then came second in the 250 at Brands. At the halfway stage he led the 350s by eight points from Martin Bennett and was one point behind Dave Butler in the 250 class. But he lost two months through injury which wrecked his chances.

Meanwhile, Andy Godber was making a charge on his 250. Fifth place at Brands began a brilliant run of five wins and a second which brought him a well-deserved championship. Hitter came back to second at Pembrey, putting him third in the table behind Dennis Wisdom.

Bennett also made his presence felt in the 350 division. Wins at Cadwell and Mallory hoisted him to second but it was another Midlander, Chris Galatowicz, who took the honours when these circuits hosted their second meetings.

Galatowicz led by 11 points as they went into the final showdown when he made sure of the title by leading home Bennett, who claimed second in the table from Hitter.

Londoners Ricky McMillan and Terry Rymer, were the stars of the 375–1000 cc class. But it was McMillan's remarkable consistency which paid off in the end. He began with a win at Snetterton and scored points at every round, his placings being 1-2-2-2-3-2-2-1-2. Rymer had four wins in a

**James Hitter managed third place in both the 250 and 350cc MCA Clubmans titles despite missing three rounds through injury** (top). **Convincing MCA 1300cc Clubmans Champion Ricky McMillan who scored in all nine rounds** (above).

row but fell at Mallory after taking full points there, and he did not figure again. Green's strong performances in the second half of the series included wins at Cadwell and Brands, elevating him to second overall in front of Rymer.

There were no holds barred all the way in the production classes. With two wins, two seconds and a third, Liverpool's John Corrin set the 250 pace in the first half of the season. Then Steve Spray, Ray Stringer, Andy Muggleton and Rod Harwin got their acts together and the sparks really began to fly.

Corrin lost his second place at Brands through a rules infringement but his third place behind Harwin and Spray at Mallory brought him back into contention and he finished with a champion's ride at Pembrey.

Third and fourth respectively in the first round, Gary Thrush and Mike Edwards fought tooth-and-nail in the 350 class. Edwards took over with a win at Carnaby but after two more rounds, Thrush had the advantage. Edwards struck again with second at Mallory and win at Cadwell, but victories at Brands and at the second Mallory meeting put Thrush back in the driving seat and he made it three in a row by leading home Graham Read and Edwards in South Wales.

Rob Shepherd, from Kirkcaldy, led the 1300 Production class from start to finish. But Dave Browne was always in the hunt and as they lined up for the Pembrey decider, he was only two points in arrears. Shepherd was not to be denied, however, and led home his rival to scoop the championship. Ian Green followed up his second place in the Open class with third overall in the Production series.

# SEWARD'S

# RECORD

The 1986 Manx Grand Prix maintained its place as the top British amateur road race meeting and for once was mainly favoured by good weather. Nearly 400 individual competitors responded to the annual challenge of the demanding 37¾-mile Snaefell Mountain Circuit and produced some outstanding performances.

The highlight was undoubtedly the breaking of the outright lap record by Mike Seward in his dramatic attempt to snatch a last-lap Senior Race victory. He knocked 24 seconds off Dave East's previous best, which had stood since 1981.

Newcomers nowadays start by competing in a special race of their own, divided into three classes. Computer studies engineer Jim Hunter proved fastest when he won the 1000 cc class on a 750 cc Suzuki, averaging 100.35 mph for four laps of the circuit totalling 150 miles, and beating Ian Mitchell by 21 seconds after a lengthy battle. Practice favourite Nick Lynn was third, his Honda unable to match the pace of the GSX-Rs.

Usually, the 350 cc class is the fastest of the three, but this time the 1000s outgunned them, despite the stalwart endeavours of the Yamaha brigade. Ian Jones (23) from South Wirral won it, although he had quite a fright when his chain came off at Bedstead Corner a mile from home. He quickly replaced it.

Matt Drane had been leading, but crashed at Cruickshanks Corner at Ramsey on the last lap. Jones squeezed home by nine seconds at an average of 96.23 mph from Trevor Robinson.

The 250 cc race was something of a walk-over for 22-year-old George Higginson from Mossley, near Belfast. He and Stewart Rae broke the lap record by 2.2 seconds, but Rae later retired and Higginson found himself with an advantage of seven minutes.

Following last year's two local victories (Gary Radcliffe and Buddy Yeardsley), hopes were high for at least one more Manx triumph. And Ralph Sutcliffe didn't disappoint the faithful indigenous community. Riding Ray Cowles' Rotax, he swept to 250 cc victory to emulate his father Roger's Senior Manx Grand Prix win on Ray's G50 Matchless sixteen years earlier.

Initially, another local, Colin Hardman, led the four-lap race, having gained experience in the sidecar of Dennis Keen at TT time. But his solo effort lasted only as far as Windy Corner on the first lap when he spilled, without injury.

Sutcliffe took over and enjoyed a trouble-free race, although he was pressed sufficiently hard to need to lap at over 103 mph on the third lap.

Mick Robinson (33) from Eastbourne took up the chase on time, but found the task of assessing the situation difficult from his position near the front of the field. Whereas Robinson may have had a lonely ride at no. 3, Stewart Rae demonstrated the other end of the problem. He had to pass traffic constantly as he scythed through the field from no. 81. Considering he had been a newcomer two days before, his progress was remarkable and he was rewarded with third place, having overcome John Davies on the final lap.

Sean Collister had perhaps hoped for better things on the Honda used by the late Gary Padgett at the TT, but his unfamiliarity with it

slowed him down, not helped either by a loose petrol tank and two fuel stops. He was fifth and must wait at least another year to secure the elusive victory snatched from him on a previous occasion.

Mark Linton's sixth place wasn't gained without trouble either. The gearbox of his Yamaha stuck in fifth and he halted thinking he was out. But frantic roadside attention freed the lever and he was away once more.

The Manx Grand Prix is renowned today for riders returning year after year seeking to win one of the three main events. There is a gentlemen's agreement that prevents a competitor continuing in the amateur meeting. Alan 'Bud' Jackson set out in the six-lap 225-mile Junior race with a lengthy string of previous disappointments behind him. Elder brother Bob had been equally unlucky in the Manx, but had immediately taken a gallant second place when he moved to the TT without the need to do so.

Behind Bud this time was a very fast field, but underneath him was the trusty Dennis Trollope Fowler Yamaha twin. Local rider Decca Kelly led to start with, but eventually succumbed to a seized gearbox which threw him off at the Gooseneck and gave him a broken collarbone.

Jackson started relatively easily, but on his second lap he averaged 106.19 mph, despite an over-soft absorber which was already wearing through the seat and his leathers!

With fuel stops interfering with the leaderboards, it was not until late in the race that a pattern became established. But at half-distance, Kelly was 16 seconds ahead of 25-year-old Douglas joiner Ralph Sutcliffe, with yet another local, Sean Collister, third. Steve Hazlett had been challenging but developed gearbox trouble and retired.

On lap 4, Jackson took over at the front once more and was never again headed. But Sutcliffe was really flying and was only 11 seconds adrift with a lap to go.

Sutcliffe was watching out for an engine seizure because the motor had cut out earlier at Greeba on lap 4. He freewheeled for half a mile before gingerly letting out the clutch and firing up after a suspected locking.

The last lap was really exciting as Sutcliffe pressed hard and Jackson went as fast as he dared with the rear unit now red-hot and nibbling his backside on every one of the many dozen severe bumps.

At the end, Jackson took it by just over eight seconds, with the evidence of the wallowing suspension there for all to see. York's Mike Seward had been nowhere to start with but plugged away to climb from tenth to third, although three minutes down on Sutcliffe. Similar beavering rewarded Tony Martin with fourth, followed by Justin Urch and Ray Evans.

The main race of the Manx Grand Prix is always regarded as being the 1000 cc Senior, with the 1986 event continuing the recent trend towards road-going four-cylinder four-strokes and away from the more costly maintenance of the pukka racers.

Dave East's outright MGP record had stood since 1981 and critics were saying that the intervening four years had failed to produce riders capable of beating it and therefore the standard was dropping. That's as may be, but Dave set it on an RG500 two-stroke four – a real racer – while few had been able to bring such bikes in prime specification since then.

Nevertheless, the pundits were well and truly silenced by the 1986 Senior. It started comparatively gently, with 25-year-old RAF MotorSports Association runner Grant Goodings setting the pace. He led by 16 seconds after the first of the six laps, with local Paul Hunt in pursuit.

Hunt had an involuntary stop on lap 2 to investigate apparent fuel starvation, which put him out of serious contention. Up came Mike Seward, revelling in the less fussy power of the Fowler FZ750 Yamaha compared to the 350 TZ.

At half-distance Goodings enjoyed a lead of nearly a minute over Seward, little knowing what was to come. Blackpool policeman Kevin Jackson was third.

On the fourth lap, Seward clawed back over half of that and the fun began in earnest. Lap 5 saw them both averaging over 108 mph and nearing East's record. Into the last lap they were separated by 23 seconds.

That final lap saw a superhuman effort from Seward. At Ballacraine, eight miles out, the gap was down to 15 seconds. At Ballaugh (18 miles) only 13. Up the Mountain Seward thrashed the big Yamaha to the limit, cursing his over-gearing which prevented use of top gear.

At the crest of the climb only seven seconds lay between them and Goodings was under pressure, so much so that he almost crashed at Keppel Gate when the suspension bottomed out. He clung on and raced the remaining three miles down the Mountain to the finish.

He then had the agonising task of waiting for Seward to come in, the pair riding apart on the road at numbers 25 and 50. Seward broke the lap record by a staggering 24 seconds, lifting the Manx Grand Prix record into the 110 mph bracket. But it wasn't quite enough to beat Goodings, who triumphed by a mere 3.6 seconds after two hours' flat-out racing.

Almost unnoticed, Hazlett finished third, nearly four minutes behind but a good effort on a 350, with Jackson fourth, Gary Tate fifth and Roy Chapman sixth. None the less, all the talk was of that electrifying last-lap battle between the mighty four-strokes.

# 1986 RESULTS

**EDDIE LAWSON**
*1986 500 cc WORLD CHAMPION*

**CARLOS LAVADO**
*1986 250 cc WORLD CHAMPION*

## 500 cc World Championship

| Position | Rider | Nationality | Machine | Spain | Italy | Germany | Austria | Yugoslavia | Holland | Belgium | France | Great Britain | Sweden | San Marino | TOTAL |
|---|---|---|---|---|---|---|---|---|---|---|---|---|---|---|---|
| 1 | Eddie Lawson | USA | Yamaha | 12 | 15 | 15 | 15 | 15 | – | 12 | 15 | 10 | 15 | 15 | 139 |
| 2 | Wayne Gardner | AUS | Honda | 15 | – | 12 | 12 | 10 | 15 | 8 | 6 | 15 | 12 | 12 | 117 |
| 3 | Randy Mamola | USA | Yamaha | 8 | 12 | 5 | 10 | 12 | 12 | 15 | 12 | 6 | 3 | 10 | 105 |
| 4 | Mike Baldwin | USA | Yamaha | 10 | 10 | 10 | 6 | 6 | 10 | – | 8 | – | 10 | 8 | 78 |
| 5 | Rob McElnea | GB | Yamaha | 4 | – | 8 | 5 | 8 | 8 | 6 | 5 | 8 | 8 | – | 60 |
| 6 | Christian Sarron | F | Yamaha | 6 | 8 | – | 8 | 5 | 6 | 10 | 10 | – | – | 5 | 58 |
| 7 | Didier de Radigues | B | Chevallier | – | 6 | 6 | – | – | 2 | 4 | 3 | 12 | 5 | 4 | 42 |
| 8 | Raymond Roche | F | Honda | 5 | – | 4 | – | 4 | 5 | – | – | 5 | 6 | 6 | 35 |
| 9 | Ron Haslam | GB | Elf | 1 | – | 3 | – | – | 4 | – | 4 | 2 | 2 | 2 | 18 |
| 10 | Pier Francesco Chili | I | Suzuki | – | 4 | – | 2 | – | – | 5 | – | – | – | – | 11 |
| 10= | Niall MacKenzie | GB | Suzuki | – | – | – | – | – | – | – | – | 4 | 4 | 3 | 11 |
| 12 | Boet van Dulmen | NL | Honda | – | 5 | – | 1 | – | – | 2 | – | – | – | – | 8 |
| 13 | Shunji Yatsushiro | J | Honda | – | – | – | 4 | 3 | – | – | – | – | – | – | 7 |
| 14= | Fabio Biliotti | I | Honda | 2 | 3 | – | – | – | – | – | – | – | – | – | 5 |
| 14= | Gustav Reiner | D | Honda | – | – | 2 | 3 | – | – | – | – | – | – | – | 5 |
| 14= | Dave Petersen | ZIM | Suzuki | – | – | 1 | – | 2 | – | – | 2 | – | – | – | 5 |
| 17= | Juan Garriga | E | Cagiva | 3 | – | – | – | – | 1 | – | – | – | – | – | 4 |
| 17= | Paul Lewis | AUS | Suzuki | – | 2 | – | – | 1 | – | 1 | – | – | – | – | 4 |
| 19= | Roger Burnett | GB | Honda | – | – | – | – | – | – | – | 3 | – | – | – | 3 |
| 19= | Mile Pajic | NL | Honda | – | – | – | – | – | – | – | 3 | – | – | – | 3 |
| 19= | Kenny Irons | GB | Yamaha | – | – | – | – | – | – | – | – | – | 3 | – | 3 |
| 22= | Kevin Schwantz | USA | Suzuki | – | – | – | – | 1 | – | – | – | – | – | 1 | 2 |
| 22= | Wolfgang von Muralt | CH | Suzuki | – | – | – | – | – | – | – | – | – | 1 | 1 | 2 |
| 24 | Marco Papa | I | Honda | – | 1 | – | – | – | – | – | – | – | – | – | 1 |

## 250 cc World Championship

| Position | Rider | Nationality | Machine | Spain | Italy | Germany | Austria | Yugoslavia | Holland | Belgium | France | Great Britain | Sweden | San Marino | TOTAL |
|---|---|---|---|---|---|---|---|---|---|---|---|---|---|---|---|
| 1 | Carlos Lavado | YV | Yamaha | 15 | 12 | 15 | 15 | – | 15 | – | 15 | 12 | 15 | – | 114 |
| 2 | Alfonso Pons | E | Honda | 10 | 6 | – | 6 | 15 | 10 | 15 | 12 | 10 | 12 | 12 | 108 |
| 3 | Dominique Sarron | F | Honda | – | 4 | – | 5 | – | 4 | 15 | 10 | 15 | 6 | 10 | 72 |
| 4 | Anton Mang | D | Honda | 12 | 15 | 12 | – | – | 12 | – | 6 | – | – | 8 | 65 |
| 5 | Jean-François Baldé | F | Honda | 3 | 10 | 8 | 10 | 12 | 2 | – | 5 | 2 | – | 10 | 63 |
| 6 | Martin Wimmer | D | Yamaha | 8 | 8 | 10 | 12 | – | 6 | – | 5 | 2 | – | 5 | 56 |
| 7 | Jacques Cornu | CH | Honda | 6 | 5 | 4 | – | – | 3 | 10 | – | 4 | – | – | 32 |
| 8 | Fausto Ricci | I | Honda | 2 | – | 6 | 8 | 8 | – | – | – | – | – | 6 | 30 |
| 9 | Tadahiko Taira | J | Yamaha | – | – | 2 | 3 | – | 5 | 2 | 1 | – | 15 | – | 28 |
| 10 | Donnie McLeod | GB | Armstrong | 4 | – | 3 | – | – | 8 | 12 | – | – | – | – | 27 |
| 11 | Pierre Bolle | F | Parisienne | 5 | 3 | 5 | – | – | 2 | – | 4 | – | – | 2 | 21 |
| 12 | Carlos Cardus | E | Honda | – | – | – | 6 | – | 5 | – | 6 | – | – | – | 17 |
| 13= | Stéphane Mertens | B | Yamaha | – | – | – | – | 5 | – | – | – | 3 | 5 | 1 | 14 |
| 13= | Virginio Ferrari | I | Honda | – | – | – | 4 | – | – | 2 | 5 | – | 3 | – | 14 |
| 15 | Maurizio Vitali | I | Garelli | – | – | – | 1 | – | – | – | 3 | 4 | 4 | – | 12 |
| 16 | Reinhold Roth | D | Honda | – | – | – | – | 1 | 1 | – | – | 8 | – | – | 10 |
| 17= | Alan Carter | GB | Kobas | 1 | – | 1 | – | – | – | 6 | – | 1 | – | – | 9 |
| 17= | Jean-Michel Mattioli | F | Yamaha | – | 1 | – | – | – | – | – | 4 | – | 4 | – | 9 |
| 19= | Manfred Herweh | D | Aprilia | – | – | – | 4 | 3 | – | – | – | – | – | – | 7 |
| 19= | Jean Foray | F | Chevallier | – | – | – | – | – | – | 4 | – | 3 | – | – | 7 |
| 21= | Niall MacKenzie | GB | Armstrong | – | – | – | – | – | – | – | 3 | 1 | – | – | 4 |
| 21= | Siegfried Minich | A | Yamaha | – | – | – | – | 2 | – | – | – | 2 | – | – | 4 |
| 23 | Massimo Matteoni | I | Honda | – | 2 | – | – | – | – | – | – | – | – | – | 2 |
| 24 | Hans Lindner | A | Rotax | – | – | – | – | – | – | – | – | 1 | – | – | 1 |

## Past 500 cc World Champions

| | | | (Wins/ Races) |
|---|---|---|---|
| 1949 | Les Graham, GB | AJS | (2/6) |
| 1950 | Umberto Masetti, I | Gilera | (2/6) |
| 1951 | Geoff Duke, GB | Norton | (4/8) |
| 1952 | Umberto Masetti, I | Gilera | (2/8) |
| 1953 | Geoff Duke, GB | Gilera | (4/8) |
| 1954 | Geoff Duke, GB | Gilera | (5/8) |
| 1955 | Geoff Duke, GB | Gilera | (4/8) |
| 1956 | John Surtees, GB | MV-Agusta | (3/6) |
| 1957 | Libero Liberati, I | Gilera | (3/6) |
| 1958 | John Surtees, GB | MV-Agusta | (6/7) |
| 1959 | John Surtees, GB | MV-Agusta | (7/7) |
| 1960 | John Surtees, GB | MV-Agusta | (5/7) |
| 1961 | Gary Hocking, RSR | MV-Agusta | (7/10) |
| 1962 | Mike Hailwood, GB | MV-Agusta | (5/8) |
| 1963 | Mike Hailwood, GB | MV-Agusta | (7/8) |
| 1964 | Mike Hailwood, GB | MV-Agusta | (7/9) |
| 1965 | Mike Hailwood, GB | MV-Agusta | (8/10) |
| 1966 | Giacomo Agostini, I | MV-Agusta | (3/9) |
| 1967 | Giacomo Agostini, I | MV-Agusta | (5/10) |
| 1968 | Giacomo Agostini, I | MV-Agusta | (10/10) |
| 1969 | Giacomo Agostini, I | MV-Agusta | (10/12) |
| 1970 | Giacomo Agostini, I | MV-Agusta | (10/11) |
| 1971 | Giacomo Agostini, I | MV-Agusta | (8/11) |
| 1972 | Giacomo Agostini, I | MV-Agusta | (11/13) |
| 1973 | Phil Read, GB | MV-Agusta | (4/11) |
| 1974 | Phil Read, GB | MV-Agusta | (4/10) |
| 1975 | Giacomo Agostini, I | Yamaha | (4/10) |
| 1976 | Barry Sheene, GB | Suzuki | (5/10) |
| 1977 | Barry Sheene, GB | Suzuki | (6/11) |
| 1978 | Kenny Roberts, USA | Yamaha | (4/11) |
| 1979 | Kenny Roberts, USA | Yamaha | (5/12) |
| 1980 | Kenny Roberts, USA | Yamaha | (3/8) |
| 1981 | Marco Lucchinelli, I | Suzuki | (5/11) |
| 1982 | Franco Uncini, I | Suzuki | (5/12) |
| 1983 | Freddie Spencer, USA | Honda | (6/12) |
| 1984 | Eddie Lawson, USA | Yamaha | (4/12) |
| 1985 | Freddie Spencer, USA | Honda | (7/12) |

## Past 350 cc World Champions

| | | | (Wins/ Races) |
|---|---|---|---|
| 1949 | Freddie Frith, GB | Velocette | (5/5) |
| 1950 | Bob Foster, GB | Velocette | (3/6) |
| 1951 | Geoff Duke, GB | Norton | (5/8) |
| 1952 | Geoff Duke, GB | Norton | (4/7) |
| 1953 | Fergus Anderson, GB | Guzzi | (3/7) |
| 1954 | Fergus Anderson, GB | Guzzi | (4/9) |
| 1955 | Bill Lomas, GB | Guzzi | (4/7) |
| 1956 | Bill Lomas, GB | Guzzi | (3/6) |
| 1957 | Keith Campbell, AUS | Guzzi | (3/6) |
| 1958 | John Surtees, GB | MV-Agusta | (6/7) |
| 1959 | John Surtees, GB | MV-Agusta | (6/6) |
| 1960 | John Surtees, GB | MV-Agusta | (2/5) |
| 1961 | Gary Hocking, RSR | MV-Agusta | (4/7) |
| 1962 | Jim Redman, RSR | Honda | (4/6) |
| 1963 | Jim Redman, RSR | Honda | (5/7) |
| 1964 | Jim Redman, RSR | Honda | (8/8) |
| 1965 | Jim Redman, RSR | Honda | (4/9) |
| 1966 | Mike Hailwood, GB | Honda | (6/10) |
| 1967 | Mike Hailwood, GB | Honda | (5/8) |
| 1968 | Giacomo Agostini, I | MV-Agusta | (7/7) |
| 1969 | Giacomo Agostini, I | MV-Agusta | (8/10) |
| 1970 | Giacomo Agostini, I | MV-Agusta | (9/10) |
| 1971 | Giacomo Agostini, I | MV-Agusta | (6/11) |
| 1972 | Giacomo Agostini, I | MV-Agusta | (6/12) |
| 1973 | Giacomo Agostini, I | MV-Agusta | (4/11) |
| 1974 | Giacomo Agostini, I | Yamaha | (5/10) |
| 1975 | Johnny Cecotto, YV | Yamaha | (4/10) |
| 1976 | Walter Villa, I | Harley-Davidson | (5/11) |
| 1977 | Takazumi Katayama, J | Yamaha | (5/11) |
| 1978 | Kork Ballington, ZA | Kawasaki | (6/11) |
| 1979 | Kork Ballington, ZA | Kawasaki | (5/11) |
| 1980 | Jon Ekerold, ZA | Yamaha | (3/6) |
| 1981 | Anton Mang, D | Kawasaki | (5/8) |
| 1982 | Anton Mang, D | Kawasaki | (1/9) |

## Past 250 cc World Champions

| | | | (Wins/ Races) |
|---|---|---|---|
| 1949 | Bruno Ruffo, I | Guzzi | (1/4) |
| 1950 | Dario Ambrosini, I | Benelli | (3/4) |
| 1951 | Bruno Ruffo, I | Guzzi | (2/5) |
| 1952 | Enrico Lorenzetti, I | Guzzi | (2/6) |
| 1953 | Werner Haas, D | NSU | (2/7) |
| 1954 | Werner Haas, D | NSU | (5/7) |
| 1955 | Hermann-Peter Müller, D | NSU | (1/5) |
| 1956 | Carlo Ubbiali, I | MV-Agusta | (5/6) |
| 1957 | Cecil Sandford, GB | Mondial | (2/6) |
| 1958 | Tarquinio Provini, I | MV-Agusta | (4/6) |
| 1959 | Carlo Ubbiali, I | MV-Agusta | (2/6) |
| 1960 | Carlo Ubbiali, I | MV-Agusta | (4/6) |
| 1961 | Mike Hailwood, GB | Honda | (4/11) |
| 1962 | Jim Redman, RSR | Honda | (6/10) |
| 1963 | Jim Redman, RSR | Honda | (4/10) |
| 1964 | Phil Read, GB | Yamaha | (5/11) |
| 1965 | Phil Read, GB | Yamaha | (7/13) |
| 1966 | Mike Hailwood, GB | Honda | (10/12) |
| 1967 | Mike Hailwood, GB | Honda | (5/13) |
| 1968 | Phil Read, GB | Yamaha | (5/10) |
| 1969 | Kel Carruthers, AUS | Benelli | (3/12) |
| 1970 | Rod Gould, GB | Yamaha | (6/12) |
| 1971 | Phil Read, GB | Yamaha | (3/12) |
| 1972 | Jarno Saarinen, SF | Yamaha | (4/13) |
| 1973 | Dieter Braun, D | Yamaha | (4/11) |
| 1974 | Walter Villa, I | Harley-Davidson | (4/10) |
| 1975 | Walter Villa, I | Harley-Davidson | (5/11) |
| 1976 | Walter Villa, I | Harley-Davidson | (7/11) |
| 1977 | Mario Lega, I | Morbidelli | (1/12) |
| 1978 | Kork Ballington, ZA | Kawasaki | (4/12) |
| 1979 | Kork Ballington, ZA | Kawasaki | (7/12) |
| 1980 | Anton Mang, D | Kawasaki | (4/10) |
| 1981 | Anton Mang, D | Kawasaki | (10/12) |
| 1982 | Jean-Louis Tournadre, F | Yamaha | (1/12) |
| 1983 | Carlos Lavado, YV | Yamaha | (4/11) |
| 1984 | Christian Sarron, F | Yamaha | (3/12) |
| 1985 | Freddie Spencer, USA | Honda | (7/12) |

| Position | Rider | Nationality | Machine | Spain | Italy | Germany | Austria | Yugoslavia | Holland | Belgium | France | Great Britain | Sweden | San Marino | TOTAL |
|---|---|---|---|---|---|---|---|---|---|---|---|---|---|---|---|
| 1 | Luca Cadalora | I | Garelli | 8 | 8 | 15 | 15 | 15 | – | 15 | 10 | 12 | 12 | 12 | 122 |
| 2 | Fausto Gresini | I | Garelli | 15 | 15 | 12 | – | 12 | 8 | 12 | – | 15 | 10 | 15 | 114 |
| 3 | Domenico Brigaglia | I | MBA | 12 | – | – | 6 | 8 | 15 | 6 | 12 | 10 | 6 | 5 | 80 |
| 4 | August Auinger | A | Bartol | – | 10 | – | – | – | – | 10 | 15 | – | 15 | 10 | 60 |
| 5 | Ezio Gianola | I | MBA | 10 | – | 10 | 12 | 10 | 5 | – | 2 | – | – | 8 | 57 |
| 6 | Bruno Kneubühler | CH | LCR | – | – | 8 | 10 | 6 | – | 8 | – | 8 | 8 | 6 | 54 |
| 7 | Lucio Pietroniro | B | MBA | – | 5 | – | 3 | – | 12 | 5 | 6 | 6 | – | – | 37 |
| 8 | Pier Paolo Bianchi | I | Elit | 4 | 6 | – | 8 | – | 4 | 4 | 1 | 2 | 5 | – | 34 |
| 9 | Johnny Wickström | SF | Tunturi | 6 | 2 | 2 | – | 5 | – | 3 | 8 | 5 | – | 2 | 33 |
| 10 | Willy Perez | RA | Zanella | 5 | 1 | 5 | – | – | 10 | – | 5 | – | – | – | 26 |
| 11 | Olivier Liegeois | B | Assmex | – | – | 4 | 5 | – | 6 | – | 3 | – | – | 3 | 21 |
| 12 | Thierry Feuz | CH | MBA | – | – | 4 | 6 | – | 3 | 1 | 1 | – | 4 | – | 19 |
| 13 | Angel Nieto | E | Ducados | – | 12 | – | – | 1 | – | 2 | – | – | – | – | 15 |
| 14 | Paolo Casoli | I | MBA | – | – | 3 | – | 4 | 3 | – | – | – | – | 4 | 14 |
| 15 | Gastone Grassetti | I | MBA | – | 3 | – | – | 2 | – | – | – | – | 4 | – | 9 |
| 16 | Jussi Hautaniemi | SF | MBA | 2 | – | – | – | 2 | – | 4 | – | – | – | – | 8 |
| 17 | Adolf Stadler | D | MBA | – | – | – | 1 | – | – | – | – | 3 | 1 | 1 | 6 |
| 18= | Alfred Waibel | D | Real | – | – | 1 | 4 | – | – | – | – | – | – | – | 5 |
| 18= | Hakan Olsson | S | Starol | 1 | – | – | – | – | – | – | – | – | 1 | 3 | 5 |
| 20 | Marin Andreas Sanchez | E | Ducados | 3 | – | – | – | – | – | – | – | – | – | – | 3 |
| 21= | Esa Kytola | SF | MBA | – | – | – | 2 | – | – | – | – | – | – | – | 2 |
| 21= | Mike Leitner | A | MBA | – | – | – | – | – | – | – | – | – | 2 | – | 2 |

| Position | Rider | Nationality | Machine | Spain | Italy | Germany | Austria | Yugoslavia | Holland | Great Britain | San Marino | Baden-Württemberg | TOTAL |
|---|---|---|---|---|---|---|---|---|---|---|---|---|---|---|
| 1 | Jorge Martinez | E | Derbi | 15 | 12 | – | 15 | 15 | 15 | 10 | 12 | – | 94 |
| 2 | Manuel Herreros | E | Derbi | 10 | 10 | 15 | 12 | – | 12 | 8 | 10 | 8 | 85 |
| 3 | Stefan Dörflinger | CH | Krauser | 2 | 15 | 12 | 6 | 6 | 12 | 6 | 5 | 12 | 82 |
| 4 | Hans Spaan | NL | Huvo | – | 4 | 8 | 6 | 8 | 10 | 6 | 8 | 10 | 57 |
| 5 | Gerhard Waibel | D | Real | 4 | 8 | 6 | 4 | 2 | 5 | 5 | 2 | 15 | 51 |
| 6 | Ian McConnachie | GB | Krauser | 6 | – | 10 | 5 | 10 | – | 15 | 4 | – | 50 |
| 7 | Angel Nieto | E | Derbi | 12 | – | 8 | 3 | 8 | 8 | – | 6 | – | 45 |
| 8 | Pier Paolo Bianchi | I | Seel | 8 | 6 | – | 10 | 5 | – | – | 15 | – | 44 |
| 9 | Josef Fischer | A | Krauser | – | – | 4 | 2 | 3 | 4 | – | – | – | 13 |
| 10 | Gerd Kafka | A | Krauser | – | 3 | – | – | – | 2 | 4 | – | – | 9 |
| 11= | Wilco Zeelenberg | NL | Huvo | – | – | – | – | – | 2 | – | 6 | 8 |
| 11= | Hubert Abold | D | Seel | 3 | – | – | – | – | – | – | 5 | 8 |
| 13= | Juan Bolart | E | Autisa | 5 | – | – | 1 | – | – | – | – | 6 |
| 13= | Theo Timmer | NL | Huvo | – | 5 | – | – | – | – | 1 | 6 |
| 13= | Rainer Kunz | D | Ziegler | – | 2 | – | – | 4 | – | – | – | 6 |
| 13= | Alexandre Barros | BR | Autisa | – | – | – | – | – | – | 3 | 3 | 6 |
| 17= | Domingo Gil | E | Autisa | 1 | – | – | – | 3 | 1 | – | 5 |
| 17= | Henk van Kessel | NL | Krauser | – | – | 3 | – | – | – | 2 | 5 |
| 19 | Reiner Scheidhauer | D | Seel | – | – | – | – | – | – | 4 | 4 |
| 20= | Alfred Waibel | D | Real | – | – | – | – | – | – | 3 | 3 |
| 20= | Felix Rodriguez | E | Autisa | – | 2 | – | 1 | – | – | 3 |
| 22 | Luis Reyes | COL | Autisa | – | 1 | 1 | – | – | 2 |
| 23= | Salvatore Milano | I | Krauser | – | 1 | – | – | – | 1 |
| 23= | Francisco Torontegui | E | Kobas | – | – | – | 1 | – | 1 |

**JORGE MARTINEZ**
*1986 80 cc WORLD CHAMPION*

| | | | (Wins/Races) |
|---|---|---|---|
| 1949 | Nello Pagani, I | Mondial | (2/3) |
| 1950 | Bruno Ruffo, I | Mondial | (1/3) |
| 1951 | Carlo Ubbiali, I | Mondial | (1/4) |
| 1952 | Cecil Sandford, GB | MV-Agusta | (3/6) |
| 1953 | Werner Haas, D | NSU | (3/6) |
| 1954 | Rupert Hollaus, A | NSU | (4/6) |
| 1955 | Carlo Ubbiali, I | MV-Agusta | (5/6) |
| 1956 | Carlo Ubbiali, I | MV-Agusta | (5/6) |
| 1957 | Tarquinio Provini, I | Mondial | (3/6) |
| 1958 | Carlo Ubbiali, I | MV-Agusta | (4/7) |
| 1959 | Carlo Ubbiali, I | MV-Agusta | (3/7) |
| 1960 | Carlo Ubbiali, I | MV-Agusta | (4/5) |
| 1961 | Tom Phillis, AUS | Honda | (4/11) |
| 1962 | Luigi Taveri, CH | Honda | (6/11) |
| 1963 | Hugh Anderson, NZ | Suzuki | (6/12) |
| 1964 | Luigi Taveri, CH | Honda | (5/11) |
| 1965 | Hugh Anderson, NZ | Suzuki | (7/12) |
| 1966 | Luigi Taveri, CH | Honda | (5/10) |
| 1967 | Bill Ivy, GB | Yamaha | (8/12) |
| 1968 | Phil Read, GB | Yamaha | (6/9) |
| 1969 | Dave Simmonds, GB | Kawasaki | (8/11) |
| 1970 | Dieter Braun, D | Suzuki | (4/11) |
| 1971 | Angel Nieto, E | Derbi | (5/11) |
| 1972 | Angel Nieto, E | Derbi | (5/13) |
| 1973 | Kent Andersson, S | Yamaha | (5/12) |
| 1974 | Kent Andersson, S | Yamaha | (5/10) |
| 1975 | Paolo Pileri, I | Morbidelli | (7/10) |
| 1976 | Pier Paolo Bianchi, I | Morbidelli | (7/9) |
| 1977 | Pier Paolo Bianchi, I | Morbidelli | (7/12) |
| 1978 | Eugenio Lazzarini, I | MBA | (4/12) |
| 1979 | Angel Nieto, E | Minarelli | (8/13) |
| 1980 | Pier Paolo Bianchi, I | MBA | (2/10) |
| 1981 | Angel Nieto, E | Minarelli | (8/12) |
| 1982 | Angel Nieto, E | Garelli | (6/12) |
| 1983 | Angel Nieto, E | Garelli | (6/11) |
| 1984 | Angel Nieto, E | Garelli | (6/8) |
| 1985 | Fausto Gresini, I | Garelli | (3/10) |

**LUCA CADALORA**
*1986 125 cc WORLD CHAMPION*

| | | | (Wins/Races) |
|---|---|---|---|
| 1962 | Ernst Degner, D | Suzuki | (4/10) |
| 1963 | Hugh Anderson, NZ | Suzuki | (2/9) |
| 1964 | Hugh Anderson, NZ | Suzuki | (4/8) |
| 1965 | Ralph Bryans, IRL | Honda | (3/8) |
| 1966 | Hans-Georg Anscheidt, D | Suzuki | (2/6) |
| 1967 | Hans-Georg Anscheidt, D | Suzuki | (3/7) |
| 1968 | Hans-Georg Anscheidt, D | Suzuki | (3/5) |
| 1969 | Angel Nieto, E | Derbi | (2/10) |
| 1970 | Angel Nieto, E | Derbi | (5/10) |
| 1971 | Jan de Vries, NL | Kreidler | (5/9) |
| 1972 | Angel Nieto, E | Derbi | (3/8) |
| 1973 | Jan de Vries, NL | Kreidler | (5/7) |
| 1974 | Henk van Kessel, NL | Kreidler | (6/10) |
| 1975 | Angel Nieto, E | Kreidler | (6/8) |
| 1976 | Angel Nieto, E | Bultaco | (5/9) |
| 1977 | Angel Nieto, E | Bultaco | (3/7) |
| 1978 | Ricardo Tormo, E | Bultaco | (5/7) |
| 1979 | Eugenio Lazzarini, I | Kreidler | (5/7) |
| 1980 | Eugenio Lazzarini, I | Kreidler/Iprem | (2/6) |
| 1981 | Ricardo Tormo, E | Bultaco | (6/8) |
| 1982 | Stefan Dörflinger, CH | Kreidler | (3/6) |
| 1983 | Stefan Dörflinger, CH | Kreidler | (3/7) |
| 1984* | Stefan Dörflinger, CH | Zundapp | (4/8) |
| 1985* | Stefan Dörflinger, CH | Krauser | (2/7) |

# Sidecar World Championship

| Position | Driver & passenger | Nationality | Machine | Germany | Austria | Holland | Belgium | France | Great Britain | Sweden | Baden-Württemberg | TOTAL |
|---|---|---|---|---|---|---|---|---|---|---|---|---|
| 1 | Egbert Streuer/ Bernie Schnieders | NL NL | LCR-Yamaha | 15 | 15 | – | – | 15 | 15 | – | 15 | 75 |
| 2 | Alain Michel/ Jean-Marc Fresc | F F | Krauser-Yamaha | 5 | 10 | 15 | 12 | 12 | – | 15 | 6 | 75 |
| 3 | Steve Webster/ Tony Hewitt | GB GB | LCR-Yamaha | – | 12 | 12 | 15 | 10 | 12 | – | 10 | 71 |
| 4 | Markus Egloff/ Urs Egloff | CH CH | LCR-Yamaha | 4 | 5 | 8 | 5 | 5 | 10 | 12 | 2 | 51 |
| 5= | Masato Kumano/ Helmut Diehl | J D | LCR-Yamaha | – | 2 | 10 | 6 | 3 | 6 | 6 | 5 | 38 |
| 5= | Alfred Zurbrügg/ Martin Zurbrügg | CH CH | LCR-Yamaha | 8 | 4 | 2 | – | 8 | 8 | – | 8 | 38 |
| 7 | Steve Abbott/ Shaun Smith Vince Biggs | GB GB GB | Windle-Yamaha | 10 | 8 | 6 | 4 | 2 | – | 2 | 4 | 36 |
| 8 | Rolf Biland/ Kurt Waltisperg | CH CH | Krauser | 12 | – | – | 8 | – | – | – | 12 | 32 |
| 9 | Derek Jones/ Brian Ayres | GB GB | LCR-Yamaha | 6 | 6 | – | – | 4 | 5 | 8 | – | 29 |
| 10 | Derek Bayley/ Bryan Nixon | GB GB | LCR-Yamaha | – | – | – | 6 | 3 | – | 10 | 1 | 20 |
| 11 | Frank Wrathall/ Kerry Chapman | GB GB | LCR-Yamaha | – | – | – | – | 1 | 4 | 5 | 3 | 13 |
| 12 | René Progin/ Yves Hunziker | CH CH | Seymaz-Yamaha | 3 | – | – | 2 | – | 2 | 4 | – | 11 |
| 13 | Rolf Steinhausen/ Bruno Hiller | D D | Busch | – | – | – | 10 | – | – | – | – | 10 |
| 14 | Theo van Kempen/ Gerardus de Haas | NL NL | LCR-Yamaha | 2 | 3 | – | – | – | – | 3 | – | 8 |
| 15 | Mick Barton/ Fritz Buck Graham Rose Eckart Rösinger | GB D GB D | LCR-Yamaha | 1 | – | 5 | – | – | 1 | – | – | 7 |
| 16= | Barry Brindley/ Chris Jones | GB GB | Windle-Yamaha | – | 1 | 4 | – | – | – | – | – | 5 |
| 16= | Graham Gleeson/ Dave Elliott Ian Colquhoun Peter Linden | NZ GB GB S | LCR-Yamaha | – | – | – | 1 | – | 3 | 1 | – | 5 |
| 18 | Bernd Scherer/ Wolfgang Gess | D D | BSR-Yamaha | – | – | – | – | 3 | – | – | – | 3 |
| 19 | Yoshisada Kumagaya/ Kazuhiko Makiuchi | J J | LCR-Yamaha | – | – | – | – | 1 | – | – | – | 1 |

**EGBERT STREUER AND BERNARD SCHNIEDERS**
*1986 SIDECAR WORLD CHAMPIONS*

# Past Sidecar World Champions

| Year | Driver / Passenger | Machine | (Wins/ Races) |
|---|---|---|---|
| 1949 | Eric Oliver, GB/ Denis Jenkinson, GB | Norton | (2/3) |
| 1950 | Eric Oliver, GB/ Lorenzo Dobelli, I | Norton | (3/3) |
| 1951 | Eric Oliver, GB/ Lorenzo Dobelli, I | Norton | (3/5) |
| 1952 | Cyril Smith, GB/ Bob Clements, GB | Norton | (1/5) |
| 1953 | Eric Oliver, GB/ Stanley Dibben, GB | Norton | (4/5) |
| 1954 | Wilhelm Noll, D/ Fritz Cron, D | BMW | (3/6) |
| 1955 | Wilhelm Faust, D/ Karl Remmert, D | BMW | (3/6) |
| 1956 | Wilhelm Noll, D/ Fritz Cron, D | BMW | (3/6) |
| 1957 | Fritz Hillebrand, D/ Manfred Grunwald, D | BMW | (3/5) |
| 1958 | Walter Schneider, D/ Hans Strauss, D | BMW | (3/4) |
| 1959 | Walter Schneider, D/ Hans Strauss, D | BMW | (2/5) |
| 1960 | Helmut Fath, D/ Alfred Wohligemuth, D | BMW | (4/5) |
| 1961 | Max Deubel, D/ Emil Horner, D | BMW | (3/6) |
| 1962 | Max Deubel, D/ Emil Horner, D | BMW | (3/6) |
| 1963 | Max Deubel, D/ Emil Horner, D | BMW | (2/5) |
| 1964 | Max Deubel, D/ Emil Horner, D | BMW | (2/6) |
| 1965 | Fritz Scheidegger, CH/ John Robinson, GB | BMW | (4/7) |
| 1966 | Fritz Scheidegger, CH/ John Robinson, GB | BMW | (5/5) |
| 1967 | Klaus Enders, D/ Ralf Engelhardt, D | BMW | (5/8) |
| 1968 | Helmut Fath, D/ Wolfgang Kallaugh, D | URS | (3/6) |
| 1969 | Klaus Enders, D/ Ralf Engelhardt, D | BMW | (4/7) |
| 1970 | Klaus Enders, D/ Wolfgang Kallaugh, D | BMW | (5/8) |
| 1971 | Horst Owesle, D/ Peter Rutterford, GB | URS-Fath | (3/8) |
| 1972 | Klaus Enders, D/ Ralf Engelhardt. D | BMW | (4/8) |
| 1973 | Klaus Enders, D/ Ralf Engelhardt, D | BMW | (7/8) |
| 1974 | Klaus Enders, D/ Ralf Engelhardt, D | Busch-BMW | (2/8) |
| 1975 | Rolf Steinhausen, D/ Josef Huber, D | Busch-König | (3/7) |
| 1976 | Rolf Steinhausen, D/ Josef Huber, D | Busch-König | (3/7) |
| 1977 | George O'Dell, GB/ Kenny Arthur, GB Cliff Holland, GB | Yamaha | (–/7) |
| 1978 | Rolf Biland, CH/ Kenny Williams, GB B2A | Yamaha | (3/8) |
| 1979 | Rolf Biland, CH/ Kurt Waltisperg, CH B2B | Yamaha | (3/7) |
| | Bruno Holzer, CH/ Karl Meierhans, CH | Yamaha | (–/6) |
| 1980 | Jock Taylor, GB/ Benga Johansson, S | Yamaha | (4/8) |
| 1981 | Rolf Biland, CH/ Kurt Waltisperg, CH | Yamaha | (7/10) |
| 1982 | Werner Schwärzel, D/ Andreas Huber, D | Yamaha | (–/9) |
| 1983 | Rolf Biland, CH/ Kurt Waltisperg, CH | Yamaha | (6/8) |
| 1984 | Egbert Streuer, CH/ Bernie Schnieders, CH | Yamaha | (3/7) |
| 1985 | Egbert Streuer, CH/ Bernie Schnieders, CH | LCR-Yamaha | (3/6) |

# Isle of Man Tourist Trophy Races, 31 May–6 June/statistics
# Isle of Man Tourist Trophy Course, 37.73-mile/60.72-km circuit

## Senior TT

**6 laps, 226.38 miles/364.32 km**

| Place | No. | Rider | Nat. | Machine | Time & speed |
|---|---|---|---|---|---|
| 1 | 9 | Roger Burnett | GB | 500 Honda | 1h 59m 09.8s 113.98 mph/ 183.43 km/h |
| 2 | 19 | Geoff Johnson | GB | 750 Honda | 2h 00m 17.8s |
| 3 | 15 | Barry Woodland | GB | 500 Suzuki | 2h 00m 45.8s |
| 4 | 3 | Joey Dunlop | GB | 750 Honda | 2h 01m 21.2s |
| 5 | 10 | Phil Mellor | GB | 750 Suzuki | 2h 01m 41.6s |
| 6 | 11 | Roger Marshall | GB | 500 Honda | 2h 01m 48.8s |
| 7 | 59 | Dave Leach | GB | 350 Yamaha | 2h 02m 46.2s |
| 8 | 51 | Kevin Wilson | CDN | 750 Suzuki | 2h 02m 55.0s |
| 9 | 16 | Sam McClements | GB | 998 Suzuki | 2h 02m 57.2s |
| 10 | 17 | Graeme McGregor | AUS | 750 Suzuki | 2h 03m 16.6s |
| 11 | 18 | Nick Jefferies | GB | 500 Suzuki | 2h 03m 33.6s |
| 12 | 24 | Dave Dean | GB | 750 Suzuki | 2h 03m 37.6s |
| 13 | 44 | Des Barry | NZ | 500 Yamaha | 2h 04m 00.2s |
| 14 | 32 | Brian Morrison | GB | 750 Suzuki | 2h 04m 06.4s |
| 15 | 33 | Chris Martin | GB | 750 Suzuki | 2h 04m 48.8s |
| 16 | 7 | Mark Johns | GB | 500 Suzuki | 2h 04m 51.8s |
| 17 | 36 | Tony Moran | GB | 750 Yamaha | 2h 05m 14.4s |
| 18 | 29 | Bob Heath | GB | 500 Suzuki | 2h 05m 19.0s |
| 19 | 22 | Paul Iddon | GB | 750 Suzuki | 2h 06m 00.2s |
| 20 | 43 | Neil Tuxworth | GB | 350 Yamaha | 2h 06m 07.6s |

*Fastest lap:* Trevor Nation, GB (750 Suzuki), 19m 25.4s, 116.55 mph/ 187.57 km/h.

## TT Formula 1 race

**4 laps, 150.92 miles/242.88 km**

| Place | No. | Rider | Nat. | Machine | Time & speed |
|---|---|---|---|---|---|
| 1 | 3 | Joey Dunlop | GB | 750 Honda | 1h 20m 09.4s 112.96 mph/ 181.79 km/h |
| 2 | 7 | Geoff Johnson | GB | 750 Honda | 1h 21m 06.8s |
| 3 | 4 | Andy McGladdery | GB | 750 Suzuki | 1h 21m 36.8s |
| 4 | 21 | John Weeden | GB | 500 Suzuki | 1h 21m 56.0s |
| 5 | 10 | Phil Mellor | GB | 750 Suzuki | 1h 22m 12.8s |
| 6 | 5 | Trevor Nation | GB | 750 Suzuki | 1h 22m 32.6s |
| 7 | 17 | Graeme McGregor | AUS | 750 Suzuki | 1h 22m 45.6s |
| 8 | 12 | Gary Padgett | GB | 500 Suzuki | 1h 23m 13.6s |
| 9 | 36 | Glen Williams | NZ | 750 Suzuki | 1h 23m 29.2s |
| 10 | 1 | Klaus Klein | D | 750 Suzuki | 1h 23m 29.2s |
| 11 | 39 | Neil Robinson | GB | 750 Suzuki | 1h 23m 34.2s |
| 12 | 18 | Anders Andersson | S | 750 Suzuki | 1h 23m 36.6s |
| 13 | 6 | Steve Parrish | GB | 750 Yamaha | 1h 23m 40.2s |
| 14 | 63 | Roger Hurst | GB | 750 Yamaha | 1h 23m 54.3s |
| 15 | 35 | Alan Jackson | GB | 750 Suzuki | 1h 24m 03.4s |
| 16 | 33 | Chris Martin | GB | 750 Suzuki | 1h 24m 06.6s |
| 17 | 8 | Steve Cull | GB | 750 Yamaha | 1h 24m 08.2s |
| 18 | 27 | Steve Henshaw | GB | 750 Suzuki | 1h 24m 10.0s |
| 19 | 13 | Helmut Dahne | D | 750 Suzuki | 1h 24m 20.6s |
| 20 | 41 | Des Barry | NZ | 500 Yamaha | 1h 24m 30.2s |

*Fastest lap:* Dunlop, 19m 51.6s, 113.98 mph/183.43 km/h.

## Junior TT

**6 laps, 226.38 miles/364.32 km**

| Place | No. | Rider | Nat. | Machine | Time & speed |
|---|---|---|---|---|---|
| 1 | 1 | Steve Cull | GB | 250 Honda | 2h 03m 54.0s 109.62 mph/ 176.42 km/h |
| 2 | 6 | Phil Mellor | GB | 250 EMC | 2h 04m 52.8s |
| 3 | 4 | Graham Cannell | GB | 250 Honda | 2h 07m 11.6s |
| 4 | 21 | Dave Leach | GB | 250 Yamaha | 2h 07m 37.4s |
| 5 | 10 | John Weeden | GB | 250 Armstrong | 2h 07m 43.8s |
| 6 | 12 | Gary Padgett | GB | 250 Honda | 2h 08m 08.4s |
| 7 | 23 | Chris Fargher | GB | 250 Yamaha | 2h 08m 44.8s |
| 8 | 14 | Kenny Shepherd | GB | 250 Armstrong | 2h 09m 02.2s |
| 9 | 27 | Steve Hislop | GB | 250 Rotax | 2h 09m 56.8s |
| 10 | 34 | Kevin de Cruz | GB | 250 EMC | 2h 12m 24.4s |
| 11 | 20 | Bob Heath | GB | 250 Yamaha | 2h 13m 51.6s |
| 12 | 51 | Raymond Hanna | IRL | 250 Rotax | 2h 13m 59.0s |
| 13 | 43 | Jamie Rae | GB | 250 EMC | 2h 14m 09.8s |
| 14 | 40 | Derek Chatterton | GB | 250 Yamaha | 2h 14m 56.6s |
| 15 | 53 | James Hodson | GB | 250 Yamaha | 2h 15m 07.2s |
| 16 | 39 | Dave Quarmby | GB | 250 Yamaha | 2h 17m 10.4s |
| 17 | 48 | Raymond Campbell | IRL | 250 Yamaha | 2h 17m 34.8s |
| 18 | 77 | Tony Willis | IRL | 250 Rotax | 2h 19m 47.0s |
| 19 | 69 | Michael Williams | GB | 250 Yamaha | 2h 19m 47.6s |
| 20 | 74 | Charlie Antoni | GB | 250 Yamaha | 2h 21m 26.8s |

*Fastest lap:* Mellor, 20m 19.0s, 111.42 mph/179.31 km/h.

## TT Formula 2 race

**4 laps, 159.02 miles/242.88 km**

| Place | No. | Rider | Nat. | Machine | Time & speed |
|---|---|---|---|---|---|
| 1 | 3 | Brian Reid | GB | 350 Yamaha | 1h 22m 31.4s 109.72 mph/ 176.58 km/h |
| 2 | 8 | John Weeden | GB | 350 Yamaha | 1h 22m 44.8s |
| 3 | 24 | Neil Tuxworth | GB | 350 Yamaha | 1h 23m 49.2s |
| 4 | 20 | Ray Swann | GB | 600 Kawasaki | 1h 24m 09.4s |
| 5 | 10 | Eddie Laycock | IRL | 350 Yamaha | 1h 24m 26.8s |
| 6 | 47 | Steve Hislop | GB | 350 Yamaha | 1h 25m 49.2s |
| 7 | 21 | Chris Faulkner | GB | 350 Yamaha | 1h 25m 59.2s |
| 8 | 33 | Bob Heath | GB | 350 Yamaha | 1h 26m 06.2s |
| 9 | 30 | Des Barry | NZ | 350 Yamaha | 1h 26m 07.2s |
| 10 | 7 | Steve Williams | GB | 350 Yamaha | 1h 26m 40.8s |
| 11 | 27 | Ian Lougher | GB | 350 Yamaha | 1h 26m 44.6s |
| 12 | 6 | Tony Head | GB | 350 Yamaha | 1h 26m 46.2s |
| 13 | 31 | Derek Chatterton | GB | 350 Yamaha | 1h 27m 10.2s |
| 14 | 43 | Kevin Wilson | CDN | 350 Yamaha | 1h 27m 10.2s |
| 15 | 22 | Tony Moran | GB | 600 Ducati | 1h 27m 21.2s |
| 16 | 65 | James Hodson | GB | 350 Yamaha | 1h 28m 16.2s |
| 17 | 26 | Gary Radcliffe | GB | 350 Yamaha | 1h 29m 25.8s |
| 18 | 11 | Steve Murray | GB | 350 Yamaha | 1h 29m 29.8s |
| 19 | 23 | Ronan Sherry | IRL | 350 Yamaha | 1h 29m 50.8s |
| 20 | 29 | Malcolm Wheeler | GB | 600 Kawasaki | 1h 30m 14.0s |

*Fastest lap:* Reid, 20m 15.4s, 111.75 mph/179.84 km/h (record).

## AVON Production TT

**(Class A, 751 cc-1300 cc four-strokes)**

**3 laps, 113.19 miles/182.16 km**

| Place | No. | Rider | Nat. | Machine | Time & speed |
|---|---|---|---|---|---|
| 1 | 5 | Trevor Nation | GB | 1100 Suzuki | 1h 00m 38.4s 111.99 mph/ 180.23 km/h |
| 2 | 8 | Kevin Wilson | CDN | 1100 Suzuki | 1h 00m 46.8s |
| 3 | 20 | Brian Morrison | GB | 1100 Suzuki | 1h 01m 06.8s |
| 4 | 3 | Nick Jefferies | GB | 1100 Suzuki | 1h 01m 30.8s |
| 5 | 4 | Barry Woodland | GB | 1100 Suzuki | 1h 01m 31.4s |
| 6 | 15 | Helmut Dahne | D | 1100 Suzuki | 1h 01m 37.8s |
| 7 | 19 | Ian Duffus | GB | 1100 Suzuki | 1h 02m 08.4s |
| 8 | 27 | Alan Batson | GB | 1100 Suzuki | 1h 02m 08.6s |
| 9 | 18 | Dave Leach | GB | 998 Kawasaki | 1h 02m 44.8s |
| 10 | 12 | Steve Henshaw | GB | 1100 Suzuki | 1h 02m 47.2s |
| 11 | 6 | Howard Selby | GB | 998 Kawasaki | 1h 02m 52.6s |
| 12 | 11 | Dave Dean | GB | 1100 Suzuki | 1h 02m 56.4s |
| 13 | 24 | Kevin Hughes | GB | 908 Kawasaki | 1h 02m 57.0s |
| 14 | 17 | Peter Rubatto | D | 908 Kawasaki | 1h 03m 32.2s |
| 15 | 10 | Paul Iddon | GB | 1100 Suzuki | 1h 03m 41.8s |

*Fastest lap:* Nation, 19m 59.2s, 113.26 mph/182.27 km/h (record).

## AVON Production TT

**(Class B, 401 cc-500 cc two-strokes/601 cc-750 cc four-strokes)**

**3 laps, 113.19 miles/182.16 km**

| Place | No. | Rider | Nat. | Machine | Time & speed |
|---|---|---|---|---|---|
| 1 | 10 | Phil Mellor | GB | 750 Suzuki | 1h 02m 10.2s 109.23 mph/ 175.79 km/h |
| 2 | 2 | Helmut Dahne | D | 750 Suzuki | 1h 02m 24.2s |
| 3 | 33 | Kevin Wilson | CDN | 750 Suzuki | 1h 02m 34.2s |
| 4 | 5 | Trevor Nation | GB | 750 Suzuki | 1h 02m 50.2s |
| 5 | 11 | Dave Leach | GB | 750 Honda | 1h 02m 55.0s |
| 6 | 4 | Andy McGladdery | GB | 750 Suzuki | 1h 03m 09.0s |
| 7 | 9 | Dave Dean | GB | 750 Suzuki | 1h 03m 23.0s |
| 8 | 1 | Geoff Johnson | GB | 750 Honda | 1h 03m 35.6s |
| 9 | 21 | Kevin Hughes | GB | 750 Honda | 1h 03m 35.6s |
| 10 | 7 | Nick Jefferies | GB | 750 Suzuki | 1h 03m 41.6s |
| 11 | 19 | Steve Hislop | GB | 750 Yamaha | 1h 03m 49.8s |
| 12 | 25 | Brian Morrison | GB | 750 Suzuki | 1h 03m 52.8s |
| 13 | 17 | Graeme McGregor | AUS | 750 Suzuki | 1h 03m 57.2s |
| 14 | 59 | Steve Ward | GB | 750 Suzuki | 1h 04m 03.4s |
| 15 | 29 | Ian Duffus | GB | 750 Yamaha | 1h 04m 09.8s |

*Fastest lap:* Mellor, 20m 27.0s, 110.69 mph/178.14 km/h (record).

## AVON Production TT

**(Class C, 251 cc-400 cc two-strokes/401 cc-600 cc four-strokes)**

**3 laps, 113.19 miles/182.16 km**

| Place | No. | Rider | Nat. | Machine | Time & speed |
|---|---|---|---|---|---|
| 1 | 112 | Gary Padgett | GB | 400 Suzuki | 1h 05m 56.6s 102.98 mph/ 165.73 km/h |
| 2 | 111 | Malcolm Wheeler | GB | 600 Kawasaki | 1h 05m 57.6s |
| 3 | 126 | Steve Linsdell | GB | 600 Yamaha | 1h 06m 15.0s |
| 4 | 103 | Joey Dunlop | GB | 400 Honda | 1h 06m 55.4s |
| 5 | 101 | Phil Nicholls | GB | 400 Honda | 1h 07m 55.4s |
| 6 | 109 | Roger Burnett | GB | 500 Honda | 1h 07m 56.6s |
| 7 | 108 | Bob Jackson | GB | 400 Honda | 1h 08m 27.0s |
| 8 | 138 | Steve Boyes | GB | 500 Honda | 1h 08m 57.2s |
| 9 | 125 | Rob Price | GB | 600 Kawasaki | 1h 09m 01.6s |
| 10 | 122 | Alan Jackson | GB | 400 Honda | 1h 09m 02.8s |
| 11 | 130 | Cliff Tabiner | GB | 600 Kawasaki | 1h 09m 03.8s |
| 12 | 133 | Carl Fogarty | GB | 400 Honda | 1h 09m 09.8s |
| 13 | 121 | Dave Deardon | GB | 400 Honda | 1h 09m 30.6s |
| 14 | 119 | Robin Milton | GB | 400 Honda | 1h 09m 34.6s |
| 15 | 106 | Ken Dobson | NZ | 500 Honda | 1h 09m 38.8s |

*Fastest lap:* Padgett, 21m 40.6s, 104.43 mph/168.06 km/h (record).

## AVON Production TT

**(Class D, 250 cc two-strokes/400 cc four-strokes)**

**3 laps, 113.19 miles/182.16 km**

| Place | No. | Rider | Nat. | Machine | Time & speed |
|---|---|---|---|---|---|
| 1 | 106 | Barry Woodland | GB | 400 Suzuki | 1h 08m 02.0s 99.82 mph/ 160.64 km/h |
| 2 | 103 | Graham Cannell | GB | 250 Yamaha | 1h 08m 19.6s |
| 3 | 101 | Mat Oxley | GB | 250 Yamaha | 1h 08m 46.6s |
| 4 | 115 | Peter Bateson | GB | 250 Honda | 1h 09m 12.6s |
| 5 | 105 | Glen Williams | NZ | 400 Suzuki | 1h 09m 16.6s |
| 6 | 116 | Chris Fargher | GB | 250 Suzuki | 1h 09m 16.6s |
| 7 | 112 | Gary Padgett | GB | 250 Yamaha | 1h 09m 53.8s |
| 8 | 122 | Kevin Mawdsley | GB | 250 Honda | 1h 10m 27.0s |
| 9 | 118 | Steve Williams | GB | 250 Yamaha | 1h 10m 28.8s |
| 10 | 123 | Jamie Whitham | GB | 250 Kawasaki | 1h 11m 10.6s |
| 11 | 130 | Steve Boyes | GB | 250 Honda | 1h 11m 14.4s |
| 12 | 119 | Kenny Harrison | GB | 250 Yamaha | 1h 11m 26.4s |
| 13 | 126 | Richard Coates | GB | 250 Honda | 1h 11m 44.6s |
| 14 | 107 | Phil Nicholls | GB | 250 Honda | 1h 11m 44.8s |
| 15 | 127 | Steve Moynihan | GB | 250 Honda | 1h 12m 09.2s |

*Fastest lap:* Oxley, 22m 27.2s, 110.82 mph/162.25 km/h (record).

## 1000 cc Sidecar TT: Race A

**3 laps, 113.19 miles/182.16 km**

| Place | No. | Driver & passenger | Nat. | Machine | Time & speed |
|---|---|---|---|---|---|
| 1 | 6 | Lowry Burton/ Pat Cashnahan | GB GB | 750 Ironside-Yamaha | 1h 04m 58.2s 104.53 mph/ 168.22 km/h |
| 2 | 7 | Warwick Newman/ Eddie Yarker | GB GB | 750 Ireson-Yamaha | 1h 05m 50.8s |
| 3 | 20 | Michael Burcombe/ Steve Parker | GB GB | 700 Ireson-Yamaha | 1h 07m 48.2s |
| 4 | 2 | Dave Hallam/ John Gibbard | GB GB | 750 Windle-Yamaha | 1h 08m 09.6s |
| 5 | 16 | Geoff Rushbrook/ Geoff Leitch | GB GB | 700 Ireson-Yamaha | 1h 09m 20.0s |
| 6 | 19 | Eric Cornes/ Graham Wellington | GB GB | 750 Ireson-Yamaha | 1h 09m 29.0s |
| 7 | 14 | Lars Schwartz/ Leif Gustavsson | S S | 750 Ireson-Yamaha | 1h 09m 37.0s |
| 8 | 23 | Steve Pullan/ Adam Smith | GB GB | 750 Baker-Yamaha | 1h 10m 05.2s |
| 9 | 1 | Derek Bayley/ Bryan Nixon | GB GB | 700 LCR-Yamaha | 1h 10m 33.4s |
| 10 | 33 | Rod Bellas/ Geoff Knight | GB GB | 998 Suzuki | 1h 10m 35.6s |

*Fastest lap:* Burton, 21m 22.6s, 105.90 mph/170.43 km/h.

## 1000 cc Sidecar TT: Race B

**3 laps, 113.19 miles/182.16 km**

| Place | No. | Driver & passenger | Nat. | Machine | Time & speed |
|---|---|---|---|---|---|
| 1 | 5 | Nigel Rollason/ Don Williams | GB GB | 750 Barton-Phoenix | 1h 05m 25.2s 103.81 mph/ 167.07 km/h |
| 2 | 10 | Derek Plummer/ Brian Marris | GB GB | 750 Ireson-Yamaha | 1h 05m 31.4s |
| 3 | 7 | Warwick Newman/ Eddie Yarker | GB GB | 750 Ireson-Yamaha | 1h 05m 40.6s |
| 4 | 20 | Michael Burcombe/ Steve Parker | GB GB | 700 Ireson-Yamaha | 1h 06m 38.0s |
| 5 | 4 | Dennis Bingham/ Julia Bingham | GB GB | 700 Windle-Yamaha | 1h 07m 38.6s |
| 6 | 23 | Steve Pullan/ Adam Smith | GB GB | 750 Baker-Yamaha | 1h 07m 51.6s |
| 7 | 21 | Kenny Howles/ Steve Pointer | GB GB | 700 Ireson-Yamaha | 1h 08m 08.6s |
| 8 | 9 | Dennis Keen/ Colin Hardman | GB GB | 750 Yamaha | 1h 10m 04.4s |
| 9 | 29 | Helmut Lunemann/ Michael Cain | D GB | 750 Yamaha | 1h 10m 09.0s |
| 10 | 33 | Rod Bellas/ Geoff Knight | GB GB | 998 Suzuki | 1h 10m 18.2s |

*Fastest lap:* Dave Hallam/John Gibbard, GB/GB (750 Windle-Yamaha), 21m 27.8s, 105.47 mph/169.74 km/h.

# US Road Racing

## Camel Pro Road Racing Championship

**DAYTONA INTERNATIONAL SPEEDWAY, Daytona Beach, Florida, 9 March 1986.**
**Superbike**

| | | |
|---|---|---|
| 1 | Eddie Lawson | Yamaha |
| 2 | Kevin Schwantz | Suzuki |
| 3 | Fred Merkel | Honda |
| 4 | Wayne Rainey | Honda |
| 5 | Jay Springsteen | Yamaha |
| 6 | Reuben McMurter | Yamaha |
| 7 | Vesa Kultalahti | Yamaha |
| 8 | John Ashmead | Honda |
| 9 | Anders Andersson | Suzuki |
| 10 | Dan Walker | Yamaha |

**Distance:** 203 miles
**Time:** 1h 54m 49s
**Average speed:** 106.030 mph

**SEARS POINT INTERNATIONAL RACEWAY, Sonoma, California, 18 May 1986.**
**Superbike**

| | | |
|---|---|---|
| 1 | Fred Merkel | Honda |
| 2 | Bubba Shobert | Honda |
| 3 | Ottis Lance | Yamaha |
| 4 | Doug Toland | Suzuki |
| 5 | John Ashmead | Honda |
| 6 | Gary Goodfellow | Suzuki |
| 7 | Rich Arnaiz | Yamaha |
| 8 | Keith Pinkstaff | Suzuki |
| 9 | Nigel Gale | Yamaha |
| 10 | Jeff Stern | Suzuki |

**Distance:** 60 miles
**Time:** (red flag, no time)
**Average speed:** (red flag, no average speed)

**SEARS POINT INTERNATIONAL RACEWAY, Sonoma, California, 18 May 1986.**
**Formula 1**

| | | |
|---|---|---|
| 1 | Kork Ballington | Honda |
| 2 | Randy Renfrow | Honda |
| 3 | Wayne Rainey | Honda |
| 4 | Steve Trinder | Suzuki |
| 5 | Marco Greco | Honda |
| 6 | Miles Baldwin | Honda |
| 7 | Gary Goodfellow | Suzuki |
| 8 | Russ Paulk | Honda |
| 9 | Keith Pinkstaff | Suzuki |
| 10 | Doug Chandler | Honda |

**Distance:** 60 miles
**Time:** 44m 12.579s
**Average speed:** 82.179 mph

**BRAINERD INTERNATIONAL RACEWAY, Brainerd, Minnesota, 1 June 1986.**
**Superbike**

| | | |
|---|---|---|
| 1 | Wayne Rainey | Honda |
| 2 | Fred Merkel | Honda |
| 3 | Gary Goodfellow | Suzuki |
| 4 | Meril Moen | Yamaha |
| 5 | Reuben McMurter | Yamaha |
| 6 | Tom Mason | Yamaha |
| 7 | Nigel Gale | Yamaha |
| 8 | Todd Strang | Yamaha |
| 9 | Jim Tribou | Yamaha |
| 10 | Rich Arnaiz | Yamaha |

**Distance:** 60 miles
**Time:** 34m 54.206s
**Average speed:** 103.142 mph

**BRAINERD INTERNATIONAL RACEWAY, Brainerd, Minnesota, 1 June 1986.**
**Formula 1**

| | | |
|---|---|---|
| 1 | Randy Renfrow | Honda |
| 2 | Kork Ballington | Honda |
| 3 | Dale Franklin | Yamaha |
| 4 | Steve Trinder | Suzuki |
| 5 | Gary Goodfellow | Suzuki |
| 6 | Russ Paulk | Honda |
| 7 | Martin Morrison | Suzuki |
| 8 | Bob Woods | Yamaha |
| 9 | David Old | Honda |
| 10 | Henry DeGouw | Yamaha |

**Distance:** 60 miles
**Time:** 34m 46.806s
**Average speed:** 103.57 mph

**ROAD AMERICA RACEWAY, Elkhart Lake, Wisconsin, 7 June 1986.**
**Superbike**

| | | |
|---|---|---|
| 1 | Wayne Rainey | Honda |
| 2 | Fred Merkel | Honda |
| 3 | Dan Chivington | Yamaha |
| 4 | Bubba Shobert | Honda |
| 5 | Doug Polen | Suzuki |
| 6 | Gary Goodfellow | Suzuki |
| 7 | John Ashmead | Honda |
| 8 | Reuben McMurter | Yamaha |
| 9 | Rich Arnaiz | Yamaha |
| 10 | Nigel Gale | Yamaha |

**Distance:** 60 miles
**Time:** 36m 24.702s
**Average speed:** 98.869 mph

**ROAD AMERICA RACEWAY, Elkhart Lake, Wisconsin, 8 June 1986.**
**Formula 1**

| | | |
|---|---|---|
| 1 | Wayne Rainey | Honda |
| 2 | Randy Renfrow | Honda |
| 3 | Kork Ballington | Honda |
| 4 | Dale Franklin | Yamaha |
| 5 | Russ Paulk | Honda |
| 6 | Miles Baldwin | Yamaha |
| 7 | Gary Goodfellow | Suzuki |
| 8 | Doug Chandler | Honda |
| 9 | Art Robbins | Honda |
| 10 | David Reed | Yamaha |

**Distance:** 60 miles
**Time:** 35m 30.824s
**Average speed:** 101.369 mph

**BRYAR MOTORSPORTS PARK, Loudon, New Hampshire, 15 June 1986.**
**Superbike**

| | | |
|---|---|---|
| 1 | Wayne Rainey | Honda |
| 2 | Fred Merkel | Honda |
| 3 | Bubba Shobert | Honda |
| 4 | Dale Quarterley | Yamaha |
| 5 | Gary Goodfellow | Suzuki |
| 6 | Michel Mercier | Suzuki |
| 7 | Reuben McMurter | Yamaha |
| 8 | Dan Chivington | Yamaha |
| 9 | John Ashmead | Honda |
| 10 | John Kocinski | Yamaha |

**Distance:** 60 miles
**Time:** 44m 27.375s
**Average speed:** 82.058 mph

**BRYAR MOTORSPORTS PARK, Loudon, New Hampshire, 14 June 1986**
**Formula 1**

| | | |
|---|---|---|
| 1 | Randy Renfrow | Honda |
| 2 | Kork Ballington | Honda |
| 3 | Wayne Rainey | Honda |
| 4 | Gary Goodfellow | Suzuki |
| 5 | Russ Paulk | Honda |
| 6 | Dan Chivington | Suzuki |
| 7 | Marco Greco | Honda |
| 8 | Miles Baldwin | Yamaha |
| 9 | Michel Mercier | Suzuki |
| 10 | David Reed | Yamaha |

**Distance:** 60 miles
**Time:** 45m 49.55s
**Average speed:** 83.254 mph

**POCONO INTERNATIONAL RACEWAY, Mt Pocono, Pennsylvania, 21 June 1986.**
**Superbike**

| | | |
|---|---|---|
| 1 | Wayne Rainey | Honda |
| 2 | Fred Merkel | Honda |
| 3 | Kevin Schwantz | Suzuki |
| 4 | John Kocinski | Yamaha |
| 5 | Jim Filice | Yamaha |
| 6 | Dan Chivington | Yamaha |
| 7 | Michel Mercier | Suzuki |
| 8 | Ottis Lance | Yamaha |
| 9 | Lance Jones | Yamaha |
| 10 | Dale Quarterley | Yamaha |

**Distance:** 62 miles
**Time:** 35m 18.671s
**Average speed:** 93.455 mph

**POCONO INTERNATIONAL RACEWAY, Mt Pocono, Pennsylvania, 22 June 1986.**
**Formula 1**

| | | |
|---|---|---|
| 1 | Randy Renfrow | Honda |
| 2 | Wayne Rainey | Honda |
| 3 | Kork Ballington | Honda |
| 4 | Russ Paulk | Honda |
| 5 | Miles Baldwin | Yamaha |
| 6 | Gary Goodfellow | Suzuki |
| 7 | Dale Franklin | Yamaha |
| 8 | David Reed | Yamaha |
| 9 | Dan Chivington | Suzuki |
| 10 | James Adamo | Ducati |

**Distance:** 62 miles
**Time:** 34m 59.458s
**Average speed:** 94.310 mph

**LAGUNA SECA RACEWAY, Monterey, California, 12 July 1986.**
**Superbike**

| | | |
|---|---|---|
| 1 | Wayne Rainey | Honda |
| 2 | Bubba Shobert | Honda |
| 3 | Fred Merkel | Honda |
| 4 | Jim Filice | Yamaha |
| 5 | John Kocinski | Yamaha |
| 6 | Gary Goodfellow | Suzuki |
| 7 | Doug Polen | Suzuki |
| 8 | Keith Pinkstaff | Suzuki |
| 9 | Randy Renfrow | Suzuki |
| 10 | Ottis Lance | Yamaha |

**Distance:** 60 miles
**Time:** 39m 3.093s
**Average speed:** 93.415 mph

**LAGUNA SECA RACEWAY, Monterey, California, 13 July 1986.**
**Formula 1**

| | | | |
|---|---|---|---|
| 1 | Mike Baldwin | 2–1 | Yamaha |
| 2 | Randy Mamola | 1–2 | Yamaha |
| 3 | Kork Ballington | 5–3 | Honda |
| 4 | Randy Renfrow | 4–4 | Honda |
| 5 | Gary Goodfellow | 6–5 | Suzuki |
| 6 | Doug Polen | 7–6 | Suzuki |
| 7 | Dan Chivington | 9–7 | Suzuki |
| 8 | Keith Pinkstaff | 10–8 | Suzuki |
| 9 | Wayne Rainey | 3–16 | Honda |
| 10 | Marco Greco | 11–9 | Honda |

**Distance:** 125.4 miles (2 × 62.7-mile segments)

**MID-OHIO SPORTS CAR COURSE, Lexington, Ohio, 3 August 1986.**
**Superbike**

| | | |
|---|---|---|
| 1 | Fred Merkel | Honda |
| 2 | Kevin Schwantz | Suzuki |
| 3 | Dan Chivington | Yamaha |
| 4 | John Ashmead | Honda |
| 5 | Reuben McMurter | Yamaha |
| 6 | Peter Lusby | Honda |
| 7 | Ottis Lance | Yamaha |
| 8 | Jim Tribou | Yamaha |
| 9 | Jeff Farmer | Yamaha |
| 10 | Bill Kelly | Yamaha |

**Distance:** 50 miles
**Time:** 40m 47.974s
**Average speed:** 88.236 mph

**MID-OHIO SPORTS CAR COURSE, Lexington, Ohio, 3 August 1986.**
**Formula 1**

| | | |
|---|---|---|
| 1 | Randy Renfrow | Honda |
| 2 | Dan Chivington | Suzuki |
| 3 | Larry Shorts | Suzuki |
| 4 | William Knott | Suzuki |
| 5 | Russ Paulk | Honda |
| 6 | Edgar Hinton III | Suzuki |
| 7 | David Old | Honda |
| 8 | Marco Greco | Honda |
| 9 | Mark Chin | Honda |
| 10 | Dave Schlosser | Suzuki |

**Distance:** 50 miles
**Time:** 42m 20.78s
**Average speed:** 85.037 mph

**ROAD ATLANTA, Braselton, Georgia, 10 August 1986.**
**Superbike**

| | | |
|---|---|---|
| 1 | Wayne Rainey | Honda |
| 2 | Fred Merkel | Honda |
| 3 | John Kocinski | Yamaha |
| 4 | John Ashmead | Honda |
| 5 | Dan Chivington | Yamaha |
| 6 | Kevin Rentzell | Suzuki |
| 7 | Jeff Farmer | Yamaha |
| 8 | Mike Harth | Yamaha |
| 9 | James Adamo | Ducati |
| 10 | Bill Kelly | Yamaha |

**Distance:** 65 miles
**Time:** 36m 19.364s
**Average speed:** 99.904 mph

**ROAD ATLANTA, Braselton, Georgia, 10 August 1986.**
**Formula 1**

| | | |
|---|---|---|
| 1 | Kork Ballington | Honda |
| 2 | Randy Renfrow | Honda |
| 3 | Russ Paulk | Honda |
| 4 | William Knott | Suzuki |
| 5 | Dan Chivington | Suzuki |
| 6 | Larry Shorts | Suzuki |
| 7 | David Reed | Yamaha |
| 8 | James Adamo | Ducati |
| 9 | Mark Chin | Honda |
| 10 | David Old | Honda |

**Distance:** 65 miles
**Time:** 36m 13.855s
**Average speed:** 100.158 mph

## Camel Pro Road Racing Championship

**Final Points (combined from Superbike and Formula 1 race points)**

| | | |
|---|---|---|
| 1 | Fred Merkel | 146 |
| 2 | Wayne Rainey | 144 |
| 3 | Randy Renfrow | 139 |
| 4 | Kork Ballington | 101 |
| 5 | Russ Paulk | 70 |
| 6 | Dan Chivington | 65 |
| 7 | Gary Goodfellow | 61 |
| 8 | John Ashmead | 57 |
| 9 | Bubba Shobert | 56 |
| 10 | Kevin Schwantz | 45 |

## *Shell Oils Transatlantic Challenge*

**SHELL OILS TRANSATLANTIC CHALLENGE, Race 1. Donington Park Circuit, 29 March. 7 laps of the 2.500-mile/4.023-km circuit, 17.50 miles/28.16 km.**
**1** Rob McElnea, GB (750 Yamaha), 12m 52.3s, 81.57 mph/131.27 km/h.
**2** Roger Burnett, GB (750 Honda); **3** Kenny Irons, GB (750 Yamaha); **4** Steve Parrish, GB (750 Yamaha); **5** Chris Martin, GB (750 Suzuki); **6** Fred Merkel, USA (750 Honda); **7** Keith Huewen, GB (750 Suzuki); **8** Michel Mercier, CDN (750 Suzuki); **9** Roger Marshall, GB (750 Honda); **10** Dan Chivington, USA (750 Yamaha).
**Fastest lap:** McElnea, 1m 47.5s, 83.72 mph/134.73 km/h (record).
**Match points:** GB, 57; USA, 9.

**SHELL OILS TRANSATLANTIC CHALLENGE, Race 2. Donington Park Circuit, 29 March. 7 laps of the 2.500-mile/4.023-km circuit, 17.50 miles/28.16 km.**
**1** Kevin Schwantz, USA (750 Suzuki), 12m 52.4s, 81.56 mph/131.26 km/h.
**2** Fred Merkel, USA (750 Honda); **3** Kenny Irons, GB (750 Yamaha); **4** Roger Burnett, GB (750 Honda); **5** Rob McElnea, GB (750 Yamaha); **6** Dan Chivington, USA (750 Yamaha); **7** Michel Mercier, CDN (750 Suzuki); **8** Dale Quarterley, USA (750 Yamaha); **9** Roger Marshall, GB (750 Honda); **10** Reuben McMurter, CDN (750 Yamaha).
**Fastest lap:** Burnett, 1m 47.8s, 83.48 mph/134.35 km/h.
**Match points:** GB, 26; USA, 40. **Total:** GB, 83; USA, 49.

**SHELL OILS TRANSATLANTIC CHALLENGE, Race 3. Donington Park Circuit, 30 March. 7 laps of the 2.500-mile/4.023-km circuit, 17.50 miles/28.16 km.**
**1** Roger Burnett, GB (750 Honda) 14m 18.7s, 73.36 mph/118.06 km/h; **2** Roger Marshall, GB (750 Honda); **3** Ron Haslam, GB (750 Honda); **4** Fred Merkel, USA (750 Honda); **5** Chris Martin, GB (750 Suzuki); **6** Paul Iddon, GB (750 Suzuki); **7** Trevor Nation, GB (750 Suzuki); **8** Kenny Irons, GB (750 Yamaha); **9** Rob McElnea, GB (750 Yamaha); **10** Steve Parrish, GB (750 Yamaha).
**Fastest lap:** Burnett, 1m 58.4s, 76.01 mph/122.33 km/h.
**Match points:** GB, 58; USA, 8. **Total:** GB, 141; USA, 57.

**SHELL OILS TRANSATLANTIC CHALLENGE, Race 4. Donington Park Circuit, 30 March. 7 laps of the 2.500-mile/4.023-km circuit, 17.50 miles/28.16 km.**
**1** Kevin Schwantz, USA (750 Suzuki), 13m 45.7s, 76.29 mph/122.78 km/h.
**2** Fred Merkel, USA (750 Honda); **3** Roger Burnett, GB (750 Honda); **4** Roger Marshall, GB (750 Honda); **5** Trevor Nation, GB (750 Suzuki); **6** Kenny Irons, GB (750 Yamaha); **7** Steve Parrish, GB (750 Yamaha); **8** Michel Mercier, CDN (750 Suzuki); **9** Paul Iddon, GB (750 Suzuki); **10** Ron Haslam, GB (750 Honda).
**Fastest lap:** Merkel, 1m 55.5s, 77.92 mph/125.40 km/h.
**Match points:** GB, 36; USA, 30. **Total:** GB, 177; USA, 87.

**SHELL OILS TRANSATLANTIC CHALLENGE, Race 5. Donington Park Circuit, 30 March. 7 laps of the 2.500-mile/4.023-km circuit, 17.50 miles/28.16 km.**
**1** Kevin Schwantz, USA (750 Suzuki); 13m 31.1s, 77.67 mph/125.00 km/h.
**2** Rob McElnea, GB (750 Yamaha); **3** Roger Burnett, GB (750 Honda); **4** Kenny Irons, GB (750 Yamaha); **5** Roger Marshall, GB (750 Honda); **6** Michel Mercier, CDN (750 Suzuki); **7** Chris Martin, GB (750 Suzuki); **8** Dale Quarterley, USA (750 Yamaha); **9** Trevor Nation, GB (750 Suzuki); **10** Paul Iddon, GB (750 Suzuki).
**Fastest lap:** Schwantz, Merkel and McElnea, 1m 54.0s, 78.94 mph/127.04 km/h.
**Match points:** GB, 43; USA, 23. **Total:** GB, 220; USA, 110.

**SHELL OILS TRANSATLANTIC CHALLENGE, Race 6. Donington Park Circuit, 31 March. 7 laps of the 2.500-mile/4.023-km circuit, 17.50 miles/28.16 km.**
**1** Fred Merkel, USA (750 Honda); 13m 44.2s, 76.43 mph/123.00 km/h.
**2** Kevin Schwantz, USA (750 Suzuki); **3** Roger Burnett, GB (750 Honda); **4** Ron Haslam, GB (750 Honda); **5** Kenny Irons, GB (750 Yamaha); **6** Steve Parrish, GB (750 Yamaha); **7** Paul Iddon, GB (750 Suzuki); **8** Dale Quarterley, USA (750 Yamaha); **9** Chris Martin, GB (750 Suzuki); **10** Rob McElnea, GB (750 Yamaha).
**Fastest lap:** Merkel, 1m 55.8s, 77.72 mph/125.08 km/h.
**Match points:** GB, 36; USA, 30. **Total:** GB, 256; USA, 140.

**SHELL OILS TRANSATLANTIC CHALLENGE, Race 7. Donington Park Circuit, 31 March. 7 laps of the 2.500-mile/4.023-km circuit, 17.50 miles/28.16 km.**
**1** Kevin Schwantz, USA (750 Suzuki); 13m 09.5s, 79.79 mph/128.41 km/h.
**2** Fred Merkel, USA (750 Honda); **3** Rob McElnea, GB (750 Yamaha); **4** Michel Mercier, CDN (750 Suzuki); **5** Kenny Irons, GB (750 Yamaha); **6** Steve Parrish, GB (750 Yamaha); **7** Ron Haslam, GB (750 Honda); **8** Paul Iddon, GB (750 Suzuki); **9** Dan Chivington, USA (750 Yamaha); **10** Dale Quarterley, USA (750 Yamaha).
**Fastest lap:** McEnea, 1m 50.3s, 81.59 mph/131.31 km/h.
**Match points:** GB, 28; USA, 38. **Total:** GB, 284; USA, 178.

**SHELL OILS TRANSATLANTIC CHALLENGE, Race 8. Donington Park Circuit, 31 March. 7 laps of the 2.500-mile/4.023-km circuit, 17.50 miles/28.16 km.**
**1** Fred Merkel, USA (750 Honda), 13m 55.6s, 75.39 mph/121.33 km/h.
**2** Kevin Schwantz, USA (750 Suzuki); **3** Ron Haslam, GB (750 Honda); **4** Roger Burnett, GB (750 Honda); **5** Michel Mercier, CDN (750 Suzuki); **6** Paul Iddon, GB (750 Suzuki); **7** Rob McElnea, GB (750 Yamaha); **8** Kenny Irons, GB (750 Yamaha); **9** Dale Quarterley, USA (750 Yamaha); **10** John Bettencourt, USA (750 Honda).
**Fastest lap:** Merkel, 1m 57.0s, 76.92 mph/123.79 km/h.
**Match points:** GB, 30; USA, 36.

**Final match points**

| | |
|---|---|
| 1 GB | 314 |
| 2 USA | 214 |

**Individual riders' points**

| | |
|---|---|
| 1 Kevin Schwantz, USA | 84 |
| 2 Fred Merkel, USA | 79 |
| 3 Roger Burnett, GB | 73 |
| 4 Kenny Irons, GB | 51 |
| 5 Rob McElnea, GB | 50 |
| 6 Ron Haslam, GB | 33 |

**7** Roger Marshall, GB, 30; **8** Michel Mercier, CDN, 29; **9** Steve Parrish, GB, 23; **10** Paul Iddon, GB, 20; **11** Chris Martin, GB, 18; **12** Trevor Nation, GB and Dale Quarterley, USA, 12; **14** Dan Chivington, USA, 8; **15** Keith Huewen, GB, 4; **16** Reuben McMurter, CDN and John Bettencourt, USA, 1.

## *Endurance World Championship*

**24 HEURES DU MANS, Bugatti Circuit, Le Mans, France, 12/13 April. Endurance World Championship, round 1. 748 laps of the 2.635-mile/4.240-km circuit, 1970.98 miles/3171.52 km.**
**1** Gérard Coudray/Patrick Igoa/Alex Vieira, F/F/F (750 Honda), 23h 56m 14.0s, 82.33 mph/132.50 km/h.
**2** Pierre Bolle/Jean-Louis Battistini, F/F (750 Honda), 742 laps; **3** Hervé Moineau/Bruno le Bihan/Eric Delcamp, F/F/F (750 Suzuki), 736; **4** Christian Sarron/Richard Hubin/Pierre-Etienne Samin, F/B/F (750 Yamaha), 718; **5** Christian le Liard/Thierry Espié/Jean-Paul Boinet, F/F/F (750 Suzuki), 718; **6** P. Mouchet/J. Goy/C. Bouheben, F/F/F (750 Suzuki), 715; **7** Mat Oxley/Kenny Irons/Vesa Kultalahti, GB/GB/S (750 Yamaha), 712; **8** Dirk Brand/Gerard Flameling/Dirk Bemelman, NL/NL/NL (750 Yamaha), 711; **9** Jose Chevalier/Dominique Savary/Eddy Chevally, CH/CH/CH (750 Honda), 690; **10** Peter Sköld/Peter Linden/Tony Hogström, S/S/S (750 Honda), 682.
**Fastest lap:** Coudray/Igoa/Vieira, 1m 37.6s, 97.18 mph/156.39 km/h.
**Championship points:** **1** Coudray, Igoa and Vieira, 30; **4** Bolle and Battistini, 24; **6** Moineau, le Bihan and Delcamp, 20; **9** Sarron, Hubin and Samin, 16.

**MOTORRAD MARATHON 6 STUNDEN ÖSTERREICHRING, Österreichring, Austria, 22 June. Endurance World Championship, round 2. 172 laps of the 3.692-mile/5.942-km circuit, 635.02 miles/1022.02 km.**
1 Gérard Coudray/Patrick Igoa, F/F (750 Honda), 6h 02m 05.22s, 105.23 mph/169.35 km/h.
2 Hervé Moineau/Bruno le Bihan, F/F (750 Suzuki), 170 laps; 3 Mat Oxley/Vesa Kultalahti, GB/S (750 Yamaha), 166; 4 Dirk Brand/Gerard Flameling, NL/NL (750 Yamaha), 164; 5 Franz-Willi Rösnick/Peter Nebel, D/D (750 Yamaha), 163; 6 Anton Heiler/Peter Häfner, D/D (750 Yamaha), 163; 7 Peter Linden/Peter Sköld, S/S (750 Honda); 163; 8 Patrice More/Patrick Braud, F/F (750 Suzuki,) 162; 9 Piet Mantel/Siebrand Nijhuis, NL/NL (750 Honda), 161; 10 Claude Couturier/Didier Meyer, F/F (750 Honda), 161.
**Fastest lap:** Coudray/Igoa, 2m 01.91s, 109.04 mph/175.48 km/h.
**Championship points:** 1 Coudray and Igoa, 45; 3 Moineau and le Bihan, 32; 5 Vieira, 30; 6 Bolle and Battistini, 24; 8 Delcamp, 20; 9 Oxley and Kultalahti, 18.

**SUZUKA 8-HOURS, Suzuka International Racing Course, Japan, 27 July. World Endurance Championship, round 3. 197 laps of the 3.675-mile/5.914-km circuit, 723.98 miles/1165.06 km.**
1 Wayne Gardner/Dominique Sarron, AUS/F (750 Honda), 8h 01m 30.74s, 90.21 mph/145.18 km/h.
2 Michael Dowson/Kevin Magee, AUS/AUS (750 Yamaha), 195 laps; 3 Satoshi Tsujimoto/Kevin Schwantz, J/USA (750 Suzuki), 194; 4 Shoji Hiratsuka/Toshinobu Shiomori, J/J (750 Yamaha), 191; 5 Shunji Yatsushiro/Hikaru Miyagi, J/J (750 Honda), 190; 6 Christian le Liard/Thierry Espié, F/F (750 Suzuki), 189; 7 Mat Oxley/Vesa Kultalahti, GB/S (750 Yamaha), 188; 8 Kork Ballington/Rob Phillis, ZA/AUS (750 Honda), 187; 9 Kazuma Morimitsu/Shinji Hagiwara, J/J (750 Honda), 186; 10 Yukiya Oshima/Shoji Miyazaki, J/J (750 Suzuki), 186.
**Fastest lap:** Not given.
**Championship points:** 1 Coudray and Igoa, 45; 3 Moineau and le Bihan, 32; 5 Vieira, 30; 6 Bolle and Battistini, 24; 8 Oxley and Kultalahti, 22; 10 Delcamp, 20.

**24 HEURES DE LIÈGE, Spa-Francorchamps Grand Prix Circuit, Belgium, 16/17 August. World Endurance Championship, round 4. 514 laps of the 4.335-mile/6.976/km-circuit, 2228.19 miles/3585.66 km.**
1 Gérard Coudray/Patrick Igoa/Alex Vieira, F/F/F (750 Honda), 23h 58m 53.3s, 93.03 mph/149.71 km/h.
2 Jean-Louis Battistini/Richard Hubin/Thierry Espié, F/B/F (750 Honda), 507 laps; 3 Patrice More/Patrick Braud/André Lussiana, F/F/F (750 Suzuki), 488; 4 Jacky Guyon/Bernard Chateau/Pascal Dejonghe, F/F/F (750 Honda), 486; 5 Gérard Jolivet/Georges Furling/Michel Coroner, F/F/F (750 Suzuki), 486; 6 Dominique Savary/José Chevalier/Eddy Chevalley, CH/CH/CH (750 Honda), 479; 7 Hervé Moineau/Bruno le Bihan/Eric Delcamp, F/F/F (750 Suzuki), 479; 8 Renaat Vincke/Eric de Donker/Michel Simeon, B/B/B (750 Suzuki), 478; 9 Robi Schläfli/Ulrich Kallen/Christian Monsch, CH/CH/CH (750 Honda), 477; 10 David Morris/Alain Delhotellerie/Barry Middleton, GB/B/GB (750 Suzuki), 476.
**Fastest lap:** Not given.
**Championship points:** 1 Coudray and Igoa, 75; 3 Vieira, 60; 4 Battistini, 48; 5 Espié, 41; 6 Moineau, le Bihan and Hubin, 40; 9 Delcamp, 28; 10 Bolle, 24.

**ADAC MOTORRAD MARATHON 1000 KMS HOCKENHEIM, Hockenheimring, German Federal Republic, 30/31 August. World Endurance Championship, round 5. 139 laps of the 4.219-mile/6.789-km circuit, 586.44 miles/943.67 km.**
1 Patrick Igoa/Alex Vieira, F/F (750 Honda), 5h 26m 47.03s, 107.66 mph/173.26 km/h.
2 Vesa Kultalahti/Mat Oxley, S/GB (750 Yamaha), 137 laps; 3 Dirk Brand/Gerard Flameling, NL/NL (750 Yamaha), 137; 4 Ernst Gschwender/Mario Rubatto, D/D (750 Suzuki), 136; 5 Martin Wimmer/Michael Galinski, D/D (750 Yamaha), 136; 6 Christian Monsch/Patrick Loser, CH/CH (750 Honda), 136; 7 Edwin Weibel/Alfred Waibel, CH/D (750 Honda), 136; 8 Patrick Braud/Patrice More, F/F (750 Suzuki), 135; 9 Franz-Willi Rösnick/Peter Nebel, D/D (750 Yamaha), 135; 10 Robi Schläfli/Ulrich Kallen, CH/CH (750 Honda), 135.
**Fastest lap:** Igoa/Vieira, 2m 15.25s, 112.28 mph/180.69 km/h.
**Championship points:** 1 Igoa, 90; 2 Coudray and Vieira, 75; 4 Battistini, 48; 5 Espié, 41; 6 Moineau, le Bihan and Hubin, 40; 9 Oxley and Kultalahti, 34.

**JEREZ 8-HOURS, Circuito del Jerez, Spain, 28 September. World Endurance Championship, round 6. 238 laps of the 2.621-mile/4.218-km circuit, 623.80 miles/1003.88 km.**
1 Patrick Igoa/Alex Vieira, F/F (750 Honda), 238 laps (no time or speed available).
2 Juan Garriga/Marco Lucchinelli, E/I (750 Ducati), 237 laps; 3 Hervé Moineau/Bruno le Bihan, F/F (750 Suzuki), 236; 4 Franz-Willi Rösnick/Anton Heiler, D/D (750 Yamaha), 228; 5 Jorge Cavestany/Juan Cano, E/E (750 Yamaha), 226; 6 Peter Merz/Rüdi Datwyler, CH/CH (750 Suzuki), 221; 7 Klaus Zabka/Koichi Shimada, D/J (750 Yamaha), 220; 8 Pardo/Bravo, E/E (750 Suzuki), 220; 9 Dave Railton/Derrick Bates, GB/GB (750 Suzuki), 218; 10 Dirk Brand/Gerard Flameling, NL/NL (750 Yamaha), 217.
**Fastest lap:** Moineau, 1m 58.2s, 79.83 mph/128.47 km/h.

**Final Championship points**

| | | |
|---|---|---|
| 1 | Patrick Igoa, F | 105 |
| 2 | Alex Vieira, F | 90 |
| 3 | Gérard Coudray, F | 75 |
| 4= | Hervé Moineau, F | 50 |
| 4= | Bruno le Bihan, F | 50 |
| 6 | Jean-Louis Battistini, F | 48 |

7 Thierry Espié, F, 41; 8 Richard Hubin, B, 40; 9 Mat Oxley, GB and Vesa Kultalahti, S, 34; 11 Eric Delcamp, F, 28; 12 Patrice More, F and Patrick Braud, F, 26; 14 Dirk Brand, NL and Gerard Flameling, NL, 25; 16 Pierre Bolle, F, 24; 17 André Lussiana, F, 20; 18 Christian le Liard, F, 17; 19 Christian Sarron, F, Pierre-Etienne Samin, F, Franz-Willi Rösnick, D, Jacky Guyon, F, Bernard Chateau, F and Pascal Dejonghe, F, 16.

## European Championship

**AUTODROMO VALLELUNGA, Italy, 30 March, 1.988-mile/3.200-km circuit.**
**500 cc, round 1 (28 laps, 55.66 miles/89.60 km)**
1 Massimo Messere, I (Honda), 43m 00.53s, 77.65 mph/124.96 km/h.
2 Vittorio Gibertini, I (Suzuki); 3 Alessandro Valesi, I (Honda); 4 Vittorio Scatola, I (Suzuki); 5 Bernard Denis, B (Suzuki); 6 Mark Phillips, GB (Suzuki); 7 Marco Marchesani, I (Suzuki); 8 Massimo Maestri, I (Suzuki); 9 Louis-Luc Maisto, F (Honda); 10 John Brindley, GB (Yamaha).
**Fastest lap:** Messere, 1m 30.49s, 79.60 mph/128.10 km/h.
**Championship points:** 1 Messere, 15; 2 Gibertini, 12; 3 Valesi, 10; 4 Scatola, 8; 5 Denis, 6; 6 Phillips, 5.

**250 cc, round 1 (24 laps, 47.71 miles/76.80 km)**
1 Josef Hutter, A (Bartol) 36m 37.60s, 78.15 mph/125.77 km/h.
2 Franco Randazzo, I (Yamaha); 3 Jean-Philippe Ruggia, F (Yamaha); 4 Konrad Hefele, D (Honda); 5 Rüdi Gachter, CH (Yamaha); 6 Urs Lüzi, CH (Yamaha); 7 Roland Busch, D (Yamaha); 8 Kevin Mitchell, GB (Yamaha); 9 Nedy Crotta, CH (Rotax); 10 Jochen Schmid, D (Yamaha).
**Fastest lap:** Hutter, 1m 30.31s, 79.76 mph/128.36 km/h.
**Championship points:** 1 Hutter, 15; 2 Randazzo, 12; 3 Ruggia, 10; 4 Hefele, 8; 5 Gachter, 6; 6 Luzi, 5.

**125 cc, round 1 (23 laps, 45.72 miles/73.60 km)**
1 Claudio Macciotta, I (MBA), 37m 04.84s, 73.98 mph/119.06 km/h.
2 Paul Bordes, F (MBA); 3 Mario Roscioli, I (MBA); 4 Jamie Whitham, GB (MBA); 5 Flemming Kistrup, DK (MBA); 6 Thierry Feuz, CH (MBA); 7 Andrea Borgonovo, I (MBA); 8 Thomas Möller-Pedersen, DK (MBA); 9 Gilles Payraudeau, F (MBA); 10 Ernst Himmelsbach, D (MBA).
**Fastest lap:** Macciotta, 1m 34.83s, 75.96 mph/122.24 km/h.
**Championship points:** 1 Macciotta, 15; 2 Bordes, 12; 3 Roscioli, 10; 4 Whitham, 8; 5 Kistrup, 6; 6 Feuz, 5.

**80 cc, round 1 (16 laps, 31.81 miles/51.20 km)**
1 Josef Fischer, A (Krauser), 27m 08.48s, 70.32 mph/113.17 km/h.
2 Mario Scalinci, I (Kawasaki); 3 René Dünki, CH (Krauser); 4 Salvatore Milano, I (Huvo); 5 Lionel Robert, F (Scrab); 6 Paolo Scappini, I (Faccioli); 7 Michael Gschwander, D (Kiefer); 8 Thomas Engl, D (ESCH); 9 Oliver Friedrich, D (Ziegler); 10 Rainer Partl, D (PAV).
**Fastest lap:** Fischer, 1m 39.72s, 72.23 mph/116.25 km/h.
**Championship points:** 1 Fischer, 15; 2 Scalinci, 12; 3 Dünki, 10; 4 Milano, 8; 5 Robert, 6; 6 Scappini, 5.

**OMLOOP VAN ZOLDER, Belgium, 6 April. 2.648-mile/4.262-km circuit.**
**250 cc, round 2 (20 laps, 52.96 miles/85.24 km)**
1 Stéphane Mertens, B (Yamaha), 35m 20.04s, 89.94 mph/144.74 km/h.
2 Jean-Philippe Ruggia, F (Yamaha); 3 Roland Busch, D (Yamaha); 4 Karl-Thomas Grässel, D (Honda); 5 Kevin Mitchell, GB (Yamaha); 6 Andreas Preining, A (Wiwa); 7 Jochen Schmid, D (Yamaha); 8 Urs Lüzi, CH (Yamaha); 9 Reinhard Strack, D (Wiwa); 10 Eric de Donker, B (Honda).
**Fastest lap:** Mertens, 1m 43.73s, 91.91 mph/147.92 km/h.
**Championship points:** 1 Ruggia, 22; 2 Mertens and Hutter, 15; 4 Busch, 14; 5 Randazzo, 12; 6 Mitchell, 9.

**125 cc, round 2 (18 laps, 47.66 miles/76.72 km)**
1 Thierry Feuz, CH (MBA), 33m 47.92s, 84.62 mph/136.19 km/h.
2 Claudio Macciotta, I (MBA); 3 Gastone Grassetti, I (MBA); 4 Paul Bordes, F (MBA); 5 Mike Leitner, A (MBA); 6 Thomas Möller-Pedersen, DK (MBA); 7 Anton Straver, NL (Jong); 8 Gilles Payraudeau, F (Scrab); 9 Christian le Badezet, F (MBA); 10 Ernst Himmelsbach, D (MBA).
**Fastest lap:** Feuz, 1m 50.09s, 86.60 mph/139.37 km/h.
**Championship points:** 1 Macciotta, 27; 2 Feuz and Bordes, 20; 4 Grassetti and Roscioli, 10; 6 Möller-Pedersen and Whitham, 8.

**Sidecars, round 1 (18 laps, 47.66 miles/76.72 km)**
1 Dave Hallam/Mark Day, GB/GB (500 LCR-Yamaha), 33m 11.20s, 86.18 mph/138.70 km/h.
2 Christian Graf/Rudolf Ammann, CH/CH (500 LCR-Yamaha); 3 John Barker/Steve China, GB/GB (500 Windle-Yamaha); 4 John Evans/Geoff Wilbraham, GB/GB (500 LCR-Yamaha); 5 Cor van Reeuwijck/Hans Blaauw, NL/NL (500 Yamaha); 6 Gary Thomas/Geoff White, GB/GB (500 BSL-Yamaha); 7 Raphael Clerc/Marcel Mai, CH/CH (500 Seymaz-Yamaha); 8 Friedel Reinhard/Jan Schluckebier, D/D (500 LCR-Yamaha); 9 Dennis Holmes/Alan Jervis, GB/GB (500 LCR-Yamaha); 10 Mike Turrell/Brian Barlow, GB/GB (500 LCR-Yamaha).
**Fastest lap:** Ivan Nigrowski/Frédéric Meunier, F/F (500 Seymaz-Yamaha), 1m 48.21s, 88.10 mph/141.79 km/h.
**Championship points:** 1 Hallam, 15; 2 Graf, 12; 3 Barker, 10; 4 Evans, 8; 5 van Reeuwijck, 6; 6 Thomas, 5.

**MOTODROM HOCKENHEIM, German Federal Republic, 4 May. 4.218-mile/6.789-km circuit.**
**500 cc, round 2 (14 laps, 59.05 miles/95.05 km)**
1 Marco Papa, I (Honda) 31m 09.13s, 113.74 mph/183.05 km/h.
2 Massimo Messere, I (Honda); 3 Alessandro Valesi, I (Honda); 4 Mark Phillips, GB (Suzuki); 5 Georg-Robert Jung, D (Honda); 6 Fabio Barchitta, I (Honda); 7 Ray Swann, GB (Suzuki); 8 Gerold Fischer, D (Suzuki); 9 Marco Marchesani, I (Suzuki); 10 Louis-Luc Maisto, F (Honda).
**Fastest lap:** Papa, 2m 12.07s, 114.98 mph/185.04 km/h.
**Championship points:** 1 Messere, 27; 2 Valesi, 20; 3 Papa, 15; 4 Phillips, 13; 5 Gibertini, 12; 6 Scatola, 8.

**250 cc, round 3 (12 laps, 50.62 miles/81.47 km)**
1 Herbert Hauf, D (Honda), 28m 11.36s, 107.74 mph/173.39 km/h.
2 Jochen Schmid, D (Yamaha); 3 Hans Lindner, A (Rotax); 4 Alain Bronec, F (Honda); 5 Alberto Rota, I (Honda); 6 Reiner Gerwin, D (Rotax); 7 Michel Simeon, B (Yamaha); 8 Josef Hutter, A (Bartol); 9 Etienne Quartararo, F (Honda); 10 Hermann Holder, D (Yamaha).
**Fastest lap:** Lindner, 2m 18.45s, 109.68 mph/176.51 km/h.
**Championship points:** 1 Ruggia, 22; 2 Hutter, 18; 3 Schmid, 17; 4 Mertens and Hauf, 15; 6 Busch, 14.

**125 cc, round 3 (12 laps, 50.62 miles/81.47 km)**
1 Mike Leitner, A (MBA) 30m 06.09s, 100.90 mph/162.38 km/h.
2 Claudio Macciotta, I (MBA); 3 Adolf Stadler, D (MBA); 4 Dirk Hafeneger, D (LCR); 5 Thomas Möller-Pedersen, DK (MBA); 6 Christian le Badezet, F (MBA); 7 Karl Dauer, A (MBA); 8 Rolf Blatter, CH (MBA); 9 Josef Bader, D (MBA); 10 Flemming Kistrup, DK (MBA).
**Fastest lap:** Not given.
**Championship points:** 1 Macciotta, 39; 2 Leitner, 22; 3 Feuz and Bordes, 20; 5 Möller-Pedersen, 14; 6 Grassetti, Roscioli and Stadler, 10.

**80 cc, round 2 (8 laps, 33.74 miles/54.31 km)**
1 Bruno Casanova, I (Unimoto), 21m 46.38s, 92.99 mph/149.66 km/h.
2 Michael Gschwander, D (Keifer); 3 Paul Bordes, F (Scrab); 4 Thomas Engl, A (ESCH); 5 Wilco Zeelenberg, NL (Huvo); 6 Hans Koopman, NL (Ziegler); 7 Paolo Scappini, I (Faccioli); 8 Bert Smit, NL (Minarelli); 9 Josef Lutzenberger, D (Huvo); 10 Mario Scalinci, I (Kawasaki).
**Fastest lap:** Not given.
**Championship points:** 1 Gschwander, 16; 2 Fischer and Casanova, 15; 4 Scalinci, 13; 5 Engl, 11; 6 Dünki and Bordes, 10.

**Sidecars, round 2 (12 laps, 50.62 miles/81.47 km)**
1 Ivan Nigrowski/Frédéric Meunier, F/F (500 Seymaz-Yamaha), 29m 05.22s, 104.42 mph/168.04 km/h.
2 Gary Thomas/Geoff White, GB/GB (500 BSL-Yamaha); 3 Bernd Scherer/Wolfgang Gess, D/D (500 LCR-Yamaha); 4 Pascal Larratte/Jacques Corbier, F/F (500 LCR-Yamaha); 5 Ray Gardner/Tony Strevens, GB/GB (500 LCR-Yamaha); 6 Cor van Reeuwijck/Hans Blaauw, NL/NL (500 Yamaha); 7 John Barker/Steve China, GB/GB (500 Windle-Yamaha); 8 Albert Weber/Harald Schneidewind, D/D (500 LCR-Yamaha); 9 Luigi Casagrande/Adolf Hänni, CH/CH (500 LCR-Yamaha); 10 Clive Stirrat/Simon Prior, GB/GB (500 BLR-Yamaha).
**Fastest lap:** Nigrowski, 2m 23.30s, 105.97 mph/170.54 km/h.
**Championship points:** 1 Thomas, 17; 2 Hallam and Nigrowski, 15; 4 Barker, 14; 5 Graf, 12; 6 van Reeuwijck, 11.

**CIRCUIT VAN DRENTHE, ASSEN, Holland, 23/28 June. 3.812-mile/6.134-km circuit.**
**500 cc, round 3 (15 laps, 57.18 miles/92.01 km)**
1 Massimo Messere, I (Honda), 35m 41.32s, 96.12 mph/154.69 km/h.
2 Simon Buckmaster, GB (Honda); 3 Marco Papa, I (Honda); 4 Rob Punt, NL (Honda); 5 Alessandro Valesi, I (Honda); 6 Mark Phillips, GB (Suzuki); 7 Esko Kuparinen, SF (Honda); 8 Peter Linden, S (Honda); 9 Eero Hyvarinen, SF (Honda); 10 Henny Boerman, NL (Assmex).
**Fastest lap:** Messere, 2m 18.97s, 98.74 mph/158.90 km/h.
**Championship points:** 1 Messere, 42; 2 Valesi, 26; 3 Papa, 25; 4 Phillips, 18; 5 Gibertini and Buckmaster, 15.

**250 cc, round 4 (14 laps, 53.37 miles/85.88 km)**
1 Hans Lindner, A (Castrol), 37m 31.73s, 85.31 mph/137.30 km/h.
2 Eric de Donker, B (Honda); 3 Andreas Preining, A (Wiwa); 4 Jean-Philippe Ruggia, F (Honda); 5 Urs Lüzi, CH (Yamaha); 6 Mar Schouten, NL (Honda); 7 Nigel Bosworth, GB (Yamaha); 8 Herbert Besendörfer, D (Yamaha); 9 Gary Cowan, GB (Honda); 10 Urs Jucker, CH (Yamaha).
**Fastest lap:** Lindner, 2m 36.86s, 87.48 mph/140.78 km/h.
**Championship points:** 1 Ruggia, 30; 2 Lindner, 25; 3 Hutter, 18; 4 Schmid, 17; 5 Preining and Hauf, 15.

**125 cc, round 4 (12 laps, 45.74 miles/73.61 km)**
1 Mike Leitner, A (Bartol), 30m 56.05s, 88.71 mph/142.77 km/h.
2 Gastone Grassetti, I (MBA); 3 Thomas Möller-Pedersen, DK (MBA); 4 Adolf Stadler, D (MBA); 5 Andrea Borgonovo, I (MBA); 6 Norbert Peschke, D (MBA); 7 Paul Bordes, F (MBA); 8 Anton Straver, NL (MBA); 9 Robin Milton, GB (MBA); 10 Peter Sommer, CH (MBA).
**Fastest lap:** Stadler, 2m 30.05s, 91.45 mph/147.17 km/h.
**Championship points:** 1 Macciotta, 39; 2 Leitner, 36; 3 Bordes and Möller-Pedersen, 24; 5 Grassetti, 22; 6 Feuz, 20.

**80 cc, round 3 (9 laps, 34.31 miles/55.21 km)**
1 Rainer Kunz, D (Ziegler), 24m 23.88s, 84.36 mph/135.76 km/h.
2 Bruno Casanova, I (Unimoto); 3 René Dünki, CH (Krauser); 4 Bert Smit, NL (BZ); 5 Wilco Zeelenberg, NL (Huvo); 6 Josef Fischer, A (Krauser), 7 Paul Bordes, F (Scrab); 8 Stefan Brägger, CH (Huvo); 9 Chris Baert, B (Seel); 10 Reiner Koster, CH (LCR).
**Fastest lap:** Kunz, 2m 38.98s, 86.31 mph/138.90 km/h.
**Championship points:** 1 Casanova, 27; 2 Fischer and Dünki, 20; 4 Gschwander, 16; 5 Kunz, 15; 6 Bordes, 14.

**Sidecars, round 3 (12 laps, 45.74 miles/73.61 km)**
1 Yoshisada Kumagaya/Kazuhiko Makiuchi, J/J (500 LCR-Yamaha), 32m 08.44s, 85.38 mph/137.41 km/h.
2 Bernd Scherer/Wolfgang Gess, D/D (500 BSR-Yamaha); 3 Luigi Casagrande/Hans Egli, CH/CH (500 LCR-Yamaha); 4 René Progin/Yves Hunziker, CH/CH (500 Seymaz-Yamaha); 5 Erwin Weber/Klaus Kolb, D/D (500 LCR-Yamaha); 6 John Barker/Steve China, GB/GB (500 Windle-Yamaha); 7 Dave Hallam/Mark Day, GB/GB (500 LCR-Yamaha); 8 Gary Thomas/Geoff White, GB/GB (500 LCR-Yamaha); 9 Clive Stirrat/Simon Prior, GB/GB (500 BLR-Yamaha); 10 Ivan Nigrowski/Frédéric Meunier, F/F (500 Seymaz-Yamaha).
**Fastest lap:** Scherer, 2m 36.87s, 87.47 mph/140.77 km/h.
**Championship points:** 1 Scherer, 22; 2 Thomas, 20; 3 Barker and Hallam, 19; 5 Nigrowski, 16; 6 Kumagaya, 15.

**IMATRA ROAD RACE CIRCUIT, Finland, 4 August. 3.076-mile/4.950-km circuit.**
**500 cc, round 4 (20 laps, 61.52 miles/99.00 km)**
1 Eero Hyvarinen, SF (Honda), 40m 17.33s, 91.62 mph/147.45 km/h.
2 Esko Kuparinen, SF (Honda); 3 Peter Linden, S (Honda); 4 Peter Sköld, S (Honda); 5 Alessandro Valesi, I (Honda); 6 Marco Papa, I (Honda); 7 Fabio Barchitta, I (Honda); 8 Bernard Denis, B (Suzuki); 9 Louis-Luc Maisto, F (Honda); 10 Paul Ramon, B (Suzuki).
**Fastest lap:** Kuparinen, 1m 56.63s, 94.95 mph/152.81 km/h.
**Championship points:** 1 Messere, 42; 2 Valesi, 32; 3 Papa, 30; 4 Phillips, 18; 5 Hyvarinen, 17; 6 Kuparinen, 16.

**125 cc, round 5 (16 laps, 49.22 miles/79.20 km)**
1 Paul Bordes, F (MBA), 35m 01.16s, 81.99 mph/131.95 km/h.
2 Claudio Macciotta, I (MBA); 3 Gastone Grassetti, I (MBA); 4 Adolf Stadler, D (MBA); 5 Flemming Kistrup, DK (MBA); 6 Mike Leitner, A (MBA); 7 Alain Kempener, B (MBA); 8 Christian le Badezet, F (MBA); 9 Hannu Kallio, SF (MBA); 10 Peter Sommer, CH (MBA).
**Fastest lap:** Macciotta, 2m 09.03s, 85.82 mph/138.11 km/h.
**Championship points:** 1 Macciotta, 51; 2 Leitner, 41; 3 Bordes, 39; 4 Grassetti, 32; 5 Stadler, 26; 6 Möller-Pedersen, 24.

**BRNO, Czechoslovakia, 31 August. 6.788-mile/10.925-km circuit.**
**500 cc, round 5 (10 laps, 67.88 miles/109.25 km)**
1 Manfred Fischer, D (Honda), 37m 49.69s, 107.67 mph/173.82 km/h.
2 Simon Buckmaster, GB (Honda); 3 Eero Hyvarinen, SF (Honda); 4 Mile Pajic, NL (Honda); 5 Paul Ramon, B (Suzuki); 6 Marco Papa, I (Honda); 7 Pavel Dekánek, CS (Suzuki); 8 Gerold Fischer, D (Suzuki); 9 Chris Bürki, CH (Honda); 10 Maarten Duyzers, NL (Suzuki).
**Fastest lap:** Fischer (Manfred), 3m 42.51s, 109.83 mph/176.76 km/h.
**Championship points:** 1 Messere, 42; 2 Papa, 35; 3 Valesi, 32; 4 Hyvarinen, 27; 5 Buckmaster, 24; 6 Phillips, 18.

**250 cc, round 5 (9 laps, 61.09 miles/98.33 km)**
1 Hans Lindner, A (Rotax), 35m 49.13s, 102.34 mph/164.70 km/h.
2 Andreas Preining, A (Wiwa); 3 Josef Hutter, A (Bartol); 4 Alberto Rota, I (Honda); 5 Wilhelm Hörhager, A (Rotax); 6 Michel Simeon, B (Yamaha); 7 Mar Schouten, NL (Honda); 8 Stefan Klabacher, A (Rotax); 9 Cees Doorakkers, NL (Honda); 10 Nedy Crotta, CH (Armstrong).
**Fastest lap:** Hutter, 3m 56.18s, 103.48 mph/166.53 km/h.
**Championship points:** 1 Lindner, 40; 2 Ruggia, 30; 3 Hutter, 28; 4 Preining, 27; 5 Schmid, 17; 6 Mertens, and Hauf, 15.

**125 cc, round 6 (9 laps, 61.09 miles/98.33 km)**
1 Thierry Feuz, CH (MBA), 38m 00.24s, 96.46 mph/155.23 km/h.
2 Paul Bordes, F (MBA); 3 Claudio Macciotta, I (MBA); 4 Flemming Kistrup, DK (MBA); 5 Gastone Grassetti, I (MBA); 6 Rolf Blatter, CH (MBA); 7 Christian le Badezet, F (MBA); 8 Thomas Möller-Pedersen, DK (MBA); 9 Josef Bader, D (MBA); 10 Peter Baláz, CS (MBA).
**Fastest lap:** Bordes, 4m 10.00s, 97.75 mph/157.32 km/h.
**Championship points:** See final points.

**80 cc, round 4 (7 laps, 47.52 miles/76.48 km)**
1 Bruno Casanova, I (Unimoto), 32m 01.09s, 89.05 mph/143.31 km/h.
2 Wilco Zeelenberg, NL (Huvo); 3 Chris Baert, B (Seel); 4 Paul Bordes, F (Scrab); 5 Michael Gschwander, D (Kiefer); 6 Rainer Kunz, D (Ziegler); 7 Josef Fischer, A (Krauser); 8 Reiner Koster, CH (LCR); 9 Thomas Engl, D (ESCH); 10 Stefan Brägger, CH (Huvo).
**Fastest lap:** Casanova, 4m 31.24s, 90.10 mph/145.00 km/h.
**Championship points:** 1 Casanova, 42; 2 Fischer and Zeelenberg, 24; 4 Bordes and Gschwander, 22; 6 Dünki and Kunz, 20.

**Sidecars, round 4 (9 laps, 61.09 miles/98.33 km)**
1 Yoshisada Kumagaya/Kazuhiko Makiuchi, J/J (500 LCR-Yamaha), 36m 29.28s, 100.45 mph/161.66 km/h.
2 Bernd Scherer/Wolfgang Gess, D/D (500 LCR-Yamaha); 3 Ivan Nigrowski/Frédéric Meunier, F/F (500 Seymaz-Yamaha); 4 Wolfgang Stropek/Hans-Peter Demling, A/A (500 LCR-Yamaha); 5 Jean-Louis Millet/Claude Debroux, F/F (500 Seymaz-Yamaha); 6 Luigi Casagrande/Adolf Hänni, CH/CH (500 LCR-Yamaha); 7 Erwin Weber/Harald Schneidewind, D/D (500 LCR-Yamaha); 8 Christian Graf/Rudolf Ammann, CH/CH (500 LCR-Yamaha); 9 John Barker/Steve China, GB/GB (500 Windle-Yamaha); 10 Kenny Howles/Steve Pointer, GB/GB (500 Yamaha).
**Fastest lap:** Kumagaya, 3m 58.93s, 102.28 mph/164.61 km/h.
**Championship points:** 1 Scherer, 34; 2 Kumagaya, 30; 3 Nigrowski, 26; 4 Barker, 21; 5 Thomas, 20; 6 Hallam, 19.

**CIRCUITO DEL JEREZ, Spain, 21 September. 2.621-mile/4.218-km circuit.**
**500 cc, round 6 (23 laps, 60.28 miles/97.01 km)**
1 Alessandro Valesi, I (Honda), 45m 39.27s, 79.22 mph/127.49 km/h.
2 Simon Buckmaster, GB (Honda); 3 Marco Papa, I (Honda); 4 Eero Hyvarinen, SF (Honda); 5 Fabio Barchitta, I (Honda); 6 Louis-Luc Maisto, F (Honda); 7 Maarten Duyzers, NL (Suzuki); 8 Rüdi Gachter, CH (Yamaha); 9 Detlef Vogt, D (Honda); 10 Hans Klingebiel, D (Suzuki).
**Fastest lap:** Massimo Messere, I (Honda), 1m 57.18s, 80.52 mph/129.58 km/h.
**Championship points:** 1 Valesi, 47; 2 Papa, 45; 3 Messere, 42; 4 Buckmaster, 36; 5 Hyvarinen, 35; 6 Phillips, 18.

**250 cc, round 6 (20 laps, 52.42 miles/84.36 km)**
1 Jean-Philippe Ruggia, F (Yamaha), 39m 39.71s, 79.29 mph/127.61 km/h.
2 Alberto Rota, I (Honda); 3 Hans Lindner, A (Rotax); 4 Urs Lüzi, CH (Yamaha); 5 Daniel Amatrain, E (Kobas); 6 Christian Boudinot, F (Kobas); 7 Nedy Crotta, CH (Armstrong); 8 Engelbert Neumair, A (Rotax); 9 Henny Boerman, NL (Assmex); 10 Urs Jucker, CH (Yamaha).
**Fastest lap:** Ruggia, 1m 57.48s, 80.32 mph/129.26 km/h.
**Championship points:** 1 Lindner, 50; 2 Ruggia, 45; 3 Hutter, 28; 4 Preining, 27; 5 Rota, 26; 6 Lüzi, 22.

**80 cc, round 5 (12 laps, 31.45 miles/50.62 km)**
1 Luis Reyes, COL (Autisa), 25m 40.95s, 73.48 mph/118.25 km/h.
2 Bruno Casanova, I (Unimoto); 3 Chris Baert, B (Seel); 4 Paul Bordes, F (Scrab); 5 Jan Verheul, NL (JVM); 6 Reiner Koster, CH (LCR); 7 Jorge Monux, E (Autisa); 8 Joaquin Fabregas, E (Autisa); 9 Nicola Casadei, I (RB); 10 Juan Alos, E (Yamaha).
**Fastest lap:** Reyes, 2m 05.91s, 74.94 mph/120.60 km/h.
**Championship points:** See final points.

**DONINGTON PARK CIRCUIT, Great Britain, 28 September. 2.500-mile/4.023-km circuit.**
**500 cc, round 7 (25 laps, 62.50 miles/100.58 km).**
1 Richard Scott, NZ (Honda), 44m 07.61s, 84.77 mph/136.43 km/h.
2 Simon Buckmaster, GB (Honda); 3 Massimo Messere, I (Honda); 4 Trevor Nation, GB (Suzuki); 5 Fabio Barchitta, I (Honda); 6 Alessandro Valesi, I (Honda); 7 Alan Jeffery, GB (Suzuki); 8 Ray Swann, GB (Suzuki); 9 Andreas Leuthe, LUX (Honda); 10 Steve Manley, GB (Suzuki).
**Fastest lap:** Mark Phillips, GB (Suzuki), 1m 44.14s, 86.21 mph/138.74 km/h (record).

**250 cc, round 7 (20 laps, 50.00 miles/80.46 km)**
1 Nigel Bosworth, GB (Yamaha), 35m 59.74s, 83.14 mph/133.80 km/h.
2 Urs Lüzi, CH (Yamaha); 3 Konrad Hefele, D (Honda); 4 Cees Doorakkers, NL (Honda); 5 Hans Lindner, A (Rotax); 6 Nedy Crotta, CH (Armstrong); 7 Jochen Schmid, D (Yamaha); 8 Helmut Bradl, D (Honda); 9 Andy Machin, GB (Rotax); 10 Gary Cowan, GB (Honda).
**Fastest lap:** Alberto Rota, I (Honda), 1m 45.47s, 85.12 mph/136.99 km/h (record).

**Sidecars, round 6 (20 laps, 50.00 miles/80.46 km)**
1 Yoshisada Kumagaya/Kazuhiko Makiuchi, J/J (500 LCR-Yamaha), 36m 20.27s, 82.36 mph/132.54 km/h.
2 Bernd Scherer/Wolfgang Gess, D/D (500 BSR-Yamaha); 3 Ray Gardner/Tony Strevens, GB/GB (500 LCR-Yamaha); 4 Pascal Larratte/Frédéric Meunier, F/F (500 Seymaz-Yamaha); 5 Gary Thomas/Graham Rose, GB/GB (500 BSL-Yamaha); 6 Mick Burcombe/Dave Knapp, GB/GB (500 LCR-Yamaha); 7 George Hardwick/Carl Fieldhouse, GB/GB (500 Ireson-Yamaha); 8 Jean-Louis Millet/Claude Debroux, F/F (500 Seymaz-Yamaha); 9 Tony Baker/Peter Harper, GB/GB (500 Yamaha); 10 John Barker/Steve China, GB/GB (500 Windle-Yamaha).
**Fastest lap:** Kumagaya, 1m 46.77s, 84.09 mph/135.33 km/h.

**Final Championship points (500 cc)**

| | | |
|---|---|---|
| 1 | Massimo Messere, I | 52 |
| 2 | Alessandro Valesi, I | 52 |
| 3 | Simon Buckmaster, GB | 48 |
| 4 | Marco Papa, I | 45 |
| 5 | Eero Hyvarinen, SF | 35 |
| 6 | Fabio Barchitta, I | 21 |

7 Mark Phillips, GB, 18; 8 Esko Kuparinen, SF, 16; 9 Manfred Fischer, D, and Richard Scott, NZ, 15; 11 Peter Linden, S, 13; 12 Vittorio Gibertini, I, 12; 13 Louis-Luc Maisto, F, 10; 14 Bernard Denis, B, 9; 15 Vittorio Scatola, I, Rob Punt, NL, Peter Sköld, S, Mile Pajic, NL and Trevor Nation, GB, 8.

**Final Championship points (250 cc)**

| | | |
|---|---|---|
| 1 | Hans Lindner, A | 56 |
| 2 | Jean-Philippe Ruggia, F | 45 |
| 3 | Urs Lüzi, CH | 34 |
| 4 | Josef Hutter, A | 28 |
| 5 | Andreas Preining, A | 27 |
| 6 | Alberto Rota, I | 26 |

7 Jochen Schmid, D, 21; 8 Nigel Bosworth, GB, 19; 9 Konrad Hefele, D, 18; 10 Herbert Hauf, D and Stéphane Mertens, B, 15; 12 Roland Busch, D, 14; 13 Eric de Donker, B, 13; 14 Franco Randazzo, I and Nedy Crotta, CH, 12.

**Final Championship points (125 cc)**

| | | |
|---|---|---|
| 1 | Claudio Macciotta, I | 61 |
| 2 | Paul Bordes, F | 51 |
| 3 | Mike Leitner, A | 41 |
| 4 | Gastone Grassetti, I | 38 |
| 5 | Thierry Feuz, CH | 35 |
| 6 | Thomas Möller-Pedersen, DK | 27 |

7 Adolf Stadler, D, 26; 8 Flemming Kistrup, DK, 21; 9 Christian le Badezet, F, 14; 10 Mario Roscioli, I and Andrea Borgonovo, I, 10; 12 Jamie Whitham, GB, Dirk Hafeneger, D and Rolf Blatter, CH, 8; 15 Anton Straver, NL, 7.

**Final Championship points (80 cc)**

| | | |
|---|---|---|
| 1 | Bruno Casanova, I | 54 |
| 2 | Paul Bordes, F | 30 |
| 3= | Josef Fischer, A | 24 |
| 3= | Wilco Zeelenberg, NL | 24 |
| 5= | Michael Gschwander, D | 22 |
| 5= | Chris Baert, B | 22 |

7 Rainer Kunz, D and René Dünki, CH, 20; 9 Luis Reyes, COL, 15; 10 Mario Scalinci, I and Thomas Engl, D, 13; 12 Bert Smit, NL, 11; 14 Paolo Scappini, I and Reiner Koster, CH, 9.

**Final Championship points (Sidecars)**

| | | |
|---|---|---|
| 1 | Bernd Scherer, D | 46 |
| 2 | Yoshisada Kumagaya, J | 45 |
| 3= | Ivan Nigrowski, F | 26 |
| 3= | Gary Thomas, GB | 26 |
| 5 | John Barker, GB | 22 |
| 6 | Dave Hallam, GB | 19 |

7 Luigi Casagrande, CH, 17; 8 Pascal Larratte, F and Ray Gardner, GB, 16; 10 Christian Graf, CH, 15; 11 Cor van Reeuwijck, NL, 11; 12 Erwin Weber, D, 10; 13 Jean-Louis Millet, F, 9; 14 John Evans, GB, René Progin, CH and Wolfgang Stropek, A, 8.

## *Major European Meetings*

**AUTODROMO SANTAMONICA, MISANO, Italy, 6 April. 2.167-mile/3.488-km circuit.**
**F1 (24 laps, 52.01 miles/83.71 km)**
1 Massimo Matteoni, I (750 Suzuki), 34m 23.9s, 90.75 mph/146.04 km/h.
2 Davide Tardozzi, I (750 Suzuki); 3 Sergio Ballabio, I (750 Yamaha); 4 Luciano Leandrini, I (750 Yamaha); 5 Silvano Righetti, I (750 Yamaha); 6 Ferdinando de Cecco, I (750 Ducati).
**Fastest lap:** Matteoni, 1m 24.43s, 92.41 mph/148.72 km/h.

**500 cc (21 laps, 45.51 miles/73.25 km)**
1 Rob McElnea, GB (Yamaha), 29m 03.6s, 93.96 mph/151.21 km/h.
2 Pier Francesco Chili, I (Suzuki); 3 Massimo Messere, I (Honda); 4 Fabio Biliotti, I (Honda); 5 Wolfgang von Muralt, CH (Suzuki); 6 Vittorio Gibertini, I (Suzuki).
**Fastest lap:** McElnea, 1m 21.37s, 95.87 mph/154.29 km/h.

**250 cc (21 laps, 45.51 miles/73.25 km)**
1 Martin Wimmer, D (Yamaha), 29m 20.0s, 93.09 mph/149.81 km/h.
2 Fausto Ricci, I (Honda); 3 Pierre Bolle, F (Parisienne); 4 Stefano Caracchi, I (Aprilia); 5 Tadahiko Taira, J (Yamaha); 6 Manfred Herweh, D (Aprilia).
**Fastest lap:** Wimmer, 1m 21.94s, 95.21 mph/153.23 km/h.

**125 cc (18 laps, 39.01 miles/62.78 km)**
1 Pier Paolo Bianchi, I (Elit), 26m 19.7s, 88.91 mph/143.08 km/h.
2 Bruno Kneubühler, CH (LCR); 3 Luca Cadalora, I (Garelli); 4 August Auinger, A (Bartol); 5 Paolo Casoli, I (MBA); 6 Domenico Brigaglia, I (MBA).
**Fastest lap:** Cadalora, 1m 26.25s, 90.47 mph/145.59 km/h.

**80 cc (13 laps, 28.17 miles/45.34 km)**
1 Pier Paolo Bianchi, I (Seel), 21m 15.4s, 79.53 mph/127.99 km/h.
2 Vincenzo Sblendorio, I (Autisa); 3 Salvatore Milano, I (Krauser); 4 Mario Stocco, I (Huvo); 5 Paolo Scapini, I (Faccioli) 6 Claudio Granata, I (Lusuardi).
**Fastest lap:** Bianchi, 1m 35.62s, 81.60 mph/131.32 km/h.

**ST WENDEL, German Federal Republic, 19/20 April. 1.740-miles/2.800-km circuit.**
**Superbikes (18 laps, 31.32 miles/50.40 km)**
1 Andreas Hofmann, D (750 Kawasaki), 27m 26.62s, 68.47 mph/110.19 km/h.
2 Michael Galinski, D (750 Yamaha); 3 Ernst Gschwender, D (750 Suzuki); 4 Klaus Klein, D (500 Suzuki); 5 Bodo Schmidt, D (750 Yamaha); 6 Manfred Fiedler, D (750 Suzuki); 7 Heinz Eberle, D (750 Suzuki); 8 Mario Rubatto, D (750 Suzuki); 9 Rene Priebe, D (750 Suzuki); 10 Thomas Franz, D (750 Suzuki).
**Fastest lap:** Hofmann, 1m 29.00s, 70.38 mph/113.26 km/h.

**500 cc (19 laps, 33.06 miles/53.20 km)**
1 Gustav Reiner, D (Honda), 29m 23.56s, 67.48 mph/108.60 km/h.
2 Rolf Aljes, D (Suzuki); 3 Manfred Fischer, D (Honda); 4 Bodo Schmidt, D (Yamaha); 5 Josef Ragginger, A (Suzuki); 6 Bernd Steif, D (Honda); 7 Gerold Fischer, D (Suzuki); 8 Pavel Dekánek, CS (Suzuki); 9 Thomas Lange, D (Suzuki); 10 Norbert Gunther, D (Suzuki).
**Fastest lap:** Reiner, 1m 30.51s, 69.20 mph/111.37 km/h.

**350 cc (19 laps, 33.06 miles/53.20 km)**
1 Reiner Gerwin, D (Armstrong), 27m 03.20s, 73.32 mph/117.99 km/h.
2 Georg Willmann, D (Yamaha); 3 Rüdi Gachter, D (Holzer); 4 Roland Pörzgen, D (Yamaha); 5 Marco Biegert, D (Bartol); 6 Volker Klett, D (Yamaha); 7 Friedhelm Weber, D (Weber); 8 Günter Schlieper, D (Yamaha); 9 Stefan Dees, D (Yamaha); 10 Michael Simunic, D (Yamaha).
**Fastest lap:** Gerwin, 1m 22.70s, 75.74 mph/121.89 km/h.

**250 cc (19 laps, 33.06 miles/53.20 km)**
1 Jochen Schmid, D (Yamaha), 25m 26.18s, 77.98 mph/125.49 km/h.
2 Konrad Hefele, D (Honda); 3 Manfred Herweh, D (Aprilia); 4 Reinhold Roth, D (Honda); 5 Herbert Hauf, D (Honda); 6 Helmut Bradl, D (Honda); 7 Reiner Gerwin, D (Bakker); 8 Herbert Besendörfer, D (Yamaha); 9 Wolfgang Bennmann, D (Yamaha); 10 Peter Jungbauer, D (Honda).
**Fastest lap:** Hefele, 1m 17.70s, 80.61 mph/129.73 km/h.

**125 cc (19 laps, 33.06 miles/53.20 km)**
1 Alfred Waibel, D (Real), 29m 08.69s, 68.05 mph/109.52 km/h.
2 Adolf Stadler, D (MBA); 3 Dirk Hafeneger, D (LCR); 4 Rolf Blatter, CH (MBA); 5 Klaus Huber, D (Hummel); 6 Josef Bader, D (MBA); 7 Heinz Litz, D (MBA); 8 Peter Meinhardt, D (Morbidelli); 9 Erich Zürn, D (MBA); 10 Lothar Zürn, D (MBA).
**Fastest lap:** Waibel, 1m 29.38s, 70.08 mph/112.78 km/h.

**80 cc (19 laps, 33.06 miles/53.20 km)**
1 Gerhard Waibel, D (Real), 28m 23.41s, 69.86 mph/112.43 km/h.
2 Michael Gschwander, D (Huvo); 3 Reiner Scheidhauer, D (Seel); 4 Rainer Kunz, D (Ziegler); 5 Josef Lutzenberger, D (ERS); 6 Oliver Friedrich, D (Ziegler); 7 Michael Knipp, D (Huvo); 8 Roland Bosch, D (Huvo); 9 Thomas Engl, D (ESCH); 10 Anton Gevers, NL (Romer).
**Fastest lap:** Waibel, 1m 28.24s, 70.98 mph/114.23 km/h.

**Sidecars (19 laps, 33.06 miles/53.20 km)**
1 Masato Kumano/Helmut Diehl, J/D (500 LCR-Yamaha), 30m 42.41s, 64.59 mph/103.95 km/h.
2 Norbert Wild/Andreas Räcke, D/D (500 OW-Yamaha); 3 Egon Schons/Eckart Rösinger, D/D (500 Busch-Yamaha); 4 Bernd Scherer/Wolfgang Gess, D/D (500 BSR-Yamaha); 5 Friedel Reinhardt/Jan Schluckebier, D/D (500 LCR-Yamaha); 6 Reinhard Link/Walter Link, D/D (500 LCR-Yamaha); 7 Rudolf Reinhard/Karin Sterzenbach, D/D (500 LCR-Yamaha); 8 Walter Eggerstorfer/Max Mayer, D/D (500 LCR-Yamaha); 9 Fritz Stölzle/Hubert Stölzle, D/D (500 LCR-Yamaha); 10 Albert Weber/Harald Schneidewind, D/D (500 LCR-Yamaha).
**Fastest lap:** Rolf Steinhausen/Bruno Hiller, D/D (Busch), 1m 33.60s, 66.92 mph/107.69 km/h.

**CIRCUIT DE CHIMAY, Belgium, 18 May. 5.903-mile/9.500-km circuit.**
**Prix Castrol et Sonnet (34 laps, 200.70 miles/323.00 km)**
1 Hans Klingebiel, D (750 Suzuki), 1h 38m 30.95s, 122.24 mph/196.72 km/h.
2 Colin Marshall, GB (750 Yamaha); 3 Tony Moran, GB (750 Yamaha); 4 Asa Moyce, GB (750 Kawasaki); 5 Alain Delhotellerie, B (750 Suzuki); 6 Michel Simul, B (500 Yamaha); 7 John Brindley, GB (750 Yamaha); 8 Kenny Blake, GB (750 Yamaha); 9 Michel Steven, B (500 Yamaha); 10 Gerhard Gutfeld, D (750 Suzuki).
**Fastest lap:** Hervé Moineau, F (750 Suzuki), 2m 46.12s, 127.93 mph/205.88 km/h.

**Prix Kronenbourg Superbike race (10 laps, 59.03 miles/95.00 km)**
1 Michel Simul, B (500 Yamaha), 29m 46.03s, 119.05 mph/191.59 km/h.
2 Johan van Vaerenbergh, B (750 Suzuki); 3 Patrick Orban, B (500 Honda); 4 Michel Steven, B (500 Yamaha); 5 Guido Verstrepen, B (750 Yamaha); 6 Antoine Bryssinck, B (500 Yamaha); 7 Paul Delcourt, B (750 Yamaha); 8 Guy Dewaele, B (750 Honda); 9 Eric Michiels, B (750 Yamaha); 10 Renaat Vincke, B (750 Suzuki).
**Fastest lap:** Steven, 2m 53.16s, 122.73 mph/197.52 km/h.

**Grand Prix Apollinaris 250 cc (12 laps, 70.84 miles/114.00 km)**
1 Michel Simeon, B (Yamaha), 35m 10.68s, 120.82 mph/194.44 km/h.
2 Andy Watts, GB (EMC); 3 André Stamsnijder, NL (Yamaha); 4 Eric de Donker, B (Honda); 5 Martyn Jupp, GB (Yamaha); 6 Laurent Naveau, B (Yamaha); 7 Peter Schleef, D (Yamaha); 8 Ton Schuurman, NL (Yamaha); 9 Jan Vanlerbergh, B (Rotax); 10 Peter Jungbauer, D (Honda).
**Fastest lap:** Simeon, 2m 53.30s, 122.63 mph/197.35 km/h.

**Prix Bata et Ricard F2 Sidecars (8 laps, 47.22 miles/76.00 km)**
1 Colin Hopper/Norman Burgess, GB/GB (350 Armstrong), 27m 34.42s, 102.76 mph/165.38 km/h.
2 Dave Saville/Dave Hall, GB/GB (350 Sabre); 3 John Coates/Gary Gibson, GB/GB (350 Yamaha); 4 Joe Heys/Ray Burns, GB/GB (350 Yamaha); 5 Andre Witherington/John Jackson, GB/GB (350 Yamaha); 6 Stan Stephens/Colin Igleston, GB/GB (350 Yamaha).
**Fastest lap:** Heys, 3m 18.73s, 106.93 mph/172.09 km/h.

**HUNGARORING, Hungary, 15 June. 2.494-mile/4.013-km circuit.**
**250 cc (20 laps, 49.88 miles/80.26 km)**
1 Wilhelm Hörhager, A (Yamaha), 45m 45.50s, 65.40 mph/105.25 km/h.
2 Neil Tuxworth, GB (Armstrong); 3 Arpád Harmati, H (Yamaha); 4 Bogdan Nikolov, BG (Yamaha); 5 Manfred Binder, A (Yamaha); 6 Anatolij Galanskij, SU (Vihur); 7 Jan Bartunek, CS (Jawa); 8 Janos Szabo, H (Yamaha); 9 Stefan Tennstädt, DDR (Sporret); 10 Laszlo Nagy, H (Yamaha).
**Fastest lap:** Not available.

**AUTODROM MOST, Czechoslovakia, 22 June. 2.577-mile/4.148-km circuit.**
**Superbikes (15 laps, 38.66 miles/62.22 km)**
1 Fritz Haussener, CH (750 Suzuki), 27m 12.02s, 85.29 mph/137.26 km/h.
2 Jörg Borck, D (908 Kawasaki); 3 Elmer Geulen, D (500 Fischer); 4 Thomas Grunwald, D (750 Suzuki); 5 Gerhard Gutfeld, D (750 Suzuki); 6 Josef Hofmann, D (750 Suzuki); 7 Franz Heller, D (750 Suzuki); 8 Martin Grein, D (750 Suzuki); 9 Arnold Teucher, D (750 Yamaha); 10 Hans-Peter Reichl, D (750 Honda).
**Fastest lap:** Not given.

**500 cc (15 laps, 38.66 miles/62.22 km)**
1 Bohumil Stasa, CS (Honda), 26m 51.65s, 86.37 mph/139.00 km/h.
2 Neil Tuxworth, GB (Yamaha); 3 Sepp Doppler, A (Honda); 4 Harry Heutmekers, NL (Suzuki); 5 Peter Smolik, A (Suzuki); 6 Stefan Slootjes, NL (Yamaha); 7 Ladislav Junek, CS (Suzuki); 8 Norbert Gunther, D (Suzuki); 9 Marien Troliga, CS (Suzuki); 10 Imrich Majoros, CS (Yamaha).
**Fastest lap:** Not given.

**250 cc (13 laps, 33.50 miles/53.92 km)**
1 Andrew Stamsnijder, NL (Honda), 24m 02.96s, 83.61 mph/134.55 km/h.
2 Arpád Harmati, H (Yamaha); 3 Neil Tuxworth, GB (Armstrong); 4 Laois Haersfai, H (Yamaha); 5 Zdravko Leljak, YU (Sever); 6 Janos Szabo, H (Yamaha); 7 Ton Schuurman, NL (Yamaha); 8 Willi Buhler, CH (Yamaha); 9 Miro Habat, YU (Yamaha); 10 Stefan Tennstädt, DDR (Sporret).
**Fastest lap:** Not given.

**125 cc (11 laps, 28.35 miles/45.63 km)**
1 Rolf Blatter, CH (MBA), 21m 03.11s, 81.44 mph/131.06 km/h.
2 Bogdan Nikolov, BG (MBA); 3 Peter Balaz, CS (MBA); 4 Werner Steege, D (Bender); 5 Karel Hanika, CS (MBA); 6 Werner Schmid, A (Rotax); 7 Heinz Pristavnik, A (MBA); 8 Uwe Heider, D (MBA); 9 Jiri Safranek, CS (MBA); 10 Robert Zwidl, A (Rotax).
**Fastest lap:** Not given.

**80 cc (9 laps, 23.19 miles/37.33 km)**
1 Janez Pintar, YU (Eberhardt), 18m 46.96s, 74.11 mph/119.26 km/h.
2 Kvetoslav Samak, CS (Huvo); 3 Otto Krmicek, CS (MOK); 4 Jan Vanecek, CS (Huvo); 5 Gunther Maussner, D (Krauser); 6 Eduard Klimek, CS (Eberhardt); 7 Zybnek Havrda, CS (Kreidler); 8 Jürgen Hofmann, DDR (Simson); 9 Reiner Czech, DDR (EGB); 10 Gerold Maissner, DDR (MN).
**Fastest lap:** Not given.

**SACHSENRING, German Democratic Republic, 13 July. 5.355-mile/8.618-km circuit.**
**250 cc twins (11 laps, 58.91 miles/94.80 km)**
1 Arpád Harmati, H (Yamaha), 33m 33.7s, 105.30 mph/169.47 km/h.
2 Janos Szabo, H (Yamaha); 3 Johannes Kehrer, DDR (EGB); 4 Laszlo Nagy, H (Yamaha); 5 Jose Lazo, C (Yamaha); 6 Marian Srna, CS (Yamaha); 7 Jan Bartunek, CS (Jawa); 8 Andreas Brandt, DDR (EGB); 9 Thomas Wittig, DDR (EGB); 10 Ladislav Majores, CS (Yamaha).
**Fastest lap:** Kehrer, 3m 00.3s, 106.92 mph/172.07 km/h.

**250 cc singles (8 laps, 42.84 miles/68.94 km)**
1 Jose Lazo, C (MZ), 27m 55.2s, 92.06 mph/148.16 km/h.
2 Niro Rivero, C (MZ); 3 Günter Hossell, DDR (MZ); 4 Jesus la Rosa, C (MZ); 5 Eduardo Cencano, C (MZ); 6 Karel Chaloupka, CS (Jawa); 7 Lutz Brandenburger, DDR (MZ); 8 Gert Brandenburger, DDR, (MZ); 9 Andreas Weiske, DDR (MZ); 10 Pavel Nechanicky, CS (CZ).
**Fastest lap:** Lazo, 3m 24.7s, 94.18 mph/151.56 km/h.

**125 cc (10 laps, 53.55 miles/86.18 km)**
1 Roland Rentzsch, DDR (Rentzsch), 33m 18.9s, 96.44 mph/155.21 km/h.
2 Attila Csosz, H (MBA); 3 Frank Rein, DDR (EGB); 4 Ladislav Polak, CS (MBA); 5 Zbynek Havrda, CS (MBH); 6 Jiri Safranek, CS (MBA); 7 Karel Hanika, CS (MBA); 8 Zdenak Zidlik, CS (MBZ); 9 Andreas Neudert, DDR (EGB); 10 Jürgen Hofmann, DDR (EGB).
**Fastest lap:** Rentzsch, 3m 15.0s, 98.86 mph/159.10 km/h.

**OKRUH ZAVODU, Hradec Czechoslovakia, 19/20 July. 2.858-miles/4.600-km circuit.**
**1000 cc (12 laps, 34.30 miles/55.20 km)**
1 Jürgen Müller, D (750 Suzuki), 21m 11.76s, 97.10 mph/156.26 km/h.
2 Jörg Borck, D (998 Kawasaki); 3 Ernst Riepel, D (900 BMW); 4 Hans Wallnsdorfer, A (750 Suzuki); 5 Günter Heil, D (998 Kawasaki); 6 Franz Heller, D (750 Suzuki); 7 Günter Norbert, (750 Suzuki); 8 Martin Grein, D (750 Suzuki); 9 Gyvla Porkolab, H (750 Yamaha); 10 Andreas Bertel, A (750 Suzuki).
**Fastest lap:** Müller, 1m 44.17s, 98.78 mph/158.97 km/h.

**500 cc (12 laps, 34.30 miles/55.20 km)**
1 Ari Rämö, SF (Suzuki), 20m 51.50s, 98.67 mph/158.79 km/h.
2 Imrich Majoros, CS (Yamaha); 3 Jack Dekkers, NL (Suzuki); 4 Rudolf Zeller, A (Suzuki); 5 Milan Pecen, CS (Yamaha); 6 Ladislav Junek, CS (Suzuki); 7 Dietmar Marehard, D (Suzuki); 8 Hans-Peter Reichl, D (Suzuki); 9 Peter Smolik, A (Suzuki); 10 Rudolf Mitosinka, CS (Yamaha).
**Fastest lap:** Rämö, 1m 41.96s, 100.92 mph/162.42 km/h (record).

**250 cc (10 laps, 28.58 miles/46.00 km)**
1 Detlef Karthin, D (Yamaha), 18m 25.21s, 93.11 mph/149.84 km/h.
2 Heinz Simentke, D (Siku); 3 Karl-Heinz Reigl, A (Yamaha); 4 Marian Srna, CS (Yamaha); 5 Jan Bartunek, CS (Jawa); 6 Rudolf Mitosinka, CS (Yamaha); 7 Pavel Sevcik, CS (Yamaha); 8 Stefan Bernard, D (Yamaha); 9 Ladislav Junek, CS (Yamaha); 10 Peter Chábera, CS (Yamaha).
**Fastest lap:** Karthin, 1m 49.17s, 94.26 mph/151.69 km/h.

**125 cc (9 laps, 25.72 miles/41.40 km)**
**1** Bogdan Nikolov, BG (MBA), 17m 52.38s, 86.34 mph/138.95 km/h.
**2** Werner Steege, D (Bender); **3** Zbynek Havrda, CS (MBA); **4** Karel Hanika, CS (Juventa); **5** Jiri Safranek, CS (MBA); **6** Heinz Pristavnik, A (MBA); **7** Dusan Petr, CS (MBA); **8** Alexander Eschig, A (MBA); **9** Jan Dobias, CS (Rotax); **10** Ladislav Polak, CS (MBA).
**Fastest lap:** Nikolov, 1m 56.18s, 88.57 mph/142.54 km/h.

**80 cc (7 laps, 20.01 miles/32.20 km)**
**1** René Dünki, CH (Krauser), 14m 53.06s, 80.65 mph/129.80 km/h.
**2** Karoly Juhasz, H (Huvo); **3** Jan Vanecek, CS (HH); **4** Günter Maussner, D (Krauser); **5** Kvetoslav Samak, CS (Juventa); **6** Otto Krmicek, CS (MOK); **7** Ladislav Solc, CS (Kreidler); **8** Karel Rathousky, CS (AHRA); **9** Miroslav Sedlák, CS (Kreidler), **10** Kurt Lidner, CS (Yamaha).
**Fastest lap:** Dünki, 2m 03.53s, 83.30 mph/134.06 km/h.

**PRIX OF SLOVAKIA, PIESTANY, Czechoslovakia, 16/17 August. 2.734-mile/4.400-km circuit.**
**500 cc (15 laps, 41.01 miles/66.00 km)**
**1** Pavel Dekánek, CS (Suzuki), 26m 40.47s, 92.25 mph/148.46 km/h.
**2** Sepp Doppler, A (Honda); **3** Hans Klingebiel, D (Suzuki); **4** Rüdi Gachter, CH (Yamaha); **5** Marco Biegert, D (Suzuki); **6** Fredy Gangelberger, A (Yamaha); **7** Helmut Schuster, A (Suzuki); **8** Karl Wolleitner, A (Yamaha); **9** Erich Kober, D (Yamaha); **10** Peter Smolik, A (Suzuki).
**Fastest lap:** Not available.

**250 cc (13 laps, 35.54 miles/57.20 km)**
**1** Siegfried Minich, A (Honda), 22m 54.93s, 93.05 mph/149.75 km/h.
**2** Andreas Preining, A (Rotax); **3** Arpád Harmati, H (Yamaha); **4** Zdravko Leljak, YU (Yamaha); **5** Rüdi Gachter, CH (Yamaha); **6** Fredy Gangelberger, A (Yamaha); **7** Karoly Juhász, H (Yamaha); **8** Dario Marchetti, I (Yamaha); **9** Engelbert Neumair, A (Rotax); **10** Jan Bartunek, CS (Jawa).
**Fastest lap:** Not available.

**125 cc (11 laps, 30.07 miles/48.40 km)**
**1** Pier Paolo Bianchi, I (Elit), 21m 03.95s, 85.65 mph/137.84 km/h.
**2** Peter Baláz, CS (MBA); **3** Bogdan Nikolov, BG (MBA); **4** Janez Pintar, YU (MBA); **5** Werner Steege, D (MBA); **6** Karl Bubenicek, A (MBA); **7** Karel Hanika, CS (Juventa); **8** Shaun Simpson, GB (MBA); **9** Heinz Pristavnik, A (MBA); **10** Jiri Safranek, CS (MBA).
**Fastest lap:** Not available.

**HOCKENHEIMRING, German Federal Republic, 30/31 August. 4.2183-mile/6.7886-km circuit.**
**350 cc (8 laps, 33.75 miles/54.31 km)**
**1** Marco Biegert, D (Bartol), 19m 25.59s, 104.23 mph/167.74 km/h.
**2** Michael Simunic, D (Yamaha); **3** Roland Pörzgen, D (Yamaha); **4** Ulli Gläser, D (Yamaha); **5** Herbert Besendörfer, D (Yamaha); **6** Bernd Roth, D (Yamaha); **7** Georg Willmann, D (Yamaha); **8** Jörg Pfaff, D (Rotax); **9** Walter Seufert, D (Yamaha); **10** Heinrich Kunzer, D (Yamaha).
**Fastest lap:** Besendörfer, 2m 19.01s, 109.24 mph/175.81 km/h.

**250 cc (8 laps, 33.75 miles/54.31 km)**
**1** Anton Mang, D (Honda), 18m 27.06s, 109.73 mph/176.60 km/h.
**2** Reinhold Roth, D (Honda); **3** Harald Eckl, D (Honda); **4** Frank Wagner, D (Honda); **5** Helmut Bradl, D (Honda); **6** Herbert Hauf, D (Honda); **7** Hermann Holder, D (Yamaha); **8** Hans Becker, D (Yamaha); **9** Herbert Besendörfer, D (Yamaha); **10** Martin Fueg, D (Wiwa).
**Fastest lap:** Mang, 2m 16.30s, 111.41 mph/179.30 km/h.

**125 cc (8 laps, 33.75 miles/54.31 km)**
**1** Adolf Stadler, D (MBA), 20m 14.87s, 100.00 mph/160.93 km/h.
**2** Norbert Peschke, D (MBA); **3** Dirk Hafeneger, D (LCR); **4** Stefan Prein, D (MBA); **5** Heinz Litz, D (MBA); **6** Ernst Himmelsbach, D (Ziegler); **7** Wilhelm Lücke, D (MBA); **8** Erich Zürn, D (Seel); **9** Lothar Zürn, D (MBA); **10** Jean-Dany Leuba, D (MBA).
**Fastest lap:** Stadler, 2m 30.32s, 101.02 mph/162.58 km/h.

**PAUL RICARD CIRCUIT, France, 20/21 September. 3.610-mile/5.810-km circuit.**
**Bol d'Or (640 laps, 2310.40 miles/3718.40 km)**
**1** Dominique Sarron/Pierre Bolle/Jean-Louis Battistini, F/F/F (750 Honda), 97.92 mph/157.59 km/h.
**2** Christian Sarron/Jacques Cornu/Richard Hubin, F/CH/B (750 Yamaha), 638 laps; **3** Eric Delcamp/Jean Monin/Eric Sabatier, F/F/F/ (750 Suzuki), 623; **4** Guy Bertin/Roger Sibille/Christian Berthod, F/F/F (750 Honda), 623; **5** Christian le Liard/Thierry Espié/Hervé Guilleux, F/F/F (750 Suzuki), 620; **6** Hervé Moineau/Bruno le Bihan/Jean-Pierre Oudin, F/F/F (750 Suzuki), 619; **7** Davide Tardozzi/Mario Rubatto/F. Pirovanno, I/D/I (750 Yamaha), 604; **8** Gérard Jolivet/Georges Furling/Michel Simeon, F/F/B (750 Suzuki), 602; **9** M. Graziano/F. Battistini/Gabriel Grabia, I/F/F (750 Suzuki), 601; **10** Jacky Guyon/Bernard Chateau/Pascal Dejonghe, F/F/F (750 Honda), 600.
**Fastest lap:** Sarron (Christian), 2m 04.1s, 104.72 mph/168.53 km/h.

# World TT F1/F2 Championship

**AUTODROMO SANTAMONICA, MISANO, Italy, 6 April. 2.167-mile/3.488-km circuit.**
**TT F1, round 1 (75 laps, 162.53 miles/261.60 km)**
**1** Marco Lucchinelli, I (750 Ducati), 1h 48m 11.85s, 90.14 mph/145.07 km/h.
**2** Anders Andersson, S (750 Suzuki); **3** Rob Phillis, AUS (750 Suzuki); **4** Henrik Ottoesen, DK (750 Yamaha); **5** Walter Cussigh, I (750 Ducati); **6** Mario Rubatto, D (750 Suzuki); **7** Patrick Orban, B (750 Kawasaki); **8** Peter Rubatto, D (750 Suzuki); **9** Tony Moran, GB (750 Yamaha); **10** Christian Monsch, CH (750 Honda).
**Fastest lap:** Joey Dunlop, GB (750 Honda), 1m 24.3s, 92.56 mph/148.96 km/h.
**Championship points: 1** Lucchinelli, 15; **2** Andersson, 12; **3** Phillips, 10; **4** Ottoesen, 8; **5** Cussigh, 6; **6** Rubatto, 5.

**MOTODROM HOCKENHEIM, German Federal Republic, 4 May. 4.218-mile/6.789-km circuit.**
**TT F1, round 2 (23 laps, 97.01 miles/156.15 km)**
**1** Joey Dunlop, GB (750 Honda), 52m 38.50s, 110.58 mph/177.96 km/h.
**2** Paul Iddon, GB (750 Suzuki); **3** Anders Andersson, S (750 Suzuki); **4** Kenny Irons, GB (750 Yamaha); **5** Mario Rubatto, D (750 Suzuki); **6** Christian Monsch, CH (750 Honda); **7** John Weeden, GB (500 Suzuki); **8** Bernd Caspers, D (750 Suzuki); **9** Bodo Schmidt, D (750 Yamaha); **10** Michael Galinski, D (750 Yamaha).
**Fastest lap:** Dunlop, 2m 14.09s, 113.25 mph/182.26 km/h.
**Championship points: 1** Andersson, 22; **2** Lucchinelli and Dunlop, 15; **4** Iddon, 12; **5** Rubatto (Mario), 11; **6** Phillis, 10.

**ISLE OF MAN TT CIRCUIT, Great Britain, 31 May/6 June. 37.73-mile/60.72-km circuit.**
**TT F1, round 3 (4 laps, 150.92 miles/242.88 km)**
**1** Joey Dunlop, GB (750 Honda), 2h 20m 09.4s, 112.96 mph/181.79 km/h.
**2** Geoff Johnson, GB (750 Honda); **3** Andy McGladdery, GB (750 Suzuki); **4** John Weeden, GB (500 Suzuki); **5** Phil Mellor, GB (750 Suzuki); **6** Trevor Nation, GB (750 Suzuki); **7** Graeme McGregor, AUS (750 Suzuki); **8** Gary Padgett, GB (500 Suzuki); **9** Glen Williams, NZ (750 Suzuki); **10** Klaus Klein, D (750 Suzuki).
**Fastest lap:** Dunlop, 19m 51.6s, 113.98 mph/183.43 km/h.
**Championship points: 1** Dunlop, 30; **2** Andersson, 22; **3** Lucchinelli, 15; **4** Iddon, Weeden and Johnson, 12.

**TT F2, round 1 (4 laps, 150.92 miles/242.88 km)**
**1** Brian Reid, GB (350 Yamaha), 1h 22m 31.4s, 109.72 mph/176.58 km/h.
**2** John Weeden, GB (350 Yamaha); **3** Neil Tuxworth, GB (350 Yamaha); **4** Ray Swann, GB (600 Kawasaki); **5** Eddie Laycock, IRL (350 Yamaha); **6** Steve Hislop, GB (350 Yamaha); **7** Chris Faulkner, GB (350 Yamaha); **8** Bob Heath, GB (350 Yamaha); **9** Des Barry, NZ (350 Yamaha); **10** Steve Williams, GB (350 Yamaha).
**Fastest lap:** Reid, 20m 15.4s, 111.75 mph/179.84 km/h (record).
**Championship points: 1** Reid, 15; **2** Weeden, 12; **3** Tuxworth, 10; **4** Swann, 8; **5** Laycock, 6; **6** Hislop, 5.

**CIRCUIT VAN DRENTHE, ASSEN, Holland, 23/28 June. 3.812-mile/6.134-km circuit.**
**TT F1, round 4 (25 laps, 95.30 miles/153.35 km)**
**1** Joey Dunlop, GB (750 Honda), 59m 39.17s, 95.84 mph/154.24 km/h.
**2** Kevin Schwantz, USA (500 Suzuki); **3** Paul Iddon, GB (750 Suzuki); **4** Kenny Irons, GB (750 Yamaha); **5** Anders Andersson, S (750 Suzuki); **6** Ernst Gschwender, D (750 Suzuki); **7** Marco Lucchinelli, I (750 Ducati); **8** Klaus Klein, D (750 Suzuki); **9** Trevor Nation, GB (750 Suzuki); **10** Jari Suhonen, SF (750 Yamaha).
**Fastest lap:** Neil Robinson, GB (750 Suzuki), 2m 19.83s, 98.14 mph/157.94 km/h (record).
**Championship points: 1** Dunlop, 45; **2** Andersson, 28; **3** Iddon, 22; **4** Lucchinelli, 19; **5** Irons, 16; **6** Weeden, Johnson and Schwantz, 12.

**CIRCUITO DEL JEREZ, Spain. 13 July. 2.621-mile/4.218-km circuit.**
**TT F1, round 5 (36 laps, 94.36 miles/151.85 km)**
**1** Paul Iddon, GB (750 Suzuki), 1h 11m 35.67s, 79.07 mph/127.26 km/h.
**2** Graeme McGregor, AUS (750 Ducati); **3** Neil Robinson, GB (750 Suzuki); **4** Anders Andersson, S (750 Suzuki); **5** Joey Dunlop, GB (750 Honda); **6** Jorge Cavestany, E (750 Yamaha); **7** Martin Decker, CH (750 Yamaha); **8** Patrick Loser, CH (750 Honda); **9** Andy McGladdery, GB (750 Suzuki); **10** Peter Rubatto, D (750 Suzuki).
**Fastest lap:** Not given.
**Championship points: 1** Dunlop, 51; **2** Iddon, 37; **3** Andersson, 36; **4** Lucchinelli, 19; **5** Irons and McGregor, 16.

**TT F2, round 2 (30 laps, 78.63 miles/126.54 km)**
**1** Graeme McGregor, AUS (600 Ducati), 47m 57.21s, 98.38 mph/158.33 km/h.
**2** Jorge Cavestany, E (350 Yamaha); **3** Des Barry, NZ (350 Yamaha); **4** Mark Westmorland, GB (350 Yamaha); **5** Tony Head, GB (350 Yamaha); **6** Eddie Laycock, IRL (350 Yamaha); **7** Brian Reid, GB (350 Yamaha); **8** Richard Peers-Jones, GB (350 Yamaha); **9** Tony Moran, GB (600 Ducati); **10** Andres Fernandez, E (350 Yamaha).
**Fastest lap:** Not given.
**Championship points: 1** Reid, 19; **2** McGregor, 15; **3** Weeden, Barry and Cavestany, 12; **6** Laycock, 11.

**VILA REAL, Portugal, 20 July, 4.36-mile/7.02-km circuit.**
**TT F1, round 6 (25 laps, 109.00 miles/175.50 km)**
**1** Joey Dunlop, GB (750 Honda), 1h 09m 33.25s, 94.03 mph/151.33 km/h.
**2** Paul Iddon, GB (750 Suzuki); **3** Anders Andersson, S (750 Suzuki); **4** Patrick Bettendorf, LUX (750 Suzuki); **5** Neil Robinson, GB (750 Suzuki); **6** Glen Williams, NZ (750 Suzuki); **7** Christian Vannieuwenhuyse, LUX (750 Suzuki); **8** Graeme McGregor, AUS (750 Ducati); **9** Franz Kaserer, A (500 Suzuki); **10** Eric Bragard, B (750 Suzuki).
**Fastest lap:** Dunlop, 2m 42.34s, 96.69 mph/155.61 km/h (record).
**Championship points: 1** Dunlop, 66; **2** Iddon, 49; **3** Andersson, 46; **4** Lucchinelli and McGregor, 19; **6** Irons and Robinson, 16.

**IMATRA ROAD CIRCUIT, Finland, 3 August. 3.076-mile/4.950-km circuit.**
**TT F1, round 7 (31 laps, 95.36 miles/153.45 km)**
**1** Joey Dunlop, GB (750 Honda), 1h 01m 12.10s, 93.49 mph/150.46 km/h.
**2** Paul Iddon, GB (750 Suzuki); **3** Neil Robinson, GB (750 Suzuki); **4** Anders Andersson, S (750 Suzuki); **5** Jari Suhonen, SF (750 Yamaha); **6** Michael Galinski, D (750 Yamaha); **7** Andy McGladdery, GB (750 Suzuki); **8** Patrick Bettendorf, LUX (750 Suzuki); **9** Peter Linden, S (750 Honda); **10** Bo Granath, S (750 Yamaha).
**Fastest lap:** Dunlop, 1m 55.83s, 95.60 mph/153.85 km/h.
**Championship points: 1** Dunlop, 81; **2** Iddon, 61; **3** Andersson, 54; **4** Robinson, 26; **5** Lucchinelli and McGregor, 19.

**DUNDROD CIRCUIT, Northern Ireland, 16 August. 7.401-mile/11.911-km circuit.**
**TT F1, round 8 (13 laps, 96.21 miles/154.84 km)**
**1** Neil Robinson, GB (750 Suzuki), 52m 16.9s, 110.42 mph/177.70 km/h.
**2** Joey Dunlop, GB (750 Honda); **3** Andy McGladdery, GB (750 Suzuki); **4** Phil Mellor, GB (750 Suzuki); **5** Sam McClements, GB (750 Suzuki); **6** Patrick Bettendorf, LUX (750 Suzuki); **7** Anders Andersson, S (750 Suzuki); **8** Graeme McGregor, AUS (750 Ducati); **9** Dave Griffith, GB (750 Suzuki); **10** Steve Linsdell, GB (750 Yamaha).
**Fastest lap:** Robinson, 3m 57.9s, 111.99 mph/180.23 km/h.

**Final TT F1 Championship points**

| | | |
|---|---|---|
| **1** | Joey Dunlop, GB | 93 |
| **2** | Paul Iddon, GB | 61 |
| **3** | Anders Andersson, S | 58 |
| **4** | Neil Robinson, GB | 41 |
| **5** | Andy McGladdery, GB | 26 |
| **6** | Graeme McGregor, AUS | 22 |

**7** Marco Lucchinelli, I, 19; **8** Kenny Irons, GB and Patrick Bettendorf, LUX, 16; **10** Phil Mellor, GB, 14; **11** John Weeden, GB, Geoff Johnson, GB and Kevin Schwantz, USA, 12; **14** Mario Rubatto, D, 11; **15** Rob Phillis, AUS, 10.

**TT F2, round 3 (11 laps, 81.41 miles/131.02 km)**
**1** Eddie Laycock, IRL (350 Yamaha), 46m 24.2s, 105.27 mph/169.42 km/h.
**2** Brian Reid, IRL (350 Yamaha); **3** Steve Hislop, GB (350 Yamaha); **4** Tony Moran, GB (600 Ducati); **5** Ian Lougher, GB (350 Yamaha); **6** John Weeden, GB (350 Yamaha); **7** Steve Williams, GB (350 Yamaha); **8** Graeme McGregor, AUS (600 Ducati); **9** Marc Carter, IRL (350 Yamaha); **10** Robert Dunlop, GB (350 Yamaha).
**Fastest lap:** Laycock, 4m 08.6s, 107.18 mph/172.49 km/h.

**Final TT F2 Championship points**

| | | |
|---|---|---|
| **1** | Brian Reid, IRL | 31 |
| **2** | Eddie Laycock, IRL | 26 |
| **3** | Graeme McGregor, AUS | 18 |
| **4** | John Weeden, GB | 17 |
| **5** | Steve Hislop, GB | 15 |
| **6=** | Des Barry, NZ | 12 |
| **6=** | Jorge Cavestany, E | 12 |

**8** Neil Tuxworth, GB and Tony Moran, GB, 10; **10** Mark Westmorland, GB and Ray Swann, GB, 8; **12** Tony Head, GB and Ian Lougher, GB, 6; **14** Steve Williams, GB, 5; **15** Chris Faulkner, GB, 4.

# ACU British TT F1 Championship

**THRUXTON CIRCUIT, 13 April. 2.356-mile/3.792-km circuit.**
**ACU British TT F1 Championship, round 1 (12 laps, 28.27 miles/45.50 km)**
**1** Ray Swann, GB (750 Suzuki), 18m 59.9s, 89.28 mph/143.67 km/h.
**2** Trevor Nation, GB (750 Suzuki); **3** Martin Taylor, GB (750 Suzuki); **4** Steve Bonhomme, GB (750 Suzuki); **5** Mark Phillips, GB (500 Suzuki); **6** Andy Green, GB (750 Suzuki); **7** Keith Huewen, GB (750 Suzuki); **8** Richard Scott, NZ (750 Honda); **9** Ian Redley, GB (750 Yamaha); **10** Phil Mellor, GB (750 Suzuki).
**Fastest lap:** Swann, 1m 32.8s, 91.39 mph/147.05 km/h.
**Championship points: 1** Swann, 15; **2** Nation, 12; **3** Taylor, 10; **4** Bonhomme, 8; **5** Phillips, 6; **6** Green, 5.

**MALLORY PARK CIRCUIT, 20 April. 1.370-mile/2.205-km circuit.**
**ACU British TT F1 Championship, round 2 (15 laps, 20.55 miles/33.08 km)**
**1** Mark Phillips, GB (500 Suzuki), 13m 28.8s, 91.47 mph/147.21 km/h.
**2** Paul Iddon, GB (750 Suzuki); **3** Kenny Irons, GB (750 Yamaha); **4** Trevor Nation, GB (750 Suzuki); **5** Keith Huewen, GB (750 Suzuki); **6** Steve Parrish, GB (750 Yamaha); **7** Neil Robinson, GB (750 Suzuki); **8** Phil Mellor, GB (750 Suzuki); **9** Richard Scott, NZ (750 Honda); **10** Steve Williams, GB (750 Yamaha).
**Fastest lap:** Phillips, 52.7s, 93.58 mph/150.60 km/h.
**Championship points: 1** Phillips, 21; **2** Nation, 20; **3** Swann, 15; **4** Iddon, 12; **5** Taylor, Huewen and Irons, 10.

**DONINGTON PARK CIRCUIT, 22 June. 2.500-mile/4.023-km circuit.**
**ACU British TT F1 Championship, round 3 (8 laps, 20.00 miles/32.18 km)**
**1** Kenny Irons, GB (750 Yamaha), 14m 17.8s, 83.93 mph/135.07 km/h.
**2** Steve Parrish, GB (750 Yamaha); **3** Trevor Nation, GB (750 Suzuki); **4** Neil Robinson, GB (750 Suzuki); **5** Richard Scott, NZ (750 Honda); **6** Keith Huewen, GB (750 Suzuki); **7** Andy McGladdery, GB (750 Suzuki); **8** Ray Swann, GB (750 Suzuki); **9** Des Barry, NZ (750 Suzuki); **10** Martin Taylor, GB (750 Suzuki).
**Fastest lap:** Irons, 1m 45.6s, 85.22 mph/137.15 km/h (record).
**Championship points: 1** Nation, 30; **2** Irons, 25; **3** Phillips, 21; **4** Swann, 18; **5** Parrish, 17; **6** Huewen, 15.

**OLIVER'S MOUNT CIRCUIT, 14 September. 2.4136-mile/3.8843-km circuit.**
**ACU British TT F1 Championship, round 4 (10 laps, 24.14 miles/38.83 km)**
**1** Andy McGladdery, GB (750 Suzuki), 18m 04.6s, 80.11 mph/128.92 km/h.
**2** Keith Huewen, GB (750 Suzuki); **3** Phil Mellor, GB (750 Suzuki); **4** Mark Phillips, GB (500 Suzuki); **5** Trevor Nation, GB (750 Suzuki); **6** Steve Parrish, GB (750 Yamaha); **7** Glen Williams, NZ (750 Suzuki); **8** Ian Bell, GB (750 Yamaha); **9** Steve Linsdell, GB (750 Yamaha); **10** Michael Seward, GB (750 Yamaha).
**Fastest lap:** Kenny Irons, GB (750 Yamaha), 1m 46.8s, 81.36 mph/130.94 km/h (record).
**Championship points: 1** Nation, 36; **2** Phillips, 29; **3** Huewen, 27; **4** Irons, 25; **5** Parrish, 22; **6** McGladdery, 19.

**SILVERSTONE GRAND PRIX CIRCUIT, 21 September. 2.927-mile/4.711-km circuit.**
**ACU British TT F1 Championship, round 5 (7 laps, 20.49 miles/32.98 km)**
**1** Paul Iddon, GB (750 Suzuki), 10m 57.60s, 112.16 mph/180.50 km/h.
**2** Richard Scott, NZ (750 Honda); **3** Steve Parrish, GB (750 Yamaha); **4** Kenny Irons, GB (750 Yamaha); **5** Andy McGladdery, GB (750 Suzuki); **6** Mark Phillips, GB (500 Suzuki); **7** Keith Huewen, GB (750 Suzuki); **8** Ray Swann, GB (750 Suzuki); **9** Steve Williams, GB (750 Yamaha); **10** Gary Lingham, GB (750 Suzuki).
**Fastest lap:** Iddon, 1m 32.80s, 113.54 mph/182.72 km/h.
**Championship points: 1** Nation, 36; **2** Phillips, 34; **3** Irons, 33; **4** Parrish, 32; **5** Huewen, 31; **6** Iddon, 27.

**CADWELL PARK CIRCUIT, 5 October. 2.250-mile/3.621-km circuit.**
**ACU British TT F1 Championship, round 6 (10 laps, 22.50 miles/36.21 km)**
**1** Mark Phillips, GB (500 Suzuki), 16m 24.8s, 82.25 mph/132.37 km/h.
**2** Kenny Irons, GB (750 Yamaha); **3** Paul Iddon, GB (750 Suzuki); **4** Richard Scott, NZ (750 Honda); **5** Steve Parrish, GB (750 Yamaha); **6** Trevor Nation, GB (750 Suzuki); **7** Keith Huewen, GB (750 Suzuki); **8** Ray Swann, GB (750 Suzuki); **9** Geoff Fowler, GB (750 Suzuki); **10** Steve Williams, GB (750 Yamaha).
**Fastest lap:** Phillips, 1m 36.6s, 83.85 mph/134.94 km/h.

**Final Championship points**

| | | |
|---|---|---|
| **1** | Mark Phillips, GB | 49 |
| **2** | Kenny Irons, GB | 45 |
| **3** | Trevor Nation, GB | 41 |
| **4** | Steve Parrish, GB | 38 |
| **5** | Paul Iddon, GB | 37 |
| **6** | Keith Huewen, GB | 35 |

**7** Richard Scott, NZ, 31; **8** Andy McGladdery, GB, 25; **9** Ray Swann, GB, 24; **10** Phil Mellor, GB, 14; **11** Neil Robinson, GB, 12; **12** Martin Taylor, GB, 11; **13** Steve Bonhomme, GB, 8; **14** Andy Green, GB, 5; **15** Steve Williams, GB and Glen Williams, NZ, 4.

# ACU British TT F2 Championship

**THRUXTON CIRCUIT, 13 April, 2.356-mile/3.792-km circuit.**
**ACU British TT F2 Championship, round 1 (12 laps, 28.27 miles/45.50 km)**
**1** Ray Swann, GB (600 Kawasaki), 18m 36.8s, 91.13 mph/146.64 km/h.
**2** Neil Tuxworth, GB (350 Yamaha); **3** Ian Lougher, GB (350 Yamaha); **4** Steve Williams, GB (350 Yamaha); **5** Ian Newton, GB (350 Yamaha); **6** Ian Burnett, GB (350 Yamaha); **7** Tony Head, GB (350 Yamaha); **8** Adrian Jupp, GB (350 Yamaha); **9** Mark Edge, GB (350 Yamaha); **10** Gary Dickinson, GB (350 Yamaha).
**Fastest lap:** Tuxworth, 1m 31.5s, 92.69 mph/149.14 km/h.
**Championship points: 1** Swann, 15; **2** Tuxworth, 12; **3** Lougher, 10; **4** Williams, 8; **5** Newton, 6; **6** Burnett, 5.

**MALLORY PARK CIRCUIT. 19 April. 1.370-mile/2.205-km circuit.**
**ACU British TT F2 Championship, round 2 (15 laps, 20.55 miles/33.08 km)**
**1** Ian Newton, GB (350 Yamaha), 13m 40.6s, 90.15 mph/145.08 km/h.
**2** Carl Fogarty, GB (350 Yamaha); **3** Tony Head, GB (350 Yamaha); **4** Neil Tuxworth, GB (350 Yamaha); **5** Ray Swann, GB (600 Kawasaki); **6** Mark Westmorland, GB (350 Yamaha); **7** Ian Burnett, GB (350 Yamaha); **8** Steve Williams, GB (350 Yamaha); **9** Steve Hislop, GB (350 Yamaha); **10** Ian Lougher, GB (350 Yamaha).
**Fastest lap:** Newton and Fogarty, 53.6s, 92.01 mph/148.08 km/h.
**Championship points: 1** Swann and Newton, 21; **3** Tuxworth, 20; **4** Head, 14; **5** Fogarty, 12; **6** Lougher and Williams, 11.

**DONINGTON PARK CIRCUIT, 22 June. 2.500-mile/4.023-km circuit.**
**ACU British TT F2 Championship, round 3 (8 laps, 20.00 miles/32.18 km)**
**1** Carl Fogarty, GB (350 Yamaha), 14m 43.7s, 81.47 mph/131.11 km/h.
**2** Ray Swann, GB (600 Kawasaki); **3** Tony Head, GB (350 Yamaha); **4** Des Barry, NZ (350 Yamaha); **5** Steve Hislop, GB (350 Yamaha); **6** Ian Newton, GB (350 Yamaha); **7** Ian Burnett, GB (350 Yamaha); **8** Steve Williams, GB (350 Yamaha); **9** Mark Edge, GB (350 Yamaha); **10** Phil Usher, GB (350 Yamaha).
**Fastest lap:** Fogarty, 1m 48.1s, 83.25 mph/133.98 km/h (record).
**Championship points: 1** Swann, 33; **2** Fogarty, 27; **3** Newton, 26; **4** Head, 24; **5** Tuxworth, 20; **6** Williams, 14.

**OLIVER'S MOUNT CIRCUIT, 13 September. 2.4136-mile/3.8843-km circuit.**
**ACU British TT F2 Championship, round 4 (8 laps, 19.31 miles/31.07 km)**
**1** Steve Hislop, GB (350 Yamaha), 15m 10.2s, 76.37 mph/122.91 km/h.
**2** Graeme McGregor, AUS (600 Bimota); **3** Tony Head, GB (350 Yamaha); **4** Ray Swann, GB (600 Kawasaki); **5** Steve Henshaw, GB (350 Yamaha); **6** Ian Newton, GB (350 Yamaha); **7** Ian Lougher, GB (350 Yamaha); **8** Hugh Robertson, GB (350 Yamaha); **9** Eric McFarlane, GB (350 Yamaha); **10** Gary Dickinson, GB (350 Yamaha).
**Fastest lap:** Hislop and McGregor, 1m 52.2s, 77.49 mph/124.71 km/h.
**Championship points: 1** Swann, 41; **2** Head, 34; **3** Newton, 31; **4** Fogarty, 27; **5** Hislop, 23; **6** Tuxworth, 20.

**SILVERSTONE GRAND PRIX CIRCUIT, 21 September. 2.4136-mile/4.711-km circuit.**
**ACU British TT F2 Championship, round 5 (7 laps, 20.49 miles/32.98 km)**
**1** Steve Hislop, GB (350 Yamaha), 11m 32.30s, 106.54 mph/171.46 km/h.
**2** Ray Swann, GB (600 Kawasaki); **3** Tony Head, GB (350 Yamaha); **4** Ian Newton, GB (350 Yamaha); **5** Des Barry, NZ (350 Yamaha); **6** Eric McFarlane, GB (350 Yamaha); **7** Steve Williams, GB (350 Yamaha); **8** Chris Lake, GB (350 Yamaha); **9** Barry Stanley, GB (350 Yamaha); **10** Rob Talton, GB (350 Yamaha).
**Fastest lap:** Williams, 1m 37.10s, 108.51 mph/174.63 km/h.
**Championship points: 1** Swann, 53; **2** Head, 44; **3** Newton, 39; **4** Hislop, 38; **5** Fogarty, 27; **6** Tuxworth, 20.

**CADWELL PARK CIRCUIT, 5 October. 2.250-mile/3.621-km circuit.**
**ACU British TT F2 Championship, round 6 (10 laps, 22.50 miles/36.21 km)**
**1** Steve Hislop, GB (350 Yamaha), 16m 53.8s, 79.89 mph/128.57 km/h.
**2** Ray Swann, GB (600 Kawasaki); **3** Des Barry, NZ (350 Yamaha); **4** Eric McFarlane, GB (350 Yamaha); **5** Ian Lougher, GB (350 Yamaha); **6** Mark Edge, GB (350 Yamaha); **7** Steve Williams, GB (350 Yamaha); **8** Rob Talton, GB (350 Yamaha); **9** Barry Stanley, GB (350 Yamaha); **10** Mark Ward, GB (600 Ducati).
**Fastest lap:** Hislop, 1m 40.1s, 80.91 mph/130.21 km/h.
**Championship points: 1** Swann, 65; **2** Hislop, 53; **3** Head, 44; **4** Newton, 39; **5** Fogarty, 27; **6** Williams, 22.

**DARLEY MOOR CIRCUIT, 12 October. 1.500-mile/2.414-km circuit.**
**ACU British TT F2 Championship, round 7 (12 laps, 18.00 miles/28.97 km)**
**1** Ray Swann, GB (600 Kawasaki), 13m 01.7s, 82.89 mph/133.40 km/h.
**2** Tony Head, GB (350 Yamaha); **3** Steve Williams, GB (350 Yamaha); **4** Mark Ward, GB (600 Ducati); **5** Tony Moran, GB (600 Ducati); **6** Gary Dickinson, GB (350 Yamaha); **7** Kevin Mawdsley, GB (600 Honda); **8** Richard Peers-Jones, GB (350 Yamaha); **9** S. Richardson, GB (350 Yamaha); **10** Ian Dugdale, GB (350 Yamaha).
**Fastest lap:** Not available.

**Final Championship points**

| | |
|---|---|
| **1** Ray Swann, GB | 80 |
| **2** Tony Head, GB | 56 |
| **3** Steve Hislop, GB | 53 |
| **4** Ian Newton, GB | 39 |
| **5** Steve Williams, GB | 32 |
| **6** Carl Fogarty, GB | 27 |

**7** Des Barry, NZ, 24; **8** Ian Lougher, GB, 21; **9** Neil Tuxworth, GB, 20; **10** Eric McFarlane, GB, 15; **11** Ian Burnett, GB, 13; **12** Graeme McGregor, AUS, 12; **13** Mark Edge, GB, 10; **14** Mark Ward, GB, 9; **15** Gary Dickinson, GB, 7.

## ACU 125 cc British Championship

**DONINGTON PARK CIRCUIT, 22 June. 2.500-mile/4.023-km circuit.**
**ACU 125 cc Championship, round 1 (6 laps, 15.00 miles/24.14 km)**
**1** Steve Mason, GB (MBA), 12m 04.6s, 74.52 mph/119.93 km/h.
**2** Robin Appleyard, GB (MBA); **3** Dave Lowe, GB (MBA); **4** Gary Buckle, GB (MBA); **5** Mark Carkeek, GB (Honda); **6** Ian Jones, GB (MBA); **7** Nigel Robinson, GB (Honda); **8** Cliff Peart, GB (MBA); **9** Dave Collinson, GB (Honda); **10** Gordon Ashton, GB (MBA).
**Fastest lap:** Mason, 1m 58.7s, 75.81 mph/122.00 km/h (record).
**Championship points: 1** Mason, 15; **2** Appleyard, 12; **3** Lowe, 10; **4** Buckle, 8; **5** Carkeek, 6; **6** Jones, 5.

**ACU 125 cc Championship, round 2 (6 laps, 15.00 miles/24.14 km)**
**1** Robin Appleyard, GB (MBA), 11m 49.0s, 76.16 mph/122.57 km/h.
**2** Dave Lowe, GB (MBA); **3** Steve Mason, GB (MBA); **4** Cliff Peart, GB (MBA); **5** Ian Jones, GB (MBA); **6** Gary Buckle, GB (MBA); **7** Mark Carkeek, GB (Honda); **8** Doug Flather, GB (Honda); **9** Nigel Robinson, GB (Honda); **10** Danny Habel, GB (MBA).
**Fastest lap:** Appleyard, 1m 56.1s, 77.50 mph/124.73 km/h.
**Championship points: 1** Appleyard, 27; **2** Mason, 25; **3** Lowe, 22; **4** Buckle, 13; **5** Jones and Peart, 11.

**MALLORY PARK CIRCUIT, 27 July. 1.370-mile/2.205-km circuit.**
**ACU 125 cc Championship, round 3 (6 laps, 8.22 miles/13.32 km)**
**1** Robin Milton, GB (MBA), 5m 49.2s, 84.74 mph/136.38 km/h.
**2** Gary Dickinson, GB (MBA); **3** Cliff Peart, GB (MBA); **4** Gordon Ashton, GB (MBA); **5** Gary Buckle, GB (MBA); **6** Dave Lowe, GB (MBA); **7** Steve Mason, GB (MBA); **8** Steve Carlisle, GB (MBA); **9** Ian Jones, GB (MBA); **10** Doug Flather, GB (Honda).
**Fastest lap:** Milton, 56.5s, 87.29 mph/140.48 km/h.
**Championship points: 1** Mason, 29; **2** Appleyard and Lowe, 27; **4** Peart, 21; **5** Buckle, 19; **6** Milton, 15.

**ACU 125 cc Championship, round 4 (8 laps, 10.96 miles/17.64 km)**
**1** Jamie Whitham, GB (MBA), 7m 32.4s, 87.40 mph/140.66 km/h.
**2** Robin Milton, GB (MBA); **3** Dave Lowe, GB (MBA); **4** Steve Carlisle, GB (MBA); **5** Gary Dickinson, GB (MBA); **6** Gary Buckle, GB (MBA); **7** Gordon Ashton, GB (MBA); **8** Shaun Simpson, GB (MBA); **9** Mark Carkeek, GB (Honda); **10** Steve Mason, GB (MBA).
**Fastest lap:** Whitham, 54.9s, 89.93 mph/144.57 km/h (record).
**Championship points: 1** Lowe, 37; **2** Mason, 30; **3** Appleyard and Milton, 27; **5** Buckle, 24; **6** Peart, 21.

**SILVERSTONE GRAND PRIX CIRCUIT, 20/21 September. 2.927-mile/4.711-km circuit.**
**ACU 125 cc Championship, round 5 (7 laps, 20.49 miles/32.98 km)**
**1** Robin Milton, GB (MBA), 12m 20.7s, 99.58 mph/160.26 km/h.
**2** Gary Buckle, GB (MBA); **3** Dave Lowe, GB (MBA); **4** Gary Dickinson, GB (MBA); **5** Gordon Ashton, GB (MBA); **6** Doug Flather, GB (Honda); **7** Steve Carlisle, GB (MBA); **8** Mark Carkeek, GB (Honda); **9** Ian Jones, GB (MBA); **10** Danny Habel, GB (MBA).
**Fastest lap:** Lowe, 1m 43.4s, 101.91 mph/164.01 km/h.
**Championship points: 1** Lowe, 47; **2** Milton, 42; **3** Buckle, 36; **4** Mason, 30; **5** Appleyard, 27; **6** Dickinson, 26.

**ACU 125 cc Championship, round 6 (7 laps, 20.49 miles/32.98 km)**
**1** Jamie Whitham, GB (MBA), 12m 01.5s, 102.23 mph/164.52 km/h.
**2** Robin Milton, GB (MBA); **3** Gary Buckle, GB (MBA); **4** Dave Lowe, GB (MBA); **5** Gary Dickinson, GB (MBA); **6** Doug Flather, GB (Honda); **7** Gordon Ashton, GB (MBA); **8** Tim Salveson, GB (MBA); **9** Dave Bowman, GB (EMC); **10** Danny Habel, GB (MBA).
**Fastest lap:** Whitham, 1m 41.3s, 104.01 mph/167.39 km/h.

**Final Championship points**

| | | |
|---|---|---|
| 1 | Dave Lowe, GB | 55 |
| 2 | Robin Milton, GB | 54 |
| 3 | Gary Buckle, GB | 46 |
| 4 | Gary Dickinson, GB | 32 |
| 5= | Steve Mason, GB | 30 |
| 5= | Jamie Whitham, GB | 30 |

**7** Robin Appleyard, GB, 27; **8** Gordon Ashton, GB, 23; **9** Cliff Peart, GB, 21; **10** Mark Carkeek, GB, Ian Jones, GB and Steve Carlisle, GB, 15; **13** Doug Flather, GB, 14; **14** Nigel Robinson, GB, 6; **15** Danny Habel, GB, Shaun Simpson, GB and Tim Salveson, GB, 3.

## 750 cc Metzeler Production Championship

**DONINGTON PARK CIRCUIT, 31 March. 2.500-mile/4.023-km circuit.**
**750 cc Metzeler Production Championship, round 1 (10 laps, 25.00 miles/40.23 km)**
**1** Trevor Nation, GB (750 Suzuki), 20m 25.4s, 73.44 mph/118.19 km/h.
**2** Dave Hill, GB (750 Suzuki); **3** Geoff Johnson, GB (750 Honda); **4** Eric McFarlane, GB (750 Suzuki); **5** Gordon Allott, GB (750 Yamaha); **6** Phil Mellor, GB (750 Suzuki); **7** Ian Green, GB (750 Suzuki); **8** Steve Sherbird, GB (750 Suzuki); **9** Richard Rose, GB (750 Suzuki); **10** Andy Green, GB (750 Suzuki).
**Fastest lap:** Richard Scott, NZ (750 Honda), 1m 54.6s, 78.53 mph/128.38 km/h.
**Championship points: 1** Nation, 15; **2** Hill, 12; **3** Johnson, 10; **4** McFarlane, 8; **5** Allott, 6; **6** Mellor, 5.

**MALLORY PARK CIRCUIT, 18 May. 1.370-mile/2.205-km circuit.**
**750 cc Metzeler Production Championship, round 2 (12 laps, 16.44 miles/26.46 km)**
**1** Richard Scott, NZ (750 Honda), 11m 12.3s, 88.03 mph/141.67 km/h.
**2** Phil Mellor, GB (750 Suzuki); **3** Eric McFarlane, GB (750 Suzuki); **4** Trevor Nation, GB (750 Suzuki); **5** Geoff Johnson, GB (750 Honda); **6** Ken Dobson, NZ (750 Honda); **7** Ian Green, GB (750 Suzuki); **8** Graham Grubb, GB (750 Suzuki); **9** J. Brown, GB (750 Yamaha); **10** John Swingler, GB (750 Suzuki).
**Fastest lap:** Scott, 53.9s, 91.50 mph/147.25 km/h.
**Championship points: 1** Nation, 23; **2** McFarlane, 18; **3** Mellor, 17; **4** Johnson, 16; **5** Scott, 15; **6** Hill, 12.

**SNETTERTON CIRCUIT, 19/20 July. 1.917-mile/3.085-km circuit.**
**750 cc Metzeler Production Championship, round 3 (12 laps, 23.00 miles/37.02 km)**
**1** Trevor Nation, GB (750 Suzuki), 15m 00.3s, 91.98 mph/148.03 km/h.
**2** Phil Mellor, GB (750 Suzuki); **3** Richard Scott, NZ (750 Honda); **4** Ian Green, GB (750 Suzuki); **5** Eric McFarlane, GB (750 Suzuki); **6** Andy Green, GB (750 Suzuki); **7** Graham Grubb, GB (750 Suzuki); **8** Geoff Johnson, GB (750 Honda); **9** Kevin Hughes, GB (750 Honda); **10** Zen Marseilles, GB (500 Suzuki).
**Fastest lap:** Mellor, 1m 13.6s, 93.76 mph/150.89 km/h.
**Championship points: 1** Nation, 38; **2** Mellor, 29; **3** Scott, 25; **4** McFarlane, 24; **5** Johnson, 19; **6** Green (Ian), 16.

**SILVERSTONE GRAND PRIX CIRCUIT, 2/3 August. 2.927-mile/4.711-km circuit.**
**750 cc Metzeler Production Championship, round 4 (10 laps, 29.27 miles/47.11 km)**
**1** Phil Mellor, GB (750 Suzuki), 16m 49.92s, 104.33 mph/167.89 km/h.
**2** Richard Scott, NZ (750 Honda); **3** Kenny Irons, GB (750 Yamaha); **4** Ian Green, GB (750 Suzuki); **5** Mark Plato, GB (750 Suzuki); **6** Geoff Johnson, GB (750 Honda); **7** Brian Morrison, GB (750 Suzuki); **8** Steve Parrish, GB (750 Yamaha); **9** Jon Holmes, GB (750 Suzuki); **10** Ken Dobson, NZ (750 Honda).
**Fastest lap:** Scott, 1m 39.70s, 105.68 mph/170.08 km/h.
**Championship points: 1** Mellor, 44; **2** Nation, 38; **3** Scott, 37; **4** Johnson, McFarlane and Green (Ian), 24.

**OULTON PARK CIRCUIT, 25 August. 2.356-mile/3.792-km circuit.**
**750 cc Metzeler Production Championship, round 5 (8 laps, 18.85 miles/30.34 km)**
**1** Trevor Nation, GB (750 Suzuki), 14m 22.2s, 78.69 mph/126.64 km/h.
**2** Phil Mellor, GB (750 Suzuki); **3** Howard Selby, GB (750 Suzuki); **4** Ian Duffus, GB (750 Yamaha); **5** Eric McFarlane, GB (750 Suzuki); **6** Geoff Johnson, GB (750 Honda); **7** Ken Dobson, NZ (750 Honda); **8** Steve Bastow, GB (750 Suzuki); **9** Graham Grubb, GB (750 Suzuki); **10** Ian Green, GB (750 Suzuki).
**Fastest lap:** Mellor, 1m 45.9s, 80.09 mph/128.89 km/h.
**Championship points: 1** Mellor, 56; **2** Nation, 53; **3** Scott, 37; **4** McFarlane, 30; **5** Johnson, 29; **6** Green (Ian), 25.

**THRUXTON CIRCUIT, 7 September. 2.356-mile/3.792-km circuit.**
**750 cc Metzeler Production Championship, round 6 (6 laps, 14.14 miles/22.75 km)**
**1** Phil Mellor, GB (750 Suzuki), 9m 08.40s, 92.80 mph/149.35 km/h.
**2** Trevor Nation, GB (750 Suzuki); **3** Geoff Johnson, GB (750 Honda); **4** Brian Morrison, GB (750 Suzuki); **5** Eric McFarlane, GB (750 Suzuki); **6** Steve Parrish, GB (750 Yamaha); **7** Richard Scott, NZ (750 Honda); **8** Graham Grubb, GB (750 Suzuki); **9** Ian Green, GB (750 Suzuki); **10** Howard Selby, GB (750 Suzuki).
**Fastest lap:** Nation, 1m 29.10s, 95.19 mph/153.19 km/h.
**Championship points: 1** Mellor, 71; **2** Nation, 65; **3** Scott, 41; **4** Johnson, 39; **5** McFarlane, 36; **6** Green (Ian), 27.

**OLIVER'S MOUNT CIRCUIT, 13 September. 2.4136-mile/3.8843-km circuit.**
**750 cc Metzeler Production Championship, round 7 (8 laps, 19.31 miles/31.07 km)**
**1** Phil Mellor, GB (750 Suzuki), 14m 54.3s, 77.73 mph/125.09 km/h.
**2** Trevor Nation, GB (750 Suzuki); **3** Andy McGladdery, GB (750 Suzuki); **4** Brian Morrison, GB (750 Suzuki); **5** Eric McFarlane, GB (750 Suzuki); **6** Steve Parrish, GB (750 Yamaha); **7** Richard Scott, NZ (750 Honda); **8** Geoff Johnson, GB (750 Honda); **9** Ken Dobson, NZ (750 Honda); **10** Ian Martin, GB (750 Suzuki).
**Fastest lap:** Nation, 1m 50.1s, 78.92 mph/127.01 km/h.
**Championship points: 1** Mellor, 86; **2** Nation, 77; **3** Scott, 45; **4** Johnson and McFarlane, 42; **6** Green (Ian), 27.

**CADWELL PARK CIRCUIT, 5 October. 2.250-mile/3.621-km circuit.**
**750 cc Metzeler Production Championship, round 8 (8 laps, 18.00 miles/28.97 km)**
**1** Trevor Nation, GB (750 Suzuki), 13m 44.9s, 78.55 mph/126.41 km/h.
**2** Eric McFarlane, GB (750 Suzuki); **3** Brian Morrison, GB (750 Suzuki); **4** Phil Mellor, GB (750 Suzuki); **5** David Browne, GB (750 Suzuki); **6** Richard Scott, NZ (750 Honda); **7** Andy Green, GB (750 Suzuki); **8** Simon Sloan, GB (750 Suzuki); **9** Geoff Johnson, GB (750 Honda); **10** Andy McGladdery, GB (750 Suzuki).
**Fastest lap:** Nation 1m 41.3s, 79.96 mph/128.68 km/h.

**Final Championship points**

| | |
|---|---|
| **1** Phil Mellor, GB | 94 |
| **2** Trevor Nation, GB | 92 |
| **3** Eric McFarlane, GB | 54 |
| **4** Richard Scott, NZ | 50 |
| **5** Geoff Johnson, GB | 44 |
| **6** Ian Green, GB | 31 |

**7** Brian Morrison, GB, 30; **8** Dave Hill, GB, Ken Dobson, NZ and Graham Grubb, GB, 12; **11** Howard Selby, GB and Andy McGladdery, GB, 11; **13** Kenny Irons, GB, 10; **14** Steve Parrish, GB and Ian Duffus, GB, 8.

## 1300 cc Metzeler Production Championship

**DONINGTON PARK CIRCUIT, 31 March, 2.500-mile/4.023-km circuit.**
**1300 cc Metzeler Production Championship, round 1 (10 laps, 25.00 miles/40.23 km)**
**1** Trevor Nation, GB (1100 Suzuki), 21m 04.5s, 71.17 mph/114.54 km/h.
**2** Glen Williams, NZ (1100 Suzuki); **3** Phil Mellor, GB (1100 Suzuki); **4** Geoff Johnson, GB (1100 Suzuki); **5** David Browne, GB (1100 Kawasaki); **6** Ian Wilson, GB (1100 Kawasaki); **7** Rob Shepherd, GB (1100 Suzuki); **8** Ian Duffus, GB (1100 Suzuki); **9** John Swingler, GB (908 Kawasaki); **10** Jeff Donovan, GB (1100 Suzuki).
**Fastest lap:** Mellor, 2m 02.6s, 73.40 mph/118.13 km/h.
**Championship points: 1** Nation, 15; **2** Williams, 12; **3** Mellor, 10; **4** Johnson, 8; **5** Browne, 6; **6** Wilson, 5.

**MALLORY PARK CIRCUIT, 18 May. 1.370-mile/2.205-km circuit.**
**1300 cc Metzeler Production Championship, round 2 (12 laps, 16.44 miles/26.46 km/h)**
**1** Trevor Nation, GB (1100 Suzuki), 11m 10.9s, 88.21 mph/141.96 m/h.
**2** Phil Mellor, GB (1100 Suzuki); **3** Brian Morrison, GB (1100 Suzuki); **4** Glen Williams, NZ (1100 Suzuki); **5** Geoff Johnson, GB (1100 Suzuki); **6** John Swingler, GB (908 Kawasaki); **7** Ian Duffus, GB (1100 Suzuki); **8** Peter Davies, GB (1100 Suzuki); **9** Rob Shepherd, GB (1100 Suzuki); **10** Tony Thompson, GB (1100 Suzuki).
**Fastest lap:** Nation and Mellor, 54.8s, 90.00 mph/144.84 km/h.
**Championship points: 1** Nation, 30; **2** Mellor, 22; **3** Williams, 20; **4** Johnson, 14; **5** Morrison, 10; **6** Duffus and Swingler, 7.

**SNETTERTON CIRCUIT, 19/20 July. 1.917-mile/3.085-km circuit.**
**1300 cc Metzeler Production Championship, round 3 (12 laps, 23.00 miles/37.02 km)**
**1** Phil Mellor, GB (1100 Suzuki), 14m 43.1s, 93.77 mph/150.91 km/h.
**2** Brian Morrison, GB (1100 Suzuki); **3** Trevor Nation, GB (1100 Suzuki); **4** Barry Woodland, GB (1100 Suzuki); **5** Tony Thompson, GB (1100 Suzuki); **6** Ian Duffus, GB (1100 Suzuki); **7** Geoff Johnson, GB (1100 Suzuki); **8** Steve Bonhomme, GB (1100 Suzuki); **9** Rob Shepherd, GB (1100 Suzuki); **10** Peter Ashbolt, GB (1100 Suzuki).
**Fastest lap:** Woodland, 1m 12.2s, 95.58 mph/153.82 km/h.
**Championship points: 1** Nation, 40; **2** Mellor, 37; **3** Morrison, 22; **4** Williams, 20; **5** Johnson, 18; **6** Duffus, 12.

**SILVERSTONE GRAND PRIX CIRCUIT, 2/3 August. 2.927-mile/4.711-km circuit.**
**1300 cc Metzeler Production Championship, round 4 (8 laps, 23.42 miles/37.69 km)**
**1** Keith Huewen, GB (1100 Suzuki), 15m 28.54s, 90.78 mph/146.10 km/h.
**2** Alan Batson, GB (1100 Suzuki); **3** Trevor Nation, GB (1100 Suzuki); **4** Rob Shepherd, GB (1100 Suzuki); **5** Geoff Johnson, GB (1100 Suzuki); **6** Brian Morrison, GB (1100 Suzuki); **7** Phil Mellor, GB (1100 Suzuki); **8** Barry Woodland, GB (1100 Suzuki); **9** Eric McFarlane, GB (908 Kawasaki); **10** Ian Wilson, GB (1100 Suzuki).
**Fastest lap:** Batson, 1m 52.55s, 93.62 mph/150.67 km/h.
**Championship points: 1** Nation, 50; **2** Mellor, 41; **3** Morrison, 27; **4** Johnson, 24; **5** Williams, 20; **6** Shepherd, 16.

**OULTON PARK CIRCUIT, 25 August. 2.356-mile/3.792-km circuit.**
**1300 cc Metzeler Production Championship, round 5 (6 laps, 14.14 miles/22.75 km)**
**1** Trevor Nation, GB (1100 Suzuki), 10m 44.8s, 78.92 mph/127.01 km/h.
**2** Phil Mellor, GB (1100 Suzuki); **3** Keith Huewen, GB (1100 Suzuki); **4** Brian Morrison, GB (1100 Suzuki); **5** Geoff Johnson, GB (1100 Suzuki); **6** Ian Duffus, GB (1100 Suzuki); **7** Tony Thompson, GB (1100 Suzuki); **8** Peter Davies, GB (1100 Suzuki); **9** Alan Batson, GB (1100 Suzuki); **10** Peter Ashbolt, GB (1100 Suzuki).
**Fastest lap:** Nation, 1m 45.7s, 80.24 mph/129.13 km/h.
**Championship points: 1** Nation, 65; **2** Mellor, 53; **3** Morrison, 35; **4** Johnson, 30; **5** Huewen, 25; **6** Williams, 20.

**THRUXTON CIRCUIT, 7 September. 2.356-mile/3.792-km circuit.**
**1300 cc Metzeler Production Championship, round 6 (6 laps, 14.14 miles/22.75 km)**
**1** Brian Morrison, GB (1100 Suzuki), 8m 57.40s, 94.70 mph/152.40 km/h.
**2** Phil Mellor, GB (1100 Suzuki); **3** Ian Duffus, GB (1100 Suzuki); **4** Tony Thompson, GB (1100 Suzuki); **5** Trevor Nation, GB (1100 Suzuki); **6** Geoff Johnson, GB (1100 Suzuki); **7** Rob Shepherd, GB (1100 Suzuki); **8** Peter Davies, GB (1100 Suzuki); **9** Barry Woodland, GB (1100 Suzuki); **10** David Pickworth, GB (1100 Suzuki).
**Fastest lap:** Morrison, 1m 28.30s, 96.05 mph/154.58 km/h (record).
**Championship points: 1** Nation, 71; **2** Mellor, 65; **3** Morrison, 50; **4** Johnson, 35; **5** Duffus, 27; **6** Huewen, 25.

**OLIVER'S MOUNT CIRCUIT, 14 September. 2.4136-mile/3.8843-km circuit.**
**1300 cc Metzeler Production Championship, round 7 (8 laps, 19.31 miles/31.07 km)**
**1** Phil Mellor, GB (1100 Suzuki), 14m 56.3s, 77.55 mph/124.80 km/h.
**2** Brian Morrison, GB (1100 Suzuki); **3** Ian Duffus, GB (1100 Suzuki); **4** Eric McFarlane, GB (1100 Suzuki); **5** Ian Wilson, GB (1100 Suzuki); **6** Tony

Thompson, GB (1100 Suzuki). No other finishers.
**Fastest lap:** Mellor, 1m 50.9s, 78.35 mph/126.09 km/h.
**Championship points:** **1** Mellor, 80; **2** Nation, 71; **3** Morrison, 62; **4** Duffus, 37; **5** Johnson, 35; **6** Huewen, 25.

**CADWELL PARK CIRCUIT, 5 October. 2.250-mile/3.621-km circuit.**
**1300 cc Metzeler Production Championship, round 8 (8 laps, 18.00 miles/28.97 km)**
**1** Trevor Nation, GB (1100 Suzuki), 13m 34.4s, 79.56 mph/128.04 km/h.
**2** Brian Morrison, GB (1100 Suzuki); **3** Phil Mellor, GB (1100 Suzuki); **4** Ian Duffus, GB (1100 Suzuki); **5** Paul Ruckledge, GB (1100 Suzuki); **6** Tony Thompson, GB (1100 Suzuki); **7** Ian Wilson, GB (1100 Suzuki); **8** Richard Scott, NZ (750 Honda); **9** David Browne, GB (750 Suzuki); **10** David Pickworth, GB (1100 Suzuki).
**Fastest lap:** Not given.

**Final Championship points**

| | |
|---|---|
| **1** Phil Mellor, GB | 90 |
| **2** Trevor Nation, GB | 86 |
| **3** Brian Morrison, GB | 74 |
| **4** Ian Duffus, GB | 45 |
| **5** Geoff Johnson, GB | 35 |
| **6** Tony Thompson, GB | 29 |

**7** Keith Huewen, GB, 25; **8** Glen Williams, NZ and Rob Shepherd, GB, 20; **10** Ian Wilson, GB, 16; **11** Alan Batson, GB, 14; **12** Barry Woodland, GB, 13; **13** Eric McFarlane, GB, 10; **14** David Browne, GB, 8; **15** John Swingler, GB, 7.

## Motor Cycle News/ EBC Brakes Superstock Series

**BRANDS HATCH INDY CIRCUIT, 4 May. 1.2036-mile/1.9370-km circuit.**
**MCN/EBC Brakes Superstock Series, round 1 (15 laps, 18.05 miles/29.06 km)**
**1** Trevor Nation, GB (750 Suzuki), 13m 19.8s, 81.26 mph/130.77 km/h.
**2** Phil Mellor, GB (750 Suzuki); **3** Roger Marshall, GB (750 Honda); **4** Keith Huewen, GB (750 Suzuki); **5** Dale Robinson, GB (750 Suzuki); **6** Richard Scott, NZ (750 Honda); **7** Steve Parrish, GB (750 Yamaha); **8** Kenny Irons, GB (750 Yamaha); **9** Paul Iddon, GB (750 Suzuki); **10** John Brindley, GB (750 Yamaha).
**Fastest lap:** Marshall, 51.5s, 84.13 mph/135.39 km/h.
**Championship points:** **1** Nation, 15; **2** Mellor, 12; **3** Marshall, 10; **4** Huewen, 8; **5** Robinson, 6; **6** Scott, 5.

**MALLORY PARK CIRCUIT, 15 June. 1.370-mile/2.205-km circuit.**
**MCN/EBC Brakes Superstock Series, round 2 (15 laps, 20.55 miles/33.08 km)**
**1** Trevor Nation, GB (750 Suzuki), 13m 32.2s, 90.97 mph/146.40 km/h.
**2** Kenny Irons, GB (750 Yamaha); **3** Neil Robinson, GB (750 Suzuki); **4** Keith Huewen, GB (750 Suzuki); **5** Richard Scott, NZ (750 Honda); **6** Steve Parrish, GB (750 Yamaha); **7** Roger Marshall, GB (750 Honda); **8** Phil Mellor, GB (750 Suzuki); **9** Paul Iddon, GB (750 Suzuki); **10** Roger Burnett, GB (750 Honda).
**Fastest lap:** Nation, 53.1s, 92.88 mph/149.48 km/h.
**Championship points:** **1** Nation, 32; **2** Huewen and Marshall, 16; **4** Mellor and Irons, 15; **6** Scott, 11.

**SNETTERTON CIRCUIT, 19/20 July. 1.917-mile/3.085-km circuit.**
**MCN/EBC Brakes Superstock Series, round 3 (12 laps, 23.00 miles/37.02 km)**
**1** Kenny Irons, GB (750 Yamaha), 14m 14.8s, 96.88 mph/155.91 km/h.
**2** Keith Huewen, GB (750 Suzuki); **3** Richard Scott, NZ (750 Honda); **4** John Lofthouse, GB (750 Suzuki); **5** Phil Mellor, GB (750 Suzuki); **6** Roger Hurst, GB (750 Suzuki); **7** Chris Breeze, GB (750 Yamaha); **8** Roger Marshall, GB (750 Honda); **9** Roland Brown, GB (750 Suzuki); **10** Mark Plato, GB (750 Suzuki).
**Fastest lap:** Irons and Huewen, 1m 10.3s, 98.16 mph/157.97 km/h.
**Championship points:** **1** Nation and Irons, 32; **3** Huewen, 30; **4** Mellor and Scott, 21; **6** Marshall, 19.

**CADWELL PARK WOODLAND CIRCUIT, 10 August. 1.000-mile/1.609-km circuit.**
**MCN/EBC Brakes Superstock Series, round 4 (20 laps, 20.00 miles/32.18 km)**
**1** Keith Huewen, GB (750 Suzuki), 15m 29.0s, 77.50 mph/124.72 km/h.
**2** Richard Scott, NZ (750 Honda); **3** Kenny Irons, GB (750 Yamaha); **4** Trevor Nation, GB (750 Suzuki); **5** Phil Mellor, GB (750 Suzuki); **6** Steve Parrish, GB (750 Yamaha); **7** Roger Marshall, GB (750 Honda); **8** John Lofthouse, GB (750 Suzuki); **9** Mark Boughton, GB (750 Suzuki); **10** Ray Swann, GB (750 Suzuki).
**Fastest lap:** Huewen, 45.2s, 79.65 mph/128.18 km/h.
**Championship points:** **1** Huewen, 45; **2** Irons, 42; **3** Nation, 40; **4** Scott, 35; **5** Mellor, 27; **6** Marshall, 23.

**OULTON PARK CIRCUIT, 24 August. 2.356-mile/3.792-km circuit.**
**MCN/EBC Brakes Superstock Series, round 5 (8 laps, 18.85 miles/30.34 km)**
**1** Kenny Irons, GB (750 Yamaha), 11m 32.8s, 97.38 mph/156.72 km/h.
**2** Richard Scott, NZ (750 Honda); **3** Neil Robinson, GB (750 Suzuki); **4** Trevor Nation, GB (750 Suzuki); **5** Steve Parrish, GB (750 Yamaha); **6** Phil Mellor, GB (750 Suzuki); **7** John Lofthouse, GB (750 Suzuki); **8** Roger Hurst, GB (750 Yamaha); **9** Roger Marshall, GB (750 Honda); **10** Ray Swann, GB (750 Suzuki).
**Fastest lap:** Irons, 1m 25.8s, 98.85 mph/159.08 km/h (record).
**Championship points:** **1** Irons, 59; **2** Nation, 48; **3** Scott, 47; **4** Huewen, 45; **5** Mellor, 32; **6** Marshall, 25.

**THRUXTON CIRCUIT, 7 September. 2.356-mile/3.792-km circuit.**
**MCN/EBC Brakes Superstock Series, round 6 (8 laps, 18.85 miles/30.34 km)**
**1** Kenny Irons, GB (750 Yamaha), 11m 40.60s, 96.85 mph/155.86 km/h.
**2** Richard Scott, NZ (750 Honda); **3** Trevor Nation, GB (750 Suzuki); **4** John Lofthouse, GB (750 Suzuki); **5** Neil Robinson, GB (750 Suzuki); **6** Phil Mellor, GB (750 Suzuki); **7** Keith Huewen, GB (750 Suzuki); **8** Steve Parrish, GB (750 Yamaha); **9** Roger Marshall, GB (750 Honda); **10** Geoff Fowler, GB (750 Yamaha).
**Fastest lap:** Scott, 1m 26.02s, 98.62 mph/158.71 km/h (record).
**Championship points:** **1** Irons, 74; **2** Scott, 61; **3** Nation, 58; **4** Huewen, 49; **5** Mellor, 37; **6** Marshall, 27.

**OLIVER'S MOUNT CIRCUIT, 14 September. 2.4136-mile/3.8843-km circuit.**
**MCN/EBC Brakes Superstock Series, round 7 (10 laps, 24.14 miles/38.84 km)**
**1** Kenny Irons, GB (750 Yamaha), 18m 14.2s, 79.41 mph/127.80 km/h.
**2** Phil Mellor, GB (750 Suzuki); **3** Richard Scott, NZ (750 Honda); **4** Andy McGladdery, GB (750 Suzuki); **5** Steve Henshaw, GB (750 Suzuki); **6** John Lofthouse, GB (750 Suzuki); **7** Richard Crossley, GB (750 Suzuki); **8** Steve Ward, GB (750 Suzuki); **9** John Brindley, GB (750 Yamaha); **10** John Swingler, GB (750 Suzuki).
**Fastest lap:** Mellor, 1m 47.6s, 80.75 mph/129.95 km/h (record).
**Championship points:** **1** Irons, 89; **2** Scott, 71; **3** Nation, 58; **4** Mellor, 51; **5** Huewen, 49; **6** Lofthouse, 28.

**DONINGTON PARK CIRCUIT, 28 September. 2.500-mile/4.023-km circuit.**
**MCN/EBC Brakes Superstock Series, round 8 (10 laps, 25.00 miles/40.23 km)**
**1** Kenny Irons, GB (750 Yamaha), 17m 52.10s, 83.74 mph/134.77 km/h.
**2** Keith Huewen, GB (750 Suzuki); **3** Steve Parrish, GB (750 Yamaha); **4** Trevor Nation, GB (750 Suzuki); **5** Richard Scott, NZ (750 Honda); **6** Roger Hurst, GB (750 Yamaha); **7** Roger Marshall, GB (750 Honda); **8** John Lofthouse, GB (750 Suzuki); **9** Ray Swann, GB (750 Suzuki); **10** Chris Martin, GB (750 Suzuki).
**Fastest lap:** Irons, 1m 45.61s, 85.01 mph/136.81 km/h (record).
**Championship points:** **1** Irons, 106; **2** Scott, 77; **3** Nation, 64; **4** Huewen, 61; **5** Mellor, 51; **6** Marshall and Lofthouse, 31.

**BRANDS HATCH INDY CIRCUIT, 19 October. 1.2036-mile/1.9370-km circuit.**
**MCN/EBC Superstock Series, round 9 (15 laps, 18.05 miles/29.06 km)**
**1** Keith Huewen, GB (750 Suzuki), 13m 37.7s, 79.48 mph/127.91 km/h.
**2** Richard Scott, NZ (750 Honda); **3** Paul Iddon, GB (750 Suzuki); **4** John Lofthouse, GB (750 Suzuki); **5** Kenny Irons, GB (750 Yamaha); **6** Trevor Nation, GB (750 Suzuki); **7** Mark Plato, GB (750 Suzuki); **8** Jamie Whitham, GB (750 Suzuki); **9** Roger Marshall, GB (750 Honda); **10** Chris Martin, GB (750 Suzuki).
**Fastest lap:** Scott, 52.0s, 83.32 mph/134.09 km/h.

**Final Championship points**

| | |
|---|---|
| **1** Kenny Irons, GB | 118 |
| **2** Richard Scott, NZ | 105 |
| **3** Keith Huewen, GB | 91 |
| **4** Trevor Nation, GB | 74 |
| **5** Phil Mellor, GB | 51 |
| **6** John Lofthouse, GB | 47 |

**7** Roger Marshall, GB, 35; **8** Steve Parrish, GB, 33; **9** Neil Robinson, GB, 26; **10** Paul Iddon, GB 24; **11** Roger Hurst, GB, 13; **12** Mark Plato, GB, 9; **13** Andy McGladdery, GB, 8; **14** Dale Robinson, GB, Steve Henshaw, GB and Jamie Whitham, GB 6.

## Shell Oils British Transnational Championship

**CADWELL PARK CIRCUIT, 9 March. 2.250-mile/3.621-km circuit.**
**1300 cc round 1 (8 laps, 18.00 miles/28.97 km)**
**1** Roger Burnett, GB (500 Honda), 14m 22.7s, 75.11 mph/120.88 km/h.
**2** Roger Marshall, GB (500 Honda); **3** Niall MacKenzie, GB (350 Armstrong); **4** Trevor Nation, GB (500 Suzuki); **5** Mark Phillips, GB (500 Suzuki); **6** Gary Padgett, GB (500 Suzuki); **7** Ray Swann, GB (500 Suzuki); **8** Joey Dunlop, GB (500 Honda); **9** Kenny Irons, GB (500 Suzuki); **10** Neil Stafford, GB (350 Yamaha).
**Fastest lap:** MacKenzie, 1m 43.6s, 78.18 mph/125.82 km/h.
**Championship points:** **1** Burnett, 15; **2** Marshall, 12; **3** MacKenzie, 10; **4** Nation, 8; **5** Phillips, 6; **6** Padgett, 5.

**1300 cc, round 2 (8 laps, 18.00 miles/28.97 km)**
**1** Roger Burnett, GB (500 Honda), 13m 10.2s, 82.00 mph/131.97 km/h.
**2** Roger Marshall, GB (500 Honda); **3** Trevor Nation, GB (500 Suzuki); **4** Niall MacKenzie, GB (350 Armstrong); **5** Alan Jeffery, GB (500 Suzuki); **6** Steve Manley, GB (500 Suzuki); **7** Mark Phillips, GB (500 Suzuki); **8** Paul Simmonds, GB (350 Yamaha); **9** Dave Griffith, GB (500 Suzuki); **10** Steve Henshaw, GB (500 Suzuki).
**Fastest lap:** Burnett, 1m 35.3s, 84.99 mph/136.78 km/h.
**Championship points:** **1** Burnett, 30; **2** Marshall, 24; **3** Nation and MacKenzie, 18; **5** Phillips, 10; **6** Jeffery, 6.

**250 cc, round 1 (8 laps, 18.00 miles/28.97 km)**
**1** Niall MacKenzie, GB (Armstrong), 14m 03.2s, 76.85 mph/123.68 km/h.
**2** Donnie McLeod, GB (Armstrong); **3** Kevin Mitchell, GB (Honda); **4** Darren Dixon, GB (Honda); **5** Mick Crick, GB (Rotax); **6** Ian Newton, GB (Armstrong); **7** Carl Fogarty, GB (Yamaha); **8** Dudley Bell, GB (Armstrong); **9** Dave Butler, GB (Yamaha); **10** Stu Melen, GB (Honda).
**Fastest lap:** MacKenzie, 1m 43.0s, 78.64 mph/126.56 km/h.
**Championship points:** **1** MacKenzie, 15; **2** McLeod, 12; **3** Mitchell, 10; **4** Dixon, 8; **5** Crick, 6; **6** Newton, 5.

**250 cc, round 2 (8 laps, 18.00 miles/28.97 km)**
**1** Donnie McLeod, GB (Armstrong), 13m 13.6s, 81.65 mph/131.40 km/h.
**2** Mick Crick, GB (Rotax); **3** Kevin Mitchell, GB (Honda); **4** Niall MacKenzie, GB (Armstrong); **5** Darren Dixon, GB (Honda); **6** Steve Patrickson, GB (Rotax); **7** Ian Young, GB (Armstrong); **8** Carl Fogarty, GB (Yamaha); **9** Peter Hubbard, GB (Rotax); **10** Dave Butler, GB (Yamaha).
**Fastest lap:** MacKenzie, 1m 34.7s, 85.53 mph/137.65 km/h (record).
**Championship points:** **1** McLeod, 27; **2** MacKenzie, 23; **3** Mitchell, 20; **4** Crick, 18; **5** Dixon, 14; **6** Fogarty, 7.

**Sidecars, round 1 (8 laps, 18.00 miles/28.97 km)**
**1** Steve Webster/Tony Hewitt, GB/GB (500 LCR-Yamaha), 13m 45.1s, 78.53 mph/126.38 km/h.
**2** Steve Abbott/Shaun Smith, GB/GB (500 Windle-Yamaha); **3** Derek Bayley/Bryan Nixon, GB/GB (500 LCR-Yamaha); **4** Derek Jones/Brian Ayres, GB/GB (500 LCR-Yamaha); **5** Barry Brindley/Chris Jones, GB/GB (500 Windle-Yamaha); **6** Yoshisada Kumagaya/Kazuhiko Makiuchi, J/J (500 LCR-Yamaha); **7** Ray Gardner/Tony Strevens, GB/GB (500 LCR-Yamaha); **8** Mick Barton/Peter Brown, GB/GB (500 LCR-Yamaha); **9** Geoff Young/Jimmy Cochrane, GB/GB (500 Yamaha); **10** Dennis Holmes/Alan Jervis, GB/GB (500 LCR-Yamaha).
**Fastest lap:** Webster, 1m 39.1s, 81.73 mph/131.53 km/h.
**Championship points:** **1** Webster, 15; **2** Bayley, 12; **3** Abbott, 10; **4** Jones, 8; **5** Brindley, 6; **6** Kumagaya, 5.

**Sidecars, round 2 (8 laps, 18.00 miles/28.97 km)**
**1** Derek Bayley/Bryan Nixon, GB/GB (500 LCR-Yamaha), 13m 05.0s, 82.54 mph/132.83 km/h.
**2** Steve Webster/Tony Hewitt, GB/GB (500 LCR-Yamaha); **3** Steve Abbott/Shaun Smith, GB/GB (500 Windle-Yamaha); **4** Derek Jones/Brian Ayres, GB/GB (500 LCR-Yamaha); **5** Barry Brindley/Chris Jones, GB/GB (500 Windle-Yamaha); **6** Mick Barton/Peter Brown, GB/GB (500 LCR-Yamaha); **7** Mick Boddice/Chas Birks, GB/GB (500 LCR-Yamaha); **8** Yoshisada Kumagaya/Kazuhiko Makiuchi, J/J (500 LCR-Yamaha); **9** Ray Gardner/Tony Strevens, GB/GB (500 LCR-Yamaha); **10** Barry Smith/Dave Smith, GB/GB (500 Yamaha).
**Fastest lap:** Abbott, 1m 36.3s, 84.11 mph/135.36 km/h.
**Championship points:** **1** Webster, 27; **2** Bayley, 25; **3** Abbott, 22; **4** Jones, 16; **5** Brindley, 12; **6** Kumagaya and Barton, 8.

**BRANDS HATCH INDY CIRCUIT, 28 March. 1.2036-mile/1.9370-km circuit.**
**1300 cc, round 3 (20 laps, 24.07 miles/38.74 km)**
**1** Niall MacKenzie, GB (350 Armstrong), 18m 29.4s, 78.11 mph/125.71 km/h.
**2** Donnie McLeod, GB (350 Armstrong); **3** Roger Marshall, GB (500 Honda); **4** Roger Burnett, GB (500 Honda); **5** Trevor Nation, GB (500 Suzuki); **6** Gary Padgett, GB (500 Suzuki); **7** Steven Veasey, GB (998 Kawasaki); **8** Neil Robinson, GB (750 Suzuki); **9** Roland Brown, GB (750 Suzuki); **10** Terry Rymer, GB (500 Suzuki).
**Fastest lap:** McLeod, 52.7s, 82.21 mph/132.30 km/h.
**Championship points:** **1** Burnett, 38; **2** Marshall, 34; **3** MacKenzie, 33; **4** Nation, 24; **5** McLeod, 12; **6** Phillips and Padgett, 10.

**1300 cc, round 4 (20 laps, 24.07 miles/38.74 km)**
**1** Roger Marshall, GB (500 Honda); 17m 22.7s, 83.11 mph/133.75 km/h.
**2** Roger Burnett, GB (500 Honda); **3** Trevor Nation, GB (500 Suzuki); **4** Neil Robinson, GB (750 Suzuki); **5** Donnie McLeod, GB (350 Armstrong); **6** Howard Selby, GB (500 Suzuki); **7** Terry Rymer, GB (500 Suzuki); **8** Les Burgen, GB (500 Suzuki); **9** Steve Henshaw, GB (500 Suzuki); **10** Ricky McMillan, GB (998 Kawasaki).
**Fastest lap:** Marshall, 50.1s, 86.48 mph/139.18 km/h.
**Championship points:** **1** Burnett, 50; **2** Marshall, 49; **3** Nation, 34; **4** MacKenzie, 33; **5** McLeod, 18; **6** Robinson, 11.

**250 cc, round 3 (20 laps, 24.07 miles/38.74 km)**
**1** Darren Dixon, GB (Honda), 20m 44.4s, 69.63 mph/112.06 km/h.
**2** Steve Patrickson, GB (Rotax); **3** Niall MacKenzie, GB (Armstrong); **4** Tony Rogers, GB (Yamaha); **5** Carl Fogarty, GB (Yamaha); **6** Mark Barker, GB (Rotax); **7** James Rae, GB (EMC); **8** Gary Weston, GB (Yamaha); **9** Gary Padgett, GB (Yamaha); **10** Chris Fargher, GB (Yamaha).
**Fastest lap:** MacKenzie, 1m 00.4s, 71.73 mph/115.44 km/h.
**Championship points:** **1** MacKenzie, 33; **2** Dixon, 29; **3** McLeod, 27; **4** Mitchell, 20; **5** Crick, 18; **6** Patrickson, 17.

**250 cc, round 4 (20 laps, 24.07 miles/38.74 km)**
**1** Gary Noel, GB (EMC), 19m 52.0s, 72.70 mph/117.00 km/h.
**2** Donnie McLeod, GB (Armstrong); **3** Darren Dixon, GB (Honda); **4** Niall MacKenzie, GB (Armstrong); **5** Steve Patrickson, GB (Rotax); **6** Joey Dunlop, GB (Honda); **7** Peter Hubbard, GB (Rotax); **8** Gary Weston, GB (Yamaha); **9** Mick Crick, GB (Rotax); **10** Dave Quarmby, GB (Yamaha).
**Fastest lap:** Noel, 55.9s, 77.51 mph/124.74 km/h.
**Championship points:** **1** MacKenzie, 41; **2** McLeod and Dixon, 39; **4** Patrickson, 23; **5** Mitchell and Crick, 20.

**Sidecars, round 3 (20 laps, 24.07 miles/38.74 km)**
**1** Steve Webster/Tony Hewitt, GB/GB (500 LCR-Yamaha), 17m 04.4s, 84.59 mph/136.13 km/h.
**2** Steve Abbott/Shaun Smith, GB/GB (500 Windle-Yamaha); **3** Barry Brindley/Chris Jones, GB/GB (500 Windle-Yamaha); **4** Mick Barton/Peter Brown, GB/GB (500 LCR-Yamaha); **5** Tony Baker/Peter Harper, GB/GB (500 Yamaha); **6** Yoshisada Kumagaya/Kazuhiko Makiuchi, J/J (500 LCR-Yamaha); **7** Judd Drew/Andrew Wadsworth, GB/GB (500 BLR-Yamaha); **8** Gary Thomas/Geoff White, GB/GB (500 BSL-Yamaha); **9** Dave Carnell/Andy Peach, GB/GB (500 Windle-Yamaha). No other finishers.
**Fastest lap:** Webster, 49.7s, 87.18 mph/140.30 km/h.
**Championship points:** **1** Webster, 42; **2** Abbott, 34; **3** Bayley, 25; **4** Brindley, 22; **5** Jones and Barton, 16.

**Sidecars, round 4 (16 laps, 19.26 miles/30.99 km)**
**1** Steve Abbott/Shaun Smith, GB/GB (500 Windle-Yamaha), 14m 52.0s, 77.72 mph/125.08 km/h.
**2** Barry Brindley/Chris Jones, GB/GB (500 Windle-Yamaha); **3** Steve Webster/Tony Hewitt, GB/GB (500 LCR-Yamaha); **4** Tony Baker/Peter Harper, GB/GB (500 Yamaha); **5** Mike Turrell/Brian Barlow, GB/GB (500 LCR-Yamaha); **6** Judd Drew/Andrew Wadsworth, GB/GB (500 BLR-Yamaha). No other finishers.
**Fastest lap:** Webster, 50.0s, 86.65 mph/139.45 km/h.
**Championship points:** **1** Webster, 52; **2** Abbott, 49; **3** Brindley, 34; **4** Bayley, 25; **5** Jones and Barton, 16.

**OULTON PARK CIRCUIT, 31 March. 2.356-mile/3.792-km circuit.**
**1300 cc, round 5 (10 laps, 23.56 miles/37.92 km)**
**1** Niall MacKenzie, GB (350 Armstrong), 16m 37.8s, 85.00 mph/136.79 km/h.
**2** Howard Selby, GB (500 Suzuki); **3** Gary Lingham, GB (500 Suzuki); **4** Steve Henshaw, GB (500 Suzuki); **5** Joey Dunlop, GB (500 Honda); **6** Andy McGladdery, GB (750 Suzuki); **7** Michael Seward, GB (750 Yamaha); **8** Paul Simmonds, GB (350 Yamaha); **9** Dave Griffith, GB (500 Suzuki); **10** Trevor Herrington, GB (997 Suzuki).
**Fastest lap:** MacKenzie, 1m 36.5s, 87.89 mph/141.44 km/h.
**Championship points:** **1** Burnett, 50; **2** Marshall, 49; **3** MacKenzie, 48; **4** Nation, 34; **5** McLeod, 18; **6** Selby, 17.

**1300 cc, round 6 (10 laps, 23.56 miles/37.92 km)**
**1** Howard Selby, GB (500 Suzuki), 16m 27.4s, 87.08 mph/140.14 km/h.
**2** Joey Dunlop, GB (500 Honda); **3** Steve Henshaw, GB (500 Suzuki); **4** Andy McGladdery, GB (750 Suzuki); **5** Gary Lingham, GB (500 Suzuki); **6** Dave Griffith, GB (500 Suzuki); **7** Terry Rymer, GB (500 Suzuki); **8** Andy Coldwell, GB (500 Suzuki); **9** Tony Moran, GB (750 Yamaha); **10** Michael Seward, GB (750 Yamaha).
**Fastest lap:** Donnie McLeod, GB (350 Armstrong), 1m 35.2s, 89.08 mph/143.36 km/h.
**Championship points:** **1** Burnett, 50; **2** Marshall, 49; **3** MacKenzie, 48; **4** Nation, 34; **5** Selby, 32; **6** Dunlop and Henshaw, 21.

**250 cc, round 5 (10 laps, 23.56 miles/37.92 km)**
**1** Niall MacKenzie, GB (Armstrong), 16m 14.9s, 86.99 mph/140.00 km/h.
**2** Gary Noel, GB (EMC); **3** Ian Newton, GB (Armstrong); **4** Andy Watts, GB (Decorite); **5** Mick Crick, GB (Rotax); **6** Keith Nicholls, GB (Yamaha); **7** Ian Young, GB (Armstrong); **8** Peter Hubbard, GB (Rotax); **9** Steve Patrickson, GB (Rotax); **10** James Rae, GB (EMC).
**Fastest lap:** MacKenzie, 1m 34.8s, 89.46 mph/143.97 km/h.
**Championship points:** **1** MacKenzie, 56; **2** McLeod and Dixon, 39; **4** Noel, 27; **5** Crick, 26; **6** Patrickson, 25.

**250 cc, round 6 (10 laps, 23.56 miles/37.92 km)**
**1** Niall MacKenzie, GB (Armstrong), 15m 47.6s, 89.50 mph/144.04 km/h.
**2** Donnie McLeod GB (Armstrong); **3** Ian Newton, GB (Armstrong); **4** Gary Noel, GB (EMC); **5** Ian Young, GB (Armstrong); **6** Carl Fogarty, GB (Yamaha); **7** Peter Hubbard, GB (Rotax); **8** Kevin Mawdsley, GB (Armstrong); **9** Andy Watts, GB (Decorite); **10** Steve Patrickson, GB (Rotax).
**Fastest lap:** MacKenzie, 1m 32.7s, 91.49 mph/147.24 km/h.
**Championship points:** **1** MacKenzie, 71; **2** McLeod, 51; **3** Dixon, 39; **4** Noel, 35; **5** Crick and Patrickson, 26.

**Sidecars, round 5 (10 laps, 23.56 miles/37.92 km)**
**1** Steve Webster/Tony Hewitt, GB/GB (500 LCR-Yamaha), 16m 05.9s, 87.81 mph/141.32 km/h.
**2** Steve Abbott/Shaun Smith, GB/GB (500 Windle-Yamaha); **3** Derek Bayley/Bryan Nixon, GB/GB (500 LCR-Yamaha); **4** Mick Boddice/Chas Birks, GB/GB (500 LCR-Yamaha); **5** Barry Brindley/Chris Jones, GB/GB (500 Windle-Yamaha); **6** Yoshisada Kumagaya/Kazuhiko Makiuchi, J/J (500 LCR-Yamaha); **7** Ray Gardner/Tony Strevens, GB/GB (500 LCR-Yamaha); **8** Kenny Howles/Steve Pointer, GB/GB (500 LCR-Yamaha); **9** John Phillips/Malcolm Hollis, GB/GB (500 Yamaha); **10** Judd Drew/Andrew Wadsworth, GB/GB (500 BLR-Yamaha).
**Fastest lap:** Webster, 1m 35.0s, 89.27 mph/143.68 km/h.
**Championship points:** **1** Webster, 67; **2** Abbott, 61; **3** Brindley, 40; **4** Bayley, 35; **5** Kumagaya, 18; **6** Jones and Barton, 16.

**Sidecars, round 6 (10 laps, 23.56 miles/37.92 km)**
**1** Steve Abbott/Shaun Smith, GB/GB (500 Windle-Yamaha), 15m 56.7s, 88.65 mph/142.67 km/h.
**2** Steve Webster/Tony Hewitt, GB/GB (500 LCR-Yamaha); **3** Derek Bayley/Bryan Nixon, GB/GB (500 LCR-Yamaha); **4** Ray Gardner/Tony Strevens, GB/GB (500 LCR-Yamaha); **5** Geoff Young/Jimmy Cochrane, GB/GB (500 Yamaha); **6** Yoshisada Kumagaya/Kazuhiko Makiuchi, J/J (500 LCR-Yamaha); **7** John Phillips/Malcolm Hollis, GB/GB (500 Yamaha); **8** Dennis Holmes/Alan Jervis, GB/GB (500 LCR-Yamaha); **9** Judd Drew/Andrew Wadsworth, GB/GB (500 BLR-Yamaha). No other finishers.
**Fastest lap:** Webster, 1m 33.6s, 90.61 mph/145.82 km/h.
**Championship points: 1** Webster, 79; **2** Abbott, 76; **3** Bayley, 45; **4** Brindley, 40; **5** Kumagaya, 23; **6** Gardner, 18.

**BRANDS HATCH INDY CIRCUIT, 4 May. 1.2036-mile/1.9370-km circuit.**
**1300 cc, round 7 (20 laps, 24.07 miles/38.74 km)**
**1** Roger Burnett, GB (500 Honda), 20m 02.6s, 72.05 mph/115.95 km/h.
**2** Neil Robinson, GB (750 Suzuki); **3** Gary Lingham, GB (500 Suzuki); **4** Terry Rymer, GB (500 Suzuki); **5** John Brindley, GB (500 Yamaha); **6** Dennis Ireland, NZ (500 Suzuki); **7** Peter Dalby, GB (500 Suzuki); **8** Phil Mellor, GB (750 Suzuki); **9** Mark Boughton, GB (500 Yamaha); **10** John Swingler, GB (500 Suzuki).
**Fastest lap:** Roger Marshall, GB (500 Honda), 57.2s, 75.75 mph/121.91 km/h.
**Championship points: 1** Burnett, 65; **2** Marshall, 49; **3** MacKenzie, 48; **4** Nation, 34; **5** Selby, 32; **6** Lingham, 26.

**1300 cc, round 8 (20 laps, 24.07 miles/38.74 km)**
**1** Roger Burnett, GB (500 Honda), 16m 43.8s, 86.33 mph/138.93 km/h.
**2** Roger Marshall, GB (500 Honda); **3** Trevor Nation, GB (500 Suzuki); **4** Steve Henshaw, GB (500 Suzuki); **5** Neil Robinson, GB (750 Suzuki); **6** John Brindley, GB (500 Yamaha); **7** Gary Lingham, GB (500 Suzuki); **8** Steve Manley, GB (500 Suzuki); **9** Dennis Ireland, NZ (500 Suzuki); **10** Mark Boughton, GB (500 Yamaha).
**Fastest lap:** Burnett, 48.8s, 88.79 mph/142.89 km/h.
**Championship points: 1** Burnett, 80; **2** Marshall, 61; **3** MacKenzie, 48; **4** Nation, 44; **5** Selby, 32; **6** Lingham, 30.

**250 cc, round 7 (20 laps, 24.07 miles/38.74 km)**
**1** Donnie McLeod, GB (Armstrong), 20m 50.6s, 69.29 mph/111.51 km/h.
**2** Darren Dixon, GB (Honda); **3** Ian Young, GB (Armstrong); **4** Andy Watts, GB (Decorite); **5** Gary Weston, GB (Yamaha); **6** Dave Quarmby, GB (Yamaha); **7** Colin Wainwright, GB (Rotax); **8** Ian Muir, GB (Yamaha); **9** Peter Hubbard, GB (Rotax); **10** Chris Fargher, GB (Yamaha).
**Fastest lap:** Young, 1m 00.9s, 71.14 mph/114.49 km/h.
**Championship points: 1** MacKenzie, 71; **2** McLeod, 66; **3** Dixon, 51; **4** Noel, 35; **5** Crick and Patrickson, 26.

**250 cc, round 8 (20 laps, 24.07 miles/38.74 km)**
**1** Nigel Bosworth, GB (Yamaha), 17m 20.0s, 83.32 mph/134.09 km/h.
**2** Carl Fogarty, GB (Yamaha); **3** Darren Dixon, GB (Honda); **4** Mick Bridges, GB (Yamaha); **5** Ian Newton, GB (Armstrong); **6** Bob Haynes, GB (Yamaha); **7** Peter Hubbard, GB (Rotax); **8** Dave Quarmby, GB (Yamaha); **9** Barry Seward, GB (Armstrong); **10** Colin Wainwright, GB (Rotax).
**Fastest lap:** Donnie McLeod, GB (Armstrong), 50.2s, 86.31 mph/138.90 km/h.
**Championship points: 1** MacKenzie, 71; **2** McLeod, 66; **3** Dixon, 61; **4** Noel, 35; **5** Newton, 31; **6** Fogarty, 30.

**Sidecars, round 7 (15 laps, 18.05 miles/29.06 km)**
**1** Steve Webster/Tony Hewitt, GB/GB (500 LCR-Yamaha), 13m 36.5s, 79.60 mph/128.10 km/h.
**2** Derek Bayley/Bryan Nixon, GB/GB (500 LCR-Yamaha); **3** Steve Abbott/Shaun Smith, GB/GB (500 Windle-Yamaha); **4** Derek Jones/Brian Ayres, GB/GB (500 LCR-Yamaha); **5** Barry Brindley/Chris Jones, GB/GB (500 Windle-Yamaha); **6** Tony Baker/Peter Harper, GB/GB (500 Baker-Yamaha); **7** Barry Smith/Dave Smith, GB/GB (500 Windle-Yamaha); **8** Mick Barton/Fritz Buck, GB/D (500 LCR-Yamaha); **9** Lowry Burton/Pat Cashnahan, GB/GB (500 Yamaha); **10** George Hardwick/Carl Fieldhouse, GB/GB (500 Ireson-Yamaha).
**Fastest lap:** Bayley, 52.1s, 83.16 mph/133.83 km/h.
**Championship points: 1** Webster, 94; **2** Abbott, 86; **3** Bayley, 57; **4** Brindley, 46; **5** Jones, 24; **6** Kumagaya, 23.

**Sidecars, round 8 (15 laps, 18.05 miles/29.06 km)**
**1** Steve Webster/Tony Hewitt, GB/GB (500 LCR-Yamaha), 12m 44.6s, 85.00 mph/136.79 km/h.
**2** Derek Bayley/Bryan Nixon, GB/GB (500 LCR-Yamaha); **3** Steve Abbott/Shaun Smith, GB/GB (500 Windle-Yamaha); **4** Barry Brindley/Chris Jones, GB/GB (500 Windle-Yamaha); **5** Dennis Bingham/Julia Bingham, GB/GB (500 LCR-Yamaha); **6** Tony Baker/Peter Harper, GB/GB (500 Baker-Yamaha); **7** Lowry Burton/Pat Cashnahan, GB/GB (500 Yamaha); **8** George Hardwick/Karl Fieldhouse, GB/GB (500 Ireson-Yamaha); **9** Dave Carnell/Andy Peach, GB/GB (500 Yamaha); **10** Tony Croft/Carl Firmin, GB/GB (350 Yamaha).
**Fastest lap:** Webster, 49.9s, 86.83 mph/139.74 km/h.
**Championship points: 1** Webster, 109; **2** Abbott, 96; **3** Bayley, 69; **4** Brindley, 54; **5** Jones and Baker, 24.

**DONINGTON PARK CIRCUIT, 22 June, 2.500-mile/4.023-km circuit.**
**1300 cc, round 9 (8 laps, 20.00 miles/32.18 km)**
**1** Richard Scott, NZ (750 Honda), 15m 38.0s, 76.75 mph/123.52 km/h.
**2** Kenny Irons, GB (500 Yamaha); **3** Trevor Nation, GB (500 Suzuki); **4** Steve Henshaw, GB (500 Suzuki); **5** Roger Burnett, GB (500 Honda); **6** Neil Robinson, GB (750 Suzuki); **7** Roger Marshall, GB (500 Honda); **8** Gary Lingham, GB (500 Suzuki); **9** Terry Rymer, GB (500 Suzuki); **10** Mike Lomas, GB (500 Suzuki).
**Fastest lap:** Irons, 1m 54.5s, 78.59 mph/126.48 km/h (record).
**Championship points: 1** Burnett, 86; **2** Marshall, 65; **3** Nation, 54; **4** MacKenzie, 48; **5** Henshaw, 37; **6** Robinson, 34.

**1300 cc, round 10 (8 laps, 20.00 miles/32.18 km)**
**1** Kenny Irons, GB (500 Yamaha), 14m 16.6s, 84.05 mph/135.27 km/h.
**2** Roger Marshall, GB (500 Honda); **3** Roger Burnett, GB (500 Honda); **4** Trevor Nation, GB (500 Suzuki); **5** Steve Henshaw, GB (500 Suzuki); **6** Neil Robinson, GB (750 Suzuki); **7** Steve Parrish, GB (750 Yamaha); **8** Terry Rymer, GB (500 Suzuki); **9** Richard Scott, NZ (750 Honda); **10** Andy McGladdery, GB (750 Suzuki).
**Fastest lap:** Marshall and Nation, 1m 44.5s, 86.12 mph/138.60 km/h (record).
**Championship points: 1** Burnett, 96; **2** Marshall, 77; **3** Nation, 64; **4** MacKenzie, 48; **5** Henshaw, 43; **6** Robinson, 39.

**250 cc, round 9 (8 laps, 20.00 miles/32.18 km)**
**1** Niall MacKenzie, GB (Armstrong), 15m 23.3s, 77.97 mph/125.48 km/h.
**2** Donnie McLeod, GB (Armstrong); **3** Kevin Mitchell, GB (Yamaha); **4** Carl Fogarty, GB (Yamaha); **5** Tony Head, GB (Armstrong); **6** Andy Machin, GB (Rotax); **7** Darren Dixon, GB (Honda); **8** Rob Orme, GB (Yamaha); **9** Andy Watts, GB (Decorite); **10** Peter Hubbard, GB (Rotax).
**Fastest lap:** MacKenzie, 1m 52.5s, 80.00 mph/128.75 km/h (record).
**Championship points: 1** MacKenzie, 86; **2** McLeod, 78; **3** Dixon, 65; **4** Fogarty, 38; **5** Noel, 35; **6** Newton, 31.

**250 cc, round 10 (8 laps, 20.00 miles/32.18 km)**
**1** Niall MacKenzie, GB (Armstrong), 14m 29.7s, 82.78 mph/133.22 km/h.
**2** Donnie McLeod, GB (Armstrong); **3** Kevin Mitchell, GB (Yamaha); **4** Andy Watts, GB (Decorite); **5** Carl Fogarty, GB (Yamaha); **6** Rob Orme, GB (Yamaha); **7** Peter Hubbard, GB (Rotax); **8** Andy Godber, GB (Yamaha); **9** Darren Dixon, GB (Honda); **10** Mark Farmer, GB (Honda).
**Fastest lap:** McLeod, 1m 46.2s, 84.74 mph/136.38 km/h (record).
**Championship points: 1** MacKenzie, 101; **2** McLeod, 90; **3** Dixon, 67; **4** Fogarty, 44; **5** Mitchell, 40; **6** Noel, 35.

**Sidecars, round 9 (8 laps, 20.00 miles/32.18 km)**
**1** Steve Webster/Tony Hewitt, GB/GB (500 LCR-Yamaha), 14m 40.1s, 81.80 mph/131.64 km/h.
**2** Derek Bayley/Bryan Nixon, GB/GB (500 LCR-Ricardo); **3** Barry Brindley/Chris Jones, GB/GB (500 Windle-Yamaha); **4** Frank Wrathall/Phil Spendlove, GB/GB (500 LCR-Yamaha); **5** Lowry Burton/Geoff Leitch, GB/GB (500 Yamaha); **6** Dennis Bingham/Julia Bingham, GB/GB (500 LCR-Yamaha); **7** Geoff Young/Jimmy Cochrane, GB/GB (500 Yamaha); **8** George Hardwick/Carl Fieldhouse, GB/GB (500 Ireson-Yamaha); **9** Warwick Newman/Eddie Yarker, GB/GB (500 Ireson-Yamaha); **10** Stewart Rich/Steve Groves, GB/GB (500 Hempsall-Yamaha).
**Fastest lap:** Webster, 1m 46.2s, 84.74 mph/136.38 km/h (record).
**Championship points: 1** Webster, 124; **2** Abbott, 96; **3** Bayley, 81; **4** Brindley, 64; **5** Jones and Barker, 24.

**Sidecars, round 10 (8 laps, 20.00 miles/32.18 km)**
**1** Derek Bayley/Bryan Nixon, GB/GB (500 LCR-Ricardo), 14m 22.0s, 83.52 mph/134.41 km/h.
**2** Frank Wrathall/Phil Spendlove, GB/GB (500 LCR-Yamaha); **3** Barry Brindley/Chris Jones, GB/GB (500 Windle-Yamaha); **4** Graham Gleeson/Dave Elliott, NZ/GB (500 LCR-Yamaha); **5** Lowry Burton/Geoff Leitch, GB/GB (500 Yamaha); **6** Dennis Bingham/Julia Bingham, GB/GB (500 LCR-Yamaha); **7** Geoff Young/Jimmy Cochrane, GB/GB (500 Yamaha); **8** George Hardwick/Carl Fieldhouse, GB/GB (500 Ireson-Yamaha); **9** Warwick Newman/Eddie Yarker, GB/GB (500 Ireson-Yamaha); **10** Mick Smith/Kevin Webster, GB/GB (500 Yamaha).
**Fastest lap:** Bayley, 1m 45.6s, 85.22 mph/137.15 km/h (record).
**Championship points: 1** Webster, 124; **2** Abbott and Bayley, 96; **4** Brindley, 74; **5** Jones and Barker, 24.

**SNETTERTON CIRCUIT, 19/20 July. 1.917-mile/3.085-km circuit.**
**1300 cc, round 11 (12 laps, 23.00 miles/37.02 km)**
**1** Roger Marshall, GB (500 Honda), 13m 51.8s, 99.56 mph/160.23 km/h.
**2** Trevor Nation, GB (500 Suzuki); **3** Kenny Irons, GB (500 Suzuki); **4** Richard Scott, NZ (750 Honda); **5** Steve Manley, GB (500 Suzuki); **6** Barry Woodland, GB (500 Suzuki); **7** Mark Phillips, GB (500 Suzuki); **8** Dennis Ireland, NZ (500 Suzuki); **9** Mark Phillips, GB (500 Suzuki); **10** Mark Stone, GB (500 Suzuki).
**Fastest lap:** Marshall and Nation, 1m 08.2s, 101.19 mph/162.85 km/h.
**Championship points: 1** Burnett, 96; **2** Marshall, 77; **3** Nation, 64; **4** MacKenzie, 48; **5** Henshaw, 43; **6** Irons and Robinson, 39.

**1300 cc, round 12 (12 laps, 23.00 miles/37.02 km)**
**1** Roger Burnett, GB (500 Honda), 13m 55.4s, 99.13 mph/159.53 km/h.
**2** Roger Marshall, GB (500 Honda); **3** Mark Phillips, GB (500 Suzuki); **4** Trevor Nation, GB (500 Suzuki); **5** Richard Scott, NZ (750 Honda); **6** Barry Woodland, GB (500 Suzuki); **7** Dennis Ireland, NZ (500 Suzuki); **8** Ricky McMillan, GB (1260 Kawasaki); **9** Mark Phillips, GB (500 Suzuki); **10** Zen Marseilles, GB (500 Suzuki).
**Fastest lap:** Marshall, 1m 08.2s, 101.19 mph/162.85 km/h.
**Championship points: 1** Burnett, 111; **2** Marshall, 104; **3** Nation, 84; **4** MacKenzie, 48; **5** Henshaw, 43; **6** Irons and Robinson, 39.

**250 cc, round 11 (12 laps, 23.00 miles/37.02 km)**
**1** Andy Watts, GB (EMC), 14m 27.0s, 95.50 mph/153.69 km/h.
**2** Carl Fogarty, GB (Yamaha); **3** Kevin Mitchell, GB (Yamaha); **4** Nigel Bosworth, GB (Yamaha); **5** Steve Chambers, GB (Yamaha); **6** Ian Newton, GB (Armstrong); **7** Martyn Jupp, GB (Yamaha); **8** Steve Patrickson, GB (Rotax); **9** Barry Seward, GB (Armstrong); **10** Rob Orme, GB (Yamaha).
**Fastest lap:** Fogarty, 1m 09.09s, 98.72 mph/158.87 km/h.
**Championship points: 1** MacKenzie, 101; **2** McLeod, 90; **3** Dixon, 67; **4** Fogarty, 56; **5** Mitchell, 50; **6** Watts, 43.

**250 cc, round 12 (12 laps, 23.00 miles/37.02 km)**
**1** Andy Watts, GB (EMC), 14m 19.8s, 96.31 mph/155.00 km/h.
**2** Carl Fogarty, GB (Yamaha); **3** Nigel Bosworth, GB (Yamaha); **4** Steve Chambers, GB (Yamaha); **5** Kevin Mitchell, GB (Yamaha); **6** Rob Orme, GB (Yamaha); **7** Peter Hubbard, GB (Rotax); **8** Ian Newton, GB (Armstrong); **9** Martyn Jupp, GB (Yamaha); **10** Darren Dixon, GB (Honda).
**Fastest lap:** Watts, 1m 10.1s, 98.44 mph/158.42 km/h.
**Championship points: 1** MacKenzie, 101; **2** McLeod, 90; **3** Dixon and Fogarty, 68; **5** Watts, 58; **6** Mitchell, 56.

**Sidecars, round 11 (12 laps, 23.00 miles/37.02 km)**
**1** Yoshisada Kumagaya/Kazuhiko Makiuchi, J/J (500 LCR-Yamaha), 14m 53.6s, 92.67 mph/149.14 km/h.
**2** Dave Hallam/Mark Day, GB/GB (500 LCR-Yamaha); **3** Gary Thomas/Geoff White, GB/GB (500 BSL-Yamaha); **4** Mick Burcombe/Steve Parker, GB/GB (500 LCR-Yamaha); **5** Tony Baker/Peter Harper, GB/GB (500 Yamaha); **6** Warwick Newman/Eddie Yarker, GB/GB (500 Ireson-Yamaha). No other finishers.
**Fastest lap:** Kumagaya, 1m 11.8s, 96.11 mph/154.67 km/h.
**Championship points: 1** Webster, 124; **2** Abbott and Bayley, 96; **4** Brindley, 74; **5** Kumagaya, 38; **6** Baker, 30.

**Sidecars, round 12 (12 laps, 23.00 miles/37.02 km)**
**1** Yoshisada Kumagaya/Kazuhiko Makiuchi, J/J (500 LCR-Yamaha), 14m 56.3s, 92.38 mph/148.67 km/h.
**2** Dave Hallam/Mark Day, GB/GB (500 LCR-Yamaha); **3** Tony Baker/Peter Harper, GB/GB (500 Yamaha); **4** Mick Burcombe/Steve Parker, GB/GB (500 LCR-Yamaha); **5** George Hardwick/Carl Fieldhouse, GB/GB (500 Ireson-Yamaha); **6** Gary Thomas/Geoff White, GB/GB (500 BSL-Yamaha); **7** David Lee/Richard Lee, GB/GB (500 Yamaha). No other finishers.
**Fastest lap:** Kumagaya, 1m 12.1s, 95.71 mph/154.03 km/h.
**Championship points: 1** Webster, 124; **2** Abbott and Bayley, 96; **4** Brindley, 74; **5** Kumagaya, 53; **6** Baker, 40.

**MALLORY PARK CIRCUIT, 27 July. 1.370-mile/2.205-km circuit.**
**1300 cc, round 13 (12 laps, 16.44 miles/26.46 km)**
**1** Roger Burnett, GB (500 Honda), 10m 37.7s, 92.80 mph/149.35 km/h.
**2** Roger Marshall, GB (500 Honda); **3** Mark Phillips, GB (500 Suzuki); **4** Richard Scott, NZ (750 Honda); **5** Dennis Ireland, NZ (500 Suzuki) and Steve Henshaw, GB (500 Suzuki); **7** Alan Jeffery, GB (500 Suzuki); **8** Dave Griffith, GB (500 Suzuki); **9** Steve Ward, GB (500 Suzuki) and Michael Seward, GB (750 Yamaha).
**Fastest lap:** Marshall, 51.9s, 95.02 mph/152.92 km/h.
**Championship points: 1** Burnett, 126; **2** Marshall, 116; **3** Nation, 84; **4** Henshaw, 49; **5** MacKenzie, 48; **6** Irons, Robinson and Scott, 39.

**1300 cc, round 14 (12 laps, 16.44 miles/26.46 km)**
**1** Roger Burnett, GB (500 Honda), 10m 32.3s, 93.60 mph/150.63 km/h.
**2** Roger Marshall, GB (500 Honda); **3** Mark Phillips, GB (500 Suzuki); **4** Alan Jeffery, GB (500 Suzuki); **5** Richard Scott, NZ (750 Honda); **6** Dennis Ireland, NZ (500 Suzuki); **7** Steve Henshaw, GB (500 Suzuki); **8** Mike Lomas, GB (500 Suzuki); **9** Steve Manley, GB (500 Suzuki); **10** Dave Griffith, GB (500 Suzuki).
**Fastest lap:** Burnett and Marshall, 51.9s, 95.02 mph/152.92 km/h.
**Championship points: 1** Burnett, 141; **2** Marshall, 128; **3** Nation, 84; **4** Henshaw, 53; **5** MacKenzie, 48; **6** Scott, 45.

**250 cc, round 13 (10 laps, 13.70 miles/22.05 km)**
**1** Niall MacKenzie, GB (Armstrong), 8m 56.6s, 91.91 mph/147.91 km/h.
**2** Donnie McLeod, GB (Armstrong); **3** Kevin Mitchell, GB (Yamaha); **4** Andy Watts, GB (EMC); **5** Nigel Bosworth, GB (Yamaha); **6** Martyn Jupp, GB (Yamaha); **7** Peter Hubbard, GB (Rotax); **8** Ian Newton, GB (Armstrong); **9** Darren Dixon, GB (Honda); **10** Gary Noel, GB (EMC).
**Fastest lap:** MacKenzie, 52.3s, 94.30 mph/151.76 km/h.
**Championship points: 1** MacKenzie, 116; **2** McLeod, 102; **3** Dixon, 70; **4** Fogarty, 68; **5** Mitchell and Watts, 66.

**250 cc, round 14 (8 laps, 10.96 miles/17.64 km)**
**1** Donnie McLeod, GB (Armstrong), 7m 08.0s, 92.18 mph/148.35 km/h.
**2** Carl Fogarty, GB (Yamaha); **3** Kevin Bosworth, GB (Yamaha); **4** Kevin Mitchell, GB (Yamaha); **5** Darren Dixon, GB (Honda); **6** Niall MacKenzie, GB (Armstrong); **7** Ian Newton, GB (Armstrong); **8** Steve Patrickson, GB (Rotax); **9** Martyn Jupp, GB (Yamaha); **10** Tony Rogers, GB (Yamaha).
**Fastest lap:** Mcleod, 52.4s, 94.12 mph/150.96 km/h.
**Championship points: 1** MacKenzie, 121; **2** McLeod, 117; **3** Fogarty, 80; **4** Dixon, 76; **5** Mitchell, 74; **6** Watts, 66.

**Sidecars, round 13 (10 laps, 13.70 miles/22.05 km)**
**1** Steve Abbott/Vince Biggs, GB/GB (500 Windle-Yamaha), 8m 53.6s, 92.42 mph/148.74 km/h.
**2** Derek Bayley/Bryan Nixon, GB/GB (500 LCR-Yamaha); **3** Dennis Bingham/Julia Bingham, GB/GB (500 LCR-Yamaha); **4** Tony Baker/Peter Harper, GB/GB (500 Yamaha); **5** Yoshisada Kumagaya/Kazuhiko Makiuchi, J/J (500 LCR-Yamaha); **6** Lowry Burton/Geoff Leitch, GB/GB (500 Ironside-Yamaha); **7** Gary Thomas/Geoff White, GB/GB (500 BSL-Yamaha); **8** George Hardwick/Carl Fieldhouse, GB/GB (500 Ireson-Yamaha); **9** Mick Burcombe/Steve Parker, GB/GB (500 LCR-Yamaha); **10** Kenny Howles/Steve Pointer, GB/GB (500 Yamaha).
**Fastest lap:** Steve Webster/Tony Hewitt, GB/GB (500 LCR-Yamaha), 51.0s, 96.70 mph/155.62 km/h (record).
**Championship points: 1** Webster, 124; **2** Abbott, 111; **3** Bayley, 108; **4** Brindley, 74; **5** Kumagaya, 59; **6** Baker, 48.

**Sidecars, round 14 (10 laps, 13.70 miles/22.05 km)**
**1** Steve Webster/Tony Hewitt, GB/GB (500 LCR-Yamaha), 8m 46.3s, 93.71 mph/150.81 km/h.
**2** Derek Bayley/Bryan Nixon, GB/GB (500 LCR-Yamaha); **3** Steve Abbott/Vince Biggs, GB/GB (500 Windle-Yamaha); **4** Yoshisada Kumagaya/Kazuhiko Makiuchi, J/J (500 LCR-Yamaha); **5** Tony Baker/Peter Harper, GB/GB (500 Yamaha; **6** Dennis Bingham/Julia Bingham, GB/GB (500 LCR-Yamaha); **7** Lowry Burton/Geoff Leitch, GB/GB (500 Ironside-Yamaha); **8** Gary Thomas/Geoff White, GB/GB (500 BSL-Yamaha); **9** Kenny Howles/Steve Pointer, GB/GB (500 Yamaha); **10** George Hardwick/Carl Fieldhouse, GB/GB (500 Ireson-Yamaha).
**Fastest lap:** Webster, 51.0s, 96.70 mph/155.62 km/h (equals record).
**Championship points: 1** Webster, 139; **2** Abbott, 121; **3** Bayley, 120; **4** Brindley, 74; **5** Kumagaya, 67; **6** Baker, 54.

**OULTON PARK CIRCUIT, 24/25 August. 2.356-mile/3.792-km circuit.**
**1300 cc, round 15 (8 laps, 18.85 miles/30.34 km)**
**1** Roger Burnett, GB (500 Honda), 11m 19.3s, 99.88 mph/160.74 km/h.
**2** Kenny Irons, GB (500 Yamaha); **3** Steve Henshaw, GB (500 Suzuki); **4** Andy McGladdery, GB (750 Suzuki); **5** Dennis Ireland, NZ (500 Suzuki); **6** Paul Iddon, GB (750 Suzuki); **7** Roger Hurst, GB (750 Yamaha); **8** Dave Griffith, GB (500 Suzuki); **9** Steve Manley, GB (500 Suzuki); **10** Gary Lingham, GB (750 Suzuki).
**Fastest lap:** Burnett, 1m 23.3s, 101.82 mph/163.86 km/h.
**Championship points: 1** Burnett, 156; **2** Marshall, 128; **3** Nation, 84; **4** Henshaw, 63; **5** MacKenzie, 48; **6** Irons, 51.

**1300 cc, round 16 (6 laps, 14.14 miles/22.75 km)**
**1** Neil Robinson, GB (750 Suzuki), 9m 55.5s, 85.45 mph/137.52 km/h.
**2** Roger Marshall, GB (500 Honda); **3** Roger Burnett, GB (500 Honda); **4** Mark Phillips, GB (500 Suzuki); **5** Trevor Nation, GB (500 Suzuki); **6** Dave Griffith, GB (500 Suzuki); **7** Ray Swann, GB (500 Suzuki); **8** Geoff Fowler, GB (750 Yamaha); **9** Gary Lingham, GB (750 Suzuki); **10** Julian Scott, GB (750 Suzuki).
**Fastest lap:** Marshall, 1m 37.3s, 87.16 mph/140.27 km/h.
**Championship points: 1** Burnett, 166; **2** Marshall, 140; **3** Nation, 90; **4** Henshaw, 63; **5** Robinson, 54; **6** Phillips, 52.

**250 cc, round 15 (8 laps, 18.85 miles/30.34 km)**
**1** Rob Orme, GB (Yamaha), 11m 55.9s, 94.77 mph/152.52 km/h.
**2** Ian Newton, GB (Honda); **3** Nigel Bosworth, GB (Yamaha); **4** Darren Dixon, GB (Honda); **5** Steve Chambers, GB (Yamaha); **6** Martyn Jupp, GB (Yamaha); **7** Kevin Mitchell, GB (Yamaha); **8** Jamie Hodson, GB (Rotax); **9** Tony Rogers, GB (Yamaha); **10** Tony Head, GB (EMC).
**Fastest lap:** Orme, 1m 27.8s, 96.60 mph/155.46 km/h.
**Championship points: 1** MacKenzie, 121; **2** McLeod, 117; **3** Dixon, 84; **4** Fogarty, 80; **5** Mitchell, 78; **6** Watts, 66.

**250 cc, round 16 (6 laps, 14.14 miles/22.75 km)**
**1** Kevin Mitchell, GB (Yamaha), 10m 17.5s, 82.41 mph/132.63 km/h.
**2** Rob Orme, GB (Yamaha); **3** Tony Head, GB (Honda); **4** Darren Dixon, GB (Honda); **5** Geoff McConnell, GB (Kimoco); **6** Ian Young, GB (Armstrong); **7** Graham Cannell, GB (Honda); **8** Peter Hubbard, GB (Rotax); **9** Tony Rogers, GB (Yamaha); **10** Jamie Hodson, GB (Rotax).
**Fastest lap:** Orme, 1m 40.1s, 84.73 mph/136.36 km/h.
**Championship points: 1** MacKenzie, 121; **2** McLeod, 117; **3** Mitchell, 93; **4** Dixon, 92; **5** Fogarty, 80; **6** Watts, 66.

**Sidecars, round 15 (8 laps, 18.85 miles/30.34 km)**
**1** Steve Webster/Tony Hewitt, GB/GB (500 LCR-Yamaha), 11m 29.8s, 98.36 mph/158.29 km/h.
**2** Derek Bayley/Bryan Nixon, GB/GB (500 LCR-

Yamaha); **3** Steve Abbott/Shaun Smith, GB/GB (500 Windle-Yamaha); **4** Frank Wrathall/Kerry Chapman, GB/GB (500 LCR-Yamaha); **5** Yoshisada Kumagaya/Kazuhiko Makiuchi, J/J (500 LCR-Yamaha); **6** Dennis Bingham/Julia Bingham, GB/GB (500 LCR-Yamaha); **7** Tony Baker/Peter Harper, GB/GB (500 LCR-Yamaha); **8** Lowry Burton/Pat Cashnahan, GB/GB (500 Yamaha); **9** George Hardwick/Carl Fieldhouse, GB/GB (500 Ireson-Yamaha); **10** John Coles/Graham Mapletoft, GB/GB (500 Yamaha).
**Fastest lap:** Webster, 1m 23.9s, 101.09 mph/162.69 km/h.
**Championship points: 1** Webster, 154; **2** Bayley, 132; **3** Abbott, 131; **4** Brindley, 74; **5** Kumagaya, 73; **6** Baker, 58.

**Sidecars, round 16 (8 laps, 18.85 miles/30.34 km)**
**1** Steve Abbott/Shaun Smith, GB/GB (500 Windle-Yamaha), 13m 13.9s, 85.46 mph/137.53 km/h.
**2** Derek Bayley/Bryan Nixon, GB/GB (500 LCR-Yamaha); **3** Frank Wrathall/Kerry Chapman, GB/GB (500 LCR-Yamaha); **4** Steve Webster/Tony Hewitt, GB/GB (500 LCR-Yamaha); **5** Tony Baker/Peter Harper, GB/GB (500 Yamaha); **6** Yoshisada Kumagaya/Kazuhiko Makiuchi, J/J (500 LCR-Yamaha); **7** George Hardwick/Carl Fieldhouse, GB/GB (500 Ireson-Yamaha); **8** Dennis Bingham/Julia Bingham, GB/GB (500 LCR-Yamaha); **9** Mick Boddice/Chas Birks, GB/GB (500 LCR-Yamaha); **10** Mike Salmon/Roy Swellwood, GB/GB (500 Yamaha).
**Fastest lap:** Webster, 1m 35.9s, 88.44 mph/142.33 km/h.
**Championship points: 1** Webster, 162; **2** Abbott, 146; **3** Bayley, 144; **4** Kumagaya, 78; **5** Brindley, 74; **6** Baker, 64.

**THRUXTON CIRCUIT, 6/7 September. 2.356-mile/3.792-km circuit.**
**1300 cc, round 17 (8 laps, 18.85 miles/30.34 km)**
**1** Roger Burnett, GB (500 Honda), 11m 23.70s, 99.24 mph/159.71 km/h.
**2** Niall MacKenzie, GB (500 Suzuki); **3** Roger Marshall, GB (500 Honda); **4** Kenny Irons, GB (500 Yamaha); **5** Neil Robinson, GB (750 Suzuki); **6** Trevor Nation, GB (500 Suzuki); **7** Mark Phillips, GB (500 Suzuki); **8** Richard Scott, NZ (750 Honda); **9** Dennis Ireland, NZ (500 Suzuki); **10** Steve Henshaw, GB (500 Suzuki).
**Fastest lap:** Burnett, 1m 24.10s, 100.85 mph/162.25 km/h (record).
**Championship points: 1** Burnett, 181; **2** Marshall, 150; **3** Nation, 95; **4** Henshaw, 64; **5** MacKenzie and Robinson, 60.

**1300 cc, round 18 (8 laps, 18.85 miles/30.24 km)**
**1** Roger Burnett, GB (500 Honda), 11m 20.10s, 99.78 mph/160.58 km/h.
**2** Roger Marshall, GB (500 Honda); **3** Niall MacKenzie, GB (500 Suzuki); **4** Neil Robinson, GB (750 Suzuki); **5** Trevor Nation, GB (500 Suzuki); **6** Alan Jeffery, GB (500 Suzuki); **7** Paul Iddon, GB (750 Suzuki); **8** Ray Swann, GB (500 Suzuki); **9** Mark Phillips, GB (500 Suzuki); **10** Steve Henshaw, GB (500 Suzuki).
**Fastest lap:** Burnett, 1m 24.00s, 100.97 mph/162.50 km/h (record).
**Championship points: 1** Burnett, 196; **2** Marshall, 162; **3** Nation, 101; **4** MacKenzie, 70; **5** Robinson, 68; **6** Henshaw, 65.

**250 cc, round 17 (8 laps, 18.85 miles/30.24 km)**
**1** Niall MacKenzie, GB (Armstrong), 11m 33.06s, 97.83 mph/157.44 km/h.
**2** Donnie McLeod, GB (Armstrong); **3** Nigel Bosworth, GB (Yamaha); **4** Gary Noel, GB (EMC); **5** Rob Orme, GB (Yamaha); **6** Kevin Mitchell, GB (Yamaha); **7** Gary Cowan, GB (Honda); **8** Darren Dixon, GB (Honda); **9** Steve Chambers, GB (Yamaha); **10** Martyn Jupp, GB (Yamaha).
**Fastest lap:** MacKenzie, 1m 24.30s, 100.61 mph/161.92 km/h (record).
**Championship points: 1** MacKenzie, 136; **2** McLeod, 129; **3** Mitchell, 98; **4** Dixon, 95; **5** Fogarty, 80; **6** Bosworth, 69.

**250 cc, round 18 (8 laps, 18.85 miles/30.24 km)**
**1** Nigel Bosworth, GB (Yamaha), 11m 29.70s, 98.38 mph/158.33 km/h.
**2** Donnie McLeod, GB (Armstrong); **3** Gary Noel, GB (EMC); **4** Niall MacKenzie, GB (Armstrong); **5** Rob Orme, GB (Yamaha); **6** Gary Cowan, GB (Honda); **7** Tony Head, GB (Armstrong); **8** Steve Chambers, GB (Yamaha); **9** Martyn Jupp, GB (Yamaha); **10** Ian Young, GB (Armstrong).
**Fastest lap:** Noel, 1m 24.06s, 100.26 mph/161.35 km/h.
**Championship points: 1** MacKenzie, 144; **2** McLeod, 141; **3** Mitchell, 98; **4** Dixon, 95; **5** Bosworth, 84; **6** Fogarty, 80.

**Sidecars, round 17 (6 laps, 14.14 miles/22.75 km)**
**1** Steve Webster/Tony Hewitt, GB/GB (500 LCR-Yamaha), 8m 45.90s, 96.77 mph/155.74 km/h.
**2** Derek Bayley/Bryan Nixon, GB/GB (500 LCR-Yamaha); **3** Frank Wrathall/Kerry Chapman, GB/GB (500 LCR-Yamaha); **4** Barry Brindley/Simon Birchall, GB/GB (500 Windle-Yamaha); **5** Dave Hallam/Mark Day, GB/GB (500 LCR-Yamaha); **6** Yoshisada Kumagaya/Kazuhiko Makiuchi, J/J (500 LCR-Yamaha); **7** Mick Boddice/John Hennigan, GB/GB (500 LCR-Yamaha); **8** Clive Stirrat/Simon Prior, GB/GB (500 Yamaha); **9** Warwick Newman/Eddie Yarker, GB/GB (500 Ireson-Yamaha); **10** Dave Carnell/Andy Peach, GB/GB (500 Windle-Yamaha).
**Fastest lap:** Webster, 1m 24.10s, 100.73 mph/162.11 km/h (record).
**Championship points: 1** Webster, 177; **2** Bayley, 156; **3** Abbott, 146; **4** Kumagaya, 83; **5** Brindley, 82; **6** Baker, 64.

**Sidecars, round 18 (8 laps, 18.85 miles/30.24 km)**
**1** Steve Webster/Tony Hewitt, GB/GB (500 LCR-Yamaha), 11m 35.60s, 97.55 mph/156.99 km/h.
**2** Derek Bayley/Bryan Nixon, GB/GB (500 LCR-Yamaha); **3** Frank Wrathall/Kerry Chapman, GB/GB (500 LCR-Yamaha); **4** Steve Abbott/Shaun Smith, GB/GB (500 Windle-Yamaha); **5** Yoshisada Kumagaya/Kazuhiko Makiuchi, J/J (500 LCR-Yamaha); **6** Dave Hallam/Mark Day, GB/GB (500 LCR-Yamaha); **7** Lowry Burton/Pat Cashnahan, GB/GB (500 Yamaha); **8** Mick Boddice/John Hennigan, GB/GB (500 LCR-Yamaha); **9** Mick Burcombe/Dave Knapp, GB/GB (500 LCR-Yamaha); **10** Clive Stirrat/Simon Prior, GB/GB (500 Yamaha).
**Fastest lap:** Webster, 1m 24.50s, 100.37 mph/161.53 km/h.
**Championship points: 1** Webster, 192; **2** Bayley, 168; **3** Abbott, 154; **4** Kumagaya, 89; **5** Brindley, 82; **6** Baker, 64.

**SILVERSTONE GRAND PRIX CIRCUIT, 20/21 September. 2.927-mile/4.711-km circuit.**
**1300 cc, round 19 (10 laps, 29.27 miles/47.11 km)**
**1** Roger Burnett, GB (500 Honda), 15m 31.90s, 113.07 mph/181.97 km/h.
**2** Roger Marshall, GB (500 Honda); **3** Kenny Irons, GB (500 Yamaha); **4** Mark Phillips, GB (500 Suzuki); **5** Trevor Nation, GB (500 Suzuki); **6** Paul Iddon, GB (750 Suzuki); **7** Mike Lomas, GB (500 Suzuki); **8** Glen Williams, NZ (750 Suzuki); **9** Andy McGladdery, GB (750 Suzuki); **10** Steve Manley, GB (500 Suzuki).
**Fastest lap:** Marshall, 1m 31.30s, 115.41 mph/185.73 km/h.
**Championship points: 1** Burnett, 211; **2** Marshall, 174; **3** Nation, 107; **4** MacKenzie, 70; **5** Irons, 69; **6** Robinson, 68.

**1300 cc, round 20 (10 laps, 29.27 miles/47.11 km)**
**1** Roger Burnett, GB (500 Honda), 15m 27.90s, 113.55 mph/182.74 km/h.
**2** Roger Marshall, GB (500 Honda); **3** Kenny Irons, GB (500 Yamaha); **4** Mark Phillips, GB (500 Suzuki); **5** Paul Iddon, GB (750 Suzuki); **6** Steve Parrish, GB (750 Yamaha); **7** Glen Williams, NZ (1100 Suzuki); **8** Trevor Nation, GB (500 Suzuki); **9** Andy McGladdery, GB (750 Suzuki); **10** Steve Manley, GB (500 Suzuki).
**Fastest lap:** Marshall, 1m 31.20s, 115.53 mph/185.93 km/h.

**250 cc, round 19 (10 laps, 29.27 miles/47.11 km)**
**1** Donnie McLeod, GB (Armstrong), 16m 03.20s, 109.39 mph/176.05 km/h.
**2** Niall MacKenzie, GB (Armstrong); **3** Nigel Bosworth, GB (Yamaha); **4** Steve Chambers, GB (Yamaha); **5** Rob Orme, GB (Yamaha); **6** Ian Newton, GB (Honda); **7** Darren Dixon, GB (Honda); **8** Martyn Jupp, GB (Yamaha); **9** Tony Rogers, GB (Yamaha); **10** Andy Machin, GB (Rotax).
**Fastest lap:** McLeod, 1m 34.70s, 111.26 mph/179.06 km/h.
**Championship points: 1** MacKenzie and McLeod, 156; **3** Dixon, 99; **4** Mitchell, 98; **5** Bosworth, 94; **6** Fogarty, 80.

**250 cc, round 20 (10 laps, 29.27 miles/47.11 km)**
**1** Niall MacKenzie, GB (Armstrong), 16m 00.70s, 109.68 mph/176.51 km/h.
**2** Gary Noel, GB (EMC); **3** Donnie McLeod, GB (Armstrong); **4** Steve Chambers, GB (Yamaha); **5** Ian Newton, GB (Honda); **6** Rob Orme, GB (Yamaha); **7** Martyn Jupp, GB (Yamaha); **8** Nigel Bosworth, GB (Yamaha); **9** Steve Patrickson, GB (Rotax); **10** Tony Rogers, GB (Yamaha).
**Fastest lap:** MacKenzie, 1m 34.10s, 111.97 mph/180.20 km/h.

**Sidecars, round 19 (10 laps, 29.27 miles/47.11 km)**
**1** Steve Webster/Tony Hewitt, GB/GB (500 LCR-Yamaha), 15m 45.40s, 111.46 mph/179.38 km/h.
**2** Derek Bayley/Bryan Nixon, GB/GB (500 LCR-Yamaha); **3** Frank Wrathall/Kerry Chapman, GB/GB (500 LCR-Yamaha); **4** Dennis Bingham/John Gibbard, GB/GB (500 LCR-Yamaha); **5** Yoshisada Kumagaya/Kazuhiko Makiuchi, GB/GB (500 LCR-Yamaha); **6** Mick Boddice/John Hennigan, GB/GB (500 LCR-Yamaha); **7** Tony Baker/Peter Harper, GB/GB (500 Yamaha); **8** Lowry Burton/Pat Cashnahan, GB/GB (500 Yamaha); **9** George Hardwick/Carl Fieldhouse, GB/GB (500 Ireson-Yamaha); **10** Warwick Newman/Eddie Yarker, GB/GB (500 Ireson-Yamaha).
**Fastest lap:** Bayley, 1m 32.30s, 114.16 mph/183.72 km/h.
**Championship points: 1** Webster, 207; **2** Bayley, 180; **3** Abbott, 154; **4** Kumagaya, 95; **5** Brindley, 82; **6** Baker and Wrathall, 68.

**Sidecars, round 20 (10 laps, 29.27 miles/47.11 km)**
**1** Steve Webster/Tony Hewitt, GB/GB (500 LCR-Yamaha), 15m 43.60s, 111.67 mph/179.71 km/h.
**2** Barry Brindley/Simon Birchall, GB/GB (500 Windle-Yamaha); **3** Mick Boddice/John Hennigan, GB/GB (500 LCR-Yamaha); **4** Yoshisada Kumagaya/Kazuhiko Makiuchi, J/J (500 LCR-Yamaha); **5** Dave Hallam/Mark Day, GB/GB (500 LCR-Yamaha); **6** Ray Gardner/Tony Strevens, GB/GB (500 LCR-Yamaha); **7** Dennis Bingham/John Gibbard, GB/GB (500 LCR-Yamaha); **8** Tony Baker/Geoff Leitch, GB/GB (500 Yamaha); **9** Mick Burcombe/Dave Knapp, GB/GB (500 LCR-Yamaha); **10** Kenny Howles/Steve Pointer, GB/GB (500 Yamaha).
**Fastest lap:** Webster, 1m 32.60s, 113.79 mph/183.13 km/h.

**Final Championship points (1300 cc)**

| | |
|---|---|
| **1** Roger Burnett, GB | 220 (226) |
| **2** Roger Marshall, GB | 186 |
| **3** Trevor Nation, GB | 110 |
| **4** Kenny Irons, GB | 79 |
| **5** Mark Phillips, GB | 74 |
| **6** Niall MacKenzie, GB | 70 |

**7** Neil Robinson, GB, 68; **8** Steve Henshaw, GB, 65; **9** Richard Scott, NZ, 48; **10** Gary Lingham, GB, 36; **11** Dennis Ireland, NZ, 33; **12** Howard Selby, GB, 32; **13** Andy McGladdery, GB, 26; **14** Alan Jeffery, GB, 23; **15** Terry Rymer, GB, 22.

**Final Championship points (250 cc)**

| | |
|---|---|
| **1** Niall MacKenzie, GB | 171 |
| **2** Donnie McLeod, GB | 166 |
| **3** Darren Dixon, GB | 99 |
| **4** Kevin Mitchell, GB | 98 |
| **5** Nigel Bosworth, GB | 97 |
| **6** Carl Fogarty, GB | 80 |

**7** Ian Newton, GB, 69; **8** Gary Noel, GB and Andy Watts, GB, 66; **10** Rob Orme, GB, 64; **11** Steve Chambers, GB, 41; **12** Peter Hubbard, GB, 35; **13** Steve Patrickson, GB, 34; **14** Ian Young, GB, 30; **15** Martyn Jupp, GB, 28.

**Final Championship points (Sidecars)**

| | |
|---|---|
| **1** Steve Webster, GB | 222 |
| **2** Derek Bayley, GB | 180 |
| **3** Steve Abbott, GB | 154 |
| **4** Yoshisada Kumagaya, J | 103 |
| **5** Barry Brindley, GB | 94 |
| **6** Tony Baker, GB | 71 |

**7** Frank Wrathall, GB, 68; **8** Dennis Bingham, GB, 51; **9** Dave Hallam, GB, 41; **10** Lowry Burton, GB, 37; **11** Mick Boddice, 36; **12** George Hardwick, GB, 28; **13** Gary Thomas, GB, 25; **14** Derek Jones, GB, 24; **15** Ray Gardner, GB, 23.

## *Major British Meetings*

**CADWELL PARK CIRCUIT, 9 March. 2.250-mile/3.621-km circuit.**
***See also* Shell Oils British Transnational Championship results.**
**350 cc (8 laps, 18.00 miles/28.97 km)**
**1** Donnie McLeod, GB (Armstrong), 13m 42.1s, 78.91 mph/126.99 km/h.
**2** Andy Machin, GB (Yamaha); **3** Paul Simmonds, GB (Yamaha); **4** Barry Stanley, GB (Yamaha); **5** Steve Wright, GB (Yamaha); **6** Gary Cowan, GB (Yamaha).
**Fastest lap:** McLeod, 1m 41.0s, 80.19 mph/129.05 km/h.

**BRANDS HATCH INDY CIRCUIT, 28 March. 1.2036-mile/1.9370-km circuit.**
***See also* Shell Oils British Transnational Championship results.**
**TT F1/F2 (10 laps, 12.04 miles/19.37 km)**
**1** Asa Moyce, GB (750 Kawasaki), 11m 01.0s, 65.55 mph/105.49 km/h.
**2** Tony Moran, GB (750 Yamaha); **3** Roland Brown, GB (750 Suzuki); **4** Mark Linscott, GB (750 Kawasaki); **5** Michael Seward, GB (750 Yamaha); **6** Vince Cundle, GB (350 Yamaha).
**Fastest lap:** Moyce, 1m 03.9s, 67.80 mph/109.11 km/h.

**350 cc (15 laps, 18.05 miles/29.06 km)**
**1** Donnie McLeod, GB (Armstrong), 14m 18.3s, 75.72 mph/121.86 km/h.
**2** Vince Cundle, GB (Yamaha); **3** Marek Nofer, GB (Yamaha); **4** Roddy Taylor, GB (Yamaha); **5** John Wells, GB (Yamaha); **6** Chris Branneck, GB (Yamaha).
**Fastest lap:** McLeod, 52.5s, 82.53 mph/132.82 km/h.

**DONINGTON PARK CIRCUIT, 29 March. 2.500-mile/4.023-km circuit.**
***See also* Shell Oils Transatlantic Challenge results.**
**1300 cc (10 laps, 25.00 miles/40.23 km)**
**1** Roger Marshall, GB (500 Honda), 20m 08.9s, 74.44 mph/119.80 km/h.
**2** Roger Burnett, GB (500 Honda); **3** John Swingler, GB (500 Suzuki); **4** Steve Parrish, GB (750 Yamaha); **5** Julian Scott, GB (750 Suzuki); **6** Howard Selby, GB (500 Suzuki).
**Fastest lap:** Burnett, 1m 55.0s, 78.26 mph/125.95 km/h.

**Sidecars (10 laps, 25.00 miles/40.23 km)**
**1** Steve Webster/Tony Hewitt, GB/GB (500 LCR-Yamaha), 19m 08.0s, 78.39 mph/126.16 km/h.
**2** Steve Abbott/Shaun Smith, GB/GB (500 Windle-Yamaha); **3** Derek Bayley/Bryan Nixon, GB/GB (500 LCR-Yamaha); **4** Dave Hallam/Mark Day, GB/GB (500 LCR-Yamaha); **5** Graham Gleeson/Dave Elliott, NZ/GB (500 LCR-Yamaha); **6** John Phillips/Malcolm Hollis, GB/GB (500 Yamaha).
**Fastest lap:** Webster, 1m 52.0s, 80.35 mph/129.31 km/h.

**DONINGTON PARK CIRCUIT, 30 March. 2.500-mile/4.023-km circuit.**
***See also* Shell Oils Transatlantic Challenge results.**
**1300 cc (8 laps, 20.00 miles/32.18 km)**
**1** Roger Burnett, GB (500 Honda), 15m 53.7s, 75.49 mph/121.49 km/h.
**2** Roger Marshall, GB (500 Honda); **3** Trevor Nation, GB (500 Suzuki); **4** John Swingler, GB (500 Suzuki); **5** Julian Scott, GB (750 Suzuki); **6** Paul Lewis, AUS (500 Suzuki).
**Fastest lap:** Burnett, 1m 55.8s, 77.72 mph/125.08 km/h.

**TT F1 (8 laps, 20.00 miles/32.18 km)**
**1** Trevor Nation, GB (750 Suzuki), 16m 13.0s, 73.99 mph/119.08 km/h.
**2** Julian Scott, GB (750 Suzuki); **3** Steve Parrish, GB (750 Yamaha); **4** Dave Hill, GB (750 Suzuki); **5** Ray Swann, GB (750 Suzuki); **6** Brian Morrison, GB (750 Suzuki).
**Fastest lap:** Nation, 1m 58.9s, 75.69 mph/121.81 km/h.

**TT F2 (8 laps, 20.00 miles/32.18 km)**
**1** Carl Fogarty, GB (350 Yamaha), 16m 19.9s, 73.47 mph/118.24 km/h.
**2** Ian Newton, GB (350 Yamaha); **3** Tony Head, GB (350 Yamaha); **4** Ray Swann, GB (600 Kawasaki); **5** Mark Johns, GB (350 Yamaha); **6** Mark Westmorland, GB (350 Yamaha).
**Fastest lap:** Newton, 1m 59.1s, 75.56 mph/121.60 km/h.

**250 cc (8 laps, 20.00 miles/32.18 km)**
**1** Niall MacKenzie, GB (Armstrong), 16m 13.6s, 73.95 mph/119.01 km/h.
**2** Donnie McLeod, GB (Armstrong); **3** Carl Fogarty, GB (Yamaha); **4** Keith Nicholls, GB (Yamaha); **5** Ian Newton, GB (Armstrong); **6** Gary Noel, GB (EMC).
**Fastest lap:** McLeod, 2m 01.0s, 74.38 mph/119.70 km/h.

**125 cc (8 laps, 20.00 miles/32.18 km)**
**1** Reg Lennon, GB (MBA), 17m 59.2s, 66.71 mph/107.36 km/h.
**2** Shaun Simpson, GB (MBA); **3** Rob Blow, GB (Honda); **4** Gary Buckle, GB (MBA); **5** Dave Bowman, GB (EMC); **6** Dave Brown, GB (MBA).
**Fastest lap:** Lennon, 2m 11.8s, 68.28 mph/109.89 km/h.

**Sidecars (8 laps, 20.00 miles/32.18 km)**
**1** Steve Webster/Tony Hewitt, GB/GB (500 LCR-Yamaha), 16m 33.5s, 72.47 mph/116.63 km/h.
**2** Barry Brindley/Chris Jones, GB/GB (500 Windle-Yamaha); **3** Dave Hallam/Mark Day, GB/GB (500 LCR-Yamaha); **4** Steve Abbott/Shaun Smith, GB/GB (500 Windle-Yamaha); **5** Dennis Holmes/Alan Jervis, GB/GB (500 LCR-Yamaha); **6** Gary Thomas/Geoff White, GB/GB (500 BSL-Yamaha).
**Fastest lap:** Webster, 2m 00.4s, 74.75 mph/120.30 km/h.

**DONINGTON PARK CIRCUIT, 31 March. 2.500-mile/4.023-km circuit.**
***See also* Shell Oils Transatlantic Challenge, 1300 cc Metzeler Production Championship and 750 cc Metzeler Production Championship results.**
**1300 cc (10 laps, 25.00 miles/40.23 km)**
**1** Roger Burnett, GB (500 Honda), 19m 38.5s, 76.36 mph/122.89 km/h.
**2** Trevor Nation, GB (500 Suzuki); **3** Steve Parrish, GB (750 Yamaha); **4** Julian Scott, GB (750 Suzuki); **5** John Swingler, GB (500 Suzuki); **6** Neil Robinson, GB (750 Suzuki).
**Fastest lap:** Roger Marshall, GB (500 Honda), 1m 54.5s, 78.60 mph/126.49 km/h.

**Superstock (10 laps, 25.00 miles/40.23 km)**
**1** Trevor Nation, GB (750 Suzuki), 19m 48.5s, 75.72 mph/121.86 km/h.
**2** Neil Robinson, GB (750 Suzuki); **3** Julian Scott, GB (750 Suzuki); **4** Martin Taylor, GB (750 Suzuki); **5** Steve Parrish, GB (750 Yamaha); **6** Kenny Irons, GB (750 Yamaha).
**Fastest lap:** Scott, 1m 57.4s, 76.66 mph/123.37 km/h.

**350 cc (10 laps, 25.00 miles/40.23 km)**
**1** Andy Machin, GB (Yamaha), 20m 37.4s, 72.73 mph/117.05 km/h.
**2** Dave Leach, GB (Yamaha); **3** Mark Westmorland, GB (Yamaha); **4** Mark Johns, GB (Yamaha); **5** Phil Usher, GB (Yamaha); **6** Gary Cowan, GB (Yamaha).
**Fastest lap:** Machin, 1m 59.2s, 75.50 mph/121.51 km/h.

**250 cc (10 laps, 25.00 miles/40.23 km)**
**1** Geoff Fowler, GB (Yamaha), 21m 09.1s, 70.91 mph/114.12 km/h.
**2** Ian Redley, GB (Yamaha); **3** Ian Muir, GB (Yamaha); **4** Geoff Larney, GB (Yamaha); **5** Gary Cowan, GB (Honda); **6** Mick Preston, GB (EMC).
**Fastest lap:** Fowler, 2m 01.7s, 73.95 mph/119.01 km/h.

**F2 Sidecars (10 laps, 25.00 miles/40.23 km)**
**1** Andre Witherington/John Jackson, GB/GB (350 Yamaha), 21m 16.6s, 70.49 mph/113.44 km/h.
**2** Dave Saville/Dave Hall, GB/GB (350 Yamaha); **3** John Coates/Gary Gibson, GB/GB (350 Yamaha); **4** Alan Delmont/Tim Johnson, GB/GB (350 Yamaha); **5** Cliff Pritchard/Ken Morgan, GB/GB (350 Yamaha); **6** Pat Gallagher/Andrew Cawdell, GB/GB (350 Yamaha).
**Fastest lap:** Witherington, 2m 05.7s, 71.59 mph/115.21 km/h.

**OULTON PARK CIRCUIT, 31 March. 2.356-mile/3.792-km circuit.**
***See also* Shell Oils British Transnational Championship results.**
**Wirral '100' TT F1/F2 (10 laps, 23.56 miles/37.92 km)**
**1** Andy McGladdery, GB (750 Suzuki), 15m 48.7s, 89.40 mph/143.87 km/h.
**2** Carl Fogarty, GB (350 Yamaha); **3** Stuart Jones, GB (750 Yamaha); **4** Steve Henshaw, GB (750 Suzuki); **5** Trevor Herrington, GB (750 Suzuki); **6** Tony Moran, GB (750 Yamaha).
**Fastest lap:** McGladdery, 1m 33.4s, 93.40 mph/150.31 km/h.

**350 cc (10 laps, 23.56 miles/37.92 km)**
**1** Donnie McLeod, GB (Armstrong), 15m 23.4s, 91.85 mph/147.82 km/h.
**2** Carl Fogarty, GB (Yamaha); **3** Ian Newton, GB (Yamaha); **4** Dean Robinson, GB (Yamaha); **5** Roddy Taylor, GB (Yamaha); **6** Jamie Hitter, GB (Yamaha).
**Fastest lap:** McLeod, 1m 31.0s, 93.20 mph/149.99 km/h.

**CADWELL PARK CIRCUIT, 6 April, 2.250-mile/3.621-km circuit.**
**See also Motoprix UK 86 results.**
**King of Cadwell 1300 cc (10 laps, 22.50 miles/36.21 km)**
**1** Ron Haslam, GB (500 Honda), 16m 05.4s, 83.90 mph/136.02 km/h.
**2** Roger Marshall, GB (500 Honda); **3** Roger Burnett, GB (500 Honda); **4** Mark Phillips, GB (500 Suzuki); **5** Dave Griffith, GB (500 Suzuki); **6** Alan Jeffery, GB (500 Suzuki).
**Fastest lap:** Haslam, 1m 34.3s, 85.89 mph/138.23 km/h.

**Superstock Challenge (8 laps, 18.00 miles/28.97 km)**
**1** Trevor Nation, GB (750 Suzuki), 13m 22.1s, 80.78 mph/130.00 km/h.
**2** Kenny Irons, GB (750 Yamaha); **3** Keith Huewen, GB (750 Suzuki); **4** Phil Mellor, GB (750 Suzuki); **5**

Steve Parrish, GB (750 Yamaha); **6** Ray Swann, GB (750 Suzuki).
**Fastest lap:** Nation, 1m 38.1s, 82.56 mph/132.87 km/h.

**THRUXTON CIRCUIT, 13 April. 2.356-mile/3.792-km circuit.**
***See also*** **ACU British TT F1 Championship, ACU British TT F2 Championship and Motoprix UK 86 results.**
**International Spring Cup (12 laps, 28.27 miles/45.50 km)**
**1** Mark Phillips, GB (500 Suzuki), 19m 15.0s, 88.12 mph/141.79 km/h.
**2** Paul Lewis, AUS (500 Suzuki); **3** Trevor Nation, GB (500 Suzuki); **4** Ron Haslam, GB (500 Honda); **5** Neil Robinson, GB (750 Suzuki); **6** Dave Griffith, GB (500 Suzuki).
**Fastest lap:** Phillips, 1m 34.0s, 90.22 mph/145.16 km/h.

**MALLORY PARK CIRCUIT, 19 April. 1.370-mile/2.205-km circuit.**
***See also*** **ACU British TT F2 Championship results.**
**500 cc Spring Cup (15 laps, 20.55 miles/33.08 km)**
**1** Roger Burnett, GB (Honda), 13m 19.4s, 92.54 mph/148.93 km/h.
**2** Kevin Schwantz, USA (Suzuki); **3** Roger Marshall, GB (Honda); **4** Paul Lewis, AUS (Suzuki); **5** Mark Phillips, GB (Suzuki); **6** Trevor Nation, GB (Suzuki).
**Fastest lap:** Burnett and Schwantz, 52.3s, 94.30 mph/151.76 km/h.

**250 cc Spring Cup (15 laps, 20.55 miles/33.08 km)**
**1** Donnie McLeod, GB (Armstrong), 13m 24.7s, 91.93 mph/147.95 km/h.
**2** Kevin Mitchell, GB (Yamaha); **3** Ian Newton, GB (Armstrong); **4** Andy Watts, GB (Decorite); **5** Nigel Bosworth GB (Yamaha); **6** Alan Carter, GB (Kobas).
**Fastest lap:** McLeod and Mitchell, 52.7s, 93.58 mph/150.60 km/h.

**Sidecar Spring Cup (15 laps, 20.55 miles/33.08 km)**
**1** Steve Webster/Tony Hewitt, GB/GB (500 LCR-Yamaha), 13m 03.8s, 94.38 mph/151.89 km/h.
**2** Steve Abbott/Shaun Smith, GB/GB (500 Windle-Yamaha); **3** Barry Brindley/Chris Jones, GB/GB (500 Windle-Yamaha); **4** Dave Hallam/Mark Day, GB/GB (500 LCR-Yamaha); **5** Ray Gardner/Tony Strevens, GB/GB (500 LCR-Yamaha); **6** Dennis Holmes/Alan Jervis, GB/GB (500 LCR-Yamaha).
**Fastest lap:** Webster, 51.2s, 96.32 mph/155.01 km/h (record).

**MALLORY PARK CIRCUIT, 20 April. 1.370-mile/2.205-km circuit.**
***See also*** **ACU British TT F1 Championship and Motoprix UK 86 results.**
**Race of the Year (25 laps, 34.25 miles/55.13 km)**
**1** Roger Marshall, GB (500 Honda), 22m 01.5s, 93.30 mph/150.15 km/h.
**2** Kevin Schwantz, USA (500 Suzuki); **3** Mark Phillips, GB (500 Suzuki); **4** Kenny Irons, GB (500 Suzuki); **5** Ron Haslam, GB (500 Honda); **6** Paul Lewis, AUS (500 Suzuki).
**Fastest lap:** Marshall, 51.5s, 95.76 mph/154.11 km/h (record).

**OLIVER'S MOUNT CIRCUIT, 27 April. 2.4136-mile/3.8840-km circuit.**
**Ken Redfern Trophy (8 laps, 19.31 miles/31.07 km)**
**1** Mark Phillips, GB (500 Suzuki), 15m 18.8s, 75.65 mph/121.75 km/h.
**2** Trevor Nation, GB (500 Suzuki); **3** Steve Henshaw, GB (500 Suzuki); **4** Phil Mellor, GB (750 Suzuki); **5** Dave Leach, GB (350 Yamaha); **6** Steve Hislop, GB (350 Yamaha).
**Fastest lap:** Mellor, 1m 52.7s, 77.10 mph/124.08 km/h.

**350 cc (6 laps, 14.48 miles/23.30 km)**
**1** Dave Leach, GB (Yamaha), 11m 44.3s, 74.02 mph/119.12 km/h.
**2** Mark Phillips, GB (Yamaha); **3** Steve Hislop, GB (Yamaha); **4** Richard Coates, GB (Yamaha); **5** Dave Brown, GB (Yamaha); **6** Andy Machin, GB (Yamaha).
**Fastest lap:** Leach, 1m 55.6s, 75.16 mph/120.96 km/h.

**250 cc (8 laps, 19.31 miles/31.07 km)**
**1** Peter Hubbard, GB (Rotax), 15m 40.5s, 73.91 mph/118.95 km/h.
**2** Andy Machin, GB (Rotax); **3** Mick Preston, GB (EMC); **4** Dudley Bell, GB (Armstrong); **5** Martin Burkenshaw, GB (Armstrong); **6** Mark Barker, GB (Rotax).
**Fastest lap:** Machin, 1m 55.4s, 75.29 mph/121.17 km/h.

**125 cc (5 laps, 12.07 miles/19.42 km)**
**1** Cliff Peart, GB (MBA), 10m 49.6s, 66.88 mph/107.63 km/h.
**2** Gary Dickinson, GB (MBA); **3** Rob Blow, GB (Honda); **4** Ken Beckett, GB (MBA); **5** Steve Wright, GB (Waddon); **6** David Reid, GB (MBA).
**Fastest lap:** Steve Carlisle, GB (MBA), 2m 06.8s, 68.52 mph/110.27 km/h.

**F2 Sidecars (6 laps, 14.48 miles/23.30 km)**
**1** Eddie Wright/Ian Marchant, GB/GB (350 Yamaha), 12m 50.6s, 67.65 mph/108.87 km/h.
**2** Andre Witherington/John Jackson, GB/GB (350 Yamaha); **3** Dave Saville/Dave Hall, GB/GB (350 Yamaha); **4** John Coates/Gary Gibson, GB/GB (350 Yamaha); **5** Colin Hopper/Colin Burgess, GB/GB (350 Armstrong); **6** Dick Fletcher/N. Roche, GB/GB (350 Yamaha).
**Fastest lap:** Witherington, 2m 06.6s, 68.63 mph/110.45 km/h.

**MALLORY PARK CIRCUIT, 18 May. 1.370-mile/2.205-km circuit.**
***See also*** **1300 cc Metzeler Production Championship and 750 cc Metzeler Production Championship results.**
**1300 cc (12 laps, 16.44 miles/26.46 km)**
**1** Alan Jeffery, GB (500 Suzuki), 10m 51.1s, 90.89 mph/146.28 km/h.
**2** John Swingler, GB (500 Suzuki); **3** Terry Rymer, GB (500 Suzuki); **4** Dale Robinson, GB (750 Suzuki); **5** Richard Scott, NZ (750 Honda); **6** Chris Galatowicz, GB (350 Yamaha).
**Fastest lap:** Swingler, 53.3s, 92.53 mph/148.91 km/h.

**350 cc (10 laps, 13.70 miles/22.05 km)**
**1** Martin Bennett, GB (Yamaha), 9m 19.3s, 88.18 mph/141.91 km/h.
**2** Chris Galatowicz, GB (Yamaha); **3** Steve Bevington, GB (Yamaha); **4** Phil Rawson, GB (Yamaha); **5** J. Brown, GB (Yamaha); **6** Barry Stanley, GB (Yamaha).
**Fastest lap:** Bennett, 54.8s, 90.00 mph/144.84 km/h.

**250 cc (10 laps, 13.70 miles/22.05 km)**
**1** Nigel Bosworth, GB (Yamaha), 9m 08.3s, 89.95 mph/144.76 km/h.
**2** Darren Dixon, GB (Honda); **3** Andy Godber, GB (Yamaha); **4** Mick Preston, GB (EMC); **5** Dave Wisdom, GB (Yamaha); **6** Mark Barker, GB (Rotax).
**Fastest lap:** Bosworth, 53.5s, 92.18 mph/148.35 km/h.

**80 cc (8 laps, 10.96 miles/17.64 km)**
**1** Steve Dale, GB (Huvo), 8m 38.1s, 76.15 mph/122.55 km/h.
**2** Dave Shields, GB (Huvo); **3** Dennis Batchelor, GB (Huvo); **4** Graham Grubb, GB (Yamaha); **5** Dean Hodgson, GB (Yamaha); **6** M. Harrison, GB (Yamaha).
**Fastest lap:** Dale, 1m 03.1s, 78.16 mph/125.79 km/h.

**Sidecars (10 laps, 13.70 miles/22.05 km)**
**1** Dave Hallam/Mark Day, GB/GB (500 LCR-Yamaha), 9m 19.8s, 89.95 mph/144.76 km/h.
**2** Roger McCall/Stephen Wilson, GB/GB (750 Yamaha); **3** Kenny Howles/Steve Pointer, GB/GB (700 Yamaha); **4** George Hardwick/Carl Fieldhouse, GB/GB (500 Ireson-Yamaha); **5** John Evans/Geoff Wilbraham, GB/GB (500 Yamaha); **6** Derek Bayley/Bryan Nixon, GB/GB (700 LCR-Yamaha).
**Fastest lap:** Hallam, 54.3s, 90.82 mph/146.16 km/h.

**F2 Sidecars (10 laps, 13.70 miles/22.05 km)**
**1** Andre Witherington/John Jackson, GB/GB (350 Yamaha), 9m 45.6s, 84.22 mph/135.54 km/h.
**2** Keith Galtress/Neil Shelton, GB/GB (350 Yamaha); **3** Mike Hamblin/Wally Brammer, GB/GB (350 Yamaha); **4** Steve Judkins/Robert Gater, GB/GB (350 Yamaha); **5** Colin Broadstock/Robert Bradford, GB/GB (350 Yamaha); **6** P. Wilkinson/K. Lowe, GB/GB (350 Yamaha).
**Fastest lap:** Witherington, 57.4s, 85.92 mph/138.27 km/h.

**OLIVER'S MOUNT CIRCUIT, 6 July. 2.4136-mile/3.8840-km circuit.**
**Cock o' the North First Leg (10 laps, 24.14 miles/38.84 km)**
**1** Trevor Nation, GB (500 Suzuki), 18m 13.6s, 79.45 mph/127.86 km/h.
**2** Keith Huewen, GB (750 Suzuki); **3** Phil Mellor, GB (750 Suzuki); **4** Michael Seward, GB (750 Yamaha); **5** Steve Hislop, GB (350 Yamaha); **6** Dave Leach, GB (350 Yamaha).
**Fastest lap:** Nation, 1m 46.9s, 81.28 mph/130.81 km/h.

**Cock o' the North Second Leg (10 laps, 24.14 miles/38.84 km)**
**1** Trevor Nation, GB (500 Suzuki), 18m 02.7s, 80.25 mph/129.15 km/h.
**2** Keith Huewen, GB (750 Suzuki); **3** Phil Mellor, GB (750 Suzuki); **4** Michael Seward GB (750 Yamaha); **5** Steve Hislop, GB (350 Yamaha); **6** Dave Leach, GB (350 Yamaha).
**Fastest lap:** Nation, 1m 46.0s, 81.97 mph/131.92 km/h (record).
**Overall: 1** Nation; **2** Huewen; **3** Mellor; **4** Seward; **5** Hislop; **6** Leach.

**SNETTERTON CIRCUIT, 19/20 July. 1.917-mile/3.085-km circuit.**
***See also*** **MCN/EBC Brakes Superstock Series, 1300 cc Metzeler Production Championship and 750 cc Metzeler Production Championship results.**
**Snetterton Race of Aces (12 laps, 23.00 miles/37.02 km)**
**1** Roger Burnett, GB (500 Honda), 13m 49.6s, 99.82 mph/160.64 km/h.
**2** Kenny Irons, GB (500 Suzuki); **3** Roger Marshall, GB (500 Honda); **4** Mark Phillips, GB (500 Suzuki); **5** Richard Scott, NZ (750 Honda); **6** Barry Woodland, GB (500 Suzuki).
**Fastest lap:** Burnett, 1m 08.0s, 101.48 mph/163.32 km/h (record).

**MALLORY PARK CIRCUIT, 27 July. 1.370-mile/2.205-km circuit.**
***See also*** **Shell Oils ACU Transnational Championship and ACU 125 cc Championship results.**
**350 cc (10 laps, 13.70 miles/22.05 km)**
**1** Steve Bevington, GB (Yamaha), 9m 10.7s, 89.55 mph/144.12 km/h.
**2** Chris Branneck, GB (Yamaha); **3** Dave Leach, GB (Yamaha); **4** Ian Burnett, GB (Yamaha); **5** Steve Patrickson, GB (250 Rotax); **6** Dougie Black, GB (Yamaha).
**Fastest lap:** Niall MacKenzie, GB (Armstrong), 53.2s, 92.70 mph/149.19 km/h (record).

**SILVERSTONE GRAND PRIX CIRCUIT, 2/3 August. 2.927-mile/4.711-km circuit.**
***See also*** **Shell Oils British Grand Prix, 1300 cc Metzeler Production Championship and 750 cc Metzeler Production Championship results.**
**Sidecars (8 laps, 23.42 miles/37.69 km)**
**1** Steve Webster/Tony Hewitt, GB/GB (500 LCR-Yamaha), 14m 32.95s, 95.56 mph/153.79 km/h.
**2** Rolf Steinhausen/Bruno Hiller, D/D (500 Busch); **3** Derek Bayley/Bryan Nixon, GB/GB (500 LCR-Ricardo); **4** Tony Baker/Peter Harper, GB/GB (500 Yamaha); **5** Mick Boddice/Don Williams, GB/GB (500 LCR-Yamaha); **6** Dennis Bingham/Julia Bingham, GB/GB (500 LCR-Yamaha).
**Fastest lap:** Steinhausen, 1m 47.09s, 98.39 mph/158.34 km/h.

**CADWELL PARK WOODLAND CIRCUIT, 10 August. 1.000-mile/1.609-km circuit.**
***See also*** **MCN/EBC Brakes Superstock Series results.**
**Bill Ivy Trophy (20 laps, 20.00 miles/32.18 km)**
**1** Roger Burnett, GB (500 Honda), 15m 07.40s, 79.35 mph/127.70 km/h.
**2** Roger Marshall, GB (500 Honda); **3** Richard Scott, NZ (750 Honda); **4** Kenny Irons, GB (750 Yamaha); **5** Ray Swann, GB (750 Suzuki); **6** Phil Mellor, GB (750 Suzuki).
**Fastest lap:** Burnett, 44.6s, 80.72 mph/129.91 km/h (record).

**OLIVER'S MOUNT CIRCUIT, 13/14 September. 2.4136-mile/3.8843-km circuit.**
***See also*** **ACU British TT F1, ACU British TT F2, MCN/EBC Brakes Superstock Series, 1300 cc Metzeler Production Championship and 750 cc Metzeler Production Championship results.**
**International Gold Cup (10 laps, 24.14 miles/38.84 km)**
**1** Steve Henshaw, GB (500 Suzuki), 18m 08.6s, 79.82 mph/128.46 km/h.
**2** Andy McGladdery, GB (750 Suzuki); **3** Michael Seward, GB (750 Yamaha); **4** Dave Griffith, GB (500 Suzuki); **5** Eero Hyvarinen, SF (500 Honda); **6** Richard Crossley, GB (750 Suzuki).
**Fastest lap:** Henshaw, 1m 47.3s, 80.98 mph/130.32 km/h.

**1000 cc (8 laps, 19.31 miles/31.07 km)**
**1** Trevor Nation, GB (500 Suzuki), 14m 25.5s, 80.31 mph/129.25 km/h.
**2** Mark Phillips, GB (500 Suzuki); **3** Steve Henshaw, GB (500 Suzuki); **4** Phil Mellor, GB (750 Suzuki); **5** Steve Parrish, GB (750 Yamaha); **6** Roger Hurst, GB (750 Yamaha).
**Fastest lap:** Nation, 1m 46.3s, 81.74 mph/131.55 km/h.

**350 cc (8 laps, 19.31 miles/31.07 km)**
**1** Kevin Mitchell, GB (Yamaha), 15m 00.9s, 77.16 mph/124.18 km/h.
**2** Steve Hislop, GB (Yamaha); **3** Tony Head, GB (Yamaha); **4** Ray Hutchison, GB (Yamaha); **5** Mark Westmorland, GB (Yamaha); **6** Steve Henshaw, GB (Yamaha).
**Fastest lap:** Mitchell, 1m 50.4s, 78.70 mph/126.66 km/h.

**250 cc (8 laps, 19.31 miles/31.07 km)**
**1** Kevin Mitchell, GB (Yamaha), 14m 53.5s, 77.80 mph/125.21 km/h.
**2** Tony Head, GB (Honda); **3** Andy Machin, GB (Rotax); **4** Dave Leach, GB (Yamaha); **5** Mark Barker, GB (Rotax); **6** Mick Preston, GB (EMC).
**Fastest lap:** Mitchell, 1m 50.2s, 78.85 mph/126.90 km/h.

**F2 Sidecars (8 laps, 19.31 miles/31.07 km)**
**1** Eddy Wright/Ian Marchant, GB/GB (350 Yamaha), 16m 28.9s, 70.29 mph/113.12 km/h.
**2** John Coates/Gary Gibson, GB/GB (350 Yamaha); **3** Dave Seville/Dave Hall, GB/GB (350 Yamaha); **4** Andre Witherington/John Jackson, GB/GB (350 Yamaha); **5** Mick Hamblin/Robert Smith, GB/GB (350 Armstrong); **6** Paul Hanson/Andy Graves, GB/GB (350 Yamaha).
**Fastest lap:** Wright, 2m 01.4s, 71.57 mph/115.18 km/h.

**DONINGTON PARK CIRCUIT, 28 September. 2.500-mile/4.023-km circuit.**
***See also*** **European Championship and MCN/EBC Superstock Series results.**
**1300 cc (10 laps, 25.00 miles/40.23 km)**
**1** Roger Marshall, GB (500 Honda), 17m 23.81s, 86.01 mph/138.42 km/h.
**2** Roger Burnett, GB (500 Honda); **3** Richard Scott, NZ (750 Honda); **4** Trevor Nation, GB (500 Suzuki); **5** Glen Williams, NZ (750 Suzuki); **6** Steve Manley, GB (500 Suzuki).
**Fastest lap:** Marshall, 1m 42.62s, 87.49 mph/140.80 km/h (record).

**CADWELL PARK CIRCUIT, 5 October. 2.250-mile/3.621-km circuit.**
***See also*** **ACU British TT F1 Championship, ACU British TT F2 Championship, 1300 cc Metzeler Production Championship and 750 cc Metzeler Production Championship results.**
**Superstocks (10 laps, 22.50 miles/36.21 km)**
**1** Kenny Irons, GB (750 Yamaha), 16m 26.4s, 82.11 mph/132.14 km/h.
**2** Steve Parrish, GB (750 Yamaha); **3** Keith Huewen, GB (750 Suzuki); **4** Trevor Nation, GB (750 Suzuki); **5** Geoff Fowler, GB (750 Suzuki); **6** Chris Breeze, GB (750 Yamaha).
**Fastest lap:** Irons, 1m 37.4s, 83.16 mph/133.83 km/h.

**350 cc (8 laps, 18.00 miles/28.97 km)**
**1** Paul Simmonds, GB (Yamaha), 13m 37.0s, 79.31 mph/127.64 km/h.
**2** Ian Lougher, GB (Yamaha); **3** Andy Machin, GB (Yamaha); **4** Steve Spray, GB (Yamaha); **5** Des Barry, NZ (Yamaha); **6** Rob Talton, GB (Yamaha).
**Fastest lap:** Simmonds, 1m 38.9s, 81.90 mph/131.80 km/h.

**250 cc (8 laps, 18.00 miles/28.97 km)**
**1** Andy Machin, GB (Rotax), 13m 20.0s, 80.49 mph/129.54 km/h.
**2** Tony Rogers, GB (Yamaha); **3** Peter Hubbard, GB (Armstrong); **4** John Gainey, GB (Yamaha); **5** Michael Otter, GB (Yamaha); **6** Tony Couzens, GB (Yamaha).
**Fastest lap:** Rogers, 1m 38.8s, 81.98 mph/131.93 km/h.

# Motoprix UK 86 Championship

**CADWELL PARK CIRCUIT, 6 April. 2.250-mile/3.621-km circuit.**
**500 cc Motoprix, round 1 (15 laps, 33.75 miles/54.32 km)**
**1** Ron Haslam, GB (Honda), 23m 44.5s, 85.29 mph/137.26 km/h.
**2** Roger Burnett, GB (Honda); **3** Roger Marshall, GB (Honda); **4** Mark Phillips, GB (Suzuki); **5** Alan Jeffery, GB (Suzuki); **6** Trevor Nation, GB (Suzuki); **7** Steve Henshaw, GB (Suzuki); **8** Gary Lingham, GB (Suzuki); **9** Eero Hyvarinen, SF (Suzuki); **10** John Brindley, GB (Yamaha).
**Fastest lap:** Burnett, 1m 33.0s, 87.09 mph/140.16 km/h (record).
**Championship points: 1** Haslam, 15; **2** Burnett, 12; **3** Marshall, 10; **4** Phillips, 8; **5** Jeffrey, 6; **6** Nation, 5.

**250 cc Motoprix, round 1 (15 laps, 33.75 miles/54.32 km)**
**1** Donnie McLeod, GB (Armstrong), 25m 23.7s, 79.74 mph/128.33 km/h.
**2** Gary Noel, GB (EMC); **3** Carl Fogarty, GB (Yamaha); **4** Peter Hubbard, GB (Yamaha); **5** Alan Carter, GB (Honda); **6** Andy Watts, GB (Decorite); **7** Ian Newton, GB (Armstrong); **8** Brent Jones, NZ (Yamaha); **9** Darren Dixon, GB (Honda); **10** Gary Cowan, GB (Honda).
**Fastest lap:** McLeod, 1m 39.9s, 81.08 mph/130.49 km/h.
**Championship points: 1** McLeod, 15; **2** Noel, 12; **3** Fogarty, 10; **4** Hubbard, 8; **5** Carter, 6; **6** Watts, 5.

**125 cc Motoprix, round 1 (12 laps, 27.00 miles/43.45 km)**
**1** Steve Mason, GB (MBA), 22m 53.6s, 70.76 mph/113.88 km/h.
**2** Robin Appleyard, GB (MBA); **3** Mark Barker, GB (MBA); **4** Reg Lennon, GB (MBA); **5** Cliff Peart, GB (MBA); **6** Neil Tuxworth, GB (Honda); **7** Doug Flather, GB (Honda); **8** Hilary Musson, GB (Yamaha). No other finishers.
**Fastest lap:** Mason, 1m 50.6s, 73.23 mph/117.85 km/h.
**Championship points: 1** Mason, 15; **2** Appleyard, 12; **3** Barker, 10; **4** Lennon, 8; **5** Peart, 6; **6** Tuxworth, 5.

**80 cc Motoprix, round 1 (12 laps, 27.00 miles/43.45 km)**
**1** Hans Koopman, NL (Ziegler), 23m 54.3s, 67.76 mph/109.05 km/h.
**2** Steve Dale, GB (Huvo); **3** Dennis Batchelor, GB (Huvo); **4** Henk van Kessel, NL (Krauser); **5** Raimo Lipponen, SF (Huvo); **6** Steve Lawton, GB (Eberhardt); **7** John Cresswell, GB (Lusuardi); **8** Ian Laycock, GB (Yamaha); **9** Alistair Stanway, GB (KTM); **10** Jan Verheul, NL (Huvo).
**Fastest lap:** Ian McConnachie, GB (Krauser), 1m 53.7s, 71.24 mph/114.65 km/h.
**Championship points: 1** Koopman, 15; **2** Dale, 12; **3** Batchelor, 10; **4** van Kessel, 8; **5** Lipponen, 6; **6** Lawton, 5.

**Sidecar Motoprix, round 1 (15 laps, 33.75 miles/54.32 km)**
**1** Steve Webster/Tony Hewitt, GB/GB (500 LCR-Yamaha), 24m 25.9s, 82.88 mph/133.38 km/h.
**2** Derek Bayley/Bryan Nixon, GB/GB (500 LCR-Yamaha); **3** Derek Jones/Brian Ayres, GB/GB (500 LCR-Yamaha); **4** Barry Brindley/Chris Jones, GB/GB (500 Windle-Yamaha); **5** Markus Egloff/Urs Egloff, CH/CH (500 LCR-Yamaha); **6** Warwick Newman/Eddie Yarker, GB/GB (500 Ireson-Yamaha); **7** Steve Sinnott/Geoff Leitch, GB/GB (500 Yamaha); **8** John Phillips/Malcolm Hollis, GB/GB (500 Yamaha); **9** Helmut Lingen/Jutta Naus, D/D (500 Yamaha). No other finishers.
**Fastest lap:** Webster, 1m 36.0s, 84.37 mph/135.78 km/h.
**Championship points: 1** Webster, 15; **2** Bayley, 12; **3** Jones, 10; **4** Brindley, 8; **5** Egloff, 6; **6** Newman, 5.

**THRUXTON CIRCUIT, 13 April, 2.356-mile/3.792-km circuit.**
**500 cc Motoprix, round 2 (12 laps, 28.27 miles/45.50 km)**
**1** Ron Haslam, GB (Honda), 18m 31.3s, 91.58 mph/147.36 km/h.
**2** Paul Lewis, AUS (Suzuki); **3** Roger Marshall, GB (Honda); **4** Mark Phillips, GB (Suzuki); **5** Roger Burnett, GB (Honda); **6** Trevor Nation, GB (Suzuki); **7** Ray Swann, GB (Suzuki); **8** Eero Hyvarinen, SF (Suzuki); **9** Neil Tuxworth GB (350 Yamaha); **10** Steve Henshaw, GB (Suzuki).
**Fastest lap:** Haslam, 1m 29.8s, 94.44 mph/151.99 km/h.
**Championship points: 1** Haslam, 30; **2** Marshall, 20; **3** Burnett, 18; **4** Phillips, 16; **5** Lewis, 12, **6** Nation, 10.

**250 cc Motoprix, round 2 (12 laps, 28.27 miles/45.50 km)**
**1** Carl Fogarty, GB (Yamaha), 19m 22.0s, 87.58 mph/140.95 km/h.
**2** Andy Watts, GB (Decorite); **3** Andy Machin, GB (Rotax); **4** Gary Noel, GB (EMC); **5** Donnie McLeod, GB (Armstrong); **6** Ian Redley, GB (Yamaha); **7** Alan Carter, GB (Kobas); **8** Kevin Mitchell, GB (Yamaha); **9** Paul Williams, GB (Yamaha); **10** Phil Mellor, GB (EMC).
**Fastest lap:** Fogarty, 1m 34.2s, 90.03 mph/144.90 km/h.
**Championship points: 1** Fogarty, 25; **2** McLeod, 21; **3** Noel, 20; **4** Watts, 17; **5** Carter and Machin, 10.

**125 cc Motoprix, round 2 (12 laps, 28.27 miles/45.50 km)**
**1** Robin Appleyard, GB (MBA), 20m 15.2s, 83.75 mph/134.78 km/h.
**2** Steve Mason, GB (MBA); **3** Gary Dickinson, GB (MBA); **4** Doug Flather, GB (Honda); **5** Gary Buckle, GB (MBA); **6** Reg Lennon, GB (MBA); **7** George Higginson, GB (Waddon). No other finishers.
**Fastest lap:** Appleyard, 1m 38.6s, 86.02 mph/138.44 km/h.

**Championship points: 1** Appleyard and Mason, 27; **3** Lennon, 13; **4** Flather, 12; **5** Barker and Dickinson, 10.

**80 cc Motoprix, round 2 (12 laps, 28.27 miles/45.50 km)**
**1** Henk van Kessel, NL (Krauser), 20m 34.4s, 82,45 mph/132.69 km/h.
**2** Ian McConnachie, GB (Krauser); **3** Hans Koopman, NL (Ziegler); **4** Chris Baert, B (Seel); **5** Jan Verheul, NL (Huvo); **6** Steve Dale, GB (Huvo); **7** Jarmo Piepponen, SF (Kiefer); **8** Stuart Edwards, GB (Huvo); **9** Steve Lawton, GB (Eberhardt); **10** Raimo Lipponen, SF (Huvo).
**Fastest lap:** McConnachie, 1m 38.9s, 85.75 mph/138.00 km/h (record).
**Championship points: 1** Koopman, 25; **2** van Kessel, 23; **3** Dale, 17; **4** McConnachie, 12; **5** Batchelor, 10; **6** Baert, 8.

**Sidecar Motoprix, round 2 (12 laps, 28.27 miles/45.50 km)**
**1** Steve Webster/Tony Hewitt, GB/GB (500 LCR-Yamaha), 18m 50.8s, 90.00 mph/144.84 km/h.
**2** Barry Brindley/Chris Jones, GB/GB (500 Windle-Yamaha); **3** Derek Bayley/Bryan Nixon, GB/GB (500 LCR-Ricardo); **4** Mick Boddice/Chas Birks, GB/GB (500 ORS-Yamaha); **5** Yoshisada Kumagaya/Kazuhiko Makiuchi, J/J (500 LCR-Yamaha); **6** Steve Abbott/Shaun Smith, GB/GB (500 Windle-Yamaha); **7** Warwick Newman/Eddie Yarker, GB/GB (500 Ireson-Yamaha); **8** Ray Gardner/Tony Strevens, GB/GB (500 LCR-Yamaha); **9** Mick Burcombe/Steve Parker, GB/GB (500 LCR-Yamaha); **10** Dave Hallam/Mark Day, GB/GB (500 LCR-Yamaha).
**Fastest lap:** Webster, 1m 32.6s, 91.59 mph/147.40 km/h.
**Championship points: 1** Webster, 30; **2** Bayley, 22; **3** Brindley, 20; **4** Jones, 10; **5** Newman, 9; **6** Boddice, 8.

**MALLORY PARK CIRCUIT, 20 April. 1.370-mile/2.205-km circuit.**
**500 cc Motoprix, round 3 (20 laps, 27.40 miles/44.10 km)**
**1** Roger Burnett, GB (Honda), 17m 49.5s, 92.23 mph/148.43 km/h.
**2** Roger Marshall, GB (Honda); **3** Mark Phillips, GB (Suzuki); **4** Kevin Schwantz, USA (Suzuki); **5** Trevor Nation, GB (Suzuki); **6** Alan Jeffery, GB (Suzuki); **7** Steve Henshaw, GB (Suzuki); **8** Ray Swann, GB (Suzuki); **9** Kenny Irons, GB (Suzuki); **10** Simon Buckmaster, GB (Honda).
**Fastest lap:** Burnett and Schwantz, 52.3s, 94.30 mph/151.76 km/h.

**250 Motoprix, round 3 (20 laps, 27.40 miles/44.10 km)**
**1** Donnie McLeod, GB (Armstrong), 18m 10.3s, 90.47 mph/145.60 km/h.
**2** Alan Carter, GB (Kobas); **3** Ian Newton, GB (Armstrong); **4** Nigel Bosworth, GB (Armstrong); **5** Andy Watts, GB (Decorite); **6** Gary Noel, GB (EMC); **7** Darren Dixon, GB (Honda); **8** Mick Crick, GB (Rotax); **9** Peter Hubbard, GB (Rotax); **10** Gary Cowan, GB (Rotax).
**Fastest lap:** McLeod, 52.4s, 94.12 mph/151.47 km/h (record).

**125 cc Motoprix, round 3 (12 laps, 16.44 miles/26.46 km)**
**1** Jamie Whitham, GB (MBA) 11m 40.2s, 84.52 mph/136.02 km/h.
**2** Robin Milton, GB (MBA); **3** Steve Carlisle, GB (MBA); **4** Steve Mason, GB (MBA); **5** Gary Buckle, GB (MBA); **6** Gordon Ashton, GB (MBA); **7** Doug Flather, GB (Honda); **8** Cliff Peart, GB (MBA); **9** Pete Banks, GB (MBA); **10** Bill Robertson, GB (MBA).
**Fastest lap:** Whitham, 56.3s, 87.60 mph/140.98 km/h (record).

**80 cc Motoprix, round 3 (12 laps, 16.44 miles/26.46 km)**
**1** Ian McConnachie, GB (Krauser), 12m 18.7s, 80.57 mph/129.66 km/h.
**2** Henk van Kessel, NL (Krauser); **3** Hans Koopman, NL (Ziegler); **4** Steve Mason, GB (Huvo); **5** Jamie Whitham, GB (Wicks); **6** Steve Lawton, GB (Eberhardt); **7** Steve Dale, GB (Huvo); **8** Dennis Batchelor, GB (Huvo); **9** Raimo Lipponen, SF (Huvo); **10** Jarmo Piepponen, SF (Kiefer).
**Fastest lap:** McConnachie, 59.8s, 82.72 mph/133.12 km/h (record).

**Sidecar Motoprix, round 3 (15 laps, 20.55 miles/33.08 km)**
**1** Steve Abbott/Vince Biggs, GB/GB (500 Windle-Yamaha), 13m 42.1s, 89.98 mph/144.81 km/h.
**2** Dave Hallam/Mark Day, GB/GB (500 LCR-Yamaha); **3** Dennis Bingham/Julia Bingham, GB/GB (500 LCR-Yamaha); **4** Mick Boddice/Chas Birks, GB/GB (LCR-Yamaha); **5** Yoshisada Kumagaya/Kazuhiko Makiuchi, J/J (500 LCR-Yamaha); **6** Mick Burcombe/Steve Parker, GB/GB (500 LCR-Yamaha); **7** Warwick Newman/Eddie Yarker, GB/GB (500 Ireson-Yamaha); **8** Barry Brindley/Chris Jones, GB/GB (500 Windle-Yamaha). No other finishers.
**Fastest lap:** Abbott and Brindley, 53.3s, 92.53 mph/148.91.

**Final Motoprix points (500 cc)**
| | | |
|---|---|---|
| **1** | Roger Burnett, GB | 33 |
| **2** | Roger Marshall, GB | 32 |
| **3** | Ron Haslam, GB | 30 |
| **4** | Mark Phillips, GB | 26 |
| **5** | Trevor Nation, GB | 16 |
| **6** | Paul Lewis, AUS | 12 |

**7** Alan Jeffery, GB, 11; **8** Steve Henshaw, GB, 9; **9** Kevin Schwantz, USA, 8; **10** Ray Swann, GB, 7.

**Final Motoprix points (250 cc)**
| | | |
|---|---|---|
| **1** | Donnie McLeod, GB | 36 |
| **2=** | Gary Noel, GB | 25 |
| **2=** | Carl Fogarty, GB | 25 |
| **4** | Andy Watts, GB | 23 |
| **5** | Alan Carter, GB | 22 |
| **6** | Ian Newton, GB | 14 |

**7** Andy Machin, GB, 11; **8** Peter Hubbard, GB, 10; **9** Nigel Bosworth, GB, 8; **10** Darren Dixon, GB, 6.

**Final Motoprix points (125 cc)**
| | | |
|---|---|---|
| **1** | Steve Mason, GB | 35 |
| **2** | Robin Appleyard, GB | 27 |
| **3** | Doug Flather, GB | 16 |
| **4** | Jamie Whitham, GB | 15 |
| **5** | Gary Buckle, GB | 14 |
| **6** | Reg Lennon, GB | 13 |

**7** Cliff Peart, GB, 12; **8** Mark Barker, GB, Gary Dickinson, GB and Steve Carlisle, GB, 10.

**Final Motoprix points (80 cc)**
| | | |
|---|---|---|
| **1=** | Hans Koopman, NL | 35 |
| **1=** | Henk van Kessel, NL | 35 |
| **3** | Ian McConnachie, GB | 27 |
| **4** | Steve Dale, GB | 21 |
| **5** | Dennis Batchelor, GB | 13 |
| **6** | Steve Lawton, GB | 12 |

**7** Raimo Lipponen, SF, 9; **8** Chris Baert, B and Steve Mason, GB, 8; **10** Jan Verheul, NL, 7.

**Final Motoprix points (Sidecars)**
| | | |
|---|---|---|
| **1** | Steve Webster, GB | 30 |
| **2** | Barry Brindley, GB | 23 |
| **3** | Derek Bayley, GB | 22 |
| **4** | Steve Abbott, GB | 20 |
| **5** | Mick Boddice, GB | 16 |
| **6=** | Warwick Newman, GB | 13 |
| **6=** | Dave Hallam, GB | 13 |

**8** Yoshisada Kumagaya, J, 12; **9** Derek Jones, GB and Dennis Bingham, GB, 10.

# Manx Grand Prix

**MANX GRAND PRIX, Isle of Man, 30 August/4 September. 37.73-mile/69.72-km circuit.**
**Senior Race 1000 cc (6 laps, 226.38 miles/364.32 km)**
**1** Grant Goodings, GB (750 Suzuki), 2h 07m 26.2s, 106.58 mph/171.52 km/h.
**2** Michael Seward, GB (750 Yamaha); **3** Stephen Hazlett, GB (350 Yamaha); **4** Kevin Jackson, GB (750 Suzuki); **5** Gary Tate, GB (750 Yamaha); **6** Roy Chapman, GB (750 Honda); **7** Geoff Martin, GB (750 Suzuki); **8** Paul Hunt, GB (750 Suzuki); **9** Tom Knight, GB (750 Ducati); **10** David Montgomery, GB (750 Suzuki).
**Fastest lap:** Seward, 20m 26.4s, 110.75 mph/178.23 km/h (record).

**Junior Race 350 cc (6 laps, 226.38 miles/364.32 km)**
**1** Alan Jackson, GB (Yamaha), 2h 10m 55.0s, 103.75 mph/166.97 km/h.
**2** Ralph Sutcliffe, GB (Yamaha); **3** Michael Seward, GB (Yamaha); **4** Tony Martin, GB (Yamaha); **5** Justin Urch, GB (Yamaha); **6** Ray Evans, GB (Yamaha); **7** Chris Harris, GB (Yamaha); **8** Richard Rogers, GB (Yamaha); **9** Henry Januszewski, GB (Yamaha); **10** Alan Douglas, GB (Yamaha).
**Fastest lap:** Jackson, 21m 19.0s, 106.19 mph/170.90 km/h.

**Lightweight Race 250 cc (4 laps, 150.92 miles/242.88 km)**
**1** Ralph Sutcliffe, GB (Armstrong), 1h 28m 58.4s, 101.77 mph/163.78 km/h.
**2** Mick Robinson, GB (Yamaha); **3** Stewart Rae, GB (Rotax); **4** John Davies, GB (Yamaha); **5** Sean Collister, GB (Honda); **6** Mark Linton, GB (Yamaha); **7** Pete Wakefield, GB (Maxton); **8** George Higginson, GB (Decorite); **9** Dave Grigson, GB (Yamaha); **10** Nick Turner, GB (Rotax).
**Fastest lap:** Sutcliffe, 21m 54.2s, 103.35 mph/166.33 km/h.

**Newcomers Race 1000 cc four-stroke/750 cc two-stroke (4 laps, 150.92 miles/242.88 km)**
**1** Jim Hunter, GB (750 Suzuki), 1h 30m 13.8s, 100.35 mph/161.50 km/h.
**2** Ian Mitchell, GB (750 Suzuki); **3** Nick Lynn, GB (750 Honda); **4** David Goodley, GB (908 Kawasaki); **5** Steve Wickes, GB (908 Kawasaki); **6** Russ Jones, GB (750 Yamaha); **7** Frank Guymer, GB (750 Suzuki); **8** Chris Petty, GB (908 Kawasaki); **9** Joe Toner, GB (750 Suzuki); **10** Paul Evans, GB (600 Ducati).
**Fastest lap:** Hunter, 21m 58.0s, 103.05 mph/165.84 km/h (record).

**Newcomers Race 350 cc (4 laps, 150.92 miles/242.88 km)**
**1** Ian Jones, GB (Yamaha), 1h 34m 05.4s, 96.23

mph/154.87 km/h.
**2** Trevor Robinson, GB (Yamaha); **3** Vaughan Smith, GB (Yamaha); **4** Cliff Peart, GB (Yamaha); **5** Phil Matulja, GB (Yamaha); **6** Roy Richardson, GB (Yamaha); **7** Des Senior, GB (Yamaha); **8** Derek Wagstaffe, GB (Yamaha); **9** Chris Hayden, GB (Yamaha); **10** Tony Anderson, GB (Yamaha).
**Fastest lap:** Matt Drane, GB (Yamaha), 22m 47.6s, 99.31 mph/159.82 km/h.

**Newcomers Race 250 cc (4 laps, 150.92 miles/242.88 km)**
**1** George Higginson, GB (Decorite), 1h 32m 28.2s, 97.92 mph/157.59 km/h.
**2** Tony Tuttle, GB (Yamaha); **3** Eddie Edmunds, GB (Yamaha); **4** Tony Hutchison, GB (Yamaha); **5** Carl Marsh, GB (Yamaha); **6** Phil Pennington, GB (Suzuki); **7** Kevin Bowran, GB (Armstrong); **8** Nigel Barton, GB (Armstrong); **9** Michael Thompson, GB (Honda); **10** Bill Norris, GB (Rotax).
**Fastest lap:** Higginson and Stewart Rae, GB (Rotax), 22m 44.4s, 99.55 mph/160.21 km/h (record).

**Classic Race 500 cc (3 laps, 113.19 miles/209.16 km)**
**1** Alan Dugdale, GB (Matchless), 1h 09m 04.8s, 98.31 mph/158.21 km/h.
**2** Dave Pither, GB (Matchless); **3** John Goodall, GB (Matchless); **4** Tony Russell, GB (Matchless); **5** John Knowles, GB (Seeley); **6** Dave Davies, GB (Matchless); **7** Phil Woodall, GB (Seeley); **8** Ken Inwood, GB (Norton); **9** Brian Richards, GB (Seeley); **10** Richard Cutts, GB (Matchless).
**Fastest lap:** Dugdale, 22m 54.0s, 98.85 mph/159.08 km/h (record).

**Classic Race 350 cc (3 laps, 113.19 miles/209.16 km)**
**1** Bill Swallow, GB (Honda), 1h 11m 51.6s, 94.50 mph/152.08 km/h.
**2** John Kidson, GB (Aermacchi); **3** John Stephens, GB (Aermacchi); **4** Mark Linton, GB (Aermacchi); **5** James Porter, GB (Aermacchi); **6** Rob Brewer, GB (Honda); **7** Tony Ainslie, GB (Ducati); **8** Bob Millinship, GB (Ducati); **9** Les Trotter, GB (Suzuki); **10** Richard Tree, GB (Aermacchi).
**Fastest lap:** Swallow, 23m 44.0s, 95.38 mph/153.50 km/h.

# North-West 200

**NORTH-WEST 200 INTERNATIONAL ROAD RACES, Portstewart-Coleraine-Portrush Circuit, Northern Ireland, 10 May. 8.924-mile/14.362-km circuit.**
**North-West 200 (6 laps, 53.54 miles/86.17 km)**
**1** Joey Dunlop, GB (750 Honda), 29m 43.9s, 108.05 mph/173.89 km/h.
**2** Roger Marshall, GB (500 Honda); **3** Steve Cull, GB (500 Honda); **4** Sam McClements (998 Suzuki); **5** Trevor Nation, GB (500 Suzuki); **6** Tony Moran, GB (750 Yamaha); **7** Neil Robinson, GB (750 Suzuki); **8** Alan Irwin, GB (500 Suzuki); **9** Geoff Johnson, GB (750 Honda); **10** Johnny Rae, GB (750 Yamaha).
**Fastest lap:** Dunlop, 4m 50.1s, 110.74 mph/178.22 km/h.

**Superbikes (6 laps, 53.54 miles/86.17 km)**
**1** Roger Marshall, GB (500 Honda), 29m 15.4s, 113.69 mph/182.97 km/h.
**2** Gene McDonnell, GB (500 Suzuki); **3** Mark Phillips, GB (500 Suzuki); **4** Dennis Ireland, NZ (500 Suzuki); **5** Sean McStay, GB (500 Suzuki); **6** Alan Irwin, GB (500 Suzuki); **7** Paul Cranston, GB (500 Suzuki); **8** Tony Moran, GB (600 Ducati); **9** Sam McClements, GB (750 Suzuki); **10** Barry Woodland, GB (500 Suzuki).
**Fastest lap:** Marshall, 4m 38.7s, 115.27 mph/185.51 km/h.

**Superstocks (6 laps, 53.54 miles/86.17 km)**
**1** Trevor Nation, GB (750 Suzuki), 29m 08.0s, 110.27 mph/177.46 km/h.
**2** Kenny Irons, GB (750 Yamaha); **3** Steve Parrish, GB (750 Yamaha); **4** Andy McGladdery, GB (750 Suzuki); **5** Steve Henshaw, GB (750 Suzuki); **6** Glen Williams, NZ (750 Suzuki); **7** Mark Farmer, GB (750 Yamaha); **8** Rob Marchant, GB (750 Suzuki); **9** Chris Martin, GB (750 Suzuki); **10** Bill McCormack, IRL (750 Suzuki).
**Fastest lap:** Nation, 4m 54.4s, 112.57 mph/181.16 km/h.

**350 cc (6 laps, 53.54 miles/86.17 km)**
**1** Robert Dunlop, GB (Yamaha), 29m 29.4s, 108.94 mph/175.32 km/h.
**2** Gene McDonnell, GB (Yamaha); **3** Neil Tuxworth, GB (Yamaha); **4** Steve Cull, GB (Yamaha); **5** Brian Reid, GB (Yamaha); **6** Gary Cowan, GB (Yamaha); **7** Courtney Junk, GB (Yamaha); **8** Tony Moran, GB (Yamaha); **9** Denis Todd, GB (Yamaha); **10** Mick McGarrity, GB (Yamaha).
**Fastest lap:** Dunlop, 4m 47.4s, 111.78 mph/179.89 km/h.

**First 250 cc (6 laps, 53.54 miles/86.17 km)**
**1** Eddie Laycock, IRL (EMC), 30m 07.1s, 106.67 mph/171.67 km/h.
**2** Andy Watts, GB (EMC); **3** Gary Cowan, GB (Honda); **4** Steve Cull, GB (Yamaha); **5** Gene McDonnell, GB (EMC); **6** Kevin de Cruz, GB (EMC); **7** Gene McDonnell, GB (EMC); **8** Tony Head, GB (Armstrong); **9** Robert Dunlop, GB (EMC); **10** Courtney Junk, GB (EMC).
**Fastest lap:** Joey Dunlop, GB (Honda), 4m 55.1s, 108.87 mph/175.21 km/h.

**Second 250 cc (6 laps, 53.54 miles/86.17 km)**
**1** Andy Watts, GB (EMC), 29m 56.3s, 107.31 mph/172.70 km/h.
**2** Eddie Laycock, IRL (EMC); **3** Gary Cowan, GB (Honda); **4** Courtney Junk, GB (EMC); **5** Tony Head, GB (Yamaha); **6** Gene McDonnell, GB (EMC); **7** Kevin de Cruz, GB (EMC); **8** Robert Dunlop, GB (EMC); **9** Brian Reid, GB (Kimoco); **10** Mick McGarrity, GB (Honda).
**Fastest lap:** Cowan, 4m 54.1s, 109.24 mph/175.80 km/h.

# Ulster Grand Prix

**ULSTER GRAND PRIX, Dundrod Circuit, Northern Ireland, 16 August. 7.401 mile/11.911-km circuit.**
*See also* World TT F1/F2 Championship results.
**Classic race (8 laps, 59.21 miles/95.29 km)**
**1** Joey Dunlop, GB (500 Honda), 30m 01.9s, 118.29 mph/190.37 km/h.
**2** Roger Marshall, GB (500 Honda); **3** Andy McGladdery, GB (500 Suzuki); **4** Alan Irwin, GB (500 Suzuki); **5** Steve Cull, GB (500 Suzuki); **6** Johnny Rae, GB (500 Suzuki); **7** Sam McClements, GB (750 Suzuki); **8** Dave Cowan, GB (500 Suzuki); **9** Des Barry, NZ (500 Yamaha); **10** Glen Williams, NZ (750 Suzuki).
**Fastest lap:** Dunlop, 3m 40.5s, 120.83 mph/194.46 km/h (record).

**Superstock (8 laps, 59.21 miles/95.29 km)**
**1** Phil Mellor, GB (750 Suzuki), 31m 49.9s, 111.60 mph/179.60 km/h.
**2** Andy McGladdery, GB (750 Suzuki); **3** Ken Dobson, NZ (750 Honda); **4** Neil Robinson, GB (750 Suzuki); **5** Steve Linsdell, GB (750 Yamaha); **6** Glen Williams, NZ (750 Suzuki); **7** Dave Griffith, GB (750 Suzuki); **8** Bill McCormack, GB (750 Suzuki); **9** Asa Moyce, GB (750 Suzuki); **10** George Linder, GB (750 Suzuki).
**Fastest lap:** McGladdery, 3m 54.1s, 113.81 mph/183.16 km/h.

**350 cc (10 laps, 74.01 miles/119.11 km)**
**1** Eddie Laycock, IRL (Yamaha), 39m 49.3s, 111.51 mph/179.46 km/h.
**2** Gary Cowan, GB (Yamaha); **3** Dennis Todd, GB (Yamaha); **4** Dave Leach, GB (Yamaha); **5** Mark Farmer, GB (Yamaha); **6** Sean McStay, GB (Yamaha); **7** Geoff McConnell, GB (Yamaha); **8** Donnie Robinson, GB (Yamaha); **9** Barry Stanley, GB (Yamaha); **10** Mick Chatterton, GB (Yamaha).
**Fastest lap:** Laycock, 3m 57.1s, 112.37 mph/180.84 km/h.

**250 cc (10 laps, 74.01 miles/119.11 km)**
**1** Steve Cull, GB (Honda), 43m 17.0s, 102.60 mph/165.12 km/h.
**2** Ian Newton, GB (Honda); **3** Mark Farmer, GB (Honda); **4** Joey Dunlop, GB (Honda); **5** Tony Head, GB (Armstrong); **6** Gary Cowan, GB (Honda); **7** Martin Barr, IRL (Armstrong); **8** Paul Williams, GB (Yamaha); **9** Woolsey Coulter, GB (ECM); **10** Brian Hewitt, GB (Spondon).
**Fastest lap:** Cull, 4m 13.4s, 105.15 mph/169.22 km/h.